The
Warwick Guide
to British Labour Periodicals
1790–1970

The Warwick Guide to British Labour Periodicals 1790–1970

A Check List

Arranged and compiled by
ROYDEN HARRISON
GILLIAN B. WOOLVEN
ROBERT DUNCAN

Centre for the Study of Social History,
University of Warwick

HARVESTER PRESS
HUMANITIES PRESS

First published in 1977 by
THE HARVESTER PRESS LIMITED
Publisher: John Spiers
2 Stanford Terrace, Hassocks,
Sussex, England
and in the USA by
HUMANITIES PRESS INC.,
Atlantic Highlands, New Jersey 07716

Harvester Press Limited
British Library Cataloguing in Publication Data
Harrison, Royden
    The Warwick guide to British labour
    periodicals, 1970–1970
    Index.
    ISBN 0-901759-76-7
    1. Title   2. Woolven, Gillian B
    3. Duncan, Robert
    016.355'1'0941 Z 7164.L1
    Labor and laboring classes – Great Britain – History
    Periodicals – Bibliography

Humanities Press Inc.
Library of Congress Cataloging in Publication Data
Harrison, Royden John.
    The Warwick guide to British labour periodicals,
    1790–1970.
    Includes index.
    1. Labor and laboring classes – Great Britain – Periodicals –
    Bibliography.   I. Woolven, G. B., joint author.   II. Duncan, R.,
    joint author.
    III. Title.
    Z7164.L1H37   1976   [HS8383]   016.30144'42'0941
    ISBN 0-391-99589-8   76-4577

Printed in Great Britain by
Redwood Burn Limited,
Trowbridge, Wiltshire

Contents

Acknowledgements

I am indebted to the Social Science Research Council for a grant which allowed me to employ Miss Woolven and Mr Duncan for a two-year period. I am also indebted to the University of Warwick for a grant of £500 which allowed the work to be completed, if not 'on time', then very nearly.

In relation to a project which depended for its success upon the co-operation of so many individuals and institutions it may seem invidious to single out anyone for special mention. Yet it is surely proper that those who contributed time or learning or both, not to one or two items, but to whole classes of them or to the project as such, should receive some pride of place. Accordingly, thanks are particularly due to:

Professor George Bain for valuable advice and material encouragement: John Battye for exceptional generosity with time and learning: Dr Joyce Bellamy for allowing us to draw so freely upon the published and unpublished findings of the **Dictionary of Labour Biography**: Michael Brook for generosity with his knowledge and enthusiasm: David Englander for clearing up problems regarding housing journals and deposits in the Library of the London School of Economics: Hywel Francis for guiding us to items in the South Wales Miners' Library: Edmund Frow for acquainting us with the contents of his own remarkable collection and helping us with workshop papers; and to his wife, Ruth, for help and hospitality: John Halstead for detailed help on particular items as well as for an enlightened editorial policy in the **Bulletin for the Society for the Study of Labour History**: Else Hibburd for her partnership in preparing the original Harrison-Hibburd checklist: Deian R. Hopkin for his learning respecting the journals of the ILP: R. Mervyn Jones for help and advice with Welsh-language publications: Dr Henry Katz for particular help with respect to other non-English-language publications: J. Kinaken for his particular helpfulness about sailor's journals: Dr Tony Mason for sacrificing two weeks' sabbatical leave in order to allow us to clear up some 'ultimate questions': Jim Roche for co-operation with respect to several unique items in his collection: John B. Smethurst for similar services: Mary White for preparing the index: Special thanks to Mr H. O. Roth for assisting in checking the index and making a number of amendments.

It is also a pleasure to acknowledge the help of the following persons with respect to particular entries or classes of entry:

Dr Geoff Brown, Dr Alan Clinton, Roy Davies, Diana Dickson, Fred Donnelly, Janet Druker, Jim Epstein, W. Fishman, Brian Graham, Dr

Robert Grey, Dr W. A. Hampton, M. Harkin, Professor J. F. C. Harrison, P. Hay, Nick Howard, Dr R. Hyman, Charles McCarthy, Lionel Madden, John Mahon, Lawrence Marlow, Richard McKay, Victor E. Neuberg, R. G. Neville, A. S. Newens, Sir Frederic J. Osborn, A. J. Peacock, H. Pollins, Thomas W. Porter, Dr Richard Price, Raphael Samuel, Eric Shaw, Stan Shipley, Richard Storey, E. Taplin, Eric Tartakover, Dorothy Thompson, Gary Thorn, V. M. Thornes, Nigel Todd, Angela Tuckett, Bob Turner

The help of librarians and their staff in many public, university and specialised libraries has been indispensable. Particular thanks are due to our long-suffering friends in the British Library — both at Bloomsbury and at Colindale; to Bodley's librarian and his staff; to the librarian of Nuffield College who allowed Miss Woolven working space and a locker in the Library. The librarians of the Trades Union Congress, the Co-operative Union and the Labour Party endured innumerable interrogations and answered many requests with unfailing helpfulness and good humour. Librarians and staff at the Bishopsgate Institute, London, the Sheffield Public Library and Swansea University Library gave us exceptional assistance in terms of prompt and comprehensive replies to enquiries about unique holdings.

It is a pleasure to acknowledge the help of the following public libraries:

Altrincham, Avon County (Bristol), Barnet, Bebington, Belfast, Blackpool, Bolton, Bradford, Bromley, Buckhaven and Methil, Buckinghamshire, Bury, Calderdale, Cambridgeshire, Cardiff, Chelmsford, Cheshire, Cleveland, Clywyd, Colchester, Cornwall, Coventry, Croydon, Cumbria, Darlington, Derbyshire, Devon, Doncaster, Dorset, Dumbarton, Dundee, Dunfermline, Durham (Darlington), Durham, Dyfed, Ealing, East Sussex, Epsom, Esher, Essex, Gateshead, Glasgow (Mitchell Library), Hammersmith, Haringey, Havering, Hemel Hempstead, Hertfordshire, Hounslow, Ipswich, Islington, Keighley, Kensington and Chelsea, Kent, Kettering, Kirkless, Knowsley, Lambeth, Lancashire, Lancaster, Leamington, Leicestershire, Lewisham, Lincolnshire, Liverpool, Manchester, Merton, Newcastle-upon-Tyne, North Yorkshire, Northampton, Northumberland, Nottingham, Oldham, Oxford, Poole, Portsmouth, Preston, Reading, Richmond upon Thames, Rochdale, Sefton, Sheffield, Shoreditch, Somerset, Southampton, Southwark, Staffordshire, Stirling, Stockport, Stratford (London Borough of Newham), Surrey, Sutton, Tower Hamlets, Trafford, Wakefield, Waltham Forest, Wandsworth, Watford, Westminster, Weymouth, Wiltshire, Wirral, Wolverhampton

It is a pleasure to acknowledge the help of the following university libraries, specialised libraries and the libraries or research departments of the following organisations:

Aberdeen University Library, Amalgamated Union of Engineering Workers, Technical, Administrative and Supervisory Section, Associated Society of Locomotive Engineers and Firemen, Association of Acrobats, Association of Assistant Mistresses, Association of Broadcasting Staff, Association of First Division Civil Servants, First Division Association, Association of Government Supervisors and Radio Officers, Association of Her Majesty's Inspectors of Taxes, Association of Local Government Engineers and Surveyors, Associated Metalworkers' Society, Association of Officers of the Ministry of Labour, Association of Professional, Executive Clerical and Computer Staff, Association of Professional Scientists and Technologists Pharmaceutical Group, Bakers' Union, Birmingham Trades Council, Bishopsgate Foundation Librarian, Brighton, Hove and District Trades Council, Britannic Field Staff Association, British Actors' Equity Association, British Association of Colliery Management, British Council Staff Association, British Fire Services' Association, City Museum Bristol, Civil and Public Services Association — Newcastle Central Office Branch, Communist Party of Great Britain (James Klugmann, Betty Reid), Conservative Research Department, Co-operative College, Co-operative Societies: Ashton-under-Lyne, Bolton and Wigan, Bristol and Bath, Failsworth, Ipswich, Lancastria, Oxford, Perth and Swindon, Wollaston, Co-operative Union — Scottish Section, Cusworth Hall Museum, Deal and District Trades Council, Department of Health and Social Security Library, Derbyshire Area Trades Union Council, Economic League. Edinburgh University Library, Electrical, Electronic Telecommunication and Plumbing Union, Fabian Society, Farnworth, Worsley and District Trades Council, Faversham Constituency Labour Party, Fire Brigades' Union, Firth-Brown Shop Stewards' Committee, Glasgow University Library, Grimsby and District Trades Union Council, Grimsby Evening Telegraph, Headmasters' Association, Huddersfield and Kirkburton Central Labour Party, Inland Revenue Staff Association — PD Cardiff (Taxes) Branch, Institution of Professional Civil Servants, International Co-operative Alliance, Kingston Constituency Labour Party, Labour Party Library (Mrs Irene Wagner), Labour Parties: Ipswich, Sudbury and Woodbridge, Lancashire Records Office, Leeds University Library, Linen Hall Library Belfast, Liverpool Trades Council, London Co-operative Society, London Federation of Trades Councils, Manchester and Salford Trades Council, Manx Museum and National Trust, Marx Memorial Library, Metropolitan Motor Cab Co-operative Society Limited, Mole Valley District Council, National Association of Fire Officers, National Association of Probation Officers, National and Local Government Officers Association — Newcastle upon Tyne Metropolitan District Branch, National Library of Scotland, National Society of Operative Printers, Graphical and Media Personnel, National Union of Mineworkers, National Union of the Footwear, Leather and Allied Trades, National Union of Insurance Workers: Royal London Section, Liverpool Victoria Section, Prudential Section, National Union of Journalists (R. Knowles), National Union of Public Employees, National Union of Scalemakers,

National Union of Tailors and Garment Workers, Newcastle East Constituency Labour Party, North Ayrshire Museum, North Staffordshire Trades Council, Nottingham and District Trades Council, Peterborough Trades Council, Peterborough Trades Union Council, Prison Officers' Association, Post Office Engineering Union — Metropolitan North West Branch, Professional Footballers' Association, Radio and Electronic Officers' Union, Retail Book, Stationery and Allied Trades Employees' Association, Rossendale Union of Boot, Shoe and Slipper Operatives, Royal Arsenal Co-operative Society, Royal College of Nursing Library, Royal Commission on Historical Manuscripts, Royal Society Library, St Bride Institute, William Salt Library — Stafford, Scottish Schoolmasters' Association, Society of Civial Servants, Customs and Excise Group, the **Stage** (periodical), Society of Lithographic Artists, Designers, Engravers and Process Workers, Eye (Suffolk) Constituency Labour Party, Sheffield Trades and Labour Club, Surbiton Constituency Labour Party, Taxes (Inland Revenue Staff Federation), Transport Salaried Staffs' Association, Trinity College Dublin, Library, Tunbridge Wells Trades Council, United Road Transport Union, University College, Cork, University College, Dublin, Warwick University Library, Windsor Trades Council, Yeovil and District Trades Council.

Some respondents to our questionnaire failed to add a name and address. I apologise for not acknowledging them adequately. Equally, I ask all those who participated in the inaugural conference held at Warwick University in the summer of 1972 to forgive me for not mentioning each of them by name.

The responsibility for any errors or shortcomings in this **Guide** is shared by me with Mr Duncan and Miss Woolven. It does not extend to any of the individuals or institutions referred to above.

RH

Introduction

This **Guide** has its origin in a suggestion which one of us made at the Inaugural Conference of the Society for the Study of Labour History held in London in May 1960. On that occasion it was argued that 'the "Labour" press was the one great institution of the British Working Class that had yet to find its historian'. Moreover, this institution was the one most likely to tempt the student beyond the limits of merely institutional history. Such an undertaking ought, so it was contended, to lead to a far closer approximation to the history of a class than would be the case with such other institutional starting points as parties, unions or co-operative societies. The preparation of a guide appeared as the indispensable preliminary to such a monumental task. The appearance of Mr Stanley Harrison's valuable **Poor Men's Guardians** (London 1947) has not diminished the force of the argument.

Assured of the support of the Social Science Research Council, we began with a conference held at the University of Warwick in mid-summer 1972. Here we enlisted the help of many high authorities on the history of this or that aspect of the Labour press. Their contributions enabled us to discern the balance that had to be struck between what we might hope to accomplish and what ideally needed to be done. In October of that year we set about consolidating everything that could be found in existing bibliographies. An unpublished listing prepared by Royden Harrison and Else Hibburd had already brought together the pioneering work of Foxwell, the important contribution of J. Brophy and of others. The invaluable work of J. Weiner, **A Descriptive Finding List of Unstamped British Periodicals, 1830–1836** (London 1970) supplemented it. Then Professor Chimen Abramsky was persuaded to publish a rough check list of his own, which appeared in the **Bulletin of the Society for the Study of Labour History**, 26, (Oxford 1973). Members of the Society were invited to supplement it, although few proved able to do so.

The next stage was an attempt to comb books, articles and unpublished theses dealing with all aspects of British Labour History in search of every reference to periodicals. This large task was made all the more difficult by inadequate indexes and the occasional thesis which was unobtainable. We then examined existing bibliographical guides, notably the **British Union Catalogue of Periodicals** and **Mitchell's Newspaper, Press Directory**. There followed a search through the catalogue of the British Library and other major libraries in the hope of locating what we had already heard of and with the intention of catching the scent of what remained to be discovered. Finally, we had recourse to specialised appeals to particular groups and institutions. Questionnaires were devised for Trades Councils, University Extramural Departments, members of the National Union of

Journalists, local Labour Parties, Trade Unions, Co-operative Societies, public libraries and other bodies. The extent of our success can be measured, if only approximately, by inspecting the list of persons and institutions which it has been our pleasure to acknowledge.

The reader will occasionally discover that volume and issue numbers are missing. This may be because no complete set can be traced, and it was not clear when the last issue appeared, or when the number and title changed. In some cases volume numbers were not used at certain periods in the life of a journal and sometimes volumes may be numbered but not individual issues. Upon occasion information was sent to us which was incomplete, or the periodical itself was not available and only incomplete information relating to it could be found in library catalogues.

It was not to be expected that we would personally examine every page of every issue of every run of a periodical in all the locations listed. However we have been depressed to discover how often the **British Union Catalogue of Perodicals** gave rise to hopes that were disappointed. Even if the holding was correctly described at the time of **BUCOP**'s compilation, it was, at the time of our examinations missing or incomplete. Nor is BUCOP's listing exhaustive. Moreover, we discovered, to our dismay, that reprints published by reputable companies were sometimes imperfect. Accordingly, we tried to inspect personally at least one holding of every journal listed, even if this meant no more than establishing the presence of the first and the last issue. The holding so inspected is indicated by a dagger (†) and its type (original, reprint or photo-copy) identified. We remind the reader that our information was gathered between October 1972 and January 1975. Items may have been lost or misplaced or destroyed after those dates. Moreover, in a small minority of cases we have not managed to meet even this austere requirement. Time and money were exhausted before we could conduct a direct inspection. This applies, in particular, to the very numerous local journals produced by the National Association of Local Government Officers and to particular local publications linked by a syndicate as in the case of the **Citizen** or **Voice** 'papers. This matter of periodicals which we have not troubled to locate, introduces the more important question of what we were to do about ones which we were unable to locate even after diligent looking. Where we have strong reason to believe that such journals were actually published — and not merely projected — we have tended to include them. We have done so in the hope that other scholars may be alerted to their presence and succeed in tracking them down although we have failed to do so. Finally, a brief reference must be made to a small but important class of items where we have been denied the opportunity of checking out our entries. This refers particularly to the archive of the Independent Labour Party.

What has been said above should have sufficiently established the distinction between our check list and a bibliography properly so called. By a Check List we understand a mere alphabetically ordered listing of a particular class of publication: provisional in its extent and modest in the information which it carries about each item listed. In this case the usefulness of the list is somewhat enhanced by the addition of an index. It is by consulting the index that the reader may hope to discover 'Labour periodicals' associated with a particular period or place; occupation or calling; institution or ideological tendency.

The *Standard Entry* is, as indicated, austere. It normally contains nothing beyond the title, starting and finishing dates, the corresponding numbers and volumes, if any; an indication of the frequency of issue, the place of publication, if other than London; the price, the category in which it has been deemed to fall (see below), and a location or locations (subject to the qualifications referred to above). Sometimes, the reader may find rather more than this. For example, a note may be appended drawing attention to a periodical's affiliations, its publishers, its printers, editors or contributors. No attempt has been made to record the exact dates of any such associations; we have treated these annotations as mere 'acts of supererogation'.

By *'British'* we refer to any Labour periodical published in the United Kingdom, or what is now the Irish Republic, irrespective of the language in which it appeared. Thus, we have tried to include not only journals published in Welsh, but others which were published during all or part of their lifetime in the United Kingdom so long as they had the required association with Labour. In addition, we have attempted to locate journals published outside the United Kingdom which appeared in English and which were connected with or directed towards British Labour.

By a *Periodical* we understand any paper, journal, commentary or record – whether printed or not – which was published with the evident intention that it should appear at regular intervals for an indefinite period of time (the length of the intended interval might change). We thus exclude as 'ephemera' all strike bulletins, election addresses or similar occasional appeals produced in response to what was seen as a passing occurrence. We have also excluded mere balance sheets or statistical returns appearing periodically.

By a *Labour periodical* we understand one which falls into one or other of the following three categories: First, one which was produced by an organised body consisting wholly or mainly of wage-earners or collectively dependent employees. Such periodicals which we deem to fall within this category are indicated by placing the letter 'A' at the beginning of an annotation. Thus we aspired to include all national, regional and pit or factory journals produced by trade unions. If periodicals produced by salaried employees were wholly or largely concerned with topics which might be the subject of collective bargaining these, too, were brought into our list. Our belief about the social character of the great majority of co-operative societies or working men's clubs led us to bring them in through this door.

Second, we tried to include all periodicals which were produced in the avowed interest of the working class – where that class was thought to have interests exclusive of the interests of other social classes or actively opposed to them. Although not necessarily produced by organised bodies of workers or collectively dependent employees, such periodicals present themselves as being 'on the side of Labour' as against Capital, or of the

Employee as against the Employer. Items deemed to fall within this category are designated by the letter 'B' placed at the beginning of an annotation. Through this door we sought to admit all Communist, Socialist or Anarchist journals. The sharpness with which they identify with the 'proletariat' or recognise its involvement in a 'class struggle' varies greatly from case to case. We have tried not to be too exacting. Communist, Socialist, Syndicalist and Anarchist periodicals almost always incline to espouse the special interests of the working class, if only seen as those of the most long suffering or deserving class.

Third, we have thought it right to include within the community of 'Labour Periodicals' those which were produced for wage-earners by members of other social classes who sought to improve them, instruct them, or entertain them. Whereas our first category of 'Labour Periodical' was produced *by* the class and the second *for* the class in the sense of taking its side, this last group consisted of periodicals directed *towards* the working class with an eye to 'bettering' it from the stand-point of non-working class values. For two reasons the number of items brought into our list in this way is relatively small. It was not enough for us that a proprietor or editor was apparently aiming at a popular or plebeian audience: — we required that he should think of his readership as *wage-earners.* Further, we came to the conclusion that one of the leading forms taken by this type of periodical had already been the subject of adequate bibliographic description and that there was no point in repeating the references which can be found in **British House Journals** (1956) or in the **Annual Press Directory** (1846–). Nevertheless, a significant number of our entries fall into this category which is marked by the letter 'C' placed at the beginning of the annotation. In our opinion such periodicals are by no means necessarily barren ground in relation to the needs of the kind of social historian we have had in mind in preparing this *Guide.*

From the foregoing it will be apparent that this *Guide* does not attempt to direct the **Labour** or Social historian to all the periodical literature which may be of service to him. There is a vast and as yet unnumbered population of newspapers and journals which contain articles and reports of as much concern to him as anything included in our list. To take a leading example, Henry Mayhew's marvellous series of letters which appeared in the **Morning Chronicle** between 19 October 1849 and 12 December 1850 do not suffice to lift that paper into any of our categories. Nor is it enough for us that a paper should have been editied by acknowledged friends of Labour or by acknowledged Labour leaders to ensure its automatic inclusion in our *Guide.* Thus, we have not included the **Barnsley Chronicle** under Frost nor the **Leamington Advertiser** under Vincent since their editorial control did not prevent the papers from having the predominant characteristics of the conventional local or family journal. Of course, there were many local papers published in areas where proletarians were concentrated in large numbers which reported in depth on local Labour conditions and Labour Movements. Frequently such papers expressed a general sympathy and understanding of the claims of

Labour. One recalls the **Oldham Standard** at least during the early years after its foundation in August 1859 when it still espoused the values associated with the names of Richard Oastler or J. R. Stephens. Papers that served coal mining communities, such as the **Hamilton Advertiser** or the **Mexborough and Swinton Times**, are further cases in point. *Mitchell* frequently referred to such publications as produced 'for or 'in the interests of the working classes'. On inspection most of these periodicals will be found to have appeared in the mid-Victorian period: to have been Liberal in their politics, never to have been owned or managed by wage-earners, and rarely to have articulated any conception of distinct working class interest opposed to those of other classes or seen to be clearly distinct from them. Nor did they address themselves to wage-earners as such, except incidentally or occasionally. The greater part of this population fits the account offered of them in Professor J. R. Vincent's **Formation of the British Liberal Party 1857—1868** (revised edition 1976 Harvester Press, Hassocks) pp. 58—65. Accordingly, they fall outside our self-imposed terms of reference.

Of course, there are particular papers which have presented us with the greatest difficulty. For instance, we were tempted to include the **Newcastle Weekly Chronicle** for the years when it was controlled by Joseph Cowan. Its sympathy for craft unionism, co-operation, and working class self-help in general, recommended it. Moreover, the temper of its radicalism, even if middle class, went beyond that of the conventional Manchester School. Along with peace, retrenchment and reform, it advocated a particular form of class alliance linked to the claims of continental radicalism and nationalism. In the end we concluded that it failed to meet the requirements for inclusion in any of our three categories. This decision, like many others, will properly become the subject of debate. We will be content if our categories are clear enough to allow that the rules of the debate are not in doubt and the conclusion one which will be essentially dependent upon empirical considerations.

Rather than multiply particular instances of difficulty akin to that presented by the case of the **Newcastle Weekly Chronicle**, we prefer to identify three or four large problems. We believe that these large problems are all related to one another as manifestations of one master difficulty: that of doing justice to historical development. At the simplest level this 'master difficulty' is present when a periodical evolves from one of our catergories to another. Thus to confine ourselves to two of the most famous Labour Papers: it is arguable that the **Bee-Hive** began in category 'A'. Then, under the Reverend Henry Solly in 1870—1 it passed into category 'C', until finally, under George Potter, it joined category 'B'. **The Daily Herald** began as a mix of 'A' and 'B': became predominantly 'A' before becoming a mix of 'B' and 'C'. We have not allowed ourselves to become too distressed by these complexities and we would be surprised if they delayed our readers for very long. We consider that only a small minority of our total entries were affected by such changes. We could hardly be expected to record every change in ownership or editorial style. In practice we have been content — in most cases — to try to determine predominant characteristics of our periodicals at the time of birth and of death without attempting to record all the vicissitudes that might have occurred between these two events.

A more interesting and important problem is presented by periodicals produced during the gestation of the British working class. We assume that this process was going on in England roughly between the years 1790 and 1832. We recognise that it occurred rather later in other parts of the United Kingdom. Moreover, we acknowledge that what happened in Ireland, Wales and Scotland ought not to be reduced to the model of the 'Making of the English Working Class' with no differences other than that the making tends to be deferred in these more backward countries!

So far as England is concerned, we have adopted a thoroughly 'Whiggish' solution. We have included those journals of 'the Democracy' which most clearly anticipated what were subsequently to become the characteristic demands of organised Labour. We have sought out the Jacobin, the ultra-radical and the ultra-democratic papers, while gratefully including such forerunners of our tradition as John Gast's **Trade Newspaper** which plainly belongs in our first category since it was managed by eleven delegates recruited from different trades. To the objection that the more temperate attitudes of other reforming journals might equally be seen as anticipating attitudes to be adopted by sections of the Labour world, we are content to reply that if these attitudes were shared with other classes and frequently more influential for being so shared, they were also necessarily less distinctive. But if we are pressed about the matter we will simply have to reply with the *ad hominem* argument that the periodicals we have listed are of the type which G. D. H. Cole or E. P. Thompson treated as formative and precursive of a distinct working class or Labour standpoint.

Despite the distance which we have just acknowledged between English experience and experience in the 'Celtic fringe', we believe that the same kind of solution is possible. With the help of our Irish, Scottish and Welsh friends we have tried to distinguish between those periodicals of the pre-proletarian world which anticipated the future of the British working class and those which were permanently locked within the terms of a rebellious, outcast, national, plebeian nonconformity. It is here that we are most conscious that we have displayed our ignorance while perhaps giving gravest offence. We can only add that, in this matter as in others, we will welcome correction.

Then there was a related problem which was hardly less difficult than the ones referred to above: what were we to do with periodicals related to institutions whose class significance changed over time? For instance, there is the problem of the infidel press. Nobody doubts that it played a great part in shaping working class consciousness at the beginning of the nineteenth century. Equally, nobody doubts that once it was transformed — during the mid-Victorian years — into the Secularist press it was frequently found in opposition to Labour movements. Our policy has been to seek out the infidel press while being much more sparing when it came to be an attack on God divorced from the defence of Labour. Periodicals which proclaimed disbelief or contempt for the Almighty were not admitted if they avowed their support for 'Labour' in the context of a mere eclectic jumble in which pacificism, vegetarianism, Humanism and the prevention of cruelty to animals were allowed admittance on the same terms as working men and women. This has meant that the anti-religious periodical has been more sympathetically considered in the early than in the late Victorian period. Nor has mere defiance of authority, whether in theory or in practice, been taken as a sufficient condition for inclusion at all times. To be 'unstamped' or 'underground' is not necessarily enough. Analogous difficulties arise in relation to the history of Mechanics Institutes or subsequent developments in the history of Workers' Educational Movements. Difficulties present themselves once more when it comes to the uncertain and changing frontier that divides genuine attempts at the foundation of producers' co-operatives from 'co-partnership' schemes. These generalisations do not exhaust the difficulties.

This *Guide* is a provisional check list, not a definitive bibliography. Our aim has been to provide historians with a tool of the trade, but we do not pretend that it is a precision instrument. It is our hope that those who use our *Guide* will nominate fresh entries: correct or update our information: and supply supplementary notes. If this is done then we may make our way, perhaps through the publication of supplementary lists, to a second edition which will be 'definitive'.

Yet we are confident that even in its present form our work will be found to have some usefulness for the student of particular places and periods, occupations or callings, institutions or ideological tendencies. We also consider that it will suggest questions which have been left unasked — as valuable a function in its way, as disclosing material which has been left unexamined.

Royden Harrison
Jill Woolven
Bob Duncan
Centre for the Study of Social History, University of Warwick

Abbreviations

Most of the abbreviations in this *Guide* are taken from those used in the first volumes of the **British Union Catalogue of Periodicals. (BUCOP)**. Abbreviations with an asterisk are our own inventions, not to be found in BUCOP but following BUCOP's conventions where appropriate. Thus in the statement on holdings we follow BUCOP i.e. a = first title and sequence of numbering, b = second title and sequence of numbering, etc.; i = first series, ii = second series, etc.

The reader should note that some abbreviations in BUCOP relate to institutions and libraries which may have changed their names since they were first listed and that public libraries have amended their titles after local government re-oranization.

As explained in the Introduction, the archive of the Independent Labour Party was not open to public inspection while this **Guide** was being prepared, and is the subject of litigation as we go to press. The Warwick University (MRC) refers to the Modern Records Centre established in the University in October 1973. Its aim is to ensure the preservation and collection of primary sources for British Labour Social and Industrial History. A number of accessions of importance in this field have already been received by the Centre, and some periodical publications within these deposits are noted in the text. As the Centre has had only a brief existence it is not possible to list all runs of periodicals which have been included within the deposits there.

LIBRARIES

AP	Aberdeen Public Libraries
AU	Aberdeen University
AbN	National Library of Wales
AbU	University College of Wales, Aberystwyth
BP	Birmingham Public Libraries
BS	Selly Oak College
BU	Birmingham University
BdP	Bradford City Library
BeP	Bermondsey Public Libraries
BiP	Brighton Public Library
BkP	Birkenhead Public Library
BlU	Belfast University
BnU	University College of North Wales, Bangor
BrP	Bristol Public Libraries
BrU	Bristol University

C	Cambridge University
CME	Marshall Library of Economics, Cambridge
*CPGB	Communist Party of Great Britain
CnP	Croydon Public Libraries
CoU	Cork University College
CrP	Cardiff Public Libraries
*CrU	Cardiff University
CvP	Coventry Public Libraries
D	Trinity College, Dublin
DnP	Dundee Public Libraries
E	National Library of Scotland
EP	Edinburgh Public Libraries
EU	Edinburgh University
EdP	Edmonton Public Libraries, London
ExU	Exeter University
FiP	Finsbury Public Libraries
GE	Institution of Engineers and Shipbuilders in Scotland
GM	Glasgow Public Libraries (Mitchell Library)
GU	Glasgow University
GaU	Galway University College
GrP	Gloucester City Library
GwP	Greenwich Public Libraries
*HO	Home Office papers, Public Record Office
HU	Hull University
HsP	Hammersmith Public Libraries
*ILP	Independent Labour Party Archive
IpP	Ipswich Borough Libraries
KB	Royal Botanic Gardens, Kew
KeP	Kensington Public Libraries
L	British Library (Bloomsbury)
L(Col)	British Library (Newspaper Library, Colindale)
L(Place Coll.)	Place Collection, British Library
LA	Royal Army Medical Cllege
LAM	Ministry of Agriculture and Fisheries Library
LAP	Association for Planning and Regional Reconstruction
LBE	National Institute of Adult Education
LCH	Charing Cross Hospital Medical School
LCI	Chartered Insurance Institute
LCR	Institute of Commonwealth Studies
LDA	British Dental Association
LDS	Department of Scientific and Industrial Research
LDW	Dr Williams's Library, London

LE	London School of Economics and Political Science
LFE	Fuel Research Station
LFI	British Film Institute
LFS	Society of Friends
LGU	Guildhall Library, London
LIA	Royal Institute of British Architects
LIE	Institute of Education, London University
LII	Royal Institute of International Affairs
LJ	Jew' College Library
LMD	Royal Society of Medicine
LME	Institute of Marine Engineers
LMH	Ministry of Health *now* Department of Health and Social Security
LR	Royal Society of London
*LRD	Labour Research Department
LS	Royal College of Surgeons of England
LSC	Science Library
LSF	St Bride Printing Library
LSL	School of Slavonic and East European Studies
LU	London University
LUC	University College, London
LWL	Wiener Library, London
*LabP	Labour Party Library
*LaU	Lancaster University
LcP	Leicester City Libraries
LdP	Leeds Public Libraries
LdU	Leeds University
LdW	Wool Industries Research Association, Leeds
LvP	Liverpool Public Libraries
LvU	Liverpool University
*MML	Marx Memorial Library
MP	Manchester Public Libraries
MR	John Rylands Library, Manchester
MTB	Taylor Brothers and Company, Manchester
MU	Manchester University
MUC	Manchester Unitarian College
NDR	Dr R. Neville, 11 Scotland Way, Horsforth, Leeds LS18 5SQ
NP	Nottingham Public Libraries
NU	Nottingham University
NoP	Northampton Public Libraries
NpP	Newport (Mon.) Public Libraries
NrP	Norwich Public Library
NwA	King's College, Durham University
NwIE	Institute of Education, Newcastle University
NwP	Newcastle upon Tyne City Libraries

O	Bodleian Library, Oxford
O(JJ)	John Johnson Collection, Bodleian Library
OAC	Agricultural Economics Research Institute, Oxford
OCS	Institute of Commonwealth Studies, Oxford
OMA	Manchester College, Oxford
ONC	Nuffield College, Oxford
OR	Radcliffe Science Library, Oxford
ORH	Rhodes House Library, Oxford
OW	Fawcett Library (This has been deposited on permanent loan in Westfield College, London)
PlP	Plymouth Public Libraries
PmP	Portsmouth Public Libraries
RU	Reading University
SP	Sheffield City Libraries
SaU	St Andrews University
ShP	Shoreditch Public Library
SmP	St Marylebone Public Libraries
SoU	Southampton University
SptP	Southport Public Libraries
StP	Stoke-on-Trent Public Libraries
*StrU	Strathclyde University
SwU	Swansea University College
SyP	Stepney Public Libraries
TUC	Trades Union Congress Library
TUC, John Burns Lib.	Trades Union Congress, John Burns Library
USDAW	Union of Shop, Distributive and Allied Workers
*WCML	Working Class Movement Library, Manchester. Mr E. Frow, 111 Kings Road Old Trafford, Manchester M16 9NU
WdK	Kodak Limited, Research Library
WhP	West Ham Public Libraries
WiP	Wigan Public Libraries
WmP	Westminster Public Libraries
WnP	Wimbledon Public Library
WtB	Building Research Station (Building Research Establishment, Department of the Environment).
Warwick U(MRC)	Warwick University, Modern Records Centre
*YU	York University

FREQUENCY ABBREVIATIONS

a	annual
bi-m	every two months
d	daily
fortn	fortnightly
irreg	irregular
m	monthly
q	quarterly
s-a	twice annually
s-m	twice monthly
s-w	twice weekly
3-m	three times a month
3-yr	three times a year
tri-w	every three weeks
w	weekly

Check List

1 AA: the official organ of the Actors' Association I, 1 (Jan. 1917)–II,11 (Dec. 1918); then **Actor**: I, 1 (Jan. 1919)–III, 8 (July 1922); m
    A
    L (destroyed)

ABS see **ABS Bulletin**

2 ABS Bulletin [Jan. 1947?]–177 (Nov./Dec. 1969); then **ABS**: 1, (May 1970)–(30 Dec. 1972); bi-m
    A   BBC Staff Association, then Association of Broadcasting Staff. Superseded by **Broadcast**. 1, (Jan. 1973)–.
    L† 2 (March 1947)–(w occ. nos); ONC 162, Nov./Dec. 1967–

AC.DC. Current News see **Factory News**

3 AEI Voice 1 (May/June 1964)–? Manchester
    B   Workers' Northern Publishing Society. One of the 'Voice newspapers' series.
    TUC 1

4 AEI Worker [193–?]
    A   'of Metro Vick, Manchester.' (Daily Worker, 20 May 1932)

AEU Journal see Amalgamated Society of Engineers **Monthly Journal**
AEU Monthly Journal see Amalgamated Society of Engineers **Monthly Journal.**

5 ALGES Bulletin 1 (24 May 1948)– ; frequency varies
    A   Association of Local Government Engineers and Surveyors. Information Bulletin.
    L† The Association

ALGFO Journal see Association of Local Government Financial Officers' **Journal**

6 ALGFO News 1965– ; q
    A   Association of Local Government Financial Officers. (**Willings Press Guide, 1970.**)

AMA Journal of the Incorporated Association of Assistant Masters in Secondary Schools see Assistant Masters' Association **Circular to Members**

7 AOS **Journal**: the Organ of the Agricultural Organisation Society I, 1 (1 July 1907)–IV, 1 (Jan. 1910); then **Co-operation in Agriculture**: IV, 2 (Feb. 1910)–IX, 10 (Sept./Oct. 1915); m

      B   1d. Printed and published by The Stepney Press for the AOS.
      AbN VI–VIII; L(Col)†; LAM; LSC VI–IX; LdU; OR IX

APAC **Progress** see United Patternmakers Association. **Monthly Trade Report**

8 ARC [19--?]–?
      A   Issued by the Amalgamated Union of Engineering Workers shop stewards of Crompton Parkinson.
      TUC† June 1958

AScW Journal see **Scientific Worker**

9 AScW **Stop-Press**: Monthly News Broadcast of the Association of Scientific Workers 1 (March 1965)–Jan. 1968; m
      A   There are discrepancies in the numbering of the publication. Continued as **ASTMS Gains**.
      HU†

ASE Monthly Journal see Amalgamated Society of Engineers **Monthly Journal**

10 ASSET [195-? 196-?]–Nov./Dec. 1964; then **ASSET Journal**: 1965–7; then **ASTMS Journal**: 1968– ; bi-m
      A   Association of Supervisory Staffs, Executives and Technicians, then Association of Scientific, Technical and Managerial Staffs. Changed to newspaper format in 1970.
      E 1968– ; HU 1968– ; LE 1968– ; O 1968– ; ONC*†

ASSET Journal see **ASSET**

11 ASTE **Report** I, 1 (July/Aug. 1910)–?; bi-m; m
      A   1d. etc. Official organ of the Amalgamated Society of Telephone Employees. Printed and published by W. Speaight and Sons. No issue for March/April 1912.
      O† I, 1–V, 47 (Oct. 1915)

ASTMS Journal see **ASSET**

12 ASTMS **Gains** May 1968–Dec. 1968; m
      A   Association of Scientific, Technical and Managerial Staffs Superseded **AScW Stop-Press**.
      HU†

13 ASW Viewpoint Jan. 1969–Dec. 1969; then **Woodworkers and Painters Viewpoint**: Jan. 1970–March 1971; then **Viewpoint**: Journal of the Amalgamated Society of Woodworkers and Painters: April 1971– ; m

    A   The sub-title varies according to changes in the name of the union. In February 1972 the Society was amalgamated into the Union of Construction, Allied Trades and Technicians, and the sub-title became 'Newspaper of the Union of Construction, Allied Trades and Technicians'.

    ONC†

AUCE Journal see **Co-operative Employe**

14 **AUT Bulletin** 1 (Oct. 1962)– ; bi-m; q

    A   Association of University Teachers. For members only.

    E; LaU; LUC; NwIE; SoU

15 Aberavon, Port Talbot and District Trades' and Labour Journal: the Official Organ of the Trades and Labour Council I, 1 (Sept. 1901)–Aug. 1902? Aberavon; m

    A   1d. 'A journal devoted to the moral and intellectual advancement of the Workers.' Printed for the proprietors by T. M. Jones and Son. Edited by George T. Owen. Local political news, notes and comments. To represent the Trades and Labour Council in municipal politics.

    O(JJ) 1, 2 (Oct. 1901); SwU

16 Aberdare Division Labour News

    B   (J. Bellamy and J. Saville, eds. **Dictionary of Labour Biography**, Vol. I, Macmillan 1972, p. 312.)

17 Aberdeen Citizen 1 (24 May 1926)–622 (24 Aug. 1928). Aberdeen; d

    A   1d; 2d. Printed for and published by The Citizen (Aberdeen) Publishing Society. Proprietors: Aberdeen Trades and Labour Council? '. . established by the Central Strike Committee, decided to attempt an evening newspaper to assist in the fight against non-unionism in newspaperdom.' The only paper in the North of Scotland produced by trade-union labour.

    AP 190, Jan. 1927–239, Feb. 1927; E (Microfilm of AP holding); L(Col)†

18 Aberdeen Clarion 1 (Nov. 1958)–? Aberdeen; m

    B   Published by Aberdeen City Labour Party.

    AU MSS. Coll. 83 (Aug./Sept. 1966); TUC† 1, 3 (Jan. 1959)

19 Aberdeen Labour Elector: a Weekly Record of the Labour Movement 1 (7 Jan. 1893)—35 (31 Aug. 1893); then **Aberdeen Standard**: 36 (7 Sept. 1893)—[59, 17 Feb. 1894?]. Aberdeen; w

B   Printed and published for the proprietor by John Avery. Aberdeen ILP organ. Proprietor: H. H. Champion. Editor: G. Gerrie. Arose out of **The Fiery Cross** (qv). For the first three months published as a supplement to the London **Labour Elector**.

AU*†; AbU (Microfilm of L(Col) holding); L(Col) 7 Sept. 1893—3 Feb. 1894

Aberdeen Monitor see **Artizan**, 1834

20 Aberdeen Patriot 1 (Nov. 1838)—3 (Feb. 1839). Aberdeen; irreg

B   2d. Conducted and published by the Working Men's Association, President: John Legge, Treasurer: Joseph Rowell, Secretary: John Freaser. Printed by G. Mackay. (**Scottish Notes and Queries**, Sept. 1891, pp. 53—5.)

21 Aberdeen Review and North of Scotland Advertiser 1 (1843)—91 (31 Dec. 1844). Aberdeen; w

B   Printed by George Mackay. Edited by John Mitchell. For complete suffrage; addressed to Radical and Chartist working men.

L(Col)†. 39—91

Aberdeen Standard see **Aberdeen Labour Elector**

22 Abingdon Constituency Labour Party Digest I (1960—?) Abingdon; irreg?

B   Edited and published by Ernie Murphy (1963). 'For members of the Abingdon Constituency Labour Party with the compliments of the General Management Committee.' Short articles, some signed, some reprinted from other sources.

LabP† II, 5 (March/April), 7(Aug. 1963)—11 (1964); TUC 1960—1

23 Account Rendered [19—?] — . Hastings

A   National Association of Local Government Officers, later National and Local Government Officers' Association, Hastings Branch.

L 154 (Feb. 1953—)

24 Acornian 1964?— . Sevenoaks

A   National and Local Government Officers' Association, Sevenoaks Urban Branch. Reproduced from typewriting.

L 1964—

25 Action for Peace 1 [1963?]—12 (1 Jan. 1964); m

B   Bulletin of the London Committee of the Committee of One Hundred. 'Libertarian', for 'direct action'. On means of achieving peace. Also deals with tenants' struggles. Reproduced from typewriting.

L† [8] (22 Sept. 1963)—12 (w 10)

26 Action Keynote Chord 1, June 1926–?

    A   Free; ½d. Printed and published by the Communist Party of Great Britain, except the Strike Edition which was published by the Communist Group of Piano Workers. A factory sheet, reproduced from typewriting, produced at Herrburger Brooks, piano manufacturers.

    O(JJ)† Chord 1, Chord 2 (17 June 1926); Special Strike Edition (12 July 1926)

27 Acton Citizen 1 (March 1930)–114 (Sept. 1939); [ns] 1 (Jan. 1947)

    B   Gratis. Published by the London Co-operative Society Education Committee.

    L(Col)†

Actor see 'AA'

28 Address from Henry Hunt to the Radical Reformers of England, Ireland & Scotland on the Measures of the Whig Ministers since They Have Been in Power 1 (20 Oct. 1831)–13 (9 Jan. 1832); w

    B   1d. Printed Robinett. For annual parliaments, universal suffrage, secret ballot. (Note also **Addresses to Radical Reformers**, by Henry Hunt (1820–1), a collection of single addresses in one volume.)

    LU† ; WCML†

29 Address from One of the 3730 Electors of Preston, to the Labouring Classes of Great Britain and Ireland 1 (24 Dec. 1831)–[56?] (5 Jan. 1833). Preston (24 Dec. 1831–Oct. 1832); Bolton; w

    B   1d. Printed by W. P. Staines, then R. Holden. 'A radical miscellany whose democratic political views closely parallel those of Henry Hunt. It was widely circulated among the working classes of South Lancashire'. (Wiener) The title is varied slightly each week to evade the stamp duty.

    Harvard UL, 11 occ. nos; LU (21 April 1832); Lancashire Public Record Office 42 occ. nos; PrH (31 March, 7 April, 14 April 1832)

30 Adult Student: Workers' Educational Association, **Glasgow Branch Review** I, 1 (Dec. 1931)–II, 2 (Nov. 1936). Glasgow; irreg

    B   3d. Editor: Thomas L. MacDonald.

    E: GM; GU; L; O†

31 Advance [18--?] –?; m

    B   Organ of Chatham and District Trades and Labour Council. (**Labour Annual**, 1899.)

    ILP March 1910

32 Advance 1 (Dec. 1935)–6 (May 1936); ns. I, 1 [June 1936]–III, 12 (July/Aug. 1939); m

    B   1d. First series reproduced from typescript, then published by Ted Willis for 'Advance'. 'Owned and controlled by members of the Labour Party League of Youth.'

    L(Col)† ns. 1, 3–III, 12; LabP† (w 2)

33 Advance [1969?] –? [Gosport?]

    B   'A commentary edited by John Hales and produced by our local Young Socialists.' (First number described in **Gosport's Socialist Spotlight**, Oct. 1969.)

34 Advance News [196-?] –?

    B?   Ex-Service Movement for Peace.

    ILP 9 (1968)

35 Advance, Towards the Workers' Industrial Republic September 1936. Glasgow

    B   Glasgow Anarchist Anti-Parliamentary Communist Federation. Includes extracts from **Boletin de Information** issued by the CNT and FAI, on Spain.

    WCML†

36 Adversaria 1 [195-?] – . Tipton

    A   National Association of Local Government Officers, later National and Local Government Officers' Association, Midland Electricity Board, South Staffordshire and North Worcestershire Sub-Area Branch.

    L 14 (Jan. 1953)– (w 20)

37 Advocate [19--?] Nuneaton; m

    B?   Gratis. Published at the **Observer** Office. 'Official organ of the Warwickshire miners and other workers.' (Mitchell, 1900.)

38 Advocate and Merthyr Free Press July 1840–April 1841. Merthyr Tydfil; m

    B?   2d. 10 issues. Editors, printers, publishers: David John, Jr and Morgan Williams, Unitarian and weaver.

39 Advocate of the Working Classes 1826–7. Edinburgh

    B   Editor: George Mudie. (J. Bellamy and J. Saville, eds. **Dictionary of Labour Biography**, Vol. I, 1972, p. 250; R. G. Garnett, **Cooperation and the Owenite Socialist communities in Britain, 1825–45**, 1972, p. 242.)

40 Advocate, or, Artizans' and Labourers' Friend, Including a Review of Arts, Science and Literature 1 (16 Feb. 1833)–10 (20 April 1833); w

    A   1d. Published by George Bright. Printed by P. P. Thomas. Editor: John Ambrose Williams and managed by a committee of the Printers' Protection Society. 'A miscellany which deplores the effects of machinery, and advocates compensation for those workers adversely affected by the introduction of machinery' (Wiener).

    BP 1–9; Columbia U, New York; LU 1–2, 6, 7; O 1–2; O(JJ) 1; ONC† 1; Yale U

Aegis see **Blanketteer, and People's Guardian**

41 AEolus: Esher Branch NALGO Staff Magazine 1964?– . Esher
    A   National and Local Government Officers' Association. Reproduced from typewriting.
    L 1964–

42 After Work: a Magazine for Workmen's Homes I, 1 (Jan 1874)–IV, 12 (Dec. 1877); ns 1878–80; ns 1882–7; m
    C   1d. Published W. Macintosh. Promotes Christian values, devotion to work, duty to home, family and superiors. Includes illustrations, fiction.
    C; E (w III–IV, ii VIII); L†; O (w 1885)

43 Agenda: a Quarterly Magazine Devoted to the Special Interests of Members of Co-operative Committees I, 1 (June 1953)–XV, 3 (Dec. 1967). Manchester; q
    A   2s 6d. etc. To develop the best techniques of committee management and ensure a successful enterprise.
    Co-op.; Union; E; L†; MP

Agents' Journal and Official Gazette see **Life Assurance Agents' Journal**

44 Agitator 1 (9 March 1833)–5 (13 April 1833). Glasgow; w
    B   1d. Published and printed by John Sharp for the proprietor. 'A working-class political miscellany that advocates the abolition of monarchy and aristocracy, universal suffrage, the common ownership of land, and, if necessary, a "moral revolution" to enforce the demands of the people' (Wiener). To turn the Whigs out of Glasgow Political Union.
    GM†; LU 1

45 Agitator [1, 9? Nov. 1965] –fifth year, 2 (Nov. 1969); approx. s-w during term
    B   6d. Published by the London School of Economics and Political Science, Socialist Society. Reproduced from typewriting.
    LE†; (The Left in Britain – microfilm – Harvester Press Ltd.)

46 Agitator, and Political Anatomist. Established in the Cause of Trade Unions and the People 1 (Nov. 1833)–2 (Dec. 1833); m
    B   1d. Publisher and printer: J. Canning. Editor: William Benbow. 'Contains political essays, primarily written by Benbow, which advocate the division of land, a minimum daily wage, repeal of the Union with Ireland, and a general strike to enforce the workers' demands' (Wiener). Also advocates the eight-hour day.
    L(Place Collection, Set 51)†; LU 1; ONC 1

47 Agitator for Workers' Power I, 1 [1961]–I, 5 ½1961]; then **Solidarity for Workers' Power**: I, 6 [1961] – . London etc.: irreg
    B   6d. Organ of rank and file syndicalist group, later of **Solidarity**. Reproduced from typewriting.
    E II, 9 (1963)– ; L; ONC V (1968)– ; (The Left in Britain – microfilm – Harvester Press Ltd.)

48 Agricultural and Industrial Magazine [of the Society for the Encourage
ment of Domestic Industry, and for Promoting Effectual Relief from the
General Distress] I, (1 Oct. 1834)– II (1 Dec. 1836); fortn
    C   2d. Volume numbers only. Publisher: James Cochrane and
Company. Printer: W. Nicol. Managed by a Commitee of twenty-one MPS.
'Features essays on agricultural subjects, many of them deploring the
widespread economic distress.' (Wiener)
     Co-op. Coll.; L; O 1834–5

Agricultural Economist see **Co-operative Prices Current**

49 Alarm, for Your Liberty and Ours 1 (26 July 1896)–10 (22 Nov.
1896); irreg
    B   ½d. Written, printed and published by a London Anarchist
Group. The Associated Anarchists. Editor: Carl Quinn. First issued for the
Hyde Park Demonstration, International Socialist Congress, 26 July 1896.
'Teaches anarchy, "when every man shall have his own," but whilst
believing in revolutionary economic action, refuses to advocate deeds of
violence.' (**Labour Annual**)
     L(Col)†; O(JJ)† 1–5

50 Aldis [19--?] –?
    A   Union of Post Office Workers, Amalgamated London Districts P
& TO Branch. (W. Dunlop, 'Local journals', **Belpost**, IV, 5 (May 1965)

51 Alexander [1941?] –? Watford; m
    A   'Since 1941 the **Co-operative News** has been sent weekly to
each member of the Society's staff serving in the Forces, and financial help
given to the magazine for them (Alexander), sent monthly.' (H. Afford,
**The Golden Year, being the Jubilee History of the Watford. Co-operative
Society Ltd., 1895–1945**, Reading 1945; p. 130.)

52 Alloa Co-operative Herald [187-? 188-?] –? Alloa; q
    A   'In order to keep the members interested in the affairs of the
Alloa Society particularly, the Education Committee published, for a time,
a quarterly magazine called the **Alloa Co-operative Herald**. The **Herald**
published reports of the quarterly meetings of the Society and of the
Wholesale Society, directed attention specially to the educational agencies
controlled by the Society, presented reports of the educational meetings
and biographical sketches of the leaders of co-operation in Alloa, and
offered open columns in which members of the Society could ventilate
their views upon matters of general interest to co-operators. It was edited
by Mr David Liddell, a member of the Education Committee; but, like
most editors, he found that the public taste in literature was a variable
measure. The **Herald** had a quarterly circulation of over 2,000 copies.'
(**Alloa Co-operative Society Ltd., 1862–1912: a Historical Survey on the
Occasion of the Society's Jubilee, 1912**, Alloa 1912, pp. 45–6.)

53 All Power: the Official Organ of the Red International of Labour Unions I, 1 (Jan. 1922)–III, 30 (July 1924); m

    A   1d. British Bureau of RILU. Editor: Harry Pollitt. Opposed the Amsterdam (Yellow) International. Aimed at making the trade unions a revolutionary instrument for the taking of working-class power. Insisted on need for alternative leadership in the unions. Supported the work of the National Minority Movement. Contributors: Tom Mann, J. T. Murphy, Tom Quelch, J. T. Walton Newbold, Frank Smith, W. McLaine, Nat Watkins, R. M. Fox, Wal Hannington, Ellen Wilkinson.

    L(Col)†; MML 6–28;* ONC I*

54 Alnwick Local Labour Party's **Magazine** I, 1 (Dec. 1958)–I, 2 (Feb. 1959). Alnwick; m

    B   6d. Duplicated and published by Ronald Allan. Editor: Ronald Allan.

    L†

55 Altrincham Express [193-?]. Altrincham; m

    B   Labour Party. (Labour and Socialist International. **The Socialist Press**, 1933.)

Amalgamated Engineering Union **Monthly Journal** see Amalgamated Society of Engineers. **Monthly Journal**

56 Amalgamated Society of Carpenters and Joiners. **Monthly Report** [18--?]–[1920?] London; Manchester; m

    A   1d. Union affairs, branch news. See also Amalgamated Society of Woodworkers' **Monthly Journal**, 1921– .

    Bishopsgate Institute 1863–9, 1873–1918; O† ns 73 (Jan. 1869)–84 (Dec. 1869), 97 (Jan. 1871)–311 (Nov. 1888)

57 Amalgamated Society of Coopers. **Quarterly Report** 1 (Jan. 1920)–? Burton-on-Trent; Glasgow; Clydebank; q

    A

    TUC† Jan. 1920–63*

58 Amalgamated Society of Engineers. **Monthly Journal** [1895?] – ; m

    A   Amalgamated Society of Engineers; Amalgamated Engineering Union; Amalgamated Union of Engineering and Foundry Workers; Amalgamated Union of Engineering Workers, Engineering Section. Title varies: **ASE Monthly Journal and Report**; **AEU Monthly Journal**; **AEU Monthly Journal and Report**; **AEU Journal**; **AUEW Journal** etc. Preceded by a **Monthly Report** (1851?–), which was sometimes published separately after the start of the **Journal**.

    AbN 1913– ; Bishopsgate Institute*; L 1897– ; LE 1897–; NU 1939– *; LU*; ONC*; TUC*; the Union*

59 Amalgamated Society of Farriers and Blacksmiths. **Quarterly Journal** [19--?] –? St Helens; q
    A
    TUC† 1931–5*

60 Amalgamated Society of Gas, Municipal and General Workers. **Monthly Journal** I, 1 (July 1915)–IV, 12 (Dec. 1920). Birmingham; m
    A   Gratis. Continued militant wages and conditions policy of its predecessor, the **Municipal Employees Monthly** (qv) and defended trade-union rights in wartime. At the end of 1920 the union was amalgamated into the National Union of General Workers, and its journal was absorbed by the **Journal** of the larger union.
    BP†

61 Amalgamated Society of House Decorators and Painters ('London Amalgamated'). **Monthly Circular** [18–?] –?
    A   (R. W. Postgate. **The Builders' History**. London: National Federation of Building Trades' Operatives, 1923.)

62 Amalgamated Society of Leather Workers. **Quarterly Journal** [19–?] –? Leeds; q
    A
    TUC† 81 (1932)–178 (May 1962*)

63 Amalgamated Society of Tailors. **Journal** I, 1 (April 1898)–XXXI, 231 (Dec. 1931); then b **Tailor and Garment Worker**: I, 1 (Feb. 1932)–   . Manchester; Leeds;. m; q
    A   1d. etc. The Society later added **and Tailoresses** to its name. The **Tailor and Garment Worker**, later **Garment Worker**, is published by the National Union of Tailors and Garment Workers. The journal gradually extended its range of interests.
    AU 1944–52*; L(Col)† a, b XVII, 1948–   ; NU XXI, 10 (1952)–XXIV, 6 (1955), XXXI, 1962–   ; ONC Nov. 1949–   ; ShP b XXIII, 1954–

64 Amalgamated Society of Woodcutting Machinists. **Trade Report** 1917– . Manchester; m
    A   After a few years became **Monthly Report**
    BU Feb. 1955–   ; L 1962–   ; TUC*

Amalgamated Society of Woodcutting Machinists. **Monthly Report** see Amalgamated Society of Woodcutting Machinists. **Trade Report**

65 Amalgamated Society of Woodworkers. **Monthly Journal** (Jan. 1921)–
(Dec. 1947); then **Woodworkers' Journal**: Official Organ: (Jan. 1948)–
(Oct. 1969); then **Woodworkers' and Painters' Journal**: (Jan. 1970)–(April
1971); then **Woodworkers', Painters' and Buildingworkers' Journal**: (July
1971)–1 (1972); then **Union of Construction, Allied Trades and Technicians' Journal**: 2 (1972)–   . Manchester; London; m; q
      A   2d. etc. Extensive record of union affairs. Support for Labour
Party.
       L†; NU 1954–   ; ONC† Nov. 1949–   ; TUC; Warwick U (MRC)
1924–72

66 Amalgamated Toolmakers **Monthly Record** [18–?] –? Birmingham; m
      A
  Bishopsgate Institute July 1892–1903, 1905–14; ILP Jan., March
  1906; WCML† XXXVIII, 378 (Sept. 1913)

67 Amalgamated Union of Building Trade Workers. **Monthly Report**
1921–35?; m
      A
  Warwick U (MRC) 1921–35

68 Amalgamated Union of Building Trade Workers. **Circular to Branches**
1921–?
      A
  Warwick U (MRC) 1921–65

Amalgamated Union of Building Trade Workers of Great Britain and
Ireland. **Quarterly Report** see Amalgamated Union of Building Trade
Workers of Great Britain and Ireland. **Trade Circular and General Reporter**

69 Amalgamated Union of Building Trade Workers of Great Britain and
Ireland. **Trade Circular and General Reporter** 1 [19–?] –179 (Sept. 1953);
then Amalgamated Union of Building Trade Workers of Great Britain and
Ireland. **Quarterly Report**: 180 (Dec. 1953)–2nd quarter, 1971; q
      A   For use of members only. The Union merged with the Amalg-
amated Society of Woodworkers in 1971.
      BU 190 (1956)–   ; ONC† 164 (Nov. 1949)–   ; TUC 1921–   ;
Warwick U (MRC) 1921–65

Amalgamated Union of Engineering Workers, Engineering Section.
Monthly Journal see Amalgamated Society of Engineers. **Monthly Journal**

Amalgamated Union of Engineering and Foundry Workers. **Monthly
Journal** see Amalgamated Society of Engineers. **Monthly Journal**

70 Amalgamated Union of Foundry Workers. **Monthly Journal and Report** (April 1950)–(Dec. 1952); then **Foundry Workers' Journal**: (Jan. 1953)– (Dec. 1961); then **Foundry Worker** (Jan. 1962)–   ; m

    A   Amalgamated Union of Foundry Workers; Amalgamated Union of Engineering and Foundry Workers; Amalgamated Union of Engineering Workers, Foundry Section.

    BU March 1955–   ; NU 1954–   ; ONC†; TUC; Warwick U (MRC)

71 Ambulance Driver: the Official Organ of the National Ambulance Services Association I, 1 (July 1955)–?; m

    A   Organ of the Association's campaign to gain the status of a profession for ambulance drivers, then classified as manual workers, and to have pay and status raised to those of firemen and police.

    L†

Amddiffynydd y Gweithiwr see **Workman's Advocate**, 1873–75

72 Amusement Workers News: official organ of Theatrical Employees, 1 [19--?] –?

    A   1d. Published by William Johnson, Editor and General Secretary, for the Association.

    TUC† 1, 8 (Nov. 1914)

Amusement Workers' News see **NATE Journal**

73 Anarchist: a Revolutionary Review I, 1 (March 1885)–ns II, 6 (Aug. 1888); m

    B   1d. Printed and published by The International Publishing Company. Editor: Henry Seymour. The first anarchist journal in England. Anti-political Socialism advocated, and abolition of the State (Brophy). Contributors: G. B. Shaw, Henry Appleton, Henry Glasse

    L(Col)†; LE*; O; O(JJ) April, May 1887

74 Anarchist: Communist and Revolutionary I, 1 (18 March 1894)–II, 24 (18 April 1896). Sheffield; m; fortn; irreg

    B   1d. Published by David Nicoll. To build support for Anarchism. Articles, news of anarchist groups.

    L(Col) (Jan.–Nov. 1895 microfilm); LdP 1895*; O† II, 21, Aug. 1895; ONC† I, 1–6 (24 June 1894)–13 (16 Dec. 1894), II 22 (Oct 1895)

75 Anarchist I, 1 (3 May 1912)–I, 34 (17 Jan. 1913). Glasgow; w

    B   1d. Printed and published by the Anarchist Press. Editor: George Barrett. Favoured Syndicalism, revolution by direct action, not by political means (Brophy).

    E*; L(Col)†; LE*; ONC*

76 Anarchist 1, [1964] –? London; Bristol (4); Birmingham (5); Edinburgh (6, 7)

    B   1s.6d. Reproduced from typewriting. No. 7 states '**Anarchist** first appeared early in 1964 as a London based polemical journal for Freedom readers. Its reputation spread under the editorship of Jack Stevenson.'

    LE† 6 (1 Feb. 1965); 7, undated

77 Anarchist Labour Leaf 1 (May 1890)–4 (Aug. 1890); m

    B   Gratis. Issued by East-London Communist-Anarchist Group. Editor: H. Davis. Promulgated principles of Anarchist Communism in opposition to other tendencies, especially 'State Socialism'

    LE†; ONC 1–2

78 Anarchy: a Journal of Anarchist Ideas 1 (March 1961)– ; m

    B   1s.6d. Published by Freedom Press. Volume numbering adopted as from III, 1963? Articles by a variety of contributors, academics and workers, on the contemporary relevance of Anarchism in society and culture

    E 11 (1962)– ; HU 1966– ; L†; LdP; LE; LUC 92 (1968)– ; O 11 (1962)– ; SwU III (1963)–

Anglo-Russian News Bulletin see Anglo-Russian Parliamentary Committee. **Weekly Bulletin**

79 Anglo-Russian Parliamentary Committee. Weekly Bulletin [1927?] –?; then **Anglo-Russian News Bulletin**: ?–(July 1963); w; irreg

    B   Reproduced from typewriting.

    LE† (June 1927)–(July 1963*), TUC† 1927–39*

80 Anti-Cobbett, or the Weekly Patriotic Register I, 1 (15 Feb. 1817)–I, 8 (5 April 1817); w

    C   1½d. Published at 112 Strand, and occasional numbers also by W. Bulgin, Bristol, Effingham Wilson, London, and R. Jabet, Birmingham. From Number 2, the title was **Anti-Cobbett, or the Weekly Patriotic Pamphlet**. In the form of addresses to the people, the primary purpose was to criticise, from the standpoint of a constitutional agitation for reform, the allegedly dangerous and inflammatory journalism of Cobbett in the **Political Register**.

    L†; MP 1–6; O

81 Anti-Dear Beef Journal and Working Man's Friend: Organ of the Anti-Dear Beef, Mutton and Coal Association 1 (5 Aug. 1872). Manchester; s-w

    C

    MP†

Antidote see **Anti-Socialist Gazette and Christian Advocate**

82 Anti-Imperialist Review I, 1 (July 1928). Paris; Berlin; London; q
  B   2s.6d. A quarterly journal edited and published by the International Secretariat of the League Against Imperialism (President: Henri Barbusse, Bhairman: James Maxton). Contributors: Maxton, Gorki, Barbusse.
   MML†; WCML†

83 Anti-Imperialist Review I, 1 (Sept. Oct. 1931)—II, 1 (Nov. Dec. 1932). Berlin; bi-m
  B   6d. Edited and published by the International Secretariat of the League Against Imperialism.
   MML†; WCML†

84 Anti-Persecution Union. Circular 1 (1 May 1845)—4 (1 Aug. 1845); m
  B   1d. Publisher: James Watson. Printer: J. Griffin Hornblower. Preceded by **The Movement and Anti-Persecution Gazette** (qv). To publicise the activities of the Anti-Persecution Union set up as defence fund for victims of blasphemy laws etc. and to campaign for right of free speech and free thought. Important for its association with radicalism and Chartism. Discontinued because of heavy expenses.
   Bishopsgate Institute†; LU

85 Anti-Socialist Gazette and Christian Advocate, Exposing and replying to the Blasphemous and Seditious Errors of Socialism, Mormonism & Chartism 1 (Oct. 1841)—8 (May 1842); then b **Antidote**: a Monthly Magazine for the Refutation of Modern Delusions, and for the Defence of Christian Truth: 1 (July 1842)—6 (Dec. 1842). Chester; m
  C   4d. Published and edited by John Brindley. The objects of the paper were to expose socialist missionaries and their influence, and to report 'Mr. Brindley's course of counter-operations'.
   LU† (w b 2)

86 Anti-Sweater: a Journal Devoted to the Exposition of the Sweating System, and for the Organization of the Journeyman Tailors and Machinists 1 (July 1886)—8 (Feb. 1887); m
  B   1d. Printed, published and edited by Lewis Lyons, 'one who has worked in the sweater's den, and is well versed in the working of the system'. After the first number subtitled: 'A Journal Devoted to the Exposure of the Sweating System in All Trades and for the Organization of Working Men and Women'. The last two numbers are more overtly political, and advocate independent Labour representation.
   L(Col)†

87 Anti-Tithe Journal 1 (15 Nov. 1881)
  C   1d. Organ of the Anti-Tithe League. Editor: John Bedford Leno. Sole object of the League 'to improve the present alarming condition of British Agriculture, by assisting to abolish all tithings'.
   L†

Anvil, 1936–60 see Associated Blacksmiths' Forge and Smithy Workers' Society. Official Journal

88 Anvil: the Official Organ of the Hammersmith Branch of NALGO I, 1 (Jan./Feb. 1953)–Christmas 1963; bi-m
    A   National Association of Local Government Officers. Reproduced from typewriting. Editor: Miss P. M. Webster.
    L†

89 Anvil: a Forum for Discussion by Dorman Long Workers Sept. 1954–May 1961; m
    A   1d. Shop stewards' factory paper at Dorman Long, Nine Elms, a constructional engineering company. Edited and published by Mick Kavanagh. Reproduced from typewriting.
    WCML†

Apex see **Clerk, 1908–73**

90 Apostle and Chronicle of the Communist Church I. 1 (1 Aug. 1848)–? Douglas, Isle of Man
    B   Gratis. Financed from the proceeds of the Propaganda Fund of the Communist Church. Printed by Shirrefs and Russell, Manx Steam Press. Editor: Goodwyn Barmby. To record the 'doctrinal development' of the Communist Church and register the progress of the movement.
    LU† 1

91 Appeal to the Common Sense of the Whole World. 1 (2 Sept. 1859); then **Correspondence of a Man Out of Work**: 2–3 (16 Sept. 1859); w
    B   1d. By L. Poncet. Printed and published by P. Grant and Company. Editor: P. P. [P. Parmel]. Advances theories for the removal of misery and poverty from the world. Appeals to reformers like Roebuck, to prominent politicians and even to Louis Napoleon.
    L†

92 Apprentice and Trades' Weekly Register: a Weekly Journal of Art, Science and Literature I, 1 (3 Feb. 1844)–Dec. 1844; ns I, 1 (Jan. 1845–Dec. 1845; w
    A   from August 1845. 1½d. Edited by the Artizan Club. Initially a technical and scientific magazine for skilled working men, non-political in content. From August 1845 it changes character completely and becomes organ of the National Association of United Trades, the directors of that body having secured a controlling interest in the magazine. Its columns now 'thrown open to all parties who seek for the emancipation of labour'.
    L†; LU i

93 Aquarius: Magazine of the MWB Staff Association I, 1 (Aug. 1905)– ; m
    A   1d. Printed and published by James Truscott for the Metropolitan Water Board Staff Association.
    FiP XIV–XXIV;* L†; the Association

94   Arbaiter [Worker]. Robotnik 1 (4 Dec. 1898)–7 (Nov. 1902). London; irreg

B   A paper published by J. Kamiowski on behalf of the Polish Socialist Party, for Jewish workers. Yiddish.

L(Col)† (w 7)

95 Arbaiter Fraind. [Workers' Friend] (15 July 1885)–(26 March 1897); (14 Oct. 1898)–(21 July 1916); (April 1920)–(23 Dec. 1923); ns I, 1 (15 May 1930)–III, 1 (Dec. 1931/Jan. 1932). London; m; w; m

B   1d. etc. Published by the International Workingmen's Educational Club. Later subtitled: 'Anarchistish-Komunistisher Organ', and published by the Federation of Yiddish Speaking Anarchists. Yiddish. Also 1904–5 published a supplement: **Wochentliche Literarisze Bailage Tsum Arbaiter Fraind. [Weekly Literary Supplement to Workers' Friend]**.

L(Col)*†; O XXVI, 1–8 (1912)

96 Arbaiter Fraind: [Anarchistish-Komunistischer Buletin] (The Workers' Friend: Anarchist-Communist Bulletin). 1924

B   Published by the reorganised group Workers' Society and Red Cross. Yiddish.

L(Col)† 22 March 1924

97 Arbaiter Fraind Buletin 1 [April 1930]. (The Workers' Friends' Bulletin). London

B   Published by the Group 'Workers' Friend' and Anarchist Red Cross in London. Yiddish.

L(Col)†

98 Arbaiter Vort. [Workers' Word] I. 1 (28 March 1915)–III, 38 (July 1917). London; fortn; m

B   1d.; 2d. Organ of the Jewish-Social Democratic Organisation in England. Probably suspended between January and June 1917. Yiddish.

L(Col)†

Arbeiter Ring see **Circle**

99 Arbekay: Official Journal of the Royal Borough of Kensington Branch of NALGO 1959?–

A   National and Local Government Officers' Assocation.

L Dec. 1959–

100 Arbitrator: Organ of the Workmen's Peace Association [18--?] – [19--?]; w? m

C?   ½d. etc. Long-time editor: W. R. Cremer. The Association changed its name in 1889 to International Arbitration League.

LE 155 (1884)–444 (1916*)

101 Archontes: the Aldershot NALGO Magazine 1961?–   . Aldershot
    A   National and Local Government Officers' Association. Reproduced from typewriting.
    L 1961–

102 Ardleigh Labour News. [194–?]. Ardleigh, Essex; irreg
    B   1d. Duplicated. Labour Party. (Labour Party. **Your own Journal**, 1948.)

103 Ardwick Pioneer. [193–?]. Manchester; m
    B   Labour Party. (Labour and Socialist International. **The Socialist Press**, 1933.)

104 Arena: the Official Journal of the National Association of Registration Officers 1 (Summer 1953)–26 (Aug. 1961). Plymouth; 3-yr
    A   Published for members by the Executive Council of NARO. Internal information.
    L†

105 Argus. [19-?]–Bootle
    A   National and Local Government Officers' Association, Bootle Branch.
    L 1954–

106 Argus and 'Demagogue' 1 (2 Aug. 1834)–? Huddersfield; w
    B   1d. Published, printed and edited by Joshua Hobson. 'A political miscellany that advocates universal suffrage and factory legislation, and continually attacks Edward Baines, the publisher of the **Leeds Mercury**. Each issue features a lengthy article by Richard Oastler' (Wiener). Succeeds **The 'Demagogue'**.
    Huddersfield PL 4 (23 Aug. 1834 [photocopy]); LU 1–3 (in Oastler Collection in a volume entitled **Oastler's Letters and Cuttings. White Slavery 1835–6**); Tolson Memorial Museum, Huddersfield 4 (23 Aug. 1834)

107 Arrael Griffin X-Ray
    A   Organ of the Arrael Griffin Miners' Minority Movement. (R. G. Neville.)

108 Artisan; or, Mechanic's Register 1, (1825)–2, (1825)
    C   Edited by G. C. Carey
    BlU 1; C 1; LR

109 Artizan. 1 ([March?] 1834)–?; then **Aberdeen Monitor:** 1 (Aug. 1834)–2 (Sept. 1834?). Aberdeen; m?

    B   2d. Printed and sold by J. Watt. Motto: 'I seek no recompense – I fear no consequences. Fortified by that proved integrity which disdains to triumph or to yield, I will advocate the rights of man.' A note states that 'at the suggestion of a number of Friends, we have substituted the title **The Aberdeen Monitor** in place of **The Artizan**, the former being thought a more appropriate title to our publication.' A political paper of radical principles. (J. M. Bulloch, 'A bibliography of local periodical literature'. **Scottish Notes and Queries,** I.)

Artizan's London and Provincial Chronicle see **Journeyman and Artizan's London and Provincial Chronicle**

110 Artizan's Miscellany, or **Journal of Politics and Literature** I, 1 (28 May 1831)–I, 10 (30 July 1831). Edinburgh; w

    B   2d; 1d. 'Published and conducted by several members of the working classes.' Printer: W. Reid. Literary varieties and moderate reform articles dealing with such subjects as parliamentary suffrage, slavery and Ireland; also the place of the working class in society and politics.

    EP†

111 Artizan's News and Temperance Reporter 1 (1 Sept. 1875)–13 (25 Dec. 1875); w

    C   1d. Printed and published by the proprietor, Arthur George Newton. Addressed to the 'Artizan and Labouring Classes'. Considers the 'mutual interests of Capital and Labour, which are identical to a very large extent'. Special promotion of temperance, with other measures of self-improvement.

    L(Col)†

Ascoll see **Ascoll Review**

112 Ascoll Review June 1923–Nov. 1933; then **Ascoll:** Jan. 1934–Dec. 1935; q; m

    A   Official publication of the National Association of Assessors and Collectors of Taxes, later National Association of the Taxes Assessing and Collecting Services. Incorporated in Taxes.

    Inland Revenue Staff Federation

113 Ashton Chronicle, and **District Advertiser** 1 (March 1848)–73 (3 Nov. 1849). Ashton; w

    C   Started by Joseph Raynor Stephens. 'Dedicated to the promotion of Tory humanitarianism.' Contributor: Oastler. Replaced by **Champion.** From No. 48 the title was the **Ashton Chronicle.**

    MR*†; WCML†

114 Ashton-under-Lyne Co-operator [189-?] Manchester; m

    A   Gratis. (**Labour Annual,** 1897; Mitchell, 1905.)

115 Ashton-under-Lyne Workingmen's Co-operative Society **Record**
[19--?] Ashton-under-Lyne; m
    A   Gratis. Issued and edited by the Educational Committee
(International Directory of the Co-operative Press, 1909.)

116 Askern Turn Point. Askern
    A   Organ of the Askern Communist Pit Group. (R. G. Neville)

117 Aspirex (July 1914)–[1924?] ; m
    A   3d. (1924). National Association of Employment and Clerical
Officers. Succeeded by **Civil Service Argus,** when the Association became
the Ministry of Labour Staff Association. **(Whitley Bulletin,** [Aug. 1948].)

118 Ass, or **Weekly Beast of Burden** 1 (1 April 1826)–16 (15 July 1826);
w
    B   4d. Printed and published by G. Cowie and Company. Dedi-
cations to mechanics and labourers, expressing sympathy with them.
Comment on current affairs, often satirical. Articles signed 'The Ass'.
    EU; MP; O†; WCML†

119 Assistant Masters' Association; then Incorporated Association of
Assistant Masters in Secondary Schools. **Circular to Members**: 1 (July
1898)–59 (Nov. 1905); then b AMA: the **Journal** of the Incorporated
Association of Assistant Masters in Secondary Schools: I, 1 (Feb. 1906)–
; m; bi-m; m
    A   Gratis. The Association changed its name in 1905.
    C   b XXXII–(XLI*); L†; LIE b XXXIV–XLIII;* LU b I–XXIII; O
b XXXIII–   ; OTT b XIX–   ; the Association

120 Assistant Masters' **Year Book** 1922/3–43; a
    A   2s.6d. Incorporated Association of Assistant Masters in Second-
ary Schools.
    C   1937–43; L; O 1937, 1939–43

121 Associate 1 (1 Jan. 1829)–9 (1 Jan. 1830); then **Associate and
Co-operative Mirror**: 10 (1830)–12 (1830); irreg
    A   1d. Publisher: Cowie and Strange. Printer: W. Johnston.
Inspired by the original 'Benevolent Fund Association', a co-operative
venture set up by some working men in Brighton in 1827. To promote the
ideal and practice of co-operation.
    Bishopsgate Institute; LU† (w 10, 12)

122 Associate: Organ of the Brotherhood Association 1 (Feb. 1903)–?; q
    B   'The Brotherhood Association is a Propagandist Body formed to
further the ideals of the Co-operative Brotherhood Trust, Limited.' Printed
by George Frankland, 'The Fraternity Press'. A leaflet for communication
among members.
    ILP Nov. 1903; O(JJ)† 1–17 (Feb. 1907) (w 12)

Associate and Co-operative Mirror see **Associate, 1829–1830**

123 Associated Blacksmiths' and Ironworkers' Society of Great Britain and Ireland. **Quarterly Report** [18--?] –? Glasgow; q

    A

    L† ns 8 (1918 ['First quarterly report, 61st year'])

124 Associated Blacksmiths' Forge and Smithy Workers' Society. **Official Journal** [19--?] –1935; then **Anvil**: 1 (March 1936)–ns 12 (Dec. 1960). Glasgow; q

    A   Contents gradually expanded.

    GM Sept.–Dec. 1949; NU June 1954–60 (w Sept. 1960); TUC 1936–45; Amalgamated Society of Boilermakers, Shipwrights, Blacksmiths and Structural Workers, Newcastle [193-?] – (at present held by Angela Tuckett).

125 Associated Carpenters and Joiners. **Monthly Report** [18–?] –? [Glasgow?] ; m

    A   (R. W. Postgate, **The Builders' History**, London: National Federation of Building Trades Operatives, 1923.) Warwick U (MRC) 1872–6, 1880–5, 1910–11

126 Associated Ironmoulders of Scotland. **Monthly Report** I, [1875–1-919] –[1920?]. Glasgow; m

    A   Editorial, financial returns, correspondence etc.

    Bishopsgate Institute 1893–1920; LE† 1891–1918*; TUC 1912, 1914, 1918; Warwick U (MRC) 1875–1919

127 Associated Metalworkers' Society. **Quarterly Report** Jan. 1957– Manchester; q

    A

    The Society

128 Associated Shipwrights' Society. **Quarterly Report** [18–?] –?; q

    A

    TUC 92 (Jan./March 1905)–(July/Sept. 1907)

129 Association for Promoting the Repeal of the Taxes on Knowledge. **Gazette** 1 [185-?] –33 (May 1861); irreg

    C   Gratis. Published at the office of the Association. A record of the parliamentary and extra-parliamentary campaign of the Committee to effect the repeal of 'Taxes on Knowledge'. Association headed and patronised by MPs, public persons, publishers of literature for the working class, eg, Holyoake, Cassell, Charles Knight. Secretary: C. D. Collet.

    L† 21, 23–7, 29–31, 33

130 Association Notes I, 1 (Dec. 1916)–IV, (Dec. 1920)

    A   Association of Post Office Women Clerks.

    OW

131 Association of Assistant Masters. **Journal** 1 (April 1869)–2 (June 1869); q

A   6d. Publisher: Longmans, Green and Company. No. 1 states that the journal is 'specially intended to provide for the wants and to further the interests of Assistant Masters' who are overworked and underpaid. However, No. 2 contains purely scholastic matters.

L†

132 Association of Assistant Mistresses. **Journal** I, 1 (Spring 1950)–; 3-yr

A   A record of Association affairs, policy and interests.

LIE., Warwick UL 1973–; the Association

133 Association of Cine-Technicians. **Journal** I, 1 (May 1935)–II, 8 (Feb./March 1937); then **Cine-Technician**: III, 9 (April/May 1937)–XXII, 144 (Dec. 1956); then **Film and TV Technician**: XXIII, 145 (Jan. 1957)–   ; q; m; bi-m

A   9d. etc. Later, organ of the Association of cinematograph (Television) and Allied Technicians 'to provide a link between film technicians, provide an outlet for their views, help them in their work and benefit the Film Industry generally.'

C; E; FiP XVIII (1952)–   ; L; LFI; LSC; TUC 4 (1936)–   ; WdK

134 Association of Civil Service Designers and Draughtsmen. **Monthly Circular** [1946?]–[1948? 1949?] ; then **Right Angle**: 1949–?; m

A   Free. The **Right Angle** is the organ of the Society of Technical Civil Servants.

TUC 1946–8,* 1949–July 1970

135 Association of Engineering and Shipbuilding Draughtsmen. **Vacancy List** [19--?]–2004 (July 1963); then **DATA News**: 2005 (11 July 1963)–(Dec. 1971); then **TASS News**: (Jan. 1972)–   ; w

A   Originally mainly concerned with employment opportunites for members, it increasingly carried advice and news. The union became the Draughtsmens and Allied Technicians Association, then Amalgamated Union of Engineering Workers, Technical, Administrative and Supervisory Section.

TUC 1963–   ; the Union 1949–

136 Association of Engineering and Shipbuilding Draughtsmen, Coventry East Branch. **Newsletter** I, 1 [1960?]–1961; then Draughtsmen's and Allied Technicians' Association, Coventry East Branch. **Newsletter**: 1961–?; m

A

Warwick U (MRC) II, 3 (March), II, 9 (Sept. 1961)

Association of First Division Civil Servants. **Monthly Notes** see Association of First Division Civil Servants. **Occasional Notes**

137 Association of First Division Civil Servants. **Occasional Notes**
1946–48; then **Monthly Notes**: I, 1 (Nov. 1949)–XII, 3 (May/Aug. 1960);
then **FDA Association Notes**: XII, 4 (Sept./Nov. 1960)–XIV, 2 (Aug.
1962); then **FDA Monthly Notes**: XIV, 3 (Nov. 1962)–   ; irreg; m
    A   'concerned with domestic matters and is confidential to
members.'
    L 1949–   ; the Association

138 Association of HM Inspectors of Taxes. **Quarterly Record** 1904–   ; q
    A   'mainly professional in character.' 'Supplemented by news-
sheets issued at more or less regular intervals.' (**Whitley Bulletin**, Nov.
1947, p. 172.)
    The Association

139 Association of Local Government Financial Officers. **Journal**
1920–[19–?]; then ALGFO **Journal**: [19–?]–   ; q
    A   For members only.
    L XVII (Jan. 1966)–

140 Association of Officers of the Ministry of Labour. **Journal** 1924–
[London?]; m
    A   Free to members.
    The Association (w 1)

141 Association of Professional Fire Brigade Officers. **Journal** [c1920]; m
    A   6d. (Mitchell, 1920.)

142 Association of Scientific Workers. Leeds and District Branch. **Bulletin**
1 [1944?] –?; Leeds
    A   No. 1 was a single duplicated sheet.
    LdP† 2 (Oct. 1944)

143 Association of Teachers in Technical Institutions. **Journal** I, 1 (April
1908)–III, 4 (Oct. 1910); then **Technical Journal**: IV, 1 (Jan.
1911)–XXXIX, 9 (Nov. 1947); q
    A   Gratis. Published by the Association, to inform members more
closely of its work.
    AbN VIII–*; BP XII–; L†; LIE 1949–*; LSC 1924–

144 Association of Tutors in Adult Education and Co-operative Wholesale
Society. Joint Consultative Committee. **Economic Information** 1 (Oct.
1933)–4 (Oct. 1934). Manchester; q
    A   Published by the Co-operative Wholesale Society. 'Designed to
provide teachers and students with up-to-date information about the
consumers' Co-operative Movement.'
    L†

Assurance Agents' **Chronicle** see Assurance Agents' Union **Chronicle,
Advocate and Critic**

Assurance Agents' Review see Assurance Superintendents' and Agents'
Review

145 Assurance Agents' Union Chronicle, Advocate and Critic 1 (9 April
1889)–LXXV, 12 (Dec. 1963). Manchester (I–IV); London; Manchester;
w; m
    A   1d. Official organ of the National Union of Life Assurance
Agents, later of the National Amalgamated Union of Life Assurance
Workers. Rival of the **Life Assurance Agents Journal**, the original official
organ, which, it was claimed, no longer represented the members, as the
directors had secured it for their own ends. Later entitled **Assurance
Agents' Chronicle**.
    L(Col)† (w 1894): LCI 50–*

Assurance Review see Assurance Superintendents' and Agents' Review

146 Assurance Superintendents' and Agents' Review 1 (15 March 1888)–9
(15 Nov. 1888); then **Assurance Agents' Review**: 10 (15 Dec. 1888)–261
(15 Dec. 1909); then **Assurance Review**: [262 (15 Jan. 1910?)]–613 (15
Dec. 1939). Wolverhampton; m
    C   2d. Publisher and proprietor: Wm. Henry Hilton, later
Assurance Review Co. 'A monthly magazine devoted to the interests of the
outside staff of Assurance Companies and Collecting Friendly Societies.'
In opposition to the **Life Assurance Agents' Journal**. 'We are
conscientiously of the opinion that trade unionism is completely
inapplicable to Industrial Assurance Agency.' In 1912 sub-titled: An
Independent Monthly Journal Devoted to Assurance Generally, and the
Elucidation and Criticism of the Affairs of Public Companies'.
    L(Col)† (w 1892, 1894, 1910, 1911)

147 Aston Forward: the Monthly Organ of the Aston Divisional Labour
Party I, 1 (April 1946)–II, 13 (July 1947). Birmingham; m
    B   2d. Editor: Jim Meadows, Divisional Agent; Contributor:
Woodrow Wyatt.
    BP†·

148 Asylum News: the Journal of the Asylum Workers' Association I, 1
(Jan. 1897)–XXIII, 4 (Dec. 1919). Lancaster (Jan. 1897–Feb. 1898);
Richmond, Surrey; m
    A   1d; 2d. Editor: G. E. Shuttleworth. The Association was
founded in 1895 to improve the status of asylum nurses and attendants.
    L(Col)†

149 'At Your Service': the Journal of the Doncaster and District Branch of
the National Association of Local Government Officers I [1948?]–?
Doncaster
    A   Later, National and Local Government Officers' Association.
Reproduced from typewriting.
    L VI, 1 (March 1953)–IX, 2 (July 1956)

150 Athro: Cylchgrawn dau-fisol Undeb Athrawon Cymreig I, 1 (Jan. 1928)– . Wrexham etc.; bi-m; m (1937–)

   A   6d. Union of Welsh Teachers.

   AbU;* BnU; CrU I–XVIII; L XXVI–XXX (w XXVIII, 42–8); SwU I–XVIII, 2

151 Attack: an Organ of Working Class Thought and Challenge I, 1 (May 1936). Glasgow

   B   1d. Edited, published and printed by Guy Aldred on behalf of the United Socialist Movement. Launched against the 'betrayals' of the Labour Party, the Communist Party and their support for the League of Nations. Also in opposition to the 'sanctionist trade unions'.

   L(Col)†

152 Austrian Socialist News: London Information of the Austrian Socialists in Britain Feb. 1940–41?; then London-Information of the Austrian Socialists in Great Britain: 1942?–(15 April 1946); fortn

   B   Published by the London Bureau of the Austrian Socialists. During 1942 published alternately in English and German. Reports news about events in Austria and about activities of Austrian Socialists in Great Britain.

   O1944–46*; ONC† 1941–46*

153 Autonomie: Anarchistisch-Communistisches Organ 1 (6 Nov. 1886)–211 (22 April 1893); w

   B   1d. In German. Printed by The International Publishing Company. Printed and published by R. Gunderson. Anarchist. Includes an international review of socialist and working-class events.

   L(Col)†; LE 1886–8

154 Auxiliary Postman I, 1 (March 1912)–II, 4 (May 1913)

   A   1d. Published by H. Hulland. Official journal of the National Union of Auxiliary Postmen. Edited by Thomas F. Easthope, President of the Union. Founded by H. Hulland, an auxiliary postman. See themselves as a branch of the Civil Service drive for Unionism.

   L(Col)†

155 Avenue: a Monthly Magazine Devoted to Association, Education, and Social Progress I, 1 (Oct. 1896)–I, 8 (May 1897); m

   B   3d. Publisher: Simpkin, Marshall. Editors: Phineas Briggs, Bradford, Owen Greening. News and articles on Co-operation at home and abroad, fiction, women's page, children's page. Contributors: G. J. Holyoake, Margaret Macmillan.

   LE†; O†

156 Aviation Voice [196-?] –? Manchester; q

   B   6d. Workers' Northern Publishing Society. One of the 'Voice' series of newspapers. (Mitchell, 1965.)

157 Ayrcobra I [1952?] –? Ayr
   A   National Association of Local Government Officers, later,
National and Local Government Officers' Association. Reproduced from
typewriting.
      L II, 1 (July 1953)–IV, 4 (April 1956)

158 Ayrshire Democrat 1 (1839)–8 (1840). Paisley
   B   Chartist newspaper (A. Wilson, **The Chartist Movement in
Scotland**, 1970, p. 183.)

159 Ayrshire Examiner July 1838–Nov. 1839. Kilmarnock
   B   'a Chartist newspaper conducted . . . by J. R. Robertson . . . the
first of the Scottish Chartist journals outside of Glasgow.' Published by
James Quigley. (Cowan.) 'Present **Ayrshire Examiner** owes its existence
almost solely to him [ie Hugh Craig] as well as the **Ayrshire Reformer**.'
(**Operative**, II, 17 [24 Feb. 1839].)

Ayrshire Forward see **New Forward**

160 Ayrshire Reformer and **Kilmarnock Gazette** 1833. Kilmarnock
   B   Radical. 'Now notable chiefly as Dr John Taylor's
stepping-stone towards the Glasgow **Liberator** and Chartism' (Cowan).

161 BDC Worker: the Paper of the BDC Workers 1 [Nov. 1931?] –?
Manchester
   A   Duplicated Communist Party factory paper at British Dyestuffs
Corporation (now ICI, Blockley Works, Manchester).
      WCML 2 (18 Dec. 1931), 3 (15 Jan. 1932)

162 BFYC: a Year's Work I (1931)–XII (1942); then **Work in Wartime**:
XIII, 1943/4–1953/4; a
   A   British Federation of Co-operative Youth, later British
Federation of Young Co-operators.
      L† 1942–54

163 BMA News 1966–   ; bi-m
   A   Free. '**BMA News** is published by the British Medical
Association as a contribution to discussion, particularly of medical
politics, and as a medium of expression'.
      Department of Health and Social Security Library. 2 years only kept

BW Review see **Leeds Monthly**

164 Bacup Report [194–?] Bacup; q
   B   Free. Labour Party (Labour Party. **Your own Journal**, 1948.)

Bagshot and Egham Clarion see **Egham Clarion**

165 Baker [192-?]

    A   National Minority Movement (National Minority movement conference reports.)

166 Bakers' Record and General Advertiser 1864–1954?; w

    C   2d. Printed for the proprietors by Peter McCallum and Company. Published by the News Agents Publishing Company A full-size newspaper for master bakers and operatives. Trade news and general news. Reports meetings of the Master Bakers' Association, and the Amalgamated Society [of operative bakers]. The editor is independent but recommends the paper to the support of the Union. Lays open its columns to contributions from operative bakers and unions in the provinces. Advocates conciliation. In 1889 sub-titled: 'The only national weekly organ of baking trade recognised by employers and operatives'. In later years given over to trade interests, and no longer observes the separate identity of the operatives.

    L(Col)†. IX, 275, (10 July 1869)–4743 (30 Sept. 1954)

167 Bakery Trades Journal: a Quarterly Devoted to the Interests of All Bakery Operatives I, 1 (28 Jan 1936)–? Dublin; q (1936); m (1937–Oct. 1938); q (1939)

    A   3d. Irish Bakers', Confectioners', and Allied Workers' Amalgamated Union. At first run from the Dublin No. 1 Branch, then recognised by the National Organisation and began to publish news from branches. Officially adopted by the National Union in October 1938. Contents reflect the aim of disseminating the idea of education and culture through the trade union movement. 'Along with trade items, general literaty matter, including articles, poems, short stories and other features will appear in its pages. Tendentious matter, such as criticism of the Union's Officials etc., will not be published.' Also includes news of workers' education, and political and economic articles.

    L(Col)† I, 1–IV, 4 (Oct./Dec. 1939).

Bakery Worker see **Journeyman Bakers' Magazine**

168 Balance [189–?]–? Edinburgh

    B   Issued by the Socialist movement in Edinburgh, sometime in the 1890s? (**Labour Standard**, [5 Oct. 1929].)

169 Balham and Tooting Citizen 1 (Feb. 1933)–78 (Sept. 1939); m

    A   Published by London and Royal Arsenal Co-operative Societies. L(Col)

170 Ballot 1 (2 Jan. 1831)–97 (4 Nov. 1832), w

    B   7d. Editor: Thomas Wakley before becoming Radical MP for Finsbury. A general paper, radical reformist, reporting meetings of Political Unions and of National Union of the Working Classes. Correspondence columns. Incorporated **Political Letter** (qv).

    L(Col)†; 0 2

171 Banba Review 1 (1962)–   . Dublin; m
   A   Irish National Union of Vintners, Grocers and Allied Trades'
Assistants.
   University College, Dublin

172 Banbury Co-operative Record 1871–94. Banbury
   A   Editors: Thomas Proverbs, John Butcher, and William Bunton,
bookseller and newsagent, Owenite and Chartist. 'It is claimed that this
was the first local Co-operative Journal introduced into the Movement . . .'
(W. H. Lickorish, 'Our Jubilee story' or fifty Years of Co-operation in
Banbury & the Neighbourhood, 1916, pp. 51–5.) Replaced by **The
Wheatsheaf.**
   Banbury PL

173 Bandstaff I, 1 (July 1953)–I, 8 (Feb. 1955). Bolton
   A   National and Local Government Officers' Association, Bolton
and District Branch.
   L†

174 Bank Clerks' Review I, 1 ([registration issue] , May 1914); I, 1, (July
1914)–II, 11 (Sept. 1915)
   A   2d. Official organ of the National Association of Bank Clerks,
representing an estimated 120,000 bank clerks throughout the United
Kingdom.
   L(Col)†

175 Bank Officer: the Official Organ of the Bank Officers' Guild I, 1 (Aug.
1919)–([unnumbered] Winter 1969); superseded by **NUBE News**; 1 (Jan.
1970)–   ; m; q; m
   A   2d. Sub-title became: **'Journal of the National Union of Bank
Employees'.**
   C   V–VII*, VIII–; L†; LE; NU May 1955–   ; O VII, 6–; ONC
1960–; the Union; Warwick U (MRC)

176 Banner [19--?] –?; m
   B   Hounslow Independent Labour Party.
   ILP Aug. 1936

177 Banner. 1962?–. Banstead
   A   National and Local Government Officers' Association, Banstead
Branch. Reproduced from typewriting.
   L 1962–

178 Baptist Pioneer and Poor Man's Friend [I] (1, July 1846)–[I], 5
(Nov. 1846); then **Christian Pioneer and Poor Man's Friend**: [1, 6 (Dec.
1846)–XXXVII, 450 (Dec. 1883); m
   C   ½d. Editor: Joseph Foulkes Winks. A Baptist magazine specially
priced to reach 'poor congregations', ' the poor of our people'. For the
'cottage homes of England'.
   C   [I], 6–XXXVII (XIX*); L†

179 Bargeman: the Magazine of the Bargemen's Brotherhood 1 (Feb. 1914)–III, 1 (June 1916). Sittingbourne

    C   Editor: Rev. Parry Evans. To promote the spiritual welfare of bargemen.

    L†

180 Barmaid 1 (17 Dec. 1891)–6 (21 Jan. 1892); w

    C   1d. Illustrated weekly produced by a group of middle-class sympathisers to promote 'the interests' of the 80,000–90,000 (estimated) barmaids of the United Kingdom.

    L(Col)† ; O(JJ)† 1

181 Barman and Barmaid: a Newspaper Devoted to the Interests of Public House Employees 1 (5 July 1879)–5 (2 Aug. 1879), [ns], 1 (29 May 1880)–5 (26 June 1880); w

    B   1d. Published by the proprietor, 7 Bolt Court, Fleet Street, London EC4. Edited by 'Caerau'. An organ designed to express and make known the grievances of public house employees. Also 'gossip' and job advertisements. (The new series is primarily 'gossip'.)

    L(Col)† O i]

182 Barnet, Boreham Wood, Elstree and Hatfield Citizen 1, 1 [1952?]–37 (Jan. 1956); irreg

    B   Issued by the Political Committee of the London Co-operative Society. Preceded by Barnet Parliamentary Constituency Citizen

    L(Col) 16 (Jan. 1954)–37

183 Barnet East Bulletin [194-?] East Barnet, Hertfordshire; m

    B   Labour Party. Duplicated. (Labour Party. **Your own Journal**, 1948.)

184 Barnet Labour Review [194-?] Barnet, Hertfordshire; m

    B   Labour Party. Duplicated. (Labour Party. **Your own Journal**, 1948.)

185 Barnet Parliamentary Constituency Citizen ns 1 (Nov. 1950)–16 (March 1952); m

    B   Issued by the Political Committee of the London Co-operative Society.

    L(Col)

186 Barnsley Main Spark [193-?] Barnsley

    A   Communist factory paper printed and published by the militant miners at Barnsley Main. (H. Wilde,'The Factory Paper'. **Communist Review** III, 4 [April 1931], pp. 140–4.)

187 Barnsley Schoolmaster I, 1 (Oct. 1964)–? Barnsley
    A   Issued by the Barnsley Branch of the National Association of Schoolmasters.
        LdP† 1–2 (Dec. 1965)

Barons Court Citizen see **South Hammersmith Citizen**

188 Barrow Guardian 1 (24 Sept. 1910)–2118 (28 june 1947). Barrow-in-Furness; w
    B   2d. (1932). Began publication as an organ of the Barrow Labour Party. Later its allegiance appears to vary. Merged with the **Barrow News**.
        Barrow PL; L(Col) 209 (21 Sept. 1912)–

189 Barrow ILP Journal 1 (10 March 1895)–[28 July 1895?]. Barrow-in-Furness; w
    B   Free. Printed for the proprietors by T. Hull. Editor: 'Nemo Vulgus', then 'Henri'.
        AbU 1–19 (w15) (microfilm); O(JJ) 1–19 (w15)

191 Barrow Pioneer: the Official Organ of the Labour Representation Committee 1 [19–5?] –? Barrow-in-Furness; m
    B   1d. Later, organ of the Barrow Labour Party. Published by Barrow-in-Furness Co-operative Printing and Publishing Society (No. 8). Local news, women's column.
        Barrow PL (Sept. 1905)–(Jan. 1908), (Oct. 1908); LabP† 34 (Oct. 1908); ONC† 8 (Feb. 1906)

192 Barry Herald, Conducted in Democratic and Labor [sic] Interests 1 (21 Feb. 1896)–3516 (21 June 1962). Barry; w
    B   1d; ½d; 1d. Published and owned by the Barry Herald Newspaper Publishing Co-operative Society Ltd. Partly in Welsh. 'The purpose of the paper shall be the furtherance of Democratic and Labour Principles . . . So far the bulk of the Shares has been taken up by the working men of the district . . .' Founded by socialists, Trade Unionists, and Radicals, the paper loses much of its Labour emphasis in later years. Incorporated with **Barry and District News**.
        L(Col)† (w 1897, 1912)

193 Basildon Brentwood Citizen [1950?] –?; m
    B   Issued by the Political Committee of the London Co-operative Society.
        L(Col) 63 (July 1955)–67 (Nov. 1955)

194 Basildon Urban District Circular [1959?] –? Billericay
    A   National and Local Government Officers' Association, Basildon Urban District Branch. Reproduced from typewriting.
        L 4 (Jan. 1960)–

195 Bass Drum: the Official Gazette of the NFPM 1 (March 1912)–13 (March 1913); m
    A   1d. National Federation of Professional Musicians.
    L†

196 Bath: Voice of Bath Labour [194-?] Bath; m
    B   Labour Party. Duplicated. (Labour Party. **Your own Journal**, 1948.)

197 Bath NALGO Branch Magazine I, 1 [1962?] –I (3, Jan. 1963); then b Mosaic. I, 1 (1963)–? Bath
    A   National and Local Government Officers' Association.
    L† I, 2 (Sept. 1962), I, 3 b I, 3 (May 1963)–

198 Battersea South News Letter [194-?)] ; m
    B   Labour Party. Duplicated. (Labour Party. **Your own Journal**, 1948.)

199 Battersea Vanguard [c 1908]
    B?   1d. (**Reformers' Year Book**, 1908.)

200 Battle I, 1 (May 1938)–I, 4 (Feb. 1939). Heaton Chapel, Stockport
    A   1d. Published by Fairey Aviation Shop Stewards' Committee. Discontinued in favour of **The New Propellor** which gave national coverage.
    WCML†

201 Bayonet, Being the Official Organ of the National Association of Discharged Sailors and Soldiers I, 1 (Sept. 1920)–I, 5(Jan. 1921); m
    A   2d. Published by the Association. Disclaims connection with any political party or group. Especially opposed to the National Union of Ex-Service Men. Aims: to safeguard the interests of dependants, assist cases of hardship, secure redress for grievances regarding pensions etc., educate public opinion that it is the State's duty to care for dependants and disabled ex-servicemen, seek to arrange employment. Contains news from headquarters, and from branches and divisions, through lack of practical support.
    L(Col)†

    Be and Cee see **NALGO Newsletter** [Brentford and Chiswick Branch]

202 Be–Em 1962?– . Hemel Hempstead
    A   National and Local Government Officers' Association, Hemel Hempstead and District Branch.
    L1962–

203 Beacon: a Weekly Journal of Politics and Literature 1 (26 Oct. 1853)–12 (9 Jan. 1854); w

    B   1½d. Published by J. P. Crantz. Printed by S. Taylor then by Kenny, Finch and Company Supports universal suffrage, 'the claims of labour', republicanism of continental movements. Apparently associated with Fraternal Democrats. Supported workers during Preston 'lock out'.

    Bishopsgate Institute†; MP†; NwA (Cowen Coll.); O(JJ)1–2†

204 Beacon [18--?]; w

    B   See account by Francis Place in **Trades' Newspaper** and **Mechanics' Weekly Journal**, (9 July 1826).

205 Beam: Magazine of the BEA, Midlands Division Branch I, 1 (Jan. 1954)– ; m

    A   National and Local Government Officers' Association. From April 1966 entitled **Beam News**.

    L†

206 Beam: the Official Publication of the Birmingham and District Electricity Branch of NALGO 1966– . Birmingham

    A   National and Local Government Officers' Association. Reproduced from typewriting.

    L†

Beam News see **Beam**: Magazine of the BEA, Midlands Division Branch

207 Bebington Citizen. Bebington

    A   Issued jointly by the Bebington Trades Council and the Bebington Co-operative Party. Incorporating **Bebington Review**.

    L(Col)† ns 1 (Aug. 1949)–25 (Nov. 1951)

208 Bebington Review [194-?] Wirral; m

    B   Free. Labour Party. (Labour Party. **Your own Journal**, 1948.)

Beckenham and Penge Discussion see **Penge Discussion**

209 Beckenham Labour Chronicle [194-?]; m

    B   2d. Labour Party. (Labour Party. **Your own Journal**, 1948.)

210 Becontree, Chadwell Heath and Dagenham Citizen 1 (April 1930)–112 (mid-Aug. 1939); m

    A   Gratis. Published London Co-operative Society Ltd. Local edition in the Co-operative 'Citizen' series.

    L(Col)†

211 Beddington and Wallington Monthly Notice [194-?] Wallington, Surrey; m

    B   Labour Party. Duplicated. (Labour Party. **Your own Journal**, 1948.)

212 Bedford and District NALGO Branch Magazine I, 1 (Jan. 1953)—[195-? 196-?]; then **Pilgrim**: Magazine of the Bedford Borough & District Branch, NALGO: [195-? 196-?]— . Bedford

A   National and Local Government Officers' Association. Reproduced from typewriting.

L Jan. 1953—9 (Sept. 1953), 1962—

Bee see Keighley **Co-operative Bee**

213 Bee 1 (22 Dec. 1832)—2 (29 Dec. 1832). Liverpool; w

B   1d. Published and edited by John Finch. Other editors: M. J. Falvey and Rev. C. B. Dunn. 'A radical miscellany that advocates Owenite co-operative doctrines, including the need for a Labour Exchange Bank in Liverpool' (Wiener).

L 1; MP; O 1

214 Bee Hive 1 (19 Oct. 1861)—794 (30 Dec. 1876); then **Industrial Review, Social and Political**: 795 (6 Jan. 1877)—898 (28 Dec. 1878); w

A then B.   2d. except for Feb.—Dec. 1870 when it came close to C and was entitled **Penny Bee Hive**. Published by the Trades Newspaper Company, subsidised by various trade unions. Founded and later edited by George Potter 'in the interests of the working classes'. First editors: G. Troup and then Robert Hartwell. Editor in 1870: H. Solly. Regarded as official organ of London Trades Council until September 1865; and for a while British organ of the First International. Advocated universal suffrage, supported Reform League and more particularly the London Workingmen's Association's, 'rights of labour'. Forum for discussion of Labour issues. In 1870s carried regular articles by Lloyd Jones. Peak circulation 8,000, March/April 1865.

Bishopsgate Institute 1870—6; GU 436—898*; L(Col) 51—898; LE No. 51—1870 (photocopy); ONC (microfilm of L(Col) holding)

215 Beehive: London Co-operative Society Staff Magazine [c1920]—[195-?]; m

A   Gratis. Superseded by **Now**.

L XXXIV, 10 (Oct. 1955)—XXXV, 10 (Oct. 1956)

216 Behold! Branch Magazine of Beverley and District NALGO 1964—

A   National and Local Government Officers' Association. Reproduced from typewriting.

L

217 Belfast Citizen: a Journal Advocating Labour, Temperance, and Social Progress [c1896]—? Belfast; m

A   1d. Published by the Trades Council. (**Labour Annual**, 1898; Mitchell, 1900.)

218 Belfast Co-operative Advocate: the Journal of the Belfast Co-operative Trading Association 1 (Jan. 1830)–? Belfast

    A

    LDW

219 Belfast Labour Chronicle: the Organ of the Belfast Trades Council and Labour Representation Committee [1904?]–? Belfast; m

    B   1d. Printed for the publishers by John Adams. Local and national concerns, short articles, news, poem.

    ONC† I, 9 (June 1905 [imperfect])

220 Belper Recorder [194-?] Belper; m

    A   1d. Labour Party. (Labour Party. **Your own Journal**, 1948.)

221 Belpost: Official Organ of the Belfast Amalgamated Branch, Union of Post Office Workers I (1962–6?) Belfast; m

    A   Reproduced from typewriting. Editor: W. Dunlop. News of union, conditions of employment, humour, verse.

    ONC† 29, [IV, 5] (May 1965), 38, [V, 3] (March/April 1966); TUC 1962–6

Ben Bull or the Benwell Bulletin see **Benwell Bulletin**

222 Benefit Societies' Herald I, 1 (Jan. 1866)–I, 2 (Feb. 1866); m

    B   1d. Printed and published by Sarah Johns. Editor: Robert Desborough. News of benefit societies of all kinds, co-operative, trade union, and other working-class bodies. 'Benefit societies are the pride of British Working Men . . .'

    L; O†

223 Benefit Societies' Magazine, and Mechanics' and Labourers' Adviser I (22 Feb. 1834); ns 1 (1 Nov.–1 Dec. 1834); m?; fortn

    C   3d; 1d. Printer: W. Clowes; J. Jacques. Publisher? (No. 1): R. Groombridge. 'Serves as an organ of communication for the Benefit Societies by publishing extensive information about their activities as well as correspondence relating to them' (Wiener).

    BP ns 1; O 1; ONC† 1

224 Benefit Societies' Penny Magazine 1 (17 Nov. 1832); w

    B   1d. Publisher: George Berger under the direction of a Benefit Societies Committee. 'Its primary aim is to strengthen the laws relating to Benefit Societies' (Wiener).

    BP; O(JJ)

225 Bentley Turnplate [193-?]

    A   Organ of the Bentley militant miners. (**Daily Worker**, [20 May 1932].)

226 Benwell Bulletin [1] (Easter 1951–[18] (Summer 1955). then **Ben Bull or the Benwell Bulletin**: 19 (Autumn 1955)–(Winter 1957). Sunbury; q

    A   National Association of Local Government Officers, later National and Local Government Officers' Association. Sunbury Branch. Reproduced from typewriting.

    L†

227 Berkshire Co-operative Leader I, 1 (Dec. 1939)–I, 7 (June 1940). Reading; m

    A   Free. Published by the Reading Co-operative Society, Ltd. and printed by the Co-operative Press, Ltd. London. One of the 'Citizen' series.

    L(Col)†

228 Bermondsey Citizen 1 (April 1961)

    A   Published by the Co-operative Press. One of the 'Citizen' series.

    L(Col)†

229 Bermondsey Labour Magazine 1 (Oct. 1923)–184 (Sept. 1940); ns 1 (Nov. 1946)–?; m

    B   1d. Labour Party.

    BeP

230 Bermondsey Labour News 1 (1920)–22 (1922); m

    B   Labour Party.

    BeP

231 Berthold's Political Handkerchief 1 (3 Sept. 1831)–10 (5 Nov. 1831); w

    B   4d. Published, printed, edited by Henry Berthold. 'A working-class newspaper that is printed on cotton to evade the payment of the stamp duty. It strongly endorses the Reform Bill, but advocates the use of "physical power" if sufficient concessions are not made to the working classes' (Wiener).

    E 1; HO 64/17 1; L Place Coll. Set 70 2; L(Col); LU 4; O 1–4, 6; O(JJ) 1–2, 4

Bethnal Green and Hackney South Citizen see **Bethnal Green Citizen**

232 Bethnal Green Citizen ns 1 (Jan. 1947)–129 (July/Aug. 1958). then **Bethnal Green and Hackney South Citizen**: 130 (Sept. 1958)–164 (March 1963); m

    B   Gratis. Issued by the Political Committee of the London Co-operative Society.

    L(Col)

Better Business see **Co-operative Reference Library. Bulletin**

233 Between Ourselves: ILP Internal Bulletin [19--?] —?; bi-m?
    B   Independent Labour Party
    GU, Broady Coll. Nov.–Dec. 1948, Nov.–Dec. 1950, May–June
1951

234 Between Ourselves I [1949?] —[1963?] ; then **Catalyst**: 1964— .
Ewell; Epsom
    A   National Association of Local Government Officers, later,
National and Local Government Officers' Association. Reproduced from
typewriting.
    L V, 1 (May 1953)–

235 Betwixt: Midland NFS Report 1 (1941)–14 (Oct./Nov. 1942).
Birmingham; m
    A   1d. Published by. The Fire Brigades Union, Birmingham Office.
Trade union reports, correspondence.
    BP† 10 (May, 1942)–14

236 Bexley Citizen ns 1 (Oct. 1949)–27 (March 1953); irreg
    B   Issued by the Political Purposes Committee of the Royal
Arsenal Co-operative Society.
    L(Col)

237 Bexley News I, 1 (Feb. 1947–I (30, Aug. 1949). Bexleyheath; m
    B   1d. Bexley Divisional Labour Party.
    N. Todd, c/o Dept. of History, Univ. of Lancaster; A. Scutt, 50
Normanhurst Avenue, Bexleyheath; Warwick U (MRC)

238 Bialostoczanin, Wydawnictwo Polskiej Partyi Socyalistycznej (**The
Bialystok-Man**, Publication of the Polish Socialist Party). 1899–May 1905.
London
    B
    L* (mislaid)

239 Big Flame: Merseyside's Rank and File Newspaper 1 (26 Feb.
1970)–[1972?]; [ns], 1 (June 1972)–. Wallasey; Liverpool; frequency
varies
    B   6d.; 3d. First series claims it is not run by a group or party, but
will be written and run by its readers. No sectarian allegiance to the
Labour Party, Communist Party, or any of the 'ideologically differing
trotskyist groups which go to make up the Left'. The second series is
sub-titled: 'Merseyside's Revolutionary Socialist Newspaper'; '**Big Flame**
consists of groups of militants working with a common approach at Fords,
Standards, in the committees etc.'
    LvP† 1–7, [ns] *

240 Big Stick: a Journal of Industrial Unionism Voicing the View-Point of the Rank and File in Factory, Field, Ship, Shop and Job I, 1 (1 Oct. 1920)–I, 2 (15 Oct. 1920); fortn
    A   1d. Published and edited by Tom Walsh, Secretary of the National Federation of Shop Stewards. Printed at Agenda Press.
    L(Col)†

241 Billericay Citizen; m; irreg
    A   Issued by the Political Committee of the London Co-operative Society. One of the 'Citizen' series.
    L(Col) ns 1 (July 1949)–62 (June 1955); ns 1 (Oct. 1957)–26 (June/July 1964); LabP June/July 1964

242 Bird's Eye View [19--?] –?
    A   Union of Post Office Workers, Western Post Office. (W. Dunlop, 'Local Journals', Belpost, IV, 5 [May 1965])

243 Birkbeck Magazine, Conducted by Members of the London Mechanics' Institution I, 1 (May 1852)–I, 3 (July 1852)
    A
    L (holding destroyed)

244 Birkenhead Citizen: Official Organ of the Birkenhead Labour and Co-operative Movement ns 1 (Aug. 1949)–7 (April 1950); irreg
    B   One of the 'Citizen' series.
    L(Col)†

245 Birkenhead Labour Bulletin [194-?] m
    B   1d. Labour Party. Duplicated. (Labour Party. **Your own Journal**, 1948.)

246 Birkenhead Labour Monthly 1 (Nov. 1896)–? Birkenhead; m
    B   ½d. Printed for Birkenhead Independent Labour Party. Localised edition of a newspaper launched in 1896 by Allen Clarke.
    AbU Nov., Dec. 1896 (microfilm); O(JJ) Nov., Dec. 1896

247 Birmingham and District Trades Journal March 1896–June 1899. Birmingham; m
    A   Published by the Secretary of the Birmingham Trades Council, S. G. Middleton. Editor: Allan Grainger. '. . . it mirrored rather than inspired the movement' (J. Corbett, **The Birmingham Trades Council 1866–1966**, 1966, pp. 174–5.)

248 Birmingham Argus 1818–19. Birmingham; w
    B   7d. Printed and edited by George Ragg, Vice-President of the Radical Union Society (prosecuted 1819). (W. H. Wickwar, **The Struggle for the Freedom of the Press 1819–1832**, Allen & Unwin, 1928, pp. 108–9. Also in Appendix to Asa Briggs, 'Press and public in early 19th-century Birmingham', **Dugdale Society Occasional Papers**, 8, 1949.)
    L(Col) 3 (31 Oct. 1818), (21 Nov. 1818 [incomplete]), (16 Jan. 1819 [incomplete])

249 Birmingham Citizen ns 1 (Jan./Feb. 1955)–30 (Dec. 1963.
Birmingham; irreg
    B   Issued by the Birmingham and District Co-operative Party.
    L(Col)

250 Birmingham Co-operative Citizen I, 1 (Dec. 1934)–? Birmingham
    B
    L(Col) I, 1

251 Birmingham Co-operative Herald 1 (1 April 1829)–19 (1 Oct. 1830).
London; m
    B   1d. Published by Cowie and Strange. Printed by William Talbot.
Edited by William Pare. Details the progress of working-class co-operative
societies. Articles on the theory of co-operation, causes of social distress
and their remedy in co-operation.
    Bishopsgate Institute†; BP (photocopy); LU

252 Birmingham District Commonwealth 1 (Jan. 1922)–9 (Oct. 1922).
Birmingham; m
    A   1d. Printed and published for the Birmingham and District
Co-operative Party. Reissued in 1930 as **The Deritend Commonwealth**
(qv).
    BP†

253 Birmingham Inspector 1 (4 Jan. 1817)–16 (23 Aug. 1817).
Birmingham; fortn
    B   4d. Printer, publisher, editor: W. Hawkes Smith. Organ of
radical reform in Birmingham. Supports Hampden Club and 'general
suffrage'. George Edmunds, leading reformer, a frequent contributor.
    BP; L†; LU

Birmingham Journal see Birmingham Trades Council. **Journal**

Birmingham Journal see **Birmingham Journal and General Advertiser**

254 Birmingham Journal and General Advertiser 1 (4 June 1825)–2050
(19 Nov. 1859); then **Birmingham Journal**: 2051 (26 Nov. 1859)–2530
(13 Feb. 1869). Birmingham; w
    B. 1830–9.   4½d. In 1830s the unofficial organ of the Birmingham
Political Union and under the editorship of R. K. Douglas supported the
early phase of the Chartist movement, withdrawing in 1839 to become a
moderate reforming and commercial newspaper. Incorporated with the
Birmingham Daily Post.
    L(Col)†

255 Birmingham Labour Exchange Gazette 1 (16 Jan. 1833)–5 (9 Feb.
1833). Birmingham; w
    B   Publisher: W. Cooper. Printer: Thomas Wood. Editor: William
Pare. Promoted Owenite scheme of equitable labour exchanges as solution
to the errors in society.
    BP†, LU†

256 Birmingham Trades Council. **Journal** I, 1 (Oct. 1946)–I, 12 (Oct. 1947); then **Birmingham Journal**: Organ of the Birmingham Trades Council: II, 13 (Nov. 1947)–IX, 161 (April 1960); then **Journal**: IX, 162 (May 1960)– . Birmingham; m

    A   First published as a magazine, then in newspaper format. An open forum for opinion of trade unions and Labour. Reports of trade union, trades council, and political meetings.

       BP†; ONC 1956–

257 Birmingham West Labour News [194-?] Hockley, Birmingham; q

    B   Free. Labour Party. (Labour Party. **Your own Journal**, 1948.)

258 Birmingham Workman's Times 1 (6 June 1890)–17 (26 Sept. 1890). Birmingham; w

    B   Then merged in **Workman's Times** (qv).

    L(Col)

259 Black Cat: a Socialist Paper for the District 1895–? Dundee; m

    B   1d. (**Labour Annual**, 1896.)

260 Black Dwarf I, 1 (29 Jan. 1817)–XII, 21 (Dec. 1824); w

    B   4d; 6d. Edited, printed and published by Thomas Wooler. One of the most important unstamped ultra-radical periodicals. Advocated universal suffrage; a consistent antagonist of 'Old Corruption'.

       BP; BdP i–IX; EU I–II; L; LE I–IV; LU I–V, VII; LUC I, II*, III; O; NwP; MP I–III, 49; ONC I, II, IV, VII, IX, X; Greenwood reprint and microfiche: microfiche distributed in Britain and Europe by the Harvester Press Ltd

261 Black Dwarf Pre-issue, May Day, 1968; XIII, 1 (1 June 1968)–XIV, 37 (5 Sept. 1970); fortn

    B   2s., 1s. 6d., 2s. Supposedly in continuation of the periodical of 1817–24. Editor: Tariq Ali, revolutionary Socialist.

       L; LE*; O

262 Blackburn Labour Journal 1 (Oct. 1897)–118 (Aug. 1907?) Blackburn; m

    B   Gratis. Published: Labour Educational League. Editor: Luke Bates (1904–6).

       Blackburn PL† 4 (Jan. 1898)–(Aug. 1907*); L(Col) 4 (Jan. 1898)–118 (Aug. 1907) (w 94, 99, 100, 105, 106, 109, 110) (microfilm); ONC 4–118* (microfilm)

263 Blackburn Labour Monthly 1 (Oct. 1896)–4 (Jan. 1897). Blackburn;
m
    B   Free. Published for the proprietor at 41 Wynne Street,
Liverpool; then from November 1896 published for the Blackburn
Independent Labour Party, in Manchester.
    O(JJ) 1–2, 4

264 Blackburn Workers' Tribune [c1909]. Blackburn; m
    B   ½d. Independent Labour Party. Editor: R. F. Morse.
(Reformers' Year Book, 1909.)

265 Blackley Co-operative Citizen 1 (May 1940). Manchester
    A
    L(Col)

266 Blackley Div[isional] Bulletin [194-?] Manchester; m
    B   Free. Labour Party. (Labour Party. **Your own Journal,** 1948.)

267 Blackpool Co-operative Pioneer 1893; I, 1 (Jan. 1894)–? Blackpool;
m
    A   Gratis. Blackpool Co-operative Society. Reports, occasional
articles.
    L† XXI, 11–XXV, 12 (Dec. 1918); the Society (7 [31 July], 12 [30
Dec.] 1893)

268 Blackpool Co-operative Pioneer 1 (Oct. 1936)–2 (Dec. 1936); 3 (Feb.
1938)–4 (Oct. 1938). Blackpool; m
    A   Published by the Blackpool Co-operative Society.
    L(Col)

269 Blackpool Labour's Voice [195-?]–? [Manchester?; m?]
    B   Workers' Northern Publishing Society?
    L(Col) II, 56 (July 1959)–II, 93 (Oct. 1962)

270 Blandford News and Views [194-?] Blandford; m
    B   Labour Party. Duplicated. (Labour Party. **Your own Journal,**
1948.)

271 Blanketteer, and People's Guardian: a New Moral and Political Work,
Devoted Solely to the People's Cause 1 (23 Oct. 1819)–6 (27 Nov. 1819).
Leeds; w
    B   3d. Owner and publisher: Joseph Mitchell. In the form of
weekly letters. Ultra-radical. First announced under the name of **The
Aegis.**
    L† 1–3, 5; ONC 1–3; SP (Wentworth Muniments F 52/45) 1–6

272 Blast Pipe [192-?] Fife
    A   Rank-and-file paper. (**The Signal,** 18 [22 April 1926])

273 Blaydon-on-Tyne Co-operative Record 1 [190-?]−155 (Nov. 1915). Blaydon-on-Tyne; m

    A   Gratis. Blaydon District Co-operative Society. Issued by the Educational Association, Northern Section. Printed by the Co-operative Newspaper Society, Ltd., Manchester.

    L† 98 (Feb. 1911), 140 (Aug. 1914)−155

274 Bleachers' Monthly Journal March 1906−? Bolton; m

    A   Official organ of the Operative Bleachers', Dyers' and Finishers' Association (Bolton Amalgamation). Printed and published by George S. Ikin.

    J. Smethurst, 81 Parrin Lane, Winton, Eccles, Manchester M30 8AY. IV (March 1909)−X (Feb. 1916)

275 Blind Advocate: Organ of the National League for the Blind of Great Britain and Ireland I (1 Sept. 1898)−. Manchester; London; m; q

    A   1d. Editor (1898): Ben Purse, General Secretary. Contested Poor Law boards; agitated for State aid for the blind, a living wage for blind employees, and suitable work accommodation.

    L†; O LII−

276 Blue Dwarf 1−6. [1819]. Yarmouth

    C   2d. Printed for the author by Barnes and Webster. 'The production of a junta of eminent literary characters'. Anti-Cobbett, but pro-Burdett and parliamentary reform. Highly satirical.

    L†; NrP

277 Blue Riband 1 [196-?]−?

    A   Civil and Public Services Association, Supreme Court Branch Magazine. Duplicated.

    Warwick U (MRC) 11 (Feb. March 1969)

278 Blyth, Ashington and Broomhill Co-operative Citizen 1 (July 1935)−6 (Dec. 1935). Blyth; m

    A

    L(Col)

279 Board Teacher I, 1 (2 July 1883)−XXI, 231 (1 April 1904); then **London Teacher and London Schools Review**: XXI, 232 (1 May 1904)−1348 (Jan. 1967); m

    A   1d. Metropolitan Board Teachers' Association; London Teachers' Association; Inner London Teachers' Association.

    L(Col)†; LU XLVIII−

280 Boilermaker 1 (March 1928)−II, 4 (June 1929); m

    A   1d. National Minority Movement. Edited by Harry Pollitt. Dealt almost exclusively with problems in the Boilermakers' Society from the Minority Movement standpoint. Later issues expanded to cover more general trade union questions.

    WCML*†

281 Bollettino Socialista-Rivoluzionario 1 (6 Marzo 1879)–4 (2 Maggio 1879). London; irreg

    B   5 centesimi. Edited, printed and published by P. Magno. Four open letters, single sheets, printed on one side only. For the social emancipation of the working class.

        L† 2; L(Col)†

282 Bolton and District Independent Labour Party Pioneer I, 1 (4 Oct. 1894)–? Bolton; m

    B   ½d. Edited by Fred Brocklehurst. Published by James Sims, for the Bolton ILP.

        L(Col)† I, 4 (Jan. 1895)–12 (Sept. 1895)

283 Bolton Citizen I, 1 (Nov. 1913)–I, 7 (June 1914). Bolton; m

    B   Published by the Progressive League. Expresses socialist ideals and egalitarian aims.

        Bolton PL

284 Bolton Citizen: Official Organ of the Bolton Labour Party I, 1 (Oct. 1928)–9; then **Citizen**: Jan. 1930–X, 8 (Feb. 1938). Bolton; m

    B

        Bolton PL*; ILP April 1932

285 Bolton Co-operative Record I, 1 (Dec. 1899)–XLI, 9 (Sept. 1930). Bolton; m

    A   Gratis. Issued by the Education Committee of Bolton Co-operative Society. Began as a record of the work and objects of the Society; contents later expanded to include fiction, reviews, and pages for women and children. After September 1930 local pages were taken in the **Wheatsheaf**, and the publication was entitled **Bolton Co-operative Record and the Wheatsheaf.**

        L† XXVI, 4 (April 1915)–; the Society

286 Bolton Socialist Dec. 1902–? Bolton; m

    B   ½d. Edited by W. A. Seaton.

        O(JJ) 14 (Jan. 1904)

287 Bolton Trotter 1 (9 Jan. 1891)–68 (22 April 1892); then **Trotter**: 69 (29 April 1892)–129 (23 June 1893). Bolton; w

    C   ½d. Founded and edited by Teddy Ashton, ie Allen Clarke. A local weekly designed to amuse working men. There was also a '**Trotter**' Christmas Annual, 1893, then **Teddy Ashton's Christmas Annual** etc. 1 (1894)–45 (1935/6), published in Manchester, then Blackpool.

        L(Col)† (microfilm 1892); Christmas Annual† C 35–45; E 39, 45; L; MP 1932/3–1933/4; O 1–2, 35–

288 Bolton Voice I, 1 (March 1965)–? Bolton; m

    B   Journal of the Bolton Labour Party.

        Bolton PL March–Aug. 1965

289 Bonnet Rouge: the Republican Magazine 1 (16 Feb. 1833)–8 (30 March 1833); then **Republican** 9 (6 April 1833)– 10 (13 April 1833); w

B 1d. Published, printed and edited by Benjamin Franklin and Company, ie James Henry Lorymer, as a new series of **The Republican**. 'An extreme working-class miscellany that hints at revolution if such grievances as reform of the Church of England and repeal of the assessed taxes are not redressed. It also advocates the non-payment of taxes until universal suffrage is implemented' (Weiner). There is also an earlier No. 1, dated 2 Feb. 1833, located in Nuffield College.

BP 1–4; H.O. 64/19 2, 9; LU† 1–3; NwP; 0 1–2; ONC 1, [2 Feb]; 1, [16 Feb], 1833; WCML [16 Feb]–[9 March] 1833

290 Bookbinders' and Machine Rulers' Consolidated Union Monthly Circular [18--?]–? Glasgow; m

A (R. A. Peddie, 'Bibliography' in S. and B. Webb, **The History of Trade Unionism**, Longmans Green, 1894. Peddie states that 1885–94 were in the trade union office).

291 Bookbinders' Consolidated Union Friendly Circular [1846?]–? Dublin

A

LU† 4 (1 Oct 1846)

292 Bookbinders' Consolidated Union Trade Circular I, 1 (Feb. 1848)–? Liverpool; Manchester; Glasgow; Bradford; irreg; q

A Reports, discussion, correspondence.

LU† I, 1–VII, 26 (March 1896*)

293 Book-Binders' Provident Asylum Society. Quarterly Circular 1 (Sept. 1840)–ns 43 (Oct. 1855); a

A Quarterly single sheet report on the upkeep of an 'asylum' (old people's home) for 'decayed' binders.

L† (w ii 19–20, 22)

294 Bookbinders' Trade Circular I, 1 (Oct. 1850)–VI, 22 (Nov. 1877); bi–m

A 1d. Issued by the London Consolidated Society of Journeymen Bookbinders. Editor and author of many articles was T. J. Dunning, Secretary of the Society until July 1873. Contents include articles on Labour and conditions, wage movements, Labour law, philosophy of Trade Unionism, current disputes and events.

L†; LSF; LU

295 Book-Binding Trades Journal I, 1 ([no month] 1904)–II, 16 (July 1914). Manchester; q

A Bookbinders' and Machine Rulers' Consolidated Union; National Union of Bookbinders and Machine Rulers (1911–14). Printed by Co-operative Printing Society; James Collins. Editor: William Mellor News, notes, articles, verse, correspondence. Hyphen dropped from title in Vol. II.

GU; L; LSF II, 1–11; LvP; MP; O†

296 Book-Finishers' **Friendly Circular** 1 (Aug. 1845)—19 (Sept. 1850);
-yr

    A   Gratis to members. 'Conducted by a committee of the Finish-
rs' Friendly Association.' Printed for the Association by the Working
Printers' Association. The Association of Finishers belonged to the
Friendly Society of Journeymen Bookbinders of London and Westminster.
Encourages friendly society benefit principles, social improvement;
erialises the early history of the Journeyman Bookbinders' Friendly
Society; provides details of current disputes over hours etc.

    Lt; LU

297 Bookshelf [196-?] —? Sheffield; q?

    C   Issued by the University of Sheffield, Department of Extra-
mural Studies. Directed at day-release students on the course run by the
Department for miners and steel workers.

    R. Harrison 14 (Spring 1969)

Boot and Shoe Maker see St. Crispin

Boot and Shoe Trades Journal see St. Crispin

298 Border City 1 (June 1863)—14 (July 1864). Carlisle; m

    B   Sponsored by a group of 'Working Men' within the city. Edited
by John Lowry. 'A medium through which the working men in this
part of the world could express their opinions on the various topics which
are frequently and often ably discussed among them' (T. B. Graham,
Department of Adult Education, University of Nottingham).

    Jackson Library, Tullie House, Carlisle 1—13; T. B. Graham 1—13

299 Border City Socialist [19--?] —? Carlisle; m

    B

    ILP April—June, Aug.—Oct. 1908

300 Borderer [196-?] —. Petersfield

    A   National and Local Government Officers' Association,
Petersfield Branch. Reproduced from typewriting.

    L II (Nov. 1963)—

301 Borough Council Worker ns 1 (Nov. 1933)—7 (May 1934); m

    A   1d. Originally issued in stereotyped form, confined to Stepney
borough. Received such a response that it became an organ of public
cleansing workers in other boroughs within London. Issued for all London
municipal workers. Fighting for 100% Trade Unionism, against
rationalisation and redundancy. Editorial committee consists of 'workers
on the job'. Militant, lively, rank-and-file journal.

    L(Col)t

Borough of Woolwich Labour Journal see Woolwich and District Labour
Notes

Borough of Woolwich **Pioneer** see Woolwich and District **Labour Notes**

Borough of Woolwich **Pioneer and Labour Journal** see Woolwich & District **Labour Notes**

Bournemouth and Poole, **The Worker**: a Socialist and Labour Journal see **Worker**: a Socialist and Labour Journal

302 Bow and Bromley Citizen 1 (May 1932–80 (Dec. 1938); m
    A   Gratis. Published by the London Co-operative Political Committee.
    L(Col); Tower Hamlets Local History Library 1933–8

303 Bow and Bromley Socialist 1 [1897] –10 (Feb. 1898); m
    B   Gratis. Social Democratic Federation branch organ. Leader, local notes, comments.
    L(Col)† 9–10; LE 7–10?

304 Bow and Bromley Worker 1 (27 Nov. 1909)–?; then b Worker; w; m
    B   ½d. 'The organ of the Borough of Poplar Trades and Representation Committee.'
    ILP occ. nos; Tower Hamlets Local History Library 1–9, b 19–30, 35–7 (Sept. 1912)

305 Box, Packing Case Makers', and **Coopers' Gazette** 1 (1 Jan 1901)–?
    A?   (BUCOP)
    L (not traced in catalogue)

306 Boxers' Bulletin: Official Organ of the National Union of Boxers I, 1 (July 1936)–8 (Feb./March 1937); m
    A   2d. Printed and published by the Woodstock Press. The Union, registered in July 1935, was started by Jimmy Wilde, Len Harvey and a group of boxers and supporters 'to promote the interests of the professional boxer and to fight to remove the exploitation rampant in the boxing world'. Trustees: Ben Tillett, Jack Tanner, Arthur J. Gillian.
    L†; ONC Feb/March 1937

307 Boy Clerk I, 1 (Feb. 1912)–I, 5 (June 1912); m
    A   1d. A short-lived magazine issued for boy clerks in the Civil Service. It discusses the question of the formation of a 'Boy Clerks' Association' to press for continuing employment in the profession. By May, a Civil Service Boy Clerks' Association had been formed. It put its case before the Royal Commission investigating Civil Service employment. The last number of the journal is sub-titled; 'the Official Organ of the Boy Clerks' Association'.
    L(Col)†

308 Boy Messenger 1 (Feb. 1910)–20 (Feb. 1915); q

C　1d. Telegraph Messengers Christian Association. Successor to The Boys' Mail Bag (qv).

L†

309 Boys' Mail Bag, or the Messengers' Mail Bag I, 1 (Oct. 1892)–XVII, 81 (Oct. 1909); m

C　Postal and Telegraph Christian Association, Junior Branch. Editor: Miss A. F. Synge. Succeeded by **Boy Messenger** (qv).

L†

310 Bracknell Bulletin: the Bulletin of the Bracknell, New Town, Branch of NALGO 1964?–. Bracknell

A　National and Local Government Officers' Association' Bracknell (New Town) Branch. Reproduced from typewriting.

L 1964–

311 Bradford Courier 1 (Jan. 1936)–8 (Sept. 1936). Bradford; m

A　Gratis. Published by the City of Bradford Co-operative Society. Printed by the Co-operative Press, London. News and information about 'your Co-op. store'. Monthly circulation, 10,000.

L(Col)†

312 Bradford East Ward Labour Club Bulletin [1900?]–? Bradford; m

B　Independent Labour Party. (D. Hopkin, 'Local Newspapers of the Independent Labour Party, 1893–1906. Society for the Study of Labour History. **Bulletin**, 28 [Spring 1974].)

313 Bradford ILP News [19–?]–? Bradford; w

B　Independent Labour Party.

ILP (4 Oct. 1935), 1940 (17 occ. nos.) 13 Aug., 10 Dec. 1943, 29 Jan. 16 July, 13 Aug., 10 Dec. 1943.

314 Bradford Labour Echo. I, 1 [Oct. 1894?]–V, 265 (4 Nov. 1899). Bradford; w

B　½d. First published by the Bradford Labour Church; from 1898 the official organ of the Bradford and District Independent Labour Party, F. W. Jowett; Edwin Halford. 'the only journal in this district which speaks with authority for the Masses of the People.' Regular contributor on theoretical questions: E. D. Girdlestone.

BdP I, 25 (28 March 1895)–V, 265 (4 Nov. 1899*); L(Col)† 169 (1 Jan 1898)–264; ONC II, 25

315 Bradford Labour Record [1930?] Bradford; m

B　Gratis. (Mitchell, 1930).

316 Bradford Labour's Voice I, 1 (Jan. 1959)–? Manchester; m

B   3d. Published for Bradford City Labour Party by the Workers' Northern Publishing Society, Ltd. A serious monthly journal for presentation of issues and policy, and a forum for discussion. Some articles in common with **Labour's Voice**, and local news and contributions.

L(Col)† I, 1, – II, 19 (Aug. 1963); LabP II, 15

317 Bradford News [19–?] –   . Bradford; m

B   Printed and published by Bradford Independent Labour Party. Duplicated. See also **Bradford ILP News**. Is this the same journal?

TUC† xxxiii, 36 (28 Jan. 1972)–51 (July 1973*)

318 Bradford Pioneer [I], 1 (17 Jan. 1913)–XXII, 1161 (13 Dec. 1935); ns 1 (Jan. 1936)–10 (Oct. 1936). Bradford; w

B   ½d; 1d. Published at the Labour Institute, as organ of the Independent Labour Party, Trades Council, and Workers Municipal Federation. Later, organ of Bradford Labour Party. Editor and contributor: F. W. Jowett. Socialist. Emphasis on municipal politics.

BdP; ILP*, L(Col)† (w occ. nos.)

319 Bradford Socialist Vanguard 1 (Sept. 1908)–142 (Oct. 1920). Bradford; m

B   ½d; 1d. Published and edited by C. A. Glyde. Object: to 'make Socialists'. No. 142 says started originally as **The Tong Pioneer** (qv).

BdP Aug. 1920; ILP July 1915, Oct. 1920; L(Col)† (w 1911); O(JJ) O‹ 1920

320 Brass Check [I, 1, 1925?] –II, 5/6 (27 June 1925). Dundee; w

A   ½d. Metalworkers' Section, National Minority Movement. 'Organ of the Shipyard Communist Group', Caledon and Stannergate. Duplicated foolscap.

MML† (10 April 1925); II, 1 (May 22)–II, 5/6 (w 3)

321 Brass Tacks: Monthly Notes for LCS Employees 1939–   ? Leicester; m

A   Leicester Co-operative Society
L (main entry not traced in catalogue)

Brassworkers' Quarterly Journal see National Society of Amalgamated Brassworkers and Metal Mechanics **Quarterly Report**

322 Bread Basket 1 (24 Dec. 1842)–10 (25 Feb. 1843); w

C   1d. Printed and published by George Peirce. An 'unofficial' Anti-Corn Law League organ designed with illustration and argument aimed at enlisting working-class support against aristocratic monopoly. There is a regular feature entitled 'A Word with the Working Classes'.

MP 1–8; O† 1–9

323 Braille Tape [19--?] –?; m
   A   Issued to blind members of the Civil Service Clerical Association
for many years (**Whitley Bulletin**, Sept/Oct. 1963).

324 Branch Brevities [1962?] –[196-?] ; then b NALGO **Branch Magazine**:
Bulletin of the Stafford Branch of NALGO: [196-?] –. Stafford
   A   National and Local Government Officers' Association, Stafford
Borough Branch. Reproduced from typewriting
   L a July 1962–July 1964, b 1966–

325 Branch Lines [19--?] –   . Gloucester
   A   National and Local Government Officers' Association,
Gloucestershire Branch
   L X, 5 (June 1958)–

Branch Lines, 1964–   see·National Association of Local Government
Officers. Hereford City Branch. **Newsletter**

Branch Lines [c1970?] see Sheffield Municipal Officers' **Journal**

326 Brecon and Radnor Labour Campaigner; [194-?] [Builth Wells?] ; m
   B   3d. Labour Party. (Labour Party. **Your own Journal**, 1948.)

327 Brentford and Chiswick Citizen 1 (Dec. 1930)–?; m
   A   Published by the London Co-operative Society
   L(Col) 1–18, (June 1932)

328 Brentford and Chiswick Labour News [194-?] ; m
   B   2d. Labour Party. (Labour Party. **Your own Journal**, 1948.)

329 Brick: a Paper for the Railwaymen at Bricklayers' Arms No. 0 [*sic*] (5
June 1926)–?
   A   London Communist Railwaymen's Committee. No. 0 is 'an
advance sheet', free, reproduced from typewriting. It announces the
intention, as **Bricklets** is not to appear again, of producing **Brick** fort-
nightly, at ½d, for 4 pp. Asks readers to stand by the miners, support the
Minority Movement, change the leadership.
   O(JJ)† No. 0

330 Bricklets ?–[1926?]
   A   A paper for railwaymen at Bricklayers' Arms. See **Brick**

Bridge see National Association of local Government Officers. Staines
Branch. **Magazine**

331 Bridgeton Advertiser and Single Tax Review I, 1 (7 Sept. 1889)—I, 2(Oct. 1889); then **Bridgeton Single Tax Review and Advertiser**: I, 3 (Nov. 1889)—II, 6 (Feb. 1891). Bridgeton, Glasgow; m
    C   ½d. Scottish Land Restoration League, Eastern Branch, Bridgeton. Conducted on Georgeite principles. For the removal of class legislation bearing on industry and upon the wage-earning community. A local organ for Glasgow's East End.
    GM†; ILP (1 Feb. 1890)

Bridgeton Single Tax Review and Advertiser see **Bridgeton Advertiser and Single Tax Review**

332 Bridgwater Excelsior 1 (June 1923)— ? Bridgwater; m
    B   Labour Party. (Labour and Socialist International. **The Socialist Press**, 1933).
    ILP 1

333 Brighter Day 1900. Bradford
    B   (**ILP News**, Jan. 1900, p. 2.)

Brighton Co-operator see **Co-operator**

334 Brighton Labour News [194—?] Brighton; m
    B   2d. Labour Party. (Labour Party. **Your own Journal**, 1948.)

335 Brighton Patriot and **Lewes Free Press** 1 (24 Feb. 1835)—71 (28 June 1836); then **Brighton Patriot** and **South of England Free Press**: 72 (5 July 1836)—234 (13 Aug. 1839). Brighton; w
    B   6d. Printed and published by the proprietor, William Heaves Smithers. Until late 1838 a Liberal/Radical commercial paper, then became a supporter of Chartism and acted as the organ of the Brighton Radical Registration and Patriotic Association. Also defended Trade Unionism. But dropped Chartism in 1839.
    BiP March—Oct. 1835*; L(Col)†

336 Brightside and Carbrook Co-operative Citizen 1 (March 1939)—9 (Nov. 1939). Sheffield m
    A   Published by Brightside and Carbrook Co-operative Society.
    L(Col)

337 Briove Post [19--?] —? Brighton
    A   Union of Post Office Workers, Brighton Amalgamated Branch. (W. Dunlop, 'Local Journals'. **Belpost**, IV, 5 [May 1965].)

338 Bristol Citizen 1 (Dec. 1931)—2 (Jan. 1932); then Bristol Co-operative Citizen; 3 (Feb. 1932)—128 (July 1942); ns 1 (Jan. 1946)—89 (Sept. 1953); then Bristol Citizen: ns 90 (Oct. 1953)—98 (July 1954). Bristol; m
    A   One of the 'Citizen' series.
    L(Col)†

Bristol Co-operative Citizen see **Bristol Citizen**

339 Bristol Forward 1 (Dec. 1915)–8 (July 1916). Bristol; M
    B   ½d. Published by the Bristol Indepndent Labour Party. Printed by the National Labour Press, Manchester and London. ILP, trade union, and Labour notes. Anti-war.
      ILP 2, 6, 7 L(Col)† 2–8

340 Bristol Job Nott or **Labouring Man's Friend** 1 (15 Dec. 1831)–107 (26 Dec. 1833). Bristol; w
    C   1½d. Published and printed by J. and W. Richardson. Expounds political Conservatism to the lower orders.
      BrP; BrU; GM; L†; LU; 0 1, 5

Bristol Labour Herald see **East Bristol Election Labour Herald**

341 Bristol Labour Weekly: Official Organ of the Bristol Labour and Trade Union Movement [192-?]–[194-?]. Bristol w
    B   1d. Printed and published by the Bristol Printers Ltd. and the Bristol Newspaper Society Ltd. Labour Party in Bristol. Editor: A. W. S. Burgess.
      BrP XIV, 4 (16 Sept. 1939)–XXII, 13 (8 Nov. 1947*); O(JJ)† II, 12 (26 Nov. 1927)

342 Bristol North Forward; m
    B?
      ILP Dec. 1921, Jan., Feb. 1922

343 Bristol Poor Man's Magazine, and **Cottager's Friend**: a Weekly Paper, Devoted to the Amusement, and Domestic, Social, and Moral Improvement of the Labouring Classes 1 (25 July 1829). Bristol; w
    C   1d. Printed and published by Philip Rose.
      BrP

344 Bristol Rails Worker [1952?]–? Bristol
    B   1d. Reproduced from typewriting. Issued by Bristol Rails Branch, Communist Party
      Warwick U (MRC)† 10 occ. nos between 4 (May 1953) and July 1955

345 Bristol Reporter [1832?–3?]. Bristol; w
    B   'Lent to read six months, without deposit for 1½d'; 1d. from 4 May 1833; unstamped. Printers and publishers: H. Onion; J. Keegan; Robert Peake; J. G. Powell; John Chappell; J. Sullivan. Title varied slightly to evade Stamp Laws. Explicitly Radical (A. Hart, **A Catalogue of Periodicals printed in Bristol 1820–40**, University of Leicester Victorian Studies Centre, 1972).
      BrU (1 Sept. 1832); BrP(15 Sept. 1832)–(4 May 1833*)

346 Bristol Retaliator 1832. Bristol; w?

B 1½d. Unstamped. Proprietor, editor, publisher, printer: John Charles Fitzgerald. Radical, anti-Church, pro-Reform, anti- Taxes on Knowledge.

BrP I, 5 (7 April, 6 (12 May ['after a severe illness'] 1832)

347 Britannic Journal: Official Organ of the Brittannic Field Staff Association. Jan. 1926–   . Birmingham; m; q. (June 1971–   )

A For members only. 'The basic object of our Journal is one of conveying current reports and items of interest of basically domestic issues, with occasional references to national items, though unrelated to party politics'.

LCI XXII–; the Association*

348 British Association of Colliery Management **National News Letter**. June 1947–   . Nottingham; q

A Free to members. Matters relating to conditions of employment, salaries etc.

ONC June 1965; the Association

349 British Citizen and Empire Worker I, 1 (25 Aug. 1916)–X, 237 (12 March 1921); then b **Empire Citizen**: I, 1 (Dec. 1921)–V, 70 (Sept. 1927); w; m

C 1d; 2d. Organ of British Workers' National League. Some leading officials included John Hodge, Will Crooks. Later, organ of the National Democratic and Labour Party. David Gilmour, ed. Stridently anti-Bolshevik. **Empire Citizen** published by Empire Citizen League, whose slogan was 'Down with the Bolshies – For Britain & Empire!' For peace in industry and class collaboration.

C; L(Col)†; O a–b I, 5, V, 70

350 British Committee for the Defence of Leon Trotsky. **Information Bulletin.** [1937?] –?

B Warwick U.L. Maitland/Sara Papers 2 (July 1937).

British Co-operator see **Co-operative Magazine** and **Monthly Herald**

351 British Equity: the Official Organ of the British Actors' Equity Association I, 1 (Feb. 1934)–   ; m

A 6d

L*; TUC† 1934

British Gardener see British Gardeners' Association. **Journal**

352 British Gardeners' Association; then National Union of Horticultural Workers **Journal**: I 1 (May 1907)–   X, 109 (Nov. 1917); then **British Gardener**: XI, 110 (March 1918)–XII, 123 (Feb. 1920); then **Horticultural Worker**: the Journal of the National Union of Horticultural Workers: XII, 124 (March 1920)–XIII, 134 (March 1921;) m

A 1d; 3d.

L†

353 British Labourer's Protector, and Factory Child's Friend 1 (21 Sept. 1832)–31 (19 April 1833). Leeds; w

    C   ½d. Published and printed by R. Inchbold. Editor: Rev. George Stringer Bull, Vicar of Brierley, Bradford ('Parson Bull of Brierley'). 'Exposes factory abuses and strongly agitates for a ten-hours factory act. It is written from a Christian point of view' (Weiner).

    BdP; L; LU†; LdP; MP 1–21; ONC; Greenwood reprint and microfiche: microfiche distributed in Britain and Europe by the Harvester Press Ltd

354 British Miner and General Newsman 1(13 Sept. 1862)–25 (28 Feb. 1863); then **Miner**: ns 1 (7 March 1863)–14 (6 June 1863); then **Miner and Workman's Advocate**: 15 (13 June 1863)–130 (2 Sept. 1865); then **Workman's Advocate**: 131 (9 Sept. 1865)–152 (3 Feb. 1866); then **Commonwealth**: 153 (10 Feb. 1866)–226 (20 July 1867); w

    C; B; A.   3d; 1d. 'A publication devoted to the Interests of the Working Miners of the United Kingdom.' Editor until 5 Aug. 1865 was John Towers, who opposed Alexander Macdonald, miners' leader and subsequently MP. Exposes abuses and accidents, tommy-shop and truck systems. Consistently promotes the British Miners' Benefit Association. Attempts to inculcate the assertion of manly independence; promotes co-operative stores, friendly societies, but also class conciliation. Aug. 1865–Feb. 1866 editor and proprietor: John Bedford Leno. The paper becomes more political, supports universal suffrage programme of Reform League, and London Trades Council. The **Commonwealth** was 'managed by working men' but their control was often in doubt in relation to a circle of middle-class radicals and noncomformist employers. Proprietors: The Industrial Newspaper Company, one of whose directors was George Odger. Published by Arthur Miall. From Sept. 1866 'The Organ of the Reform Movement', and campaigns for universal suffrage. Contributors include Frederic Harrison, Professor Beesly, and J. G. Eccarius, who, for a time had editorial control.

    L(Col)†; O i

355 British Monarchy 1 (20 June 1867)–11 (31 Aug. 1867); w

    C   2d. Printed for the proprietors by Charles William Bradley, and published by him, then printed by Joseph Bruton and published at the Newsagents Publishing Company. At No. 3 sub-titled: 'a Conservative Journal for the Working Classes', but then changed to be 'for all classes'. Contains specific anti-trade union and anti-Reform League propaganda aimed at working-class readers, and correspondence by working men on these issues.

    L(Col)† (w 2)

356 British Railway Employee's Privilege Ticket Movement. Continental Club. Members Journal I, 1 (1958/9). Southport

    A   Issued as supplement to the Continental Club Brochure. Reproduced from typewriting.

    L†

357 British Revolutionary Socialist [193–?] Edinburgh; m

    B   1d. Printed and published by the Revolutionary Socialist Party. Reproduced from typewriting. Trotskyist.

    E† III, (2 July 1937)

358 British Seafarer I, 1 (Jan. 1913)–X, 1 (Jan. 1922). Southampton; m

    A   Free. Organ of the British Seafarers' Union. A militant journal, in conflict with Havelock Wilson and the National Sailors' and Firemen's Union. Editor?: Tommy Lewis, trade unionist, Borough alderman, MP. Jan. 1922 incorporated with the **Marine Caterer** and a new journal issued, entitled the **Marine Worker**

    LE† III, 4 (April 1915), III, 7 (July 1915)–X, 1; National Union of Seamen 1913, 1914, 1916

359 British Seamen's Advocate 1 (1825)– 2 (1825)

    C?

    LUC

360 British Seamen's Magazine, or, **Church of England Maritime Guardian** I, 1 (Feb. 1931); q

    C   4d. Published by James Nisbet. Caters for the spiritual welfare of merchant seamen.

    BP†

British Socialist see **Social — Democrat**

361 British Socialist News 1899–?; w

    B   Editors: Tom Mann, Ben Tillett. (There is reference in the **Reformers' Year Book**, 1901, to the closing of a journal of this title, published in Accrington).

British Soviet Newsletter see **Russia Today Newsletter**

362 British Statesman: a Journal Devoted to the Interests of the People 1 (13 March 1842)–46 (21 Jan. 1843); w

    B   4d., 5d. etc. Printed and published by Robert Chambers. Initially advocated Corn Law repeal and franchise extension. Bronterre O'Brien became editor in June, changing its content, promoting and extensively reporting Chartist and complete suffrage agitation in the regions.

    L(Col)†

363 British Steel Smelters Amalgamated Association. Monthly Report [188–?]– ? [London?] ; m

    A

    TUC† 117, Jan.–Dec. 1899; Warwick U (MRC) 1, 1919–(50), 1968–9

364 British Trades Union Review: a Monthly Review of Trade Union Activity [1], 1 (Aug. 1919)– III, 9 (April 1922); m

A   Issued by the Parliamentary Committee of the Trades Union Congress. Medium for circulating up-to-date information in the trade union world. Then merged in **Labour Magazine** (qv).

BP; L†; LE; LdU

365 British Worker: Official Strike News Bulletin, Published by the General Council of the Trades Union Congress 1 (5 May 1926)– 11 (17 May 1926); d

A   There were also local editions published in Aberdeen, Cardiff, Leicester, Manchester, Newcastle, and a **Scottish Worker**.

London edition. BeP; BlU 10; BrU 3; C; E; L(Col)*; LGU; LdU 2, 3, 8; O; ONC; local editions ONC; Manchester edition WCML†; Newcastle edition L(Col)*

366 British Worker: Official Trade Union Defence Campaign Bulletin 1 (29 April 1927)–9 (24 June 1927); w

A   1d. Revived by the National Trade Union Defence Committee to organise opposition to the anti-trade union legislation of 1927. 'Kill the Bill' campaign.

C; L(Col)†

367 British Worker [c Sept. 1941]

B   Issued by the **Daily Worker** Defence League. Preceded by **Workers Gazette**, Aug. 1941. 'Produced by members of the **Daily Worker** staff' during the ban on the **Daily Worker**.

ONC†; 1 undated no. [c Sept. 1941]; TUC†

368 British Workman and Friend of the Sons of Toil 1 (Feb. 1855)–801 (Sept. 1921); m

C   1d. Publishers: W. and R. Chambers; S. W. Partridge. Editor (1899): Sam Woods, MP. Title varies: Feb. 1855–March 1856 as above; April 1856–Feb. 1921 **The British Workman**; March–Sept. 1921 **The British Workman and Home Monthly**. An illustrated monthly addressed to workers and their families, anxious to promote their welfare through the encouragement of the virtues of hard work, prudence, temperance, godliness. Latterly, mainly religious. Some editions in foreign languages were published from time to time, e.g. **L'Ouvrier française**, 1–9 [1868–72], located in the British Museum. There were also German, Polish, Dutch and Italian editions.

BP 1–60; BdP 1855–74; C 1860–1921*; L(Col)†; LE 73–96; LU 2–60, 241–88; MP 1855–69; O 1903–21; PmP 1855–96; SwU 1873, 1875–6

369 British Workwoman Out and at Home 1 (1 Nov. 1863)–?; m
C   1d. Illustrated monthly, counterpart of **British Workman and Friend of the Sons of Toil**, calculated to promote the social and moral improvement of the working-class woman.
L (1–390), (503–Aug. 1905); O (1863–96)

370 Briton 1 (25 Sept. 1819)–9 (20 Nov. 1819); w
B   1d. Published and printed by J. Turner. For radical political reform. The People versus the Aristocracy. For the Rights of Man, but also in defence of Holy Scripture against Atheists and Deists.
L†; ONC 3–6, 8–9

371 Brixton Citizen ns 1 (Oct. 1950)–(29 [April 1953]); [ns], 1 [195-?] –; m
B   Published by the Co-operative Press.
L(Col) ns 1–[29], [ns] 28 (Oct. 1960)–

372 Brixton News Letter [194-?] ; m
B   Labour Party. Duplicated. (Labour Party. **Your Own Journal**, 1948.)

373 Broadsheet [19–?] –. Salisbury.
A   National and Local Government Officers' Association, Salisbury Branch. Reproduced from typewriting.
L 38 (mid-summer 1959)–

374 Broadside 1903. Newcastle
B   Newcastle Socialist Society. (**Labour Leader**, [4 April 1903].)

375 Bromley (Kent) Divisional Labour Chronicle [192-?] ; m
B
ILP July 1926

376 [Bronterre O'Brien's European Letters and Tracts for the National Reform League] 1 (6 Dec. 1851)–2 (13 Dec. 1851); w
B   (A. Plummer, **Bronterre: a political biography of Bronterre O'Brien 1804–1864**, London 1971.)

377 Bronterre's National Reformer in Government, Law, Property, Religion and Morals I, 1 (7 Jan. 1837)–I, 11 (18 March 1837); w
B   1d. Unstamped. Publisher: J. Oldfield. Printer: Lee; G. H. Davidson. Editor: Bronterre O'Brien. Advocated universal suffrage and 'a reformation in favour of the great mass of the community', by the peaceful or 'physical force' mobilisation 'of the great majority'.
L†; LE; LU 1; MP

378 Brotherhood: a Weekly Paper Designed to Help the Peaceful Evolution of a Juster and Happier Social Order I, 1 (22 April 1887)–(Oct. 1935). Limavady; London; Letchworth; Limavady; w; m; q

    B   1d. etc. Printed and published by the Circle Co-operative Printing Company, Limavady, then by the Botherhood Press, London etc. Editor: J. Bruce Wallace. Advocated nationalisation of land, a co-operative commonwealth, Christian Socialist ideals. From 1893 was the organ of the Nationalisation of Labour Society. Sub-title varies. There was also a 'Northern Counties edition', (11 May 1889)–(31 May 1890), published at Limavady.

    E I–VI; L†; L(Col)† Northern Counties edition; LE 1887–1903*; O 1892–1901*

379 Buff 1959? –   Orpington

    A   National and Local Government Officers' Association, Orpington Branch. See also 'Running Buff-et a News Supplement to the **Buff**.

    L June 1959–

380 Bugle 1959? –   Croydon

    A   National and Local Government Officers' Association, Croydon Hospitals Branch. Reproduced from typewriting.

    L 1959–

381 Builders Standard 1 (Jan. 1960)–36 (Dec. 1962); then **Federation Builders Standard**: 1 (Jan. 1963)–78 (Dec. 1968); m

    A   2d; 3d. 1960–2 published by the Amalgamated Union of Building Trade Workers, and during those years replaced the **Building Worker**. Transferred to the National Federation of Building Trades Operatives in January 1963. A newspaper containing union and general news, women's column, correspondence etc.

    HU; ONC†; TUC Jan. 1963–Dec. 1968

382 Building and Monumental Workers' **Trade Journal** I, 1 (March 1921)–? Glasgow; m

    A   Building and Monumental Workers' Association of Scotland.

    WCML† I (March 1921)–(Dec. 1923), VI (Jan. 1936)–(Dec. 1938). Warwick U (MRC) 1924–40

383 Building Guildsman I, 1 (15 Dec. 1921)–I, 7 (July 1922). Manchester; m

    A   1d. Printed at the Cloister Press for the National Building Guild. Guild Socialist. To state the case for the National Building Guild and to urge the Guild idea generally. Contains Guild notes and reports, and short signed articles on aspects of the movement. Contributors: S. G. Hobson, Malcolm Sparkes and other Guild Socialists.

    MP; O(JJ) 1, 3; ONC†

384 Building Operatives' **Bulletin** I (1933–46); m

    A   National Federation of Building Trade Operatives. An information bulletin.

    L† III, 5 (May 1935)–9, 11–12, IV, 2–VII, 10 (Oct. 1939); TUC 1937–Sept. 1939

385 Building Trades' News I, 1 (Sept. 1894)–I, 12 (Aug. 1895); then **National Building Trades' Gazette**: II, 1 (Sept. 1895); m

    A   1d. Issued by the London Building Trades Federation; National Federation of the Building Industry. Editor: J. Verdon, Secretary of the Federation. Trade-union Journal, to serve the interests of all workers in the building trades.

    L(Col)†

386 Building Worker 1 (April 1932)–3 (July 1932); m

    A   1d. Published by William Zak. Printed by the Utopia Press. Succeeded **London Building Worker**. 'Monthly Supplement of **The Weekly Worker**, published in conjunction with the Building Workers' Minority Movement.' Wide coverage of trade-union issues and Communist Party industrial and political agitation.

    L(Col)†

387 Building Worker I, 1 (March 1947)–XIII, 12 (Dec. 1959); [ns], I, 1 (Jan. 1963)–IX, 7 (July 1971); m

    A   Amalgamated Union of Building Trade Workers of Great Britain and Ireland. Merged July 1971 with the Amalgamated Society of Woodworkers. The journal was replaced 1960–62 by **Builders' Standard** (qv).

    BU IX, 3 (1955)– ; HU 1963– ; L 1963– ; LvP 1963– ; ONC† III, 11 (Nov. 1949)– ; TUC

388 Building Workers' Charter: Organ of the Rank and File Building Workers 1 ([July] 1970)– ; bi-m?

    A   6d.; 3p. Published by Building Workers' Charter.

    L(Col)†

389 Building Workers' Industrial Union. **Weekly Bulletin**

    A   Postgate says (5 Sept. 1914)–(16 July 1915) (w nos 14–16) were in Hamilton College, property of John Hamilton, Chairman, National Council of Labour Colleges.

390 Building Workers' **Industrial Union's Record** 1 (7 July 1920)– ?

    A   1d. Published by the Executive Committee of the Building Workers' Industrial Union. Editor: J. V. Wills, General Secretary. No. 1 consists of statement, copies of correspondence, and account of events, head-lined 'The cause of the dock dispute!' Protesting against the action of the Building Trades Federation.

    ONC† 1

391 Bulletin, Issued by the London District Committee of the Communist Party [19--?] –?; w?

     B

     TUC† (8 Feb. 1946), (1 April 1949)

392 Bulletin: the Official Organ of the Headquarters of the National Federation of Discharged and Demobilised Sailors and Soldiers I, 1 (13 March 1919)–III, 46 (April 1921); fortn

     C   1d. Published by the NFDDSS. Branch and divisional reports. Campaigns for pensions for ex-servicemen and their dependants, and for employment opportunities. The Federation was non-political. Then merged in **The Comrades Journal.** Sometime title: **DSS Bulletin.**

     L†

393 Bulletin: the Organ of the St Pancras LPC 1 (Aug. 1925)–   ?; m

     B   'For members only.' Reproduced from typewriting. Title varies: **Bulletin of the St Pancras Local CPGB; Bulletin of the St Pancras LPC** Communist Party of Great Britain. See also **CP Bulletin; St Pancras Local.**

     O(JJ)† 1, 2 (Sept. 1925), 4 (Nov. 1925), (Feb. 1926), (April 1926).

Bulletin: the Official Organ of the WUEA, European Division [1932?] – see **WUEA Review**

Bulletin: the Official Journal of the Printing and Kindred Trades

Federation see **Printing Federation Bulletin**

Bulletin, 1947–54 see **Lancashire News**

394 Bulletin: a Monthly Newsletter I (1957)–   . Reading; m

     A   National and Local Government Officers' Association, Reading and District Branch.

     L

395 Bulletin: a Journal for Road Passenger Transport Workers I, 1 (March 1958)–I, 2 (April 1958). Brighton; m

     A   3d. Reproduced from typewriting. A rank-and-file paper 'produced by a joint Committee of working busmen employed by the three Brighton Passenger Transport Undertakings'.

     L†

396 Bulletin: Journal of the Wolverhampton and District Branch 1961?–   . Wolverhampton

     A   National and Local Government Officers' Association. Reproduced from typewriting.

     L 1961–

397 Bulletin for Leaders of Communist Children's Groups (I, 1 [1923?])–1925

    B   3d. English edition published by the Executive Committee of the Young Communist International. Printed in Sweden. Instruction on how to organise Pioneer Groups and educate children in Communist teaching and practice, drawing on Soviet youth experiences and on the promotion of Children's Sections internationally. Includes children's letters.

    MML† II, 2 (1924) 3/4 (Jan. 1925)

398 Bulletin of Marxist Studies I, 1 ([Summer?] 1968)–? Rugeley, Staffordshire; London; q

    B   1s. 6d. Printed and published by K. Tarbuck; later published by BMS Publications. Editors: Ken Tarbuck, Chris Arthur etc. Early ones reproduced from typewriting. No. 5 (and later?) title on cover is **Marxist Studies**. Articles and reviews on United Kingdom and abroad.

    E I, 4 (1969)–   ; LE I, 1–II, 3 (Autumn 1970); O† I, 3–5 Warwick (UL) (MRC) I, 1–15, II, 1–3

Bulletin of the Busmen's Minority Movement see **Busman's Voice**: Bulletin of the Busmen's Minority Movement

Bulletin Officiel du Parti Socialiste Polonais see **Parti Socialiste Polonais, Bulletin Officiel**

399 Bulletins for Socialists [193–?] Leeds

    B   6d. Reproduced from typewriting. No. 5 consists of 'The cry of the Chartists, 1839–1939' issued to commemorate Chartism. It is a collection of poems 'written roughly between 1830 and 1850, which have a direct or indirect connection with the politics of the period'.

    ONC† 5 (May 1939)

400 Bull's Eye, Issued by the National Union of Police and Prison Officers I, 1 ([Aug.] 1920)–III, 25 (8 Dec. 1922); fortn

    A   2d. Printed by the National Labour Press. Edited by J. H. Hayes, General Secretary of the Union. Militant, politically left-wing. Outlawed by Police Act of 1919 following police strike, agitated for right to trade-union organisation.

    L(Col)† ; TUC*

401 Bumbledom: a Quarterly Review and Miscellany of Municipal Matters I, 1 [Spring 1957?]– . Farnham; q

    A   National and Local Government Officers' Association, Farnham Branch. Reproduced from typewriting.

    L II, 1 (Spring 1958)–

402 Burnley and District **Labour Standard** 1, [May 1934?] –280 (7 May 1942). Burnley; w

    B   ½d.; 1d. Published by Burnley Trades and Labour Council, later printed and published by the 'Padiham Advertiser, Ltd.'. Later sub-title: 'Official Organ of the Burnley Trades and Labour Council'. Newspaper format, with leader, short news items, local and national, correspondence, occasional short signed article, and by 1942 a serial story. Incorporated with **East Lancashire Sentinel.**

    L(Col)†31 (4 Jan. 1935)–280

403 Burnley Citizen Sept. 1937. Burnley

    A   Published by the Co-operative Press.

    L(Col)

404 Burnley Co-operative Record 1894–? Burnley; m

    A   Gratis. Burnley Equitable Co-operative Society. Issued by the Education Committee.

    L†XV, 185 (Jan. 1911)–XXII, 255 (Jan.–March 1918)

405 Burnley Labour News [19–?] –? Burnley

    B   Printed and published for Burnley Trades and Labour Council by Nuttal and Company.

    Burnley PL 1 no. undated [Dec. 1918?]

Burnley Pioneer see **Pioneer, 1896–1917**

Burnley Socialist see **Socialist and North-East Lancashire Labour News**

406 Burton's Red Leader 1933–[1935?]. Leeds; fortn

    A   1d. Published by Burton's Communist Group. Editor: J. Roche. Reproduced from typewriting. Rank-and-file reporting and agitational paper and clothing workers.

    Priv. Coll.† 10 (2 Aug. 1933), 14, 16; Warwick UL (MRC) (5 July), (2 Aug.), (30 Aug.), (27 Sept.), 25 Oct. 1933 (Xerox copies).

407 Bury Co-operative Quarterly [Quarterly Co-operative?] Review 1892–? Bury; q

    A   Bury and District Co-operative Society. 'To be published in connection with the Balance Sheet. In this Review an opportunity is given to the members to read what is said and done at all the meetings, together with any matter that is pertinent to the welfare of the movement.' Editors: John Collins; James Edward Wolstenholme; Sam Kay, William Mitchell; James Clegg Hill. (T. Rigby, **The Origin and the History of Co-operation in Bury**, 1905, pp. 60–1.) Then incorporated in **Home Magazine.**

408 Bury St Edmunds **Labour News and Views.** [194-?]. Bury St Edmunds; m

    B   Labour Party. Duplicated. (Labour Party. **Your Own Journal,** 1948.)

Bury-Go-Round see **NALGO Bury Branch Magazine**

409 Bus: a Paper for the London Bus Fleet Workers No. 0 (11 June 1926); then **Bus Worker**: a Paper for the London Bus Fleet: 1 (19 June 1926)— ?; fortn; m

A ½d. Issued by the London Communist Busmen (also referred to as the Communists' Group, and the Communist Busmen). Militant. No. 0 is the advance issue.

O(JJ)† No. 0, 1, (2 [July] 3, 5 [Aug.], 6 [Sept.] 1926)

[Bus and Tram?] Voice [193–?]. [Manchester?]

A **Daily Worker**, (20 May 1932).

411 Bus, Tram and Cab Trades' Gazette I, 1 (22 Oct. 1898)—I, 4 (12 Nov. 1898); w

C 1d. Printed and published for the Proprietors by A. H. Reid. Not an organ of the General Tram and Bus Workers' union. Policy is 'strictly impartial', 'Columns open to all, to Unionist, Non-Unionist, Employer, or Employee'.

L(Col)†

Bus Worker see **Bus**

412 Business Girl: the Official Organ of the Institution of Women Shorthand Typists I, 1 (Feb. 1912)—I, 2 (March 1912); m

A 1d. Published by the editor, Helen Houston. To improve status of typists. Institution will promote social intercourse, open debating societies, reading clubs, make workers more proficient. Also founds the Business Girls' League, to promote the interests of commercial women workers generally, 'and particularly to secure for them special advantages under the Insurance Act and in other legislation that may be proposed'. All IWST members became members automatically of the League.

L(Col)†

413 Busman's Voice: Bulletin of the Busman's Minority Movement [192–?]

A Reproduced from typewriting. Special numbers bear the sub-title only. All the numbers seen are concerned with a dispute at Barking.

O(JJ)† (5 Oct. [1929]); Special No. 7 (7 Oct. 1929); Special No. 8 (8 Oct. 1929)

414 Busmen's Bulletin. [1936]–?

A 1d. No. 2 was dated 26 June 1936.

415 Busmen's Clarion: a Paper for all Passenger Workers I, 1 (July 1954)—16 (Feb. 1956). Manchester; m or bi-m

A From No. 11, May 1955 the sub-title changes to: 'A Militant Paper for All Busworkers'.

WCML†

416 Busman's Punch 1 (July 1931–Dec. 1931); [ns], 1 (15 July 1932–Oct. 1932); [ns], 1 (4 Nov. 1932)–55 (May 1937); m

    A   1d. First issued by militant busmen at Cricklewood Garage, then by militant busmen at a number of London garages. Later 'the Official Paper of the London Busmen's Rank and File Movement'. At first reproduced from typewriting. Sometimes **Busmen's Punch?**

    CPGB; MML*; O(JJ) 15 July 1932; ONC Dec. 1932, March 1933, May 1937; WCML May 1933

Busmen's Punch see **Busman's Punch**, 1931–1937

417 Busman's Punch: the Official Paper of the Provincial Busmen's Rank and File Movement 1 [Oct. 1936?] –?; m

    A   1d. Published by C. F. Yeowell, Southall.

    WCML 7 (April 1937)

418 'Buzz' [19--?] –? Fleetwood; q

    A   2d. etc. National and Local Government Officers' Association, Fleetwood and District Branch, Office of Public Relations. Official bulletin. Reproduced from typewriting.

    L† June 1958–Dec. 1958

419 Buzzard 1966?–   . Trowbridge

    A   National and Local Government Officers' Association, Wiltshire County Branch. Reproduced from typewriting.

    L 1966–

420 Buzzer: the Official Organ of the Leeds Branch of the National Union of Disabled Ex-Servicemen I, 1 (June 1926). Leeds

    A   1d. Published by the Leeds Branch at their office. Secretary of the Branch: J. Potts. To help the disabled and safeguard his future, with regard to pensions, treatment, employment, legislation.

    L; O†

421 Buzzer: Organ of the Militant Miners of Glencraig

    A   1d. Communist Party. Abe Moffat was concerned with the publication. Reproduced from typewriting.

    E† 29 Aug. 1930 (photocopy)

422 CAA Magazine, Being the Official Organ of the Concert Artistes' Association I (1938)–?

    A?

    L (destroyed)

423 CANDRA: Organ of the Coney Hall and District Residents' Association 1939–41

    B

    LRD

424 CGM Clerical Grades Monthly: Official Organ of the Civil Service Clerical Association, Ministry of Health Branch 1 (1920)–251 (Dec. 1945/Jan. 1946); m

    A   Gratis. A branch journal to supplement the general **CSCA** journal **Red Tape**. Issues before No. 202 were duplicated and copies issued to members only. Reports, articles, some political, correspondence.

    L† 202 (Jan. 1941)–251

425 CHA Holiday Abroad [19   ?]– . Manchester

    A?   Co-operative Holidays Association.

    L 1957–

426 CO's Hansard: a Weekly Report of Parliamentary Proceedings etc. 1 (27 July 1916)–90 (10 April 1919); w

    B   No-Conscription Fellowship. A record of debates on cases of conscientious objectors, treatment and imprisonment.

    BP; BS 18–90*; L†; LFS

    Also retrospective series. 1–6. L

COSA Bulletin see National Union of Mineworkers, Colliery Officials and Staffs Area. **Area News Service**

COSA News Bulletin see National Union of Mineworkers, Colliery Officials and Staffs Area. **Area News Service**

427 CP Bulletin: St Pancras Local

    B   See also Bulletin: the Organ of the St Pancras LPC.

    O(JJ)† 26 Aug. 1926

428 CPSA Norm 1 [1969?]–?

    A   Civil and Public Services Association, Treasury Branch. Reproduced from typewriting.

    Warwick U (MRC)† 8 (Nov. 1970), and 2 further nos **CSM News** see **New Crusader**

429 CTO and London City District Telephones Chronicle 1 [1923?]–?

    A   1d. Published by the London Central Telegraphs and Telephones Branch, Union of Post Office Workers.

    TUC† 4 (12 Oct. 1923)

430 CW News Letter I, 1 (1 May 1950)–VI, 55 (June 1954) New Malden; fortn

    B   2d. etc. Common Wealth [party]. Editor: Douglas Stuckey.

    L*

CW Quarterly see **Common Wealth Review**

431 CYM Youth Clubs Bulletin 1 (1956)–? Loughborough

    A   Co-operative Youth Movement.

    L† 1

432 Cab 1 (3 March 1832)–20 (14 July 1832); w

B   ½d. Published by G. Berger (1–16); G. Cowie (17); and George Edmonds (18–20). Printed at Elliot's Literary Salon (1–16); then printed and edited by George Edmonds (17–20). 'Initially a slight illustrated miscellany of satire and anecdotes (1–16), then a radical political journal that condemns the aristocracy and monarchy, and advocates the use of force to rectify abuses' (17–20) (Wiener).

BP 1–4, 6–8; L (destroyed); O 1, 5; O(JJ) 1; Press Club, London 2; Tolson Memorial Museum, Huddersfield 20

433 Cabinet Newspaper 1 (27 Nov. 1858)–65 (18 Feb 1860); w

B   2d., 3d. stamped. Published by Wicks and Company, then by Ernest Jones. Printed and edited by Ernest Jones. Supported manhood suffrage, reported on the Chartist movement, advocated a New Reform Movement.

L(Col)†

434 Cabman: a Monthly Journal and Review I, 1 (Sept. 1874)–II, 6 (Feb. 1876); m

C ½d. Printed and published for the proprietors, the Dupee brothers, by R. Higginbottom. Issued from the London Cabmen's Mission Hall, Minister and Superintendent, John Dupee. Promotion of moral and spiritual welfare of cabmen.

L†

435 Cabman's Chronicle 1 (15 Oct. 1895)–2 (1 Nov. 1895)

A?   C?

L (not traced)

436 Cabman's Punch: Official Organ of Cabmen's Joint Branch (Rank and File) Committee 1 (Sept. 1935)–10 (Sept. 1936); m

A   1d. Published by the Committee's Editorial Board. Main contributor: R. Bailey.

L†

437 Cabmen's Weekly Messenger 1 (1 Jan. 1898)–22 (Sept. 1898). Brighton; w

C   'Christian paper issued free to all engaged in the Public Vehicle Traffic everywhere.' 'Published by the Brighton Mission to Wheelchairmen, Cabmen, Busmen, Tramcarmen, and others similarly occupied.'

L(Col)

438 Cab Trade News I [19   ?]–?; m

A   Organ of the branches of the Cab Section of the Transport and General Workers' Union. Absorbed the **Co-operative Cabman's Gazette**.

TUC† XIV, 172 (June 1947)–Jan. 1953

439 Cab Trade Record: the Official Journal of the London Cab Drivers' Trade Union [1897?]–128 (Aug. 1908); m

A   1d. Published by Messrs Simmons and Thorpe. Reports of branch meetings, cab trade gossip, special reports of Police Court cases involving cabmen. Contributor: Fred Hill, General Secretary.

L(Col)† 45 (Sept. 1901)–128; Transport and General Workers' Union 1897–1908? (as **Cab Drivers' Record**)

440 Cainscross and Ebley **Co-operative Economist** 1 (Jan. 1893)–? Stroud; m

A   Gratis. Cainscross and Ebley Co-operative Industrial and Provident Society. Reports of meetings, articles on co-operation and other matters, editorial jottings, poems, miscellanea.

Co-op Coll†. VII (1900), XI (1903); L 241 (1913)–?; MML occ. vols

441 Call: 'an Organ of International Socialism' 1 (24 Feb. 1916)–225 (29 July 1920); fortn; w (1 June 1916–   )

B   1d.; 2d. 1916–20 published by members of the British Socialist Party, then by the Executive Committee. From 5 Aug. 1920 incorporated in **The Communist** (qv).

L(Col)†; MML; ONC 39–126, 187

442 Call of the Socialist Anti-War Front 1 (Nov. 1939)–6 (April 1940); m

B   1d. Published by Hugo Dewar. Revolutionary socialist. Socialist Anti-War Front formed in September 1938 by 'a group of seasoned Socialist workers in London' in an effort to organize working-class opposition to imperialist war, and to achieve unity among Socialists in the Labour Movement. Looks to the Trades Councils and Shop Stewards movement for leadership. Contributors: Reg. Groves, H. Dewar, Secretary of the SAWF.

L(Col)†

443 Call, of the Workers and Peasants of Russia, to Their English Speaking Fellow Workers [Sept. 1918?]–? Moscow; w

A   Published by the Central Executive Committee of the Council of Workmen's and Peasants' Deputies 'with the object of convincing its English-speaking fellow workers that the interests of the workers of all lands are the same'. It urged the 'solidarity of international labour' and sought to give news of the international class struggle.

L(Col)† (4, 5 Oct; 9, 9 Nov. 1918)

444 Calling Croydon: the Official Organ of the Croydon Branch of NALGO [194–?] Croydon

A   National Association of Local Government Officers, later National and Local Government Officers' Association. Reproduced from typewriting.

L 45 (Jan. 1953)–

445 Camaraderie: the Monthly Record of the Bourneville Works Youths' Club 1 (Nov. 1901)–7 (June 1902). [Bourneville?] ; m
    C   Catering for mental and physical improvement, and for 'good fellowship' among Club members.
    L†

446 Camberwell Gazette [193–?] ; m
    B   Labour Party. (Labour and Socialist International. **The Socialist Press**, 1933).

447 Cambria: a Journal of Adult Education and Social Service in Wales 1 (Spring 1930)–9 (1933). Cardiff; 3-yr
    C   3d. Magazine of the South Wales District of the Workers' Educational Association. Editor: David E. Evans.
    BnU; CrU; SwU

448 Cambridge Citizen ns 1 (May 1950)–1 (Nov. 1954). Cambridge; m
    A   Issued by the Cambridge Trades Council and Labour Party. Sub-title in 1954: 'Official Organ of Cambridge City Labour Party'. Printed and published by the Co-operative Press. One of the 'Citizen' series. Replaced **Cambridge Review**.
    L(Col)† ns

449 Cambridge Intelligencer 1 (20 July 1793)–234 (1803). Cambridge
    B
    C; L(Col) (27 July 1793)–(27 Dec. 1800*)

450 Cambridge Left I, 1 (Summer 1933)–II, 1 (Autumn 1934). Cambridge; 3-yr
    B   9d. (1–2); 6d. Published by **Cambridge Left** (1–2), W. Heffer. Printed by Leicester Co-operative Printing Society. A University magazine containing articles on politics and literature, reviews, poetry. Contributors: W. H. Auden, J. D. Bernal, J. Cornford, M. Dobb.
    C; E; O†

451 Cambridge Newsletter 1964?– . Cambridge
    A   National and Local Government Officers' Association, Cambridge Branch. Reproduced from typewriting.
    L 1964–

452 Cambridge Socialist [c1954]. Cambridge
    B   (**Oxford Left**, Hilary 1954, sends fraternal greetings.)

453 Cambridge University Socialist Club. Bulletin [19   ?]–? Cambridge
    B
    C ii 14, IV, 1–8, V, 1–14 (1940–1)

454 Camden and Granby St Spark [1924?] —?; fortn
    A   ½d. Printed and published by the Communist Party of Great Britain. For all grades of railway workers. Communist Party and Minority Movement. Single sheet.
    O(JJ)† occ. nos 1925—6

455 Camden NALGO News 1967—
    A   National and Local Government Officers' Association.
    L 1967—

Camden Star and LMS Railway Worker see LMS Railway Worker

456 Camera Principis: Official Magazine of the Coventry Branch of the National and Local Government Officers' Association. Coventry
    A
    L XXIII, 200 (April 1953)—

457 Campaign 1 (Jan. 1961)—[1964?] ; m
    B   Issued by the Campaign for Democratic Socialism from May 1962, previously by the Labour Manifesto Group, Campaign for Democratic Socialism. 'CDS is not a formally constituted organisation and has no members. It relies for its income solely on the sale of **Campaign** and on donations from its supporters.' (34.) Its support was said to come from 'informed and moderate opinion determined to rescue Labour from the consequences of militant and unrepresentative minorities, and put the Party back on the road to power'. Sought to 'attack the illusions and irresponsibility of the so-called Left'.
    LE† 1—35; LabP† 2—36 (June/July 1964); ONC occ. nos

458 Campaigner, in the Interests of the United Association of Ex-Naval and Military Civil Servants 1 (25 Nov. 1913)—149 (15 Oct. 1931); fortn
    A   1d. Printed and published by R. E. Gordon and Company for the Association whose object was to gain recognition of Naval and Military Service as a qualification for Civil Service pensions. Superseded **The Sentinel**.
    L(Col)†; O 1—12

459 Campsie Quarterly Report [194-?] Lennoxtown, Glasgow; q
    B   Labour Party. Duplicated. (Labour Party. **Your own Journal**, 1948.)

460 Camshaft: the Journal of the PO Railway Branch, POEU I, 1 (Oct. 1928)—(Jan. 1932); ns I, 1, (June 1932); m
    A   Post Office Engineering Union, Post Office Railway Branch. Edited by the Branch Secretary. Reproduced from typewriting.
    L†

461 Canal Boatman's Magazine I, 1 (April 1829)—ns III, 12 (Dec. 1832);
m

    C   1d. Printed and published by A. Snell. Published under the
patronage of the Paddington Society for Promoting Christian Knowledge
among Canal Boatmen, and Others. 'To circulate among boatmen, carmen,
dustmen and labourers at the Wharfs (particularly at Paddington).'
Alternative title for Vol. I. **Paddington Canal Boatman's Magazine.**

    L†; O ii I—II

462 Candlestick 1 (31 Jan. 1900)—17 (March 1903). Derby; Leicester;
bi-m

    B   2d. Issued by Francis Riddel Henderson. Printed by the
Leicester Co-operative Printing Society. Edited by William L. Hare. Ethical
socialist and Christian pacifist with Tolstoyan influences. Contributors:
John Kenworthy, Leo Tolstoy, Ernest Crosby, Percy Redfern.

    L†

463 Cannock Chase Examiner: a Journal of General Intelligence, Devoted
to the Interests of Labour 1 (Aug. 1873)—214 (5 Oct. 1877). Hednesford,
Staffordshire; w

    B   1d. Publishers: Benjamin Evans; proprietor, William Owen;
Charles Smith. Printed by the Co-operative Newspaper and General
Printing Society; by the proprietor, William Owen. One of a series of local
papers owned by Owen, promoting the interests of Labour and the trade
unions in the Midlands localities, mainly miners and ironworkers. Then
incorporated with the **Midland Examiner and Wolverhampton Times.**

    L(Col)† 55 (2 Jan. 1875)—214

464 Cannock Labour Gazette [194-?] Cannock, Staffordshire; m

    B   1d. Labour Party. (Labour Party. **Your own Journal**, 1948.)

465 Cap of Liberty: a London Weekly Political Publication 1 (8 Sept.
1819)—18 (5 Jan. 1820); w

    B   2d. Printed and published by and for Thomas Davison, London.
Editor: James Griffin. An ultra-radical unstamped paper, for Henry Hunt,
universal suffrage.

    L†; LE 2—18; LU 3; MR; MUC

466 Capital and Labour Preliminary issue, 31. Dec. 1873; I, 1 (25 Feb.
1874)—IX, 461 (20 Dec. 1882); w

    C   4d. Issued by the Council of the National Federation of
Associated Employers of Labour, set up to counteract organised Trade
Unionism. 'Specifically designed to establish among Employers and among
non-union workmen a channel of intercommunication.' Advocates 'free
labour'; seeks to counteract agitation for repeal of Master and Servant Act,
Criminal Law Amendment Act, and Law of Conspiracy. Sub-title on
frontispiece of No. 1: 'a Weekly Journal of Facts and Arguments on
Questions Relating to Employers and Employed'. Later sub-title: 'an
Economic, Financial, and Mechanical Journal'.

    EU I—VI; L(Col)†; LU I—V; MP

467 Card, and Blowing Room and Ring Frame Operatives Association. Bolton and District. **Quarterly Report** [19--?] --? Bolton; q
    A
    TUC† May 1959--Sept. 1964*

468 Card, and Blowing Room and Ring Frame Operatives' Association. Oldham Provincial. **Quarterly Report** [19--?] --? Oldham; q
    A
    TUC† Dec. 1960, 1961, 1962

469 Cardiff Citizen 1 (Sept. 1935)--2 (Oct. 1935). Cardiff; m
    B
    L(Col)

470 Cardiff Co-operative Citizen 1 (April 1933)--? Cardiff; irreg?
    B
    L(Col) April, June 1933, June 1935

471 Cardiff Pioneer [19--?] --?
    B   Published by the Co-operative Press.
    L(Col) (1 Nov. 1937)

472 Cardiff South Clarion [194-?] Cardiff; m
    B   Free. Labour Party. (Labour Party. **Your own Journal**, 1948.)

473 Cardiganshire Labour News and Views [194-?]. Llandyssul; irreg
    B   Labour Party. Duplicated. (Labour Party. **Your own Journal**, 1948.)

Caretaker see **Caretakers' Monthly Journal**

474 Caretakers' Monthly Journal [1910?] --76 (April 1916); then **Caretaker**: 77 (May 1916)--84 (Dec. 1916); m
    A   1d. Official organ of the National Federation of Caretakers. Motto: 'Justice for Duty'. For amelioration of wages and conditions.
    L(Col)† 68 (Aug. 1915)--84

475 Carlile's Journal for 1830: a Companion to the Newspapers 1 (1 Jan. 1830)--4 (21 Jan. 1830); irreg
    B   Published, printed and edited by Richard Carlile. 'Carlile seeks to evade stamp duty by means of these unnumbered "pamphlets" which express his free-thought and republican views' (Wiener).
    H.O. 64/16 No. 4; L; LU; MP

476 Carlile's Political Register 1 (19 Oct. 1839)--9 (14 Dec. 1839); w
    B   2d. Edited by Richard Carlile. Continues his strident advocacy of republicanism and rationalism, the appropriation of Church estate for universal secular education, rejecting political agitations like Chartism, asserting instead the primacy of the education of the masses.
    L† 1, 3--5, 7--9; MP

477 Carpenters' and Joiners' Amalgamated Review: a Monthly Journal
Devoted to Promote the Interests of the Amalgamated Society of
Carpenters and Joiners 1 (March 1904)–[1904?] ; m
     A   1d. Edited by Evan T. Jones, Camden Town Branch. Urges
100% Trade Unionism and support for Labour candidates. Illustrated.
     L† 1–3 (May 1904); O† 1; O(JJ)† 1

478 Carpenter's London Journal 1 (13 Feb. 1836)–12? (30 April 1836?);
w
     B   2d. Proprietor: J. Taylor. Editor: William Carpenter. 'A political
and literary miscellany that expresses Carpenter's moderate pro-reform
outlook with its emphasis upon education and voluntary change' (Wiener).
     L Place Collection, Set 651; O 1; O(JJ) 1

479 Carpenter's Monthly Political Magazine I, 1 (Sept. 1831)–II(Sept.
1832); m
     B   Published by William Strange. Edited by William Carpenter.
Articles on political and social reform questions. Support for Political
Unions, and the National Union of the Working Classes, annual parliaments, ballot vote and adult suffrage.
     L I (Sept. 1831–July 1832); LE† Greenwood reprint and microfiche:
microfiche distributed in Britain and Europe by the Harvester Press Ltd;
LU I; MP 1–2; ONC I

480 Carpenter's Political and Historical Essays (1 (April 1831)–9 ([c.
June?] 1831); w
     B   1d. Published, printed and written by William Carpenter. 'Each
number consists of a full-length essay by Carpenter on one aspect of
reform, such as trade unionism and the extension of the Parliamentary
franchise.' (Wiener).
     LU 1–8; Columbia University Library, New York 4, 6, 9

Carpenter's Political Letters and Pamphlets see [**Political Letters and
Pamphlets**]

481 Carshalton Labour Herald: the Official Organ of the Carshalton
Labour Party 1 (Sept. 1935)–4 (Dec. 1935)–(Jan. 1936); m
     B   1d. Published by Mr Stocking. To 'rejuvenate' the Carshalton
Labour Party.
     L(Col)†

482 Cartel: a Review of Monopoly Developments and Consumer
Protection; a Publication of the International Co-operative Alliance I
(1950)– ;q
     A
     C; CME; E; L; LE; LII; MP VIII– ; O

Castle Guardian see National Association of Local Government Officers.
Hinckley Branch. **Newsletter**

Catalyst see **Between Ourselves** [1949?] –[1963?]

483 Catering Trade Worker: International Journal for the Interests of All Employees of the Catering Trade I, 1 (1 Jan. 1913)–II, 8 (1 Aug. 1914); m

    A 1d. Official organ of the Amalgamated Union of Hotel, Club and Restaurant Workers, and of the syndicate des Cuisiniers, Patissiers, Glaciers, Confisiers de Londres, and of the Section des Garçons de Cuisine Plongeurs etc. Printed and published by the Joint Unions, then by the Kitchen Workers' Union, when with Vol. I, No. 10, October 1913 it becomes the organ of that Union. A militant section within the General Federation of Trade Unions. Leader: Percy A. Young. Revolutionary syndicalist, advocating direct action. In English, French, German and Italian.

    L(Col)†

484 Catering Worker: Official Organ of the Amalgamated Union of Hotel, Club and Restaurant Workers I, 1 (Oct. 1913)–I, 11 (Sept. 1914); ns 1 (July 1915); m

    A 1d. Printed and published by the Union. Ns No. 1, monthly journal of the National Union of Catering Workers. Militant industrial Unionism. General Secretary: Percy A. Young. In English, French, German and Italian.

    L(Col)†

485 Catholic Crusader: a Challenge to Capitalism [19–?] [Thaxted]

    B Christian Socialist. Organ of the Catholic Crusade, 'the Catholic Creed expressed in the Socialist Faith'. Started by Conrad Noel and others who had broken from the Church Socialist League (C. Noel, **Autobiography**, 1945, p. 107; P. d'A. Jones, **The Christian Socialist revival, 1877–1914**, Princeton 1968, p. 301).

486 Cause of the People: a Political History of Nine Weeks 1 (20 May 1848)–9 (15 July 1848). Douglas, Isle of Man; w

    B 2d. Printed and published by William Shirrefs and Andrew Russell. London agent: James Watson. Editors: W. J. Linton and George Holyoake. Object: to make Chartists, by educating the people in the principles and the duty of the Charter. Promoted the People's Charter Union. Opposed to O'Connor and the National Charter Association. Chartist news and news of international liberation movements, e.g. Poland, France, Ireland.

    Bishopsgate Institute† ; NwA Cowen Coll.

487 Caveat Emptor: the Magazine of the West Kent Branch of NALGO I, 1 (June 1953)–? Dartford; m

    A National Association of Local Government Officers. Reproduced from typewriting.

    L† I, 1,–V, 7 (Dec. 1957)

488 Centaur: a Record of the Road 1 (22 March 1879)–348 (2 Nov. 1885); w

A 1d. Printed and published for the Amalgamated Cab-Drivers Society by H. W. Rowland, General Secretary. Advocates working-class MPs elected by the power of the trade unions, and pledged to an advanced radical political programme and pro-Labour legislation. Includes news of other working-class bodies such as friendly societies. Later sub-title: 'the Cab Trade Gazette'.

L(Col)†

489 Central Hackney Citizen 1 (May 1930)–?; m

B Published by the London Co-operative Society.

L(Col) 1–17 (Nov. 1931)

490 Central London Review: the Official Organ of the Central London Postmen's Association [19–?]–?; w

A Printed by the Co-operative Printing Society.

ONC IX, 10 (6 Feb. 1915) [missing]

491 Central Southwark Citizen 1 (May 1935)–?; m

A Published by the Royal Arsenal Co-operative Society's Political Committee.

L(Col) 1–52 (Sept. 1939)

492 Central Southwark Sentinel 1 (July 1924)–?; m

B Published and edited by Frank Roberts, Secretary of Central Southwark Labour Party. Puts forward Labour Party policy in local and national affairs.

L(Col)† 1–ns 23 (Nov. 1926)

493 Central Southwark Sentinel [193-?] ; m

B Labour Party. (Labour and Socialist International. **The Socialist Press**, 1933.)

494 Centre Lines. I, 1 (1 June 1958)–

A Organ of the Association of Engineering and Shipbuilding Draughtsmen, Stretford Branch.

TUC I, 1

495 Centre Point: the Journal of the London Teachers I, 1 (30 June 1967)–; 3-yr

A 1s. Inner London Teachers' Association (NUT).

O†

Ceramic and Allied Trades Union. **News Letter** see Potter's Union. **News Letter**

496 Cert: the NALGO Magazine for Members of Central Electricity Board Transmission Project Group and Research Laboratories 1965?–.
Guildford
    A   National and Local Government Officers' Association. Reproduced from typewriting.
    L 1965–

497 Chain Makers' Journal and Trades' Circular I, 1 (July–1858)–?
Newcastle-upon-Tyne; m
    A   Published by the Chain Makers' Trade Union. Edited by Charles Blake. Title from No. 12, May 1859: **Chain Makers' Journal and Trades' Circular of the North, Staffordshire, and Wales.**
    LE†

498 Chalk: the Young Teacher Newsletter of the Liverpool Teachers Association, NUT [1970?]– . Liverpool
    A   National Union of Teachers. No. 4 was March 1971

499 Challenge: Official Organ of the Socialist Labour Party I, 1 (May [1932?4?]) Edinburgh
    B   1d. Printed and published by the Socialist Labour Press. De Leonist.
    E†

500 Challenge: the Official Organ of the Wellingborough Divisional Labour Party ns 1 (Sept. 1934)–45 (Nov. 1935); ns Sept. 1936–July 1939. Wellingborough; m
    B   1d. Printed and published by Stanley L. Hunt for the Labour Party. Contributor: George Dallas.
    L(Col)†

501 Challenge [Special number, undated]; I, 1 (March 1935)– ; fortn; m
    B   1d. etc. Communist youth paper. Publishers: Young Communist League; S. Bristow; Challenge Publications.
    L(Col)†; MML; O 1940–

502 Champion and Weekly Herald I, 1 (18 Sept. 1836)–ns 52 (5 May 1838); w
    B   4d. Title of the first few numbers was simply **The Champion**. Printer: Mills and Son, then printed and published by Richard Cobbett. A democratic journal and review of the developing political situation in Parliament especially. Consistently attacks the Poor Law system and defends trade unions against the witch hunt of 1838. Pro-Chartist, demanding the right of the labouring classes to full political representation. Merged in **The Northern Liberator.**
    L†; MP; O(JJ)† I, 1; ONC (13 May 1837)–(5 May 1838)

503 Champion of What is True and Right and for the Good of All I 1 (10 Nov. 1849)—26 (4 May 1850); II, 1 ([May 1850?])—II, 26 ([Oct. 1850?]). Manchester, London; w

C Publisher: J. Ollivier, London; Abel Heywood, John Heywood, J. Pavey, Manchester. Printer: E. Hobson, Ashton. Official organ of the Fielden Society. Editor: Rev J. R. Stephens. Contributor: Oastler. Promotes factory reform. Contains reports of factory conditions, articles dealing with Factory Acts, emigration, the Ten-Hours Bill, wages.

Ashton PL; ONC†

Chariot see **Railway Servants' Chariot**

Chart and Compass see **Pilot**

504 Charter; Established by the Working Classes 1 (27 Jan. 1839)—60 (15 March 1840); w

A 6d. An organ of the London Working Men's Association. Publisher: Robert Hartwell, a leading member of the Association. Printer: William Summerfield. Editor: William Carpenter. Financed by subscriptions from the London trades societies. Gave full reports of proceedings of the National Chartist Convention held in London and brief coverage of Chartism in the regions. According to the last number it started favourably with a circulation of nearly 6,000 per week. Incorporated 22 March 1840, with the Liberal paper **The Statesman and Weekly True Sun**.

Bishopsgate Institute; L(Col)†; LE (Microfilm; 17—49 originals); ONC

505 Chartist 1 (2 Feb. 1839)—23 (7 July 1839); w

B 2½d. Printed and published by Messrs Thompson. 'To serve the producers, the mighty many.' Employing the rhetoric of 'physical force', it sought to intimidate the middle class into joining with the masses to win universal suffrage and bring down the aristocracy.

L(Col)†; ONC

506 Chartist Circular 1 (28 Sept. 1839)—146 (9 July 1842). Glasgow; w

B ½d. Organ of the Universal Suffrage Central Committee for Scotland. Editor William Thomson, 'advocate of retail co-operation, former secretary of the Scottish National Association for the Protection of Handloom Weavers, former editor of **Weavers' Journal** and secretary of the Universal Suffrage Central Committee for Scotland.' (T. M. Kemnitz. 'Chartist newspaper editors.' **Victorian Periodicals Newsletter**, 18 [December 1972], 1—11.) Propagated Chartist and democratic principles. Contributors: Dr. John Taylor, O'Brien, Lovett, Collins etc.

BrU; DnP; E; EP; GM; GU; L 1—104; LE; LU 1841; NpP; O; Greenwood reprint and microfiche: microfiche distributed in Britain and Europe by the Harvester Press Ltd.

507 Chartist Circular 1858

    B   Editor: Ernest Jones.

    Bishopsgate Institute, Howell Coll. 6, 9

508 Chartist Pioneer 1—2. 1842. [Leicester?]

    B   ½d. Editor and proprietor: Thomas Cooper. Cooper refers to this, his last venture into Chartist journalism, in **Northern Star**, 9 July 1842, and says 'poverty in ranks' brought it to an untimely end.

509 Chatham Co-operative Citizen 1 (Oct. 1936)—36 (Sept. 1939); ns 1 (Jan 1946)—66 (June 1951); m

    B   Published by the Co-operative Press.

    L(Col)

510 Chatterton's Commune: the Atheistic Communistic Scorcher 1 (Sept. 1884)—42 (April 1895); irreg.

    B   1d. Printed, published, edited and written by Daniel Chatterton, ('Old Chat'). In hand-written and then on printed sheets (from I, 7), this aged communist exhorts the working class to make the social revolution. The system which breeds violence has to be overthrown by violent means. No. 40, Oct. 1894, contains a brief biographical sketch of the author.

    L†

512 Cheadle and Gatley NALGO Branch Magazine 1962?— Cheadle and Gatley

    A   **Magazine** becomes **News and Views**. National and Local Government Officers' Association, Cheadle and Gatley Branch. Reproduced from typewriting.

    L 1962—

513 'Cheerio.': a Magazine Produced and Published by the Unemployed Workers in the Occupational Centres of Birkenhead I, 1 (Dec. 1932)—II, 5 (March 1934). Birkenhead; fortn

    A   1d. 'A medium for interchange of experience and pooling of ideas' concerning work of the occupational centres for the mental and physical upkeep of unemployed workmen. From II, 2, produced and published by the Unemployed Clerical Workers at Beechcroft Settlement. Non-political party. Reproduced from typewriting.

    L† (w I, 9)

514 Chelmsford Clarion [194-?]; m

    B   1d. Labour Party. (Labour Party. **Your own Journal**, 1948.)

515 Chelmsford ILP Journal [189-?]. Chelmsford

    B   Independent Labour Party. (D. Hopkin, 'Local Newspapers of the Independent Labour Party, 1893—1906'. Society for the Study of Labour History, **Bulletin**, 28 [Spring 1974].)

16 Chelsea DS and S Gazette and Services Sentinel: the Official Organ of
ne Chelsea and South Kensington Branch of the National Federation of
Discharged and Demobilised Sailors and Soldiers, the Only Registered
x-Service Man's Organisation in Chelsea 1 (11 Oct. 1919)– ns I, 10
Aug.1920); fortn

    A   1d. Published by the Ex-Service Press. Non-party political,
on-sectarian. To place the true position of the work of the NFDDSS
efore the public. To secure economic justice for the ex-serviceman in
rms of employment and good wages.

    L†

17 Chelsea Pick and Shovel 1 (Jan. 1900)–13 (Jan. 1901); m

    B   Gratis. Published by the Chelsea Branch of the Independent
abour Party. Editor: Florence Groves. Emphasis on municipal politics as
ney affect the lives of working-class families, as in housing, sanitation, and
rovision for the poor. Publicises meetings of the Chelsea Vigilance
ommittee, a body to protect the rights of working people to decent
ousing. The paper was a localisation of a newspaper published by Fred
heppard. A similar one was **Hammersmith Searchlight** (D. Hopkin).

    KeP; L(Col)† 1–12; LE*

18 Chelsea Review 1 (March 1928)–2 (April 1928)

    B   1d. Organ of the Chelsea Labour Party and Trades Council
nd published by them. Printed by the Blackfriars Press. Editor: J. M. R.
tudholme. Emphasis on housing conditions and unemployment. No. 1
as London County Council election number. Boast circulation of nearly
0,000.

    L(Col)†

19 Chelsea Searchlight 1900

    B?   Issued by Florence Grove. Discontinued in December because
f insufficient support **(Reformers' Year Book**, 1901).

20 Chelsea, South Kensington, North Kensington Labour News July
965–Sept. 1965; m

    B   Labour Party. Reproduced from typewriting. Replaced **Labour
Report: South Kensington Labour Party Journal (qv).**

    ONC†

21 Cheltenham Working Men's College Magazine I, 1 (Oct. 1884)–I, 12
Sept. 1885); then b **Philistine**: I, 1 (Oct. 1885)–I, 6 (March 1886).
heltenham; m

    C   Literary offerings.

    L†; O b

522 Chemical Workers' Herald: Bulletin of the International Chemical Workers Committee for Propaganda and Action I, 1 (Jan. 1929)—I, 4 (Aug. 1929); bi-m

A   1d. English edition published by the Chemical Workers Minorit Movement. Reproduced from typewriting. Useful for 'speakers and Workers' press men'; special information on the chemical industry.

O(JJ)†

523 Chemical Worker: Official Journal of the National Union of Drug and Chemical Workers [19--?]—? fortn; m

A   1d. Editor: Arthur J. Gillian (1931). Short articles, notes, correspondence, serial story, women's column, gardening column, reviews (1931). Socialist (1931).

BU ns XXXVI, 11 (1955)—; ONC† ns IX, 6 (21 March 1931); TUC† ns XXIV, 8 (Aug. 1944)—(April 1967)

524 Chemist's Assistant: the Official Organ of the Chemists' Assistants' Association I, 1 (March 1900)—46 (Dec. 1903); m

A   2d. Printed and published by The Farringdon Press. Urges necessity for combination. Association notes etc., and technical material. Also reports on the Chemists' Assistants' Union of Great Britain. Succeeded by **Pharmaceutical Review**, a trade journal, not within our categories.

L(Col)†

525 Chepstow Bulletin [194-?] Chepstow; m

B   Labour Party. Reproduced from typewriting. (Labour Party. **Your own Journal**, 1948.)

526 Chester Co-operative Chronicle and Magazine for the Working Classes 1 (10 July 1830)— ? Chester; w; m

B   1d., 2d. Published 'at the Store in St Werburgh Street'.

Bishopsgate Institute 1—6 (1 Oct 1830) (w 2)

527. Chevrons: the Organ of the NFDDS & S, Paddington Branch I, 1 (July 1919)—I, 9 (April 1920); m

A   2d. National Federation of Discharged and Demobilised Sailors and Soldiers. Formed to present the case of the discharged and pensioned ex-serviceman. 'The only live ex-service man's and Labour paper in the West of London.'

L†

528 China News 1 (July 1939)

B   1d. Published by the China Campaign Committee. Edited by J. B. Priestley. To gain support for China after Japan's undeclared war on the country.

L(Col)†

529 Chingford Advertiser and Labour News 1 (Jan. 1925); then **Chingford Advertiser**: 2 (Feb. 1925)–188 (Aug. 1940); m

    B   Free. Published first by the Chingford Branches of the Independent Labour Party. Continues support for the Labour Movement. Later sub-title: 'an Independent Journal of Local, National and International Citizenship'. News of local affairs; fiction (eg, 'The Bakers: a complete short story by the miner-author, Harold Heslop', Jan. 1933).

    L(Col)† (w 7)

530 Chingford Challenger [193-?]–?

    B   Guild of Youth.

531 Chingford Clarion: Organ of the Chingford Labour Party I, 1 (Sept. 1946)–III, 10 (Nov. 1949); m

    B   2d. Reports work of Chingford Labour Party and of the Labour Group on Chingford Council.

    L†

532 Chippenham Socialist [194-?]. Chippenham; m

    B   2d. Labour Party. (Labour Party. **Your own Journal**, 1948.)

533 Chisel 1 (Jan. 1929)–11 (Nov. 1929); m

    A   1d. Published by the Furnishing Trades Minority Movement. CPGB 2, 11

534 Chorley Citizen. [194-?] Chorley, Lancashire; m

    B   2d. Published by **Voice**. Labour Party. (Labour Party. **Your own Journal**, 1948.)

535 Chorley Co-operative Society. **Monthly Record** I (1896)–XXIII, 11 (Jan. 1920); then **Quarterly Record**: XXIV, 1 (April 1920)–(Jan. 1921). Chorley; m; q

    A   Gratis. 'In January 1896, the first number of the society's monthly **Record** was published. This was intended to be the medium through which matters of business and items of interest connected with things co-operative in Chorley and elsewhere, were communicated to the members, and it served that purpose – amongst others – until the end of 1920, when it was superseded by the **Wheatsheaf** . . . Whether the **Record** was published regularly through the years that followed [ie after 1901] until 1920 I have not discovered, but it was appearing in 1920, and also appeared in January 1921, when the **Wheatsheaf** was also issued, but that was the last issue' (F. Longton, **Fifty years of co-operation in Chorley 1887–1937**, Chorley 1937, p. 69, pp. 71–2).

    L XVIII, 11–XXIV, 4 (Dec. 1920); Lancashire County Lib V, 1 (Feb. 1900)–V, 12 (Jan. 1901)

Chorley Co-operative Society. **Quarterly Record** see Chorley Co-operative Society. **Monthly Record**

536 Chorlton Ward Labour Party Bulletin 1 (Sept. 1969)—16 (Jan. 1971). Manchester; m

B   Reproduced from typewriting. Distributed to members.

537 Christian Corrector 1 [c April 1831?]—61 (June 1832); w; fortn

B   1d.—4d. Published, printed and edited by Thomas Parkin, then published and printed by William Arnold. 'A radical miscellany in which Parkin denounces organized religion, supports the appropriation of church property, and repeatedly employs Christian doctrine to sanction revolution' (Wiener).

GM*; HO 64/18 42—3, 45, 48—9, 57; O(JJ) 61

538 Christian Commonwealth I, 1 (20 Oct. 1881)—(1919), (24 Sept. 1919); then b **New Commonwealth**: I, 1 (Oct. 1919)—III, 1 (Jan. 1922); w; m

B   1d. Starts as the organ of the Baptist Spurgeon movement, later coming closer to the Labour Movement. Editors: Henry Varley, W. T. Moore, John Kirton, A. Dawson. Contributors: Philip Snowden, Margaret MacMillan, Annie Besant. Supporters in the Independent Labour Party. Fenner Brockway was on the staff, c1907—1910. Absorbed **The Fountain**

L(Col)†; LDW a XVIII—XIX*; O b I—II, 8; ONC b II, 3 (May 1920)—8 (Oct. 1920)

539 Christian Democrat I (1921)—? Oxford

B?   Catholic Social Guild.

CoU;* L; O XIX, 1939—

Christian Pioneer and Poor Man's Friend see **Baptist Pioneer and Poor Man's Friend**

540 Christian Social Economist I, 1 (22 Nov. 1851)—6 (27 Dec. 1851). Dublin; w

B   4d. To 'ameliorate the condition of the masses', drastically to alter the Poor Law, encourage the universal diffusion of a sound practical industrial education and elevate the position and condition of teachers. Also seeks overhaul of Irish fisheries and manufactures. Editor: Thadeus O'Malley. Christian Socialist. Printed and published for the proprietor at the Office by Patrick Walsh.

L(Col)†

541 Christian Socialist: a Journal of Association, Conducted by Several of
the Promoters of the London Working Men's Associations I, 1 (2 Nov.
1850)—II, 61 (27 Dec. 1851); then b **Journal of Association**, Conducted
by Several of the Promoters of the London Working Men's Associations: I,
1 (3 Jan. 1852)—I, 27 (28 June 1852); w
    B   1d.; 2d. (last number.) 'Organ of the Society for Promoting
Working Men's Associations' Publishers: James Watson, Millbank and
Shorter of the SPWMA, J. Tupling. Printed by Working Printers'
Association. Editor: J. M. Ludlow. Other promoters included F. D.
Maurice.
      BP; C b; Co-op. Coll. II (1851); EU b; L a; LDW a II, 56; LE a; LU†;
ONC (19 July—8 Nov. 1851*)

542 Christian Socialist: a Journal for Thoughtful Men [I], 1 (June
1883)—IX, 103 (Dec. 1891); m
    B   1d. Published by William Reeves. 1884—6 sponsored by the
Land Reform Union; in January 1887 became the organ of the Christian
Socialist Society. Fought for independent Labour representation,
co-operated with other socialist movements. Editors: H. H. Champion,
Rev. C. L. Marson, James Leigh Joynes, Alfred Howard, William Howard,
Paul Campbell. Sub-title from June 1884: 'A Journal for Those Who Work
and Think'. Then incorporated in **Brotherhood**.
      Co-op. Coll. (w 1884); GM 1884—91; L; LabP June 1885—May
1886; LE*; LU I—II; O†

543 Christian Socialist. [19--?]; m
    B?   Christian Socialist Fellowship.
    ILP Jan. 1910

Christian Socialist, 1963— see **New Crusader**

544 Christmas Cracker: the Co-operator's Christmas Journal 1 (Dec.
1928)—? Manchester; a
    A   3d.
    L† 2—8, (1935)

Chronicle Nalgo see National Association of Local Government Officers.
Caernarvon and District Branch. **Newsletter**

545 Chronicle: the Official Organ of the Beckenham and Penge Labour
Party I, 1 (May 1936)—I, 6 (Oct. 1936); then **Labour Chronicle**: I, 7 (Nov.
1936)—V, 6 (June 1938); m
    B   1d. Joined by Bromley Labour Party when title changed.
    L†

546 Chronicle I, 1 (July 1956)–I, 4 (June 1957). Bournemouth; s-a

    A   National and Local Government Officers' Association, Bournemouth and District Health Services Branch. Reproduced from typewriting.

    L†

547 Chronicle for South and Mid-Glamorgan 1 (4 Jan. 1895)–1091 (28 June 1912). Bridgend, Glamorgan; w

    B   ½d. From 1906 supports Labour, contains 'Labour notes', and has regular columns by Labour contributors. A local general paper and advertiser.

    L(Col)† (1910*, 1911*)

548 Chronicler of the Times; or, **Hypocrisy Unmasked** 1 (12 Jan. 1833); w?

    B   1d. Published and printed (and edited?) by H. J. Record. 'A radical political miscellany that attacks the aristocracy, the fundholders, the Anglican Church, parish abuses, and the inadequacy of poor relief' (Wiener).

    BP; LU; ONC (photocopy)

549 Church Examiner and Ecclesiastical Record I, 1 (19 May 1832)–I, 21 (1 Dec. 1832); w (1–18); m (19–21)

    B   1d.; 2d. Publisher: George Cowie (1–4, 6); William Strange (5, 7–21). Printer: W. Johnston. Editors: John Cleave, William Carpenter. 'A radical political and satirical miscellany that repeatedly attacks the Church of England and counsels a refusal to pay church rates' (Wiener). Successor to **A Slap at the Church**.

    Co-op. Union; HO 64/18; 1, 4, 8–9, 11, 13–20; O 1–18, 20; O(JJ) 1; L 1

550 Church of Our Fathers: the Official Organ of the Church of England Working Men's Society 1 (June 1892)–II, 14 (July 1893). Oxford, London (and Bournemouth, 13–14); m

    A   1d. Published by Mowbray and Company. Editor: E. Mason Ingram. The Society worked among working men by means of voluntary agents 'who work for daily bread at factory or office' and taught by example and precept.

    L; O†

551 Church Reformer: an Organ of Christian Socialism and Church Reform I, 1 (Jan. 1882)–XIV, 12 (Dec. 1895); m

    B   1d.; 2d. Published for the proprietor by F. Verinder. Editor: Stuart D. Headlam. Took part in debate over basis of Socialism with secularists and scientific socialists.

    L†; LE 1884–1895*; O III–XIV

552 Church Socialist I, 1 (Jan./Feb. 1912)–IX, 96 (Nov./Dec. 1921); m

     B   1d.; 2d. Published by the Propaganda Committee of the London Branch, then by the Central Literature Committee, of the Church Socialist League. Chairman, 1912– : George Lansbury. Contributors: Conrad Noel, Egerton Swann.

     L; LdU; LE†

Church Socialist Quarterly see **Optimist**

553 Chwaral Teg; ['Fair Play'] : Official Organ of the South Wales District of the UPW [19--?] –? Cardiff, Newport

     A   1d. Union of Post Office Workers.

     TUC† July 1937

554 Chwarelwr Cymreig. [Welsh Quarryman] 1893–(27 March 1902). Bangor; w

     C   A Tory paper dominated by Lord Penrhyn directly aimed at Welsh quarrymen. Had little influence. Merged in **Clorianydd**.

     L(Col)

555 Cigarette-Maker: Organ of the United Cigarette-makers', Cutters', Packers', and Strippers' Union I, 1 (1 July 1906)–8 (22 Dec. 1906); fortn

     A   Organ of a newly organised union, with around 600 paying members. Journal conceived as an organiser, an educator, and teacher, campaigning for shorter hours, abolition of home and piece work, for decent wages and humane working conditions. Circulated mainly in the East End of London. In English and Yiddish.

     L(Col)†

Cine-Technician see Association of Cine-Technicians. **Journal**

556 Circle, for Friendly Society and Educational Purposes: Official Organ of the Workers' Circle I, 1 (April 1934)–X, 1 (April 1943); XI, 1(April 1945)–ns XII, 1 (April 1946); q

     A A 'working-class organisation' which encompasses all views and trends in the Socialist movement. Contents include reports and accounts, and general articles on political affairs, fiction, correspondence. Parallel texts in English and Yiddish. Yiddish title: **Arbaiter Ring**.

     L(Col)†

557 Circuit 1 (April 1897)–4 (July 1897); m

     B   Reproduced from manuscript, a journal of news items for socialist editors, with material from all over the world, with emphasis on election statistics. 'Arranged by L. Archilutte, illustrated by Chilli'.

     O(JJ)†

Circular of the Anti-Persecution Union see Anti-Persecution Union.

558 Circulator: the journal of the Babcock and Wilcox Staff Association
[19--?]—   ; s-a
  A Free to members.
  L 102 (Spring 1963)—

559 Citizen 1 (July 1894)—[June 1896?]. Leeds; m
  B   Published by Leeds North-West Ward Independent Labour
Party. (D. Hopkin, 'Local Newspapers of the Independent Labour Party,
1893—1906'. Society for the Study of Labour History **Bulletin**, 28 [Spring
1974].

560 Citizen [1896?]. Manchester; w
  B   ½d. Published by Manchester Citizen Newspaper and Publishing
Company. 'There is no evidence that the **Citizen** (Manchester) . . . ever
actually appeared. There was some confusion . . . when the Manchester
Labour Press, who had decided to launch a Citizen in 1896, discovered
that an independent group of ILP members were advertising a forthcoming
newspaper with the identical title the same time. After some acrimonious
correspondence, the breach was healed but there is some doubt about the
survival of either scheme' (D. Hopkin, 'Local Newspapers of the
Independent Labour Party, 1893—1906'. Society for the Study of Labour
History, **Bulletin**, 28 [Spring 1974]).

561 Citizen 1 (Feb. 1897)—? County Durham; m
  B   Independent Labour Party. (D. Hopkin, 'Local Newspapers of
the Independent Labour Party, 1893—1906'. Society for the Study of
Labour History, **Bulletin**, 28 [Spring 1974]).

  562 Citizen [19--?] —1963? irreg?
    B   Free. Published by the Co-operative Press.
    L(Col) 148 (June 1960)—178 (Nov. 1963)

563 Citizen Specimen copy (Feb. 1928); 1 (March 1928)—76 (Aug. 1934);
m
    B   8s. 6d. per 1,000. Published by the Labour Party. A
propagandist sheet, announcing the policies, and recording the
achievements of the Labour Party.
    L†; LabP (w 75); 0 1—30

Citizen 1930—1938 see **Bolton Citizen**: Official Organ of the Bolton
Labour Party

Citizen, 1966—   see **Leeds and District Weekly Citizen**

564 Citizen and Irish Artisan [1877?] —135 (27 Dec. 1879); then **Citizen
and Artisan**; 136 (3 Jan. 1880)—151 (17 April 1880). Dublin; w
    B   1d. Established 'in the interests of Labour, and for the Main-
tenance and Revival of Industries'. Material on agricultural labourers,
Saturday closing of shops; supported National Land League, and Parnell.
    L(Col)† III, 105 (31 May 1879)—III, 151

565 Citizen, Circulating in the City and County of Nottingham [19--?] –?
West Bridgford; w
    B   ½d. Printed and published by J. B. Pollard. A local Labour Party
paper.
    L(Col)† 6 occ. nos between 15 March and 26 July 1919

566 Citizen, into the Sixties, with Sudbury and Woodbridge Labour Party
1 (Feb./March 1961)–13 (May 1962); m
    B   Printed and published by the Co-operative Press. One of the
'Citizen' series.
    L(Col)†

567 City Clerk: a Monthly Journal Devoted to the Discussion of Subjects
Relating to the Intellectual, Moral, and Social Interests of the Employés in
Banking and Mercantile Establishments I, 1 (Nov. 1867); m
    C 3d. Published for the proprietors by Thomas Murby. For clerks
in London and the provinces.
    L†

568 City Counter Chronicle [19–?] –?
    A   Union of Post Office Workers, London City Counter Branch.
(W. Dunlop, 'Local Journals'. **Belpost**, IV, 5 [May 1965].)

569 City of Manchester Independent Labour Party. **Branch News** [19–?];
m
    B
    ILP March 1911

570 City of Perth Co-operative Pioneer: a Record of Social and
Educational Progress [18--?] –? Perth; m
    A   Free. City of Perth Co-operative Society.
    L† 340, (1905)–716 (ns 65) (July 1939);O(JJ)†242 (Aug. 1897);
Perth and Kinross County Lib. Jubilee issue Dec. 1932

571 City Waiters' Provident Society's Journal 1 (1 Sept. 1867)–4(March
1868); q
    A   Printed and published for the Society by J. Horsey. To promote
the newly founded City Waiters' Provident and Protection Society, which
was to provide sickness and retirement benefits for the 6,000 or so waiters
in London. Secretary: J. W. Wilford, a working waiter; President: J.
Bennett, middle-class philanthropist.
    L†

572 Civil and Public Services Association. Blackpool Central Office
[19--?] – . Blackpool
    A   Reproduced from typewriting.
    Warwick U (MRC)† 207 (May/June 1971)

573 Civil and Public Services Association. British Museum Branch.
Newsletter 1 (Sept. 1968)–   ; irreg?
    A
    Warwick U (MRC)†

574 Civil and Public Services Association. Diplomatic Service Branch.
Newsletter [19–?] –
    A
    Warwick U (MRC)† occ. nos. from Sept. 1970

575 Civil and Public Services Association. Ministry of Agriculture,
Fisheries and Food Section. **London Branch News** [19–?] –?
    A   Reproduced from typewriting.
    Warwick U (MRC)† Dec. 1969

576 Civil Servant 1930–   . Dublin; m
    A   6d. Official organ of the Civil Service Clerical Association.
(Mitchell, 1965.)

577 Civil Service Argus: the Journal of the Ministry of Labour Staff
Organization I [1925?] –; m
    A   Later, journal of the Civil and Public Services Association,
Department of Employment Section.
    L† VII (Jan. 1931)–X, 4, X, 6–; NU XXIX, (1953)–; ONC XXXVI,
(1960)–

578 Civil Service Clerical Association. Air Ministry (Headquarters) Branch.
Official Organ I, 1 (July 1939); then **Contact**: the Official Organ of the Air
Ministry (Headquarters) Branch of the Civil Service Clerical Association,
[etc] : I, 2 (Aug. 1939)–? m
    A   I, 1 dated 1938 in error. Successively the organ of the CSCA,
Air Ministry (Headquarters) Branch, Air Ministry and Ministry of Aircraft
Production Headquarters' Branches, Ministry of Aircraft Production
Branch, Air Ministry, Kinsway Branch. Several series of numbering.
    L† July 1939–Sept. 1955 (1952–3*)

579 Civil Service Clerical Association. Air Ministry (Headquarters) Branch.
[**Bulletin**] 1938–
    A
    L (not traced)

580 Civil Service Clerical Association. British Museum Branch. **Bulletin.**
Preliminary number, Dec. 1947; then **Under the Dome,** for the Diffusion
of News Among the Staff of the British Museum: 2 (Jan. 1948)–
XXXVIII, 29 (June 1958); m
    A Reproduced from typewriting.
    L†

581 Civil Service Clerical Association. **Confidential News**: Monthly Circular of the Civil Services Clerical Association 1 (March 1948)–? m etc.

    A   Information bulletin. Though 'monthly' always appears in the sub-title, the frequency varies.

      NU† 1–132 (June/Sept. 1961*)

582 Civil Service Clerical Association. Ministry of Food London Head-quarters. **Review** 1 (1950)–?; irreg

    A   Reproduced from typewriting.

    L†4 (Oct. 1950)–7 (April 1951)

583 Civil Service Clerical Association. Ministry of National Insurance (Newcastle) Branch. **News Bulletin** [pre- 1939–45 war]

    A   Preceded **Headway** (qv).

584 Civil Service Clerical Association. **Post Office Section News** 1 [19--?]–?

    A

    TUC 254 (Dec. 1966/Jan. 1967)

585 Civil Service Courier: Organ of the Birmingham Civil Service Association. 1 (Feb. 1932)–II, 15(Sept. 1941). Birmingham; m; q; s-a

    A   1d. Publisher and editor: John R. Hetherington. 'Founded to formulate the views of the Service as a whole in its relation with the nation'. Party politics rigidly excluded, but concern with conditions and prospects.

      BP; L†

586 Civil Service Gazette. 1, (1 Jan. 1853)–LXXIII, 3416 (Nov. 1926); w

    A   5d; 6d. Publishers: Edward West Jameson, Charles James Cadogan, E. Owen. 'Established to advocate the cause, and protect the interests of all civil clerks, officers and clerks in the employ of the govern-ment . . .' (Mitchell, 1856).

      L(Col)†

587 Civil Service Magazine 1[1902?] –IV, 7 (July 1905); m

    A   1d. Charles H. Garland, ed. Mainly Postal and Telegraph sections of the Civil Service.

    L(Col)† Jan. 1903–July 1905

Civil Service Observer see **Union Observer**

588 Civil Service Opinion: a Monthly Journal for Civil Servants I, 1 (Oct. 1923)– ; m

    A   2d. Association of Executive Officers and other Civil Servants; Society of Civil Servants (Executive, Directing and Analogous Grades).

    L(Col)†; LDS 1947–

589 Civil Service Review I, 1 (3 May 1873)–V, 243 (29 Dec. 1877); w
  A   3d. Published for the proprietors by Charles M. Heseltine. To
give consideration to the interests and grievances of Civil Service
employees: 'the lordly ambassador and the humble letter carrier, the
governor of a colony and the telegraph clerk, Downing Street officials and
dockyard employees'.
  L(Col)†

590 Civil Service Review I (1943)–   . Dublin; bi-m
  A   Civil Service Executive (and Higher Officers) Association.
  D I (1943)–XXI (1962), XXVIII, 10 (1970)–

591 Civil Service Socialist : the Organ of the Civil Service Socialist Society
[I], 1 (Feb. 1908)–VIII, 2 March 1915); m
  A   1d. Printed by the Clarion Newspaper Company, then by the
National Labour Press. J. G. Newlove; Arthur E. Shaw, eds. To educate
members of the Civil Service in the principles of Socialism.
  L(Col)† (wl); LabP†

592 Civil Service Times; with Supplement for Civil Service Candidates I, 1
(13 Feb. 1886)–XIII, 310 (23 Jan. 1892); w
  B   2d; 6d. Printed and published by Pardon and Sons for the
proprietors. Discusses such topics as bad supervisors, pay, promotion,
exams, and supports case of lower grades.
  L(Col)†

Civil Service Whip see Government Minor and Manipulative Grades
Association. **Bulletin**

593 Civilian: a Bulletin of News and Views ns 1 (1946)–? bi-m
  A   Civil Service Clerical Association, War Department Section.
No. 23 was the last to be called 'New Series'.
  NU† 1 (1946)–109 (Feb. 1962*)

594 Civist: the Organ of the Glasgow Branch, National Association of
Local Government Officers I, 1 (Feb. 1934)–(Dec. 1950); ns I, 1 (April
1951)–   . Glasgow; m; q
  A   Later National and Local Government Officers' Association.
  GM†; L ii

595 Civitas Calling: the News Bulletin of the City of Worcester Branch of
NALGO 1965?–   . Worcester
  A   National and Local Government Officers' Association,
Worcester City Branch. Reproduced from typewriting.
  L 1965–

Clanger see **Margate Mirror**

596 Clapham Independent and Labour News 1 (Nov. 1900)–[1901?]; m
B   ½d. Independent Labour Party. C. H. Chapman, ed. **(ILP News,**
Jan. 1901; **Reformers' Year Book,** 1901.)

597 Clarion I 1 (12 Dec. 1891)–ns IV, 6 (June 1932); then b **New**
Clarion: I, 1 (11 June 1932)–IV, 92 (10 March 1934) Manchester;
London; w
B   1d. Printed and published for the proprietors by the
Co-operative Newspaper Printing Society, then by the Clarion Press Ltd.
Robert Blatchford, ed. Socialist newspaper with varied contents.
Supported the Independent Labour Party, but thought the ILP and the
Social Democratic Party should work together. Clarion Scouts formed in
1894 and Clarion Vans in 1896 to disseminate socialist ideas.
BdP 1892–1934; C Nov. 1895–1902*; L(Col)†; LE*; LU† 1891–5;
LabP*; LdU 1892–3, b 1–89; MP (microfilm); 0 1927–; ONC
1891–1916

598 Clarion: the Journal of the Shipley Divisional Labour Party 1 (Nov.
1936)–9 (July 1937). Shipley; m
B   1d. Contributor: A. Creech–Jones.
L(Col)†

599 Clarion: a Fortnightly News Letter Issued by the Finsbury
Communist Party 1 (1946)–53 (4 June 1948); then **Finsbury Clarion**: 54
(July 1948)–62 (March 1949); fortn; m
B
FiP 11–13, 31–54, 60, 62

600 Clarion: Journal of the Oxford University Labour Club April
1947–[1950?]; then **Oxford Clarion**: [1951?]–[1958?]; then **Clarion**: ns
1 (Oct. 1958)–? Oxford etc.; fortn in term; termly; irreg.
B   4d. etc. Publishers: Oxford University Labour Club; National
Association of Labour Student Organisations. Format, price, frequency,
place of publication, vary.
L 3 (Nov. 1958)–(w 13); LabP† 8 (June 1959)–17 (Spring 1961)
(w 12. 16); O† 2, (Hilary 1951)–10 (Dec. 1959*); ONC† III, 3 (Hilary
1948), IV, 3 (Trinity 1948)

601 Clarion I, 1 (April 1949)–I, 7 (Oct. 1949); m
B   3d. A Common Wealth [party] organ. 'We believe in: Common
Ownership, Workers' Control, Political Democracy, Individual Liberty,
Ethics in Politics, International Unity'.
O†

602 Clarion: Organ of the BMC Joint Shop Stewards Committee I, 1
(Jan./Feb. 1957)–II, 5 [undated; Oct. 1959?]
A   Printed at Halesowen. Editor: A. Bate, Birmingham.
WCML†

603 Clarion: the Official Magazine of the Cumberland County Branch of NALGO 1966?— . Carlisle

    A   National and Local Government Officers' Association. Reproduced from typewriting.

    L 1966—

Clarion 1967—   see **South Kensington Clarion**

604 Clarion Cyclists' Journal 1 (Aug. 1896)—11 (Oct. 1898). Manchester; irreg

    B   1d. Printed and published for the proprietors by J. Taylor Clark. To amuse comrades with Clarion Club gossip, and keep readers in touch with the doings of other Clarion Clubs . . . 'a Club journal', 'not a miniature edition of the Clarion'. See also **King of the Road**.

    L(Col)† 1 (Aug. 1896)—4 (Nov. 1896), 7 (June 1898)—11 (Oct. 1898)

605 Clarionette: an Organ Devoted to Social Progress 1 (Dec. 1896)—(II, 1 [Dec. 1897?]). Darlington; m

    B   ½d. Published by John Fisher for the 'Clarionette' Publishing Company, ILP Club, Darlington. Editor: Norman Swift. 'There is no clear indication in the paper of a formal link with the ILP but the local branch did regard it as its own paper' (D. Hopkin).

    AbU Dec. 1897 (microfilm); O(JJ) Dec. 1897; ONC† I, 6 May; 10, Sept.; 12, Nov. 1897

606 Class Teacher: Organ of the National Federation of Assistant Teachers I, 1 (May 1902)—? London; Leicester; Derby; q

    A   1d. The Federation was a 'supporter' of the National Union of Teachers, and its object was to secure adequate representation of Assistant Teachers on the Executive of the NUT.

    L(Col)† May 1902—Sept. 1914, Nov. 1919, Feb., July 1930

607 Class Teachers' Pamphlet I, 1 (March 1900)—III (1907); then **Scottish Class Teacher**: IV, 1 (Feb. 1908)—XVIII, 5 (Nov. 1917). Aberdeen; Dundee; etc.; irreg; q; bi-m

    A   1d. Scottish Assistant Teacher's Association; Scottish Class Teachers' Federation. 'To win attention of members and non-members to unquestioned need for combination, amelioration of conditions' (R. Murdoch, **Scottish Notes and Queries**, Oct. 1903, p. 52).

    GM† 1912—15; L(Col) 1908—17

608 Clear Light 1 (June 1923)—25 (July 1925). Hebden Bridge; m

    B   2d. Sub-title from No. 17 (24 Oct. 1924): 'Organ of the National Union for Combating Fascism'. Editor: Alfred Holdsworth. Printed for him by William Ackroyd. A non-party working-class international paper. Urges front of Labour, Communist, Anarchist against the threat of Fascism.

    L(Col)†; ILP Sept. 1923

609 Cleave's London Satirist and Gazette of Variety 1 (14 Oct. 1837)–9 (9 Dec. 1837); then **Cleave's Penny Gazette of Variety (and Amusement)**: 10 (16 Dec. 1837)–327 (20 Jan. 1844); w

    B   1d. Publisher: John Cleave. An amusement miscellany for working-men, while expressly non-political in content, occasionally has leading articles dealing with the franchise for working-men, and other matters of social reform.

        L(Col)†; O(JJ)† (10 Feb. 1838); ONC 1841–2*

Cleave's Penny Gazette of Variety (and AMusement) see **Cleave's London Satirist and Gazette of Variety**

610 Cleave's Weekly Police Gazette I, 1 (11 Jan. 1834)–III, 36 (3 Sept. 1836); then **Cleave's Weekly Police Gazette and Journal of News, Politics, and Literature**: ns 1 (17 Sept. 1836)–3 (24 Sept. 1836); w

    B   2d.; 3½d. Published, printed and edited by John Cleave. 'A comprehensive working-class newspaper with an estimated weekly circulation of 30,000–40,000. Strongly agitated for factory reform, repeal of newspaper duty, and repeal of Poor Law Amendment Act of 1834' (Wiener). Contributor: Richard Oastler. Merged with Hetherington's **London Dispatch**, a stamped paper.

        HO 64/15 (26 April 1834); L(Col) occ. nos

611 Clerical and Administrative Workers' Union. North West Area. Gillmoss Branch. **Newsletter** [19–?]–? Fazakerley

    A   Single sheet reproduced from typewriting.

        TUC† 1 undated issue [196-?]

612 Clerical News: Bulletin of the Tyne, Wear and Tees District Committee [1950? 1951?]–? Newcastle

    A   Clerical and Administrative Workers' Union. Reproduced from typewriting.

        TUC† 5 (Oct. 1951)

613 Clerk I, 1 (April 1890)–I, 4 (July 1890); m

    A   2d. Published by Scott and Montague. Discusses the formation of a Clerks' Union, and agitation as a trade-union organisation for shorter hours and higher wages.

        L†

614 Clerk: Organ of the National Union of Clerks I, 1 (Jan. 1908–(Aug./Sept. 1921); (Jan. 1923)(July 1973); then **Apex**: (Aug. 1973)–; frequency varies.

    A Later sub-title: 'Official Organ of the Clerical and Administrative Workers Union'; then organ of the Association of Professional, Executive, Clerical and Computer Staff. First editor: Walter J. Read. New series started in 1961.

        L(Col); LE; LvP III, 9 (1963)– ; NU 1951– ; the Association. TUC† Dec. 1914–1921*, 1923–73

615 Clerk's Gazette: the Official Organ of the Scottish Clerks' Association
I, 1 (31 Jan. 1895)–III, 2 (31 May 1897). Glasgow; m
    A   Free to members. Published by Thomas Berrie, the General
Secretary, on behalf of the Association.
    GM†

616 Clerks' Journal I, 1 (1 March 1888)–III, 33 (1 Nov. 1890); then b
Quill: III, 34 (8 Nov. 1890). Liverpool; m
    A   1d. Published for the National Clerks' Journal Company. To
serve as an organ for the clerks throughout the country. Inspired mainly
by members of the Liverpool Clerks' Association, a mutual benefit society.
With the **Quill**, it became the organ of the newly founded National Union
of Clerks.
    L;†; O a; O(JJ)† 1

617 Cleveland Democrat [189-?]. Cleveland, Yorkshire
    B   Published by Cleveland Independent Labour Party, or North
East Division ILP. (D. Hopkin, 'Local Newspapers of the Independent
Labour Party, 1893–1906'. Society for the Study of Labour History,
Bulletin, 28 [Spring 1974].)

618 Clitheroe Labour Bulletin [194-?] ; m
    B   Labour Party. Duplicated. (Labour Party. **Your own Journal**,
1948.)

619 Clothiers Operatives Amalgamated Union Gazette [19–?] Leeds; m
    A   (**Reformers' Year Book**, 1908)

620 Clothing Worker: the Official Organ of the United Clothing Workers'
Trade Union I, 1 (May 1929)–?
    A   1d. Militant rank-and-file organ of the newly formed Union;
General Secretary: Sam Elsbury, Chairman: Dave Cohen. Breakaway from
the bureaucratically led "Mondist" Tailors' and Garment Workers' Union.
Formed after the Rego strike in East London. Branches in London; Leeds;
Glasgow etc.
    L(Col)† 1–2 (June 1929); MRC, Warwick U April 1930

621 Club and Institute Union Journal 1 (6 July 1883)– ; fortn
    A   ½d. etc. Organ of the Working Men's Club and Institute Union.
Succeeded **Workman's Club Journal**. Club and Institute Union 1883–8*; L
1883–5;
    L(Col)† 6 Sept. 1890; 3 Jan. 1891–

622 Club Life I, 1 (7 Jan. 1899)– XXXIX, 39 (25 Sept. 1937); w
    A   1d.; 2d. Club and Institute Union. 'Written for clubmen by
clubmen'. Editors: E. Garrity; Alf Watkins. For the London area.
    L(Col)†

Club News see **Our Youth**: Discussion Magazine of the Young Communist League

623 Club World: a Journal for Clubs and Kindred Societies I, 1 (7 July 1894)–XXI, 2247 (24 Sept. 1898); then **Club World and Trade Unionists' Record**: ns 1 (1 Oct. 1898–12 (17 Dec. 1898); ns 1 (7 Jan 1924)–8 (23 Feb. 1924); w

    A   1d., 2d. Organ of working-men's clubs in London. Chiefly social matters. Published by the proprietor R. Gaston.

    L(Col)†

Club World and Trade Unionists' Record see **Club World**

624 Clubbist, Consisting Chiefly of a Selection of Poems from the Pages of the Suppressed Journals 1–3. [1849]. Dublin

    B 1d. Mathew Fannin. Dedicated to Liberty and the Young Men of Ireland. To provide the 'patriotic poor' with 'Irish literature at the cheapest rate'. Poetry of the Irish freedom movement, extracted from journals like **The Irish Felon**.

    L†

625 Clubman. [19--?] – . Newcastle-upon-Tyne; m

    A?   8d. 'Covers working men's clubs in the North East.' (Mitchell, 1970.)

Coal and Iron Miners' Journal see **Colliers' and Miners' Journal**

626 Coalville Workingmen's Co-operative Society. **Record** [188-? 189-?] –? Coalville

    A   The **Record** appears as an item in the educational account for 1892 (A. Lockwood and C. W. Brown, **History of Coalville Workingmen's Co-operative Society Ltd., established 1882**, Leicester 1932, p. 21).

627 Coatbridge Labour Bulletin [194-?] ; m

    B   2d. Labour Party. (Labour Party. **Your own Journal**, 1948.)

Cobbett's American Political Register see **Cobbett's Annual Register**

Cobbett's American Weekly Political Register see **Cobbett's Annual Register**

628 Cobbett's Annual Register I, 1 (Jan. 1802)–IV, [26] (Dec. 1803); then **Cobbett's Political Register**: V, 1 (Jan. 1804)–LXXXIX, 12 (20 Feb. 1836); w

    B   Various running titles used: **Cobbett's Weekly Political Register**; **Cobbett's Weekly Political Pamphlet**; **Cobbett's Weekly Register**. There was also an American edition, 1816–18.

    BP; E I–LXXIX, 11 (w XXXIV); L (w XXIX); LU 1–88; MP; O I–LXXXVIII; ONC; see BUCOP for further holdings.

629 Cobbett's Evening Post 1 (29 Jan. 1820)—55 (1 April 1820); d

B   7d. Printed and published by William Cobbett, junior. A daily radical and general newspaper. Campaigns for free press, against National Debt, for parliamentary reform, universal suffrage and short parliaments.

L(Col)†

630 Cobbett's Genuine Two-Penny Trash 1 (Feb. 1831)

B   1½d. Publisher: Roake and Varty. A pamphlet hitting out at tithes, the clergy and 'Parson' Malthus. Addressed to 'The Labourers of England'. An answer to the 'sneaking thief' who had written in his name, issuing **Cobbett's Twopenny Trash**, a bogus publication. See also **Cobbett's Penny Trash**.

L†

631 Cobbett's Magazine: a Monthly Review of Politics, History, Science, Literature, and Rural and Domestic Pursuits I, 1 (Feb. 1833)—III, 15 (April 1834); then **Shilling Magazine**: [I, 1] (1834); m

B   Editors: John and James Cobbett, then William Cobbett, from III, 14 (March 1834). Radical periodical devoted to the cause of the people, universal suffrage, annual parliaments, secret ballot. Also a literary review.

C (w 5—8); EU Feb.—July 1833; L†; ONC I—II, 12 (12 Jan. 1834)

632 Cobbett's Penny Trash 1 (Feb. 1831)—3 (April 1831); m

B   Printed by T. C. Hansard. Mainly a personal and retrospective look at Cobbett's opinions on political reform. No. 1 is a reissue of **Cobbett's Genuine Two-Penny Trash**.

L†; LU; MR

Cobbett's Political Register see **Cobbett's Annual Register**

633 Cobbett's Twopenny Trash, or, Politics for the Poor I, 1 (July 1830)—II, 12 (July 1832); m

B   Written, printed and published by Cobbett. Personal addresses to his wide audience of working-men on the issues of the day, parliamentary and economic reform etc.

BU I—II, 8; Co-op. Coll.; KeP; L†; LU; LdU 1831—2; MP; WnP

Cobbett's Weekly Political Pamphlet see **Cobbett's Annual Register**

Cobbett's Weekly Political Register see **Cobbett's Annual Register**

Cobbett's Weekly Register see **Cobbett's Annual Register**

Cog see Craftsmen's Club, Birmingham. **Monthly Journal**

634 Colchester Citizen ns 1 (Nov. 1949)—10 (Aug. 1950); m

B   Issued by the Colchester and East Essex Co-operative Political Party.

L(Col)

635 Colchester Times [193-?]. Colchester m

    B   Labour Party. (Labour and Socialist International. **The Socialist Press**, 1933.)

636 College Clarion. [Llais y Werin] [1938?]−? Aberystwyth

    B   Aberystwyth University Labour Club. Reproduced from typewriting. In Welsh and English.

    TUC† [3?] (Feb. 1939)

637 College Herald 1913−17. Manchester; m

    A   'Issued by the Co-operative College Herald Circle.' Motto: 'Fellowship in learning and learning in fellowship'. News of summer schools etc., notes on education. Absorbed by **Co-operative Educator**.

    Co-op Coll.† Nov. 1914, May 1916

638 Colliers' and Miners' Journal [April?] 1842−[Aug.?] 1842

    A   Scottish miners' paper. Edited by William Cloughan, Lanarkshire. 'Conducted by a collier himself.' Mentioned in the **British Statesman** (13 Aug. 1842) as the **Coal and Iron Miners' Journal**.

639 Colliery Workers' magazine: the Official Organ of the South Wales Miners' Federation 1 (Jan. 1923)−V, 10 (Oct. 1927). Cardiff; m

    A   2d. Editor: Oliver Harris. Issued to supply Lodge members with 'first-hand knowledge of the work of the Federation'. Reports of meetings, articles by miners' leaders, trade-union leaders, and Labour MPs on working-class politics and the claims and conditions of the miners.

    CrP; L†; South Wales Miners' Library (w 1923−4); SwU; TUC

640 Colliery Workman's Times I, 1 (2 Dec. 1893)−I, 7 (13 Jan. 1894). Manchester; w

    A   1d. Printed for the proprietors, The Workman's Times Company, by J. Heywood, and published by him. 'Property of a number of working men, who, 22 September 1893, formed themselves into a limited liability company to acquire copyright of **The Workman's Times**, now in its 4th year as a labour paper.' Chairman: James Heaviside, compositor. One of the ten directors was Joseph Burgess. Object: 'to advocate the nationalisation of mines, by and through the independent representation of Labour in Parliament'. Has Independent Labour Party, Social-Democratic Federation and Fabian Society columns. Coverage of international working-class movement; correspondence.

    L(Col)†

641 Colwyn Comment 1965?−Colwyn Bay

    A   National and Local Government Officers' Association, Colwyn Bay Branch. Reproduced from typewriting.

    L   1965−1

642 Combine News, 1 (June 1962)– [4?]. Coventry; q

    A   3d. Issued by the Massey Ferguson Joint Shop Stewards Combine Committee. Factories at Manchester, Coventry, Kilmarnock. Editor: J. R. Stynes.

    WCML† 1–2 (Oct. 1962)

643 Comet: the Organ of the Aberdeen Social–Democrats 1 (25 June 1898)–9 (March 1908). Aberdeen; irreg

    B 1d. Published by the Aberdeen Branch of the Social-Democratic Federation. Printed by: James Blair; G. Leslie; James Leatham, Peterhead. Propagandist paper which campaigned on local issues from a socialist standpoint.

    AP†; AU† 1

644 Comisco Information Service. International Socialist Conference I, 1 (6 Jan. 1951)–I, 26 (30 June 1951); then **Socialist International Information**: I, 27/28 (7 July 1951)–XX, 12 (Dec. 1970); then **Socialist Affairs**: XXI, 1 (Jan. 1971)–; w;m

    B   Committee of the International Socialist Conference; Socialist International. Reproduced from typewriting, then printed. Journal of political analysis, Labour and international relations, with internal reports. I, 1 dated 1950 in error.

    CrU 8–; L†; LE; LII; ONC† 1051–60*

645 Comment: a Communist Weekly Review I, 1 (5 Jan. 1963)– ; w; fortn

    B 9d. Communist Party of Great Britain. Published by S. C. Easton

    O; ONC†

Commentary see Vanguard, 1934–1936

646 Commercial Service Gazette: a Weekly Paper Devoted to the Interests of Clerks, Commercial Travellers, Warehousemen, and All Employed in Banking Houses, Mercantile, Commercial and Professional Establishments, Railway and Other Companies, the Customs and Port Office Department 1 (7 Feb. 1874)–12 (25 April 1874); w

    C   1d. Printed by W. Sully. [The Paper] 'will endeavour to promote perfect harmony between Principals and Employees while it devotes its columns to the well-being of the latter.' Discusses wages and conditions. Includes a fictional serial, 'John Jones's Clerk Days'.

    L(Col)†

647 Commercial Traveller I, 1 (1 July 1908)–I, 6 (1 Dec. 1908). Southport; m

    A   2d. United Kingdom Commercial Travellers' Association. Not a rival of **On the Road**. Written by working commercial travellers of 'long and wide experience'. Its object is 'to stimulate commercial men', and to strengthen them in their sometimes depressing work. Includes news from branches of the Association.

    L(Col)†

648 Commercial Traveller: the Official Organ of the National Union of Commercial Travellers I, 1 (Sept. 1922)–XV, 55 (Dec. 1938); q

    A   2d. Printed by Twentieth Century Press. Trade union news sheet. Brief notes and reports.

    L†

649 Common Good I, 1 (9 Oct. 1880)–I, 20 (19 Feb. 1881); w

    C; A   2d. Published for the proprietor by Brook and Company. Editors: Rev. Henry Solly, George Howell. Aims at the promotion of a better understanding and more mutually profitable relations between Capital and Labour, and the political education of the people; also 'sound working-class organisations' such as Working-Men's Clubs and Institutes, friendly societies, mutual improvement and discussion societies. Addressed to working men. No. 9 announces the formation of 'Common Good' Newspaper Company, Ltd. in shares of £1 each with George Howell as Secretary and supported by leaders of trade unions. Incorporated with **Capital and Labour** (qv).

    Co-op Union; L†; LE; LU

650 Common Sense, for People with Brains and Hearts 1 (May 1887)–10 (March 1888); m

    B   1d. Editor? H. H. Champion. 'Advocated socialism brought about by organized political power of workers, rather than by physical force; favoured drawing up political platform with immediate proposals of adult suffrage, annual parliaments, payment of MPs, free education, 8-hour day, free meals in schools, prison and workhouse reform. Last issue says Champion will write in future for **Christian Socialist** and **Democrat'** (Brophy). Supports the Labour Electoral Association.

    L(Col)†; LE*; TUC, John Burns Lib

651 Common Sense, Vox Populi 1 (20 Nov. 1830)–5 (25 Dec. 1830); w

    B   2d. (1); 1½d. (2); 1d. (3–5). Published and printed by A. Poplett. 'Consists of abstract radical essays, both original and excerpted. Several essays endorse universal suffrage, annual Parliaments, and a co-operative economic system' (Wiener).

    LU; Tolson Memorial Museum, Huddersfield 3

652 Commonsense I, 1 (19 Jan. 1934)

    B   2d. Printed and published by the Gunpowder Press Association, for the Civil Defence League, which 'offers a common platform and a common Press where Progressive and Democratic movements can unite to defeat the menace to Freedom' [ie fascism, nazism]. Organising Secretary: J. George Stone.

    L(Col); ONC†

Common Weal see **Glasgow Commonweal**

653 Common Wealth Information Bulletin 1 (1943)–8 (Nov. 1944); irreg
    B   6d. Common Wealth [party]. Published by C. W. Publishing, Ltd. Printed by the Co-operative Printing Society, Newcastle. There were also revised editions of 1 and 2. Each number deals with a particular topic, eg, No. 1, 'Education'. 'Designed to provide speakers with a factual basis for their speeches, and to supply study groups in the Branches with material for discussion. It is produced by the Research Department under the authority of the Working Committee and any views expressed in it are not necessarily those of Common Wealth as a whole'
    C; L; O†

654 Common Wealth Review. I, 1 (March 1944)–VII, 3 (March 1949); then **CW Quarterly:** 1 (Autumn 1949)–?; m; q
    B   6d., Is. Common Wealth [party]. Came into being after the Ministry of Supply suppressed the **Town and Country Review** for infringement of Paper Control Orders. Published by C.W. Publishing, Ltd., then by Common Wealth. Contributors: Tom Driberg, Kingsley Martin, Honor Balfour.
    BP a II, 2–VII; C; L a I, 2–; 0 1944–Autumn 1949

655 Common Wealth Yearbook 1951/2–1952/3; a
    B   Published by the National Committee of Common Wealth. To provide a record of decisions taken at conferences, and to give information on the work and organisation of the party.
    L†

656 Commonweal 1 (May [1845])–18 (Nov. 1846); m
    B   2d.: stamped 3d. Printed, published and edited by James Hill. 'Record of the proceedings and exponent of the measures of the National Land and Building Association' presided over by Thomas Wakley, Radical MP. Aimed at making working-men electors by enabling them to become land and house freeholders.
    L† 14–18; LUC 1–2

657 Commonweal: the Official Journal of the Socialist League I, 1 (Feb. 1885)–ns II, 27 (12 May 1894); m and w; fortn (ns)
    B   1d. From Jan. 1891 journal of the London Socialist League. Editors: 1885–9, William Morris; November 1889–January 1891, Franz Kitz and David Nicoll; 1891–2, C. W. Mowbray; May 1892– , H. B. Samuels. Advocated revolutionary international Socialism, latterly Anarchism-Communism.
    L(Col)†; LE I–VII*; MP (Microfilm); O I 2–14; ONC 1885–91: TUC, John Burns Lib*

658 Commonweal I, 1 (6 May 1896)–2 (June 1896); [ns] I, 1 (20 June 1897)–17 (5 Oct. 1901). Sheffield; London; irreg

    B   1d. Printed and published by D. J. Nicoll. An Anarchist journal. David Nicoll's intention was 'to revive **The Commonweal**' founded by William Morris; 'to explain in a plain and simple way for working people, the truths of Anarchist and Revolutionary Socialism'. Succeeded **The Anarchist.**

    L(Col)†; ONC† 1

659 Commonweal I, 1 (26 April 1919)–(April/May 1922); (20 Jan. 1923)–XV, 50, (15 Dec. 1934); (1 March 1939)–(April 1941); (Jan. 1948)–(Feb./March 1950); w; m

    B   1d. Commonwealth League; Commonwealth Land Party. Editors: R. L. Outhwaite; J. W. Graham. Continuation of 'Henry Georgism'. Started as a pressure group within the Independent Labour Party. Asserts the common right to the ownership of land as the foundation of a co-operative commonwealth.

    C VI–XV, 50; L(Col)†; LE*; O IV–XV; ONC occ. nos

660 Commonwealth: Journal of Rights 1 (20 May 1848)–2 (27 May 1848); w

    B   6d. Printed and published by Henry Francis Doyle. An impressive paper which advocated universal suffrage. Extensive reportage of the May events in France.

    L(Col)†

Commonwealth, 1866–1867 see **British Miner and General Newsman**

661 Commonwealth 1 (June 1880)–2 (July 1880). Birmingham; m

    B   1d. Organ of the National Commonwealth League. Editor: Robert Harper. 'The mission of this periodical is to make known to the common people what are their rights, as founded in the Principles of Nature (unperverted).' To promote a socially responsible order by preaching about the need for progress and elimination of abuses both materially and spiritually. Includes unsigned articles on nationalisation, and dialogues on Communism.

    L†; O†

662 Commonwealth: a Social Magazine I, 1 (Jan. 1896)–XLI, 453 (April 1941); m; q (from Oct. 1933)

    B   3d. etc. Publisher: Thomas Hibberd. Editors: Canon Henry Scott Holland; G. W. Wardman. Supported Labour Movement. Early contributors include J. A. Hobson, Beatrice Webb. Sub-title varies.

    AU; C; L; LdU VII–XII*, XVI*; XXVII–XXXV*; O†; SwU I–XII*

663 Commonwealth: a Socialist Review for the Common Wealth Socialist Association 1 (Jan./March 1959)–? q

    B   Published by the Labour Party of the Association. Reproduced from typewriting.

    TUC† 1–Jan.–May 1966

664 Commonwealthsman; or Chartist Advocate 1–20. 1842. Leicester
    B   Editor and proprietor: Thomas Cooper. Succeeded his **Midland Counties Illuminator, Rushlight,** and **Extinguisher.** In **Northern Star,** (9 July 1842), Cooper says it 'was started with a view to renewing the existence of a paper as useful as the **Illuminator** had been . . . terminated at the 20th number, owing to poverty in the ranks'
    HO Staffordshire bundle OS 242 occ. nos

665 Commune: a Herald of the Coming Storm I, 1 (May 1923)–II, 12 (Aug. 1925); ns I, 1 (Sept. 1925)–II, 13 (April/May 1929). Glasgow; m
    B   1d.; 2d. Printed and published by the Bakunin Press. Edited by Guy Aldred. Anarchist organ of Aldred's Anti-Parliamentary Communist Federation (founded 1912). Analysis of the developing political situation, continuous exposure of the Labour and trade-union leaders; critical of the Communist Party.
    E 1925–7*; GM*; Lt; TUC 1925–9

666 Commune: Special Anti-Parliamentary Communist Gazette 1 (16 May 1926)–7 (May 1929). Glasgow; irreg
    B   1d. Printed and published by the Bakunin Press. Edited by Guy Aldred. Anarchist. Occasional leaflets published 'in place of **The Commune** [qv]' lambasting the policies of the official Labour leadership.
    Lt

667 Communist: an Organ of the Third (Communist) International 1 (5 Aug. 1920)–131 (3 Feb. 1923); w
    B   2d. Published by the Executive Committee of the Communist Party.
    C; L(Col)t; LE Sept. 1920–April 1922; MML; ONC occ. nos

Communist, 1927–1928 see Communist Review

668 Communist [1968?] – . Belfast; m
    B   Issued by the British and Irish Communist Organisation, formerly (until 1971) the Irish Communist Organisation. Theoretical journal.
    D 37 (1971)–

669 Communist: Bulletin of British Section of Left Opposition 1 (May 1932)–8 ([June ?] 1933); irreg?
    B   (R. Groves, **The Balham Group,** 1974.)
    ILP June 1933

670 Communist Chronicle and Communitarian Apostle 1843
    B   Editor: J. Goodwyn Barmby. A continuation of The **Promethean.** (J. F. C. Harrison, **Robert Owen and the Owenites in Britain and America,** 1969).

Communist Church: the Apostle and Chronicle of the Communist Church
see **Apostle and Chronicle of the Communist Church**

671 Communist Comment I, 1 (July 1969)– . Cork; fortn
    B   Issued by the Irish Communist Organisation, which became the British and Irish Communist Organisation.
    LE (not traced)

672 Communist Daily 1 (13 Nov. 1922)–3 (15 Nov. 1922); d
    B   1d. Published by the Communist Party of Great Britain. 'The first number of the Worker's Daily of the future is here.' Focus on the election; for the return of a workers' government with a full programme of socialist nationalisation.
    LE†; WCML† 2–3

673 Communist International 1 (1919)–ns XVII, 6 (1939). Moscow; London; frequency varies
    B   First series 1919–24 was published in Moscow, and some issues were reprinted in London. Then published by the Communist Party of Great Britain. 1938 was numbered Vol. XVI in error; there was no Vol. XV.
    C*; L*; LE*; O*; ONC 1923–39*; MML*; WCML† (w 30 occ. nos)

674 Communist International. Executive Committee. Bulletin 1 (8 Sept. 1921). Petrograd
    B   English edition. Editor: Zinoviev. Contains appeals of the Executive Committee to all branches of Comintern. Resolutions and strategy.
    MML†

675 Communist International 1 (Jan. 1940)–10 (Oct. 1940); m
    B   6d. Published by Modern Books, in London. Printed in the USA. Editor: Earl Browder. 'Theoretical' journal. Contributors: Dimitroff, Manuilsky, Varga, Marty, Thorez etc. Succeeded by **International Review**.
    E† (w 2–3, 7–8); MML; ONC† 1, 5

676 Communist Party. High Wycombe Branch. Bulletin 1 (Dec. 1949)– . High Wycombe; m
    B   Published by S. Smith.
    Abe Lazarus Memorial Library and Archive, Ruskin College, Oxford*

677 Communist Party of Great Britain. London District Committee. Bulletin [19--?] –?: w?
    B
    CPGB 1951–62; L XIII, 50 (31 Dec. 1954)– ; ONC (7 July 1944)

678 Communist Party of Great Britain. **Economic Bulletin**
[1957–1958?]; ns 1 (Sept. 1961)–[1970?]; q
    B   Published by the Economic Committee of the Communist
Party. Reproduced from type-script. On economic affairs, economic
theory and method etc.
    E ns. 4 (1964)– ; EU ns 7 (Sept.1965)– ; L ns; O† ns 4 (Jan.
1964)–19/20 (Aug. 1970)

679 Communist Party of Great Britain. **Information for Speakers** (28 Aug.
1946)–(17 March 1948); w
    B   Reproduced from typewriting. Title changed to **Information**.
Then printed each week in **World News and Views**.
    E (28 Aug. 1946)–(10 Sept. 1947*; O† 28 Aug. 1946)–(17 March
1948*); TUC (3 Dec. 1947)–(17 March 1948)

680 Communist Party of Great Britain. **Speakers' Notes** 1936–?; w
    B
    CPGB

681 Communist Review I, 1 (May 1921)–VII, 9, (Jan. 1927); then
Communist: I, 1 (Feb. 1927)–III, [unnumbered] (Dec. 1928); then
Communist Review: ns I, 1 (Jan. 1929)–VIII, 8 (Aug. 1935); ns (March
1946)–(Dec. 1953); m
    B   4d.; 6d. Communist Party of Great Britain. Dealt with a wide
range of international and domestic affairs, economic, political, ideological
and historical. During part of the period between 1935 and 1946 its place
was taken by **Discussion**. Superseded by **Marxist Quarterly**.
    C1921–35; E*; L*†; MML; O 1921–8; ONC 1921–35*; 1946–53;
WCML†

682 Communist Student: International News Bulletin 1 (April 1962)–?
    B   Printed and published by ULU [University of London Union]
Communist Society. Reproduced from typewriting. No. 1 dealt with the
22nd Congress of the Communist Party of the Soviet Union; documents,
speeches etc.
    O† 1

683 Communist Youth: Theoretical and Organisational Bulletin of the
Central Committee of the YCL 1 (April 1934)–?; m?
    B   4d.; 1d. News of the Young Communist League. Party-building.
Anti-militarist and anti-Fascist agitation. International perspectives; open
forum. 'To clarify members on political questions and organise League for
carrying out the decision and line of the Central Committee'. Includes
book reviews. Reproduced from typewriting.
    MML† April, June, Oct., Dec. 1934; Jan. 1935

Compass see National Association of Local Government Officers. Ashford
and District Branch. **Branch Newsletter**

684 Composite Section Standard 1 ([April?] 1969)–33 (Dec. 1971); m

    A   Published by the Composite Section of the National Federation of Building Trades Operatives. Newspaper format. Editor: Harry Clack. Occasional errors in numbering.

    ONC† 4–33

685 Compositors' Chronicle 1 (7 Sept. 1840)–37 (1 Aug. 1843); m

    A   2d. Published by R. Thompson. Printed by J. Campbell. Trade-union news and correspondence from London and the provinces, Scotland and Ireland. Comment on disputes, apprenticeship regulations etc. Published at the offices of the London Union of Compositors. A precursor of the **London Typographical Journal**. Sub-title on fly-leaf of volume: 'An Epitome of Events Interesting to Printers'.

    LSF†

Comrade see **Co-operative Youth**

686 Comradeship: Organ of the Royal Arsenal Co-operative Society's Education Department 1 (1 Oct. 1897)–273 (Dec. 1921); then **Comradeship and Wheatsheaf**: ns 1 (Jan. 1922)–292 (July 1946); then **Comradeship and Co-operative Home Magazine**: 293 (Aug. 1946)–(1958?); 1; m

    A   Gratis. Royal Arsenal Co-operative Society. Latterly, a local edition of **Wheatsheaf**, and **Co-operative Home Magazine**.

    L i 60–(not traced), LU i 3–4, 8–43; MP 1910–; O ii 379–; the Society's Education Department*

687 Comradeship: the Magazine of the Co-operative Holidays Association in connection with the National Home Reading Union I (1907)–XI, 2 (Dec. 1917); then b **Co-operative Holiday Association General Notes**: 1 (Oct. 1918)–3 (Feb. 1919); then **Comradeship**: XI, 3 (Feb. 1920)–XLIV, 3 (Summer 1953?) Manchester; bi-m.

    A   Published at the offices of the Co-operative Holidays Association. Reports of activities and meetings, 'rambling clubs', educational items, biographies, sketches, correspondence.

    L† a III, 2 (Nov. 1909)–XLIV, 3 (Summer 1953); LvP a XL–; MP a XXXI–

Comradeship and Co-operative Home Magazine see **Comradeship**

Comradeship and Wheatsheaf see **Comradeship**

688 Conciliator, or the Cotton Spinners Weekly Journal 1 (22 Nov. 1828)–5 (20 Dec. 1828). Manchester; w

    A   Printed, published and edited by John Doherty, Secretary of the Cotton Spinners' Union.

    MP†

689 Conflict, for All Progressive People March 1944–Dec. 1948. Glasgow; irreg

    B   2d. etc. Published by Glasgow University Socialist Club, 'bringing together all shades of Left-Wing opinion'.

    GM†

690 Congress of Peoples Against Imperialism. Information Bulletin [194–?]

    B?   6d. Published at the London Centre, Congress of Peoples (Clarion, 3 [June 1949].)

691 Consett Labour Monthly 1 (Oct. 1896)–2 (Nov. 1896). Consett, Co. Durham; m

    B   ½d. Published for the proprietors, who can be assumed to be the local Independent Labour Party branch, in Liverpool. Localised edition of a newspaper launched in 1896 by Allen Clarke.

    O(JJ) 2 (Nov. 1896)

692 Considerer 1 (Oct. 1898)–1900; m

    B   Free. Publisher: Edwin O. Catford. 'Reform through love'. The new series stated that it was intended to be run on a communistic basis. A large part of ns, No. 1, consists of an obituary of Chichele Lingham, a 'Considerer' and a socialist, and an article by the latter, 'Furniture and Socialism'.

    ILP 1 (March 1900); O(JJ) 1, w (Nov. 1898); ns 1 (Aug. 1899)

693 Consolidator [1918]

    A   River Thames shop stewards' movement. Edited by J. Gilchrist, a member of the Amalgamated Society of Woodworkers. Was being published in October 1918. (E. and R. Frow, 'Papers of Engineering Shop Stewards'. Marx Memorial Library. **Quarterly Bulletin**, 66 [April–June 1973].)

694 Constitutional Labour Journal [19--?] Walsall; m

    B   2d. Published by H. J. Sabin. 'For the welfare of the working classes, trade unionists and community generally.' (Mitchell, 1920).

695 Constructional Engineering Union. **Journal** [19--?] –1970; then **Amalgamated Union of Engineering Workers, Construction Section**: [1970? 1971?] – ; q

    A

    L ns I, 17 (March 1962)–; TUC† 41 (May 1935)–*

696 Consumer [19--?] –? [Manchester?]

    A?   Co-operative Wholesale Society? Incorporated in **The Producer** (qv).

697 Contact [19--?] –?

    A   Union of Post Office Workers, Paddington No. 2 Branch. (W. Dunlop, 'Local Journals', **Belpost**, IV, 5 [May 1965])

698 Contact: Kingsway Branch Magazine [19--?] –?
    A   Civil and Public Services Association, Ministry of Defence
Section.
    Warwick UL† 2 nos 1971

699 Contact: the Journal of the National Association of Supervising
Electricians I, 1 (Oct. 1920)–XII, 3 (Dec. 1931); then **Electrical
Supervisor**: the Official Organ of the National Association of Supervising
Electrical Engineers. XII, 4 (Jan. 1932)– ; m
    A
    C XV, 9, XVI– ; L III, 2–IX, 6, 8– ; LIA XI–*; LP; LSC XI– ; LvP
XXVII–*; MP VIII–(w XXV)

Contact, 1939–? see Civil Service Clerical Association. Air Ministry
(Headquarters) Branch. **Official Organ**

700 Contact [Oct. 1946?] –? Bristol; m?
    A   Official organ of the joint shop stewards of the BAC, Ltd.
Aircraft and AED Development Departments, Bristol. In No. 15, the joint
shop stewards recommended that it be the official organ for the trade
union movement throughout the British Aircraft Corporation works.
    WCLM† 15 (Dec. 1947)

701 Contact ?194-?] –?; m
    B   Independent Labour Party, London and Southern Counties
Division.
    ILP Jan., March 1949; July–Aug., Oct.–Dec. 1950; Jan., April 1951

702 Contact [c1950]. Nottingham
    B   Central Nottingham Labour Party, League of Youth paper.
(**Socialist Advance**, April 1950.)

Contact, 1951– see NALGO **News Sheet, 1951**

703 Contact: Newsheet of Central Sussex Electricity Branch of NALGO. 1
(Jan. 1955)–? Haywards Heath; m
    A   National Association of Local Government Officers.
    L 2 (Feb. 1955)–

704 Contact 1 [196-?] –? Stoke-on-Trent
    A   Post Office Engineering Union, Stoke-on-Trent.
    TUC 34 (Oct. 1970)–36 (Dec. 1970)

705 Contact: Journal of the Epsom Constituency Labour Party 1
[1960?] –? Great Bookham; q.
    B   Published for the Party by L. G. R. Pinchen. Newspaper with
mainly local news and comment.
    LabP† 3, New Year 1961–7 (New Year 1962)

706 Contact, 1961?– . Stockport
    A   National and Local Government Officers' Association,
Stockport Branch. Reproduced from typewriting.
    L 1961–

707 Contact 1962?– . Cheltenham
    A   National and Local Government Officers' Association,
Gloucestershire Co-ordinating Committee. Reproduced from typewriting.
    L 1962– ; TUC 1967–9?

708 Contact: the Newsheet of the Bedford County Branch of NALGO;
1963– . Bedford
    A   National and Local Government Officers' Association.
Reproduced from typewriting.
    L

709 Contact: the Monthly News-Sheet of Wycombe, Marlow and District
Branch of NALGO 1963?– . High Wycombe; m
    A   National and Local Government Officers' Association.
Reproduced from typewriting.
    L 1963–

710 Contact 1963?– . Swansea
    A   National and Local Government Officers' Association, Swansea
Branch. Reproduced from typewriting.
    L 1963–

711 Contact: NALGO City of Cardiff Branch Magazine 1967?– . Cardiff
    A   National and Local Government Officers Association.
    L 1967–

Contact, 1969 – see **Eltradion**

712 Contact Point I, 1 (Spring 1970)– . Kingsbridge; s-a
    A   British Dental Association, Western Counties Branch. News of
activities of the branch, comment on the profession, conditions etc.
    OR†

713 Contact Quarterly: the Magazine of the Guildford and District Branch
of NALGO 1 [1960?] –[196-?] ; then b **Focus**: [196-?] – . Guildford; q
    A   National and Local Government Officers' Association.
Reproduced from typewriting.
    L a 3 (July 1961)–7 (Dec. 1962), b 1964–

714 Contrast: the Magazine of Windsor and District Branch of NALGO
1966?– . Windsor
    A   National and Local Government Officers' Association.
Reproduced from typewriting.
    L 1966–

715 Control: Hackney and Transport Drivers' Co-operative Journal 1 (May 1924)–6 (Oct. 1924); then **Transport Topics and Accident Review**: 1 (1 Dec. 1924). Bournemouth; m

    B   3d. Printed and published for the proprietor, J. H. Boutcher Cody, by J. Looker, Poole. For the 'entertainment, good and advancement' of the thousands of workers in transport driving. Covers all issues affecting drivers including conditions of work and trade-union intervention. Also runs a benefit society. 'With which is incorporated the **Taxi Driver, Bus Driver, Tram Driver, Transport Driver, Charabanc Driver, Ford Driver, The Conductor, The Home**'.

    L(Col)†

716 Controlling Officers' Journal: the Accredited Organ of the Postal, Telegraph, and Telephone Supervising Forces I (1911)–III (1913); then **PO Controlling Officers' Journal**: IV (1913)–X (1917). Leeds; Lincoln

    A   Postal, Telegraph, and Telephone Controlling Officers' Association.

    L II, 15–X, 6 (w II, 20, III, 24); LE V–IX

717 Controversy: the Monthly Forum for Socialist Discussion 1 (Oct. 1936)–32 (May 1939); then **Left Forum**: 33 (June 1939)–36 (Sept. 1939); then **Left**: 37 (Oct. 1939)–156 (May 1950); m

    B   3d. Issued by the Independent Labour Party leadership. Printed by the National Labour Press. 'Established to meet the most urgent need of Left journalism in Britain – a genuine Left Socialist Forum'. First editor: C. A. Smith. Contributor: A. Fenner Brockway.

    L†; LabP† 32–143*

718 Controversy ; a Quarterly Political Forum : the Theoretical Journal of the Independent Labour Party I, 1 (Autumn 1962)–3 (Spring 1963); q

    B   2s. 6d. Printed by the National Labour Press.

    E; L; LE; O†; SoU

719 Conveyor [1934?] –? Reading

    A   Shop stewards' paper, Pressed Steel, Oxford.

    Abe Lazarus Memorial Library and Archive, Ruskin College, Oxford 7 (Sept. 1934 [photocopy]); Oxford PL 7

    WCML† 7

720 Co-op: Journal for Local Co-op. Employees etc. [19–?] –?

    A

    TUC June 1947 (missing)

Co-operation in Agriculture see **AOS Journal**

Co-operative and Anti-Vaccinator see **Co-operator, 1860–1871**

721 Co-operative and Financial Review: a Journal for the Office, the Family, and the Fireside I, 1 (20 Feb. 1875)–?; w

B   3d. Printed and published for the proprietor at the **Anglo-American Times** Press (I, 1), then by John Augustus Campion. 'Conducted by R. B. Oakley . . . Manager of the Co-Operative Credit Bank.' 'Circulated amongst that very large and influential class, the members of Co-operative Societies, as also in general domestic circles. It will also be used in lieu of a Prospectus in introducing the various financial operations advocated by the Co-Operative Credit Bank, with which this journal is associated.' 'As each new form of co-operative enterprise appears it will be duly chronicled and discussed in these columns by accomplished writers, who will remember that they write for the general public as well as for City men.' Aim – to become 'a great Family, Financial, and Co-operative newspaper'. News, reports of public meetings, articles of general interest to workers, literature.

L(Col)† I, 1; II, 44 (18 Dec. 1875)

722 Co-operative Brotherhood Trust, Ltd. Monthly Circular; m

A?   Committees' reports and price lists

O(JJ)† June, July 1899

723 Co-operative Citizen I, 1 (May 1940)–II, 15 (July 1942); ns 1 (Jan. 1946)–122 (March 1956); m

B   Gratis. Issued by the Educational Department of Grays Co-operative Society. Printed and published by the Co-operative Press. One of the 'Citizen' series.

L(Col)†

724 Co-operative College Magazine I, 1 (June 1946)–[1956?]. Loughborough; a

A   'First magazine of the New Co-operative College'. Successor to the **Stokehole**.

Co-op. Coll† 1946–56 (w 1, 2, [1947?])

725 Co-operative Commercial Circular Published under the Direction of the Executive Committee Appointed by the General Conference 1 (Nov. 1853)–17 (March 1855); m

A ½d.; 1d. Printed and published by R. Isham, Manager of the Working Printers' Association. Each issue has 'Address of the Executive Committee', 'Co-operative news', 'Market intelligence', other news of the Labour Movement, and relevant information. Published one or two supplements, eg, June 1854, 'The probable future of the labouring classes', by John Stuart Mill.

Co-op. Coll† 2–17 (w 13, 16)

726 Co-operative Consumer [195-?]. Reading; s-a

A   3d. Articles, information etc. relating to the Co-operative Movement. (Mitchell, 1955.)

727 Co-operative Cultivator I, 1 (Nov. 1923)–?; q

B   3d. Published by the Allotments Organisation Society and Smallholders, Ltd. Periodical of the 'allotment and smallholding co-operative movement'. For communication between the various constituent bodies.

L† I, 1–II, 10 (April 1926)

728 Co-operative Education Bulletin 1 (Dec. 1948)–45 (Dec. 1960). Loughborough; irreg

A   6d. Issued by the Co-operative Union, Education Department. 'It has kept under review all areas of Co-operative education and the relation to them of general social and educational developments' (No. 45). No. 1 reproduced from typewriting. From January 1961 included in Co-operative Review.

Co-op. Union†; E 10 (Dec. 1951)–; L 10–; O 10–

729 Co-operative Educator I, 1 (Jan. 1917)–XXIII, 2 (April 1939). Manchester; q

A   2d. Published by the Co-operative Union. To further the formation of co-operative character and opinions'. Absorbed Co-operative College Herald. Merged in **Co-operative Review**.

Co-op. Coll.*; Co-op. Union; MP; O

730 Co-operative Employé: Monthly Journal of the Amalgamated Union of Co-operative Employés 1 (June 1908)–109 (June 1917); then **AUCE Journal**: Official Organ of the Amalgamated Union of Co-operative and Commercial Employees and Allied Workers: 110 (July 1917)–151 (Dec. 1920). Manchester; m

A   1d. Published by the Co-operative Newspaper Society, Ltd., 'as a means of communication between the various sections of the union: the councils, districts, branches etc.' Information and articles on trade union, Co-operative and general Labour topics. Editor: A. Hewitt. Superseded by **New Dawn**. Preceded by **Gleanings**.

Co-op. Coll† 26–55; L(Col)† (w July 1908, Nov. 1909, June 1911); USDAW

Co-operative Gazette see **War Emergency Circular**

731 Co-operative Grocer: Monthly Journal for the Retail Co-operative Grocery Executive I, 1 (Feb. 1963)– ; m

A   1s. 6d. Publisher: St. Martin's Press; Co-operative Marketing Services, Ltd. Illustrated magazine.

L; O† (w occ. nos)

732 Co-operative Guildman: the Official Organ of the National
Co-operative Men's Guild I, 1 (March 1925)–[194-?]; then **Guildman**:
[194-?]–XXV, 6 (June/July 1954). Manchester; m: bi-m

    A   1d. etc. At first published for the Guild by the Co-operative
Union. 'To clarify and promulgate co-operative principles.' Editor: Edward
Topham. Official reports and news, short articles, book reviews.

    Co-op. Union† I, 1–I, 12 (March 1926), IV, 1 (Jan. 1931)–IV; 10
(Dec. 1931), XIX, 4 (April 1946)–XXV, 6 (June/July 1954); L† I,
1–XIV, 4 (April 1941); OI–III, 27; ONC† occ. nos 1950–4

Co-operative Holiday Association General Notes see **Comradeship,
1907–1917**

Co-operative Home Magazine see **Wheatsheaf**

733 Co-operative Labour Clarion [19--?] –? Bristol; m
    B   Issued by Bristol Co-operative Society and Bristol North East
Constituency Labour Party.
    L(col) [ns] 1 (Nov. 1949)–4 (Feb. 1950)

Co-operative Magazine see **Co-operative Magazine and Monthly Herald**

734 Co-operative Magazine and Monthly Herald: I, 1 (Jan. 1826)–ns II, 12
(Dec. 1827), then **Co-operative Magazine**: ns III, 1 (Jan. 1828)–III, 10
(Oct. 1829); then **London Co-operative Magazine**: ns IV, 1 (1 Jan.
1830)–IV, 3 (1 March 1830); then **British Co-operator, or, Record and
Review of Co-operation and Entertaining Knowledge**: 1 (April 1830)–7
(Oct. 1830); m; q (April 1828–)

    A   6d. Publisher: Knight and Lacey; Hunt and Clarke. Organ of the
London Co-operative Society. Led by James Watson and William Lovett.
Contributors: Abram Combe, William Thompson, William Maclure,
William kng. Details of Owenite communities and institutions, eg, New
Harmony, Orbiston, New Lanark. Theoretical articles on the philosophy of
the Co-operative ideal. For the independence of Mechanics Institutes from
middle-class control. The **Co-operative Magazine** printed the lectures of
Francis Wright, Robert Owen and Robert Dale Owen.

    Bishopsgate Institute† I–III; C I–II; Co-op Coll.† Jan. 1826–April
1828; GM I; GU I–II; L; LU (w Nov.–Dec. 1929); SaU 1–II; Greenwood
reprint I–IV, 3

**735 Co-operative Management and Marketing: the Official Co-operative
Management and Marketing Journal** I, 1 (April 1968)– . Manchester; m
    A   5s. Published by the Co-operative Press. Journal for
Co-operative Society boards of directors and officials. Illustrated
magazine. Superseded **Agenda** and **Co-operative Official**.
    Co-op. Union; O†

736 Co-operative Manager and Secretary: the Organ of the National Co-operative Managers' Association [19–?] –ns VI, 23 (April 1919). Warrington; m

    A   Forerunner of the **Co-operative Official**. Branch reports and correspondence.

    L† ns V, 17 (Oct. 1918)–VI, 23

737 Co-operative Miscellany 1830

    A?   (H. H. Sparling in **Notes and Queries**, 23 April 1892, p. 333; A. Bonner, **British co-operation**, rev. ed. 1970.)

Co-operative Monthly see **Co-operative Union Quarterly Review**

738 Co-operative News and Journal of Associated Industry I, 1 (2 Sept. 1871)–L, 17 (26 April 1919); ns I, 1, (old series 2501) (3 May 1919)– . London; Manchester; w   ·

    A   The leading organ of the British Co-operative movement. Later, **Co-operative News**. Deals with Co-operation in all its aspects.

    Co-op. Coll. 1939–*; Co-op Union†: Gu i I–II; L(Col) (microfilm 1892, 1893); LE i VII–VIII, XIX, XXVIII, XXXIX–; LU i L–XXXVII*; LvP 1903–30; MP (w 1913–30); NU 1966– : O ns 2,435, 1966–

Co-operative Newsletter see **Leeds Co-operative Record**

Co-operative Newspaper see **National Co-operative Leader**

739 Co-operative Official I, 1 (Nov. 1919)–XLIX, 2 (Feb./March 1968). Manchester; m

    A   2d.   Published by the Co-operative Union. Official organ of the National Co-operative Managers' Association, the Co-operative Secretaries' Association and the National Union of Co-operative Officials; Co-operative Officials' Management Association. First editor: Thomas Mercer. Preceded by **The Co-operative Manager**. Then published as part of **Co-operative Management and Marketing**.

    Co-op. Union; L†; LE I; MP I–XIX*; O (II*); ONC occ. vols

740 Co-operative Party. Monthly Letter to Parties I, 1 (Dec. 1944)–1965; m

    B   Replaced by **Platform** Title varies: **Monthly Letter to Party Organisations; Monthly Letter**.

    Co-op Party 1945–65; E IX, 11 (Nov. 1952)–; L† I, 1–XV, 1 (Jan. 1958); O IX, 11–XXII, 8 (Aug. 1965); ONC VIII, 8 (Aug. 1951)–XIV, 9 (Sept. 1957)

741 Co-operative Party Citizen: Monthly Journal of the Co-operative Party 1 (April 1937)–4 (July 1937); then **The Pioneer**: Official Organ of the Co-operative Party: 5 (Sept. 1937)–11 (March 1938); m

    B   Printed and published by the Co-operative Press.

    L(Col)†

742 Co-operative Party Notes. [19–?] –; m; irreg

B   In 1952 consisted of single cards stapled together, 10 or 12 each month. Issued by the Co-operative Union for the Co-operative Party. Later, reproduced from typewriting. Information on current politics.

Co-op. Union 1965–*; ONC† 309 (Feb. 1952)–318 (Dec. 1952*); [ns], 55 (Oct. 1970)–; TUC [ns], 44 (April 1969)–48 (Oct. 1969)

743 Co-operative Prices Current: Journal of the Agricultural and Horticultural Association Nov. 1869–Dec. 1869; then **Agricultural Economist and Horticultural Review**: I, 1 (Jan. 1870)–XLIX, 554 (March 1916); m

C   6d. Editor: E. O. Greening etc. A co-operative wholesale company dealing mainly in agricultural implements and materials. Members are tenant farmers and agriculturists. Becomes a specialised agricultural review, to promote better agriculture etc.

AbN 1912–16; AbU 1900–15*; BU 1905–16; GM 1908–15; GU 1909–14; L(Col)†; LAM 1893–1904*; LP; LSC 1910–12; LU XLI–XLVII; LdP 1910–14; LvU 1910–14; MU 1908–14; O 1895–1916 SaU 1908–14

744 Co-operative Productive Federation. Year Book 1897–9. Leicester; then **Co-operators' Year Book**: 1900–[1960?] London; a

A   Published by the Federation. Articles and information. Produced by Thomas Blandford. Not published in 1944 and 1945.

Co-op. Coll.*; L; LE*; NP 1943, 1946; ONC*; O 1900; Plunkett Foundation*

745 Co-operative Productive Review: Official Organ of the Co-operative Productive Federation, Ltd I (1925)–XXXV, 4 (April 1960). Leicester; m

A   Articles on the philosophy of Co-operation and on everyday activities.

Co-op. Coll. 1925–42, 1946–60; Co-op. Union Feb. 1935– ; L† IX 5 (Jan. 1935)– ; ONC Oct. 1942–April 1960

746 Co-operative Record of the Birmingham District 1 (Oct. 1892)–24 (July 1898). Birmingham; q

A   Gratis. Editor: William Cope. News of local Co-operative endeavour, with some articles, eg. by Holyoake.

BP; Co-op. Coll.; LU†

747 Co-operative Reference Library. Bulletin 1 (July 1914)–12 (June 1915); m; then b **Better Business**: a Quarterly Journal of Agricultural and Industrial Co-operation: I, 1 (Oct. 1915)–VII, 1 (Nov. 1921); then **Irish Economist**: a Quarterly Journal of Co-operative Thought and Progress: VII, 2 (Feb. 1922)–VIII, 4 (Oct. 1923). Dublin; q

B   6d. Irish Agricultural Organisation Society. Promotes ideals and work of Horace Plunkett. Articles also on international rural Co-operation schemes.

C; CoU b I–III, V–VI; D; L; LAM b; LE b; MP b VII, 4–VIII; O b

748 Co-operative Review I, 1 (Aug. 1926)– . Manchester; bi-m; m
    A   6d. etc. Owned and published by the Co-operative Union.
Editors: Thomas Mercer; Edward Topham; K. Hulse. 'To reflect the policy
of the Co-operative Union, Britain's national federation of co-operative
societies; to provide information and comment to co-operative committees.
officials . . . ' Signed articles. From Vol. XL issued as a monthly
supplement to **Co-operative News.**
    C; Co-op. Coll.; Co-op. Union; D; L†; MP I–II; NU XXX, 4 (April
1956)–XXXIX (1965); O; ONC 1927–65*; TUC 1961–5

749 Co-operative Union. Trade Advisory Bulletin 1 (23 Nov. 1962)–49 (9
June 1970). Manchester; irreg
    A   Internal bulletin, for members. Also, **Trade Advisory Bulletin
Management Series**, 1–18, undated, reprinted as chapters in **Manual on
co-operative management**, edited by John Jacques, 1969.
    Co-op. Union†

750 Co-operative Union Quarterly Review 1 (March 1914)–23 (Oct.
1919). Manchester; q
    A   Free to members. Published by the Co-operative Union. For
members of the Union and members of the various executive committees
of district associations. 'Matters of general interest to officials of
co-operative societies.'
    Co-op. Union†

751 Co-operative Union Quarterly Review: Reports of Items of Interest to
Co-operative Societies in Connection with the Work of the United Board,
its Committees and Sectional Boards 1 (March 1914)–24 (March 1920);
then b **Co-operative Monthly**: the Official Journal for Co-operative
Officials and Committeemen: 1 (Jan. 1921). Manchester; q
    A   a, no price; b, 3d. Issued by the Co-operative Union. Instruction
and information.
    L†; LE a 20–4

752 Co-operative Wholesale Societies, Ltd. Almanack and Diary 1880–2;
then **Annual**: 1883–1918; then b **People's Year Book and Annual of the
English and Scottish Wholesale Societies**: 1 1918–50. Manchester; a
    A   In earlier years, a substantial volume containing not only
statistical and other information on the Co-operative Movement, and
additional reference material, but sometimes also long signed articles on
economic, social, political, historical topics, fiction, numerous
illustrations. Latterly, reduced in size.
    BP 1900– ; BS b 17; BU 1893; 1896; 1900, 1902– ; B1U b 4, 6;
Brechin PL 1943–50; Co-op. Coll. 1881– ; DnP 1922– ; E 1895–1950;
EU 1887–1918; GM 1921–50; GU b 4–*; GrP 1937; IpP 1930; L; LE; LU
1883–1920; LdP 1925– ; LvP 1906–50*; MP; MU 1890–1916*; NU
1893, 1902, 1905, 1908, 1910–43; O b; ONC† 1882–1949; Plunkett
Foundation, Oxford 1883–1950; Sp 1923– ; SwU 1903–9, 1915–16;
Scottish CWS 1896–1926*

753 Co-operative Women's Guild. **Monthly Bulletin** [19–?] –?
   A   (London School of Economics and Political Science. Political Records Project.)

754 Co-operative Yearbook 1968– . London; Brighton; a
   A   Published by Co-operative Marketing Services, Ltd. Reference book for the Co-operative Movement, including information and articles.
   O†

755 Co-operative Youth: the Organ of the British Federation of Co-operative Youth I, 1 (Oct. 1930)–X, 108 (Oct. 1939). Manchester; then b **Comrade**: I, 1 (July 1942)–VIII, 11 (June 1950). London; then **Young Co-operator**: IX, 1 (July 1950)–XIX, 2 (June 1960). London; m
   A   2d. etc. Later issued by the British Federation of Young Co-operators. Printed and published by the National Co-operative Publishing Society. Gets increasingly slimmer and more limited in content.
   L†; ONC 1942–5*

756 Co-operative Youth Leader: Co-operative Monthly for Leaders of Youth Club, Pathfinder and Rainbow Playway Groups of the Youth Movement [I], 1 (Oct. 1946–VII, 6 (June 1952); ns [I], 1 (Jan. 1953)–[1969?]. Manchester; Loughborough; m; bi-m; s-a; 3-yr
   A   3d.; free to Co-operative Youth Movement members. Published first by the Co-operative Union in a printed form, then by the Education Department of the Co-operative Union as a more modest publication, reproduced from typewriting.
   E ns; L† (w occ. nos); O† ns I, 1–II, 3 (Feb. 1969)

757 Co-operative's Magazine [18–?]. [Edinburgh?]
   A?   W. J. Couper asks for information about this in **Scottish Notes and Queries**, March 1900, p. 142.

758 Co-operator 1 (1 May 1828)–38 (1 Aug. 1830). Brighton; sometimes London; m
   B   1d. Publishers: Cowie and Strange, London; Taylor and Son, Brighton. Editor: Dr. William King. A series of tracts, most of which were written by King, each of which discussed a particular aspect of Co-operation. Also known as **The Brighton Co-operator**. Reprinted in 1922, with introduction and notes by T. W. Mercer, as **Dr Wm King and The Co-operator**; and in 1947 in T. W. Mercer, **Co-operation's Prophet**.
   BiP; Co-op. Union; L; LU; O† (w 27)

759 Co-operator: a Record of Co-operative Progress, Conducted Exclusively by Working Men I, 1 (June 1860)–XI (1871). Manchester; m; fortn; w

    A   1d. Published by Abel and John Heywood. Issued by Manchester and Salford Co-operative Society as a general organ for the movement. For the encouragement and support of working men's co-operative societies and stores. Editors: Edward Longfield (I), Henry Pitman (II–XI). Ceased to be a local magazine after Pitman succeeded as editor and it became a national co-operative newspaper. 'It became **The Co-operator and Anti-Vaccinator**, and ere its last appearance, on 2nd December 1871, ceased to include any co-operative news whatever' (T. W. Mercer, 'Early Ventures in Co-operative Journalism'. **People's Year Book** (1928), pp. 14–16).

    BP I–III, VIII; Co-op. Coll.; Co-op. Union; L† I, 1–Aug. 1871 (w June 1865–Dec. 1867); LE I, V, VI*, VII, VIII–IX*; LU. MP

Co-operator [1886?] see **Lincoln Co-operative Record**

760 Co-operator [1926?] Feb. 1944; then **Co-operator and Home Review**: March 1944–224 (Nov. 1944); then **Home Review**: 225 (Dec. 1944)–287 (Feb. 1950). Manchester; m

    A   1d. Organ of Co-operative retail societies.

    L(Col) II, 84 (Nov. 1934)–287*

Co-operator, 1974 see **Leeds Co-operative Record**

761 Co-operator: the Official Organ of the Manchester District Co-operative Party 1 (Dec. 1927)–? Manchester; m

    B   Published by the Party.

    Eccles PL 24 (Nov. 1929), 33 (Aug. 1930)–36 (Nov. 1930)

762 Co-operator [1931?] –? Guildford; m

    A   Guildford and District Co-operative Society. 'In December, 1930, our Society issued a Christmas magazine of its own, as a result of which it was decided to commence our own monthly journal in place of the **Wheatsheaf**. This we named **The Co-operator** . . . We are proud of the fact that this journal continued publication during the difficult war years . . .' (L. Codd, **Acorn to Oak: a short History of Guildford and District Co-operative Society**, Guildford 1948, p. 9.)

Co-operator and Home Review see **Co-operator** [19--?] –?

Co-operators' Year Book see **Co-operative Productive Federation. Year Book**

763 Coopers Federation of Great Britain and Ireland. **Quarterly Report** [19--?] –? q

    A

    TUC† Aug. 1926–May 1946*

764 Cooper's Journal; or, **Unfettered Thinker and Plain Speaker for Truth, Freedom, and Progress** 1 (5 Jan. 1850)—30 (26 Oct. 1850); w

    B   1d. Printed and published by James Watson. Founded and edited by Thomas Cooper as an organ to promote the revival of Chartism under new auspices. Heavy slant towards need for a national system of secular education to prepare the people to exercise their democratic rights. Items of radical verse and prose. Contributors: Samuel Kydd, Gerald Massey, Frank Grant, Thomas Shorter, George Hooper, Richard Otley.

    L; LE†; LU; LcP; MP; ONC

Co-Partnership see **Labour Co-Partnership**

765 Copyists' Own Journal 1 (Nov. 1900)—2 (Dec. 1900); m

    A   Editor: F. W. Field. A light-hearted boy copyists' magazine, written by copyists. Then merged in **The Union Observer**

    L(Col)†

766 Cordwainers' Companion: a Miscellany of Trade and General Information 1844—?; w

    A   Mentioned in **The Northern Star**, 1846.

    MP† 3 (April)—14 (Sept. 1844) (originals and microfilm)

767 Cornwall Power 1960?— . Newquay

    A   National and Local Government Officers' Association, Cornwall Electricity Branch. Reproduced from typewriting.

    L Jan. 1960—

Correspondence of a Man Out of Work see **Appeal to the Common Sense of the Whole World**

768 Cosme 1895—1903. Colonia Cosme, Paraguay m

    A   2s. 6d. yearly. Editor: W. Lane. Deals with the work and interests of the Cosme Fellowship, described as a co-operative association of English speaking people holding Communism, teetotalism, marriage and the colour line as principles.

    L Jan.—March, Aug.—Dec. 1896; LE*; WCML† April 1897, Jan. 1899

769 Cosmopolite: a London Weekly Newspaper 1 (10 March 1832)–ns 32 (23 Nov. 1833); w

    B   1d.; 1½d. Printed and published by James Knight; George Pilgrim; Joseph Walker, Richard Carlile, Jr. Editors: George Pilgrim, Richard Carlile, Alexander Somerville. 'One of the best-known radical newspapers of the decade with probable weekly circulation of 5,000. Attacks the aristocracy and monarchy, the "taxes on knowledge", the Church of England, and the national debt, and advocates "physical force", if necessary, as a means of securing reforms' (Wiener). Publicity for the National Union of the Working Classes and for Political Unions. Merged with **The Man**. Sub-title of new series: 'A Cheap Substitute for a Stamped Newspaper'.

    Co-op. Union ii 1 (22 April 1833)–2; GM ii 9, 30; H.O. 64/18 i 1, 4, 6–11, 18–19, 23, 25, 27–39, 43–4, 46–50, 52–7; HO 64/19 ii 3–7, 11, 20; L† i 1–30; L Place Newspaper Coll. Set 65 i 1–55; LU i 25; O i 1, ii 21; O(JJ) i 1

770 Cottager in Town and Country I, 1 (Jan. 1861)–V, 53 (May 1865); then **Cottager and Artisan**: V, 54 (June 1865)–LIX, 708 (Dec. 1919); m

    C   1d.; 1½d. Published by the Religious Tract Society. An improvement magazine with instructive readings for the homes of working-men. Advocates Christian values, honesty, industriousness, thrift, moral rectitude and useful leisure. Illustrated.

    C III–LIX; L†

771 Cotton Factory Times 1 (16 Jan. 1885)–2733 (2 July 1937). Manchester; Ashton-under-Lyne; w

    B   1d. Editors: Joseph Burgess; A. W. Humphrey; James Haslam. Founded by John Andrew. 'Proclaimed itself advocate of operatives of cotton factories of Manchester area and of their trade unions; against "communist ideas which occasionally dribble over from the Continent".' (Brophy.) Registration issues were published monthly as follows: 2734 (9 July 1937)–3191 (July 1967).

    L(Col)†

772 Cotton Strike Leader 1 (10 Sept. 1931)–5 (24 Sept. 1932); then **Cotton Workers' Leader**: 6 (22 Oct. 1932)–10 (July 1933). Rawtenstall, Lancashire (printed); m

    A   1d. Published by the Cotton Strikers' Solidarity Movement. Aims: not a penny off wages, no more looms, re-instatement of all displaced workers. News of strike and its aftermath.

    WCML†

Cotton Workers' Leader see **Cotton Strike Leader**

Coulsdon and Purley Review see **NALGO Local Gazette**

773 Councillor: a Local Government Publication of the London Labour Party 1 (Sept. 1920)–3 (April 1921); q

    B   2d. Published by Herbert Morrison for the London Labour Party. Editor: Herbert Morrison. 'Produced for party information only.' Incorporated into **The Labour Chronicle**.

    L†

774 Counsellor; a Journal of the Friends of Labour Associations I, 1 (1 Dec. 1859)–I, 4 (4 April 1860); m

    C   1d. Printed and published by the proprietor, Richard Howe. Friends of Labour Associations were a mainly working-class body. The last number has a leader on the late strike and lockout in the building trades, and a copy of an address signed by George Potter. The leader is opposed to Potter and the Nine Hours Movement as being rash. No March issue

    L†

775 Counsellor, on Secular, Co-operative and Political Questions 1 (Aug. 1861)–5 (Dec. 1861); m

    B   1½d. Printed and published by A. Holyoake. Edited by G. J. Holyoake. Short-term successor to **The Reasoner**. To offer advice 'on certain proletarian or working class questions', to present secular principles in an intelligible form, promote theory and practice of working-class Co-operation, and claims of working class to enfranchisement.

    Bishopsgate Institute†

776 Counter Point: Official Staff Magazine of the Bristol Co-operative Society, Ltd [1948?]–XVII, 2 (July 1964). Bristol; m

    A

    L† X, 9 (Nov. 1957)–XVII, 2

777 Counterblast: a New Journal for Labour Youth 1 (April/May 1962)–3 (Oct./Nov. 1962)

    B   1s. Editor: Christopher Cowling. Journal of an 'informal' group within the Labour Party Young Socialists, who follow Party policy, but are not dependent on the parent body for funds etc., as was the case with the official Young Socialists paper **New Advance**. Violently opposed to the Trotskyist Young Socialist paper **Keep Left**.

    L†

778 Counterpunch I, 1 (Jan. 1955)–XI, 7 (July 1965). Manchester; m

    A   Published by CWS Publications. For Co-operative Wholesale Society shopkeepers. Hints on display, selling etc. Competitions.

    Co-op. Union

779 Country Standard 1935– ; m

    B   1d. etc. 'For peace and socialism in the countryside.' News and discussion of agricultural unions, puts forward socialist views on subjects of interest to country dwellers and workers. In 1940s includes articles on Russian agriculture.

    L(Col)† occ. nos Dec. 1939–Aug. 1944, 1946–; LAM 1949–; MML*; ONC Feb. 1950

780 Country Worker I, 1 (Jan. 1935). Mendlesham, Suffolk

    B   Duplicated and published by D. Jefferies on behalf of an independent Editorial Board of Suffolk Socialists, 'for those who work in the country districts, for farm workers, small working farmers, shoemakers, carpenters, wheelwrights, postmen, carriers, roadmen, blacksmiths'. Fights for Socialism, against war, Fascism and reduction in living standards.

    L†

781 County and Westminster Magazine; then **County, Westminster and Parr's Magazine**: [19--?] , bi-m

    A?   3d.; 4d. Organ of the staff of the LC and W Bank (then L,C, W and P Bank). (Mitchell, 1915, 1920.)

County Comment see National Association of Local Government Officers. Nottinghamshire County Council Branch. **Branch News**

782 County Court Officer: Journal of the County Court Officers' Association [19--?].

    A

    ONC† XXXVIII, 13 (15 July 1964), 15 (23 Oct. 1964)

783 County Courts Gazette: the Organ of the County Courts (Clerks and Officers) Association I, 1 (Aug. 1912)–III, 6 (Nov. 1917). Coventry etc; m

    A   2d

    L†; ONC I, 1

784 County Derry Liberal I, 1 (13 Oct. 1888)–I, 30 (4 May 1889) Limavady; w

    B   ½d. Printed and published by the Circle Co-operative Printing Company. Editor: J. Bruce Wallace. 'Our sympathies are with the people, the workers – with "the masses" rather than with "the classes".' Promoted idea of an International Democratic Federation. Declared 'we call ourselves "Liberal" ', but was Radical in outlook, especially on Land Question, when it favoured nationalisation. Published Bellamy's **Looking backward** in serial form. Then incorporated in **Brotherhood**.

    L(Col)†

785 County NALGO I, 1 (1955)—III, 4 [1959]; then **County NALGO Journal** ser. 2,1 (March/April 1959)—ser. 7,1 (Spring 1964); then **NALGO Herefordia**: [1] (May 1968)— . Hereford; irreg?
    A   National and Local Government Officers' Association.
Reproduced from typewriting.
    La I, 1, 2, II, I III, 1—4, b, c

County NALGO Journal see **County Nalgo**

786 County Officers' Gazette: the Official Organ of the NUCO I, 1 (17 Feb. 1930)—XI, 22 (27 May 1940); w
    A   1d. National Union of County Officers. Then merged in **NA-WU Magazine**.
    L(Col)†

787 County Service Journal: Official Journal of the West Riding County Officers' Association I, 1 [1957]—III, 6 [1960]; then **News and Views**: 1 (Feb. 1960)—17 (Feb. 1961); then **White Rose**: (Sept. 1962)—(Dec. 1963); then **New White Rose**: (March 1964)— . Wakefield; irreg
    A   National and Local Government Officers' Association.
Reproduced from typewriting. **The White Rose** sometimes called **The White Rosette**.
    L

County, Westminster and Parr's Magazine see **County and Westminster Magazine**

788 Courier [19--?]—? [Sheffield?]
    A   Union of Post Office Workers, Sheffield and District Branches.
(W. Dunlop, 'Local Journals'. **Belpost**, IV, 5 (May 1965).)

789 Courier 1 [1952?]—? Preston
    A   National Association of Local Government Officers, later National and Local Government Officers' Association, Ribble Motors (Preston) Branch. Reproduced from typewriting.
    L 6 (Oct. 1952)—12 (Dec. 1953)

Courier International see **International Courier**

790 Court Chronicle I, 1 (Sept. 1955)—? (Dec. 1962). Lyndhurst
    A   National and Local Government Officers' Association, New Forest Branch
    L†

791 Coventry Citizen 1 (Jan. 1960)—18 (Aug. 1961)
    B   Published by the Co-operative Press.
    L(Col)

792 Coventry Clerks Bulletin: the Clerical and Administrative Union Branch Publication 1 (May 1943)–? Coventry; q?

    A

    TUC† 1–3 (Nov./Dec. 1943)

793 Coventry Co-operative Citizen 1, [193-?]–92 (Nov. 1940); m?

    B   Issued by the Coventry and District Co-operative Society.

    L(Col). 40 (Jan. 1936)–92

794 Coventry Labour News [193-?]. Coventry; m

    B   Labour Party. (Labour and Socialist International. **The Socialist Press**, 1933.)

795 Coventry Labour's Voice 1 [1955?]– ?

    B   A 'Voice' paper.'

    WCML† I, 3 (March 1955)

796 Coventry Perseverence Co-operative Society. Record [188-?] Coventry; m

    A   Gratis. Edited by the Education Committee. (**International Directory of the Co-operative Press**, 1909; Coventry Perseverence Co-operative Society. **Jubilee History, 1867–1917**, 1917).

797 Coventry Searchlight: Official Organ of the Coventry Labour Party 1 (June 1937)–[unnumbered] (1 Nov. 1937); (1 Nov. 1938); irreg

    B   Printed by the Co-operative Press. Edited and published by George Hodgkinson. One of the 'Citizen' series.

    L(Col)†

798 Coventry Sentinel [19--?]. Coventry; w

    A   ½d. 'Local trade union organ'. (Mitchell, 1910.)

799 Coventry Town Crier [194-?]. Coventry

    B   Coventry Labour Party. Superseded by **Coventry Tribune**.

800 Coventry Tribune 1 (12 Oct. 1946)–35 (12 June 1948). Coventry; fortn

    B   2d Issued by Coventry Labour Party. Preceded by **Coventry Town Crier**.

    CvP; L(Col)†

Cover Note see **Insurance Guild Journal**

801 Cowlairs Spanish Workers' Defence Committee. [Bulletin] 1 (16 Sept. 1936). Glasgow
    B   Subscription voluntary. Two-page sheet. Published by T. L. Anderson. Printed by Bakunin Press. Advocated General Strike action in place of Popular Frontism as best way of aiding the Spanish working class. Reproduced from typewriting.
    L(Col)†

Craftsman, 1872–1873 see **Out on Strike**

802 Craftsman: a Constitutional and Industrial Review I, 1 (April 1881)–VI, 62 (July 1886); m
    A   1d. Printed, published, edited by Richard Yeates, 'a Conservative working man'. Objects: 1) to educate the mass of the people in Constitutional Principles; 2) to supply an organ of communication between the various Working Men's Conservative Clubs throughout the United Kingdom; 3) to provide a medium for the insertion of articles and essays written by working-men, expressing their political opinions from a Constitutional point of view; 4) to form a vehicle of direct communication between the working man and MPs; 5) to check the spread and eradicate the disorders of Democracy and Communism with which the British working-man has been in too many quarters inoculated by the evil contagion of seditious demagogues and exiled foreign agitators etc. The issue for May 1886 says the journal will be succeeded by **The Central Constitutional Press**, 'a new Conservative Journal for the working classes'.
    L†; O I–III

803 Craftsmen's Club, Birmingham. **Monthly Journal** I, 1 (1901)–II 16 (Aug. 1902); then **Cog**: Craftsmen's Club Monthly Journal: II, 17 (Sept. 1902)–II, 20 (Dec. 1902). Birmingham; m
    A   1d. The Craftsmen's Club was established as a means of communication between amateurs and professionals interested in similar arts or trades, for help, advice and exchange of ideas. Also promoted the formation of a body of first-class craftsmen with the object of each member becoming a businessman, employer.
    BP† II, 16 (Aug. 1902)–II, 20

804 Craftwork Circular: Periodical of the NUT Sheffield Sub-Association of Handicraft Teachers I, 1 (Sept. 1936)–30 (Oct. 1949?). Sheffield; s-a
    A   National Union of Teachers.
    SP† 1–30

805 Credit Worker: Official Organ of the Credit Workers' Association I, 1 (Jan. 1939)–3 (Aug./Sept. 1939). Sheffield; q?
    A   1s. Union of bill-collectors and salesmen. Some employer support? Editor: H. A. Bell.
    SP†

806 Cresset [194-?]. Glasgow; m
   B   6d. Labour Party. (Labour Party. **Your own Journal,** 1948.)

807 Crewe and South Cheshire Voice. [194-?]. Crewe; m
   B   2d. Published by **Voice.** Labour Party. (Labour Party. **Your own Journal,** 1948.)

808 Crewe Cuttings. Crewe
   A   National Association of Local Government Officers. Crewe and District Branch. Reproduced from typewriting.
   L 1961–

809 Crewe Recorder [1925?] –[1928]. Crewe; m
   B   Labour Party. (Labour and Socialist International. **The Socialist Press,** 1933.)

810 Crisis, or Star to the Great Northern Union 1, [1830] –2, [11 Sept. 1830]. Preston; w?
   B   3d. Printed by I. Wilcockson. Editor: J. Mitchell. 'A radical miscellany. The second number contains an address to Henry Hunt urging him to become the active leader of all the reformers' (Wiener).
   Harvard UL

811 Crisis; or, the Change from Error and Misery, to Truth and Happiness I, 1 (14 April 1832)–II, 15 (20 April 1833); then **Crisis, and National Co-operative Trades' Union and Equitable Labour Exchange Gazette:** II, 16 (27 April 1833)–IV, 20 (23 Aug. 1834); w
   A   1d.; 1½d. Publishers: George Berger; J. Eamonson; Benjamin Cousins. Editors: Robert Owen, Robert Dale Owen (1832–4), Rev. James E. 'Shepherd' Smith (1834). Published also by Strange; Richardson; Purkiss. Printed for, and published by, 'the Association of the Intelligent and well-disposed of the Industrious Classes for Removing Ignorance and Poverty, by Education and Employment, at their Institution. . .'
Succeeded by **The Shepherd** and **The New Moral World.**
   BP; BrU; Co-op. Coll.*; Co-op. Union I; L (w II, 6); LE (Greenwood reprint and microfiche; microfiche distributed by the Harvester Press Ltd); LU; MP I–IV*; MR; O†

812 Critic: a Weekly Review of the Drama, Music and Literature 1 (2 Dec. 1874)–16 (20 Nov. 1875) then **Critic:** a Social and Political Review: 17, (nsl) (27 March 1875)–22 (1 May 1875); w
   B   1d. Not relevant until No. 17, when it changes character. Printed by the National Press Agency. Advocates 'advanced and scientific Radicalism'.
   L(Col)†

813 Crofton Ward Orpington LP [194-?] ; m
   B   Labour Party. Duplicated. (Labour Party. **Your own Journal,** 1948.)

814 Crompton LP (Royton) [194-?] ; irreg
    B   Labour Party. Duplicated. (Labour Party. **Your own Journal,**
1948.)

815 Crookesmoor Gazette [19--?] –? [Sheffield?] ; m
    B   Labour Party.
    ILP Oct. 1927

816 Crossroads [1954?] –?
    B?   **Oxford Left,** Hilary 1954, sends fraternal greetings to the
above, issued at the London School of Economics.

817 Crosstalk 1963?–   . Banbury
    A   National and Local Government Officers' Association, Banbury
and District Branch. Reproduced from typewriting.
    L 1963–

818 Crow Pie [19--?] –?; m
    A?   2d. Civil Service staff magazine. (Mitchell, 1930.)

819 Crown and Rose: the Journal of the Hampshire County Branch of the
National Association of Local Government Officers. I [1948?] –?
Winchester.
    A   Later, National and Local Government Officers' Association.
    L VI, 1 (Jan. 1953)–VII, 6 (June 1954)

820 Croxley Labour News [194-?]. Croxley Green, Hertfordshire; m
    B   Free. Labour Party. (Labour Party. **Your own Journal,** 1948.)

Croydon and Surrey Labour Outlook see **Croydon Labour Outlook**

821 Croydon Brotherhood Intelligence I, 1 (Jan. 1895)–?; then **New
Order**: III, 1 Jan. 1897–? Croydon; London; m
    B   1d. Organ of the Brotherhood Church, Croydon. Published by
the Brotherhood Trust. Editor of **New Order**: John C. Kenworthy, Pastor
of the Church. Christian Socialist, and Tolstoyan (pacifist).
    L† Jan. 1897–Dec. 1899; ONC occ. nos

822 Croydon Citizen: Advocate of the Cause of Labour 1 (8 Oct. 1904)–
235 (6 March 1909). Croydon; w
    B   ½d. Published by George Gliddon and Harry Sidney. Editor:
H. T. Muggeridge. 'The first genuine Labour newspaper that the borough
has yet seen.' Issued by the local Labour Party.
    L(Col)†

823 Croydon Labour Journal: Monthly Magazine of South Croydon
Labour Party I, 1 (May 1947)–IV, 3 (Nov. 1950). Croydon; m
    B   2d. From No. 5 becomes magazine of Croydon Labour Party
(North and South).
    CnP (w II, 4, 12); L†

824 Croydon Labour Outlook I, 1 (April 1924)–V, 53 (Aug. 1928). Croydon; m

    B   1d. Published by Croydon Labour Party. No. 1 suggests there was an earlier series, but this has not been traced. Re-started to campaign for the Labour Party in power. Branch and ward news, political analysis and articles from a Labour stronghold. Contributors: Councillor H. T. Muggeridge, Chairman, Croydon Labour Party, H. Stanley Redgrove, Organiser

    CnP; L(Col)†

825 Croydon Metro Magazine 1964?–   . Croydon

    A   National and Local Government Officers' Association, South Eastern Gas Board Headquarters. Reproduced from typewriting.

    L 1964–

826 Croydon News I, 1 (29 Dec. 1929–IV, 11 (Oct. 1933). Croydon; m

    B   1d. Published for Croydon Labour Party.

    CnP I, 1–IV, 9 (Aug. 1933); L(Col)†

827 Croydon News: Monthly Publication of the Croydon Labour Party 1 (Jan. 1951)–28 (July 1953). Croydon; m

    B   2d.

    CnP (w 3, 11, 12, 28); L(Col)†

828 Crusade Against Destitution, Being the Organ of the National Committee for the Prevention of Destitution I, 1 (Feb. 1910)–11 (Dec. 1910); then **Crusade**: I, 1 (Jan. 1911)–III, 14 (Feb. 1913); w

    B   Launched under the editorship of Fabian, Clifford Sharp. The Committee had been formed by Beatrice Webb and members of the Fabian Society to promote the recommendations of the Minority Report of the Royal Commission on the Poor Laws. Also published articles on other topics, including Syndicalism.

    L; LE; LU

Crusader see **New Crusader**

829 Cuddon's Cosmopolitan Review I 1 (April 1965)–

    A?   Produced by the same team as **Ludd**? (qv). Volume numbering abandoned after I, 1.

    LUC

830 Cumberland Labour Beacon [193-?]. Carlisle; w

    B   Labour Party. (Labour and Socialist International. **The Socialist Press**, 1933.)

831 Cumberland Miner [c1908]

    A?   (**The Metal Worker**, Nov. 1908.)

832 Current Topics: Official Journal of the Exeter and District Electricity Branch of NALGO I [1954?] —   . Exeter

    A   National and Local Government Officers' Association.

    L IV (1957)—

833 Customs and Excise Journal (Jan. 1972)—   ; m

    A   Customs and Excise Group, then Society of Civil Servants, Customs and Excise Group.

    The Union

834 Customs Journal I, 1 (9 April 1904)—LXXVIII, 1283 (Dec. 1971); m

    A   Customs and Excise Preventive Staff Association. Superseded by **Customs and Excise Journal**.

    Society of Civil Servants, Customs and Excise Group

835 Cutharian: Brownhills Branch NALGO News Bulletin 1955?— Brownhills

    A   National and Local Government Officers' Association.

    L Summer [1955] —

836 Cyffro 1969—   . Cardiff; q

    B   2s.6d. Welsh Committee of the Communist Party. Editor: Alistair Wilson. A quarterly Marxist journal for Wales.

    Sw U

Cymric Democrat see **South Wales Democrat**

837 Czechoslovak Labour Bulletin 1 (July 1939)—28 (20 Dec. 1943). London; irreg

    B   Issued by Josef Bělina. Journal of the Czechoslovak Social Democratic Party in exile. Reproduced from typewriting.

    L† (w 4, 6; 1—2 are of 2nd edition)

838 Czechoslovak Trade Union Bulletin 1 (May 1943)—[unnumbered] (28 May 1945). London; m; fortn

    A   'No fee required.' Published by the Czechoslovak Trade Union Centre? Digest of news of Czech Labour Movement. Reproduced from typewriting.

    L(Col)†

839 DATA: the Organ of the Socialist Information and Research Bureau I, 1 (June 1919)—II, 5 (Oct./Nov. 1920). Glasgow; m

    B   2d. Facts, figures, information articles.

    MML

DATA Journal see **Draughtsman**

Data News see **Association of Engineering and Shipbuilding Draughtsmen. Vacancy List**

840 DS and S Journal: Official Organ of the Luton Branch, NFDDSS I, 1 (28 May 1919)–I, 10 (28 Oct. 1919). Luton; fortn

A   2d. National Federation of Discharged and Demobilised Sailors and Soldiers, General editor: Herbert Pruden. To inform members of the progress of the branch and of the Federation. Campaigns for State pensions for ex-service men and dependants, and 'to prevent the exploitation of the discharged man's labour'.

L†

841 D. S. D. S. Kurér: Official Organ of the Amalgamated Danish Seamen's Union 1 (1 Oct. 1942)–48 (20 Dec. 1944). Newcastle-upon-Tyne; fortn

A   3d.; 6d. For the benefit of all unlicensed Danish seamen sailing under the flags of the United Nations, the journal records the activities and events inside the Danish Seamen's Union. Published by The Amalgamated Danish Seamen's Union. Editor: D. V. Aagaard. Also covers news of the international Trade Union Movement and the fight against Fascism. In Danish.

L(Col)† (w 46)

DSS Bulletin see **Bulletin**: the Official Organ of the Headquarters of the National Federation of Discharged and Demobilised Sailors and Soldiers

842 Daily Bread 1 [1933?]–?

A   1d. Nottinghamshire and Derbyshire National Unemployed Workers' Movement, Tibshelf and District. Reproduced from typewriting.

MML† 5 (3 June 1933)

843 Daily Citizen 1 (8 Oct. 1912)–830 (5 June 1915). Manchester; d

B   ½d. Published by Labour Newspapers, Ltd. Editor: Frank Dilmot. Owned by the Labour Party and the Trades Union Congress. 'Supported trade union campaigns, opposed syndicalism and guild socialism; competed with **Daily Herald** for working class support' (Brophy).

L(Col)† (Oct.–Dec. 1912 microfilm); LE; 0 1–773, 1915

844 Daily Herald 1 (25 Jan. 1911)–66 (28 April 1911); [ns] 1 (15 April 1912)–757 (19 Sept. 1914); then **Herald**: 758 (26 Sept. 1914)–993 (29 March 1919); then **Daily Herald**: 994 (31 March 1919)–15,090 (14 Sept. 1964); d; w; d

B   1d., ½d. etc. Editors included Charles Lapworth (1911); George Lansbury (1912–22). Started as the strike paper of London printers, then developed into a daily Labour paper.

E 15 April 1912, 2 July 1923–   ; L(Col) (No. 1 is a facsimile); LE; LabP. ONC   25 Jan.–28 April 1911;   29 April 1912;   15 April 1914; Warwick UL 1911–62

845 Daily Worker. 1 (1 Jan. 1930)–10, 745 (23 April 1966); then **Morning Star**: 10, 746 (25 April 1966)– ; d

    B   Communist Party of Great Britain. Suppressed by Government order between 21 Jan. 1941 and 7 Sept. 1942. There was also a Scottish edition entitled **Scottish Daily Worker**, 3370 (11 Nov. 1940)–3430 (21 Jan. 1941).

    E June 1935–*; L(Col); O; ONC occ. nos 1930–

846 Daily Worker Children's Annual 1955–7; a

    B   1s.6d.; 2s. Printed and published by the People's Press Printing Society, Ltd.

    L†

847 Daily Worker Cricket-Handbook 1949–50; a

    B   1s. Published by the People's Press Printing Society, Ltd Editor: A. A. Thomas, **Daily Worker** Cricket Correspondent.

    L†

848 Daily Worker Defence Leagues. **Campaign Notes** ?–2 Sept. 1942; w

    B   Records the campaigns for the lifting of the ban on the **Daily Worker** and for the freedom of the press.

    MML† March 1941–2 Sept. 1942

849 Daily Worker Football Annual 1 [1946/7] –?; a

    B   1s. Editors: A. A. Thomas, **Daily Worker** Sports Editor, and others.

    L*†

850 Dairy Workers' Journal I, 1 (Jan. 1949)–I, 5 (May 1949); then **Milk Worker**: I, 6 (June 1949)–II, 12 (Sept. 1950); m

    A   6d. Editor: W. J. Kindell. A well-produced lively union journal, for dairy worker members of the Transport and General Workers' Union and of the Union of Shop, Distributive and Allied Workers.

    L†

851 Dalziel Co-operative Record I, 1 (Nov. 1896)–I, 14 (Dec. 1897). Shieldhall, Govan; m

    A   Gratis. Printed by the SCWS, Ltd.

    E† ; O(JJ)† I, 8

852 Darfield Main Drifter Jan./Feb. 1929–single sheet

    A   Communist Party of Great Britain pit paper. Cusworth Hall Museum, 1 copy.

    Dr R. Neville

Darian see **Tarian y Gwithiwr**

853 Darley Abbey Monthly Report [194-?]. Darley Abbey, Derbyshire; m
  B   Labour Party. Duplicated. Supplement to **Belper Recorder**.
(Labour Party. **Your own Journal**, 1948.)

854 Darlington Labour News 1 (Oct. 1921)–? Darlington; m
  B   Labour Party.
  Darlington PL 1–12, 14, 21, 23, 26, 28, 41

855 Dartford Citizen [194-?] ; fortn
  B   1d. Labour Party. (Labour Party. **Your own Journal**, 1948.)

856 Dawn (23 Feb. 1895)–? Gorton, Manchester; w
  B   ½d. Editor: 'Semper'. 'Its aim is to give people the pill of
Socialism, coated with the sugar of other interests . . .' (**Labour Annual**,
1895.)

857 Dawn: Socialism 1 (Jan 1902)–35 (Feb. 1905). Ilkeston; m
  B   Gratis. Printed for and published by T. Mayfield. Ilkeston
branch of the Social-Democratic Federation. Emphasis on propagandist
articles in simple style, outlining the philosophy and policies of
revolutionary Socialism. Contributors: Samuel Bostock, James Morley,
H. Silburn.
  L(Col)†

858 Dawn [c1921]. Swindon; m
  B   1d. Labour Party. (**Labour Organiser**, July 1921.)

859 Dawn [193-?]. Midsomer Norton, Bath; m
  B   Labour Party. (Labour and Socialist International. **The Socialist
Press**, 1933.)

860 Daylight: an Independent Weekly Journal, Political, Social, and
Satirical 1 (5 Oct. 1878)–1727 (25 Dec. 1909). Norwich; w
  B   Publisher: Edward Burgess. 'Claimed to be independent of
political party (but was definitely pro-Liberal) with aim of shedding light
on social and political problems; criticized matters connected with local
government, social requirements, national legislation; bias on side of social,
moral and political reform. After change of editor in late '90s emphasis on
reform fades' (Brophy). Favourable mention in **Commonweal**, (23 Oct.
1886), which calls it 'a lively democratic paper', always very fair to the
Socialist movement. Publicised by the Socialist League branch in Norwich.
  L(Col); NrP

861 Daylight [193-?]. Felixstowe; m
  B   Labour Party. (Labour and Socialist International. **The Socialist
Press**, 1933.)

Daylight, 1952–1954 see **International Press Correspondence**

862 Deadly Parallel: Equal Opportunity for All, Privilege for None 1 (Oct. 1907)—3 (Dec. 1907); m

B 1d. Published at Henderson's. Printed by Wadsworth and Company, The Rydal Press, Keighley. Editor: W. B. Northrop. By means of illustration and photographs, contrasts the exploited poor of London's East End with the 'sumptuous wealth' of the West End. Urges solution via land nationalisation and Georgite land tax schemes. Advocates an Anti-Poverty Party to represent the poor.

L(Col); O(JJ)†

863 Deal and District Trades Council. **Monthly News Letter** Feb. 1954— . Deal; m

A Reproduced from typewriting.

The Council Feb. 1957—*

864 Deben View: the Magazine of the Deben and Woodbridge Branch. 1958?— . Woodbridge, Suffolk

A National and Local Government Officers' Association. Reproduced from typewriting.

L 1958—

865 Deist 1 ([17 Dec. 1842])—10 ([18 Feb. 1843]); w

B 1d. Publishers: Hetherington, Watson. A weekly organ to uphold the principles of Deism, of natural theology against the 'two contending factions of priesthood and atheism'. Discussion of social questions bearing directly on the position of the working class, eg, emigration, cheap food. No. 4 expresses support for Chartism, and, with reservations, for Socialism.

L†

866 Delphic Review: an Anarchistic Quarterly I, 1 (Winter 1949)—2 (Spring 1950). Fordingbridge; q

B 2s.6d. Published by the Delphic Press, Edited by Albert J. McCarthy. Anarchist, but 'non-sectarian' and libertarian. Mainly articles of a 'sociological and philosophical nature', also 'literary articles, poems, and book reviews'. To fill the vacuum left by the suspended **Now**. Contributors: Herbert Read, George Woodcock.

L: O

867 'Demagogue', Containing Extracts from the Unpublished Memoirs of Edward Baines, Esq., MP 1 (28 June 1834)—2 (5 July 1834). Leeds; w

B 1d. Published and printed by Alice Mann. Editor: William Rider. 'A radical miscellany that attacks local Whig reformers, notably Edward Baines, for their opposition to factory reform' (Wiener). Extremely satirical. Succeeded by **Argus and 'Demagogue'**.

LU; LdP† 1

867A Democrat: a Weekly Journal for Men and Women I, 1 (15 Nov. 1884)–VI, 9 (1 Sept. 1890); w; m

B 1d.; 2d. Editors: possibly Helen Taylor and William Saunders at first; William Saunders (Dec. 1887–Sept. 1888); J. E. Woolacott; Frederick Verinder (1889–90). 'Major emphasis on land reform and adult suffrage. In 1890 front cover regularly carries banners for land resumption, free education, eight hours labor, home rule, adult suffrage, paid Members of Parliament'. (Brophy). Continued as **Labour World**.

GM VI; L(Col)†; LE*; TUC, John Burns Lib. I, 1–V, 133 (Dec. 1889)

868 Democrat: the Organ of the National Democratic League 1 (June 1902)–6(Nov. 1902); m

B Listed its programme as adult suffrage, automatic registration with three months' qualification, one man one vote, official expenses of elections to be paid by state funds, second ballot, payment of MPs, elimination of the hereditary principle in legislation. President of the League was William Thompson, editor of **Reynolds's Newspaper**.

L(Col)†

869 Democrat 1 (10 April 1919)–323 (13 June 1925); w

C 1d. 'Founded by [W. A.] Appleton, with the object of improving relations between capital and labour.' Right-wing corporatist. Virulent anti-Bolshevik propaganda. Latterly became an organ of Conservatism. Incorporated **Federationist** (qv).

L(Col)†; LE; O; WCML*†

Democrat, 1937–1939 see **Democratic Front**

870 Democrat [194-?]; m

B 1d. Labour Party, Lewisham West. (Labour Party. **Your own Journal**, 1948.)

871 Democrat ns I, 1 (Nov. 1944)–? [Norwich?]

C Workers' Educational Association, Norfolk.

C 1949– ; NrP*

872 Democrat: South Oxfordshire Labour News [1947?]–? High Wycombe (printed); m

B 2d. Organs of the South Oxfordshire Divisional Labour Party and published by them.

ONC† III, 2 (Oct. 1949)

873 Democrat and Labour Advocate: the Rights of Labour 1 (3 Nov. 1855)–5 (8 Dec. 1855). Birmingham; London; w

A   1d. Printed and published by Edward Taylor, Birmingham, No. 5 by Holyoake and Company, London. Editor: George White, 'assisted by well-known friends of the working man'; 'brought out by operatives – shall be conducted by operatives'. 'Hopes for no support or patronage from any above the sons of toil' for whom it is expressly written and published. Advocates 'The People's Charter'.

L(Col)†

874 Democrat and Northern Recorder: a Magazine of Social, Political, and General Information for the People 1–6 (1868); ns 1 (Feb. 1869). Carlisle; w; m?

B   3d. Published by the Committee of the Carlisle Democratic Association. The first six numbers covered the 1868 election in Carlisle; speeches and letters by Ernest Jones. 'Our aim is not to set class against class, but to promote trust and confidence between the various classes of society.' 'Our efforts will be directed to promote the welfare and happiness of the People, using that term in its largest and broadest sense.' A detailed report of the Carlisle election; promised to continue publication as a radical organ for the district.

L(Col)† ns1; MP† 2 issues, Oct. 1868

875 Democratic and Social Almanac for 1850

B   'Presented to the Readers of the **Weekly Tribune** of 8 Dec. 1849'. (H. S. Foxwell, 'Bibliography of the English Socialist School' in A. Menger, **The right to the whole Produce of Labour**, Appendix II, 1899.)

876 Democrat, or Political Protestants' Register 1819. Hull

B?   Published by J. Howe. Appears to have been extreme in opinion. Was circulating in York in 1819. Mentioned in the **York Gazette** for that year. (A. Peacock)

Democrate-Socialiste see **Sotsial-Demokrat**

877 Democratic Front I, 1 (Oct. 1937); then **Democrat**: I, 2 (Dec. 1937)–II, 3 (1939). Cambridge; irreg?

B   Cambridge University Democratic Front.

C; L I, 1–2 (mislaid)

878 Democratic Recorder and Reformer's Guide: a London Weekly Publication 1 (2 Oct. 1819)–4 (23 Oct. 1819); w

B   3d.; 1½d. No. 1 published by Dolby and Carlile, and printed by W. Irvine; No. 2 edited, printed and published by E. Edmonds; Nos. 3 and 4 printed for Edmonds by R. Shorter. Inquest on the Manchester massacre, and fight for free speech and free press.

HO 42. 197 (22 Oct. 1891) 1–2; L† Place Coll. Vol. 40. i. 57, 77, 113, 129; O 1

879 Democratic Review: a Political and Literary Miscellany 1 (April 1882)

B 1s. Published by Lothop Withington and Richard Denis Butler. Edited by L. Withington. Presents a democratic critique of society. Champions the working class, the producers, against the aristocracy and 'commercial profit-mongers'. Withington is a workman, and his partner, a workman and a 'veteran in the cause of Labour (of good old Chartist blood)'.

L†

880 Democratic Review of British and Foreign Politics, History and Literature I, 1 (June 1849)–II, (Sept. 1850); m

B 3d. Editor and proprietor: G. Julian Harney. Printer: James Watson. Dedicated to the emancipation of the international working class. Represented the move leftwards of Chartism to the perspectives of social democracy, eg, February 1850, 'The Charter and something more'. A forum of Socialist thought. Articles on land nationalisation, the organisation of Labour. Contributions by continental revolutionaries and democrats, eg, Blanc, Mazzini, Ledru Rollin, Cabet, and later, Engels.

E I, 1–2, 4, 6; L; LE; LU; MP; O I*; ONC; Warwick U (Merlin Press reprint)

881 Demokracie a Socialismus: List čs. Sociální Demokracie (Democracy and Socialism: Journal of Czechoslovak Social Democracy). I, 1 (Jan. 1950)–(May 1958); m

B Published by the Czechoslovak Social Democratic Party, for Czech socialists in exile. In Czech. Reproduced from typewriting.

L†

882 Demokrata Polski (Polish Democrat). I (1853)–II ([June?] 1860)

B Organ of Polish democrats in exile. Also contributions and material on Mazzini and the French democrats and republicans. In Polish.

L†

883 Denaby and Cadeby Rebel

A Printed and published by the militant miners of Denaby and Cadeby pit. Communist Party paper. (R. G. Neville.)

884 Dental Practitioner: the Organ of the National Dental Association I, (1918)–X, 88 (March 1926); m

A 3d.; 6d. Articles on dentistry but also on matters affecting the profession, eg status, legal safeguards, Dentists' Acts. Absorbed **Dentist, Dental World** and **Panel Dentist**.

L II, 2–X, 88; LDA IX*; OR† II, 6–X, 88

885 Dental Technician I (1948)– ; m

A National Union of Gold, Silver and Allied Trades, Associated Dental Technicians' Section.

L (not traced); LdU II–

886 Departure: the Official Organ of the Thomas More Society I, 1 (June 1928)—I, 3 (Nov. 1928). Oxford; bi-m

    B   6d. Produced by J. E. Meade, Oriel College, Oxford, Labour Club member. Utopian Socialist outlook. Discussion on the nature of Socialism, individual freedom etc. Essays and book reviews.

    LE†

887 Derby Co-operative Citizen 1 (Feb. 1932)—11 (Dec. 1932); ns (Feb. 1937)—(Dec. 1939)

    B

    L(Col)

888 Derby Co-operative Provident Society. **Monthly Record** 1 (Sept. 1876)—845 (Jan. 1947). Derby; m

    A   Gratis. A substantial, wide-ranging journal. Succeeded by **Co-operative Home Magazine.**

    L† 473 (Jan. 1916)—845; the Society

889 Derby Post [19--?]—? [Derby?]

    A   Union of Post Office Workers, Derby Amalgamated Branch. (W. Dunlop, 'Local Journals'. **Belpost**, IV, 5, [May 1965]).

890 Derbyshire and Leicestershire Examiner; a Journal of General Intelligence: the Official Organ of the Miners etc. 1 [Aug. 1873?]—207 (17 Aug. 1877). Derby (1873); Burton-on-Trent (1874—5); Wolverhampton (1876—7); w

    B   1½d. Published at the Co-operative Printing Society. Proprietors: William Owen, Alexander Jeffrey. Local coverage on miners, nut and bolt workers, and trade union matters.

    L(Col)† 6 (13 Sept. 1873)—207

891 Derbyshire Miner March 1957—? Chesterfield; m

    A   2d. National Union of Miners, Derbyshire Area. (J. E. Williams, **The Derbyshire Miners** 1962, p. 886.)

892 Derbyshire Worker and Labour Leader 1 (7 June 1919)—173 (29 Sept. 1922). Ripley; w

    B   1d. Published by the Derbyshire Worker Newspaper Company. Issued by Ripley Local Labour Party and Trades Council. Labour Party news, trade union activities.

    L(Col)†

893 Deritend Commonwealth 1 (March 1930)—104 (July 1939). Birmingham; m

    B   Published by the Co-operative Party, Deritend (Birmingham). 'To give expression to the programme, the policy and the achievements of the Labour and Co-operative Parties'. Contributor: Fred Longdin, Labour MP. See also **Birmingham District Commonwealth.**

    BP†

894 Derwent: Magazine of the Derbyshire Branch of NALGO 1 (Spring 1956)– . Derby; q

    A   National and Local Government Officers' Association. To encourage freedom of opinion within the branch. 'Successor to an earlier publication **The Bulletin**'.

    L†

895 'Destructive' and Poor Man's Conservative I, 1 (2 Feb. 1833)–45 (7 Dec. 1833); then **People's Conservative and Trades' Union Gazette**: 46 (14 Dec. 1833)–II, 55 (15 Feb. 1834); then **People's Conservative**; with which is incorporated **The Reformer**: II, 56 (22 Feb. 1834)–71 (7 June 1834); w

    B   2d.; 3d. Printed and published by Henry Hetherington. Editor: Bronterre O'Brien. 'A working-class newspaper that advocates universal suffrage and an unstamped press, while repeatedly attacking the profit system and the "shopocracy" ' (Wiener). Publicises meetings of the National Union of the Working Classes and of the various Political Unions. Later, reflecting the change in sub-title, supports Trades Unionism and the Grand National Consolidated Trades Union. Succeeded by **Hetherington's Twopenny Dispatch, and People's Police Register**.

    L† HO 64/19 1, 7; L Place Coll. Set 65 63; LU 1–53; ONC 1

896 Detonator 1 (1969)–3 (1969). [Belfast?]

    B   Published by the Revolutionary Socialist Students' Federation, NI.

    Linen Hall Library, Belfast 1, 3 (photocopies)

897 Devil's Pulpit I, 1 (4 March 1831)–II, 46 (20 Jan. 1832); w

    B   2d. Published and printed by Richard Carlile. 'Contains the Rotunda discourses of the Rev. Robert Taylor which seek to demonstrate the mythological basis of Christianity. Has an estimated weekly circulation of 2,000' (Wiener).

    HO 64/18 1, 24, 26–9, 33, 37–8, 40–6; MP†; O 1

Dewsbury, Batley and District Social-Democrat see **Dewsbury Social-Democrat**

898 Dewsbury Citizen [193-?]. Dewsbury; m

    B   Labour Party. (Labour and Socialist International. **The Socialist Press**, 1933)

899 Dewsbury Social-Democrat: the Local Organ of the International Socialist Movement. I, 1 (Jan. 1907); then **Dewsbury, Batley and District Social-Democrat**: I, 2 (Feb. 1907)–III, 1 (Jan. 1909). Dewsbury; m

    B   Gratis. Published by the Social-Democratic Federation. Prominent contributor: Harry Quelch. Chiefly propagandist. Illustrated the attitude of the Social-Democratic Federation towards Trade Unionism.

    L(Col)†

900 Diamond Worker: Organ of the British Diamond Workers' Union. I, 1 (April 1921)–II, 31 (Oct./Nov. 1923); m

    A   Published for the Union by S. Green, the Secretary. Printed by Twentieth Century Press. Information and reports from British union branches and international news. 'Suspended because of the slump in the diamond industry'.

    TUC†

901 Digest [19--?] –? Blackburn

    A   National Association of Local Government Officers, then National and Local Government Officers' Association. Blackburn Group Gas Branch. Reproduced from typewriting.

    L(Dec. 1953)–(Sept. 1954)

902 Dinesydd Cymreig. [Welsh Citizen] 1, (8 May 1912)–896, (10 July 1929). Caermarfon; w

    A   2d. Set up by three members of the Typographical Association in Caermarfon following a long printers' strike. Editor: J. Hugh Williams. Became 'official organ of the North Wales Quarrymen's Union', and of Caernarvonshire Labour Council. Pro-Labour. In Welsh.

    AbN; BnU; L(Col); SwU IX–X*

903 Dion: Official Organ of the Post Office Workers' Union I, 1 (June 1923)–XIII, 12 (Dec. 1935); then **Postal Worker**: XIV, 1 (Jan. 1936)– Dublin; m

    A   3d. Published by the Post Office Workers' Union. University College, Dublin XLIX, 1971–

    L(Col)† (w Dec. 1925–Dec. 1926, 1940–8); TUC 1941–

904 Direct Action 1 (May 1945)–67 (May 1954); irreg?

    B   Anarchist Federation of Britain; Syndicalist Workers' Federation, British Section of the International Working Men's Association.

    L(Col)

905 Direct Action [1961?] –IX, 6 (June 1968); m

    B   3d; 6d. Printed and published by Bill Christopher for the Syndicalist Workers' Federation. Incorporates **Worker' Voice** . Reproduced from typewriting, then printed. Advocates direct action and workers' control. Contributor, Ken Smith.

    L(Col)† II, 1 [Jan. 1962] –IX, b; LE† 1964–8

906 Discussion: a Journal for Political Controversy Published Once a Month by the Communist Party [I], 1 (Jan. 1936)–III, 3 (April 1938); m

    B   2d. Political discussion on the issues of the day, Popular Front, anti-war, anti-Fascism. An open forum for contributions from anyone in the Labour Movement, but chiefly for Party discussion. No. 1 reproduced from typewriting.

    E; ILP*; L†; O†; ONC†; WCML

907 Discussion 1 (Feb. 1957)– 3 (Oct. 1957). Ipswich

    B   Issued by East Anglia District, Communist Party of Great Britain. Edited by Neville Carey, District Secretary. Several contributions from the minority position in the CPGB. Includes pieces by Michael Barratt Brown and W. A. Hampton, both founder members of the New Left, who left the CPGB in July 1957. Both were members of the Colchester Branch, which has a statement in **Discussion**, No. 2. Reproduced from typewriting.

    Priv. Coll. Warwick U (MRC)

908 Dispensing Optician: the Official Journal of the Association of Dispensing Opticians I, 1 (April/May/June 1934)–V, 2 (April/May/June 1939); 1946– ; frequency varies

    A   Professional association journal, to safeguard and strengthen their position as skilled men.

    L† 1934–9; the Association

Distributive Trades Journal see **Shop Assistant**

909 Distributive Worker [192-?]; m

    A   Minority Movement. (Advertised in **Red International of Labour Unions**, I, 1 [October 1928].)

910 Distributive Worker; t-Oibri Imdhala [192-?] – . Dublin; m

    A   Irish Union of Distributive Workers and Clerks.

    CoU XIII, 1934– ; University College, Dublin, Library 1943–50, 1963–

911 Diwygiwr (Reformer) I, a (Aug. 1835)–LXXV, 827 (Dec. 1911). Llanelli

    B   Editor: David Rees, Independent Nonconformist minister.

    L† AbU IV, VI–VII, XXV; BnU (1836–43*); CrU I–XXVII, LVII; L; SwU*

912 Dock and River Worker 1 (30 July 1926)–?

    A   Issued by the Communist Dock and River Group. 'A new form of the **Waterside Worker** which used to make a regular appearance in and about the South Side Dockland'. Reproduced from typewriting.

    O(JJ)† 1

913 Docker [192-?]; m

    A   Minority Movement (advertised in **Red International of Labour Unions**, I, 1 [October 1928]).

914 Docker, Salford: the Paper of the Workers in the Port of Manchester [193-?]–? Salford; m? w?

    A   Left-wing, rank-and-file paper. Reproduced from typewriting.

    J. Smethurst, 81 Parrin Lane, Winton, Eccles, Manchester M30 8AY. 47 (1 June) 1934

915 Dockers' Record: Annual Report of the Dock, Wharf, and General Workers' Union of Great Britain and Ireland I (1890)—ns VII, 1 (June/July 1921); a; q; m

A   Gratis. Later, 'Quarterly' then 'Monthly'. General Secretary: Ben Tillett. Reports from London and the provinces, articles on Trade Unionism. First owner and editor: H. W. Kay, then Executive Committee of Union took it over. Contributor: Tom Mann. Union incorporated in the Transport and General Workers' Union.

L XXXII; LE 1907—15*, 1916—21; TGWU 1901—11, 1920—1; TUC 40, 1910, 1915—21

916 Dockers' Voice [195-? 196-?] —?

B   A Voice paper.

917 Docket: an Organ for Temporary Clerks 1 (Feb. 1919)—3 (April 1919); m

A   1d. Edited by C. E. W. Young. For clerks in the Civil Service.
L†

918 Dolby's Parliamentary Register I, 1 (30 Jan. 1819)—? (30 Dec.) 1819; irreg?

B   2d. A report of parliamentary debates chiefly designed for 'persons of enlarged views, with limited pecuniary means . . . ' 'Political information having, for some time past, been circulated at a cheap rate amongst what are called the "lower orders", the said "orders" are now in a fit condition to read, and to decide upon the propriety of what is said and done by their betters.'

BP 30 Jan.—30 Dec., 1819; L 1 (Jan. 1819)—67 (9 June 1819) (w 47—52); NrP

919 Domestic Miscellany, and Poor Man's Friend 1 (Sept. 1819)—7 (21 Dec.) 1819. Leeds; irreg

C   3d. Printed and published by W. Gawtress. Conservative. An antidote to radical reform and 'anarchy' literature. Addressed to the labouring men, urging self-help and the pursuit of knowledge for self-betterment. Political essays attacking universal suffrage, annual parliaments, infidelity etc.

L† LdP

920 Domestic News I, 1 (April 1915)—VI, 12 (Dec. 1920); then **Feminine Life**: VII, 1 (Jan. 1921)—VIII, 12 (Dec. 1922;) m

    C   1d.; 2d. Published for the Domestic Servants' Insurance Society, later the Domestic Workers' Friendly Society, by the Domestic Servants' Association, later the United Women's Benevolent Association. The Domestic Servants' Insurance Society, 'composed exclusively of female domestic servants, was formed [in 1912] to administer the National Insurance Act at the suggestion of Lady St Helier and others.' The Society gives members 'the free use of an Employment Bureau when seeking a situation, a Benevolent Fund for distressed members, and a Friendly Society for providing extra benefits'. Branch reports, some literary content. Latterly less relevant.

    L†

921 Domestic Servants' Advertiser: a Journal for Mistresses and Maids, Cooks, Parlourmaids, Housemaids and 'Generals' I, 1 (20 May 1913)—I, 8 (8 July 1913); w

    C   1d. An employment register, advertising situations vacant. Advises on household proficiency and decorum, and deals with court cases concerning mistress-maid disputes.

    L(Col)†

922 Domestic Servants' Gazette: Organ of London and Provincial Domestic Servants' Union Nov. 1895—? m

    A?   1d. Edited by Thomas E. Barnes. (**Labour Annual**, 1897.)

923 Domestic Servants' Journal 1 (23 June 1875)—5 (21 July 1875); w

    C   1d. Printed and published for the proprietor by Frederick A. Gosnold. 'Edited by Mrs Stannard.' Predominantly an advertising medium detailing employment required and situations vacant for 'good domestic servants'. Includes some fictional material of a moral improvement character.

    L(Col)†

924 Dominie: Organ of the Class Teachers' Section, Fife Local Association, EIS I (1956—). Kirkcaldy; termly

    A   Educational Institute of Scotland.

    L Dec. 1956—

925 Doncaster Labour News [194-?] ; irreg

    B   Free. Labour Party. (Labour Party. **Your own Journal**, 1948.)

926 Douglas Jerrold's Weekly Newspaper 1 (18 July 1846)–129 (30 Dec. 1848); w

    C   6d. Printed and published by William Stevens. An advanced liberal, social reformist newspaper and journal advocating progressive amelioration of the conditions of the masses. Supported Chartist principles in 1848, but not an independent working-class agitation. Enthusiastically acclaimed the French Revolution of 1848, Lamartine its hero. Thereafter, as **Jerrold's Weekly News and Financial Economist**, it lapsed into a moderate newspaper.

    L(Col)†

927 Dover Divisional Herald 1 (July 1935)–20 (May 1937). Dover; m

    B   published by the Co-operative Press.

    L(Col)†

928 Draughtsman: Organ of the Association of Engineering and Shipbuilding Draughtsmen I, 1 [March 1914?]–XLVII, 12 (Dec. 1964); then **DATA Journal**: Jan. 1965–Dec. 1971; then **TASS Journal**: Jan. 1972– . Glasgow; London; Richmond; irreg; m

    A   3d. etc. Association of Engineering and Shipbuilding Draughtsman; Draughtsmen's and Allied Technicians' Association; Amalgamated Union of Engineering and Foundry Workers, Technical Adminstrative and Supervisory Section. I, 3 (1918) says the journal 'after a long suspension, again makes its bow'. See also **The Tracer**.

    AbN 1924– ; E 1938– ; GM 1927– ; GU XVIII– ; L I, 3– ; LME XXXI, 12– ; LP 1924– ; LSC XVI– ; NU 1955– ; ONC 1950– ; OR 1938– ; TUC 1943– ; the Union; Warwick U (MRC) 1918–

Draughtsmen's and Allied Technicians' Association. Coventry East Branch. **Newsletter** see Association of Engineering and Shipbuilding Draughtsmen. Coventry East Branch. **Newsletter**

Drivers' World see **Headlight Magazine**

929 Droylsden Recorder: Official Organ of the Droylsden Labour Party 1 (Jan. 1958)–Dec. 1962. Droylsden: m

    B   4d. Editor: C. S. Bussin. Items from the council minutes. Otherwise is little more than advertisements. Newspaper format.

    L†

Drug and Chemical News see **Drug Trade News and Chemical Workers' Gazette**

930 Drug Trade News and Chemical Workers' Gazette: Official Journal of the Amalgamated Society of Pharmacists, Drug and Chemical Workers I, 1 (April 1919); then **Drug Union News**: I, 2 (May 1919)–II, 10 (Jan. 1921); then **Drug and Chemical News**: II, 11 (Feb. 1921)–II, 12 (March 1921); m

    A   2d. Published by the Society. On the principle of 'unity within the trade' urges 'one craft union' for all trades in drugs and fine chemicals. Correspondence and branch reports.

    L(Col)†

Drug Union News see Drug Trade News and Chemical Workers' Gazette

931 Drum [192–?.]
    B   Communist. (Mentioned in **Pioneer News**, [192–?] qv.)

932 Drury Lane Workmen's Hall Messenger 1 (Jan. 1875)–24 (Dec. 1876); then **Workmen's Hall Messenger**: 25 (Jan. 1877)–216 (Dec. 1892); then **Workmen's Messenger**: 217 (Jan. 1893)–403 (July 1908); m
    C   ½d. etc. Printed and published by F. E. Longley etc. Editor: Henry Hambleton, Secretary of the Hall. The Hall was erected for the healthy recreation of working people after the labour and worry of the day's work; popular lectures, library, temperance and Band of Hope meetings. The journal contains articles, sermons, fiction, with emphasis on self-improvement. Preceded by **Workmen's Hall Magazine**.
    L(Col)†

933 Dublin Argus; or, **Trades' Gazette**, Under the Patronage of the Regular Trades' Association 1 (1845)–59 (29 Aug. 1846). Dublin; w
    A   1d. Opposed to working-men's political Unionism. For the retention of craft privileges. Correspondence.
    L(Col)† 27 (17 Jan. 1846)–59

934 Dudley New Citizen [194-?]. Dudley, Worcestershire; m
    B   2d. Labour Party. (Labour Party. **Your own Journal**, 1948.)

935 Dulwich Bulletin [194-?]; irreg
    B   Free. Labour Party. (Labour Party. **Your own Journal**, 1948.)

936 Dumbartonshire Labour News: Official Organ of the Dumbartonshire Divisional Labour Party [1924?] –? Helensburgh; m
    B   1d.
    E† 6 (Jan. 1925)

Dundee and District Jute and Flax Workers' Guide see **Dundee Textile Workers' Guide**

937 Dundee and District Jute and Flax Workers' Bulletin I, 1 (Jan. 1940–?). Dundee
    A   ½d. Issued by the Dundee Jute and Flax Workers' Union. Urges 100% membership of the Union.
    L† I, 1

938 Dundee Chronicle 1834–Dec. 1840; then **Dundee Herald**: [Jan. ?] 1841–(Sept. 1843). Dundee
    B   For many years a Liberal/Radical commercial paper. Became a Chartist paper only in November 1840, when it became the organ and property of the Dundee Chartists. By mid-1842 it had adopted Complete Suffrage, declining thereafter.
    DnP† 104 (5 Sept. 1835)–157 (10 Sept. 1836)

939 Dundee Citizen [194-?] ; m

    B   2d. Labour Party. (Labour Party. **Your own Journal**, 1948.)

940 Dundee Free Press: a Non-party Paper for the Community I, 1 (11 June 1926)–352 (3 March 1933). Dundee; w

    B   1d; 2d. Published by the Dundee Free Press, Ltd. Pro-Labour. Columns open to all sections of the community. Emphasis on local news and municipal politics. Support for trade unions. Produced by trade-union labour when Dundee newspaper proprietors had outlawed Trade Unionism in the trade. Contributors: Edwin Scrymgeour, Tom Johnston, Dundee MPs.

    DnP; L(Col)†

Dundee Herald. see **Dundee Chronicle**

Dundee Jute and Flax Workers' Guide see **Dundee Textile Workers' Guide**

941 Dundee Labour Year Book 1936–8; then **Labour Year Book for Dundee, Angus, Perth and Montrose Burghs**: 1939–[1947?] . Dundee; a

    B   3d. Issued on behalf of and by authority of the Dundee Trades and Labour Council, then by the Council and the Mid-East Federation of Labour Parties.

    DnP† 1936–44, 1947

942 Dundee Mill and Factory Operatives' Herald 1 (5 Sept. 1885)–2 May 1886); then **Mill and Factory Herald**: ns 1 (Sept. 1888)–11 (Dec. 1889). Dundee; irreg

    A   ½d. Edited by Henry Williamson, Unitarian Minister, Honorary President of the Dundee Mill and Factory Operatives' Union.

    DnP†

943 Dundee Municipal Officer's Guild Magazine I, 1 (May 1912)–IV, 39 (July 1915). Dundee; m

    A   Represented in the National Association of Local Government Officers.

    DnP†

944 Dundee Textile News: Official Organ of Dundee Jute and Flax Workers' Union, National Union of Dyers, Bleachers and textile Workers (Dundee Branch), Dundee Power Loom Tenters' and Under-Tenters' Society 1 (Sept. 1938)–2 (Nov. 1938). Dundee

    A   ½d. Published by the three unions. Campaigns for 100% Trade Unionism, shorter hours, holidays with pay.

    L(Col)†

45 Dundee Textile Workers' Guide: the Official Organ of the Dundee Jute and Flax Workers' Union. I, 1, [191-?] –I, 7 (19 May 1916); then **Dundee Jute and Flax Workers' Guide**: I, 8 (26 May 1916)–46 (June 1919); then **Dundee and District Jute and Flax Workers' Guide**: 47 (July 1919)–166 (March 1939). Dundee; w; m

    A   ½d. Published by J. F. Sime. In 1920s and 1930s agitated for a 40-hour week and 100% Trade Unionism among textile workers. Not published between October 1931 and December 1933; or between September 1936 and March 1939.

    L(Col) (w 1–6)

46 Dunfermline Co-operative Citizen 1 (July 1932–12 (June 1933). Dunfermline; m

    B

    L(Col)†

47 Durham City and County News 1, [5 July?] 1870–102 (21 June 1872). Durham; w

    C   1d. Printed and published by the proprietor, Francis Tindale Wharam. Called itself 'the official organ of 35,000 miners'. Preached doctrine of 'identity of interests as between masters and men'. Included much reportage of miners' social activities and union meetings, also strikes and colliery disasters.

    L(Col)† (w 1; Jan.–June 1872 microfilm)

48 Durham County NALGO News [1951?] –? Durham

    A   National Association of Local Government Officers, later National and Local Government Officers' Association, Durham County Branch.

    L 28 (July 1953)–

49 Durham Miners' Association. Monthly Circular 1896–1915. Durham; m

    A   Written by the Association's Secretaries, who included John Wilson; coverage gradually enlarged.

    Bishopsgate Institute 1896–1911; Durham County Record Office*; National Union of Miners (South Durham)

50 Durham Miners' Monthly Journal 1938–? Dawdon, Co. Durham; m

    A   1d. Durham Miners' Association. Published by George Burdess. 'Following a conference of Durham miners' lodge delegates at Herrington in January 1938 a scheme was adopted for the publication of a monthly newspaper to provide scope for news coverage at local collieries' (W. R. Garside, **The Durham miners, 1919–1960**, 1971, p. 299).

    Durham County Lib. 8 (Nov. 1938); TUC 12 (March 1939)–23 April 1940*)

951 E. Renfrewshire Co-operative Citizen 1 (April 1935)–7 (Oct. 1935). Paisley; m

    B?

    L(Col)

952 E. Willesden Citizen [193-?] –?; m

    B   Gratis. Published by the London Co-operative Society. (Mitchell, 1935, 1940.)

953 ETE Herald [19--?] –?

    A   Union of Post Office Workers, ETE P and TO Branch. (W. Dunlop, 'Local journals'. **Belpost**, IV, 5 (May 1965).)

954 Ealing Citizen 1 (Oct. 1930)–17 (March 1932); ns 1, [Feb. 1947?] –; m

    B   Gratis. Published by the London Co-operative Society.

    L(Col) 1–17, ns 12 (Jan. 1948)–

955 Ealing East News [194-?] ; m

    B   2d.   Labour Party. Duplicated. (Labour Party. **Your own Journal**, 1948.)

956 Ealing ILP Gazette 1 (Dec. 1896)–?; m

    B   Free. (D. Hopkin, 'Local Newspapers of the Independent Labour Party, 1893–1906'. Society for the Study of Labour History, **Bulletin**, 28 [Spring 1974].)

957 Early Closing Advocate and Commerical Reformer I (Jan. 1854)–7 (July 1854); m

    C   2d. Published by Houlston and Stoneman. 'The organ of the Early Closing Associations, Mechanics' Institutes, and other important Young Men's Societies throughout Great Britain and Ireland.' A miscellany. Emphasis on mutual improvement, and early closing for mental improvement and recreation.

    L†

958 East and West: a Journal of the British-Asian Socialist Fellowship I, 1 (Autumn 1953)–[1956?] ; irreg

    B   6d. Published by the Fellowship, at Transport House, 'to foster understanding and cement the solidarity between the Socialists of East and West'. Local Labour Parties and trade unions were affiliated to the Fellowship. Special issues of the journal were issued, in pamphlet form, on particular subjects, eg, Special issue, February 1955, on Burma.

    E 1953–4; O† 1953–6; TUC 1953–4

959 East Birmingham Forward [190-?] –? Birmingham; m

    B?   ½d. (**Reformers' Year Book**, 1907.)

960 East Bowling Worker [c1894.] East Bowling, Yorkshire; m

    B   Free. Published by the East Bowling ILP Clubs. (D. Hopkin, 'Local Newspapers of the Independent Labour Party, 1893–1906'. Society for the Study of Labour History, **Bulletin**, 28 [Spring 1974].)

961 East Bristol Election Labour Herald 1 (24 Dec. 1909)–3 (13 Jan. 1910); then **Bristol Labour Herald**: 4, (2 April 1910)–5, (May 1910). Bristol; w

    B   ½d.; 1d. Published by Frank Freeman. Issued by Bristol Labour Party. Started to promote the candidature of Frank Sheppard in the 1910 General Election, then enlarged with the intention of becoming a permanent newspaper of the Labour Movement in Bristol.

    L(Col)†

962 East Dorset Labour Quarterly 1 (Dec. 1925–Feb. 1926)–14 (June 1929). Parkstone; q

    B   Gratis. Published by F. C. Reeves, Secretary, East Dorset Labour Party. Main contributor: E. J. Stocker, prospective Labour candidate.

    L(Col)† 5–15; LabP† 1–3

963 East End Pioneer [1920? 1921?] –?; m?

    B   1d. Published by the Limehouse and Mile End Labour Parties. Tower Hamlets Local History Library 9 (Oct. 1921).

964 East End Worker 1 [19--?] –? ns 1 (23 Oct. 1926)–3 (22 Nov. 1926); fortn

    B   1d. Published by the Joint Committee of the Communist party in West Ham, East Ham, Walthamstow and Leyton. No. 1 of the new series says the publication previously appeared as a duplicated typewritten sheet, with a limited circulation. Agitated against the workings of the Poor Law and the Board of Guardians in West Ham Union area. The Communist Party led the Active Resistance Committee, a rank-and-file organisation.

    L(Col)† ii

965 East Fulham Citizen 1 (March 1934)–65 (Sept. 1939); m

    B   Gratis. Published by London Co-operative Society's Political Committee.

    L(Col)

966 East Ham North Citizen 1 [1928?] –127 (Sept. 1939); ns 1 (Jan. 1947)– ; m

    B   Gratis. Published by London Co-operative Society, for East Ham North Divisional Labour Party.

    L(Col) 24 (March 1930)–

East Ham South Citizen see **London Citizen**. East Ham edition

967 East Islington Citizen 1 (March 1932)–14 (May 1933); m

    B   Published by the London Co-operative Society's Political Committee.

    L(Col)†

968 East Islington Citizen 1 (April 1939)–6 (Sept. 1939); m

    B   Published by the London Co-operative Society.

    L(Col)

969 East Kenton Log: Official Organ of South Stanmore Ward, Harrow Labour Party 1 (Oct. 1935)–9 (July 1936); then **Labour Log**: 10 (Aug. 1936)–VIII, 2 (Feb. 1943). Harrow; m

    B   Gratis. H. G. Deacon, ed. A slim advertisement of local Labour Party activities, with a brief editorial. Fuller in content from April 1937. Frequent contributor: Councillor Cullington.

    L†

970 East Leicester Citizen 1 (Sept. 1931)–10 (July 1932). Leicester; m

    B   Issued by the Co-operative Party.

    L(Col)

971 East Lewisham Citizen 1 (Oct. 1931)–94 (Sept. 1939); m

    B   Published by the London and Royal Arsenal Co-operative Societies' Political Purposes Committee.

    L(Col)

972 East Lewisham News Letter [194-?] ; m

    B   Labour Party. Published for each ward. Duplicated. (Labour Party. **Your own Journal**, 1948.)

973 East Leyton Citizen 1 (Nov. 1930)–12 (Oct. 1931); m

    B   Published by London Co-operative Society, Political Committee.

    L(Col); Leyton PL 7–9

974 East London Citizen ns 1 (Jan. 1947)–17 (May 1948); then **Eastern Area Citizen**: 18 (June 1948)–62 (May 1952); m

    B   Issued by the Political Committee of the London Co-operative Society.

    L(Col)

975 East London Group Information and News 1966?–

    A   National and Local Government Officers' Association, East London Group (Hospitals) Branch. Reproduced from typewriting.

    L 1966–

976 East London News-Board [1943?] –?

    A   National Union of Teachers, East London Teachers' Association. TUC 19 (13 March 1944)

977 East London Worker 1 (April 1953)–?

    C   Issued by the City and East London Area of the Union Movement. Supported Oswald Mosley. Claimed to 'fight for the workers'. Incorporated with **The East London Blackshirt**, which began in October 1953.

    L(Col)† 1, 3 (Aug. 1953)

978 East Riding Nalgolian [19--?] –31 (Sept. 1954); ns 1 (Jan. 1955)–. Beverley

    A   National Association of Local Government Officers, later National and Local Government Officers' Association, East Riding Branch.

    L 21 (Jan. 1953)–

979 East Surrey Socialist [194-?] ; m

    B   Labour Party. Duplicated. (Labour Party. **Your own Journal**, 1948.)

980 East Ward Advertiser 1900. Bradford

    B?   (**ILP News**, Dec. 1900, p. 2.)

981 East Willesden Courier 1 (March 1934)–19 (Sept. 1935): then **East Willesden Labour and Co-operative Courier** 20 (Oct. 1935)–66 (Sept. 1939); m

    B   Published by the London Co-operative Society.

    L(Col)

East Willesden Labour and Co-operative Courier see **East Willesden Courier**

982 East Woolwich Citizen 1 [Nov. 1931?] –92 (Sept. 1939); m

    B   Published by the London and Royal Arsenal Co-operative Societies' Political Purposes Committee.

    L(Col) 10 (Aug. 1932)–92

Eastern Area Citizen see **East London Citizen**

983 Eastern Counties Link: the Journal of Expression within the Cambridge, Colchester and Norwich Areas of the Union of Post Office Workers [192-?] –? Colchester; m

    A   1d. (Mitchell, 1935.)

    TUC IV, 11 (July 1930)

984 Eastern Post 1 (18 Oct. 1868)–274 (28 Dec. 1873); w

    B   Associated with the International Working Men's Association.

    Warwick UL (microfilm)

985 Eastern Star: Monthly Bulletin to Branches in No. 4 Region FBU. [19--?] –?

    A   Fire Brigade Union.

    TUC May 1942

986 Eastern Weekly Leader 1 (27 Oct. 1894)—66 (8 Feb. 1896). Norwich; w

    B   1d. Printed and published by **Eastern Weekly Leader** Company. Editor: Rev. Charles Peach. A very full, popular and political paper. Advanced radical, collectivist. Reports activities of Norfolk and Norwich Amalgamated Labour Union (agricultural labourers). Includes cultural and literary items from a democratic standpoint. Correspondence includes debate on the Independent Labour Party and Trade Unionism.

    L(Col)† NrP

987 Eastwood and Greasley News Letter [194-?]. Eastwood, Nottinghamshire; m

    B   Labour Party. Duplicated. (Labour Party. **Your own Journal,** 1948.)

988 Eccles Co-operative Record I, 1 (Feb. 1897)—LIX, 678 (June 1954). Eccles; m

    A   Gratis. Eccles Provident and Industrial Society, later Eccles and District Co-operative Society. First editors: Thomas Guest; John A. O'Brien. Reports, announcements, news, special articles, verse, humour, biography. illustrations.

    Co-op. Union (Feb. 1933)—(Jan. 1934); L XX, 231 (April 1915)—LIX, 678; MP 1932—42; the Society

989 Eccles Division News 1 (24 Oct. 1889)—15 (7 Feb. 1890). Eccles; Walkden; w

    B   Liberal-Labour. Owner: F. H. Booth.

    L(Col)

990 Echo Printed by the Locked-Out Compositors 1 (9 Jan. 1893)—2 (11 Jan. 1893); then **Glasgow Echo**: 3—32, (14 April 1893). Glasgow; irreg

    A   Gratis. Printed and published by the strike-bound compositors; 'guaranteed circulation' 30,000 (No. 3), 40,000 (No. 8). News of the strike struggle, developing into a discussion of the role of Labour and of the need for a Labour paper. Succeeded by **Weekly Echo**, 1893—5 (qv).

991 Echo Zycia Robotniczego na Litwie: Organ Litewskiej Socyal-Demokratycznej Partyi (The Echo of the Lithuanian Workmen's Life: Organ of the Lithuanian Social Democratic Party) [19--?]—?

    B

    L III, 4 (1903)

992 Echoes 1898–? Edinburgh

A   St Cuthbert's Co-operative Association. 'In 1898 **Echoes** first appeared. It was devoted to the interests of the employees and it had a fair run before vanishing during the First World War [but see next note].' (W. E. Lawson. **One Hundred Years of Co-operation: the History of St Cuthbert's Co-operative Association, Ltd. 1859–1959**. Manchester, 1959. p. 65.) 'The **Echoes** was regularly issued for a number of years . . . the diffculty of finding an editor who could sacrifice the necessary time for the duties brought the **Echoes** to a close in December 1906.' (W. Maxwell, **First Fifty Years of St Cuthbert's Co-operative Association Ltd., 1859–1909**, Edinburgh 1909, p. 174).

993 Economic Brief [I, 1] (Nov. 1967)–III, 10 ([June] 1971); 8 or 10-yr

B   Published by the Labour party. 1s.; 5p. 'Intended primarily for Party members. Each issue will include major feature articles on the whole range of economic policy and shorter reviews giving the latest facts and figures on the economy.' Superseded by **Labour Weekly**.

E; LE; LabP†; ONC†; SoU; Warwick UL (w III, 10)

994 Economic Review I, 1 (Jan. 1891)–XXIV, 4 (15 Oct.) 1914; q

C   A scholarly economics journal published for the Christian Social Union, Oxford University Branch. The Union was generally sympathetic towards Labour, and stressed the social obligation of the Church.

AU; BP I–III, VII, 4–XXIV; BS XII–XXIV*; BU; BnU I–VIII: BrP V–XXIV; BrU (w X); C; CME; CrU I–XII; EN I–IX; EP I–V, VII–X; L; LE; LU; LUC; Lap IX–XXIV; LcU XXIV; LdP; LdU Occ. nos; LvU XVII–XVIII; MP; NU XIII–XXIV; NwA (w XII, XXIII); O; ONC (w July 1903, July 1906, July 1914); SyP II, IV, VII

995 Economist: a Periodical Paper Explanatory of the New System of Society Projected by Robert Owen, Esq., and of a Plan of Association for Improving the Condition of the Working Classes, During Their Continuance at Their Present Employments I, 1 (27 Jan. 1821)–II, 52 (9 March 1822); w

B   3d. Published at the Office, then by Mr Wright, Bookseller, then by the Co-operative and Economical Society. Printers: G. Auld; J. and C. Adlard; Mudie. Edited by George Mudie. Contributors: William Thompson, William King.

L (w II, 27); LU. O†; SaU; Greenwood reprint and microfiche: microfiche distributed in Britain and Europe by the Harvester Press Ltd.

996 Edinburgh and District Shop Assistant 1 (Sept. 1944)–['early in 1946']. Edinburgh; irreg

A   Gratis. Union of Shop, Distributive and Allied Workers, Edinburgh and District. 'A periodical devoted to News and Views of the Working Life of Shop Assistants, Warehousemen, and Clerks in Edinburgh and District.' Editor: Harry Wilkinson. Reproduced from typewriting.

EP† 1–4 (March 1945)

Edinburgh and Lothians Clarion see **Edinburgh Clarion**

997 Edinburgh Clarion 1 (Nov. 1939)–79 (May 1946); then **Clarion**: 80 (June 1946)–90 (May 1947); ns 1 (Feb. 1948)–30 (July 1950); then **Edinburgh and Lothians Clarion**: 31 (Aug. 1950)–155 (Dec. 1960). Edinburgh; m

    B   1d.; 2d. Published by Gordon Stott for the West Edinburgh Divisional Labour Party, then by the Clarion Publishing Society. Later sub-title; 'Official Organ of the East of Scotland Labour Movement'.

    E†*; EP*; LabP† occ. nos 1956–60

998 Edinburgh Co-operative Citizen 1 (Oct. 1934). London

    B   National Co-operative Publishing Society

    L(Col)

999 Edinburgh Gazetteer 1 (16 Nov. 1792)–? Edinburgh; s-w

    B   4d. Printed for Captain [W.] Johnson and other proprietors by W. G. Moffat. Later proprietor: Alexander Scott. Printer: Moir. Aim: radical reform, 'Rights of the People', defence of French revolutionary principles. reported at great length the trial of Tom Paine, advertised and reported the conventions of the Friends of the People.

    E 1, 79 (3 Dec. 1793), 80 (10 Dec. 1793), 85 (15 Jan. 1794); GM occ. nos; L 7 (25 Dec. 1792), 13 (13 Jan. 1793), 28 (8 March 1793)

1000 Edinburgh Monthly Democrat and Total Abstinence Advocate 1 (7 July 1838)–4 (Oct. 1838). Edinburgh; m

    B   2d. Printer, publisher, editor and proprietor: John Fraser. An organ of moral force Chartism. The first Chartist newspaper in Scotland. Succeeded by **True Scotsman**.

    E (w 3); LU†

1001 Edinburgh Star March 1858–1858 (month unknown). Edinburgh; w

    B   1d. Thoroughly democratic, advocated a great many changes which would be for the benefit of the working-man. Had a very short career. Not to be confused with **Edinburgh Star**, 1809–24. (R. M. W. Cowan, **The Newspaper in Scotland**, Glasgow 1946, p. 286) **Scottish Notes and Queries**, July 1903, p. 11, calls it **The Star**. Unlike its namesake of an earlier date, was a thoroughly democratic paper. Referred to by a contemporary as 'a whole-hog democratic weekly'. Says it lasted for a few weeks only.

1002 Edlington Lamp

    A   Issued by the Edlington militant miners. Communist Party pit paper. (R. G. Neville.)

1003 Edmonds's Weekly Recorder, and Saturday's Advertiser 1 (26 June 1819)–8 (8 Aug. 1819); then **Edmonds's Weekly Register:** ns I, 1 (26 Aug. 1819)–19 (8 Jan. 1820). Birmingham; w

    B   4d. Printed for the proprietor, George Edmonds, by T. J. Vale. Radical miscellany. Reports of reform meetings in Birmingham and elsewhere. Contains addresses by Edmonds to his fellow citizens, urging the need for radical reform.

    BP*; LU†

Edmonds's Weekly Register see **Edmonds's Weekly Recorder, and Saturday's Advertiser**

1004 Edmonton Citizen 1 (Dec. 1929)–112 (May 1939); ns 1 (Dec. 1960)–13 (May 1963); m

    B   Gratis. Published by the London Co-operative Society.

    L(Col); LabP† ns 6, 8

1005 Education Journal [18--?] –? Belfast

    A?   2d. Published by Allen and Johnston. 'Organ of the Irish national teachers.' (Mitchell, 1885.)

Education Today see **Educational Bulletin**

Education Today and Tomorrow see **Educational Bulletin**

1006 Educational Bulletin I, 1 (Nov. 1948)–VI, 1 (Sept./Oct. 1953); then **Education Today:** VI, 2 (Nov./Dec. 1953)–VII, 3 (March/April 1955); then **Education Today and Tomorrow:** VII, 4 (March/April 1955)–; q and bi-m

    B   6d. Communist Party. Campaigns for better conditions for teachers, educational reform. Covers teacher politics.

    WCML†

1007 Educational Circular and Communist Apostle ns 1 (Nov. 1841)–6 (May 1842); m

    B   1d. Published by J. Cleave and W. Lovett. Printed by W. Paine, Cheltenham. Editor: Henry Fry. Organ of the London Communist Propaganda Society, formed and presided over by Goodwyn Barmby. Favoured universal adult suffrage. Propagated idea of communitarianism.

    L 1; LU†

1008 Educational Commentary 1 (4 Nov. 1942)–39 (22 Oct. 1956); fortn

    B   Issued by Marx House in association with the **Daily Worker.** Later title: **Educational Commentary on Current Affairs.** An information service in the form of questions and detailed answers on a whole range of current political problems and prospects.

    E; L (w 4, 7); O; ONC occ. nos; TUC

1009 Educational Record [190-?]. Northumberland; m

    A   Gratis. 'The organ of the four societies belonging to the Northern Section' (**International Directory of the Co-operative Press**, 1909).

1010 Educational Worker: Organ of the Teachers' Labour League I, 1 (Nov. 1926)–VI, 12 (Oct. 1934); m

    A   3d. Published by A. Duncan, Secretary of the League. Later, organ of the succeeding organisation, the Educational Workers' League. For socialist teachers, promoting the ideals of the Labour Movement in education and at large. Affiliated to the Labour Party, but expelled in 1927. Later affiliated to the National Minority Movement, militant, pro-Soviet Russia. President: Stanley Redgrove. Vice-president (1926): Bertrand Russell.

    L(Col)†; WCML† (w I, 2)

1011 Egham Clarion [194-?] –250 (Jan. 1964); then **Bagshot and Egham Clarion**: 251 (Feb. 1964)–265 (April 1965); then **Egham Clarion**: 255 (May 1965)–278 (May 1966); m

    B   Issued by Egham Labour Party.

    L(Col) 166 (Dec. 1956)–278; LabP occ. nos

1012 Eight Hours Working Day 1 (7 Dec. 1889)–? Zurich

    B?   Published by the Zurich Executive Committee for the Eight-Hour Working Day. Editor and publisher: E. Wullschleger. In English. There were apparently other editions in French and German.

    L(Col)† 1

1013Eδ ηοις 1961– . Aylesbury

    A   Institution of Professional Civil Servants, Ministry of Aviation Group.

    L

1014 Electrical Power Engineer: the Official Organ of the Electrical Power Engineers' Association I, 1 (July 1919–). Manchester; London; m

    A   2d. etc. To keep members informed of the Association's activities and problems, and to be a medium of expression for members.

    BU VIII–*; BrP; GE; L; LFE 1946– ; LP VII– ; LSC XIV– ; MP IV–

Electrical Supervisor see **Contact, 1920–1931**

Electrical Trades Journal see **Eltradion**

Electrical Trades Union. **Research Bulletin**   8 May 1964–?

    A

    TUC occ nos between No. 1 and No. 16 (27 Nov. 1964)

1016 Electricity News I (1956)– . Manchester
    A   National and Local Government Officers' Association, Manchester Sub-Area Electricity Branch.
    L

1017 Electron: the Electrical Workers' Journal [I], 1 (1 July 1920)–II, 22 (May 1922); m
    A   2d. Printed by The Twentieth Century Press. Edited for the London District Committee of the Electrical Trades' Union by C. H. Stavenhagen, then by W. T. Westfallen. Intended to be a propagandist instrument in gaining 100,000 London membership in three years. Branch notes, articles, news, correspondence. Political and socialist.
    L(Col)†

Electron, 1950–1960 see **Eltradion**

1018 Eleftheros Hellene: Fortnightly Review; Organ of the Greek Maritime Co-operating Unions 1 (1 Sept. 1943)–61 (19 Dec. 1945). Cardiff; fortn
    A   3d. Published by the Greek Maritime Co-operating Unions. Printed by CAP Owners, Hermes Press, Ltd. 'Continuation of **Ergatis Thelassis, Thelassinos, Naftergatis** and **Naftilos**, the publicity organs of the Maritime Labour Movement which have contributed enormously to the organising of the seamen.' Defends economic interests, trade union and political liberties of the seamen, and the 'strengthening of the Liberation struggle'. Supports the National Liberation Front. In modern Greek and English.
    L(Col)† (w 49, 52); TUC (w 1–3)

1019 Eliza Cook's Journal I, 1 (5 May 1849)–XII (1854); w
    C   1½d. Printed and published by John Owen Clarke, then by Charles Cook. 'Let me confess that I have a distaste for the fashion so violently adopted of talking to "the people", as though they needed an army of self-sacrificing champions to do battle for them . . . I am only anxious to give my feeble aid to the gigantic struggle for intellectual elevation now going on, and fling my energies and will into a cause where my heart will zealously animate my duty . . . there is a stirring development of progressive mind in "the mass" which only requires steady and free communion with Truth to expand itself . . . ' (E. Cook) Serial fiction, poetry, articles of all kinds, including some on the conditions of the labouring population.
    C I–XI; EP I–II, V–VI; MP I–VIII; O† I–XI; SP

1020 Ellesmere Port and District New Clarion I, 1 (May 1960)–? Ellesmere Port; m
    B   1d. 2d. Published by Jeff Price, Eastham, and E. Guttridge, Ellesmere Port, on behalf of the Ellesmere Port Labour party. Newspaper format. National and local news.
    LabP† I, 1, II, 3 (March 1961); TUC I–

1021 Eltradion: the Official Organ of the Electrical Trades' Union I, 1 (April 1905)—V, 52 (July 1909). London; Manchester; m; then **Electrical Trades Journal**: I, 1 (Aug. 1909)—(July 1914): (March 1915)—XXXIX, 3 (March 1950). Manchester; London; m; then **Electron**: the Journal of the Electrical Trades' Union: XXXIX, 4 (April 1950)—LVII, 12 (Dec. 1968). Bromley; Hayes; m; superseded by **Contact** (Jan. 1969)—. Hayes; q

    A   1d. etc. The journal of the Plumbing Trades' Union was incorporated in **Contact** which was the offical organ of the Electrical, Electronic and Telecommunication Union-Plumbing Trades' Union.

    BU XKIV, 4 (1955)—; L(Col)†; NU 1962—; TUC 1944—; the Union

Emergency Circular see **War Emergency Circular**

1022 Empire: a Socialist Commentary on Colonial Affairs, Journal of the Fabian Colonial Bureau a I, 1 (June 1938)—XI, 7 (Jan. 1949); then b **Venture**: I, 1 (1 Feb. 1949)—XXIV, 7 (July/Aug. 1972); then c **Third World**: I, 1 (Sept. 1972)— ; m

    B   Fabian Society. Absorbed the Fabian Colonial Bureau's **Year's Work**.

    BS a IV—*; E; GM b II— ; HsP b I, 3— ; KB b*; L; LCR b; LIE a IV—; LII; LvP b I—*; OCS a VIII—*; ONC 1941—49 b—*; ORH; TUC; Warwick UL 1949—*

Empire Citizen see **British Citizen and Empire Worker**

1023 Employees' Gazette: a Monthly Journal of the Employees of the Drapery and Kindred Trades I, 1 (June 1893)—XI, 19 (13 Jan. 1894); w

    C   3d. Proprietor: Employees' Gazette Company, Ltd. Editor: Jonathan David. Maintains 'a conciliatory attitude towards the employer'. Promotes the mental and physical recreation of employees. Much space devoted to athletic pursuits, eg, football.

    L(Col)†; O

1024 Endeavour I (1939)— . Hendon

    A   National Association of Local Government Officers, later National and Local Government Officers' Association, Hendon Branch. Reproduced from typewriting. The first number is without title.

    L

1025 Enfield Citizen 1 (Nov. 1938)—5 (May 1939); m

    B   Published by the Co-operative Press.

    L(Col)

1026 Enfield News [193-?]. Cuffley, Hertfordshire; m

    B   Labour Party. (Labour and Socialist International. **The Socialist Press**, 1933.)

1027 Engineer 1 (Aug. 1927); then **Working Engineer**: 2 (Sept. 1927)–[Aug. 1929?]; m

   A   ½d. Published by the Minority Movement Group of Engineers. Short articles, notes, news. Contributors: W. Hannington, P. Glading, J. Tanner, etc. Reproduced from typewriting.

   ONC† (w June 1928)

1028 Engineer Surveyor 1914– . Manchester; 10-yr

   A   Engineer Surveyors' Association. Technical articles and branch notes. (Mitchell, 1965.)

1029 Engineer Surveyors' Association. **Journal** I 1 (Feb. 1933)–? Manchester?; m?

   A   Preceded by the monthly report of the Association.

1030 Engineer Surveyors' Association. **[Monthly Report]** [1914?]–1933. Manchester?; m

   A   'A monthly report from the Executive Council, published in the form of a folded sheet, dealt with the Association business until October 1929, when it was converted into magazine form, and the members were invited to write technical articles for publication in its pages . . . ' (ESA **Jubilee 1914–64 Pamphlet**) Superseded by the Association's **Journal**.

1031 Engineer Surveyors' Association. **News Letter** Jan. 1943–? Manchester?

   A

1032 Engineering Voice 1 (Summer 1965)–? (Oct. 1967); irreg

   A   6d. Published by Voice of the Unions. 'This is the first issue of a new paper designed to keep active trade unionists within the Confederation of Shipbuilding and Engineering Unions informed of events and agreements reached in various parts of the country' (No. 1). Advocates Workers' Control.

   L(Col)†; LE†

1033 Engineers' Bulletin 1 (Sept. 1934)–7 ([May 1935[); m

   A   1d. Published by the Editorial Committee. Rank-and-file paper started by Minority Movement members of the Amalgamated Engineering Union. No. 1 was reproduced from typewriting.

   ONC 2–4, 6; WCML† 2–7

1034 Enginemen and Firemen's Journal 1 (1 Aug. 1911)—29 (31 Aug. 1912). Burnley; fortn

    C   1d. 'Journal founded to help the working Engineer to efficiency and to assist the various Societies in their educational work.' Predominantly concerned with technical matters, but provision for society reports and correspondence. 'The best and surest road to better conditions of labour lies in the individual improvement of each member educationally.' Societies given space include: National Engineers' Association; Enginemen's and Firemen's Association; Steam Engine Makers' Society. Then incorporated in **Industrial Engineer**.

    L(Col)

1035 English Chartist Circular, and Temperance Record for England and Wales I, 1 (Jan. 1841)—III, 153 (10 Jan. 1844); w

    B   ½d. Published by Cleave, Hetherington, Watson and Lovett. Organ of the National Charter Association. A record of the Chartist Movement. Essays, correspondence. Contributors: Lovett, Vincent, R. J. Richardson, O'Connor.

    BP I—II, 127*; E I, 50; L; LE; LU†; NpP I, 1, 11—18; ONC I—II, 90; SP I—II; 92

1036 English Chiropodists' Association. **News-letter** [1963?] — . Cambridge etc.

    A   Registered trade union formed in 1963. Non-political. (Association leaflet.)

1037 English Labourer 1 (26 June 1875)—95 (14 April 1877); then **English Labourers' Chronicle**: 1 (21 April 1877)—1148 (8 Sept. 1894). London; Leamington; w

    A   1d. Printed, published, and conducted by Howard Evans. Organ of the National Agricultural Labourers' Union. Started after dispute with the **Labourers' Union Chronicle** (qv). Advocated franchise for rural workers, and aimed to 'expose the evils of a rural magistracy of clergymen and landowners'. Campaigned for the abolition of anti-trade union legislation, eg, Law of Conspiracy and Criminal Law Amendment Act. Continued as the organ of the National Agricultural Labourers' Union after merging with the **National Agricultural Labourers' Chronicle**. Frequent articles by the Union's President, Joseph Arch.

    BP (microfilm); L(Col) (w 1893) (1891 microfilm); Warwick County Record Office April—Dec. 1877

English Labourers' Chronicle see **English Labourer**

1038 English Leader (Oct . 1861)—?; m

    B   2d. Published by F. Farrah. Advocates the principles of Secularism as expounded by G. J. Holyoake. Mentioned by Holyoake in **Sixty Years of an Agitator's Life**. Says he was editing it about 1864, and it was read by many working-class leaders in Bradford, at the time when Holyoake was trying to enter Parliament as a working class representative. (Mitchell, 1861.)

1039 English Leader 1 (4 June 1864)—20 (15 Oct. 1864); w

    B   2d. Printed for the proprietor [Holyoake], by John Rogers Pearson and published for him by F. Farrah. To satisfy the demand, 'particularly in the provinces', for a reasonably-priced radical and progressive weekly newspaper to represent the 'interests of the industrious classes' in England and abroad, and to counter press 'misrepresentations as to the movement of the European nationalities struggling for freedom'. Contributor: Mazzini.

        L(Col)†

1040 English Leader : a Journal for the Discussion of Stationary Questions 1 (6 Jan 1866)—72 (29 Dec. 1866); ns 1 (5 Jan. 1867)—52 (28 Dec. 1867); w

    B   2d. Published at the London Book Store. Nos 1—48 edited by Holyoake, and he remained a contributor. Progressive. Support for Reform League. Publishes letters by League spokesmen. Discussions on questions of philosophy. With the new series the form of the journal was altered and the object extended. An organ of Freethought. Promotes National Secular Education.

        L(Col)† 1866; L† 1867

English Patriot and Herald of Labour and Co-operation see **English Patriot and Irish Repealer**

1041 English Patriot and Irish Repealer I, 1 (22 July 1848)—I, 8 (9 Sept. 1848); then **English Patriot and Herald of Labour and Co-operation**: I, 9 (16 Sept. 1848)—I, 20 (2 Dec. 1848). Manchester; w

    B   1d. Printed and published by James Leach. For the People's Charter and Repeal of the Irish Union. Emphasis on social rights, the protection of Labour, and Rights of Labour. Discusses working-class rights, wealth, and the fruits of labour.

        LU†

1042 English Republic: a Newspaper and Review I (1851)—IV (1855). London; Coniston (1855); m

    B   Printed by J. Watson. Edited by W. J. Linton. Aims to become the organ of a national Republican Party. For universal suffrage and the organisation of Labour. Also acts as an organ for the Central European Democratic Committee, Ledru Rollin, Mazzini, Albert Dorasz, Arnold Ruge. Makes constructive criticisms of the rump of the Chartist movement.

        BP; C 1; L†; LE I—III; LU; LdU I; ONC; reprinted in an abridged edition, edited by Kineton Parkes, 1891

1043 Englishman: a Weekly Political and Industrial Journal 1 (7 Jan. 1854)—?; w

    B   1½d. Published by Holyoake and Company (3—). Printed by Tobias Taylor. Edited by William Newton. To represent the working classes.

    James Klugmann, 16 King Street, London WC 2E 8HY No. 1 (7 Jan. 1854)—No. 12 (25 March 1854)

1044 Enterprise Club Magazine 1 (Feb. 1912)–12 (Jan. 1913); m

A   Published by The Enterprise Club Limited (for Women Clerks). The Club's 'log book or diary'. News of social activities, and discussion on the organisation of women clerks, bargaining and status. Ceased from lack of support.

L(w 6)

1045 Entertaining Press, and Journal for Advertisements: a Publication, Literary, Theatrical, Useful, and Amusing 1 (2 Nov. 1831)–13 (1 Feb. 1832); w

C   1d. Published and printed by M. F. de Berg. 'A literary and theatrical miscellany that seeks to "improve and instruct" the working classes by printing reviews, excerpts, anecdotes and various kinds of "useful knowledge" ' (Wiener).

HO 64/18 13; L (destroyed); O 9; O(JJ) 1

1046 Epping Clarion Epping; m

B   Published by Epping Divisional Labour Party.

L(Col). ns 1 (Nov. 1957)–22 (March 1960)

Equity see **Equity Letter**

1047 Equity Letter: a Bi-monthly Report to the Members of the British Actors' Equity Association (March 1947)–(Feb. 1969) then **Equity**: (Aug. 1970)– ; bi-m; q

See also **British Equity**.

L† TUC

1048 Epistle: the Only Labour and Socialist Paper in Croydon 1 [191-?] –147 (29 Jan. 1919). Thornton Heath; w

B   1d. Croydon and South Norwood Independent Labour Party. Printed by ILP Press, South Norwood, and published by Harry C. Jones. No. 85 'first printed number'. Edited by Harry C. Jones . . . 'to teach Socialism'. Trade-union news, and reports of activities of all socialist groups in the district.

L(Col)† IV, 85, (31 Oct. 1917)–147

1049 Erdington Divisional Labour Party. Quarterly Letter 1 (July/Sept. 1926)–(Dec. 1930); Birmingham

B   To enable 'the electors to consider current political and industrial questions from the Labour viewpoint'. Contributor: Jim Simmons, returned to Parliament in 1929.

BP† 1–9 (Oct./Dec. 1928); (Dec. 1929); (March, Dec. 1930)

1050 Erith and Bexley Citizen 1 (Oct. 1932)–80 (Sept. 1939); m

B   Published by the London and Royal Arsenal Co-operative Societies' Political Purposes Committee.

L(Col)

1051 Erin: an Illustrated Journal of Art and Industry for Men and Women Workers of Ireland [18--?] –? London; m

C?   1d. Published by Virtue and Company. Edited by Mrs Ernest Hart. (**Labour Annual**, 1897, 1898.)

1052 Erith and Crayford Labour Newsletter 1 [1959?] –? Erith; m

B   Issued by Erith and Crayford Constituency Labour Party. Published by W. D. Stansfield. Short notes, Party notices, correspondence.

LabP† 11 (Jan. 1960)–66 (May 1965*)

1053 Erith and District Labour Notes 1 (Aug. 1896)–? Erith, Kent; m

B   Gratis. Published under the joint auspices of the Labour Council and the Independent Labour Party to spread trade union and socialist principles among workers of the district. (**Labour Annual**, 1897; **Reformers' Year Book**, 1901) Editor: A. J. Newton (D. Hopkin). Later title? **Erith Labour Notes**

ILP Oct. 1898

1054 Erith Citizen: Organ of the Erith Labour Party ns 1 (Feb. 1952)–6 (Dec. 1952); irreg?

B

L(Col)

1055 Erith ILP Record and Labour Leader [192-?] ; m

B   Independent Labour Party.

ILP Nov. 1925

1056 Erith Socialist Leaflet 1 (March 1913). Erith

B   Printed and published by TCP Ltd. No. 1 was an election number, issued by the Erith branch of the British Socialist Party, Secretary, H. W. Hampton. Announces candidates for the urban district and Guardian elections. Intended 'to appear periodically, and [to be] systematically distributed throughout the district'.

L(Col)†

1057 Escobian [19--?] – . Lewes

A   National Association of Local Government Officers, later National and Local Government Officers' Association, East Sussex County Officers Branch. Reproduced from typewriting. Title varies: **Escobian Quarterly**; **Escobian Bulletin**.

L 26 (Jan.. 1953)–

Esher and Walton Clarion see **Esher Clarion**

1058 Esher Clarion 1 [194-?] –265 (April 1965); then **Esher and Walton Clarion**: 266 (May 1965)–292 (July 1967). Esher; m

B   Issued by the Esher Division Labour Party.

L(Col) 168 (Feb. 1957)–292; LabP occ. nos 1965–6

1059 Esher Watchman 1961?– . Esher

A   National and Local Government Officers' Association, Esher Branch. Reproduced from typewriting.

L 1961–

1060 Es-press-o: the Journal of the East Suffolk Branch, NALGO 1962?– Ipswich

A   National and Local Goverment Officers' Association. Reproduced from typewriting.

L 1962–

1061 Essex and Suffolk Co-operative Citizen 1 (April 1932)–3 (July 1932)

B

L(Col)

1062 Essex Socialist 1 (1 Jan. 1909)–? East Ham; m

B   1d. Printed and published by the South Essex Printing Company. 'Educate and inspire for Socialism.' 'Independent of party.' Includes biographical items on Jim Connell, the Countess of Warwick, signed articles, lighter material, children's column. Contributors: F. P. Morley, Halstead Branch, ILP, F. Newell, Manningtree Branch, SDP.

O(JJ)† 1

1063 Eton and Slough Rapier [194-?]. Slough; m

B   2d. Labour Party. (Labour Party. **Your own Journal**, 1948.)

1064 Europe Left: Quarterly Review of the Labour Committee for Europe 1 (Summer 1963)–5 (1964); q

B   2s. 6d. 'Succeeds the **Newsbrief** of the former Labour Common Market Committee [and] is an interpretative journal of socialist, trade union and co-operative opinion. It stands in the mainstream of socialist beliefs.' Edited by Roger Broad. Designed and produced by Leslie McCombie and Company. Contributors: Peter Hall, John Diamond, Jan van Brugge, Sir W. Carron, Stanley Henig. Articles on Europe and the Common Market.

E; O†

1065 Evening Echo 1896–? Bolton; d?

B   Described in the **Labour Leader**, 16 June 1896, p. 4, as a 'new Radical-Labour paper' and claimed that 50,000 copies of the second day's issue had been sold.

1066 Evening Herald: the Labour Evening Newspaper 1 (5 June 1912)–3 (7 June 1912); d

    B   ½d. Printed by the Victoria House Printing Company for the Daily Herald Printing and Publishing Society. Brought out, separately from the **Daily Herald**, to combat the intensified attack of the capitalist press upon the Labour press, and upon the London Transport workers' strike, by misrepresentation. 'Essentially a London paper.' Ceased publication when the strike reached the point where it would be settled or extended.

    L(Col)†

1067 Evening Star 1 (25 July 1842)–188 (28 Feb. 1843). London; Leeds; d

    B   3d. Published by George Frederick Pardon; also in Leeds by Hobson at the **Northern Star** office. Feargus O'Connor became editor and manager on 27 Aug. 1842, aiming to establish a London daily paper for the Chartist movement. Contained original reports of Chartism in the provinces and extracts from the **Northern Star**. O'Connor resigned on 1 Feb. 1843, after financial losses on the paper, which then became Tory.

    L(Col)

1068 Evening Star 1889. Belfast

    B   Edited by J. Bruce Wallace. Socialist (P. d'A. Jones, **The Christian Socialist Revival, 1877–1914**, Princeton, NJ: Princeton UP, 1968, p. 336).

1069 Evenings with the People 1856–7

    B   A series of pamphlets on separate subjects, all by Ernest Jones.
    LE† 1–6, 10–11; ONC 1–5

1070 Excelsior: a Christian Socialist Monthly I, 1 (Jan. 1922)–I, 12 (Dec. 1922); m

    B   2d. Printed by the Excelsior Press. Editor: Arthur Frank Ebert. 'Assistant': Frank E. Minter. Organ of the Excelsior Group which had ten members: 'Miss Plummer, Mrs Ledbrook, J. Jay, L. H. Plummer, A. R. Casebow, D. Mount, F. E. Minter, T. H. Ledbrook, A. S. Roberts, and A. F. Ebert.' Socialism as 'Brotherhood and Love', to be achieved by peaceful means, 'by a gradual Change'. Articles and opinion. Nos. 1–4 were not printed.

    L† 5 (May 1922)–12

1071 Exeter Co-operator (1 Jan. 1927)–? [Exeter?]; m

    A   Free to members. 'The **Exeter Co-operator**, an excellent little monthly publication, free to members, issued by the Educational Committee in preference to the long-standing arrangement whereby the Society rented a number of local pages in the **Wheatsheaf**, made its first appearance on January 1st, 1927, the initial number containing, among other features, a New Year message from the pen of the President (Mr Sam. Chilcott), and a report of the December quarterly meeting . . . ' **(History of the Society: Exeter Co-operative and Industrial Society, 1885–1935**, Plymouth 1935).

1072 Exeter Man in the Street [194-?]. [Exeter?]; m

    B   1d. Labour Party. (Labour Party. **Your own Journal**, 1948.)

1073 Exponent: a Monthly Review for the People. 1 (May 1851)—?
Cambridge; m

    C   1½d. Edited from Mr Webb's. Critical of the lack of political
rights and poor social conditions of workers.

    Cambridge PL 1—2 (June 1851)

1074 Expression: Journal of the Aireborough Branch, NALGO 1963?—
Rawdon

    A   National and Local Government Officers' Association.
Reproduced from typewriting.

    L Dec. 1963—

1075 Ex-Service Bulletin I, 1 (Jan. 1948)—[unnumbered] (Oct. 1950); m

    A   'Issued mid-monthly by the Association of Ex-Service Civil
Servants.' 'Items of interest supplementary to the contents of the monthly
journal [**Live Wire**].' Brief notices and reports.

    L†

**1076 Ex-Service Man: an Independent Journal for Those Who Haved
Served** I, 1 (11 Sept. 1918)—I 103 (30 Oct. 1920); then **Service Man: an
Independent Paper for Men and Women in the Services, Incorporating The
Ex-Service Man**: w

    C   By subscription, then 2d. Printed for the proprietors by
Spottiswoode, Ballantyne and Company. Paper 'founded to help the men
by every means within its power'. By 'the men' is meant everybody who
has played a part in the armed forces, ie officers and men. Not connected
with the three ex-service men's organisations, but quite independent.
Owned and edited by ex-service men for ex-service men. Opposes political
party interest, warns men to steer clear of socialists and demagogues, urges
claim for state benefits, pensions, and restoration of jobs and housing in
civilian life.

    L(Col)†

1077 Ex-Service News I, 1 (Jan. 1948)—I, 10 (July 1948)

    A   Association of Ex-Service Civil Servants.

    L (mislaid)

1078 Ex-Service News: Journal of the Ex-Service Movement for Peace
[1950?]—?; m

    A?B   2d. Published by ESMP. Participation of ex-servicemen trade
unionists and members of working-class political parties against call-up of
reservists etc.; anti-rearmament of Germany and Japan; Ban the Bomb. At
first reproduced from typewriting.

    L† I, 4 (Feb. 1951)—IV, 4 (1954*), and three undated nos

1079 Extinguisher 1841−2. Leicester

B 1d. Editor and proprietor: Thomas Cooper. Succeeded his **Midland Counties Illuminator**, and **Rushlight** (T. M. Kemnitz, 'Chartist newspaper editors', **Victorian Periodicals Newsletter**, 18 (Dec. 1972) p. 8).

1080 Eye: the Martin Lawrence Gazette 1 (1 Sept. 1935)−[9] (Spring 1938); m

B Analysis of newly-published Left-wing literature. Contributors: T. A. Jackson, H. Pollitt, Ellen Wilkinson, Tom Mann, Karl Radek, F. D. Klingender and others.

ILP 1; L(Col)†; WCML† (w 3)

1081 Eye: Official Organ of the Eye Constituency Labour Party I, 1 (Jan. 1961)−(Dec. 1970). Stowmarket; m

B 6d. Published by Eye Constituency Labour Party. Short notes and reports, with an occasional short article.

Eye Labour Party; LabP† 1961, −4*

1082 Eye-Opener: a Progressive Journal for the Home. 1 (Nov./Dec. 1932)−4 (March 1933). London; Croydon; m

C 2d. 'Keynesian', opposed to the economic policy of the government. Promotes house-building for the working people. Publicises the Economic Housing Association, and the Workmen's Housing Association, intended to provide houses at reasonable rentals.

L(Col)†

FDA Association Notes see Association of First Division Civil Servants. **Occasional Notes**

FDA Monthly Notes see Association of First Division Civil Servants. **Occasional Notes**

FTAT Record see Furnishing Trades Association. **Monthly Report**

1083 Fabian International Review 1 (Jan. 1953)−12 (Sept. 1956); 3-yr

B Fabian Society, Fabian International Review. Edited by Kenneth Younger, MP. 'A serious socialist commentary on world events . . . '

BP; E; GM; HsP; L†; LE; LabP†; O; ONC

1084 Fabian Journal 1 (May 1950)−28 (July 1959); 3-yr

B 1s. 3d. or 1s. 6d. Issued by the Fabian Society. Signed articles on a variety of subjects.

BP; BU*; B1U 27−28; C; E; GM; HsP; ILP 20−21; L; LE; LabP†; LdP*; MP; NwP; O; ONC†; SP

1085 Fabian News I, 1 (March 1891)– ; m

B   Fabian Society. To keep provincial members in touch with London and with one another. First published for the Fabian Society by Edward Pease. Printed by G. Standring. First Editors: Hubert Bland, E. R. Pease. Incorporated **Fabian Quarterly.**

BP LI–(w Nov. 1949); C XX, 2–12, XXI– LIV, LV 2–11, LVI, 1–8, 10–11; GM 1949– ; HsP LIX, 3– ; ILP March 1891–Feb. 1893, 1905–7*; L; LE; LU I–XII; MP XXIII*– ; O 1909– ; ONC†

Fabian Quarterly see New Fabian Research Bureau. **Quarterly Journal**

1086 Fabian Research Department. **Monthly Circular** [I], 1 (July 1917)–5 (Nov. 1917); II, 1 (25 Dec. 1917)–III, 4 (1 Oct. 1918); then Labour Research Department. **Monthly Circular**: III, 5 (1 Nov. 1918)–XIX, 5 (May 1930); then **Labour Research**: XIX, 6 (June 1930)– ; m

B   Nos. 1–5 were reproduced from typewriting, and Vol. II is called 'New Series'.

AbU XIX, 6– ; C V, 5–6, VI– ; CME XXVII– ; EdP XXII– ; HU XXXVI, 3–XXXVII*, XXXVIII– ; L II, 1– ; LE V–VI*; VII–XII; LRD; LdU XXXVIII– ; LvU XIV– ; MML; O V–*; ONC†; TUC 1917*, 1918– ; Warwick UL 1934– ; WmP XXXVII, 8–

Fabian Society. Handbook: Facts and Figures for Socialists see Fabian Society. **Speakers' Handbook**

1087 Fabian Society. Liverpool Branch. **Circular** [189–?.] Liverpool
B
L 6 (1893 [not traced])

1088 Fabian Society. **Speakers' Handbook** 1948/9–1949/50; then **Handbook: Facts and Figures for Socialists**: 1951–6; a

B   Later editor: H. J. D. Cole.
L

Fact, 1949–1956 see **Labour Party News Bulletin**

1089 Fact 1 [July 1950?] –?; m

B   Duplicated news sheet, Bethnal Green Labour Party, Young Socialists. (**Socialist Advance**, [Sept. 1950].)

1090 Factory Girl I, 1877–III, 1878: then **Factory Herald**: IV, 1 (2 Jan. 1879)–VII, 157 (5 Aug. 1880) Birmingham; w

C   1d. Latterly, printed and published by the proprietor, W. G. Proverbs. Edited by Rev. C. Leach. 'To supply pure and wholesome literature for the masses.' Serial stories, tales, advice on family matters, correspondence, coverage of the Liberal Association.

BP† I–V, VI, 137, 18 March 1880, 139, 1 April 1880, 153, 8 July 1880 (I–V temporarily not available); L I; MP V, 8, VII, 157

Factory Herald see **Factory Girl**

1091 Factory News Nov. 1942—?; then b **Yousedit**: then c **AC. DC. Current News**: [c May 1946] —(Feb. 1947). Manchester
    A   Shop stewards' paper, Vickers Armstrong. Editor: Frank Allaun.
    WCML† a (Oct. 1944), b (April 1946), c [c May 1946]. (Sept., Dec. 1946), (Feb. 1947)

1092 Facts About Fascism: Information Bulletin Published Monthly by the Relief Committee for Victims of Fascism 1 [Dec. 1936?] —?; m
    B   Reproduced from typewriting. News and information about events abroad, eg, in Spain and Germany, and about the work of the Committee in Britain.
    ONC† 2 (Jan. 1937), and 2 incomplete nos

1093 Facts and Illustrations Demonstrating the Important Benefits Which Have Been, and Still May Be Derived by Labourers from Possessing Small Portions of Land, etc. 1 (1831)—23 (1833): m
    C   Published by the Labourers' Friend Society. Philanthropic, let out small portions of land to labourers to encourage industry, 'reduce poor rates', occupy their leisure hours etc. Wished to restore the independent cottager, and promote the allotment system. This publication not addressed to labourers themselves.
    L† (w 19, 21—22); LU 1—20; MU 1832

1094 Facts for Workers 1—8. [1921]
    C   Published by the Industrial League. Each issue a single leaf; sent to trade-union branches, and intended for circulation among workers. The League's objects 'are to bring Employer and Employed together, and to create and foster harmonious relationships permitting a friendly discussion of Industrial Problems'.
    L†

1095 Failsworth Industrial Society's Monthly Messenger 1 (Sept. 1891)—(Dec. 1959). Manchester; m
    A   Gratis. Failsworth Industrial Co-operative Society. Chronicle of the affairs of the Society. Superseded by **Home Magazine**.
    L† 212 (April 1909)—(Dec. 1959); MP 329—*; the Society

1096 Falclerk [1950? 1951?] —? Falkirk
    A   Published by the Falkirk branch of the Clerical and Administrative Workers' Union. Duplicated.
    TUC† 5 (Oct. 1951)

1097 Falcon, Produced Quarterly by the Printing Craftsmen of Messrs Spottiswoode, Ballantyne and Company I, 1 (March 1919)–V, 1 (June 1929); q

A   3d. Not published between April 1922 and June 1929. Editor: R. A. Austen-Leigh. For 'co-operation, conciliation and goodwill on the part of employers and employees' in order to improve conditions. Finely printed. Signed and unsigned articles on printing, conditions of work, and on current affair etc. News of meetings, social events. Correspondence.

C; L; LSF II, 4, III, 1, 3–4; O†

1098 Family Economist: a Penny Monthly Magazine, Devoted to the Moral, Physical, and Domestic Improvement of the Industrious Classes I–VI, ns I–XI (XI ns I). 1848–60; m

C   1d.; 2d. Each vol. paginated through; individual months not numbered separately. Published by Groombridge and Sons. '. . . to help the industrious classes to improve their condition, and suggest means to increase their domestic comforts . . . We have to speak of Income and Expenditure; of Food and Cooking; Clothes and Clothing; much about Children, their training, their health, their education, and their advancement in life; of Health and Sickness, and Sanitary matters. We shall have a word of counsel for Servants, and something to say each month about the Cottage Garden, or the Cottage Farm . . .'

BS i I–VI; C*; GU i–ii VIII; L† ; LE ii II; LU; MP ii III; O† i I–IV

1099 Fan 1 (14 March 1931)–? Fife; fortn

A   Organ of the Militant Section, Muiredge Mineworkers. Reproduced from typewriting.

Buckhaven & Methil PL, Proudfoot Papers 1–3 (April 3), 6 (15 May 1931)

1100 Fan, to Ventilate Grievances and Fan the Flame of Revolt [8 March 1930] –? Glasgow; Douglas Water, Lanark; w

A   1d. United Mineworkers of Scotland. 'Organ of the militant miners of South Lanark.' At first reproduced from typewriting.

E 2, 15 March; 8, 26 April; 26, 6 Sept. 1930 (photocopies)

1101 Faradian [19--?]

A   Union of Post Office Workers, Faraday Telephonists, Cleaners and Allied Grades Branch. (W. Dunlop, 'Local Journals'. **Belpost**, IV, 5 [May 1965].)

1102 Fareham Labour Focus: a Monthly Commentary of Political Enlightenment. I, 1 (Feb. 1957)–? Southampton; m

B   Printed and published by The Warsash Press, Warsash, Southampton. Companion to **Gosport's Socialist Spotlight**. Outspoken. 'To counterbalance the Tory bias of the local press.' Edited by Lewis L. Henbridge.

Warwick UL† I, 1, 7 (Aug. 1957) (I, 1 photocopy)

1103 Farmer and Laborer: a Non-Political and Unsectarian Journal, Advocating the Agricultural Interest and the Rights of the Farmers, and Devoted to Questions of Trades Unionism, Strikes and Rural Economy. 1 (16 May 1874)–44 (13 March 1875). Sherborne, Dorset; w

    C   1d. Printed and published by H. Reader Miller. Opposes the Agricultural Labourers' Union, addresses remarks to farm labourers with the aim of winning them away from union organisation and strikes. Organ of the Farmers Defence Association, then from November 1874 of a new 'union', the District Agricultural Union, open to farmers and labourers, and led by W. Hazlett Roberts. Proposed to deal with wage adjustments, labour supply (anti-emigration), and provision for old age. For harmonious class relations.

    L(Col)†

1104 Farsley Labour Church Record 1897
    B   (**Labour Leader**, 14 Aug. 1897, p. 266)

1105 Fascism: Facts and Figures About the Dictatorships I, [1933?]–XII, 7 (31 March 1945). Kempston, Bedfordshire; fortn

    A   Published by the International Transport Workers' Federation. Reproduced from typewriting. Reports from the underground (Labour) workers' organisations in Nazi countries.

    L† VIII, (17 Jan. 1940)–XII, 7; ONC March 1942–March 1945; TUC 1934–45.

1106 Faversham Torch [194-?]. Sittingbourne; fortn
    B   1d. Labour Party. (Labour Party. **Your own Journal**, 1948.)

1107 Federal Gazette I, 1 (March 1906)–X, 50 (Dec. 1915). **Walthamstow. Federal News**: (I, 1 [1919]–I, 2 [1919]); then **Federal Gazette**: XI, 51 (March 1920)– . Ilford

    A   1d. Organ of the Essex Extra-Metropolitan Federation (in affiliation with the National Union of Teachers), then the Federated Teachers' Associations in Suburban Essex.

    HsP April 1947– ; L†

Federal News see **Federal Gazette**

1108 Fédération: Journal Révolutionnaire Socialiste, Français-Anglais. 1 (24 Aug. 1872)–8 (18 March 1875); w

    B   1d. Printed by Turner and Company. Organ of revolutionary social principles. Anarchist. Opposed to Marx's role in the International. Advocates 'republican, revolutionary, communalist and federalist principles'. Records the Federalist Congress of the International Working Men's Association, held in London in September 1872. Contributors: P. Vésinier, Lucien Geofroy. In English and French. No. 8 in French only.

    L(Col)† 1–6 (28 Sept. 1872), 8

Federation Bulletin see **Printing Federation Bulletin**

1109 Federation Chronicle: the Official Organ of the Federation of Working Men's Social Clubs and the Social Institutes' Union Women's Branch Federation I, 1 (11 Feb. 1911)—II, 6 (June 1912)

 C 1d. Printed by S. J. Forsaith and Son. Provision of leisure activities for working-men after their day's work. Contends that the leisure problem is as great as the Labour problem. Advocates wholesome recreations, temperance, thrift, educational pursuits. Chronicle of activities.

 L(Col)†

1110 Federation News I, 1 (April 1951)— ; q

 A Published by the General Federation of Trade Unions. Includes general economic and industrial articles by academics and others.

 LE; ONC†; TUC; the Federation

1111 Federation of Working Men's Social Clubs. Quarterly News Sheet I, 1 (July 1914)—I, 5 (Dec. 1915); q

 A ½d. Edited by the General Secretary. Recreational.

 L†

1112 Federation Outlook: Organ of the National Federation of Pearl Officials I, 1 (Feb. 1924)—[Jan. 1934?] ; then **New Outlook**: the Official Organ of the National Pearl Federation: (Feb. 1934)— ; m

 A For insurance officials.

 L b XXIII, 12 (Jan. 1957)—

1113 Federationist : Official Organ of the General Federation of Trade Unions 1 (Dec. 1913)—VI, 65 (April 1919); m

 A ½d. Published by the General Federation of Trade Unions, a body which 'for the last 13 years has pressed for a policy of amalgamation and federation of trade unions'. 'Also a medium of communication between British Trade Unionists and those affiliated to the International Secretariat' (i.e. the Trade Union International). Editor: Tom Quelch. Secretary: W. A. Appleton. Benefit and strike fund for members. Chauvinist stand in war effort. Opposed to conscription, but not to voluntary service. Emphasis on the work of the Trades Councils. Then incorporated in **The Federationist**(qv).

 L(Col)†; LE Dec. 1913, March 1915—April 1919; WCML†

Felling Labour News see **Gateshead Labour News**

1114 Fellowship News, for Members of the Socialist Fellowship 1 (March 1951)—?

 B 1 leaf reproduced from typewriting.

 ONC† 1

1115 Fellowship: the Organ of the Birmingham District Council, UPW I, 1 (Sept. 1921)–IV, 4 (Dec. 1924); ns I, 1 (Jan. 1925)–II, 11 (Nov. 1926). Birmingham; m

    A   1d. Union of Post Office Workers. Printed by the Midland Branch of the National Labour Press.

    BP; L†

1116 Felstead News. [194-?.] Felstead, Chelmsford; m

    B   1d. Labour Party. Duplicated. (Labour Party. **Your own Journal**, 1948.)

1117 Feltham and Spelthorne Clarion [194-?] –167 (Jan. 1957); then **Feltham Clarion**: 168 (Feb. 1957)–288 (March 1967); m

    B   Edition of the Surrey and Middlesex Clarion.

    L(Col) 166 (Dec. 1956)–288: LabP occ. nos 1964–6

Feltham Clarion see **Feltham and Spelthorne Clarion**

1118 Female Servants' Union News 1 (May 1892)

    A   Editor: Mrs M. J. Sales (**Times Tercentenary Handlist**). Proclaimed itself to be non-party and non-sectarian. Need for unionisation. Rough typescript.

    L† (Misc. periodicals. 1865.a.9 (20))

Feminine Life see **Domestic News**

1119 Festival Record 1 (July 1901)–3 (Nov. 1901); irreg

    A   1s. per year. Issued by the National Co-operative Festival Society. Intended to be issued three or four times a year 'to still further encourage the formation of choirs by working class organizations and to stimulate a love of nature among co-operators. For 13 years this has been done by means of the great annual Festivals at the Crystal Palace'.

    L†

Feuille Verte see **Green Leaf**

1120 Fiery Cross. 1 (25 June 1892)–8 (4 July 1892). Aberdeen; d

    B   ½d. Edited and issued by H. H. Champion. Published during Champion's contest as independent Labour candidate for South Aberdeen parliamentary division during the General Election of 1892.

    L(Col)†; TUC, John Burns Lib

Fifeline see **NALGO News (Glenrothes Branch), 1963**

1121 Fifth Light at Crypts: the Paper of the Crypts Workers, Issued by the Communist Group 1 (Dec. 1931)– ?; m

    A   1d. Factory news and political propaganda, from a factory which made electric lamps. Reproduced from typewriting.

    WCML† 1–8 (25 April 1932)

1122 Figaro in Chesterfield I, 1 (21 July 1832)—? Chesterfield; w
B   1d. For reform. Printed and published for the proprietors by
Thomas Ford.
SP I, 1—I, 24 (29 Dec. 1832), 40 (12 Sept. 1835)

1123 Figaro in Sheffield I 1 (15 Dec. 1832)—VI, 267 (20 Jan. 1838).
Sheffield; w
B   1d. Printed and published for the proprietors by William Slater.
Last two numbers printed and published by E. M. Charles. ' "Reform" at
all events has been his [the editor's] object.'
SP

1124 Fight: Organ of the Revolutionary Socialist League, Affiliated to the
Bureau for the Fourth International I, 1 (April 1938)—I, 4 (Aug. 1938);
then **Workers Fight**: I, 5 (Oct. 1938)—?; irreg
B   1d. Incorporates **The Red Flag**.
L(Col)†. April 1938—Jan. 1939; ONC† occ. nos 1938—40

1125 Fight, Against Superstition, Clericalism and Cultural Reaction I, 1
(Jan. 1934)—I, 4 (Dec. 1934); q
B   2d. Organ of the League of Socialist Freethinkers, Communist
Party. Secretary of League: Jack Cohen. Contributors: J. D. Bernal; T. A.
Jackson. Campaigns against religion, and Fascist ideology. The journal seen
as a weapon for penetrating the working class and building a mass
movement. I, 1 reproduced from typewriting.
L† 2—4; MML†

1126 Fight for Life I, 1, [1933?]—?
B   1d. Organ of the Socialist Workers' National Health Council.
Reproduced from typewriting.
TUC† I, 3 (Jan./Feb. 1934)

1127 Fight, for the Fourth International: Organ of the British
Bolshevik-Leninists (Trotskyists) I, 1 (10 Oct. 1936)—I, 11 (Nov. 1937); m
B   2d. Published by Robert Williams. Organ of the Marxist Group
(Trotskyist) for the building of the Fourth International. Editor: C. L. R.
James, author of **World revolution: the Rise and Fall of the Communist
International**, (1937).
L†

Fight War and Fascism see **War**: Monthly Bulletin of the British Anti-War
Council

1128 Fighter: the Official Organ of the Camberwell Branch of National Union of Ex-Service Men & Women 1 (11 Sept. 1920)

    A   2d. Edited by Frank Andrews. Leading article on unemployment, asserting the right to a decent standard of living, food, work, housing, recreation etc. Advocates socialist solutions. Bill of demands: minimum wage for all adult workers; 44-hour week for all mental and manual workers; equal pay for equal work for both sexes; abolition of piece work; pensions, welfare services. Seeks nationalisation of land and workers' committees to determine employment and conditions. Reproduced from typewriting.

    L(Col)†

1129 Fighting Call, Published in Confederacy by Freedom Group, London, and Anti-Parliamentary Communist Federation, Glasgow: **Bulletin of Information** of the National Confederation of Labour (CNT) and of the Anarchist Federàtion of Iberia (FAI) I, 1 (Oct. 1936)–I, 4 (Feb. 1937). Glasgow; London.

    B   1d. Anarchist. Campaigns for an alliance of revolutionary socialist organisations against the forces of Fascism in Spain. Publishes appeal bulletins from the Anarchists in Spain. Contributor: Emma Goldman. Absorbed **Freedom** (in 1936), and **Advance**.

    L†

Film and TV Technician see Association of Cine-Technicians. **Journal**

1130 Film Artiste I, 1 (March 1959)–?; q?

    A   Published by the Film Artistes' Association, the 'smallest Trade Union in the British Film Industry'. Illustrated magazine, to promote film-making and employment for members of the Association.

    L† occ. nos 1963; TUC I, 1–

1131 Fire Brigades' Union. Auxiliary Fire Service. **Bulletin** [1939?1940?]–?

    A   'The AFS had their own **Bulletin** which later was to be merged with the professionals' journal and called the **Firefighter**' (F. H. Radford, **'Fetch the Engine': the Official History of the Fire Brigades' Union**, The Union, 1951, p. 114).

1132 Finchley and Friern Barnet Citizen 1 (Jan. 1931)–37 (Feb. 1934); m

    B   Published by the London Co-operative Society, Political Committee.

    L(Col)

1133 Finchley Labour News [194-?] ; m

    B   2d. Labour Party. (Labour Party. **Your own Journal**, 1948.)

1134 Finsbury: Organ of the Finsbury Independent Labour Party 1 (Jan. 1900)—5 (May 1900); m

    B   Gratis. Publisher and editor: Frank Johnson; later editor: A. Halliday. Object: 'An industrial commonwealth founded upon socialisation of land and capital'; Methods: 'The industrial and political organization of workers and independent representation of socialist principles on all elective bodies'. Hopes for unity of trade unions, co-operatives and all Socialist bodies to form a united Labour Party to contest Parliament.

    Islington PL 2, 3; L(Col)†

1135 Finsbury and City Teachers' Journal [188-?]—LIV, 4 (Nov. 1936); bi-m

    A   1d. Published by Finsbury and City Teachers' Association, affiliated to the National Union of Teachers. News, notices, reports of official meetings, educational review and advertiser.

    L† XLIX (1931)—LIV, 4

1136 Finsbury Citizen 1 (Feb. 1932)—90 (Sept. 1939); m

    B   Gratis. Published by the London Co-operative Society's Political Committee.

    L(Col)

Finsbury Clarion see **Clarion, 1946—1948**

1137 Finsbury Communist: an Anti-revisionist Journal, published by Finsbury Communist Association [1966?]—; m

    B

    FiP 49 (Feb. 1969)—*

1138 Finsbury Herald I, 1 (1 Jan. 1903)—?; m

    B   Socialist.

    FiP 1—4 (1 April 1903) (w 2)

1139 Finsbury Herald 1 (Oct. 1909)—?; m

    B   Independent Labour Party.

    ILP Oct., Dec. 1909; Jan., April 1910

1140 Finsbury Herald 1 (Nov. 1946)—?

    B   Finsbury Labour Party.

    FiP 1—6 (May 1947)

1141 Finsbury Star: a Record of Social and Municipal Progress in the Borough of Finsbury 1 (20 Dec. 1924)—27 (Nov. 1927); m

    B   1d. Labour Party and trade-union paper, with emphasis on local politics, and work of Finsbury Labour Party.

    Islington PL 12, 14, 20, 26; L(Col)†; O(JJ) 15

142 Fire Officer [Dec. 1939?] –?; m

A   Gratis. Official journal of fire officers of the Fire Brigades' Union. (Mitchell, 1955.)

143 Firefighter: Journal of the Fire Brigades Union 1 [194-?] – ; m

A   Gratis.

ONC 172, (July 1960)–

144 Firth Worker 1 (June 1917)–(July 1918). Sheffield irreg?

A   1d. An organ of the Shop Stewards' Committee, Thomas Firth and Son. Printer: Jas. Neville. Produced as an antidote to a house journal, rapidly secured a wide circulation. In view of this the Sheffield Workers' Committee decided to launch another paper, the **Sheffield Worker**, which was suppressed after two issues. This led to a still stronger demand for the Firth Worker, but publication was prohibited by the authorities in July 1918. The tradition established by the **Firth Worker** and the **Sheffield Worker** was renewed after the war with the appearance of the **Worker** [1918? 19?].

Bill Moore, Sheffield Bookshop, 93 The Wicker, Sheffield 8, (Nov. 1917), 14, (March 1918), 16, (May 1918); Warwick U (MRC) 8, 14, 16 (Xerox)

145 Fisherman: the Organ of the National Federation of Fishermen of Great Britain and Ireland 1 (March 1891)–9 (Nov. 1891). Hull; m

A   1d. Printed for the Federation by Mark Taylor, Trade Societies Printer. Expected **Fisherman** 'to bring us more into unionism with each other, and to do for us what **Seafaring** has done for the Sailors' and Firemen's Union'. Information on strikes, negotiations, conditions, and reports from branches.

L†

146 Fisherman's Friendly Visitor and Mariner's Companion I 1842)–XIV (1855); then b **Seaman's and Fisherman's Friendly Visitor**: I 1858)–V (1862).

C   1d. Published by W. Mackintosh, Religious readings.

L† II*, III–XIV, b I–V

147 Flame: the Organ of the ILP Guild of Youth. I, 1 (Aug. 1925)–III, 1 (Aug. 1927); m

B   2d. Printed by the Blackfriars Press. Covers Guild activities, culture for, youth pioneers, youth movement abroad, correspondence.

LdU† Mattison Coll

148 Flare [193-?], Manchester; m

B   Labour Party. (Labour and Socialist International. **The Socialist Press**, 1933.)

1149 Flash: the Croydon and District Railwaymen's Communist Group [1926?] –?; fortn?
    A   Minority Movement. Reproduced from typewriting.
    O(JJ)† (23, [25 June], 28, [9 Sept.] 1926)

1150 Flashlight for Electricians & Plumbers. 1963– Manchester; London (printed); irreg
    A   Unofficial rank-and-file paper. Anti-Executive Council of Electrical Trades Union
    J. Smethurst, 81 Parrin Lane, Winton, Eccles, Manchester M30 8AY*

1151 Fleet 1966?– . Northfleet
    A   National and Local Government Officers' Association, Northfleet and Swanscombe Branch. Reproduced from typewriting.
    L 1966–

1152 Fleet Papers, Being Letters to Thomas Thornhill, Esq., from Richard Oastler, His Prisoner in the Fleet, With Occasional Communications from Friends I, 1 (2 Jan. 1841)–IV, 36 (7 Sept. 1844); w
    B
    BdP; L I–III; LE I*, III; LU; MP; O I, I–II, 53, ONC II–III; Greenwood reprint I–IV, 15 (13 April 1844) and microfiche: microfiche distributed in Britain and Europe by the Harvester Press Ltd

1153 Fleet Review: Quarterly Magazine of the Camden Branch of NALGO 1 (Summer 1964)–
    A   National and Local Government Offices' Association.
    L 1–3 (Spring 1965).

1154 Fleet Street: a Journal for the Advancement of Trade Unionism 1 (17 Jan. 1903)–2 (11 Feb. 1903)
    A   1d. Printed and published by Powell and Company. Critical of the actions of the London Society of Compositors. Agitates for uncompromising principled trade unionism among compositors.
    LSF† O(JJ)† 1

1155 Flint County Teachers' Association's Quarterly Review I, 1 (March 1903)–? Flint; q
    A   Free to members, 3d. to non-members. The Association was a branch of the National Union of Teachers. Record of meetings, activities, and opinion.
    L† IX (1911)–XV, 4 (Dec. 1916)

1156 Flint Glass Makers' Magazine. I, 1 (Sept. 1850)–? Birmingham etc;
    A   National Flint Glass Makers' Friendly Society of Great Britain and Ireland
    Bishopsgate Institute 1969, 1874; Warwick UL Sept. 1850–Oct. 1898 (microfilm)

157 Fo'c'stle: the Official Organ of the Seamen's Reform Movement I, 1
Oct. 1960)–(I, 15 [Nov. 1962?]). Liverpool; Salford; bi-m
    A   National Seamen's Reform Movement, Manchester Branch
1–2); National Seamen's Reform Movement (3–15). Left-wing
ntra-union ginger group
    National Union of Seamen 1–15; TUC 4–5; **WCML**† 3 (Jan. 1961)

158 Focus [19--?] –?
    A   Union of Shop, Distributive and Allied Workers, Walthamstow
Branch.
    TUC June/July 1950–

159 Focus: the Magazine of the South Gloucestershire Association of the
NUT I, 1950–New Volume, 8 (Sept. 1967). Bristol
    A   National Union of Teachers. Reports of activities. Last number
ntitled **New Focus**.
    L*

Focus, [196-?] see National Association of Local Government Officers.
Leicester and District Health Service Branch. **News-sheet**

Focus, 1964–see **Focus on NALGO**

160 Focus: West Sussex County Officers' Guild Junior Committee
Magazine 1964?– . Chichester
    A   National and Local Government Officers' Association.
Reproduced from typewriting.
    L 1964–

Focus (National and Local Government Officers' Association), 1964?– see
Contact Quarterly

161 Focus: Official Journal of City of Liverpool Branch of NALGO 1
May/June 1966)– . Liverpool; bi-m
    A   National and Local Government Officers' Association.
Successor to **Front Line**.
    LvP†*

162 Focus I, 1 (June 1966)–10 (July/Aug. 1967); irreg
    B   Labour Party.
    L; LE; LabP; O

163 Focus: Labour's Paper for Youth I, 1 (June 1966)–I, 10 (July/Aug.
1967); m
    B   4d. Published by the Labour Party.
    E; HU; LE; LabP†; O†; TUC

1164 Focus on NALGO [195-?] – ?; then **Focus**: 1 (June 1964)– .
Wokingham

    A   National Association of Local Government Officers, later
National and Local Government Officers' Association, Wokingham and
District Branch. Reproduced from typewriting.

    L 35 (Jan. 1953)–119 (Sept. 1961) (w 83, 84), June 1964–

**1165 Focus on the Malton and District Branch of the National and Local
Government Officers' Association** 1960?– . Helmsley

    A   Reproduced from typewriting.

    L 1960–

1166 Football Players Magazine: Official Journal of the Association
Players' Union I (1912)–III, 17 (April 1914). Manchester

    A   1d. Editors: F. Stacey Lintott; H. J. Newbold (from September
1913). Mainly general football news, but a separate section deals with
regular meetings of the Association Football Players' Union.

    L(Col)† II, 6–III, 17

1167 Football Referee: Official Organ of the Referees' Association
[195-?] –? Dartford; 5-yr; bi-m

    A   6d. Published and edited by Cyril Jackson for the Association,
which sees itself as an employees' organisation, taking part in Labour
relations with the Football Association (May 1965). Association and
professional matters.

    O† V, 5 (1965)–VI, 5 (1968) (w March, May 1967, VI, 2, 3)

1168 Forces 1 (April 1919)–3 (June 1919); m

    A   1d. Issued by the Sailors', Soldiers' and Airmen's Union.
Objects of Union: immediate improvements in pay, status and conditions
of the serving men and women; to demand recognition of all Soldiers' and
Sailors' Organisations by the War Office and Admiralty respectively;
immediate increase of at least 100% on all pensions and allowances; to
prevent service men from being used as strike breakers; abolition of
military and industrial conscription; release of all military and political
prisoners. Urges support for **Daily Herald**.

    L†

1169 Forces Bulletin [194-?] ; m

    B Independent Labour Party.

    ILP occ. nos 1944–5

1170 Ford Worker: Official Organ of the Ford Shop Stewards [19–?] –ns
III, 10 (Dec. 1954); then **Voice of Fords' Workers**: Official Organ of the
Joint Shop Stewards' Committee, Fords, Kelsey Hayes, Briggs: (Jan.
1955)–II, 7 (Nov./Dec. 1956); then **Ford Worker**: ns I, 1 (Oct. 1957)–?
Dagenham; irreg.

    A   Published in several series.

    TUC (Sept./Oct. 1949)–   ; WCML† (Nov. 1949)–(July 1958*)

1171 Foreman 1 [1920?]—220 (Dec. 1938); m

    A   3d. National Foremen's Association (1917—38, predecessor of the Association of Supervisory Staffs and Engineering Technicians). Trade-union reports, articles on trade-union problems and prospects, especially those affecting the position of salaried professional workers.

    L† 66 (Jan. 1926)—220

1172 Forest of Dean Examiner: a Journal of Local and General Intelligence, Organ of the Miners, Ironmongers etc. 1 (2 Aug. 1873)—214 (5 Oct. 1877). Cinderford (2 Aug. 1873—27 March 1874); Blakeney; w

    A   1d. Printed and published by George Long, then published by William Owen and printed at the Co-operative Newspaper and General Steam Printing Society's Works, Hanley. 'As a result of deliberations at miners' meetings over the last few months' it was decided that they should have a 'paper of their own'. Aimed at building up Trade Unionism generally in the region. Records activities of Forest of Dean Colliers' and Miners' Union, some news from other regions, and general Labour news of the area. Incorporated with **Midland Examiner and Times**.

    L(Col)†

1173 Forester I, 1 (26 May 1831)—[4 Aug. 1831?]. Newnham; w

    B   Published by, and editorial provided by William Birt, General Printing Officer, Newnham. 'All for each and each for all.' Birt described himself as 'the first born of a free miner' (No. 8, [4 July 1831]). An advanced reforming journal showing exceptional concern with truck, unemployment and opposition to savage repression of men resisting enclosures.

    Warwick U MRC (photocopy)

1174 Forge: Journal of the Progressive Book Society, Ltd. 1 (Oct. 1932)—March 1933; m

    A   2d. The Society was formed to buy, publish and distribute books and publications for the workers' movement, and to develop a 'workers' literature'. The Journal was 'to forge the links of the socialist culture of the future'. Reviews, and reports of progress of branches. Preceded by **Progressive Books**.

    L† 1, 2 (Nov. 1932), (March 1933)

1175 Forum [19--?]—? Leeds

    A   Union of Post Office Workers, Leeds No. 1 Branch. (W. Dunlop, 'Local Journals'. **Belpost**, IV, 5 [May 1965].)

1176 Forum: the Magazine of the West Sussex County Officers' Guild I, 1 (Jan. 1953)—60 (Dec. 1957). Chichester; m

    A   National and Local Government Officers' Association

    L†

1177 Forum: the Journal of Socialist Discussion I, 1 (Oct. 1957). London; Sheffield; m

    B   Associated with The Socialist Forum Movement. An earlier experimental number in the summer of 1957 caused confusion when it described itself as the journal of this Movement. Edited by R. Harrison and M. Segal. Left-wing Socialist, but wholly committed to discussion and research

    Warwick U (MRC)

1178 Forum: News and Views of the Wallsend Branch of NALGO. 1959?– . Wallsend

    A   National and Local Government Officers' Association. Reproduced from typewriting.

    L 1959–

1179 Foreward 1, [1895?]–[1899?]. Leeds; m

    B   Free; 1d. Published by Leeds Independent Labour Party Committee, then, in 1897, by D. B. Foster in the ILP interest, reverting to the ILP in 1898. Editor: Joseph Burgess (1898–9). Contributors: A. R. Orage, Isabella Ford, Mary Foster.

    ONC (36 [May]–41 [Oct.], 43 [Dec.] 1898), 48 (May 1899)

1180 Forward [c1900]. Edinburgh

    B   Published by Edinburgh and Leith branches, Independent Labour Party. (D. Hopkin, 'Local Newspaper of the Independent Labour Party, 1893–1906'. Society for the Study of Labour History, **Bulletin**, 28 [Spring 1974].)

1181 Forward: the Official Organ of the Bradford Independent Labour Party 1 (29 Oct. 1904)–136 (29 June 1907). Bradford; w

    B   1d. Published by A. T. Sutton, Labour Institute, Peckover Street.

    BdP; ILP (3 Dec. 1904); ONC 10 (28 Jan. 1905)

1182 Forward I, 1 [Aug. 1913?]–? Birmingham; m

    B   1d. Printed by the National Labour Press and published for the Handsworth Labour and Socialist Party. Campaigns for Norman Tiptaft, Labour and Socialist candidate for Soho Ward against the Tory caucus majority in Birmingham Town Council.

    BP† 5 (Dec. 1913)

1183 Forward: the Organ of the UPW Birmingham Branches I, 1 (June 1928)–VII, 7 (Dec. 1934); ns I, 1 (Jan. 1935)–I, 5 (May 1935); ns I, 1 (March 1936)–IV, 7 (Sept. 1939). Birmingham; m

    A   1d. Union of Post Office Workers. Successor to **The Fellowship**.
    BP†

Forward, 1935 see **Oxford Forward**

1184 Forward: the Ipswich Labour Monthly 1 (Oct. 1938)—11 (Sept. 1939). Ipswich; m
    B   Published by the Ipswich Labour Party (No. 1), then by R. F. Jackson [at the Labour Club].
    IpP (w 2, 3)

1185 Forward [c1949]. High Wycombe
    B   News sheet of High Wycombe Labour Party League of Youth. (**Socialist Advance**, Oct. 1949).

1186 Forward [c1950]. Dartford; m
    B   'Dartford [Young Socialist] branches combine in publication of a monthly news letter **Forward**.' (**Socialist Advance**, Sept. 1950.) Reproduced from typewriting.

1187 Forward! 1 (July 1954)—[Nov. 1958?]. Widnes; m
    A   National and Local Government Officers' Association, Widnes Branch. Previously **NALGO News**.
    L†

1188 Forward and Lincolnshire Labour News [193-?]. Lincoln; w
    B   Labour Party. (Labour and Socialist International. **The Socialist Press**, 1933.)

1189 Forward, to Social Democracy 1 [1963]—? Dublin
    B   Reproduced from typewriting. Organ of the National Progressive Democrats.
    L† 2 nos 1963

1190 Foundry Boy: Monthly Magazine of the Wellington Place Branch 1 (Jan. 1886)—12 (Dec. 1886). Glasgow; m
    C   ½d. Glasgow Foundry Boys' Religious Society, founded for the 'religious, educational, social and provident well-being of the Foundry Boys in Glasgow'; 'to influence the young amidst the non-church-going population in Glasgow'. Girls also admitted. Sunday School work and Bible classes.
    GM†

1191 Fountain-head: a Monthly Journal of News and Views 1966?—
    A   National and Local Government Officers Association, Wigan Branch. Reproduced from typewriting.
    L 1966—

1192 Fourth International. International Secretariat. **Internal Bulletin**
    B   For members only. Reproduced from typewriting.
    ONC† [Oct. ?] 1946.

1193 Fourth International: a Journal of International Marxism. I, 1 (Spring 1964)–; q

    B   Theoretical organ of the International Committee of the Fourth International. Editors: T. Kemp, C. Slaughter, M. Banda. Chiefly contributions from the British section, the Socialist Labour League, later Workers' Revolutionary Party. Incorporates **Labour Review**.

    BU; LE†

1194 Fraie Arbeter Velt. [Free Workers' World] 1 (10 Nov. 1905)–18 (June 1906). London; s-m

    B   1d. Published by the Society of Anarchist Press. Yiddish.

    L(Col)†

1195 Fraie Velt: Monatlicher Sotsialistisher Zhornal. **[Free World**: Monthly Socialist Journal] 1 (May 1891)–3 (July 1891). London; m

    B   2d. Published by the Group 'Fraie Velt'. Yiddish.

    L(Col)

1196 Fraie Vort. [Free Word] 1 (Sept. 1925). London

    B   Free. Published by the Anarchist Propaganda Committee. Strongly atheist. Yiddish.

    L(Col)†

1197 Fraie Vort. [Free Word] 1 (15 Sept. 1933)–65 (26 July 1935). London; irreg

    B   3d. Editor: J. N. Steinberg. Socialist-Zionist. Yiddish.

    L(Col)†

1198 France and Britain 1 [1940]; [I], 1 (1941)–IV, 9 (Aug. 1945); bi-m; m (Nov. 1942–5)

    B   2d. Prepared by the Anglo-French Co-operation Committee of the Fabian Society. To keep in touch with French Socialists, trade unionists and democrats generally, now in Great Britain, America and the French colonies, and as far as possible in France itself. No. 1 was issued as a supplement to **The New Statesman and Nation**; Nos 1–4 prepared as supplements for **The Highway**.

    BS*; C; L; LdU*; O I, 2–IV; ONC†

1199 Fraternalist: the Official Organ of the National Fraternal Association of Life Insurance Officials 1 (Nov. 1921)–36 (July 1925). Birmingham; bi-m

    A   2d. No. 1 says the Association has 'recently decided to register as a Trade Union'. Intends to be the official voice of all insurance supervisors, and to improve their professional status.

    L† (w 5, 13, 21)

1200 Free Algeria, published monthly by British Friends of the Algerian Revolution 1 (April 1960)–7 (Dec. 1960); m

    B   Published by John Baird, Labour MP. Dedicated to the support of the FLN, the Algerian Liberation Front.

    TUC†

1201 Free Commune 1 (April 1898)—3 (Oct. 1898). Manchester; Leeds No. 3 then **Free Commune**: a Quarterly Magazine of Libertarian Thought: ns 1 (April 1899)—2 (June 1899). Leeds; q
    B   1d. Leeds Free Communist Group. Anarchist.
    ILP i 1; LU ii 2; LdP ii 1; MP

Free Enquirer see **New Harmony Gazette**

1202 Free Exchange 1 (May 1892)—? m
    B   Editor: Henry Seymour. 'We have long believed that there would be found sooner or later, a single platform upon which all honest labour reformers could stand and work, and we claim to put forward a panacea which shall cement all movements having for their object the emancipation of the workman . . . We defy the whole troop of political economists, from Adam Smith to Karl Marx, to show that the exploitation of labour . . . is due to any other more primary cause than an inadequate method of exchange.' Advocates abolition of money monopoly by adoption of free currency. Sees need to abolish wage slavery completely.
    L(Col)† 1—3 (July 1892)

1203 Free Expression: a Revolutionary Socialist Monthly [1939? 1940?] —?; m
    B
    Warwick UL, Maitland/Sara papers 5th year, 10 (1944)

1204 Free Labour: a Journal Devoted to the Emancipation of Industry as a Voluntary Right 1 (15 Aug. 1896); then **Free Labour, Ashore and Afloat**: 2 (Sept. 1896)—34 (15 May 1899); then **Free Labour Press and Industrial Review**: 35 (15 June 1899)—406 (27 April 1907); m; w
    C   1d. Editor and proprietor: John C. Manning. Promotes the work of the National Free Labour Association. 'Advocates united and sympathetic relations between employer and employed' (**Labour Annual**, 1897).
    L(Col)†; LE 3—46*; O 17—38*; ONC 1—40*; 289; extracts 1899—1903 (microfilm)

Free Labour, Ashore and Afloat see **Free Labour**

1205 Free Labour Gazette: the Organ of the National Free Labour Association I, 1 (7 Nov. 1894)—II, 18 (April 1896); m
    C   1d. Conducted by W. Collison, General Secretary of the Association. Insists 'upon the right of every working man to do what he pleases with his own labour'. Especially hostile to the militant leaders of New Unionism. Claims not to be seeking to destroy trade unions, but to be freeing labour from the tyranny of the 'socialist agitators' who lead the new unions.
    L(Col)† ; LE; National Union of Seamen 2—3; ONC occ. nos; extracts (microfilm)

1206 Free Labour Journal: a Penny Weekly Newspaper for the People 1 (3 Oct. 1868)–7 (14 Nov. 1868); w

C   1d. Established to provide 'a cheap medium of communication between Employers and Operatives of all denominations'. Advocates the views of the Free Labour Society, 'which has the names of upwards of 14,000 workmen on its books, comprising no less than 154 different trades and callings'. The Journal was supported 'by some of the leading firms'. Against trade unions, and strikes. Addressed to working-men with the intention of persuading them of the benefits of eschewing trade-union organisation and making an individual contract with the employer.

L† (w 2)

Free Labour Press and Industrial Review see **Free Labour**

1207 Free Lance and Conference Daily 1 (3 April 1899)–5 (7 April 1899). Cambridge. 1 (16 April 1900)–5 (20 April 1900). York. 1 (8 April 1901)–5 (12 April 1901). Yarmouth; d

A   1d. Issued daily by the National Union of Teachers during their annual Easter conferences.

L(Col)†

1208 Free Man [c1917–8] ; m

B   Leicester Independent Labour Party.

ILP Aug., Oct.–Dec. 1917; Feb., March, May 1918

1209 Free Oxford: an Independent Socialist Review of Politics and Literature. 1 (Midsummer 1921)–6 (29 April 1922). London; fortn. (in term time)

B   9d.; 3d. 'A Communist Journal of Youth.' Successor to **The New Oxford**. Produced by Arthur E. E. Reade. A theoretical journal of the revolutionary Left in the University Socialist Federation. Articles and book reviews. Contributors: Maurice Dobb, Conrad Noel, A. E. Coppard, Louis Golding. Reade was sent down from Oxford as the paper met with the disapproval of the university authorities (M. P. Ashley and C. T. Saunders, **Red Oxford**, 2nd edition, Oxford 1933).

C; L(Col)†

1210 Free Sunday Advocate and National Sunday League Record I, 1 (3 July 1869)–LXXIII, 9 (Sept. 1939); m

C   Published by the National Sunday League. 'Addressed to those who regard interference with their rational employment of their leisure on Sunday as an intolerance which should be manfully resisted, and to the large number amongst us who are debarred the social and intellectual enjoyment of visiting our Museums, Gardens, and Galleries on Sundays.' Later 'Record' in the title is changed to 'Journal'. Less relevant in its later years.

BP (I–VI*); L(Col)†; MP I–V

[Free Word, 1925] see **Fraie Vort, 1925**

[Free Word, 1933—1935] see **Fraie Vort**

[Free Workers' World] see **Fraie Arbeter Velt**

[Free World] see **Fraie Velt**

1211 Free World: a Socialist Monthly Magazine Published by the Socialist Workmen's Association 1 (Jan. 1893)—2 (Feb. 1893); m
    B   In Yiddish.
    L(Col)

1212 Freedom: a Journal of Anarchist Socialism I, 1 (Oct. 1886)—XLI, 446 (Nov./Dec. 1927); ns I, 1 (May 1930)—74 (July—Sept. 1936); ns 1 (Aug. 1936); m
    B   1d. Founded by Kropotkin and C. M. Wilson. Published by
C. M. Wilson (1895). Editors: Charlotte M. Wilson; John Turner; Alfred Marsh. Incorporated with **Fighting Call**. Sub-title varies.
    L(Col)†; LE*; ONC occ. nos; TUC, John Burns Lib. 1891—1915*; Warwick UL 1900—21

Freedom 1947— see **War Commentary**

1213 Freedom Bulletin 1 (April 1928)—15 (Dec. 1932). London; Stroud (from Sept.—Oct. 1928); irreg
    B   1d. Published by Freedom Press. Anarchist. The main anarchist paper as a temporary substitute for **Freedom**, which was suspended because of lack of funds. Contributors: John Turner, W. C. Owen, Emma Goldman, Bessie Ward.
    L(Col)†; ONC 1

1214 Freedom Defence Committee Bulletin [194-?] —?; irreg
    B   2d.; 3d.; 4d. Issued by the Committee: Chairman: Herbert Read, Vice-chairman: George Orwell, Treasurer: George Woodcock. Anarchist. For the defence of military and political prisoners, civil liberties, freedom of the individual. Opposed to the 'Communist' National Council of Civil Liberties as 'intolerant'.
    O† 2 (Feb.—March 1946)—7 (Autumn 1948)

Freedom Through Anarchism see **War Commentary**

1215 Freethinker's Magazine and Review of Theology, Politics and Literature 1 (1 June 1850)—9 (March 1851); m
    B   2d.; 6d. Published by James Watson. Printed by Holyoake Brothers. Republican, atheistic; also a political review from Liberal/radical viewpoint.
    L†; ONC

1216 Freewoman: a Weekly Feminist Review I, 1 (23 Nov. 1911)—II, 47 (10 Oct. 1912); w

C   3d. Printed by Hazell, Watson and Viney for the proprietors. Editor: Dora Marsden BA. Critical of the Women's Social and Political Union. Sympathetic to Trade Unionism. Includes discussion and correspondence on the subject of women workers and their organisation. Latterly, 'a Weekly Humanist Review'.

C I, II, 27—156: EP I; L(Col); LE I; O†; OW

1217 Freie Generation: Dokumente zur Weltanschauung des Anarchismus (Free Generation: Documents concerning the World View of Anarchism) I, 1 (July 1906)—III, 1 (July/Aug. 1908). London (1—4 [Nov. 1906]); Berlin; m

B   3d. Anarchist political-theoretical review, with poetry. In German.

L†

1218 Freiheit: Socialdemokratisches Organ (Freedom: Social-Democratic Organ) I, 1 (4 Jan. 1879)—V, 52 (29 Dec. 1883). London; Exeter (14 Oct. 1882—18 Nov. 1882); New York (from 23 Dec. 1882); m

B   1½d. Published by the Communistischen Arbeiter-Bildungsverein. Printed by John Bale and Sons. Editor: Johann Most. Organ of German revolutionary social democracy in exile. Coverage of international social democracy and labour movements, including England's. In German.

L(Col)†

1219 Freiheit: a Journal for the Diffusion of Socialistic Knowledge Amongst the People I, 1 (24 April 1881)

B   1d. English edition. Printed and published under the auspices of the English Section of the Social Democratic Club. 'Issued to supply information to the English Working Class, and all who sympathise with the social movement in regard to the question affecting the social and economical condition of the People at home and abroad, and as an answer to the attempt to suppress our German contemporary **Freiheit** by the seizure of its plant and the arrest of its Editor.' Editor: Franz Kitz. Advertises London meetings of the **Freiheit** Defence Committee, articles on the British army, the Paris Commune, a short article by Marx on the 'Normal working day', poetry.

L(Col)†

1220 Frenchman, or Expositor of the Organization of Labour 1 (13 April 1850)—? Manchester

B?   'On co-operation and the power of labour' (**Museum Book Shop Catalogue**, 1913).

Friend of the People, 1850—1851 see **Red Republican**

1221 Friend of the People: a Journal of Social Science I, 1 (28 Jan.
1860)–II (87, [Sept. 1861?]); w
    C   4d. National Association for the•Promotion of Social Science.
Published by George Bell. Final object is that of 'social improvement'.
Philanthropic. For the 'promotion of all well-considered efforts for the
amelioration of the less fortunate portions of society', including
co-operative enterprises.
    D I; L† I, I–II, 62; LU† I, 1–II, 85; O I

**1222 Friendly Societies' Advocate and Journal of Useful Information for
the Industrious Classes** 1 (Jan. 1836)–12 (Dec. 1836); m
    C
    L

**1223 Friendly Societies' and Licensed Victuallers' Journal, Freehold Land,
Building and General Advertiser**, 1 (1 Oct. 1854)–24 (Sept. 1856); ns I, 1
(Oct. 1856)–VI, 16 (Jan. 1868); m
    A   1d. Printed and published by James Horsey. First series edited
by Horsey. New series owned by members of the Literary Society
'composed of men of the various orders', thus making it a more
representative organ than ever before, i.e. 'conducted by members of the
various societies', then latterly resumed by Horsey as **Friendly Societies'
Journal and Co-operative Guide**.
    C ii I–VI*; E i; L(Col)†; O (w ii II–V)

1224 Friendly Societies' Gazette and Advertiser: a Journal Devoted to
Friendly Societies Generally I, 1 (March 1863)–I, 10 (Dec. 1863); m
    A   1d. Published by E. W. Allen. Edited by W. Cuthbertson.
Devoted to the interests of members of the 'Odd Fellows, Foresters, Old
Friends, and other Friendly and Provident Associations'. Reports of
meetings and activities, correspondence.
    C (w I, 7); E; L† I, 1–9

Friendly Societies' Journal and Co-operative Guide see **Friendly Societies'
and Licensed Victuallers' Journal, Freehold Land, Building and General
Advertiser**

1225 Friendly Societies' Journal 1 (12 April 1889)–4 (1889). Romford;
irreg?
    A   1d. Printed and published by Wilson and Whitworth.
    L† (3–4 not traced)

1226 Friendly Societies' Monthly Magazine, for the Southern Counties 1
(1889)–14 (1890). Southsea; m
    A   Information about Friendly Society work and Lodges.
    L†

Friendly Societies' Recorder see **Oddfellows Recorder and Friendly
Societies' Journal**

1227 Friendly Society of Iron Founders of England, Ireland and Wales. **Monthly Report** 1 [18--?] –593 (1903); ns 1 (Jan. 1940)–? m

    A   Financial returns and short notes (1904).

    L 1904; LE 1894, No. 4–1915, 1916–17*; TUC ns I, 6 (June 1904)–(Aug. 1913) Warwick U (MRC) 1861–1918

1228 Friendly Society of Operative Stonemasons. **Fortnightly Circular** [18--?] –?

    A   Sometimes **Return, Return Sheet.**

    Warwick U (MRC) 1834–1910

1229 Friendly Society of Operative Stone Masons. **Journal of the Operative Stone Masons' Society**: (then **of the Operative Society of Masons, Quarrymen and Allied Trades**) I, 1 (Jan. 1911)–XI, 262 (April 1921); fortn

    A   1d. Edited by William Williams, General Secretary. Discontinued when the Society amalgamated with others to form the Amalgamated Union of Building Workers of Great Britain.

    L† Warwick U (MRC)

1230 Friends of Labour Association's **Monthly Circular of General Information, and Working Men's Advocate** 1 (March 1859)–23 (Jan. 1861); ns1 (May 1861)–27 (1 March 1863); m

    A   ½d. Printed and published by Willian Shave. Records the proceedings of the branches of the Association, 'the production entirely of Working Men (members of the Association)'. Object of the Association: to enable the working-man to lay by a small sum weekly to form a fund for tools and materials to secure himself against the evils of 'partial or non-employment', ultimately for independence. A mutual savings bank and Loan Society.

    L†

1231 **From Poll to Poll** 1 (15 April 1898)–9 (8 Sept. 1898)

    B   Socialist. Edited by E. O. Thomas. A continuation of **The Circuit.** (qv). Reproduced from typewriting.

    ONC (missing)

1232 **From UPW House** 1939?–?; w (until 7 Oct. 1939); fortn

    A   Union of Post Office Workers, Aberdeen Branch. Printed as part of **The Post**, paged separately from July 1940.

    AU, MSS Coll. July 1939–Dec. 1956

1233 **Front Line** I (1953)–(Feb. 1966). Liverpool

    A   National and Local Government Officers' Association, Liverpool Branch. Succeeded by **Focus.**

    L; LvP

1234 Fudge: Staff Magazine of the Fareham Branch, National and Local Government Officers' Association I (1953)–? Fareham
    A   Reproduced from typewriting.
    L II, 1 (Jan. 1954)–II, 2 (Feb. 1954)

1235 Fulham Citizen ns 1 (Feb. 1955)–15 (Oct. 1956)
    B   Published by the Co-operative Press. The earlier series was probably **West Fulham Citizen** (qv).
    L(Col)

1236 Fulham Labour News [193-?] ; m
    B   Labour Party. (Labour and Socialist International. **The Socialist Press**, 1933.)

1237 Fulham NALGO News: Official Magazine of the Fulham Branch of the National and Local Government Officers' Association. [195-?] –?
    A   Reproduced from typewriting.
    L II, 8 (April 1953)–III, 3 (June 1954)

1238 Funeral Workers' Journal: the Official Organ of the NUFCW [19--?] –ns XXXVIII, 141 (March 1959); Ns 1 (1959)–25 (Oct.–Dec. 1963); then **Funeral Workers' Newsletter**: ns 1 (Jan. 1964)– ; m?
    A   National Union of Funeral and Cemetery Workers, later National Union of Funeral Service Operatives.
    L ns XXXIV, 102 (Jan./Feb. 1955)–XXXVIII, 141 (March 1959) (w 117, 119, 136); ns 2 (July/Aug. 1959)–

Funeral Workers' Newsletter see **Funeral Workers' Journal**

1239 Fur Worker 1 (March 1930)
    A   Issued by the Fur Section of the United Clothing Workers' Trade Union. Reproduced from typewriting.
    MRC Warwick U

1240 Furnishing Trade Worker
    A   Incorporated with **Merseyside Building Trade Worker** (qv).

1241 Furnishing Trades Association. Monthly Report 1917–?; then **NAFTA Record**:? then **NUFTO Record**:?–XXXI, 9 (Sept. 1971): then **FTAT Record**: the Journal of the Furniture, Timber and Allied Trades Union: XXXI, 10 (Oct. 1971)– ; m
    A   National Union of Furniture Trade Operatives; Furniture, Timber and Allied Trades Union. Contents gradually broadened in scope. In January 1969 changed to newspaper format.
    L XXII, 1 (Jan. 1962)– ; LE Oct. 1971– ; NU XX, 9 (1962)–XXIV, 1965, XXV, 7 (July 1965)– ; O Oct. 1971– ; ONC† IX, 12 (Dec. 1949)– ; TUC 1947–

1242 Furniture Worker [1931] ; m

    A   1d. National Minority Movement. Reproduced from typewriting (E. Frow).

1243 Furniture Worker 1 (April 1933)–34 (May 1936). High Wycombe; m

    A   1d. Issued by the High Wycombe NAFTA [National Amalgamated Furnishing Trades' Association] Branches. A militant trade-union journal which takes up political issues, eg Anti-War Movement.

    L(Col)† ; ONC 5

1244 Furniture Worker I, 1 (June 1935)–I, 6 (Nov. 1935); m

    A   1d. Published by the Editorial Committee; Secretary and Editor, William Zak. Rank-and-file branch and shop paper for all grades of furniture workers, London based.

    L(Col)†

1245 Fusion: Organ of the London District Sheet Metal Workers [194-?] –1970? bi-m; s-a

    A   Later, National Union of Sheet Metal Workers and Braziers, London District etc.

    L IV, 1 (May/June 1949), V, 2 (Aug./Sept. 1950)–(w V, 6–7, 9–10, VII, 2); ONC† IV, 1 (May/June 1949)–XX, 1 (1970)

1246 Future: an Advocate of Social and Democratic Progress 1850

    B?   Publisher: Vickers, London. (H. S. Foxwell, 'Bibliography of the English Socialist School' in A. Menger, **The Right to the whole Produce of Labour**, 1899.)

1247 Future 1 (Nov. 1955)–(6[Sept. 1956?])

    B   6d.; 1s. A magazine for members of the Labour Party. Publisher and General Editor: William Warbey, MP. ' . . . To stimulate critical and constructuve thought within the Labour Movement . . . The articles are written primarily by members of the Labour Party for members of the Labour Party. They deal with principles, policy, organization, strategy, tactics and practical achievement.' Contributors: John Freeman, Fred Lee, Michael Stewart, Clive Jenkins etc. No. 6 states: 'For financial reasons **Future** will from now on be published at two-monthly intervals. Each issue will be in the form of a pamphlet dealing with a specific subject . . . This issue is the first of **Future** in its new guise . . . '

    E 1–3; LE; O 1–3, 5–6

1248 GPO Mail Drivers' Despatch I, 1 (Nov. 1892)–I, 3 (May 1893); then b **Mail Drivers' Despatch**: II, 1 (Summer 1893)–II, 5 (Feb. 1894). Lee Green, Kent; irreg

    C   ½d. Postal and Telegraph Christian Association, Mail Driver's Branch. Promotes self-help and religious faith, home and foreign mission work.

    L† I, 1–3, II, 3–5; O a

1249 Gadfly: a Brandsby and Easingwold Review 1 (July 1897)–6 (Dec. 1897). York; Brandsby; m

    B   ½d. An independent, democratic journal, 'a literary and political gadfly to stir up the district'. The editor is a socialist, criticises Henry George, and supports engineers in the dispute with employers.

    L(Col)†

Gadwyn see **News-Litter**: Magazine of the Merioneth Branch of NALGO

1250 Galloway Division Labour Bulletin [194-?]. Castle Douglas; q

    B   2d. Labour Party. (Labour Party. **Your own Journal**, 1948.)

1251 Garden City Co-operator's Record 1 [190-?]–ns 35 (July 1913); then **Record**: ns 36 (Aug. 1913)–39 (Nov. 1913); then **Garden City Co-operator's Record**: ns 40 (Dec. 1913)–77 (Jan. 1917). Letchworth; m

    A   Free. 'Published by the Educational Committee of the Garden City Co-operators, Ltd., and distributed gratis to every household in the Estate.'

    L(Col)† 28 (Dec. 1912), 36–9, 41–77 (w July 1916)

1252 Garment Worker I, 1 (Jan. 1923)–III, 127 (Dec. 1931). Leeds

    A   Tailors' and Garment Workers' Trade Union. Then united with Amalgamated Society of Tailors and Tailoresses, **Journal** (BUCOP).

Garment Worker [post 1932]–see Amalgamated Society of Tailors. **Journal**

1253 Garment Workers' Leader: the Paper for Militant Garment Workers [1933?]–?

    A   1d. Published by the 'GW Leader'. Anti-Bedaux system agitation, London and provinces.

    MRC Warwick U2 (Feb./March 1934), 4 (May/June 1934)

1254 Garment Worker's Voice 1 (June 1933)–? Leeds; m

    A   1d. Published by the Rank and File Clothing Workers' Movement (Leeds). Includes workers' letters. Reproduced from typewriting.

    MRC Warwick U1, 2 (July 1933)

1255 Gas Worker: the Paper of the London Gas Workers [192-?]–?

    A   ½d. 'Issued by the Communist Group'. Factory paper in action led by Beckton Shop Stewards Committee. Reproduced fom typewriting.

    O(JJ)† 14 (July 1926), 15 (July 1926)

1256 Gasette 1959?– . Perth

    A   National and Local Government Officers' Association, Perth Gas Branch. Reproduced from typewriting.

    L 1959–

1257 Glasgow: Official Magazine of Glasgow Gas Branch Of NALGO
[19--?]- . Glasgow
>A   National and Local Government Officers' Association.
>L 53 (March 1961)—

1258 Gassing to You 1958?— . Shrewsbury
>A   National and Local Government Officers' Association,
Shropshire Divisional Gas Branch.
>L† May 1958

Gateshead and District Labour News see **Gateshead Labour News**

1259 Gateshead Herald 1 (153) (Feb. 1929)—248 (353) (Sept. 1947).
Gateshead; m
>B   1d. Newspaper published by Gateshead Labour Party and
Trades Council. Succeeded **Gateshead Labour News** (qv).
>Gateshead PL 2—246* (original), 1—248* (microfilm); L(Col)†
105—248*

1260 Gateshead Labour News 1 (99) (15 Oct. 1924)—7 (105) (1 April
1925); then **Felling Labour News**: 1 (105) (1 April 1925); then **Gateshead
Labour News**: 7 (106) [sic] (15 April 1925); then **Gateshead and District
Labour News**: 8 (107) (15 May 1925)—53 (152) (Jan. 1929). Gateshead; ж
>B   Gateshead Labour Party and Trades Council. Succeeds
Gateshead Labour Party and Trades Council, **Monthly Circular** (qv) and
succeeded by **Gateshead Herald** (qv).
>Gateshead PL (w 4, 12, 21, 22, 28, 29) (microfilm); 19 (original)

1261 Gateshead Labour Party and Trades Council. **Monthly Circular** 1—26
[191-?]; 27 (Feb. 1919)—98 (Sept. 1924). Gateshead m
>B   Nos. 1—26 reproduced from typewriting; no copies known to
have survived. Succeeded by **Gateshead Labour News** (qv).
>Gateshead PL 27—98* (microfilm); 27—57 (original); ILP Feb. 1919

1262 Gateway: a Journal of Life and Literature I, 1 (July 1912)—XXX,
361 (Jan/Aug. 1945). Cottingham (I—III); Turriff; m
>B   3d. Printed, published and edited by James Leatham. An
independent, collectivist and humanist review of politics and literature
conducted by one of the early socialist pioneers.
>AU†; E I—XI, XXII, 262; L†; SwU IV—VI*

1263 Gateway: NALGO Staff Association Journal [19--?]—
>A   National Association of Local Government Officers, later
National and Local Government Officers' Association.
>L 136 (Dec. 1950)—(w 137—42, 144—6, 148—50); MP Dec. 1951—

1264 Gateway 1961– . Southampton

    A   National and Local Government Officers' Association, Southampton Branch. Reproduced from typewriting.

    L 1961–

1265 Gauntlet: a Sound Republican Weekly Newspaper. 1 (10 Feb. 1833)–60 (30 March 1834); w

    B   3d. Published, printed and edited by Richard Carlile. 'A political miscellany that champions Carlile's republican and anti-clerical views. It claims a weekly circulation of 2,500 (23 March 1834)' (Wiener). Includes correspondence on working-class action and agitation, eg, by trade unions. No. 1 had no sub-title.

    BnU; GM†; HO 64/15 56–7; HO 64/19 1, 5, 27; L; Le 39–60; O 1; Warwick UL (microfiche)

1266 Gazeta Ludowa: Organ Polskiej Partyi Socjalistyoznej [**People's Newspaper**: Organ of the Polish Socialist Party] 1 (1902)–2 (1902); s-m

    D   Publisher: J. Kaniowski. A socialist organ for Polish peasants.

    L

Gazette, 1932–1936 see **Heanor and Ripley Gazette**

Gazette: Journal of the Royal London Section, [National Union of Insurance Workers], [19--?] – see **Royal London Staff Gazette**

Gazette (Prudential Assurance Company Staff Union), 1910– see **Prudential Staff Gazette**

Gazette: Official Organ of the Pearl Section, National Union of Insurance Workers [1968?] – see **Pearl Agents' Gazette**

1267 Gazette of Labour Exchanges 1833–1834

    A?   (H. S. Foxwell, 'Bibliography of the English Socialist School'. in A. Menger, **The Right to the whole Produce of Labour**, 1899, appendix II.)

1268 Gazette of the Exchange Bazaars, and Practical Guide to the Rapid Establishment of the Public Prosperity 1 (29 Sept. 1832)–9 (24 Nov. 1832); w

    A?   1d. Printed and edited by George Mudie. 'It expounds co-operative ideas, particularly the need for Exchange Bazaars' (Wiener).

    Columbia UL, New York

Gazette of the Liverpool Guild of the NALGO see **Guild Gazette**: Official Organ of the Liverpool Municipal Officers' Guild, 1898–1920

1269 General Advertiser: a Monthly Review of Literature, History, Politics etc. 1 (Jan. 1842)—48 (Dec. 1845); then **General Advertiser and Monthly Miscellany**: ns 1 (Jan. 1846)—17 (May 1847); then **General Advertiser and Literary Review**: 18 (June 1847)—24 (Dec. 1847); m

    C   (from ns 4 [April 1846]). 3d. (4d. stamped). Printed and published by John Hasler. Sub-title from ns No. 4: 'a Journal of Literature, Science and Art, and the Advocate of an Abridgement of the Hours of Business in All Trades, With a View to the Physical, Moral and Intellectual Improvement of the Industrial Classes'. Supports the early-closing agitation, especially for drapers, dressmakers, and milliners, while retaining its character as a review and advertiser. Regular communications from the Metropolitan Drapers' Association.

    L(Col)† 1—10, 21—48, ns 1—24

General Advertiser and Literary Review see **General Advertiser**

General Advertiser and Monthly Miscellany see **General Advertiser**

General and Municipal Workers' Journal see **General Workers' Journal**

1270 General Strike 1 (1 Oct. 1903)

    B   ½d. Issued by International Libertarian Group of Correspondence 'To familiarise the workers with the idea that Direct Action is the only remedy for their grievances.'

    L(Col)†

1271 General Union of Braziers and Sheet Metal Workers. **Monthly Journal** [1911?]—?; m

    A

    TUC V, 5 (May 1915)

1272 General Union of Carpenters and Joiners. **GU Monthly Reports**

    A   [Postgate says 1863—(most incomplete) were in the office of the Amalgamated Society of Woodworkers, but we have not been able to establish where they are now.]

General Union of Textile Workers. **Monthly Record** see **Textile Record**

1273 General Workers' Journal I (1920)—XV (June 1938); ns I, 1 (July 1938)— ; m

    A   National Union of General and Municipal Workers. Title varies: **General and Municipal Workers' Journal**; **NUG and MW Journal**; National Union of General Workers, **Journal**; **GMWU Journal**.

    BP 1,6— ; NU 1951— ; NwP*; ONC (Dec. 1949)— ; the Union, Scottish District Office

Germinal, 1900—1909 see **Zherminal**

1274 Germinal: Pubblicato a Cura di Alcuni Anarchici in Londra 1,
[1903?]−2 (1 May 1903). London
    B
    L(Col)† 2

1275 Gillingham Labour Pioneer [193-?]. Gillingham; m
    B   Labour Party. (Labour and Socialist International. **The Socialist
Press**, 1933.)

1276 Glasgow and District Railwaymen's Strike Bulletin 1 (28 Sept.
1919)−9 (6 Oct. 1919)' Glasgow; d
    A   1d. Printed by Socialist Labour Press, then by Kirkwood and
Company. Issued by the strike committee of the Glasgow region
railwaymen. 'Circulation went up from 5,000 to 30,000 copies.' Urged
support for the **Daily Herald** as the only daily paper which gave unstinting
support during the strike. The success of the bulletin led to a proposal that
it should be maintained as a daily paper, but resources did not permit this.
    GM 3−9; L†

Glasgow and Paisley Weavers' Journal see **Weavers' Journal**

1277 Glasgow Commonweal: a Socialist Monthly Run by the Rank and
File 1 (April 1896)−6 (Sept. 1896); then **Common Weal**: 7 (Oct. 1896)−8
(Nov. 1896). Glasgow; m
    B   1d. Printed and published for the 'Commonweal' Society by the
Labour Literature Society. Objects: to teach the ethics and economics of
Socialism and their application to social and industrial problems in the
city, and to build a democratic Socialist Party and 'avoid the dominance of
officialdom'. News of the Independent Labour Party, the
Social-Democratic Federation, Clarion Scouts, and co-operators. Regular
monthly notes on the International Working Class Movement by Eleanor
Marx Aveling and Edward Aveling.
    L(Col)†. O(JJ) 1; ONC 1

1278 Glasgow Eastern Standard I, 1 (3 March 1923)−XL, 52 (28 April
1961). Glasgow; w
    B   1d. etc. Reports all shades of opinion in politics and life in
Glasgow's East End, but is chiefly a supporter of Labour especially in the
early years.
    GM†; L(Col)†

Glasgow Echo see **Echo**

1279 Glasgow Federation ILP Bulletin; m
    B
    ILP June, Aug.−Dec. 1919; Jan., Feb., June 1920

1280 Glasgow Labour Party Year Book: a Compendium of Useful Information for Working Class Electors and Ratepayers Generally. 1915−16. Glasgow; a

    B   1d. Printed by Civic Press, Ltd.

    GM†

1281 Glasgow Mechanics' Magazine and Annals of Philosophy I, 1 (3 Jan. 1824)−V, 143 (16 Sept. 1826). Glasgow; w

    C   Publisher: W. R. McPhun. New edition published 1829−31; and another edition in 1838. For 'instruction and amusement'. Vols. IV and V 'conducted by a committee of civil engineers and practical mechanics'. Reports on Glasgow Mechanics' Institution, and briefly on others.

    B1U I−II; C; DnP; E II−V; EU I, 19, V, 123; GU V; L†; LGU; OR; SaU I, V

    New edition: E; Gu I−IV; MU II−IV; 1838 edition

    AU

1282 Glasgow Sentinel 1 (5 Oct. 1850)−730 (24 Sept. 1864); then **Glasgow Sentinel and Scottish Banner**: 731 (1 Oct. 1864)−920 (23 May 1868); then **Glasgow Sentinel and Journal of the Industrial Interests**: 921 (30 May 1868)−1418 (29 Dec. 1877). Glasgow; w

    B   4½d.; 3d. In its time, the main working-class newpaper in Scotland. Purchased, and edited from May 1851 to 1860 by Robert Buchanan, the Owenite. Reported on trade-union and labour activities. A consistent advocate of universal suffrage, combined with extensive social reform. Particular coverage of mining affairs and miners' Trade Unionism. Editor in the 1860s was Alexander Campbell, Scottish Labour leader. Contributor of leading articles, 1850−63 was Lloyd Jones, as 'Cromwell'.

    GM (May−Dec. 1877); L(Col)†

1283 Gleanings Jan. 1898−May 1908. Manchester; m

    A   Manchester and District Co-operative Employees' Association, then Amalgamated Union of Co-operative Employees. Published as a 4−8-page section in **Wheatsheaf**. Succeeded by **Co-operative Employé**. (**Co-operative Employé**, no.1.)

1284 Glocke ein Freies Sozial-Politisches Blatt. (Freedom: Social-Democratic Organ). 1 (15 May 1881).

    B   2d. Publisher and editor: Heinrich Joachim Gehlsen. For the socialist emancipation of society. In German.

    L(Col)†

1285 Glomoa News: the Official Journal of the Gloucester Branch of NALGO I, 1 (Dec. 1953)−? Gloucester

    A   National and Local Government Officers' Association. Reproduced from typewriting.

    L I, 1−II, 8 (April 1955)

1286 Glorian I, 1 (7 Jan. 1899)—? Blaenau Ffestiniog; w

    B   ½d. Welsh radical paper. (Mitchell.)

    L(Col) (7 Jan. 1899)—(23 Aug. 1913*)

1287 Gloucester Co-operative and Industrial Society. Record 1894—?. Gloucester; m

    A   Gratis. Edited by the Educational Committee.

    GrP 7 (June 1895)—(Sept. 1948*); L XXI, 1 (1914)—

1288 Gloucester Labour News: the Official Organ of the Gloucester Labour Party I, 1 (Sept. 1937)—   . Gloucester; m

    B   1d. Published by J. E. Walsh.

    GrP II— ; L(Col)†; LabP† 1960—71*

1289 Gloucestershire Beacon [194-?]. Stroud; m

    B   3d. Labour Party. (Labour Party. **Your own Journal**, 1948.)

1290 Good Lines: the Organ of the Commercial Travellers' Christian Association 1890—(Oct./Dec. 1960); m; q

    C   1d. etc. For the moral and spiritual advancement of commercial travellers.

    L† 1896—1960

1291 Good Shopping I, 1 (Dec. 1964)—III, 10 (Oct. 1967). Manchester; m

    A   Free. Co-operative Wholesale Society. Printed for CWS Publications Department. Editor: Hugh Steele. Shopping, home interests, entertainment. Illustrated. 'Started life as **The Wheatsheaf**, and then became **Home Magazine** . . .'

    Co-op. Coll. Dec. 1964—Dec. 1966; L; MP; O†

1292 Goodwill: a Monthly Magazine for the People I, 1 (Jan. 1894)—XVII, 12 (Dec. 1910); m

    B   1d. Christian Socialist. Published and printed by Thomas Hibberd. Editors: James G. Adderley, H. Scott Holland. Sympathetic to Labour; 'sold . . . especially among working men'. Fiction, general articles, religious matters, home affairs, social questions, gardening, children's page. With Volume III, split into **The Commonwealth** and **Goodwill**, the latter being a local parish organ, and the former for more general distribution.

    L; O† III—XVII

1293 Goole Guardian: the Official Organ of the Goole Labour Party [19--?]—? Goole; m

    B   1d. Local matters, general policy, correspondence, women's column. Before and after 1920 this probably appeared as a local insert in a national Labour magazine, existing as a separate publication for a brief spell in 1920 when Goole Labour Party had its own agent. There is reference to an Independent Labour Party publication of this name in **Reformers' Year Book**, 1909, but none has been traced.

    L(Col)† 15 (July 1920)—17 (Sept. 1920)

1294 Goole Guardian I, 1 (Aug. 1937)–II, 5 (Dec. 1958). Goole; m

B ½d. Goole Labour Party. To give expression to working-class opinion on matters of public interest, and to expose injustices in Goole and campaign for remedies. Reproduced from typewriting.

L†

1295 The Gorgon: a Weekly Political Publication 1 (23 May 1818)–49 (24 April 1819); w

B 1d.; 1½d. Nos 1–9 printed and published by Richard Carlile. Working-class political newspaper started by John Wade, a woolcomber. Supported trade-union rights and struggles. Place used it as a medium for publicising his views on the need for the repeal of the Combination Laws. Advocated short parliaments and universal suffrage.

L† (with MS. notes by J. Wade and Francis Place; also prospectuses); LU; MP; NU 1–48; ONC 41; Greenwood reprint and microfiche: microfiche distributed in Britain and Europe by the Harvester Press Ltd.

Gosport and Fareham Spotlight see **Gosport's Socialist Spotlight**

1296 Gosport's Socialist Spotlight. 'After 1947 and before 1954'– Gosport; m

B Gosport Labour Party. Edited by Lewis L. Hanbidge. Most numbers are reproduced from typewriting.

LabP† May 1964–June 1971*; Warwick UL† May 1957–1973*

1297 Governess: a Ladies' Literary Monthly. I, 1 (April 1882)–II, 2 (Jan. 1883); then **Governess**: a Weekly Journal for Schoolmistresses: ns [I], 1 (27 Jan. 1883)–ns 7 (10 March 1883); then **Governess**: a Weekly Journal for Schoolmistresses and Certificated Teachers: ns 8 (17 March 1883)–33 (8 Sept. 1883); then **Governess and Head-Mistress**: a Weekly Journal for Certificated and High School teachers: ns 34 (15 Sept. 1883)–II, 17 (12 Jan. 1884); m; w

A? C? 6d. Edited and published by Joseph Hughes. Begins to be relevant with the new series, the first number of which (not traced) would probably explain the new commitment of the journal, which begins to report the activities of the National Union of Elementary Teachers, and associated issues.

L (w ii 1); O† (w ii 1)

Governess and Head-Mistress see **Governess**

1298 Government Minor and Manipulative Grades Association. Bulletin I, 1 (March 1932)–I, 12 (Feb. 1933); then **Civil Service Whip**: II, 1 (March 1933)–XVII, 3 (Nov. 1951); then **Whip**: XVIII, 1 (Feb. 1952)– ; m

A Free to members. Later, organ of the Civil Service Union.

L(Col)† I, 2– ; ONC I, 7

1299 Government Workers' Advocate: the Official Organ of the United Government Workers' Association I, 1 (Jan. 1903)–XVI, 192 (Dec. 1918); m

 A ½d. Printed for the proprietors by the Borough of Woolwich Labour Representation Printing Company, later by The Pioneer Press. For workers in government dockyards, explosives and small arms workers. Concerned with pay, conditions, workmen's compensation, and the value of Labour representation.

 L(Col)† IX, 97 (Jan. 1911)–XIV, 168 (Dec. 1916); LE† V, 60 (Dec. 1907); IX, 97 (Jan. 1911)–XVI, 192; LabP† I, 1

1300 Gracchus, or, Advocate of the People: a Political and Literary Journal 1 (27 June 1818)–?; w

 B 4d. Published by R. Carlile. Printed by W. Molineux for the editor, John Whitehead.

 O† 1

1301 Grapevine 1961?– . Poole

 A National and Local Government Officers' Association, Poole and District Branch. Reproduced from typewriting.

 L 1961–

1302 Graphical Journal: Official Organ of the National Graphical Association I, 1 (Jan. 1964)–IV, 12 (Dec. 1967). Aspley Guise, nr. Bletchley; m; then **Print**: the Official Journal of the National Graphical Association: V, 1 (Jan. 1968)– . Bedford; m

 A Union and professional affairs, letters, illustrations, book reviews. Changed to newspaper format with the new title.

 E; LE; NU; ONC†; Warwick UL

1303 Grays Co-operative Citizen 1 (mid-April 1936)–?

 B Printed and published by the Co-operative Press.

 L(Col)† 1

1304 Great Wakering News Sheet [194-?] Great Wakering, Essex; m

 B Labour Party. Duplicated. (Labour Party. **Your own Journal**, 1948.)

1305 Great Western Star: the Paper of the GWR Men of All Grades 1 ([Jan.? Feb.?] 1927)–? m

 A Produced by GWG [Great Western Group?] of Communist Railwaymen. Reproduced from typewriting. Preceded by **Paddington Star**.

 Warwick UL† 3 (March), 8 (June) 1927

1306 Greater Manchester Engineer. [196-?]. Manchester

 B Published by the Manchester Branch of International Socialists. Reproduced from typewriting.

 J. Smethurst, 81 Parrin Lane, Winton, Eccles, Manchester M30 8AY. 9 (7 June [1966?67?])

1307 Green Badge Journal. ?—ns XCI, 4 (June 1953); then **Taxi Trader**: Voice of the Taxi Trade: XCI, 5 (July 1953)— ; fortn

    A   2d. Official organ of the Motor Cab Trade Protection Society, later London Motor Cab Drivers' Co-operative Trade Union. Written by cabmen, for cabmen, in the interests of cabmen. Incorporated **The Taxi-Cab Drivers Gazette.**

    L(Col)† ns XXVI, 6 (23 March 1929)—

1308 Green Leaf. [Feuille Verte] 1 (15 Dec. 1926)—7 (15 June 1927). Paris;

    B   6d. Issued by British Labour Party, Paris Group. In English and French. Articles on British and French Labour and Trade Union Movements

    L†

1309 Greenock and Port Glasgow Co-oerative Citizen 1 (Oct. 1932)—? Greenock

    B

    L(Col)

1310 Greenock Central Co-operative Society. **Record** 1915—? Greenock; q

    A   Not published between September 1917 and September 1919. (M. S. Swan, **Jubilee History of The Greenock Central Co-operative Society Limited**, 1930, p. 108.)

1311 Greenock Commonwealth 1 (Sept. 1928)—31 (May 1931). Greenock; m

    B   Gratis. Published by The Greenock Co-operative and Labour Joint Committee. Editor: Mrs Hardstaff. Labour and Co-operative Party. Original articles. Emphasis on municipal politics. Contributor: William Leonard, prospective Co-operative and Labour candidate for Greenock

    L(Col)†

1312 Greenock Labour Bulletin [194-?]. Greenock; m

    B   2d. Labour Party. (Labour Party. **Your own Journal**, 1948.)

1313 Greenwich Citizen 1 (Oct. 1931)—94 (Aug./Sept. 1939); ns 1 (May 1949)— ; m; irreg

    B   Published by the London and Royal Arsenal Co-operative Societies' Political Purposes Committee.

    L(Col); LabP† 112 (Nov. 1961)—122 (Aug. 1963*)

1314 Greenwich Labour News [194-?] ; m

    B   Labour Party. Duplicated. (Labour Party. **Your own Journal**, 1948.)

1315 Grève Générale (General Strike). 1 (18 March 1902)–3 (2 June 1902); irreg

    B   1d. Published by Henry Cuisinier and Louis Depoilly. Propagates Anarcho-Syndicalist doctrines, and the idea of the social revolutionary nature of the general strike. In French.

    L(Col)†

1316 Grille 1 (1968). Dublin

    B   The Irish Christian Left.

    University College, Dublin

1317 Grims Journal I, 1, Feb. 1953–? Grimsby

    A   National and Local Government Officers Association, Grimsby Branch. Reproduced from typewriting.

    L I, 1–II, 1, March 1954

1318 Grocers' Assistant: Official Organ of the National Association of Grocers' Assistants I, 1, Sept. 1899–XV, 174, Feb. 1914; m

    C   1d. The Association was not a trade union, but, patronised by the traders, an early rival of the Shop Assistants' Union. Editor: J. Aubrey Rees. Object: to 'reform shop life'. Became **The Grocers' Magazine**, and no longer relevant, being devoted to general trading matters.

    L(Col)†; also a registration issue, May 17, 1899; LE 1902–10

1319 Guardian, and Tradesman's Advocate: a Weekly Literary and Industrial Journal, Specially Patronized by the Associated Trades of Dublin I, 1 (31 Oct 1846)–I, 14 (30 Jan. 1847); Dublin; w

    A   1d. Printed by John O'Donohoe for the proprietor, Cornelius R. Mahony. The journal of a Trades Association formed in 1844 for co-operation between working men. Devoted to the rights of labour, 'a fair day's wages for a fair day's work', promoted teetotalism, self-improvement ideas and institutions, early closing. Included miscellaneous gleanings and correspondence.

    L(Col)†

1320 Guerre Sociale: Journal Socialiste-Révolutionnaire (Social War: Socialist-Revolutionary Journal). 1 (2 Oct. 1878)–4 (2 Oct. 1878)

    B

    L†

1321 Guide [19--?]–?

    A   Union of Post Office Workers, Faraday Male Telephonists Branch. (W. Dunlop, 'Local Journal'. **Belpost**, IV, 5 [May 1965])

1322 Guild Broadsheet: an Official Publication of the Sheffield Municipal Officers' Guild [195-?] – . Sheffield

    A

    SP 6–

1323 Guild Gazette: Official Organ of the Liverpool Municipal Officers' Guild I, 1 (June 1898)–XX, 1 (June 1920); then National Association of Local Government Officers. Liverpool Guild. **Gazette**: XX, 2 (Jan. 1921)– . Liverpool; m

    A   Editor: H. E. Blain. Before 1920 the journal is almost exclusively concerned with social activities. In that year, the municipal officers joined the Liverpool Federated Guilds, which had a membership of 'brain workers'. This 'ill-paid class' now determined to agitate for better conditions. From Vol. XX, No. 1 (June 1920), the journal comes into category A. The Guild later amalgamated with NALGO

    L†; LvP (June 1902)–(Sept. 1917*)

Guild Gazette, 1963– see **'Guilder'**

1324 Guild Journal: the Official Organ of the Manchester Municipal Officers' Guild I, 1 (July 1906)–XLIII, 10 (Oct./Nov. 1967). Manchester; m

    A

    L†; XXXI, Nov. 1951–; MP†

Guild Journal, 1941– see **Sheffield Municipal Officers' Journal**

1325 Guild of Nurses Quarterly Review

    A?   Merged in NA-WU Magazine. (BUCOP)

Guild Socialist see **Guildsman, 1916–1921**

1326 'Guilder' I, 1 (June/July 1953)–? (Nov. 1962); then **Guild Gazette**: (Feb. 1963)–? Reading

    A   National and Local Government Officers' Association, Berks County Officers' Guild. Early issues reproduced from typewriting.

    L† I, 1–Oct. 1969.

Guildford and District Co-operator see **Co-operator, [1931?]**–?

1327 Guildhall Gazette: the Magazine of the Middlesex County Officers' Association 1 (July 1933)–87 (1959); q, 3-yr

    A   2d. 'Staff magazine.' Associated with the National Association of Local Government Officers, later National and Local Government Officers' Association

    L†

1328 Guildman: the Organ of the Leeds Municipal Officers' Guild I, 1 (June 1907)—4th ser., XVII, 8 (Aug. 1939); then **Guildman Bulletin**: 1 (Nov. 1939)—138 (March 1952); then **Guildman Newsletter**: (April 1952)—(Jan. 1956); then **Guildman Bulletin**: ns I, 1 (May 1956)— . Leeds; bi-m; m

    A   The Guild became a branch of the National Association of Local Government Officers, later National and Local Government Officers' Association. Reproduced from typewriting and printed.

    L† i I—VIII, 48 (1915) (w VII, 43—4), II, 7 (July/Aug. 1957)—; LdP† i I—IX (1916), ii I (1923)—XVII, 8, (1939)

Guildman [194-?]—1954 see **Co-operative Guildman**

Guildman Bulletin see **Guildman**

Guildman Newsletter see **Guildman**

1329 Guildsman: Journal of Social and Industrial Freedom 1 (Dec. 1916)—54 (June 1921). Paisley; London; then **Guild Socialist**: a Journal of Workers' Control: 55 (July 1921)—78 (Aug. 1923). Letchworth; then b **New Standards**: 1 (Oct. 1923)—12 (Oct. 1924). London; m

    B   1d., 2d., 3d. Organ of the National Guilds' League. at first published on behalf of the Glasgow Group of the League. Chief founder of the journal, John Paton, was editor until his death in 1920, when G. D. H. Cole and M. Cole become editors. In April 1919 the journal began to be published in London and became the organ of League. Cover title of **New Standards** was: **New Standards in Industry, Politics, Education: a Journal of Workers' Control**

    C a 54—b; L†; LE b; MP b; O a 54—b; ONC

1330 Guildsman: the Official Organ of the City of Birmingham Municipal Officers' Guild I, 1 (Sept. 1920)— . Birmingham; m

    A   From 1946 the sub-title was the **'Official Organ of the Birmingham Branch, National Association of Local Government Officers'**, later National and Local Government Officers' Association

    BP†; L XXVIII, 11 (July 1953)—

1331 Gun

    B   Issued by the Communist Party at Vickers, Ltd., Elswick. (E. Frow)

1332 Gweithiwr. [Worker] 1834. Merthyr Tydfil

    B?   Editor: Morgan Williams. Chief contributors: Morgan Williams (in English); John Thomas (in Welsh).

1333 Gweithiwr. [Worker] 1 (25 Sept. 1858)—30 (June 1860). Aberdare; w

    C   1d. Publisher: Josiah Thomas Jones. Aimed explicitly at the working class to improve their morals, education etc.

    L

[Gweriniaethwr] see **Welsh Republican**

[Gwerinwr] see **Monthly Democrat**

[Gwerinwr] see **South Wales Democrat**

HWD [Heavy Woollen District] **Textile Record** see **Textile Record**

1334 Hackney Woman Worker [1927?] —?; w
   A; B · 1d.; ½d. Published by Hackney Trades Council, Women's
Section, then, by No. 23, it is a local Communist Party woman's paper.
Nos. 24, 26, 28 have one leaf supplements inserted, on Russia, from
Hackney Local Communist Party. Reproduced from typewriting.
   O(JJ)† [20 (6 Sept.), 23 (27 Sept.), 24 (3 Oct.), 26 (18 Oct.), 28
(1 Nov.) 1927]

1335 Hailsham NALGO Branch Magazine 1966— . Hailsham
   A   National and Local Government Officers' Association.
Reproduced from typewriting.
   L 1966—

1336 Hairdresser: Official Organ of the International Union of
Journeyman Hairdressers of London 1 (15 Jan. 1912)—5 (15 May 1912);
m
   A   1d. Published for the union by F. W. Niessen, the Secretary.
The Union was 'largely composed of foreigners resident in the metropolis'.
An assistants' paper, written by assistants for assistants, deals with wages,
conditions, prices, 'living in', and campaigns for strong trade-union
organisation. Contributor: Victor Fletcher.
   L(Col)†

**1337 Halfpenny Magazine of Entertainment and Knowledge; Conducted
by the Author of Various Standard Works** I, 1 (2 May 1840)—I, 50
([March?] 1841); w
   C   ½d. Published and edited by Henry Hetherington. Printed by
Joseph Taylor, Birmingham. Useful knowledge, fiction, but also articles
discussing the 'condition of the people', and possible remedies. Editorials
by Hetherington on class and social evils etc.
   BP; L 1—36; LU†

1338 Halfpenny Weekly. 1 (21 Nov. 1885)—225 (8 March 1890).
Liverpool; w
   C;B   ½d. Intention to furnish a paper 'suitable for family reading in
the homes of the industrial classes'. Advanced Liberal and Gladstonian,
and sympathetic to the claims of Labour. Latterly, included a page headed
'Voice of Labour' conducted on behalf of the Labour Electoral
Association by its secretary, T. R. Threlfall, Southport. Also Labour notes
from the regions on this page.
   L(Col)†; LvP 53—225

1339 Halifax and District Labour News: the **Weekly Journal** of the Trades, Friendly, Co-operative and Socialist Organizations of Halifax, Elland and Sowerby Parliamentary Divisions. 1 [1907?] –111, (13 Nov. 1909). Halifax; w

    B   1d. Printed by **The Worker** Socialist Newspaper Society, Ltd., Huddersfield, and published by the Halifax and District Labour News Company. Editor: James Leatham. A popular Labour newspaper for Halifax and district, includes reports of local events, news coverage of all sections of trade-union and working-class organisations. Comprehensive review of politics, trade-union news, literary notices, contributed articles, and correspondence.

    H1P (5 Oct. 1907); L(Col)† 78 (27 March 1909)–111

1340 Halifax Labour News 1 [1893?] –(Sept. 1895). Halifax; w

    B   ½d. Published by Halifax Independent Labour Party and printed at the Central Printing and Publishing Offices, Halifax. The paper was wound up after a break-in and fire at the offices which destroyed the type and fittings (D. Hopkin, 'Local newspapers of the Independent Labour Party, 1893–1906'. Society for the Study of Labour History, **Bulletin**, 28 [Spring 1974])

1341 Hallamshire Teacher: Organ of the Sheffield and District Teachers' Association ns 1 (Jan. 1927)–53 (March 1940); ns 1 (May 1941)–107 (May 1960); [ns], 1 (Sept. 1960)– . Sheffield; q; bi-m; q

    A   National Union of Teachers.

    SP†

1342 Hammer: an Organ of Religious, Social and Political Reform 1 (21 Oct. 1893)–94 (3 Aug. 1895). Sheffield; w

    C   ½d. Published by Parker Bros. Temperance, Christian, 'anti-infidel crusade', anti-socialist, anti-anarchist, Liberal. Covers non-conformist groups in the region as well as Labour and co-operative societies. From 28 (Oct. 1893) sub-titled: 'An Organ of Reform'.

    SP† (w 20, 22–4, 48–51)

1343 Hammer: the Paper of the Workers at Hoe's 1 (16 April 1926)–?; fortn

    A   Factory paper of the Communist Group. No. 1 includes report of Minority Movement Conference of Action, and is a strike edition, but the intention was to publish the paper fortnightly.

    O(JJ)† 1

1344 Hammer: Organ of the Ewell Branch NUPE 1, [Dec. 1939] –5 [undated]. Surbiton

    A   1d. National Union of Public Employees; 'the only newspaper of the rank and file of local government workers in the Southern Counties'. Reproduced from typewriting. No. 1 appeared 'in the fourth month of the war'

    L†

1345 Hammer or Anvil: Organ of the Action Centre for Marxist-Leninist Unity I, 1 (Nov. 1965)–III, 1 (July/Aug. 1967). London; Manchester; irreg

    B   To re-organise the Communist Movement on the basis of Marxism-Leninism against revisionism and opportunism. In Manchester, printed and published by M. Scott. Superseded by **Red Front**.

    L† II, 1 (Jan/Feb. 1966); Election supplement, (March 1966); LE†

Hammersmith Labour Record see **Hammersmith Record**

1346 Hammersmith Pioneer: the Labour Journal for West London 1 (May 1921)–?; m

    B   2d. Labour Party.

    HsP 1–8 (Jan. 1922)

1347 Hammersmith Record: Organ of the Hammersmith Labour Movement 1 (Aug. 1923)–?; then **Hammersmith Labour Record**: I, 1 (June 1925), then **Record**: I, 2 (July 1925)–I, 7 (Dec. 1925); m

    B   1d.; Gratis. Hammersmith Labour Party.

    HsP I, 1 (Aug. 1923)–9 (Aug. 1924), 12 (Dec. 1924)–15 (April 1925); L(Col)† June–Dec. 1925.

1348 Hammersmith Searchlight 1 (Feb. 1900)

    B   Gratis. Socialist. Issued by the Political Committee, 'Kelmscott Club'. To demand reforms for Hammersmith borough by the pressure of the electoral body upon its representatives.

    L(Col)†

1349 Hammersmith Socialist Record 1 (Oct. 1891)–21 (June 1893); m

    B   Issued by Hammersmith Socialist Society, Kelmscott House; 'to assist in the Socialist Propaganda'. Editors: William Morris and Emery Walker. Advocates international revolutionary Socialism.

    HsP (w 2, 7, 9, 11, 19); L†

1350 Hampstead Citizen 1 (July 1931)–97 (Aug. 1939); ns 1 (Oct. 1955)–8 (Nov. 1956); m

    B   Gratis. Published by the London Co-operative Society.

    L(Col)

Hampstead Heathen see **National Association of Local Government Officers. Hampstead Branch. Official Magazine**

1351 Hampstead Tenant: Organ of the Hampstead Tenants' Defence League 1 [193-?] –?; irreg?

    B   1d. Agitation on working-class housing. Reproduced from typewriting

    MML† 5 (Sept. 1937), 6 (Feb. 1938), 8 (March 1939)

352 Hand Loom Weavers' Journal 1 (July 1840)–12 (June 1841); m

    A   1d. Printed by Thomas Stutter for the Hand Loom Weavers of London. Published by Mr. Windsor. 'Devoted entirely to the advocacy of the real interest and instruction of the Hand Loom Weavers of the United Kingdom.' Reports meetings, state of trade, parliamentary business dealing with weavers, struggle against wage reductions. In particular covers the Spitalfields silk weavers.

    BP†

353 Har Mag: a Journal for the Harlow Branch of NALGO I (1956)–? Harlow

    A   National and Local Government Officers' Association

    L (w I, 2)

354 Harborough Bulletin [194-?]. Leicester; m

    B   Labour Party. Duplicated. (Labour Party. **Your own Journal,** 1948.)

355 Haringey Citizen: the Local Voice of Labour I (Feb. 1969)– ; m

    B

    L(Col); LabP 1

356 Harp [c1910]. Dublin; m

    A   A Dublin edition of James Connolly's American monthly which for a few months before his return to Dublin [July 1910] 'had served as a kind of unofficial organ for the Union' [ie the Irish Transport and General Workers' Union] (Irish Transport and General Workers' Union. **Fifty years of Liberty Hall,** Dublin [1959?]).

357 Harpenden News Letter [194-?]. Harpenden; m

    B   Labour Party. Duplicated. (Labour Party. **Your own Journal,** 1948.)

358 Harrogate and District Co-operative Society. Record [c1891?]–? Harrogate; q

    A   Gratis. Issued and edited by the Educational Department. **International Directory of the Co-operative Press,** 1909; Harrogate and District Co-operative Society. **Twenty-one Years of Progress, 1887–1908,** 1908)

359 Harrow Citizen [194-?]. Harrow; m

    B   2d. Labour Party. (Labour Party. **Your own Journal,** 1948.)

360 Harrow Post [19--?]–? Harrow

    A   Union of Post Office Workers, Harrow Amalgamated Branch. W. Dunlop, 'Local Journals'. **Belpost,** IV, 5 [May 1965])

361 Hartlepools (LOY) Youth [194-?]

    B   3d. Labour Party League of Youth. Duplicated (Labour Party. **Your own Journal,** 1948.)

1362 Hartlepools' Labour News: the Voice of the Worker 1 (1 Nov. 1922)–3 (22 Dec. 1922). West Hartlepool; m

    B   1d. Issued by Hartlepools Labour Party. Edited by A. J. Fairey To serve as an organ for the local Labour and Trade Union Movement.

    L(Col)†

1363 Hartlepools Labour News [194-?]; m

    B   1d. Labour Party. Duplicated. (Labour Party. **Your own Journal**, 1948.)

1364 Harworth Spark

    A   Communist Party pit paper. Printed and published by the Militant Miners at Harworth Colliery. (R. G. Neville)

1365 Head Teacher I, 1 (7 April 1894)–XIV, 154 (11 June 1908); m

    A   1d. Conducted by the School Board for London Head Teachers Association. Then adopted as the organ of the National Association of Head Teachers. Covers salaries, conditions, status, as well as educational matters. Incorporated with **The Teacher**.

    L(Col); O†

1366 Head Teacher's Review I, 1 (18 Jan. 1910)–   ; m

    B   1d. etc. Official organ of the National Association of Head Teachers. The first two numbers are both numbered Vol. I, No. 1

    L(Col); O*†

1367 Headlamp: Organ of Militant Group of Priory Miners [1933?]–? Blantyre

    A   1d. Branch of the United Mineworkers of Scotland. Edited at the Social Club, Blantyre. Reproduced from typewriting.

    MML† 8 (14 July 1933)

1368 Headlight [c1934]

    A   A National Union of Vehicle Builders rank-and-file news sheet. (London School of Economics and Political Science. Historical Records Project)

Headlight, 1946–   see **Road Haulage News Letter**

1369 Headlight Magazine: Journal of the Transport Workers I, 1 (March 1953)–I, 2 (April 1953); then **Drivers' World**: I, 1 (May 1953)–I, 7 (Nov./Dec. 1953). Hornchurch; m

    C   9d. Published and edited by Eric Cant. An independent monthly 'exclusively devoted to the interests of those employed in road transport'. Encourages transport workers to become trade unionists. Prints views of workers on problems of work etc.

    L†

1370 Headmasters' Association. Review 1898–   ; 3-yr

A   The Association was founded in 1891, to safeguard the interests of its members, and three years later became the Incorporated Association of Headmasters.

L XIX, 57 (March 1920)–   ; the Association*

1371 Headway: Official Journal of the Ministry of National Insurance (Newcastle) Branch of the Civil Service Clerical Association I, 1 (Dec. 1946)–   . Newcastle; m; bi-m

A   No. 1 says it was preceded by a typed **News Bulletin**. Sub-title became: 'Official Journal of the CPSA [Civil and Public Services Association] Department of Health and Social Security, Newcastle Central Office'

L† I, 1–XVI, 2 (May 1965); TUC April 1948–65

1372 Headway: Journal of the Passenger Worker I, 1 (Jan. 1948)–3 (March 1948); m

C   4d. Editor: E. Cant. Assistant Editor: S. W. Greenwood. To encourage full, active, and militant trade-union membership among London and provincial bus and tram workers. A companion paper of **Headlight**, which was 'published primarily for commercial transport workers'.

L

Health Services Journal see **NA-WU Magazine**

Health Visitor see **Woman Health Officer**

1373 Heanor and Langley Mill Gazette [194-?]. Ripley; w

B   1d. Labour Party. Printed and published by Ripley Printing Society. (Labour Party. **Your own Journal**, 1948.)

1374 Heanor and Ripley Gazette I, 1 (29 April 1932)–31 (25 Nov. 1932); then **Gazette** 32 (2 Dec. 1932)–238 (13 Nov. 1936); then **Ripley Gazette**: 239 (20 Nov. 1936)–1021 (8 Nov. 1951). Ripley; w

B   ½d. Printed first by J. S. Reynolds and Company for the proprietors, Ilkeston Division Labour Party. For financial reasons the Party relinquished control in September 1932, but the Ripley Printing Society Ltd., as printers and publishers, claim to have carried Labour's message since then, though the paper became more of a general local one.

L(Col)†

1375 Heatwave 1 (July 1966)–2 (Oct. 1966)

B   1s. 6d. Inspired by the publication of the Chicago Industrial Workers of the World, **Rebel Worker**, this journal was said to be 'an experimental, perhaps slightly crazed libertarian socialist journal'. Favoured Direct Action. English successor to the Anglo-American edition of **Rebel Worker** which was published in London (No. 6 was May 1966). Reproduced from typewriting.

E 2; LE†; LUC

1376 Helper: the Organ of the Daily Herald Helper 1 (23 Jan. 1930)–?; w

    B   Printed by Odhams Press. To help in the campaign to promote 'the new' **Daily Herald**; encourages the 'Helpers' to secure more readers, and provides information about the business of registering new readers, subscriptions etc.

    O(JJ)† 1, 2 (30 Jan. 1930)

Hemel Hempstead & Berkhamstead Citizen see **Hemel Hempstead Citizen**

1377 Hemel Hempstead Citizen [194-?] ; m: then **Hemel Hempstead and Berkhamstead Citizen**: ns 1 (July 1954)–24 (March/April 1959); then **Hemel Hempstead Constituency Citizen**: ns 25 (July 1959)–27 (Feb. 1960); irreg?

    B   Early series 1d. (Labour Party. **Your own Journal**, 1948) Later published by the Co-operative Press.

    L(Col) July 1954–Feb. 1960.

Hemel Hempstead Constituency Citizen see **Hemel Hempstead Citizen**

1378 Hendon and Cricklewood Factory News 1 (April 1937)–?

    A

    TUC 1 (not traced)

1379 Hendon and District Citizen 1 (March 1930)-107 (Aug. 1939); m

    B   Gratis. Published by the London Co-operative Society.

    L(Col)

1380 Hendon Sentinel I, 1 (June 1926)–? m

    B   Central Hendon Labour Group.

    ILP I, 1

1381 Herald [19--?] –? Middleton; m

    B   Middleton Independent Labour Party.

    ILP Sept. 1909, Jan. 1910

Herald, 1914–1919 see **Daily Herald**

Herald and Helpmate see **International Herald**

1382 Herald and Leaguer I, 1 (April 1914)

    B   1d. Published by the proprietors, 'The Daily Herald and Leaguer'. Records and publicises the work of the Daily Herald League, which had branches throughout the country. National Secretary: W. F. Rean. On the achievement of the **Daily Herald**.

    L(Col)†

1383 Herald of Anarchy: an Organ of Social, Political and Economic Freethought I, 1 (Oct. 1890)–I, 2 (Nov. 1890); m

B   1d. Printed and published for A.Tam, at the Labour Press, Ltd. (Co-operative Society). Anarchist, advocating abolition of the State. In the formulation of its principles denies the right of the landlord, capitalist, tax collector, State socialist or Communist to interfere with the disposal of the fruits of one's labour.

L(Col)† I, 2; RU I, 1

Herald of Co-operation and Organ of the Redemption Society see **Herald of Redemption**

1384 Herald of Progress 1 (25 Oct. 1845)–16 (23 May 1846).

B   Rational Society. Editor: John Cramp. Ended when **The Reasoner** was commenced (H. S. Foxwell, 'Bibliography of the English Socialist School' in A. Menger, **The Right to the whole Produce of Labour**, 1899).

MP (missing)

1385 Herald of Redemption 1 (Jan. 1847)–3 (March 1847); then **Herald of Co-operation and Organ of the Redemption Society**: 4 (April 1847)–19 (July 1948). Douglas, Isle of Man; m

B   1d. Printed and published by William Robinson and Company. Editor: James Hole. To transform society along the lines of mutual co-operation. Organ of the Leeds Redemption Society, President: D. Green. Reports of meetings, theoretical articles, extracts from other progressive journals. Contributor: Goodwyn Barmby. Succeeded by **The Spirit of the Age** (handwritten note on copy seen).

LU†

1386 Herald of Revolt: an Organ of the Coming School Social Revolution I, 1 (Dec. 1910)–IV, 5 (May 1914); m

B   1d. Published and edited by Guy A. Aldred. Printed by the Bakunin Press. For the abolition of the wage system of capitalism. Opposed social democrats and reformist Trade Unionism.

Bishopsgate Institute April 1911–May 1914; GM Feb. 1913–May 1914; ILP 1913–14*; L(Col)† (w I, 1)

1387 Herald of the Future, and **Miscellany of Science and Literature** 1 (Oct. 1839)–6 (7 March 1840). Manchester; m

B   Published by A. Heywood. Edited by George Frederick Manley. Against the system of competition which is seen as the greatest evil afflicting the working man.

Chetham's Library; MP†; MR

1388 Herald of the Rights of Industry 1 (8 Feb. 1834)—16 (24 May 1834). Manchester; w

    B   1d. Published by the Society for Promoting National Regeneration, a group of factory reformers led by John Doherty and the champion in Parliament, John Fielden, MP for Oldham. Edited by J. Doherty. Organ of the trade-union fight, in Lancashire, for an eight-hour day, which is seen as a cure for most of society's evils.

    Co-op. Coll.; HO 64/15 1—5; L (w 15); LU 3—16; MP; ONC 1; Tolson Memorial Museum, Huddersfield (w 5, 6, 9); Warwick UL 3—16 (microfilm)

Herald to the Trades' Advocate see **Herald to the Trades' Advocate, and Co-operative Journal**

1389 Herald to the Trades' Advocate, and Co-operative Journal 1 (25 Sept. 1830)—20 (5 Feb. 1831); then **Herald to the Trades' Advocate**: 21 (12 Feb. 1831)—36 (28 May 1831). Glasgow; w

    A   2d. Organ of the Trades' Committee of Glasgow. Published by David Robertson. Printed by A. Young (1—16). Miller (17—36). Probable editors: John Tait and Alexander Campbell. 'A working-class political miscellany that is mainly devoted to encouraging trades union activities' (Wiener). For Co-operation, and political representation for the people 'full, fair and free'. Suppressed by the Solicitor of Stamps.

    E 32; GM; L 13; LE†; LU; LUC (w 5, 14, 25, 27); MP; Warwick UL; Greenwood reprint and microfiche: microfiche distributed in Britain and Europe by the Harvester Press Ltd.

1390 Hercules [c1897].

    A?   5d. 'Devoted to the agitation of the Olombia Commonwealth Campaign, the propaganda of a new political economy for the new millenial era of justice, liberty, peace, and plenty, with free land, habitation, material, production, transit, and use of all the products of the earth.' Editor: Dr W. H. von Swartwout, London. He was also President of the Campaign, with an address in New York. (**Labour Annual**, 1897).

1391 Here's Health I, (1952)—? Ipswich

    A   National Association of Local Government Officers, later National and Local Government Officers' Association, East Suffolk Health Services Branch. Reproduced from typewriting

    L IV, 1, (Christmas 1955)—

Hertford and Ware Patriot see **Ware Patriot**

1392 Hertfordshire Bulletin 1 (Oct. 1926)—33 (June 1929). Watford; m

    B   Labour Party.

    Watford PL

1393 Heston and Isleworth Borough Labour News [194-?]. Hounslow; m

    B   3d. Labour Party. (Labour Party. **Your own Journal**, 1948.)

1394 Heston and Isleworth Citizen ns 1 (Feb. 1955)

    B   Published by the Co-operative Press.

    L(Col)

1395 Heston and Isleworth Clarion Edition of the Surrey and Middlesex Clarion 1 [19--?] —268 (July 1965); then **Hounslow Borough Clarion**; 269 (Aug. 1965)—279, (June 1966); then **Hounslow Clarion**: 280 (July 1966)— ; m

    B   Heston and Isleworth Labour Party. One of a number of local 'Clarion' papers.

    L(Col)† 166 (Dec. 1956)— (w 280); LabP† Nov. 1964—Dec. 1970*

1396 Hetherington's Twopenny Dispatch, and People's Police Register 1 [14 June 1834?] —118 (10 Sept. 1836); w

    B   2d. Published and printed by Henry Hetherington. Editor: Bronterre O'Brien. The 'successor to **'Destructive'** and Poor Man's **Conservative** and succeeded in September 1836 by the stamped **London Dispatch**. . . . One of the best known working-class newspapers of the decade. It agitates for universal suffrage, factory legislation, repeal of the Poor Law Amendment Act of 1834, and repeal of the stamp duty on newspapers' (Wiener).

    L(Col) 109, 112, 114—18; LSF 69; LabP archives 109 (cuttings)

Higher Education Bulletin see **Union and Higher Education**

Higher Education Report see: **Union and Higher Education**

1397 Highway: a Monthly Journal of Education for the People I, 1 (Oct. 1908)— ; m; Oct.—April, with 1 number each summer

    C   1d. etc. Published by the Workers' Educational Association. 'Announced its purpose to supply forum where those engaged in manual labour could discuss with professional teachers problems of education of concern to the worker' (Brophy). Articles on subjects of study, course outlines, relationship of the worker to the educational world, developing his education and his contribution to society. Absorbed the WEA **Students' Bulletin.**

    AbU IV— ; BP II—*; C XII—XIII*, XIV— ; E 1916—31; EU 1939— ; GM 1933—58*; GU XVI—*; L†; LBE 1930— ; LE; LU*; LUC III—X; LdP IV—XIII; LdU XVIII—?; O XII, 11, XIII, 4— ; SaU VII—*; SoU XXXVIII— ; SwU I—IX; Warwick UL XX—Xl*

1398 Highway 1 (May 1939)— . Glasgow; s-m

    A   Scottish Horse and Motormen's Association; Scottish Commercial Motormen's Union; Transport and General Workers' Union, Glasgow

    L 1964— ; A. Tuckett, c/o Mrs. I. Gladwell, 5 Liddington Street, Swindon, Wiltshire

1399 Highway and West Midlands WEA Torch Oct. 1932—59

    C   A local supplement inserted in **The Highway** (qv). Incorporated **West Midlands WEA Torch**

    BP†; BU 1932—39

1400 Hit Back I [1964? 1965?] —

    B   Newsletter of the Greater London Regional Council of the Labour Party.

    Greater London Labour Party

1401 Hitchin Leader [19--?] —? Hitchin

    B   Issued by Hitchin Labour Party.

    L(Col) Sept. 1951

1402 Hog's Wash, or a Salmagundy for Swine I, 1 (Sept. 1793)—I, 6 (2 Nov. 1793); then **Politics for the People, or, Hog's Wash**: I, 7 (9 Nov. 1793)—II, 30 (Jan 1795); w

    B   2d. Printed for D. I. Eaton. Title varies; Nos 2 to 5 are called simply **Hog's Wash**; No. 6 is called **Hog's Wash, or, Politics for the People**; from No. 10 the title is simply **Politics for the People**. The title-pages of the two volumes have the title: **Politics for the People, or, a Salmagundy for Swine**. (These details are taken from the set in the Bodleian Library, Oxford. It appears to be the first edition; but see letter from J. Kuczynski in the **Bulletin** of the Society for the Study of Labour History, No. 26, Spring 1973.)

    C I—II, 10; L I; 3rd ed. I; 4th ed. I; LU; LUC I—II, 9; MP I—II, 6; O†; Warwick UL (microfilm); Greenwood reprint and microfiche: microfiche distributed in Britain and Europe by the Harvester Press Ltd

Holborn Inn Brief see **No Name**

1403 Holborn Outlook I, 1 (May 1936)—VIII, 9 (Nov. 1941); m

    B   1d. Published by B. Bowling, then by Raymond Birt. A working-class paper presented from a broad socialist viewpoint. To voice the feelings and grievances of the workers in the Borough of Holborn. News and analysis of the organised Labour Movement. Advocates a Popular Front against Fascism. Contributors from the Communist Party and the Labour Party.

    L†; MML*†

1404 Holbrook Tribune I, 1 (March 1952)—? Coventry; bi-m

    B   Holbrook Ward Labour Party.

    Warwick U (MRC) I, 1—2.

1405 Holloway Bus Guide [19--?] —?

    B   Communist Party factory paper. (H. Wilde, 'The factory paper'. **Communist Review**, III, 4 [April 1931])

1406 Holybrook: the Magazine of the Holybrook Fellowship [of the Workers' Educational Association] I (1925)–? Reading
    C
    L (missing)

1407 Home: the Altar, the Throne and the Cottage I, 1 (3 May 1851)–VIII, 218 (30 June 1855); w
    B   1d.; 2d. Published by Wertheim and Macintosh. Editor: Richard Oastler. Contributors: Oastler, S. Kydd. In 1853 adopted as the official organ of the Labour League of Lancashire, Yorkshire and Cheshire. 'These papers are to be mainly addressed to the Working Classes of England, to that mind, which, having been accounted worthless, has been so grossly abused, bewildered, irritated, misled.' Proposes to 'explain to them the principles on which our Christian and Protestant Institutions are founded, and to trace the suffering of the poor, and the insecurity of the rich, to a departure from those principles'. Anti-Poor Law, anti-Popery, for home agriculture and manufacture, Ten-Hours' Bill. Pages open to various trades to discuss their conditions. Articles, addresses, verse, correspondence, extracts
    L I–III, 86; LU II, 36–61; LdU I, 1–20; O† I, 1–IV, 102 (9 April 1853); O(JJ)† VIII, 214 (2 June 1855)–216 (16 June) 218 (30 June)

1408 Home Front, 1940–41
    B   National Federation of Tenants' and Residents' Associations.
    MML

1409 Home Links: Quarterly Magazine 1 (Feb. 1898)–8 (Feb. 1900); q
    B   3d. Printer, publisher, editor: A. Gottschling. Christian Socialist. Prints Independent Labour Party notes, and news of other labour and socialist groups. Communistic ideals. Advocates public control of the necessities of life. From No. 2 sub-titled: 'the Ideal Magazine'. 'The official organ of the World's League of Brotherhoods and the English National Brotherhood.' (No. 8)
    L; O†

Home Magazine see **Wheatsheaf**

Home Review see **Co-operator, [19–?]–?**

1410 Home Service: Goddington Labour News I, 1 (Oct. 1947)–   Sept. 1949. Orpington; m
    B   Produced and published for Orpington Labour Party, Women's Section, and Goddington Ward Labour Party. Succeeded by **Orpington Labour News**. Reproduced from typewriting.
    L†

1411 Homme: Journal de la Démocratie Universelle. (Man: Journal of Universal Democracy). I, 1 (30 Nov. 1853—III, 132 (23 Aug. 1856)). Saint-Hélier; London (17 Nov. 1855)—   ; w

     B   3d. Editor: Charles Ribeyrolles, ex-editor of **Réforme**. Advocated political democracy, the principles of 1848, Liberty, Equality, Fraternity. Also social democratic. Supports international and national liberation movements; linked with the English republicans and democrats. Contributors: Louis Blanc, Herzen, Victor Hugo.

     L(Col)†

1412 Hone's Reformists' Register and Weekly Commentary I, 1 (1 Feb 1817)—II, 14 (25 Oct. 1817); w

     B   2d. Published by William Hone. Printed by Hay and Turner. Advocates radical reform; agitates for parliamentary reform, suspension of Habeas Corpus etc. Reports reform agitation proceedings in the House of Commons and carries reports and analyses of out-of-doors agitation. Preceded by **Hone's Weekly Commentary**; 1, (18 Jan.)—   2, (25 Jan.) 1817 Title-page of bound volume gives title as: **Reformists' Register and Weekly Commentary**

     GM; L; MP; NpP I; O; ONC†

1413 Hope Mill Strike Bulletin 1 (20 Jan. 1933)—18 (18 May 1934). Haslingdon

     A   Printed and published by the Hope Mill Strike Committee. Reproduced from typewriting.

     WCML† (w 17)

1414 Horizon [19--?] —?; m

     A   1s. National League of the Blind. In Braille. (R. B. Suthers, One of a series of articles on unions.) **Labour Magazine** (April 1933).

1415 Hornchurch Labour News I, 1 (July 1959)—?

     B   Hornchurch Constituency Labour Party.

     London County Record Office (A/HHL/4) I, 1

1416 Hornsey Herald: the Local Voice of Labour 1, [195-?] —127 (June/July 1965); then **Hornsey Herald and Haringey Clarion**: 128 (Sept. 1965)—133 (May 1968); m

     B   Free. Published by Hornsey Labour Party. One of the 'Citizen' papers. Sometime title: **Hornsey Herald and Citizen**.

     L(Col)† 93 (Oct. 1960)—133; LabP† 88 (March 1960)—132 (March 1967*)

Hornsey Herald & Citizen see **Hornsey Herald**

Hornsey Herald and Haringey Clarion see **Hornsey Herald**

1417 Hornsey Star 1, [1925?]–?

    A   ½d. Printed and published by the Railway Communist Group. Organ of the Railway Communist Group, Communist Party of Great Britain, Hornsey Group. Reproduced from typewriting.

    O(JJ)† 23 (12 June 1926), 24, 25, 30, 39, (21 Jan. 1927)

1418 Horsham Future [194-?]. Horsham; m

    B   Labour Party. Duplicated. (Labour Party. **Your own Journal**, 1948.)

Horticultural Worker see **British Gardeners' Association Journal**

1419 Hospital: the Journal of the Inter-Hospital Socialist Society I, 1 (March 1935)–III, 4 (Nov. 1937); then **Medical Student Opinion**: IV, 1 (Lent Term, 1938)–IV, 3 (Christmas Term, 1938); m; termly

    A   3d. Published by the Inter-Hospital Socialist Council at the offices of the University Labour Federation, to which the Society was affiliated. Vol. III, Nos 3–4 published by the Inter-Hospital Socialist Council, 'representing the interests of Progressive doctors, nurses, students and all other workers in Medicine'. Urges the need for practical socialist policies for the Health Service, and encourages the organisation of strong socialist groups in hospitals and colleges. Vol. I–Vol. II, No. 4 reproduced from typewriting.

    L† III–

1420 Houghton Clarion 1 [1961?]–? Houghton-le-Spring

    B   Published and edited for the local Labour Party by Donald Cockburn. Newspaper, with national and local affairs. No. 2 was a special local election issue.

    LabP† 2, May 1961

Hounslow Borough Clarion see **Heston and Isleworth Clarion**

Hounslow Clarion see **Heston and Isleworth Clarion**

1421 House and Home: a Journal of Social and Sanitary Information for the People I, 1 (25 Jan 1879)–V, 145 (29 Sept. 1882); w

    C   1d. Published and edited by John Pearce. For all measures which would improve the condition of the masses, eg, improved dwellings, building societies, improved sanitation and diet, temperance, provident habits.

    L†

1422 Housecraft: the Official Magazine of the Association of Teachers of Domestic Science I, 1 (Jan. 1928)–   ; m

    A   6d. For the protection of professional standards

    L†; LIE XXIII (1950)–XXVIII (1955); O XXXI (1958)–

1423 Househillwood Round-About [194-?]. Nitshill, Scotland
    B   3d. Labour Party. (Labour Party. **Your own Journal,** 1948.)

1424 Housing Journal: Organ of the Workmen's National Housing Council
1 (Aug. 1900)–126 (Sept. 1929); m; irreg
    B   1d. etc. Later, organ of the Labour Housing Association
(1918–   ), the National Labour Housing Association and Federation of
Tenants' Leagues (1922–   ); Labour Housing Association (1929–   ).
Editors: Fred Knee; J. Sylas Whybrew; C. E. Longley. For State aid for
municipal housing and fair rents courts, and then for improvement on
progress already made
    L(Col); LE*; LabP*

1425 Howitt's Journal of Literature and Popular Progress I, 1 (2 Jan.
1847)–III, 78 (24 June 1948); w
    C   1½d. Vols I–II published by William Lovett, printed by Richard
Clay; Vol. III printed and published by Lovett. Editors: William and Mary
Howitt. A 'Weekly Record of Facts and Opinions Connected with General
Interests and Popular Progress'. Claims to support rights and enjoyments
of the labouring classes, but not exclusively. Articles, poetry, book
reviews, illustrations, notes on Mechanics' Institutes, meetings of trade
unions, co-operative organisations. Main contributors: William and Mary
Howitt. Then incorporated in **The People's Journal**.
    BP†; BiP; BkP; C; CSJ; I; D; EP; Eu; L I–II; LdP I; MP; O I–II

**1426 Hucknall, Bulwell and District Monthly Illustrated Labour Journal:
A Local Magazine of Useful Information and Instruction.** 1, [189-] –?
then **Hucknall Torkard and District Monthly Illustrated Labour Journal:
A Local Magazine of Useful Information and Instruction.** n.s. 2, Nov.
1890–11, Aug. 1891. Hucknall, Notts; m
    B   Printed and published by William Mellors: Each issue contains
two pages of local material, the rest consisting of fiction and general
articles quite unrelated in nature, possibly printed from stereotypes of a
popular magazine. The covers are filled with local advertisements.
    NU† 2, Nov. 1890, 6–16, March 1891–Jan. 1892, 21, June 1892

1427 Huddersfield Citizen [1926?] –[1965?]. Huddersfield; m
    B   1d. etc. Huddersfield Labour Party.
    Huddersfield Labour Party (w occ. nos); L(Col) 38 (Jan. 1935)–64
(April 1965*); LabP 1961–64*

1428 Huddersfield Co-operative Citizen 1 (Sept. 1952)–? Huddersfield
    B   Published by Huddersfield and District Co-operative Society.
    L(Col)

Huddersfield Worker see **Worker, 1905–1922**

1429 Hull Co-operative Citizen 1 (May 1932)–3 (July 1932); [ns] 1
(March 1934)–(Aug. 1936) Hull; m
    B
    L(Col)

1430 Hull Portfolio; or, Memoirs and Correspondence of an Editor I, 1 (20 Aug. 1831)–IV, 26 (15 June 1834). Hull; w; s-w

    B   2d. Vol. I, Nos. 1–6 printed and published by Joseph Noble, Secretary of Hull Political Union, then the sole proprietor and editor was James Acland, President of the Union. The voice of Radicalism in Hull; the People versus borough corruption. Includes much correspondence. Victimised by the boroughmongers for a time; Acland edited the journal from prison.

    HU; L† (w I, 4); LdP I–III, 13; ONC I, 1–22

1431 Hull Sentinel I, 1 (14 Jan. 1928)–1402 (Jan. 1963). Hull; w (1–3); m

    A   1d.; 3d. Sponsoring body: Hull and District Trades Council. Workers' press, trade unions, political. The first three numbers were entitled **The Hull Weekly Sentinel**.

    HP*†; L(Col) 34 (July 1930)–1402; LabP† 1960–1*

1432 Hull Trades Council. Labour Journal. Nov. 1893–? Hull; m

    A   1d. Later called **Monthly Labour Journal**. Support for Independent Labour Party. Includes articles on Labour politics, women's corner.

    L(Col)† 121 (Jan. 1904)–293 (May 1918) (w 1912)

Hull Trades Council. **Monthly Labour Journal** see Hull Trades Council. **Labour Journal**

Hull Weekly Sentinel see **Hull Sentinel**

1433 Hull Workmen's Times 1 (6 June 1890)–17 (26 Sept. 1890). Hull; w

    A   1d. Published for the proprietor by Joseph Burgess. Local edition of **Workmen's Times** for Hull and district Labour and Trade Union Movement. Written 'by workers for workers'.

    HP (13 June 1890); L(Col)†

1434 Humanity: Devoted to the Emancipation of the Sweated Female Worker I, 1 (May 1913)–II, 4 (Aug. 1914); m

    C   1d. Printed and published by W. Cave and Company for the British Federation for the Emancipation of Sweated Women. 'Official organ of the British Federation for the Emancipation of Sweated Women and Girls.' Philanthropic, under the patronage of Alice, Countess of Stafford and others. Founded by W. Belcher; President: Dr Beale Collins. To furnish funds for the training and rehabilitation schemes for 'broken' and 'fallen' women sweaters, as well as urging the legislature to end the sweating system.

    L†

1435 Humanity 1 (Oct. 1932)–?

    B   Issued by Helen Allan for the Women's International Matteotti Committee, Honorary Secretary: Sylvia Pankhurst. To free Matteotti's wife and children from persecution

    L(Col)† 1

1436 Humber Clarion [1948?]–[1950?]. Coventry; irreg?

   A   Shop stewards' paper at the Humber car works, Coventry.
   TUC Jan./March 1949–Feb. 1950

1437 Humberside Transport Workers' Gazette and Monthly Record 1 (Jan. 1912)–18 (June 1913). Hull; m

   A   ½d. Printed, published and edited by J. Little, 'to record the activities of the different Transport Workers' organizations and of the Labour members in Parliament' and in local municipal politics. The National Union of Dock Labourers is prominent, and the Transport Workers Union. Contributor: James Sexton, dockers' leader. 'Circulated 10,000 in Hull, Wakefield, Selby, Driffield, Beverley, Grimsby, Goole and East Coast Ports.'
   L(Col)†

1438 Humberside Voice I, 1 (Dec. 1964)–V, 1 (Dec. 1968); m

   B   6d. Published by Workers' Northern Publishing Society, Ltd. Editorial addresses in Hull. For the Labour movement.
   HU† I, 5–V, 1*; HP† I, 1–III, 9 (Aug. 1967)

Hunslet Pioneer see **Pioneer 1895**

1439 Huyton and Kirby Voice [c1965]. Manchester; m

   B   4d. Workers' Northern Publishing Society Ltd. Edited by Arthur Smith. (Mitchell, 1965.)

1440 Hyde Park: Organ of the Hyde Park Movement, London, Federated to the United Socialist Movement, Glasgow I, 1 (Sept. 1938)–?; m

   B   1d. Edited and published by Guy Aldred. For the campaign for unrestricted right to free assembly in Hyde Park, 'to secure the right to circulate the printed word as well as proclaim the spoken word'. Anarchist standpoint. Critical of the Communist Party, and of W. Gallacher in particular.
   L† 1

1441 Hyde Park Socialist [1969?]–   ; q

   B   2½p. etc. Published by J. Hughes. Articles, notes. Reproduced from typewriting.
   ONC† 11 (Spring 1971)–   ; (The Left in Britain– microfilm–Harvester Press Ltd)

ICA Co-operative News Service see International Co-operative Alliance. **Co-operative News Service**

1442 ICWPA: the Information Bulletin of the British Section, International Class War Prisoners' Aid I, 1 ([Nov.?], 1926)–? irreg?

   B   'For distribution among the district & local committees and affiliated bodies etc.' Information on the campaign here and abroad. Reproduced from typewriting.
   O(JJ)† I, 17 (3 Nov. 1927); TUC occ. nos 1926–8

1443 ILGOU Forum 1970–1 Dublin; s-a
    A   Irish Local Government Officials' Union.
    University College, Dublin

1444 ILP Advance 1 (Jan. 1910)–?; m
    B   Independent Labour Party.
    ILP 1

ILP and Socialist Year Book see **ILP Year Book**

1445 ILP Chronicle 1 (Jan. 1923)–?; m
    B   Independent Labour Party Head Office. Editor: A. Fenner
Brockway.
    ILP Jan., June–Aug. 1923

1446 ILP Gazette 1 (July 1894)–? Manchester; m
    B   Free. Printed and published for the proprietors (Gorton
Independent Labour Party) by the Labour Press Society.
    O(JJ) 5 (Nov. 1894). (D. Hopkin)

1447 ILP Journal 1 (7 Jan. 1894)–(1 April 1898); then **Keighley Labour
Journal**: (8 April 1898)–(Dec. 1902). Keighley; w (winter only until April
1896); m (1901–)
    B   Gratis. ½d. Published by Keighley Labour Union; then by
Thomas Mackley for the Union. Sub-title from 29 Sept. 1895: 'Organ of
the Keighley Labour Union., from March 1900: Organ of Municipal and
Social Reform. Editors: G. J. Wardle; Philip Snowden; Thomas Machley.
    AbU (microfilm of Keighley PL holding); Keighley PL*

1448 ILP May Day Garland: Arranged by J. Keir Hardie; the Herald of the
Socialist Daily. 1 May 1911. Manchester
    B   ½d. Printed and published by the National Labour Press. A May
Day special, anticipating the time when the **Labour Leader** be transformed
into the daily paper of the working class.
    O(JJ)†

1449 ILP News: Monthly Official Circular to the Branches I, 1 (April
1897)–VII, 81 (Dec. 1903); m
    B   1d. Issued by the National Administrative Council of the
Independent Labour Party. Printed by Twentieth Century Press (1–7)
then by Labour.Press, Ltd., Manchester. Editors: Tom Mann; Francis
Johnson.
    L(Col)†; LE*; MR I–V; ONC occ. nos; TUC, John Burns Lib.;
Warwick UL (microfilm)

1450 ILP Year Book. 1908—10; then **ILP and Socialist Year Book**: 1911; then **Socialist Year Book**: a Guide Book to the Socialist and Labour Movement at Home and Abroad: 1912—13; London; Manchester; a
    B   1d. etc. Published by the Independent Labour Party, then printed and published by the National Labour Press. Edited by J. Bruce Glasier (1911—13).
    E 1913; L 1913; LE†; O 1913; ONC 1908. 1913

1451 ILPer: the Monthly Record of the Liverpool Branch of the Independent Labour Party 1 (Jan. 1904)—? Liverpool; m
    B   Notes of meetings, finances etc.
    AbU 2 (Feb. 1904 [microfilm]); O(JJ)† 2 (Feb. 1904)

1452 IRIS News I, 1 (Sept. 1956)— ; bi-m; m (May 1959—)
    C   4d.; 3d. etc. Industrial Research and Information Services, Ltd. Directors have included: Jack Tanner, William McLaine, Charles R. Sonnex. Industrial and trade-union news. To oppose Communist infiltration in trade unions. Absorbed **Iris Fact Service**. Has supplement **IRIS News Survey**.
    L; ONC†; TUC

1453 ITF Documentation 1 [1967?]—?; q
    A   International Transport [Workers?] Federation. Reproduced from typewriting. Deals with legislation and collective bargaining affecting transport workers.
    TUC† 2 (July 1967)

1454 ITF Newsletter 1 (7 Jan. 1965)— ; fortn
    A   International Transport Workers' Federation. 'News and information about activities and achievements of the ITF and its affiliates, about wage movements, industrial disputes, legislation etc. affecting the life and work of transport workers and their unions.' Reproduced from typewriting.
    E†

1455 Idisher Traid-Yunionist [Jewish Trade Unionist] 1 (15 Jan. 1892)—4 (5 Feb. 1892). London; fortn
    A   Yiddish.
    L(Col)†

Iris, or the Sheffield Advertiser see **Sheffield Register**

1456 Idris Ginger: the Paper of the Idris Workers [192-?]—?; irreg?
    A   ½d. Published by the Idris Communist Group. Factory paper. Reproduced from typewriting.
    O(JJ)† 19 (May 1926), 2 issues dated Aug. 1926, (1 Oct. 1926), new vol., 2 (26 Nov. 1926)

1457 Ilford and Beacontree Argus [19--?] –? Ilford; w

B   1d. Labour. Contains local news and advertisements. Published by W. L. Gladwell. (Mitchell, 1925.)

1458 Ilford Citizen 1 (Jan. 1931)–102 (Sept. 1939); m

B   Gratis. Published by the London Co-operative Society.

L(Col)

1459 Ilford South Democrat [194-?]. Ilford; m

B   Free. Labour Party. (Labour Party. **Your own Journal**, 1948.)

1460 Ilkeston Division Labour Monthly 1 (Sept. 1924)–; Ripley; irreg

B   Labour Party. (Labour and Socialist International. **The Socialist Press**, 1933.)

Ilkeston PL 1, 2 (28 March 1925)

1461 Ilkley Monthly Letter [194-?]. Ilkley; m

B   Labour Party. Duplicated. (Labour Party. **Your own Journal**, 1948.)

1462 Illustrated Weekly News 1 (21 Sept. 1889)–14 (21 Dec. 1889); w

B   1d. Published for the proprietors by the Tower Publishing Company. Printed by W. Burgess. A packed popular newspaper with a large section of Labour and trade-union news, two or three pages in each number. Supported the Dock Strike and the burst of new Unionism which followed, eg, postmen, bakers, tram men, chairmakers etc. Correspondence, contributions by wage earners. Reports and analysis of contemporary labour movements in London and the provinces. Support for the Labour Electoral Association. Contributors: J. L. Mahon, Cunninghame Graham.

L(Col)†

1463 Imp 1967?–   . Leicester

A   National and Local Government Officers' Association, Leicestershire Branch. Reproduced from typewriting. Reports of branch executive meetings.

L 1967–

1464 Impact: a Journal of Labour Opinion 1 (Feb. 1951)–5 (June 1951) Dublin; m

B   6d. Published by Freeman Publications. Voice of the Irish Labour Party and trade union movement.

CoU; D; L†

1465 Impact 1964?–. Doncaster

A   National and Local Government Officers' Association. Doncaster and District Branch.

L July 1964–

1466 Impact: the Magazine of the Leicestershire Branch of the National and Local Government Officers' Association I, 1 (Dec. 1966)– Leicester; irreg?

    A   Reproduced from typewriting.

    L I, 1–II, 3 (Dec. 1967), III, 2 (May–3), (Aug. 1968), V, 1 (Sept. 1969)

1467 Impact: Maidstone Branch Magazine 1967?–   . Maidstone

    A   National and Local Government Officers' Association, Maidstone Branch. Reproduced from typewriting.

    L 1967–

1468 In and Out: Official Journal of the Ealing Branch of NALGO [193-?] – [1958?]. Ealing; m

    A   National Association of Local Government Officers, later National and Local Government Officers' Association.

    L† XVI, 7 (July 1954)–XX, 9 (Dec. 1958)

1469 In Print: the Official Journal of the Birkenhead Branch of the NALGO I, 1 (April 1939)–I, 11 (May 1940). Birkenhead; m

    A   National Association of Local Government Officers.

    BkP

1470 Incendiary: ARP Workers' Bulletin in ARP Bangor Wharf Section of the T&GWU 1 [1940] –II, 1 (Feb. 1942); irreg

    A   1d. Issued by members of the Transport and General Workers' Union at Bangor Wharf Depot. A journal of organised Air Raid Protection workers. Later journal of St Pancras ARP workers, then of Hampstead, Finsbury and St Pancras ARP workers. Founded by Paul Williams. Reproduced from typewriting.

    L†

1471 Incorporated Association of Clerks and Stewards of Mental Hospitals. **Journal** [1933?] –?; q

    A   Intended for private circulation only.

    TUC† June, Sept. 1934

1472 Independent [1865?] Ashton-under-Lyne?

    A   'The **Co-operator** for August 15th, 1865, records still another attempt to establish a co-operative society to undertake printing and publishing. This attempt was made at Ashton-under-Lyne, and a prospectus was issued headed "Ashton-under-Lyne and Stalybridge Co-operative Newspaper and General Printing Company Limited". The capital was to be £1,500 in shares of £1 each. A paper, to be named the **Independent**, was to be published, and, in regard to matters political and theological, was to be strictly neutral. Whether the company ever reached the stage of registration or ever undertook business of any kind we do not know, as the available publications contain no further reference to it.' (F. Hall, **The History of the Co-operative Printing Society, Ltd., 1869–1919**, Manchester 1919, p. 32).

1473 Independent 1 (26 June 1915)–14 (25 Sept. 1915); w

A 1d. Editor: F. D. 'Designed for the service of a special class of the community.' Addressed to the three million trade unionists to encourage the war effort in response to the appeal of the Ministry of Munitions. To present to trade unionists week by week the views of their official leaders. The main feature is the contribution by the official leaders, including Brownlie (engineers), Bromley (Locomotive Union), Hodge, MP (steelmen), Clynes (gasworkers), Thomas (railwaymen). Also trade-union news from the regions.

L(Col)†; ONC 1–4

1474 Independent Labour Party. Monthly Report 1 (March 1896)–?; m

B Free. Edited by Tom Mann. Notes from chief office to branches and unattached members. (**Labour Annual**, 1897.)

1475 Independent Labour Party. Information Committee. Monthly Notes for Speakers 1 ([March?] 1923)–?; m

B Facts and figures on a variety of topics.

LabP† 3 (June 1923)–32 (July/Oct. 1926); ONC† 1923–4*

1476 Independent Labour Party. Information Committee. Weekly Notes for Speakers [1919?]–?; w

B Facts and figures on a variety of topics.

LabP† 32 (20 Nov. 1919)–499 (21 Feb. 1929); ONC† occ. nos 1923–7

Independent Labour Party Platform see **Platform**

1477 Indian Socialist [195-?]–?; m

B Organ of the Indian Socialist Group, Great Britain. Reproduced from typewriting.

TUC† II, 1 (Nov. 1956)–3 (Jan. 1957)

1478 Indicator [c1926]

A ½d. 'Issued by the London Bridge and New Cross Communist Railwaymen.' 'We make an overdue re-appearance' (14 June 1926); production previously halted by confiscation of apparatus. Asks readers to join Communist Party, help miners, change leadership. Reproduced from typewriting.

O(JJ)† 14, June 1926

1479 Industrial Magazine and Trades' and Co-operative Record I,1 (Jan. 1862)

B 6d. Printed and published by J. Kenny. Ambition to 'make the Magazine a complete and able representative of the largest class in society'. Presents all questions affecting working-men and their organisations. Argues the workmen's case. Believes capital and labour can be brought harmoniously together but asserts the right of working-men to organise in trade unions and to form co-operative associations. Contributors: T. J. Dunning, Thomas Hughes.

LU†

1480 Industrial Magazine of the Scottish Patriotic Society for Improving the Condition of the Labouring Classes I, 1 (March 1847)–? Edinburgh; m; q

C   3d. 'By the publication of useful intelligence and hints, to point the way, and to stimulate the working classes to self-respect and self-support'. Also to provide a medium of communication among members of the philanthropic Royal Patriotic Society. The Society was established in 1846 'with the view of diminishing and preventing destitution and crime', and to inculcate self-improvement habits and 'industrial economy'. Concern about the Highland problem; discusses emigration schemes, home colonisation etc.

E*†; L† II (Oct./Dec. 1848), III, 1 (Jan. 1851)

1481 Industrial News, for the Use of the Press 1 (6 July 1926)–   ; w; irreg

A   Issued by the Trades Union Congress. Reproduced from typewriting. Not published continuously since 1926? First three numbers entitled **Industrial News Service**.

L† 1–365 (19 Sept. 1933); 1 (5 Jan. 1962)–   ; ONC (11 Jan. 1968)–   ; TUC (5 Jan. 1962)–

1482 Industrial News, for the Use of the Press. TUC Incomes Policy Bulletin 1 (May 1967)–31 (Feb. 1970); m

A   Issued by the Trades Union Congress in the same format as **Industrial News**.

ONC†; TUC

Industrial News Service see **Industrial News, for the Use of the Press**

1483 Industrial Newsletter for Women 1 (June 1938)–(Jan. 1962); m; irreg

A   Issued by the Trades Union Congress. Reproduced from typewriting.

TUC*†

Industrial Participation see **Labour Co-partnership**

1484 Industrial Partnerships' Record 1 (March 1867)–12 (1 Feb. 1868); then **Social Economist, Industrial Partnerships' Record and Co-operative Review**: ns II, 13 (1 March 1869)–III, 31 (Sept. 1869). London; Manchester; m

C   2d. Publishers: E. Pitman, London, Joun and Abel Heywood, and E. Greening, Manchester. Owned by Edward Owen Greening. To promote the principle that co-operation between employers and employed, captialists and labourers, is an actual, practical, business – profitable to all concerned because just to all. Details of existing co-partnership ventures and profit-sharing. Important correspondence. 'While Pitman's **Co-operator** appeals more particularly to the intelligent working classes, we appeal to the middle and upper, and commercial classes generally.'

L I–II, 19; LU†; MP

1485 Industrial Review I, 1 (Jan. 1927)–VII, 8 (Aug. 1933); m

    A   2d. Issued by the Trades Union Congress General Council. Declared its main purpose 'to provide a channel of communication between the General Council and the trade unions, and to continue the policy of closer co-operation with the local Trades Councils'. An information bulletin specially designed for active trade unionists and officials. Then merged in **Labour.**

    L†; LE I, 4–III, 6*; TUC

Industrial Review, Social and Political see **Bee Hive**

1486 Industrial Syndicalist I, 1 (July 1910)–I, 11 (May 1911); m

    B   1d. Published by Guy Bowman. Edited by Tom Mann. 'Series of pamphlets advocating economic organization as chief means of obtaining better conditions, but not opposed to using political methods as well; advocated abolition of wage system. Superseded by the **Syndicalist**' (Brophy).

    LE; ONC† –(w8)

1487 Industrial Unionist: Official Organ of the British Advocates of Industrial Unionism 1 (March 1908)–14 (June 1909). Manchester; m

    A   1d. Printed for the British Advocates of Industrial Unionism, later for the Industrial Workers of Great Britain. Syndicalist.

    CPGB; L(Col)†; O; Warwick UL (microfilm)

1488 Industrial Worker I, 1 (Nov. 1913)–III, 1 (Oct. 1917); m

    B   1d. Printed and published by the British Section of Industrial Workers of the World. Organ of the movement in Britain for revolutionary industrial Unionism.

    L(Col)† I, 1–I, 9 (Aug. 1914), II, 1 (July 1916)–III, 5 (Nov. 1916), II, 1

1489 Industrial World: the Official Organ of the South Wales, Monmouthshire, and Gloucestershire Tinplate Workers' Union I, 1 (8 Jan. 1892)–VII, 360 (14 Oct. 1898). Swansea; w

    A   1d. Published by John Hopkin John. Preceded by **Welsh Industrial Times**. Published also in a daily edition, February–June 1897. In Welsh and English.

    L(Col)† (w 1893); SwU

1490 Industrialist [1908?] – ?; m

    B   1d. Organ of the Industrial League, which was founded in 1908 by dissident members of the Socialist Labour Party opposed to political activity (**Reformers' Year Book**, 1909).

1491 Inklings: the Journal of the Salford Branch of the National and Local Government Officers Association I, (1952)–?; Salford; m?

    A   Reproduced from typewriting.

    L II, 3 (March 1953)–IV, 1 (April 1955).

1492 Insight: the Labour Magazine 1−2. 1924. Aberdeen

    B   Aberdeen University Labour Club.

    AU (not traced)

1493 Institute: an Illustrated Weekly Journal of the Arts and Sciences, and a Record of Literary, Scientific and Mechanics Institutions 1, (14 Dec. 1844)−9 (8 Feb. 1845); w

    C   3d. (stamped 4d.) Object 'to furnish accurate reports of the most important lectures on Literature, Science and the Fine Arts, which are delivered in the metropolitan and provincial institutions', etc., 'and diffuse this knowledge generally among the mass of the population'. Then merged in **The Apprentice**.

    L(Col)†

1494 Institute, and Lecturers' Gazette I, 1 (1 Oct. 1861)−XXIX, 338 (2 Dec. 1889). Newport Pagnell; m

    C   2d. Printed and published by Joseph Simpson. Aims, as a medium of communication between the Institutions and lecturers, to win the attention of those societies which have for their object the advancement of literature, science, art, and education of every form. Reports from Mechanics' Institutes and Mutual Improvement Associations. Chiefly for lecturers and members of the Lecturers' Association.

    L(Col)† I−VI, 70, VIII, 85−XXIX, 338

1495 Institute for Workers' Control. **Bulletin** I, 1 (1968)−   . Nottingham; q

    B   Edited by Ken Coates, then by Tony Topham. Reports, articles, discussion, reviews.

    O; ONC†; Warwick UL 1969−

1496 Institute for Workers' Control. **Monthly Digest** 1 [Aug.? 1968]−15 (Oct. 1969). Nottingham; m

    B   Reproduced from typewriting.

    ONC† 8 (March)−15 (Oct. 1969)

1497 Institute Journal: the Official Organ of the Institute of Journalists I, 1 (Nov. 1912)−XII, 7 (Dec. 1924); then Institute of Journalists. **Journal**: XIII, 110 (Jan./Feb. 1925)−L, 492 (July/Aug. 1962); then **Journal**: L, 493 (Sept./Oct. 1962)−LI, 502 (Dec. 1963); ns 1 (Jan. 1964)−12 (Oct./Dec. 1966); m; q

    A   3d. etc. Records the work of the Institute, which meets the needs of the working members of the profession. News of branches, copyright and libel cases. Preceded by the Institute's **Proceedings**.

    C XVIII−   ; L(Col)†; LE II, 7−   ; LSF VII−VIII, 3, XVII, 148−XXX, 289; LdU XIV, 116−   ; O XVIII, 160; the Institute

Institute of Journalists. Journal see **Institute Journal**

1498 Institution of Professional Civil Servants Air Ministry Engineering
Branch. **Bulletin** [19--?] –
    A
    L ser. 2, 1 (Aug. 1962)–

1499 Air Ministry Professional Staff Branch. **Newsletter** [19--?] –
    A
    L 40 (Feb. 1960)–(w 41, 44)

1500 Air Ministry Works Technical Staffs Branch 1 [195-?] –? Harlow; q?
    A
    L 5 (March 1960)–19 (Oct. 1963) (w 15)

1501 Meteorological Office Branch. **Bulletin** 1 [1955?] –. Dunstable; m
    A
    L 61, Jan; 63, (March 1960)–

1502 Ministry of Works Branch. **Bulletin** 1 (Jan. 1953?)–. Eastbourne; m
    A
    L 2 (Feb. 1953)–

1503 Scottish Branch. **Bulletin** 1960–. Edinburgh
    A
    L

1504 Institution of Professional Civil Servants. War Office Branch.
Singapore Group. **Bulletin** 1 (June 1956)–? Singapore
    A
    L†

1505 Institutional Advocate: a Monthly Record of the Proceedings of
London and Provincial Literary, Scientific and Mechanics' Institutions 1
(Jan. 1845)–3 (March 1845); m
    A   4d. (stamped 5d) Edited by members of London Institutions;
'non-party, non-political'.
    L(Col)†

Insuppressible, William O'Brien's Paper see **Suppressed** United Ireland

1506 Insurance Guild Journal I, 1 (Jan. 1920)–(July 1963); then **Cover
Note**: (Aug. 1963)–?; m
    A   3d.; free to members; 6d. Official organ of the Guild of
Insurance Officials, a national organisation formed for collective
bargaining purposes under Whitleyism. Changed to newspaper format with
Cover Note 'to give a wider, fuller coverage to the expanding activities of
the union throughout the country'.
    E (Aug. 1963)–; L†; LCI*; NU 1963–; TUC (July 1922)–

1507 Intercom 1 (Jan. 1966)–? Oxford; termly
    B   1s. Oxford University Communist Club (Comclub). Reproduced from typewriting. Discussion articles.
    LE† 1

Intercom see national Association of Local Government Officers. Sunderland Branch. **Newsletter**

1508 Interest: News Sheet of the Hyde Branch of NALGO. I, 1 (Dec. 1953)–? Hyde; m
    A   National and Local Government Officers' Association. Reproduced from typewriting. Not published between Jan. 1956 and Feb. 1959.
    L† I, 1–II, 8 (July 1955), IV, 1 (Feb. 1959)–IV, 4 (May/June 1959)

1509 Inter-links 1 (Aug. 1961)–? Lincoln
    A   National and Local Government Officers' Association, Lindsey County Council Branch. Reproduced from typewriting.
    L 1–9 (April 1962)

1510 InterNALGOssip: Journal of the East Ham Branch of Nalgo. East Ham
    A   National and Local Government Officers' Association. From April 1964 published by the Newham Branch. Reproduced from typewriting.
    L 1963– .

1511 International: the Organ of the Left Wing of the ILP 1 (10 June 1920)–[1921?]. Glasgow; fortn
    B   1d. Published for the Left Wing of the Independent Labour Party by H. C. Glass. To win the ILP over to the Third International.
    TUC† 1–8 (25 Sept. 1920)

1512 International Anarchism I, 1 (1 May 1969). Lund, Yorks; m
    B   Printed and published by C. Beadle. Reproduced from typewriting.
    E†

1513 International Book Review 1–2 (Nov. 1938)–3–4 June 1939); irreg
    B   Marx Memorial Library and Workers' School. A review and catalogue of works on Marxist philosophy and the international working-class movement.
    BP 1–2; L†

1514 International Bulletin of Metal and Engineering Workers 1952—55?; then **International Bulletin of Workers in the Metal and Engineering Industries**: Jan. 1957?—?; s-a; irreg?

    A   6d. World Federation of Trade Unions. Published by WFTU Publications. News of metal workers' activities all over the world, with reports of conferences, and articles.

    C; O 1952—5; L 1952—5 (Jan.1957)

1515 International Bulletin of Workers' Education I, 1 (Spring 1951)—? q

    B   Published by the International Federation of Workers' Educational Associations. Reproduced from typewriting. Superseded by **Teachers of the World**, World Federation of Teachers' Unions, World Federation of Trade Unions, published from Prague.

    TUC† 1—32 (Winter 1967—8*)

International Bulletin of Workers in the Metal and Engineering Industries see **International Bulletin of Metal and Engineering Workers**

1516 International Committee of the Propaganda and Action of Revolutionary Metal Workers. **Bulletin** [192-?] —? Moscow; irreg?

    A   Some discussion of British affairs. No. 8/9 is a special number for the Fifth International Conference of the Revolutionary Metal Workers. Reproduced from typewriting.

    ONC† 8/9 (May 1930), 13 (1 Aug. 1930)

1517 International Co-operative Alliance. **Co-operative News Service** 1929—; fortn?; m

    A   Subs. £1 pa (1974). Started for the purpose of distributing news, rapid information and reliable documentation on co-operative events throughout the world. Also keeps its readers informed about the work of the ICA, its auxiliary committees and working parties. Reproduced from typewriting. Present title: **ICA Co-operative News Service**.

    L 1974—; TUC May 1956—Nov. 1960*; the Alliance 1941—*

1518 International Co-operative Bulletin I, 1 (Jan. 1908)—XXI, 3 (March 1928); then **Review of International Co-operation**: Official Organ: XXI, 4 (April 1928)— m; bi-m

    A   4d. Published by the International Co-operative Alliance. News of the Co-operative Movements in all countries. Editors: Hans Muller; H. J. May. Also French and German editions;

    L† III, (Jan. 1910)— ; LE II—V, VI*— ; LII Dec. 1930— ; LU 1909—XVI, 5; IV—XXX*; OAC XXI, 4—; the Alliance

1519 International Courier 1 (Nov. 1864)–29 (July 1867); m; w

B   4d.; 2d; 1d. Originally a monthly magazine which sought to promote international co-operation with free trade and anti-war and anti-militarist sentiments, above all to unite Britain and France in an 'everlasting alliance'. Comes within our categories when, in Dec. 1866, it becomes a penny weekly, published by Joseph Collet, a Central Council member of the First International whose meetings are reported in the paper. Printed at International Co-operative Printing Office. Also entitled **Courrier International**.

L(Col)† 1–21

1520 [International Federation of Trade Unions.] **Boletin de la Federacion Sindical International** [1942?] –? London; fortn

A   Trade union news from many countries. Published from Transport House. In Spanish. Reproduced from typewriting.

L† 18 (15 Sept. 1942)–(July 1945*)

1521 International Federation of Unions of Employees in Public and Civil Services. **Bulletin** [1946?47] –   . Paris; Berlin etc.; London; irreg

A   Reproduced from typewriting.

TUC† 3 (April 1947)–

1522 International Free Trade Union Movement. **Yearbook** 1957/8–?; a

A   Published by Lincolns-Prager International Yearbook Publishing Company. Provides historical and current information on the International Confederation of Free Trade Unions, its affiliates and secretariats.

E† 1957/8–1961/2

1523 International Herald 1 (2 March 1872)–[1874?]; then **Republican Herald**: [1874?]; then **Herald and Helpmate**: [1874] –ns 18 (April 1875); fortn; w

B   1d.; 2d. First edited and published by W. Harrison Riley. Objects included universal suffrage, nationalisation of land etc., currency reform and liquidation of the National Debt. Riley hoped to make his journal 'the special organ of such societies as are not specially represented by the **Beehive** or the **National Reformer**'. Gave special notice to the International Working Men's Association, and in May 1872 declared itself the 'Official Organ of the British Section' of the Association, but did not long remain so. Riley appears to have given up the management of the paper, but resumed it again in May 1874. The **Herald and Helpmate** was the 'Official Organ of the Mutual Help Association', for promoting co-operative production and distribution in place of strikes.

L(Col)† 81, 106 (11 April 1874)–116 (20 June 1874), 124 (15 Aug. 1874)–126 (29 Aug. 1874); LE*; MP† 1 (2 March 1872)–81 (18 Oct. 1873), ns 1 (15 Aug. 1874)–18 (April 1875 [microfilm and original]); O(JJ) 48 (1 March 1873)

1524 International Hotel, Club and Restaurant Workers' Gazette I, 1 (15 July 1921)–3 (15 Sept. 1921); m

    A   2d. Issued by the Publicity Committee of the Hotel, Club and Restaurant Section, Workers' Union. Militant organ of workers in the catering trade. In French and English.

    L†; TUC

1525 International Labour Movement [1921?] –? Berlin; Moscow

    A   Bulletin of the International Council of Trade and Industrial Unions. Articles by leading members of the Third Communist International including Rosmer, Lozovsky, William Paul.

    WCML† 2 (Feb. 1921)

1526 International Labour Movement: **RILU Bulletin** I, 1 (1 May 1928)–II, 16 (1 Dec. 1929). Moscow; w

    A   Red International of Labour Unions. Reproduced from typewriting.

    L†; ONC I*

International Literature see **Literature of the World Revolution**

1527 International of Youth: Monthly Organ of the Executive Committee of the Young Communist International [1926]; ns 1 ([May?] 1927)–[1930?]; [ns] 1 (April/May 1930)–?; [ns] I, 1 (Aug./Sept. 1933)–? London; bi-m

    B   4d.; 6d. Published by the International Publishing House of the YCI. Youth version of **The Communist International**.

    MML† occ. nos 1926–30 (Aug./Sept. 1933), 5 (June 1934); WCML† 3 (Sept. 1927), 4, 7 (Aug. 1928) (April/May 1930)

1528 International Press Correspondence. (English Edition) I (1921)–XVIII, 32 (25 June 1938); then **World News and Views**: XVIII, 33 (2 July 1938)–XXXIII, 50 (19 Dec. 1953); then b **World News**: I, 1 (2 Jan. 1954)–IX, 51 (22 Dec. 1962). Vienna; Berlin; London (9 March 1933–); w

    B   Until 1943 the information organ of the Third International, 'providing material for journalists, politicians, scholars, workers' officials, etc.' 1938–62 published by the Communist Party of Great Britain. Two supplements were published: **Daylight**, I, 1 (Autumn 1952)–II, 3 (1954), a 'journal of stories, poems, songs and pictures showing the life of our people as it really is – and as it might be'; **World News Discussion Supplement**, 1 (26 Jan. 1957)–3 (23 March 1957), which included discussion on the revised draft of 'The British road to Socialism', and on Hungary, 1956.

    C a XIX (1939)–; E a XIX–; L† (w a XIX, 27); MML*; O a VII, 55–IX, 62, XIX, 2– ; ONC*

Daylight E; L†; O

International Review, 1889 see To-Day, 1883–1889

1529 International Review. [English edition] 1941. London
   B   Published by Modern Books. Printed in USA. Successor to
Communist International, 1940. Contributors: Varga, Dimitroff,
Malenkov, Zhukov, Kuznetsov.
   ONC† June 1941 (only one published?)

1530 International Seafarer: Supplement to the International Transport
Workers' Bulletin I, 1 (Sept./Oct. 1923)–[1931?] ; bi-m; q
   A   1d. Published by the Seamen's Section of the International
Propaganda Committee of Revolutionary Transport Workers (National
Minority Movement, Red International of Labour Unions). 'Advocates
ships committees as a means of controlling the job, the union, and also as a
necessary weapon for the emancipation of the seamen from wage slavery.'
   L(Col)† I, 7 (Dec. 1924/Jan. 1925)–I, 12 (Dec. 1925/Jan. 1926);
TUC I (1–Oct./Dec. 1927*)

1531 International Seamen's Gazette. Published in the Interests of the
Seafaring Community and the Official Organ of the National Amalgamated
Sailors' and Firemen's Union of Great Britain and Ireland I, 1 (29 Jan.
1892)–I, 25 (16 July 1892) Sunderland; London; w
   A   1d. Editor: J. H. Wilson. Exposed grievances of sailors,
extensive union news from 'special correspondents' in all main British
ports, news coverage of other sections of labour movement, columns for
women and young people. Some signed leaders by Shaw Maxwell; series
'Our Seamen', by S. Plimsoll.
   LE†

1532 International Socialism: Quarterly for Marxist Theory I, 1 (Autumn
1958)–3 (Jan. 1960); [ns] (Spring 1960)–   ; q
   B   Spring 1960, sub-titled **Journal for Socialist Theory** states 'a
first duplicated version appeared in autumn 1958. Nos. 2 and 3 appeared
in print as a political biography of Rosa Luxemburg by Tony Cliff in
January 1960 . . . they were the responsibility and expression of one
stream of socialist thought, that centred on **Socialist Review**. This is no
longer true. **International Socialism** is to be completely independent of
Socialist Review, financially, administratively and in personnel.' To be
forum for currents of socialist thought in the Labour Movement.
   HU Spring 1960–   ; L†; LE Spring 1960–   ; O† Spring 1960–
ONC 24, Spring 1966–   ; YU 19, 1964/5–

1533 International Socialist: a Journal of Labour Opinion I, 1 (Feb. 1952)–? q?

    B   Published and edited by E. Grant. Criticism of Labour Party policy by the Marxist Left within the Party.

    ONC† I, 1–I, 4 (Nov./Dec. 1952)

1534 International Socialist Bibliography: Supplement to the Socialist International Information I, 1 (9 Jan. 1954)–III, (Sept. 1956); fortn

    B   Reproduced from typewriting. Lists fairly recent publications under broad headings, with short notes on content and value.

    L; ONC† I, 1–III, 6 (5 May 1956); TUC I, 1–III, 6 (5 May 1956)

1535 International Socialist Bureau. **Periodical Bulletin** [19–?]–?

    B

    LabP 1909–12

1536 International Socialist Bureau. **Bulletin** [19–?]–?

    B

    LabP 1921–24

International Socialist Forum see **Left Book News**

1537 International Socialist Women's Secretariat. **Bulletin** I, 1 (Jan. 1955)–? m

    B   From I, 6 (June 1955), International Council of Social Democratic Women. News of social-democratic women's movements throughout the world. Reproduced from typewriting.

    CrU IV, 11 (1958)–   ; L I, 2 (Feb. 1955)–   ; ONC† I, 2–VI (1960)

1538 International Teachers News Nov. 1963–   ? London; Prague; irreg?; 8-yr

    A   Published for the World Federation of Teachers' Unions, by WFTU Publications, Ltd., London, until 1966, when it was reproduced from typewriting and published direct from Prague. Covers activities of teachers and teachers' organisations all over the world.

    O† Nov. 1963–May 1967*

International Trade Union Information see **International Trade Union Press Correspondence**

1539 International Trade Union Press Correspondence (English edition) I, 1 (17 June 1932)–II, 8 (21 Feb. 1933). Berlin; then **International Trade Union Information**: II, 9 (30 March 1933)–II, 12 (17 June 1933). London; irreg

    A   1d. Red International of Labour Unions. Published by Sefer, Berlin; W. Thorpe, London. Editors: Albert Zwicker (1–22), Erich Fox. Contributors: John Mahon, W. Payne.

    L I, 9–11, II, 8–12; ONC† (w I, 2, 11, 20, II, 5, 6, 11); WCML† I, 3, 10, 11, 13, 16, 19, II, 10

1540 International Trades Union Review 1 (Aug. 1918)–10 (Jan. 1922); q
    A   'Issued by the TUC Information Bureau to British Sections
Affiliated Internationally.'
    L† (w 1); TUC

1541 International Transport Worker 1 (Nov. 1924)–11 (Feb. 1926);
irreg?
    A   1d. Published by the International Propaganda Committee of
Revolutionary Transport Workers' Minority Movement, and in particular
the Railway Section of the National Minority Movement.
    L(Col)† (w 1)

1542 International Transport Workers' Federation. **Press Report** [Feb.
1924?] –Dec. 1964. Kempston; fortn
    A   Reproduced from typewriting. Superseded by **ITF Newsletter**.
    L† (27 Nov. 1939)–(6 June 1963); TUC

International Transport Workers Journal see **Transport Workers Link the
World**

1543 International Woman Co-operator I, 1 (Jan. 1945)–?
    A
    HU I, 1–XVII, 2 (March 1961*)

1544 International Working Union of Socialist Parties. **Bulletin** (English
edition) II, 1 (Jan. 1922)–III, 2 (April 1923). Vienna
    B   1d. Earlier numbers not published in an English edition. German
edition started in April 1921. British Labour represented by the
Independent Labour Party and the Labour Party. Printed and published by
Vorwärts . Discussion of strategy for the international movement and for
the youth movement.
    L†

1545 Internationale Anarchiste. (Anarchist International). **Bulletin** 1 (31
Jan. 1908)–13 (April 1910). London; m
    B   Printed and published by A. Schapiro. Mainly in French, but
some reports in English.
    L†

1546 Internazionale: Periodico Socialista-Anarchico (International:
Socialist-Anarchist periodical). 1 (12 Jan. 1901)–4 (5 May 1901); irreg
    B   1d. Printed and published on behalf of the Group
L'Internazionale, by G. Pietraroja, then by A. Galassine. A review of the
international Anarchist Movement. Contributors: Malatesta, Louise
Michel. In Italian.
    L(Col)†

1547 Investigator 1 (1 April 1843)–28 (7 Oct. 1843); 'weekly numbers and monthly parts'

    B   2d. Publisher: Hetherington. Editor: Charles Southwell. For the liberty of the press. Urges that a republic, no matter how it is based, needs 'virtue' at its foundation. Against the 'falsity' of religion.

    L† (w 26, 27); LU; ONC†

Investigator see **London Investigator**

1548 Invicta Post [19--?]–?

    A   Union of Post Office Workers, Kent and East Surrey District Council. (W. Dunlop, 'Local Journals'. **Belpost**, IV, 5 [May 1965].)

1549 Ipswich Citizen: Organ of the Ipswich Co-operative Party 1 (Oct. 1934)–3 (Dec. 1934). Ipswich; m

    B

    L(Col); East Suffolk Record Office, Ratcliffe Coll. Nov. 1934

1550 Ipswich Co-operative Advocate Dec. 1888–Dec. 1890. Ipswich; m?

    A   Ipswich Industrial Co-operative Society. Succeeded by **Ipswich Co-operative Herald** (qv).

1551 Ipswich Co-operative Herald 1 [Jan. 1891?]–? Ipswich; m

    A   Gratis. Ipswich Industrial Co-operative Society. Articles, and notes of meetings. Preceded by **Ipswich Co-operative Advocate**.

    O(JJ)† 33 (Sept. 1893)

1552 Ipswich Co-operative Pioneer Nov. 1875–? Ipswich; m; q

    A   Ipswich Industrial Co-operative Society. (G. Haines. 'Rise and Progress of the Ipswich Society' in **Opening Celebration of New Central Strores**, Ipswich, 1896.)

    Suffolk County Archives 1875–80

Iris; or, The Sheffield Advertiser, [1794?]–[18--?] see **Sheffield Register**

1553 Iris; or, the Addingham Mechanics' Institute Observer 1 (Jan. 1845)–12 (Dec. 1845). Addingham; m

    A   1d. 'The object contemplated by the present miscellany is simply the development and elevation of mind, and the dissemination of useful and interesting intelligence.'

    L†

Iris Fact Service see **IRIS News**

1554 Irish Communist 1 (Dec. 1965)–   . London; m

   B   1s. etc. Sub-title from No. 50, Feb. 1970: 'Theoretical Journal of the Irish Communist Organisation', from December 1971: 'A Theoretical Journal of the British and Irish Communist Organisation', Marxist-Leninist. Editor: Angela Clifford. Published by Patrick Murphy (1965).

   LE†

1555 Irish Co-operative Review: Official Journal of the Irish Agricultural Co-operative Movement I, 1 (Jan. 1968)–III, 1 (1970). Dublin; q

   A   Irish Agricultural Organisation Society.

   Royal Irish Academy; University College, Dublin

Irish Democrat see **Irish Freedom**

Irish Economist see Co-operative Reference Library. **Bulletin**

1556 Irish Exile: an Organ of Irish Movements in and around London 1 (March 1921)–7 (Sept. 1921); ns 1 (Nov. 1921)–8 (June 1922); m

   B   2d. Published by the London District Committee of the Irish Self-Determination League. Printed by the National Labour Press. With the new series the journal was taken over by the Central Executive of the League, as its official organ. Activities predominantly in London, but later also in the provinces. For free and independent Ireland. De Valera active.

   L(Col)†

1557 Irish Felon: Successor to the United Irishman I, 1 (24 June 1848)–5 (22 July 1848). Dublin; w

   B   5d. Editor: John Martin. In form and content a continuation of Mitchell's **United Irishman**. A Felon Club was formed, for an independent democratic Ireland to be achieved by armed insurrection.

   D; L(Col)†; NwA

1558 Irish Free State Medical Union. Journal I, 1 (July 1937)–IX, 50 (Aug. 1941); then Medical Association of Eire. **Journal**: IX, 51 (Sept. 1941)–XXVII (1950); then Irish Medical Association. **Journal**: XXVIII, 1951–   . Dublin; m; fortn

   A   6d. Covers union matters, especially in early years; later emphasis on medical matters.

   B1U XXIII, 134–   ; BrU; GaU XV–   ; L†; LA XX–XXIV; LMA; LMD I–V, XIX–   ; LS XVII–

1559 Irish Freedom I, 1 (Jan. 1939)–I, 72 (Dec. 1944); then **Irish Democrat**: ns 1 (Jan. 1945)–   ; m

   B   2d. etc. Republican, Labour and Progressive. Preceded by **Irish Front**. Connolly Club, later Connolly Association. Contributors: Desmond Ryan, Sean O'Casey.

   L(Col)†; MML 1945–*

234

1560 Irish Homestead: the Organ of Irish Agricultural and Industrial Development I, (1895)–XXX, 36 (8 Sept. 1923). Dublin; w

    A   Irish Agricultural Organisation Society. Editor: G. W. Russell (AE). Promoted creation of agricultural co-operative societies. Merged in **The Irish Statesman**.

    AbN XXVI–XXX; AbU 1901–1904*; BU 1914–15*; L(Col) II–XXIX, 51 (w March–Dec.1897); ONC III–V*

1561 Irish Independent (13 Sept. 1873)–? Dublin; w

    C   1d. Published by J. T. Quigley. 'Circulates amongst the labouring population in Dublin and Ireland generally. It advocates the interests of the trading and agricultural population of the country and the development of its natural resources. It reports the proceedings of the various labour associations in England and Scotland and gives the general news of the week.' (Mitchell, 1876)

1562 Irish Journal of Education: the Organ of the Association of Secondary Teachers, Ireland I (1911)–VII (1917). Dublin; m

    A 3d.
    L IV, 4–VII, 4

1563 Irish Journalist: Organ of the Irish Journalists' Association I, 1 (Oct. 1914)–I, 8 (May 1915). Dublin; m

    A   1d. Printed and published for the Association by Patrick Mahon. To unite Irish press men for better wages and working conditions.
    L(Col)†

1564 Irish Labour Advocate: a Representative Organ of Industrial Brotherhood Nov. 1890–? Dublin; w

    A   1d. Printed and published by the Irish Labour Printing and Publishing Company (No. 14). News of Labour Movement, unions, strikes, discussion of events, legislation, politics. Correspondence.
    L(Col)† I, (14 [14 Feb.]; I, 15 [21 Feb.] 1891)

1565 Irish Labour Party. Monthly News Bulletin I, 1 [July 1933?]–? Dublin; m

    B   1d. Published by the Administrative Council of the Irish Labour Party. Reproduced from typewriting, then printed. Title varies: **Monthly Bulletin; Labour Bulletin**. Notes, comments, reports.
    LabP† I, 4 (Oct. 1933)–IV, 11 (Nov. 1936*)

1566 Irish Labour Party and Trade Union Congress. **Weekly Labour Notes.** [19--?]–[1923? 1924?]. Dublin

    B   Superseded by **The Pioneer**, Feb. 1924–   (qv).

Irish Medical Association. **Journal** see Irish Free State Medical Union. **Journal**

1567 Irish Militant, For an Irish Workers Republic I, 1 (April 1966)–III, 7 [Aug. 1968]; m

B   6d.; 1d. Printed St Martin's Printers; Socialist Review Publishing Company (Aug. 1968). Editor: Joseph Mac Anna; Pat Flynn? Sought the ideal of an Irish Workers' Republic 'based on the needs of the Irish working class'.

LE†

Irish Nurse see **Irish Nurses' Journal**

1568 Irish Nurses' Journal: the Official Organ of [Cumann na mbanáltraí nGaedhealach], the Irish Nurses' Organization [19–?] –1963; then Irish Nurse: I, 1 (Aug. 1963)–7; then **Irish Nurses' Journal**: 1968–72; then **World of Irish Nursing**: 1972–   . Dublin; m

A   Sometimes entitled **Irish Nurses' Magazine**.

D (April 1940)–   ; L (Jan. 1949)–*

Irish Nurses' Magazine see **Irish Nurses' Journal**

1569 Irish Opinion: a Weekly Newspaper and Review 1 (17 June 1916)–46 (28 April 1917); ns I, 1 (1 Dec. 1917)–I, 20 (13 April 1918): then **Voice of Labour**: 21 (20 April 1918)–96 (20 Sept. 1919); then **Watchword of Labour**: I, 1 (27 Sept. 1919)–I, 42 (17 July 1920); then **Watchword and Voice of Labour**: ns I, 43 (24 July 1920)–I, 62 (4 Dec. 1920); then **Voice of Labour**: ns I, 1 (Oct. 1921)–IX, 19 (17 May 1927); then **Irishman**, with which is incorporated the **Voice of Labour**: I, 1 (14 May 1927)–IV, 43 (25 Oct. 1930); then **Watchword**, incorporating **The Irishman** and **The Voice of Labour**: I, 1 (1 Nov. 1930)–III, 8 (24 Dec. 1932). Dublin; w

B   1d. Irish Transport and General Workers' Union; Irish Trades Union Congress and Irish labour Party. 'Before 1917 ended Thomas Johnson, with the support of O'Brien and other colleagues took over a weekly journal, **Irish Opinion**, which had ceased publication, and converted it into a Labour organ. Early in January 1918 this took the sub-title **The Voice of Labour** and later in the year under this latter title, with O'Shannon as Editor, it became the official organ of the Union, published at Liberty Hall' (Irish Transport and General Workers' Union. **Fifty years of Liberty Hall**, Dublin [1959]). **The Voice of Labour** was suppressed in September 1919, but was soon succeeded by **The Watchword of Labour**, which was printed in Manchester. Editor: Cathal O'Shannon.

CoU 1927–32; D*; L(Col)*†

1570 Irish People: a Weekly Journal of National Politics and Literature I, 1 (28 Nov. 1863)–II, 43 (1865). Dublin; w

B   Editors: Thomas Clarke Luby and John O'Leary. Organ of Fenian agitation.

C; LCol)† 1–(19 Nov. 1864)

1571 Irish People [1875?] –? Manchester; m

   B   1d. Advocates a completely independent Ireland organised
federally, and the taking up of arms against the English oppressor. Appeals
to 'English Democracy' for solidarity.
   L(Col)† I, 9 (1 June 1876)

1572 Irish Postal and Telegraph Guardian [1904?] –X, 3 (May 1923).
Dublin; m

   A   2d. (1915). Organ of the Association of Irish Post Office Clerks,
later the Irish Postal Union
   L(Col) (Jan. 1911)–(May 1923); TUC (1921–3)

Irish Railway Review see **New Way**

Irish School Monthly see **Irish Teachers' Journal**

Irish School Weekly see **Irish Teachers' Journal**

1573 Irish Schoolmistress, and Female Teachers' Assistant I, 1 (28 Feb.
1891)–I, 6 (4 April 1891); then **absorbed by O'Byrne Correspondence
Journal**: I, 7 (11 April 1891)–[8?9], (1891): then **Irish Schoolmistress
and Female Teachers' Assistant** [9?10], 1891–? Dublin; w

   C   1d. Proprietors: Harrison and Company. Editor: Alice O'Byrne.
'The only Paper in Ireland Owned, Edited and Managed by Women, and
the only Paper exclusively devoted to the interests of the great Teaching
Body of Women.' To assist teachers in obtaining promotion through
exams, and a substantial part devoted to instruction, but also takes up the
cause of equal pay for women teachers.
   L(Col)† 1–3, 5–7, 10 (2 May 1891)

1574 Irish Socialist Review. 1970–3; Dublin; s-a
   B   10p Communist Party of Ireland.
   University College, Dublin

1575 Irish Teachers' Journal [1867?68?] –XXXVIII, 5 (30 Jan. 1904);
then **Irish School Weekly**: XXXVIII, 6 (ns I, 1) (6 Feb. 1904)–LVI, 39/40
(23/30 Oct. 1954); then **Irish School Monthly**: LVI, 41 (Nov.
1954)–LVII, 11 (Dec. 1955). Dublin; m; w; fortn

   A   1d. etc. Official organ of the Irish National Teachers'
Organisation. Superseded by **An Múinteoir Náisiunta.**
   L(Col) XXXIV, 1900–*; O III, 27–30

1576 Irish Trades' Advocate 1 (13 Sept. 1851)–7 (25 Oct. 1851). Dublin;
w
   C   2½d. Printed and published for the proprietors by William
Baird. Carried on masthead the slogan 'A Fair Day's Wages for a Fair Day's
Work', and sought support from the 'intelligent man' among all classes of
artisan.
   L(Col)†

1577 Irish Tribune I, 1 (10 June 1848)–I, 5 (8 July 1848). Dublin; w
    B   5d. Continued the democratic republican policies of the **United Irishman** after the latter was suppressed. Succeeded by **Irish Felon**.
    L(Col)†

1578 Irish Tribune: an Irish national Journal for England and Scotland 1 (13 Dec. 1884)–(28 March 1896). Newcastle-on-Tyne; w
    B   1d. Irish Press Company of Great Britain. nationalist and Catholic. Addressed to Irish on British mainland. Organ of Irish National League. Covers Irish nationalist agitation in Liverpool, Glasgow, Lancashire, Newcastle, London etc. Includes short notes, 'The cause of labour'. Merged in **Tyneside Catholic News**.
    L(Col)† 1–598 (27 Dec. 1895)

1579 Irish Worker: a Chronicle of Trade Unionism and Democratic Opinion. 1 (23 April 1892)–41 (June 1893). Dublin; m
    B   1d. Printed and published by Bernard Doyle at 'Ye Franklin Presse'. Staunch advocate of Trade Unionism and 'the only publication in the country free from political or sectarian influence'. Promoted industrial employment for Irish labour on Irish soil. Covers a wide range of trade-union news, grievances, discussion of Labour topics such as the eight-hours' day.
    L(Col)† III, 38 (March 1893)–41

1580 Irish Worker, and People's Advocate I 1 ([27 May 1911?] –? Dublin; w
    A   1d. Editor: Jim Larkin. Second part of title dropped after a few months. Several series published. Not published continuously, eg, suppressed December 1914. Coverage of trade-union organisation and agitation in Southern Ireland, resolutions, correspondence. At one time subtitled: 'Official Organ of the Irish Worker League'.
    L(Col)† III, 8 (12 July 1913)–IV, 29 (28 Nov. 1914); ONC† occ. nos 1913–31

1581 Irish Workers' Voice [19--?] –1936; then **Worker**: 1 (1936)–?
    A?
    BlU a ii 2–b IX*; MML occ. nos

1582 Irish Workers' Weekly [19--?] –? Dublin; w
    B   1d. 'Labour political journal'. (Mitchell, 1940.)
    BlU 11–12

Irishman see **Irish Opinion**

1583 Iron and Steel Trades Confederation. **Journal** I, 1 (April 1917)–VII, 2 (Sept. 1923); q; then b **Man and Metal**: the Journal of the Iron and Steel Trades Confederation: I, 1 (Oct. 1923)–   ; m
    A   1d.
    L(Col)† b; LE a I–V, VI*, b?; MTB b XVI–XXIV*.
    XXV–   ; NU 1953–   ; SwU 1954–   ; the Confederation

1584 Ironworkers' Journal 1 (2 Jan. 1869)–637 (Feb. 1916). Darlington; m; fortn; m

    A   National Association of Iron, Steel, Tin, Blastfurnace and Other Workers; Associated Iron and Steel Workers of Great Britain. For a time, used the subtitle: 'the Monthly Journal of the Amalgamated Malleable Ironworkers'.

    Batley Textile Hall 1–145; Iron and Steel Trades Confederation; L(Col) 113–637*; LE*

1585 Isca Searchlight: Organ of the Exeter and District Branch of Union of Post Office Workers [c1931]. [Exeter?]

    A   (**Forward**: Organ of the UPW Birmingham Branches, May 1931.)

1586 Isis: a London Weekly Publication, Edited by the Lady of the Rotunda I, 1 (11 Feb. 1832)–I, 39 (15 Dec. 1832); w

    B   6d. Edited by Eliza Sharples Carlile while Richard Carlile and Robert Taylor were in prison. Published by David France. Discourses delivered at the Rotunda, correspondence by Carlile and others on radical politics, free speech, free thought etc. 'The first journal produced by a women in support of sex equality and political and religious freedom ... Published in place of Carlile's **The Prompter**. Carlile contributed many articles, and in May 1832 announced his 'conversion' to Christianity.' (G. D. H. Cole, **Richard Carlile**, 1943)

    BP i, 1; BnU; L†; LU; MP

1587 Iskra 1 (1900)–112 (1905). Zürich etc.

    B   **Rossiiskaya sotsial-demokraticheskaya rabochaya partiya.** Editors: Lenin, Krupskaya etc. The editorial committee spent just over twelve months (April 1902–May 1903) in London and during this time 17 issues of the journal (Nos. 22–38) were printed at Clerkenwell Green, headquarters of the Social Democratic Federation and the Twentieth Century Press (A. Rothstein, **A House on Clerkenwell Green**, 1966).

    L(Col); LE

1588 Isle of Wight Clarion [194-?]. Wroxall; m

    B   2d. Labour Party. (Labour Party. **Your own Journal**, 1948.)

1589 Islington Citizen [c1921]; m

    B   1d. Labour Party (**Labour Organiser**, July 1921.)

1590 Islington Labour Argus: a Local Journal for All Who Work for a Living 1 (Oct. 1906)

    B   ½d. Printed and published for the proprietors by The Barnsbury Press. Promotes the National Labour Party. Edited anonymously but 'both well-known trade unionists, one of the LSC and the other of the NSAB and MM.' Focuses on the putting up of Labour candidates at local elections.

    L(Col)†; O(JJ)†

1591 Islington Woman Worker: Organ of the Islington Local CPGB 1 (July 1927)—?; m

    B   Gratis (1); ½d. (2—4). Communist Party of Great Britain. Printed and published by Dora Savage (1), J. Murray (2—4). Reproduced from typewriting. Letters, news, events, cartoons.

    O(JJ) 1—4 (Oct. 1927)

1592 Islingtonic 1967?—

    A   National and Local Government Officers Association, Islington Branch. Reproduced from typewriting.

    L(1967)—

1593 JEC Magazine 1965?—   . Walsall

    A   National Association of Local Government Officers, Walsall Branch. Reproduced from typewriting.

    L 1965—

1594 Jarrow Division Labour Herald 1 [April 1905?]—62 (15 March 1907). Jarrow-on-Tyne; m; w

    B   Gratis; ½d.; 1d. Labour Party. Local news, 'Jottings', women's column. Printed and published by the Co-operative Printing Society. Then, from No. 13, 6 April 1906 becomes **Jarrow Labour Herald**. This issue states 'the **Jarrow Division Labour Herald** has ceased to exist as the official organ of the Local Labour Party. It was freely distributed among the people for twelve months, and was kept going by the contributions, and the labour of working men and working women; but the burden was a heavy one, and the conference on March 24th decided to suspend production. We dare to affirm that the old **Herald** did useful work, and with many hold the opinion that there is a place in the public life of the district for a paper with a principle . . . The fact that we retain the title **Labour Herald** should give a fairly clear indication that the policy of the paper remains the same. But while that is so, and while we shall strongly support and advocate Independent Labour Representation, we will do our utmost to provide a newspaper in the real sense of the word.' Enlarged. Published by Tom Gibb.

    L(Col)† 13—62 (w 56); ONC† 2 (May 1905), 9 (Dec. 1905), 11 (9 Jan. 1906)

1595 Jet Sept. 1943—Dec. 1947; 1950; ([Nov.?Dec.] 1951—[mid-1971]); irreg; m; fortn; q; fortn

    A   Official journal of the National Association of Fire Officers. Incorporated in a **Yearbook**.

    The Association Sept. 1944—mid. 1971 (w occ. nos)

Jewish Clarion, April 1945 see **Jewish Opinion**

1596 Jewish Clarion 1 (Dec. 1945)—ns 12 (March 1957); m
    B   3d.; 4d. Communist Party of Great Britain, Jewish Committee.
Published by the Committee, then by A. Lazarus, and later by R. Bernard.
Started in newspaper format then gradually reduced in size.
    CPGB†; L(Col) 4 (March 1946)—ns 11 (Dec. 1956); LJ 42 (Dec.
1949)—ns 10 (Sept. 1956); LWL 1–6; O† 2 (Jan. 1946)—ns 10 (Sept.
1956)

Jewish Forum see **Jewish Opinion**

1597 Jewish Opinion Feb. 1945?—[March 1945?]; then **Jewish Clarion**:
April 1945; then **Jewish Forum**: May 1945—June 1945?; m
    B   3d. Publisher: Fred Stone; Workers' Circle, Branch No. 9.
    CPGB† Feb., April, May, June 1945

Jewish Trade Unionist see **Idisher Traid-Yunionist**

1598 Jigger Hurlford
    A   Published by Frank Moore. Pit paper. (R. G. Neville)

1599 Jogger: the Communist Party Paper for Clearing House Clerks
[1927?]—? irreg
    B   1d. Published by the Euston Rail Group of the Communist
Party. Reproduced from typewriting. News and notes, branch meetings,
letters, cartoons.
    O(JJ)† 6 (May 1928)—20 (March 1930) (w 13, 16–19)

1600 Johnson and Phillips Shop Stewards' Journal 1 (Jan. 1936)—24
(1938)
    A
    CPGB

Johnstone's Monthly Register see **Schoolmaster and Edinburgh Weekly
Magazine**

1601 Journal: Odd Fellows and Friendly Societies' Advocate 1 (4 July
1846)—(27 March 1847); w
    A   4d. Printed and published by David White. Organ of the
Manchester Unity of the Independent Order of Odd Fellows. Successor of
The London Journal and Pioneer.
    L(Col)†

Journal: the Official Organ of the National Union of Insurance, Refuge
Section [19--?]— see **RFSA Journal**

Journal, 1933— see **Working Men's College Journal**

1602 Journal: the Official Organ of the National Union of Insurance, Refuge [1915?]—XLII, 12 (Dec. 1957); then **POEU Journal**: XLIII, 1 (Jan. 1958)—   ; m

    A   Though the title on the cover changes, the masthead continues to read **The Journal** . . : Subject matter increasingly extended.

    NU XXXI (1946)—(w 1953); ONC† XXXV (1950)—   ; the Union

Journal (Birmingham Trades Council), 1946— see Birmingham Trades Council. **Journal**

1603 Journal 1 (April 1950)—?

    A   London Trades Council.

    TUC 1—May 1951*

1604 Journal: Monthly News-Sheet of the Dorset County Branch of NALGO I, 1 (Jan. 1955)—? Dorchester; m

    A   National and Local Government Officers' Association. Sometimes entitled **NALGO Chit-Chat**

    L

Journal, 1962—1966 see **Institute Journal**

Journal (Society of Graphical and Allied Trades. Division I. Natsopa), **1965—1967** see **Natsopa Journal**

Journal, 1971— see **Royal Liver Workers' Journal**

Journal of Association see **Christian Socialist, 1850—1851**

Journal of HM Customs and Excise see **Journal of HM Excise Service**

1605 Journal of HM Excise Service I, 1 (30 July 1910)—Dec 1971. Sunderland (July—Oct. 1910—); London; fortn; w; fortn; m

    A   1½d. etc. Customs and Excise Federation. Became the official organ of the Federation. News, Federation and branch notes, articles on conditions of work, general articles of interest to the profession. Later entitled **Journal of HM Customs and Excise.** Superseded by **Customs and Excise Journal.**

    L(Col)†; Society of Civil Servants, Customs and Excise Group

Journal of Hospital Pharmacy see **Public Pharmacist**

1606 Journal of Human Rights I, 1 [1866]—II, 16 (4 March 1867); w

    B   1d. Published F. Farrah. Sole contributor: John Scott, author of 'The logic of the labour problem' etc. An elaboration of the principles of political democracy during the Reform crisis of 1867. Supports working-class call for universal suffrage. Motto: 'Our country is the world, our countrymen are all mankind.'

    L† II, (14 [22 Feb.]—16 [4 March] 1867)

1607 Journal of the Operative Stone Masons [19--?.] Manchester; fortn
    A   Operative Stonemasons' Society.

1608 Journal of the Typographic Arts, Devoted to the Interests of Every Department of the Printing Profession 1 (2 Jan. 1860), 29 (May 1862); m
    A   1½d. Published by William Henry Everett. Established by '200 Shareholders' of 'independent' views. Avowedly non-political in character. Records trade disputes and analyses relations between workmen and employees. Covers events in London and the provinces. Addressed to both sides of industry. Advocates mutual relations between compositors and employers. Supports viewpoint of Thomas J. Dunning in **Trades' Unions and Strikes**. Reports meetings of Typographical Associations.
    L†; LSF Sept.–Nov. 1860, Jan.–May 1861

1609 Journal of the Working Classes 1 (1842)–15 (1842); w
    C   1d. Printed and published by William Edward Pointer. Journal for the working class. Object: union of all classes for the good of the nation and for the especial good of the working classes. Articles on home colonisation, emigration, Poor Laws, suggesting remedies for the existing distress in 1842. Opposed to those who mislead 'the people', eg 'Chartist demagogues'.
    L†

1610 Journalism: Official Organ of the National Association of Journalists 1 (Nov. 1887)–11 (Feb. 1889); m
    A   Free to members. Published and printed for the Association by Herbert Cornish, General Secretary. Debates matters such as insurance fund, and general welfare of members.
    L(Col)†

Journalist see **National Union Journal**

1611 Journeyman: an Organ Devoted to the Interests of Working Tailors 1 (Aug. 1890)–8 (March 1891); m
    A   1d. A trade-union journal 'with the desire of serving the working tailors "the wide world over".' Emphasises the need for trade-union organisation. Campaigns ardently against the sweating system in the trade. London Society of Tailors and Tailoresses. (S. Webb and A. Freeman, eds., **Seasonal trades**, 1912, p. 91).
    L†

1612 Journeyman: a Journal Devoted to the Interests of the Workers in the Clothing Industry I, 1 (23 March 1896)–II, 4 (July 1897); fortn
    A   1d. Organ of the Amalgamated Society of Tailors, International Branch. Published by Otto Matthias, Secretary. Coverage of London district and provincial Trade Unionism, including Scottish branches. Correspondence, much on the question of alien and pauper immigration. Special coverage of continental tailors' Trade Unionism and politics.
    L(Col)†

1613 Journeyman and Artizan's London and Provincial Chronicle 1 (12 June 1825)–4 (3 July 1825); then **Artizan's London and Provincial Chronicle**: 5 (10 July 1825)–7 (24 July 1825); then **Mechanic's Newspaper**: 8 (31 July 1825)–13 (4 Sept 1825); w

     A   7d. Printed and published for the proprietors by Thomas Dickie. Working-class newspaper set up as an organ of the trades delegates gathered in London to act as watchdog over the proposed legislation on the Combination Laws. Analysis of and commentary upon the findings of the Committee which recommended repeal of the laws of 1824. Also contains news of Mechanics Institutes and trade-union matters.

     L(Col)†

1614 Journeyman Bakers' Magazine, Devoted Entirely to the Interests of the Operative Bakers of Great Britain 1 (June 1885)–192 (Dec. 1927); then **Journeyman Baker**: ns I, 1 (Jan. 1928)–12 (Dec. 1968); then **Bakery Worker**: Official Organ of the Bakers' Union: XXII, 1 (Jan. 1969)–   ; m

     A   ½d.; 1d. Amalgamated Union of Operative Bakers and Confectioners (and Allied Workers); Bakers' Union. Editors: James Jenkins (1897); W. Bonfield; S. Gretton. It is believed that there may have been an earlier series of this journal but none has been traced.

     BU IX, 6 (1951)–   ; L(Col)†; TUC 1940–   ; the Union 1912–

1615 Journeymen Butchers' Gazette: a Monthly Review of the Work of the Journeymen Butchers' Federation of Great Britain and of All Workers Connected with Meat, By-products, Bacon Factory and Other Allied Trades ns I, 1 (Jan. 1922)–XI, 1 (Jan./Feb. 1932). Sheffield; m

     A   1½d. Reports and correspondence.

     TUC†

1616 Journeymen Cabinet Maker, Carver and Wood Turners' Friendly Society. Monthly Report [18--?–1915?]. Liverpool etc.; m

     A   Later Operative Cabinet Makers', Carvers' and Wood Turners' Friendly Society (1872–5), Friendly Society of Operative Cabinet and Chairmakers, Carvers and Wood Turners (1876–84), Amalgamated Union of Cabinet Makers (1885–   ).

     Warwick U (MRC) 1869–1915

1617 Juice: Organ of the 'Underground' Workers [192-?]

     A   ½d. Issued by the Communist Group [of Railway Workers]. Reproduced from typewriting.

     O(JJ)† 12 June 1926

1618 Junior: a Monthly Civil Service Paper 1 (Jan 1894)–3 (March 1894); m

     A   2d. Magazine promoting the interests of Boy Clerks, ie under 20 years of age; 'run for themselves by one of themselves'.

     L† (w 1)

1619 Junior: the Organ of the London Junior Section, UPW [1932?]–?; m

    A   Union of Post Office Workers.
    TUC† 10 (March 1933)–38 (Oct. 1935*)

1620 Junior Officer Sept. 1952–Sept. 1954; m; bi-m

    A   Bulletin of the Junior (Fire Brigade) Officers Association. 18 issues in all. Incorporated in **Jet**. National Association of Fire Officers.

1621 Justice: the Organ of the Social Democracy I, 1 (19 Jan. 1884)–XLI, 2141 (22 Jan. 1925); then **Social Democrat**: XLII, 2142 (Feb. 1925)–L, 2248 (Dec. 1933); w

    B   1d. Organ of the Social Democratic Federation, later Social Democratic Party. Editors: Hyndman; Harry Quelch; H. W. Lee.

    C 1911– ; L(Col); LE I–XX (IV, VI, XVI–XVII*); LabP 1925–33; LdU IV, 209–X, 520; MP 1884–1914 (microfilm); ONC occ. nos of a; TUC, John Burns Lib. 1884–1915; Warwick UL 1884–1902 (microfilm)

1622 Justice, Issued by the Commonwealth Labour Party (Northern Ireland) I [194-?]–? Belfast; m?

    B   2d. The Party 'stands for the creation, in Northern Ireland, of a Labour Government pledged to the maintenance of Northern Ireland as an integral part of the United Kingdom and the British Commonwealth of Nations . . .' Editorial, short signed contributions.

    LabP† IV, 11 (Feb. 1946); Linen Hall Library, Belfast II, 2 (1943)–IV, 7 (1945 [Xerox copies])

1623 K-W-A- News: the Journal of the Kalamazoo Workers' Alliance [19--?]– . Birmingham

    C   Workers at Kalamazoo, Ltd.
    L† 54 (Feb. 1957)–

1624 Keele Left 1 (Autumn 1961)–4 (Autumn 1965?) Keele; irreg

    B   6d. Independent journal of Left-wing opinion, published at Keele University.
    L†

1625 Keep Left: the Paper for Socialist Youth [1957?]–?; m; w

    B   Trotskyist Young Socialists.
    L; LE XIV, 10 (Nov. 1965)–XVII, 11 (Dec. 1968)

1626 Keighley Bulletin [194-?]. [Keighley?]; q

    B   3d. Labour Party. (Labour Party. **Your own Journal**, 1948.)

1627 Keighley Co-operative Bee (Nov. 1879)–? Keighley; q
  A   Free. Keighley Co-operative Society, Educational Committee.
'Our chief mission is to educate our members and make them not only
enthusiastic, but also intelligent Co-operators' (J. Rhodes, **Half a Century
of Co-operation in Keighley, 1860–1910**, Manchester 1911).
  L† occ. nos only

Keighley Labour Journal see **ILP Journal**

1628 (Kenneth's) Hawk
  A   Published by the Communist Party of Great Britain group of
miners in the Springside and Dreghorn area? (R. G. Neville)

1629 Kennington Labour Record: the Organ of the Kennington Labour
Party 1 (March 1929)–27 (Oct. 1931); 28 (Jan. 1934)–30 (Oct. 1934); m;
3-yr
  B   1d. Contributor: Leonard W. Matters, Kennington Labour MP.
Issued mainly for election purposes.
  L(Col)†

1630 Kensington Pioneer 1 (Feb. 1915)–? Liverpool; m
  B   ½d. Independent Labour Party, Kensington Branch.
  LvP 1–13 (Feb. 1916) (w 12)

1631 Kensington Red Letter [193-?] ; m
  B   Labour Party. (Labour and Socialist International. **The Socialist
Press**, 1933.)

1632 Kent County Chronicle: the Official Organ of the Kent County
Officers' Guild I, 1 (Oct. 1936)–V, 4 (Oct. 1941) Maidstone; q
  A   National Association of Local Government Officers.
  L†

1633 Kentish Fire: the Official Publication of Kent East Branch Post
Office Engineering Union I, 1 (Sept. 1952)–III, 1 (June 1960).
Canterbury; s-a; q; irreg
  A   2d. Articles and branch reports.
  L†

1634 Kentish Leader: Labour Journal Circulating Throughout the
South-Eastern District 1 (Oct. 1920)–17 (March 1922); m
  B   1d. Printed and published for the Labour Party by Matthews
and Company. A local district paper covering Greenwich, Lewisham and
Deptford Labour Parties. Margaret MacMillan prominent in the Women's
Section
  L(Col)†

1635 Kettering and Wellingborough Quarterly Record [189-?] –?
[Kettering] ; q
    A   Gratis. Organ of the Co-operative societies in the district.
Editor: William Betts (**Labour Annual**, 1897; **International Directory of
the Co-operative Press**, 1909).

1636 Kettering Co-operative Magazine 1910–31 Kettering; q
    A   Kettering Co-operative Society.
    Kettering PL. (w May 1917–July 1919)

Keynote see **Vox Pop**

1637 Keystone: the Journal of the Association of Architects, Surveyors
and Technical Assistants I (1925)–(April 1969); bi-m
    A   6d. to non-members. Association from 1942 named Association
of Building Technicians.
    BU*; L IV, 1 (Feb. 1928)–(April 1969); LSC*; LvP I; O*; TUC
(1934–April 1969*; WtB 1944–

1638 Kidderminster Labour and Union News [194-?]. [Kidderminster?] ;
q
    B   1d. Labour Party. (Labour Party. **Your own Journal**, 1948.)

1639 King of the Road 1 (April 1897)–13 (24 Dec. 1897); m; w
    B   1d. Printed and published by the Clarion Newspaper Company,
Ltd. ' "The smartest cycling weekly", conducted by Socialists . . .'
(**Labour Annual**, 1898) Touring notes, cycling information, local reports,
news of Clarion Clubs, humorous articles, fiction.
    L(Col); O†

1640 King's Cross Journal 1880
    A   Started by J. Greenwood. 4 issues. 'It was presumably Evans
who advocated that it should be given a new title, to be called the **Railway
Review**' (G. W. Alcock, **Fifty Years of Railway Trade Unionism**, London
1922, p. 262).

1641 Kings Cross Star [192-?] –?; fortn; w
    A   ½d. Printed and published by the Communist Party of Great
Britain. No. 46 sub-titled: 'The Paper of the King's Cross Railway Workers
of All Grades'. Ns No. 3 'Published by the King's Cross Group of
Communist Railwaymen'. Minority Movement agitational and information
sheet. Reproduced from typewriting.
    O(JJ)† 46 (28 May 1926), 47 (11 June 1926), ns 3 (1 July 1927), 4
(14 July 1927)

1642 King's Norton Labour News: Official Organ of the King's Norton Divisional Labour Party I, 1 (Jan. 1928)—ns 45 (Oct. 1946). Birmingham; m; irreg

    B   Gratis. Printed by Blackfriars Press, Leicester. Contributor: Robert Dennison, MP. From ns No. 34, September 1941 incorporates the **Northfield Messenger.**

    BP† (w 1, 43)

1643 Kings Norton News Letter [194-?]. Birmingham; m

    B   1d. Labour Party. Duplicated. (Labour Party. **Your own Journal,** 1948.)

1644 Kingston and District Citizen 1 (May 1930)—25 (June 1932); m

    B   Published by the London Co-operative Society, Political Committee.

    L(Col)†

Kingston Borough Clarion see **Malden Workers' Monthly**

1645 Kingston Citizen 1 (April 1960)—10 (May 1963); irreg

    B   Published by the Co-operative Press.

    LabP 8 (Oct. 1962); L(Col)

1646 Kingston Clarion 1 (Nov. 1938)—5 (March 1939); m

    B   Labour Party newspaper.

    L(Col)†

1647 Kinning Park Co-operator 1891—? Kinning Park; m

    A   Kinning Park Co-operative Society. 'In 1891 the Society published the **Kinning Park Co-operator**, a monthly journal of varied interest. It was edited by M. H. Cadiz, one of the Jubilee directors, and was a lively periodical, which included Keir Hardie, Robert MacNish, . . . Thomas Ritchie, D. Thomson, William Barclay, J. Campsie, and James M'Aulay among its contributors. The league of Nations was one of the reforms advocated in its columns as a means of preventing war, while other proposals favoured included mines nationalisation, a Labour-Co-operative alliance, the amalgamation of neighbour societies in competing areas, the encouragement of co-operative production. Altogether, it was a commendable enterprise which led to the starting of the Scottish Co-operator in 1893. The latter publication was edited in Kinning Park premises for many years, and received its chief support from the Society . . .' (P. J. Dollan, **Jubilee History of the Kinning Park Co-operative Society Limited,** 1923, p. 157)

1648 Kirkdale Herald [193-?]. Kirkdale; m

    B   Labour Party. (Labour and Socialist International. **The Socialist Press,** 1933)

1649 Knebworth Bulletin [194-?]. Knebworth; bi-m
    B   Labour Party. Duplicated. (Labour Party. **Your own Journal**, 1948.)

1650 Knight's Penny Magazine I, 1 (1846)—II, 30 (1846); w
    C   1d. Published and edited by Charles Knight. Printed by William Clowes. For 'all who are not specially educated', self-styled 'popular literature'. Popular education and elevation. Occasionally touches on social questions like short hours, colonisation. Analyses current political issues, favouring free trade and anti-Corn Law League. Preceded by **The Penny Magazine of the Society for the Diffusion of Useful Knowledge**, which falls outside our categories.
    BP; BU; C I; EN; GU; LU; MP; NwP; Newcastle Literary and Philosophical Society†; O

1651 Knot; Bulletin of the Staffordshire County Officers' Branch, National and Local Government Officers' Association. Newcastle-under-Lyme
    A
    L 1961—

1652 Kommunistische Zeitschrift. (Communist Magazine). 1 (Sept. 1847)
    B   2d. The proof copy, with annotations, is reprinted in **Die Londoner Kommunistische Zeitschrift und andere Urkunden aus den Jahren 1847/1848**, Leipzig 1921, pp. 35—81. This is by Carl Grünberg, and appears as **Hauptwerke des Sozialismus und der Sozialpolitik**, Neue Folge, 5 Heft. See also R. Payne, **Marx** (1968), p. 158, where it is referred to as **Kommunistische Zeitung**. 'Engels was probably the editor of the newspaper, and he was certainly responsible for the longest and most comprehensive article 'The Prussian Diet and the Prussian Proletariat, together, with the proletariat throughout Germany' [translation of the original German title]. The phrase 'Proletarians of all lands, unite!' was first printed in this journal where it appeared on the masthead.' Printed for the proprietors by Meldolas Cahn and Company, London.
    ONC† proof copy as above

1653 Krash: Kent River Authority's NALGO Branch News Sheet and Staff Magazine Gillingham
    A   National and Local Government Officers' Association, Kent River Authority Branch. Reproduced from typewriting.
    L 1966—

1654 Kropotkin Group. Buletin. (The Bulletin of Kropotkin Group). 1 (April 1925). London
    B   Yiddish
    L(Col)†

1655 LGO, Local Governmnent Officer: the Official Organ of the National Association of Local Government Officers I, 1 (8 Sept. 1906)—X, 25 (19 Aug. 1911); then **Municipal Officer**: I, 1 (Sept. 1911)—III, 10 (July 1914); ns I, 1 (Jan. 1916)—V, 14 (Feb. 1920); then **Local Government Service**: V, 15 (March 1920)—XXVII, 12 (Dec. 1952); then **Public Service**: XXVII, 13 (Jan. 1953)— ; m

    A   3d. Later, National and Local Government Officers' Association
    E I—X, XVIII— ; GM 1922—52 (w XIV—XV); L(Col)†; NU XXVII, 13 (1953)—XXXVIII, 1 (1964), XXXIX, 8 (1965)— ; ONC 1937— ; TUC 1931— ; the Association

LHTA Bulletin see London Head Teachers' Association. **Pamphlet**

LJC and M Venture see **Venture, 1920**

1656 LMS Railway Worker: the Paper of the St Pancras and Kentish Town Railway Workers 1 (28 May 1926)—?; then b **Camden Star and LMS Railway Worker**: 1 (3 Sept. 1926)—?; fortn

    A   ½d. Printed and published by the Communist Party of Great Britain. Issued by the Communist Railway Group. Minority Movement paper. Reproduced from typewriting

    O(JJ)† a 1—5 (July 1926); b 1—3 (1 Oct. 1926)

1657 LMS Rebel [c1932]. Derby

    A   (**Daily Worker**, [8 June 1932])

LPF Bulletin see Labour Peace Fellowship. **Bulletin**

LPF Newsletter see Labour Peace Fellowship. **Newsletter**

1658 LRD Fact Service 1 (1939)— ; w

    B   Labour Research Department. No. 1 is undated, No. 2 is dated 18 October 1939. Numbered in one sequence to the end of 1946, then 4 Jan. 1947 is numbered Vol. IX, No. 1. Thereafter each year sees a new volume. Economic and political information; regular indexes produced. Reproduced from typewriting.

    L; ONC† (w occ. nos)

1659 L and C Magazine: the Official Organ of the City of Edinburgh Lighting and Cleansing Department Welfare Club I, 1 (Jan. 1936)—2 (May 1936)

    A   Issued by the Club Executive Committee. Editor: William C. Williamson. 'Launched in the interests of the welfare movement amongst our members.'

    L†

1660 Labor Leader 1 (10 Oct. 1891)—11, (19 Dec. 1891); w

    B   Independent Labour Party. Editorial staff: Fred Henderson, W. B. Hodgson, J. B. Joyce.

    L(Col)

1661 Laborista Esperantisto: la Organa de Tutmonda en Britio 1
(July—Sept. 1934)—12 (April—June 1937); then **Worker Esperantist**:
Official Organ of the Workers' Esperanto Movement: 13 (July—Sept.
1937)—? Manchester; q

    B   2d. Typed and duplicated by SATEB. Organ of the British
Section of the Workers' Esperanto Movement. To promote solidarity and
understanding within the international working-class movement by means
of a 'common' language. Refers to an earlier **Bulletin**, now improved and
enlarged. In English and Esperanto.

    L† 1—14 (Oct.—Dec. 1937)

1662 Labour 1 (Jan. 1930)—3 (April 1930). Manchester; irreg

    B   2d. Printed and published by J. Hepinstall. General labour
coverage.

    MP†; O(JJ)† 1

1663 Labour: a Magazine for All Workers I, 1 (Sept. 1933)—V, 12 (Aug.
1938); ns I, 1 (Sept. 1938)—XII, 12 (Aug. 1950); ns I, 1 (Sept. 1950)—   ;
m

    A   3d. etc. Official organ of the Trades Union Congress. Absorbed
Labour Bulletin, Labour Magazine, Industrial Review.

    BP; BS ii IV, 4—   ; BnU 1959—   ; C; CoU Sept. 1948—   ; CrU
1955—   ; GM; L; MP†; NU 1949—63, 1965—   ; ONC 1938—   ; TUC;
Warwick UL

1664 Labour Abstainer: Official Organ of the Workers' Temperance
League 1 (First quarter, 1933)—20 (June 1939?); q

    B   1d. Organ of a pressure group of Labour Party members
promoting total abstinence policies in the Labour and Trade Union
Movement, and lobbying for legislative control over the 'drink traffic'.

    TUC†

1665 Labour Advertises [c1907]. Leeds; m (**Reformers' Year Book**, 1907)

1666 Labour Advocate: Ulster's Labour Monthly I, 1 (Jan. 1935)—II, 3
(March 1936). Belfast; m

    B   1d. Printed for Alderman Harry Midgley, MP, the editor, by
William Strain and Sons (March 1936). Its intention was 'to provide the
Labour and Trade Union movement with a paper which would offset the
pernicious propaganda of the old political parties, and at the same time
present the policy of the working-class movement in relation to domestic
and international affairs.' Short news items.

    B1U 1—8; LabP† II, 3

1667 Labour Advocate: the Official Organ of the Blackpool and District
Labour Representation Committee I, 1 (Jan. 1910)—I, 59, (Dec. 1914).
Blackpool; m

    B   Gratis.

    L(Col)†

1668 Labour and Socialist International **Bulletin.** I, 1 (March 1924)–Ser. IV, 2 (Aug. 1939). London; Zürich; Brussels; irreg

B   3d. etc. Also German and French editions. L I 1 (March 1924)–Ser. IV, 1 (Aug. 1937); LE;

LabP 1924–33

1669 Labour and Unity: a Monthly Journal Devoted to the Interests of Insurance, Building, Friendly, Co-operative, Loan, Trade, and Other Societies 1 (March 1868)–108 (Feb. 1877); then **Unity:** 109 (March 1877)–547 (Nov. 1916); m

A   1d. First printed and published by Thomas Williams. Organ claiming to represent the interests of 'all classes of Labourers', to point out to working-men 'the best path in which to travel, the best investments for their savings, the best course of conduct for their permanent social and political elevation'. Columns open to all matters pertaining to the 'welfare of the working masses of the community'. A clear conception of Labour as a separate identity in society is evident in the early numbers, but this disappears. Thereafter mainly a catalogue of society branch reports.

L(Col)†; O (w 1878–81)

1670 Labour Annual. 1895–1900. Manchester; then **Reformers' Year Book. 1901–9:** London; etc.; a

B   1s. etc. Publishers included Labour Press Society, Manchester, 'Clarion' Company, Ltd. London, Joseph Edwards, Glasgow, New Age Press, London (1909). Editors: Joseph Edwards, F. W. Pethwick-Lawrence (joint editor at one time), Clifford D. Sharp (1909). Much useful information on all aspects of the Labour movement. There were two editions for 1895.

BP; BkP 1895–9; C 1896, 1899–1900, 1906; E 1899–1904, 1907, 1909; L 1895–1905, 1907; LabP; LE; LU; MP 1895–1908; Q 1896, 1899–1907, 1909; ONC†; Harvester Press reprint 1895–1900

1671 Labour Book Service Bulletin 1 (Feb. 1940)–14 (April 1941); m

B   2d. Issued free to members of the Labour Book Service. Guide to forthcoming publications and discussion groups for Labour Party members. The 'function of the LBS is to provide the basis of a democratic culture.' Articles and notices of Labour literature. No number issued in January 1941.

L; TUC (w 1, 2)

1672 Labour Bookshelf: an Occasional Fly-Sheet 1 (Oct. 1924)–5 (Oct. 1926); irreg

B   Issued by the Independent Labour Party Publication and Labour Literature Department. Announcement circular and literature review.

L 1, 2 (2nd ed.), 3, 5; LdU 1–4

1673 Labour Bulletin I, 1 [Jan. 1925?] —? [m?]

    B   1d. Issued under the auspices of the Saffron Walden Divisional Labour Party. Comment on local Labour Party activities and contemporary issues.

    O(JJ)† I, 1 (April 1925)

Labour Bulletin 1929—1933 see **Labour Bulletin of Industrial and Political Information**

Labour Bulletin 1935 see Irish Labour Party. **Monthly News Bulletin**

1674 Labour Bulletin, for Service to the Labour Movement 1 (Sept. 1936)—33 (Aug. 1939); [ns] 1 (May/June 1947)—?; m; bi-m

    B   Gratis. Issued by the Labour Movement Relations Department of the **Daily Herald**. 'Our purpose is to form a link between the **Daily Herald** and those who are responsible for the Party's development in the Constituencies.' Functions: 'First, to provide for Party Leaders, Officers and Public Representatives a forum for all subjects, news and views related to Party work. Second, to remind its readers that the **Daily Herald** is Labour's own national newspaper, pledged to Labour's policy and at Labour's service to present its ideals and programme in millions of homes.' (ns 1).

    LabP† 1—[ns] 18 (May—July 1950)

1675 Labour Bulletin of Industrial and Political Information I, 1 (June 1925)—V, 1 (June 1929); then **Labour Bulletin**: V, 2 (July 1929)—([unnumbered] Aug. 1933); m

    B   3d. Prepared by the Labour Joint Research and Information Department, and published by the Trades Union Congress and the Labour Party, then prepared by the Labour Party Research (and Information) Department and published by the Labour Party. 'Service of information', 'facts and figures of current interest'. Then merged in **Labour**.

    C; E 1927—32; L; LE; LdU Feb.—March, Nov. 1931; O; TUC

1676 Labour Campaigner: the Official Organ of the 'Million Members and Power' Campaign [1932] —?

    B   Printed by Odhams Press. To support the Labour Party's nationwide campaign for a million new members and power, and an increased circulation for the **Daily Herald**. Slogan of the campaign: 'A million new members and power'. Hints for recruiting, and short encouraging contributions from Labour MPs.

    O(JJ)† First number (undated, unnumbered)

1677 Labour Candidate: Journal of the Society of Labour Candidates 1 (Sept. 1932)—?; then **Labour Representative**: 1945—?

    B   1d. Published by Ben Greene etc. for the Society of Labour Candidates. Later the organ of the Labour Parliamentary Association. A medium for Labour Party opinion and expression by prospective MPs and others, and more widely a forum for Party discussion.

    L 1—42 (Autumn 1937); LabP† 1—52 (Summer 1943*)

1678 Labour Challenge I, 1 (Sept. 1970)—?. Belfast; bi-m
    B   Northern Ireland Labour Party. Reproduced from typewriting.
Not issued for some time (**Fortnight**, 11 Jan. 1974).
    E; LabP† I, 1—7 (Sept./Oct. 1971)

1679 Labour Champion 1 (Oct. 1893)—5 (11 Nov. 1893). Leeds; w
    B   1d. Printed by J. W. Friedenson for the Leeds and County
Co-operative Newspaper Society. Edited by Tom Maguire. Independent
Labour Party. Wide interests: Labour and trade union news, poetry,
sketches, football etc.
    LdU† 2, 21 Oct.; 4, 4 Nov.; 5, 11 Nov.

1680 Labour Chronicle: the Workman's Paper for Leeds and District 1
(May 1893)—2 (June 1893). Leeds; m
    B   1d. Published by A. S. Fryer, Labour Chronicle Publishing
Company, and printed by G. O. Battye, in the interests of the Independent
Labour Party. Editors: Alf Mathison, J. Brotherton, A. S. Fryer.
Contributors: Tom Maguire, Raymond Unwin
    L(Col)† 1; LdU†

1681 Labour Chronicle: a Monthly Record of the Labour, Trade Union,
and Advanced Political Movements in Liverpool and District I, 1 (1 July
1894)—IV, 66 (Dec. 1899); then **Labour Chronicle and Trades Union
Reporter**: Official Organ of Liverpool and Vicinity United Trades and
Labour Council: I, 1 (Jan. 1900)—III, 1 (Jan. 1902). Liverpool; m
    B   1d.; ½d.; 1d. First published by Liverpool Fabian Society; from
March 1895 published by Liverpool Fabians and Independent Labour
Party under joint editorship; taken over by Liverpool Trades Council in
1899. Editors: John Edwards; Samuel Hales; Charles Doeg; Hugh
MacClare; Arthur W. Short. From February to December 1895 the title
was **Liverpool Labour Chronicle**. Sub-title varies.
    L(Col)† 1894—5, (1900—2 [microfilm]); LE (1898—9 [original])
(1894—1901* [microfilm]); LU 1 April 1896; LvP II, 7—18; ONC†
1894—8*

1682 Labour Chronicle: a Local Organ of Democratic Socialism 1 (15 Oct.
1894)—15 (Dec. 1895). Edinburgh; m
    B   ½d.; 1d. Printed by John Anderson for the proprietors, the local
branches of the Independent Labour Party and the Scottish Socialist
Federation. Published and edited by Alexander Dickinson. Regular
contributors included James Connolly, under the pseudonym 'R. Ascal'
(R. Gray — personal communication).
    AbU (microfilm); EP† 1—12; LE†; ONC 4

1683 Labour Chronicle: the Organ of the Yeadon and District ILP 1
(March 1898)—? Yeadon; m
    B   Free. Published by Yeadon Independent Labour Party.
    AbU (microfilm of O[JJ] holding); O(JJ) 1—3, 5

Labour Chronicle 1936–1938 see **Chronicle**: the Official Organ of the Beckenham and Penge Labour Party, 1936

Labour Chronicle and Trades Union Reporter see **Labour Chronicle 1894–1899**

1684 Labour Chronicle for Southampton, Portsmouth and District 1 (25 Sept. 1897)–[1898?]. Southampton; w

    B   Independent Labour Party. Edited by Joseph Clayton. 'The Paper was beset by legal troubles. An article entitled "Municipal Mismanagement", written by the editor and a colleague on the paper, Bicker Caarten, who was Chairman of the Navvies' Union, and published in the issue for 23 October 1897, led to a libel suit against the authors. After five court appearances over the next two and a half years, the men were eventually acquitted.' (D. Hopkin, 'Local Newspapers of the Independent Labour Party, 1893–1906'. Society for the Study of Labour History, **Bulletin**, 28 [Spring 1974].)

1685 Labour Church Record 1 (Jan. 1899)–[10] (Oct. 1901) Horsted Keynes, Sussex; Bolton; q

    B   Free; ½d. Published John Trevor; James Sims, **Labour Church Record** Office. Editors: John Trevor; Allen Clarke (No. 8–). Contributors: Wicksteed, A. J. Waldegrove, Raymond Unwin. Record of activities of Labour Churches. See also **Labour Prophet**.

    L Jan. 1899–July 1900, Jan. 1901; LE 1899; O 2–8, O(JJ)†; ONC 4

1686 Labour Common Market Committee. **Newsbrief** 1 [1961?]–13 (1963); irreg?

    B   Succeeded by **Europe Left**.

    TUC 2 (1961)–13; Warwick U (MRC) 5 (April 1962)

1687 London Co-operative Society. **Members Report** 1, [19–?]– ; q; s-a

    A

    The Society

1688 Labour Co-partnership I, 1 (1 Aug. 1894)–XII, 12 (Dec. 1906); then **Co-partnership**: XIII, 1 (Jan. 1907)– ; m; q

    C   Labour Co-partnership Association; Industrial Co-partnership Association; Industrial Participation Association. First published by Henry Vivian. 'Advocated form of co-operation in which a substantial share of profit of business goes to workers who can invest it in shares and thus be entitled to vote on affairs of body which employs them; equal partnership of labour and capital' (Brophy). Current title: **Industrial Participation**. Absorbed **Profit-sharing and Co-partnership**.

    Bishopsgate Institute 1894–1905; C IV, 12–(V, XIX, XXI, XXV*); Co-op. Coll. I, XV; Gu I–VI; L(Col); LE (1901, 1903–5*); LU I–IX, XIV–XX, XLIV, 411–(w 416, 425, 444); LvU XVI– ; MP XI–XIV; O V– ; ONC occ. nos; the Association

1689 Labour Councillor I, 1 (Jan. 1949)–III, 11/12 (Nov./Dec. 1951); m

    B   2d. Published by the Labour Party. Edited by the Local Government Section of the Labour Party. Relevant news and comment.

    E; L; O; ONC (w 1–3)

Labour Councillor 1973– see **Partnership**

1690 Labour Defence: Organ of the International Labour Defence I, 1 (March 1934)–?; m

    B   No. 1 contained 'Defend the Hunger Marches', Release Dimitròv', and 'Save the Scottsboro Boys'.

    WCML† 1

1691 Labour Defender: Organ of the ICWPA. 1 (Jan. 1929)–2 (March 1929)

    B   1d. Published by International Class War Prisoners Aid. Agitated for the immediate release of workers imprisoned for political acts against the capitalist State, i.e. of workers undergoing penal servitude for alleged crimes during 1926 General Strike, also of international political prisoners. President: Klara Zetkin.

    L(Col)†

1692 Labour Discussion Notes 1 (1939)–45 (June 1944?); bi-m?

    B   Published by the Socialist Clarity Group, which was founded in 1936 by several people including Austen Albu, Patrick Gordon Walker and William Warbey, who were dissatisfied with the various opposition groupings within the Labour Party, and decided to publish a journal outlining alternative policies.

    L 6, 8–   ; LabP 5 (Sept. 1939)–45 (June 1944); ONC 39–45

Labour Echo 1894–1899 see **Bradford Labour Echo**

1693 Labour Echo: Organ of the Nottingham Labour Church 1 (June 1896)–[1899?]. Nottingham; m

    B   Gratis. Printed for the Nottingham Labour Church by Nottingham Co-operative Printing Society. Editor: William Robinson. 5000 issued; 'hopes to enlarge shortly and to emulate the Bradford **Echo**' (**Labour Annual**, 1897). Monthly report, notes of meeting etc.

    NU† 7 (Dec. 1896); O(JJ)† 1–3 (Aug. 1896)

1694 Labour Elector 1 (June 1888) I, 9 (15 Dec. 1888); ns I, 1 (5 Jan. 1889)–ns 68 (18 April 1890); ns 1 (7 Jan. 1893)–102 (July 1894); m; fortn; w

    B   1d. Editor: H. H. Champion: 'With which is incorporated the sub-titled 'Organ of Gas Workers' and Dockers' Union.' June 1893 organ of the Independent Labour Party. One-time organ of the National Labour Electoral Association – **The Labour Party**. Agitates on the eight-hours' question.

    GM June 1888–March 1890; L(Col)†; TUC, John Burns Lib

1695 Labour Forum: a Quarterly Review I, 1 (Sept.–Dec. 1946)–I, 8 (July–Aug. 1948); q

B 6d. Published by the Labour Party. Edited by the Research Department. '. . . to explore the next steps in the Party's programme, to analyse current trends, and especially to develop education within the Party. . . . Material of use to the steadily growing number of Labour Discussion Groups will be included . . .'

E; L; LabP†; O; ONC

1696 Labour Fund Raiser: a Publication of the National Fund Raising Foundation I, 1 (1962)–? Oxford

B Printed Pergamon Press. Edited by Robert Maxwell. Probably only one published.

Warwick UL†

1697 Labour Gazette: the Official Organ of Warrington Trades and Labour Council 1 (Oct. 1912)–([24?] Jan. 1915). Warrington; m?

A Edited by Charles Dukes. Local trade-union and Labour news. Deals with wire workers, fustian cutters, iron workers, carters, labourers and women workers.

Warrington PL

1698 Labour Herald: an Unofficial Paper for ILPers [c1897?] ; w

B 1d. Edited by Sleigh Appleton. Prospectus for shares in **Labour Leader**, December 1896. 'There is no evidence that the . . . **Labour Herald** . . . ever actually appeared . . . The **Labour Herald** was advertised in the **Labour Leader** but it is by no means certain that it ever appeared or that it gained the approval of the ILP itself. It is included as an unique independent ILP newspaper, which, like the **Labour Monthly** scheme, sought to serve the party without being altogether tied to it . . . There are no references in any established ILP sources to Sleigh Appleton and no clear indication, therefore, what was his connection with the ILP.' (D. Hopkin, 'Local Newspapers of the Independent Labour Party, 1893–1906'. Society for the Study of Labour History, **Bulletin**, 28 [Spring 1974])

1699 Labour Herald: Organ of the Pudsey Division ILP 1 (July 1897)–? Pudsey, Yorkshire; m

B Free. Published by Pudsey Independent Labour Party. Edited by J. W. Allerton. Printed by Ogden and Company, Keighley.

AbU 30 (Dec. 1899 [microfilm]); ILP Oct. 1908, April, June, July, Nov. 1909, Feb., March 1911; O(JJ) 30

1700 Labour Herald 1899. Paisley

B Independent Labour Party. (ILP News, July 1899.)

Labour Herald 1905–1907 see **Jarrow Division Labour Herald**

1701 Labour International Handbook. 1921, 1923
B   Issued by the Labour Research Department. Editor: R. Palme Dutt. Articles and information on the international Labour Movement, international affairs and international Labour organisations.
BP; C; L 1923; LE; LvP†; O 1923; SP 1923

1702 Labour Israel: For Jewish Independence, For Socialism, For World Peace 1 (22 Oct. 1948)–128 (April/May 1959); fortn; m; bi-m
B   4d.; 3d. Published (?) by MAPAM, London.
L(Col)†; LWL; TUC*

1703 Labour Journal 1 (30 Sept. 1892)–10 (2 Dec. 1892). Bradford; w
B   ½d. Printed and published by the Labour Journal Company. Organ of the Labour movement in Bradford, the Labour Church, Fabian Society, Labour Union, Women's Labour Union, Bradford Trades and Labour Council.
L(Col)†

Labour Journal Nov. 1893–? see Hull Trades Council, **Labour Journal**

1704 Labour Journal: Organ of the Accrington Branch of the British Socialist Party 1 (June 1912)–30 (Nov. 1914). Burnley; m
B   Gratis. Printed and published for the Accrington BSP by Nuttall and Company. A popular propaganda paper which discusses in simple terms the meaning of Socialism. Advocates return of Socialist-Labour MPs. 'Woman's corner'.
L(Col)† 20 (Jan. 1914)–30

Labour Leader, 1889 see **Miner, 1887–1889**

1705 Labour Leader Jan. 1893–ns XIX, 39 (28 Sept. 1922); then **New Leader:** I, 1 (6 Oct. 1922)–XXXVIII, 24 (1946); then **Socialist Leader:** XXXVIII, 25 (1946)–   ; m; w
B   Independent Labour Party. Editors included Keir Hardie, Bruce Glasier, H. N. Brailsford.
C 2 July 1914–28 Sept. 1922; E April 1957–   ; GM 1897–*; L(Col) ns V, 1 (31 March 1894)–   ; LE 31 March, 1894–June 1922*; O 1905–   ; TUE 3 Feb. 1893–1917*; Warwick UL March 1894–1915 (microfilm)

1706 Labour Leaf, [c1886]; m
B   Socialist League, Clerkenwell.
ILP Nov. 1886

1707 Labour Leaflet 1 [1888]–? Alyth
B   1d. for 8 copies etc. Propagandist single-sheet leaflet, issued under the auspices of the Ploughmen's Club and the Socialist Union. No. 6 publicises the Scottish Socialist Federation just founded in Edinburgh. Compiled by R. Dempster.
E† 1–6

1708 Labour League; or, Journal of the National Association of United Trades, 1 (5 Aug 1848)–42 (26 May 1849). Douglas, Isle of Man; London; w

A   1d. Printed and published by William Shirrefs and Andrew Russell, later published by James Watson. Conducted the Central Committee of the National Association of United Trades for the Protection and Employment of Industry. Succeeds the **Monthly Report** previously circulated by the Committee. To create opinion among the trades for self-improvement, funds to provide employment for unemployed members, and to press for State legislation for fair wages and decent conditions. Urged the right to work.

Bishopsgate Institute †

1709 Labour League [c1950]

B   Duplicated magazine for Labour Party Young Socialists, North Paddington branch (**Socialist Advance**, April 1950).

1710 Labour League Examiner: the Organ of the Amalgamated Labour League of Lincoln, Norfolk, Suffolk, Leicester, Derby, Notts, York, Wilts, Salop, Hereford, Brecon etc 1 [1874?]–42 (12 Dec. 1874);then **Labourer**: 1 (9 Jan. 1875)–318 (26 Feb. 1881). Boston, Lincolnshire; Grantham (25 Oct. 1879–); w

A   1d. Published by William Banks, the General Secretary of the League, and from 1875 by Banks and Edward Bradbury, the Treasurer. For agricultural and general labourers, chiefly in rural districts.

L(Col)† (w 1–10)

1711 Labour Letters 1 (May Day 1896)–? [Wallasey?] ; irreg?

B   Free. Edited by Joseph Edwards, Labour Annual Office, Wallasey. No. 1 on 'Labour' is reprinted in **Labour Annual**, 1897, p. 48, opposite its description. Advertisements on the reverse helped to defray the cost of production, and special editions with local advertisement were also printed. 'The second leaflet, on the nature and effects of Landlordism, will probably be issued for May Day, 1897.' It is not known if this was published.

1712 Labour Life: Magazine of St Marylebone Labour Party 1 (Nov. 1944)–   ; irreg (1–6); m

B   3d. (1960). Published by the St Marylebone Constituency Labour Party. National and local news, short articles, correspondence, diary of events.

LabP† 153 (April 1960)–233 (Dec. 1967*); SmP (w occ. nos); TUC occ. nos

1713 Labour Light and Local Trades Unions' Journal 1 ([14 March 1890?])–?. Bolton; w

    B   Printed and published by W. and T. R. Morris for the proprietors. In **Teddy Ashton's Weekly**, 4 Jan. 1908, C. Allen Clarke says that he started the first Labour paper in Lancashire, **The Labour Light**. 'It did fairly well until I aired the piecer question in it — and then it paid for its rashness. The trade union spinners boycotted it.' Advocated Labour Representation in Parliament; most extensive coverage of strike and trade-union news from the local area to the international field. James Haslam employed on the paper.

    LU† 8 (2 May 1890)–13 (6 June 1890)

1714 Labour Link April 1958–April 1962

    B   3d. Issued by the British and Asian Overseas Socialist Fellowship, later named British-Overseas Socialist Fellowship. Editor: I. S. Campbell. One of the aims of the Fellowship was to 'make contact with groups from Asia, Africa and South America and let them see something of the side of British life that is presented by the Labour Movement'.

    LE† July 1958–April 1962; TUC April 1958–(July 1960*)

1715 Labour List, and Universal Gazette of Employment 1 (21 Nov. 1854)

    C   2d. Printed and published for the proprietor by Edward Shelton. 'Organ of that large class of people who are daily seeking to find employment for their industry.' Advertisements of situations vacant.

    L(Col)†

Labour Log see **East Kenton Log**

1716 Labour Magazine: Official Monthly Journal of the Labour Movement I, 1 (May 1922)–XII, 4 (Aug. 1933); m

    B   Published by the Trade Union Congress and the Labour Party. 'The first monthly joint journal of the TUC and the Labour Party', advocates 'the policy of the National Labour Movement as formulated from time to time by representative conferences'; 'authoritative voice of the whole Movement'. Articles by leading figures in the Trade Union and Labour Movement. Absorbed **British Trades Union Review**. Incorporated in **Labour**.

    BP; E; GM; L†; LabP; LdU; LE; ONC 1922–30*; TUC

1717 Labour Mail 1906–7

    BP (not available)

1718 Labour Mayor 1 (Dec. 1958)–   ; s-a

    B   Issued by the London Labour Mayors' Association, later the Metropolitan Labour Mayors' Association. Covers Association activities and local authority matters.

    LabP*†

1719 Labour Member [193-?]; I, 1 [Dec. 1962?] –15 (May 1963?)
Westhoughton; Manchester; m

    B   Earlier series listed in Labour and Socialist International, **The Socialist Press** (1933) but no copies traced. Later series one of the 'Labour's Voice' series. Published by the Workers' Nothern Publishing Society. Sub-title: 'Organ of Westhoughton Constituency Labour Party'. 4d. Edited by Harry Alvarez.

      L(Col)*†; LabP† 9, 10, 15

1720 Labour Monthly 1 (Oct. 1896)–[1897?]. Blackburn; m

    B   One of a series of papers supporting the Independent Labour Party founded by Allen Clarke.

      O(JJ) 1, 3 (Dec. 1896)

1721 Labour Monthly: a Magazine of International Labour I, 1 (July 1921)– ; m

    B   1s. etc. The longest serving Communist journal. Published by the Labour Publishing Company etc. Editor: R. Palme Dutt. Associate editor: R. Page Arnot. 'Notes of the month', signed articles, shorter notices, book reviews, cartoons.

    BP XV– ; BdP 1–II; C; CME XXII) ,; E; ExU II–VIII; GM; L. LE; LII, Dec. 1939– ; LU XX–XXXI; LdP L–VII; LvP I–VI; MML; O†; ONC*†; WmP XXX–

1722 Labour News: a Circular of Information on the Condition of the Labour Market in Town and Country 1 (30 Aug. 1871)– ; w

    C   1d. etc. Published at first at the Labour Agency and Employment Inquiry Office. Later titles: **Labour News and Employment Advertiser** (5 July 1873–30 April 1927); **Labour News, Public Works and Building Trades Advertiser** (7 May 1927–30 Aug. 1962); **Construction and Labour News** (6 Sept. 1962–13 June 1963); **Construction News** (20 June 1963–). But relevant only in its early years; provided information for working-men seeking jobs, for societies, and also of use to employers. Provided a 'reputable' service, ie did not advertise scabbing and cheap labour. Sometimes compiled tables of average wages for districts by trade.

      L(Col)†; LvP (July 1949)–

Labour News. 1922–1927 see **Washington Labour News**

1723 Labour News: for Kirkcaldy District of Burghs 1 (20 Jan. 1923)–23 (23 June 1923). Kirkcaldy; w

    B   1d. Published by W. C. O'Neill, the editor, for the Kirkcaldy Burgh Divisional Labour Party. Established as a much-needed local paper to represent the 'Labour point of view'; 'moderate socialist'.

      L(Col)†

1724 Labour News: Organ of the Irish Labour Movement I, 1 (28 Nov. 1936)–II, 4 (2 April 1938). Dublin; w

    B   2d. Printed and published for the proprietors by Cahill and Company. Official paper of the Irish Labour Party (Irish Free State). Claimed heritage of James Connolly, for a 'workers' republic'.
Contributor: William O'Brien, General Secretary of the Irish Transport and General Workers' Union and Chairman of the Administrative Council, Labour Party.

    L(Col)†

1725 Labour News: Official Organ of Labour Party in Dublin South-West [I, 1] (Oct. 1965)–II, 12 (Dec. 1966). Dublin; m

    B   4d.; 6d. Published by the Labour Party, Dublin South-West Constituency, then by 'Labour News'. Left-wing, militant Labour.

    L(Col)† Oct. 1965–Dec. 1965, March 1966–Dec. 1966.

1726 Labour News: the Voice of All Saints Ward Labour Party [c1969]. Manchester

    B   Single sheet reproduced from typewriting issue for July 1969 seen, in R. Williamson's possession.

1727 Labour News Letter [1940?]–? Dublin; m

    B   1d. Published by the Irish Labour Party. Reproduced from typewriting. 'Facts, figures and comments concerning politics and economics in Ireland'; then printed, **A Monthly Review of Political and Economic Affairs in Ireland.**

    LabP† 1st series, 2 (June 1940)–III, Sept./Oct. 1942), ns I, 1 (Sept. 1943)–4 (Dec. 1943)

1728 Labour Progressive [1905?]–?

    B?   Started by H. A. Sheridan Bickers. (**Reformers' Year Book**, 1906.)

1729 Labour Prophet: the Organ of the Labour Church I, 1 (Jan. 1892)–IV, 44 (Aug. 1895); then **Labour Prophet and Labour Church Record**: IV, 45 (Sept. 1895)–VI, 81 (Sept. 1898); then **Labour Church Record**: 1 (Jan. 1899)–(Oct. 1901). Manchester; London; m; q

    B   1d. Editors: John Trevor; Reginald A. Beckett; John Trevor. To represent the religious life which inspires the Labour movement, and to further the formation of a national organisation of Labour Churches. Pages offered to local Labour Churches, eg Ramsbottom. See also **The Prophet** Included a 'Cinderella' supplement for children.

    E I–VI; L(Col)† 1892–3, 1896–7 (1893 microfilm); LE*†; LU*; LdU I–II; MP I–VI; O I–VI; OMA*

1730 Labour Observer (March 1923- Jan 1928)

    B?   (BUCOP).

    GrP

1731 Labour Organiser: the Official Journal of the National Association of Labour Organisers and Election Agents I, 1 (Aug. 1920)–L, 584 (Aug./Sept. 1971). Worcester; London; m

   B   4d. Sub-title dropped after five issues when the name of the proprietors was changed to the National Association of Labour Agents. Later published by the Labour Party. First editor: H. Drinkwater; last editor: R. Haywood. 'The only Labour journal devoted to organisation, electioneering, and business matters.'

   BP I–XXXII; E Oct. 1944–L 127–   ; LE† I, 2–   ; LabP† I, 2–(w 3, 4); TUC 1953–71;* Warwick UL 1924–*

Labour Party. Economic Brief see **Economic Brief**

1732 Labour Party. General Secretary's Newsletter 1 (May 1960)–   ; irreg

   B   Printed and published by the Labour Party. 'The idea behind this newsletter is to provide you regularly with a broad picture of the things we are doing at Head Office and to fill in the background of the National Executive Committee statements and circulars which you receive from time to time.' Unnumbered after No. 4, Aug. 1960. Title of No. 1 was **Secretary's Newsletter**.

   LabP*†; ONC occ. nos

1733 Labour Party. International Briefing 1, [1970]–4 [1971]; q

   B   4s. Published by the Labour Party; 'quarterly review of International Affairs'. Numbers not dated. Pagination varies; each is devoted to a particular topic and has a separate title to indicate that, eg, 'Labour and the World, 1964–70' (No. 1); 'Labour and the UN' (No. 2). Occasional signed articles. Superseded the Labour Party's **Overseas Review**. Was superseded by **Labour Weekly**.

   LabP†; ONC†; TUC

Labour Party. Monthly Youth Letter see **Labour's Monthly Youth Letter**

1734 Labour Party. Overseas Review: Labour's View of the World [Sept. 1967?]–(May/June 1969); 9-yr

   B   1s. printed and published by the Labour Party. Reproduced from typewriting. Edited by Gwyn Morgan. News, reports (some signed). Superseded by **International Briefing**.

   ONC† Sept. 1967–   ; TUC 1968–

Labour Party. Quarterly Circular. see Labour Representation Committee. **Quarterly Circular**

Labour Party. Secretary's Newsletter see Labour Party. **General Secretary's Newsletter**

1735 Labour Party. **League of Youth. Monthly Bulletin** 1 (12 July 1929)–11 (May 1930?); ns 1 (July 1930)–? m

    B   Issued by the Labour Party Press and Publicity Department Edited by W. Arthur Peacock. 'Part of a great campaign we are launching right away to form Leagues of Youth in every Divisional Labour Party, and where advisable every local Labour Party' (No. 1). For communication between the Advisory Committee and Branches. First series reproduced from typewriting.

        LabP† 1–11 (May 1930); ns 1–28 (Oct. 1932)

1736 Labour Party. **League of Youth. Organization Bulletin** 1 (April 1938)–? irreg; 'at frequent intervals'

    B   Editor: John Huddleston, National Youth Officer.
Reproduced from typewriting. News of branches and activities, literature, propaganda work etc.

        LabP† 1–ns 4 (July 1942) (w ns 1)

1737 Labour Party and Trades Union Congress. **Notes for Speakers** [c1918]; [1924?]–1096 (7 Feb 1947); w

    B   Printed and published by the TUC and Labour Party (1925); published by the Labour Party and the TUC General Council (1947). Each number consists of several cards, and the whole set of cards is numbered in one sequence. Indexes issued from time to time. Title sometimes **Weekly Notes for Speakers**.

        E 1924; LabP [1924?]–1945*, ONC† occ. nos c1918; 29 (11 Nov. 1925)–*

Labour Party Bulletin. 1920–1921 see Labour Party Local Government. **Parliamentary and International Bulletin**

Labour Party Bulletin, 1941–1948 see **Labour Party News Bulletin**

1738 Labour Party Information Bureau Bulletin 1 (10 July 1916)–?
    B
    LabP 1–ns 3 (5 Nov. 1917) (not traced on shelf)

1739 Labour Party Local Government. **Parliamentary and International Bulletin.** I, 1 (1 March 1920)–I, 24 (1921); irreg?

    B   Produced by the Labour Party's Information Bureau. This is called 'Third series'. Earlier series may have been **Labour Party Information Bureau Bulletin**. Information, statistics, Labour Party policy on all matters. Sometimes referred to as **Labour Party Bulletin**?

        C; LabP†; O 1–3, 24

1740 Labour Party News Bulletin 1 (27 Oct. 1939(−10 (April 1940); then **Labour Party Bulletin**: ns I, 1 (Nov. 1941)−VI, 12 (Dec. 1948); then **Fact**: VII, 1 (Jan. 1949)−XV, 12 (Dec. 1956); m

    B   1d. Edited by the Labour Party Research Department. 'A war-time service of information and guidance to all sections of the Labour Party, Trade Union and political.' Policy announcements and decisions. Incorporated in **Socialist Digest**.

    BU 1955−6; HsP ii I−IV*; L; LabP 1941−56; ONC April 1949−Dec. 1956; TUC; Warwick UL 1940, 1949−56

Labour Party Year Book see **Labour Year Book**

1741 Labour Party Young Socialists Chief Officer's Newsletter 1 (May 1966)−37 (Dec. 1969); then **Young Socialists' Communiqué**: 1/70−? m; irreg

    B   Reproduced from typewriting. Two copies sent to branches, one for the Secretary, the other for display on the notice board. News, forthcoming events etc.

    LabP† 1−3/70*

Labour Peace Bulletin see Labour Peace Fellowship. **Bulletin**

1742 Labour Peace Fellowship. Bulletin (Sept. 1958)−(May 1959); then **LPF Bulletin**: ns 1 (Sept. 1959)− ns 2 (Nov. 1959); then **Labour Peace Bulletin**: ns 1 (Jan./Feb. 1960)−[1961?] ; bi-m

    B   Reproduced from typewriting at first. The Fellowship was an organisation of members of the Labour Party and the affiliated bodies, who refused to support war. Supports non-violent methods for resolving world problems. 'Against war − for international Socialism'.

    L 1−ns 9 (Oct. 1961)

1743 Labour Peace Fellowship. Newsletter (May 1962)−? Petts Wood; bi-m?

    B   Reproduced from typewriting. Sometimes **LPF Newsletter**?

    L (but only issue for Jan./Feb. 1963 seen)

1744 Labour Peace Leader: Organ of the Labour Peace Fellowship 1 (Sept./Oct. 1954)−8 (Feb./March 1956); bi-m

    B   Anti-war and anti-bomb lobby in the Labour Party.

    L; TUC*.

1745 Labour Pioneer: the Organ of the Cardiff Socialist Party I, 1 (Feb. 1900)−III, 2 (Nov. 1902). Cardiff; m

    B   ½d. Editors: A. E. Ellery, T. J. Hart (Amalgamated Society of Railway Servants), Harold Snelling. 'Favoured labour representation in Parliament, TUC policies, emancipation of labour, freedom from capitalism and landlordism. Supported by trade unions in area' (Brophy).

    L(Col)† 1900; LE† Sept. 1900−Nov. 1902*.

Labour Pioneer. 1919–1922 see **Yorkshire Factory Times**

1746 Labour Pioneer 1 (May 1921)–8 (Dec. 1921). Gloucester; m
   B?   (BUCOP).
   GrP

1747 Labour Press and Miners' and Workmen's Examiner: a Journal of
General Intelligence, Devoted to the Interests of Labour 1873–(26 Dec.
1874) then **Miner and Workmen's Examiner**: 73 (2 Jan 1875)–215
(13 Oct. 1877); then **Miner: the Organ of Underground Labour**: 216
(20 Oct. 1877)–260 (24 Oct. 1878). Hanley (1873–4); Stoke-on-Trent;
Wolverhampton (20 Feb. 1875)–(1878); w
   B   1d. Printed for the proprietors by the Co-operative Newspaper
and General Steam Printing Society, published by William Owen, the
editor; then, 1877–8, printed and published by the proprietors, Owen and
Spencer. Detailed information on iron and coal miners' unions, and in
1874 on agricultural labourers' unions in the Midlands area; some
information on general Unionism. In later years concentrates more on
conditions of labour and struggles in the mining industry, chiefly in the
Midlands.
   L(Col)† 33 (4 April)–26 Dec. 1874, 9 Jan. 1875–24 Aug. 1878

1748 Labour Press Service [1922?] –(Aug./Sept. 1961); w; m
   B   Issued by the Labour Party. Several series of numbering. Size
and format varies.
   LE*; LabP July 1922–Aug./Sept. 1961; ONC† 1936–1961*; TUC
1953–61

Labour Progress. 1941–1943 see **Northern Ireland Labour Bulletin**

Labour Prophet and Labour Church Record see **Labour Prophet**

1749 Labour Record: Official Organ of the London and Counties Labour
League 1 (1 May 1893)–20 (1 Dec. 1894); m
   A   1d. Published by Charles Beale, General Secretary of the
League, 'the oldest registered Labourers' Trades Union in the United
Kingdom'. A general trade union and member of the wide-ranging London
Building Trades Federation. Motto: 'Defence, not Defiance'. To secure
adequate wages, regulate working hours and provide protection in labour
and trade disputes. Moderate and conciliatory. No political commitment.
   L(Col)†

1750 Labour Record 1 (Sept. 1920)–4 (Dec. 1920?) Cardiff; m
   B   1d. Published by the proprietors, 'Labour Record' Press
Committee. 'Portraying Labour thought and action in Cardiff and district.'
   AbN 4 (now missing)

1751 Labour Record and Review I, 1 (March 1905)–III, 3 (May 1907); m
   B . 1d. Edited by F. W. Pethwick-Lawrence. Supported Labour
Party, reforms proposed by the Trades Union Congress, and socialist
reform to be achieved through the Labour Party. Includes character
sketches of Labour and trade union leaders. Incorporated into **New Age**
   ILP March 1905–Feb. 1907; L(Col)†; LE; O(JJ)† 1; ONC 1; TUC,
John Burns Lib.

1752 Labour Report: South Kensington Labour Party Journal [196-?] –?
m
   B   Reproduced from typewriting. Internal and local affairs as well
as more general political matters. July–September 1965 superseded by
Chelsea, South Kensington, North Kensington Labour News.
   ONC† Nov. 1962–Sept. 1967

1753 Labour Reporter [c1903]. [Wellington, Salop?] ; m
   B?   ½d. Organ of Oakengates Labour movements. (**Reformers'
Year Book**, 1903.)

1754 Labour Representation Committee. **Quarterly Circular** 1 (June
1902)–[1912?] ; q
   B   **Quarterly Circular** of the Labour Party from No. 13, April
1906. 'Head Office report', parliamentary report, parliamentary diary,
financial statements etc.
   E 3, 4; LE 1907–12*; LabP† 1–32 (July 1912); O† 20–5, 27–32

Labour Representative see **Labour Candidate**

Labour Research see Fabian Research Department. **Monthly Circular**

Labour Research Department. **Monthly Circular** see Fabian Research
Department. **Monthly Circular**

1755 Labour Review I, 1 (Jan.–March 1952)–VII, 5 (Summer 1963).
Manchester; London (3-); bi-m
   B   2s.; 2s.6d. Published by New Park Publications. Suspended
March 1954–Dec. 1956. Theoretical journal conducted by the Trotskyist
group within the Labour Party, until their expulsion. From April 1959 the
theoretical organ of the Socialist Labour League. Superseded by **Fourth
International.**
   BU 1961–2; L†; LE; ONC I, 1, 3

1756 Labour Searchlight 1 (July 1961)–? Liverpool
   B   Liverpool Trades Council and Labour Party
   TUC 1

1757 Labour Standard: an Organ of Industry 1 (7 May 1881)–V, 218 (4 July 1885); w

B   1d. Editors: George Shipton (until February 1884); William Barnett. 'Declared purpose to defend and advance interests of labour with special attention to trade societies, to express views of working people, to elicit and publish their opinion. Advocated independent Labour Party. Shipton, Secretary of London Trades Council 1871–96. From Oct. 1881 journal carried note that it was the recognised Industrial Journal of the Organized Trades of the United Kingdom. Less emphasis on political action under Barnett's editorship' (Brophy). Some coverage of American Labour. (See also F. Engels, **Articles in Labour Standard**, Moscow, Progress Publishers, 1891.)

Bishopsgate Institute 1–(29 April 1882); L(Col)†

1758 Labour Standard 1 (Specimen) (Nov. 1901)–2 (Feb. 1902). Birmingham; m

B   ½d. Published by J. Warren Owen. 'Issued monthly in support of Direct Labour Representation and in the interests of Organised Labour and Democratic Citizenship.' Labour and Democratic Alliance for Birmingham, ie National Democratic League, Trades Council, and Independent Labour Party. 'For united action on behalf of Labour' at municipal and national levels. For circulation in Birmingham and the Midlands.

BP†; O(JJ) 1

1759 Labour Standard, Circulating in Edinburgh and the Lothians. 1 (21 Feb. 1925)–VI, 304 (27 Dec. 1930). Edinburgh; w

B   1d. Published by the Labour Standard Printing and Publishing Society. A local Independent Labour Party paper

EP† (w occ. nos)

1760 Labour Teacher I, 1 (Dec. 1951)–(May 1961); q

B   6d. Published by Peter Ibbotson for the National Association of Labour Teachers later Socialist Education Association (Labour Party). Edited by P. Ibbotson and Jim Wood. Addressed to members, and to render service to all those in the Labour Movement who take an interest in education. Supports 'the social-democratic approach to education' attempting to have some influences on Labour policy. Does not deal with wages and working conditions of teachers, but with the future of education generally. Reproduced from typewriting. Superseded by **Socialism and Education**.

L†

1761 Labour Torch: a Light on Labour Matters in the Yardley Division, and Elsewhere 1 (Sept. 1924)–46 (Oct. 1936). Birmingham; m; bi-m; irreg

B   Free. Official organ of the Yardley Divisional Labour Party. Record and review of the activities of the Labour movement locally and nationally. Contributor: A. G. Gossling, local candidate and MP.

BP†

1762 Labour Tribune: Organ of Miners, Iron Workers, Nut and Bolt Forgers etc. of Great Britain 1 (6 March 1886)–435 (30 June 1894). West Bromwich; w

    A   1d. Printed and published for the proprietors by F. T. Jefferson. Main issue in its pages was the miners' struggle for an eight-hour day. Supported the Labour Electoral Association.

    L(Col)† (1893 microfilm); LE 214 (5 April 1890)–426 (28 April 1894)

1763 Labour Union Journal 1 (26 May 1892)–7 (2 July 1892). Bradford; w

    B   Free. Printed and published for the Bradford and District Labour Union by J. S. Toothill. Supports the canditature of Ben Tillett for Western Bradford constituency. Programme: eight-hour day, independent labour representation, land nationalisation etc. Contributors: Ben Tillett, Dan Irving.

    BdP; L(Col)† 1–6

Labour Voice see **Llais Llafur**

1764 Labour Weekly: the Newspaper of the Labour Party 1 (1 Oct. 1971–   ; w

    B   5p. Published by the Labour Party. Superseded **Economic Brief, International Briefing, Labour Organiser, Labour Women, Talking Points, This Week**.

    L(Col); O†; ONC†; TUC

Labour Woman see **League Leaflets**

1765 Labour Worker [1962?]–83 (May 1968); then **Socialist Worker**: 84 (June 1958)–   ; m; fortn; m

    B   4d.; 6d. etc. 'For Workers Control and International Socialism.' Published until 1968 by the Socialist Review Publishing Company, then by International Socialists. Editor (1965): Paul Foot.

    L(Col)† 29 (mid-Jan. 1965)–   ; LE 297 (11 Nov. 1972)–   ; Warwick UL 1968–

1766 Labour World 1 (21 Sept 1890)–37 (30 May 1891); w

    B   1d. Proprietors: The London World News Company. Editor: Michael Davitt. A bulky newspaper focusing attention on the Labour Movement in Britain, and abroad. Much emphasis on Irish affairs, especially the Irish land question.

    L(Col); LE†; ONC† II, 33 (2 May 1891)

1767 Labour Year Book. 1916—32: irreg; a (1924—   )

B   1s. etc. Issued first by the Parliamentary Committee of the Trades Union Congress, the Fabian Research Department, and the Executive Committee of the Labour Party; from 1924 by the General Council of the TUC and the National Executive of the Labour Party. Not published in 1917, 1918, 1920—3, 1929. Information on the Labour Movement, labour and social legislation, government etc. with special signed articles, eg 'The Triple Industrial Alliance', by Robert Smillie.

BP; BU 1916, 1925—7, 1930; BrU 1916, 1919; C;
DnP 1924—5, 1927—32; E; EU 1919; GM; HsP 1932; L 1916, 1924—32; LE; LGU 1932; LvP† 1916, 1925—31; MP*; O; ONC† 1916, 1919, 1924—6, 1931—2; SP 1924—   ; TUC 1916—31; Warwick UL*

Labour Year Book for Dundee, Angus, Perth and Montrose Burghs see **Dundee Labour Year Book**

1768 Labour Youth [1936?] —?

B   Printed and published by **Labour Youth**. Reproduced from typewriting. Two purposes: to be 'the national paper of the L. of Y' [Labour party League of Youth] ; to be a 'local paper serving the interests of the small Leagues'. Short articles on the re-organisation of the youth movement.

O(JJ)† I, 3 (July 1936)

Labour Youth. 1948 see **Young Socialist. 1946—1948**

1769 Labourer: a Monthly Magazine of Politics, Literature, Poetry etc. I, 1 (Jan. 1847)—IV, (Dec. 1848). London; Manchester; m

B   Published in London at the **Northern Star** Office, in Manchester by Abel Haywood. Joint editors: Feargus O'Connor, Ernest Jones. Chartist and 'Land Plan' organ. Articles dedicated to 'the redemption of the working classes from their thraldom'. Contains O'Connor's treatises on the land question. Vol. IV, 1848 contains material on the National Land Company. In 1847 considerable support for the National Association of Unitied Trades.

C; Co-op. Coll. I; E; GM I—III; L; LE; LU (IV*); MP; NP; O; ONC I—III; Warwick UL (microfilm); Greenwood reprint and microfiche: microfiche distributed in Britain and Europe by the Harvester Press Ltd.

1770 Labourer [1865—6?]. Edinburgh; m

12 nos published. (**Scottish Notes and Queries**, March 1904, p. 134.)

Labourer. 1875—1881 see **Labour League Examiner**

1771 Labourer 1895—? Devizes; m

1d. 'Devoted to the interests of the agricultural labourer.' (**Labour Annual**, 1896, p. 244.)

1772 Labourer [19--?] ; w

    A   National Agricultural Labourers' and Rural Workers' Union. ILP 21 March, 28 March 1914

1773 Labourer 1 (Feb. 1915)–13 (Jan. 1918). Norwich; q

    A   1d. Printed and published by the Caxton Press. Organ of the National Agricultural labourers' and Rural Workers' Union, 'to voice the needs and aspirations of its members'. Supported Labour Party. Includes branch reports, and material on the Scottish Farm Servants Union.

    L(Col)†

1774 Labourer's Friend [189-?]. (**Labour Annual**, 1897)

1775 Labourer's Friend, and Handicrafts Chronicle 1 (Jan. 1821)–14 (Feb. 1822); ns I, 1 (March 1822)–[Jan. 1825?] (**Museum Book Shop Catalogue**, 1922, p. 37).

    C   6d. 'To draw the attention of our readers to practical modes of bettering the present condition of the labouring poor, and at the same time of requiting the patronage of their benefactors.' Advocates restoration of the rural labouring poor in cottage economy, small holdings etc. Anti-Malthusian.

    L 1; LU I, III*; O Feb. 1821

1776 Labourers' Friend Magazine for Disseminating Information on the Advantages of Allotments of Land to the Labouring Classes, on Loan Funds, and on Other Means of Improving Their Condition 1 (1834)–278 (Jan. 1884); m; q

    C   3d.; 2d. Printed for the Labourers' Friend Society, later the Society for the Improvement of the Condition of the Labouring Classes, by T. C. Savill. To urge the general adoption of the cottage allotment system as being conducive to the 'welfare and happiness' of the rural labourer. Reports of branches of the Society, articles on population, the poor and the land, extracts from newspapers etc. In later years has special interest in the provision of decent housing for the urban working class and labouring poor.

    C 1844–84*; L; LE 1842–47*; LU 1836–55*; O 1844–84; ONC 1839–40

1777 Labourer's Herald: the Organ of the Federal Union of Agricultural and General labourers 1 (27 Nov. 1874)–7 (8 Jan. 1875). Maidstone; w

    A   1d. Published and printed by W. R. and F. Masters. Important paper representing the interests of agricultural workers and others organised in the Federal Union, which claims to represent the whole of Labour, in a movement of general Unionism. The Federal Union encompassed '60–70,000 labourers in counties and towns of Surrey, Sussex, Kent, Hereford, Wilts., Norfolk, Suffolk, Boston (seceded), Yorkshire, Peterborough, Radnorshire, Breconshire, Gloucester, Bristol etc.' (No. 1). Incorporated with **Kent Messenger**.

    L(Col)†

1778 Labourer's News 1 (5 Feb. 1886)–217 (29 March 1890). Cambridge; w

    C   ½d. Printed and published by W. P. Spalding and Company. Claims to be non-partisan in politics, but is definitely Conservative. Opposes Gladstone, Jesse Collings, Joseph Arch. Apparently designed to counteract the radical movement of Trades Unionism among agricultural workers. Addressed to 'English labourers', in the interests of their social improvement.

    C (w 5, 62, 64–71); Cambridge PL 48 (1 Jan. 1887)–214; L(Col)†

1779 Labourers' Union Chronicle 1 (June 1872)–(28 Aug. 1875); then **National Agricultural Labourers' Chronicle and Industrial Pioneer.** (11 Sept. 1875)–(14 April 1877); m; w

    A   Published by J. E. Matthew Vincent. Merged with **The English Labourer** to become **The English Labourers' Chronicle.**

    BP (microfilm); L(Col); Warwick County record Office*

1780 Labouring Man's Advocate 1821

    Edited by John Ovington. (H. S. Foxwell, 'Bibliography of the English Socialist School' in A. Menger, **The Right to the whole Produce of Labour**, 1899, appendix II.)

1781 Labourite: the Official Journal of the Newport Labour Representation Committe. 1 (Nov. 1905)–9 (June 1906). Newport; m

    B

    AbN; NpP

1782 Labour's Advocate, and Northern Weekly Advertiser 1 (3 April 1847)–7 (22 May, 1847). Belfast; w

    A   1½d. Printed and published by James O'Neill; 'ushered into existence for working men, by working men' to defend the rights of Labour, 'the toiling masses'. Support for ten-Hours' Bill. Suspended publication because of insufficient support from Belfast trades societies.

    L(Col)†

1783 Labour's Blackpool Voice [195-?]–? Manchester; m

    B   3d. Workers' Northern Publishing Society (Mitchell, 1960.)

1784 Labour's Broadcast [19--?] [Ipswich?]

    B   Labour Party.

    Ipswich and East Suffolk Record Office, Ratcliffe Coll. Oct. 1937; Ipswich Labour Party

1785 Labour's Call, From Behind the Iron Curtain: Bulletin of the Socialist Union of Central-Eastern Europe 1 (Sept. 1949)–?; irreg?

    B   Reproduced from typewriting. Later unnumbered. Union of the Socialist or Social-Democratic Parties of the countries of Central Eastern Europe. News and comment on events in those countries.

    LabP† Sept. 1949–Feb./March 1962*

1786 Labour's Cheshire Voice [195-?] –? Manchester; m
   B   2d. Workers' Northern Publishing Society. Merged in **Labour's Northern Voice**. (Mitchell, 1955.)

1787 Labour's Cornish Voice [195-?] –? Manchester; m
   B   3d. Workers' Northern Publishing Society. Merged in **Labour's Western Voice**. (Mitchell, 1955.)

1788 Labour's Farnworth Voice [195-?] –? Manchester; m
   B   3d. Workers' Northern Publishing Society. (Mitchell, 1955.)

1789 Labour's Merseyside Voice I, 1 (Oct. 1953)–III, 99 (April 1964?) Manchester; m
   B   2d. Workers' Northern Publishing Society. 'Views of organised labour.'
       L(Col)† I, 1–III, 99; LabP† 1960-*; LvP 1954–7*

1790 Labour's Monthly Youth Letter 1 (Oct. 1957)–18 (March 1959); then Labour Party. **Monthly Youth Letter**: 1 (Nov. 1959)–11 (Oct. 1960); m
   B   Issued by the Labour Party National Agent's Department. Edited by Alan Williams, National Youth Officer. First series reproduced from typewriting. News and accounts of activities.
       LabP†

Labour's Northern Voice see **Northern Voice**

1791 Labour's Northern Voice (Stockport Edition) XV, 69 (Jan. 1945)–XV, 89 (Sept. 1946); then **Stockport Voice**: XV, 90 (Oct. 1946)–May 1965. Manchester; m
   B   Workers' Northern Publishing Society. Numbering continues that of **Labour's Voice**. Sometimes called **Labour's Stockport Voice**?
       L(Col) XX, 142 (July 1959)–XXXVIII, 34 (Aug. 1963); LabP† 1960–3*; Stockport PL (w 1959)

1792 Labour's Oldham Voice [195-?] –? Manchester; m
   B   2d. Workers' Northern Publishing Society. (Mitchell, 1955.)

Labour's Reading Voice see **Reading Labour's Voice**

1793 Labour's Rural Bulletin 1 (Jan. 1951)–24 (Dec. 1952); m
   B   Published by the Labour Party, Press and Publicity Department. Reproduced from typewriting. Short articles, notes, information on agriculture, land etc. Material may be used by editors of Labour Party journals. Note with last number says 'we are arranging for similar space to be devoted to rural matters in **The Labour Press Service** each month . . .'
       LabP†

1794 Labour's Salford Voice I, 1 (April 1956); then **Salford Labour's Voice**: I, 2 (May 1956)—50 (March 1962?) Manchester; m
    B   3d. (1960.) Workers' Northern Publishing Society.
    L(Col) 1—50; LabP† 1960—1*

1795 Labour's Southern Voice (Bromley, Beckenham and Penge Edition) [1951?]—? Manchester; m
    B   3d. Workers' Northern Publishing Society.
    Beckenham PL March 1951—May 1953 (w Oct. 1951, March, April 1953)

1796 Labour's Southern Voice (Chislehurst Edition) Feb. 1951—Jan. 1955. Manchester; m
    B   2d. Workers' Northern Publishing Society.
    Sidcup Constituency Labour Party

Labour's Stockport Voice see **Labour's Northern Voice** (Stockport Edition)

1797 Labour's Stretford and Urmston Voice [195-?]—? Manchester; m
    B   2d. Workers' Northern Publishing Society (Mitchell, 1955.)

Labour's Voice. 1920 see **Voice of Labour. 1907—1916**

1798 Labour's Voice I, 1 May 1953—[1968?]. Manchester; m
    B   2d. Workers' Northern Publishing Society. 'The first issue of **Labour's Voice** appears 28 years after the first issue of **Labour's Northern Voice**, the parent newspaper of the 'Labour's Voice' series of newspapers . . . ' 'Socialist and trade union monthly.'
    L(Col) IV, 3 (July/Aug. 1956)—Dec. 1964; LE 1953—62; LabP† 1953—68*

1799 Labour's West Sussex Voice: Official Organ of the Worthing Divisional Labour Party. [195-?]—[1964?]. Manchester; m
    B   Workers' Northern Publishing Society. (Mitchell, 1955, notes two editions of **Labour's West Sussex Voice**: Worthing, Arundel and Shoreham Edition; Horsham and Crawley Edition.)
    L(Col) XV, 43 (July 1959)—XXXVIII, 38 (March 1964); LabP† 1960—4*

1800 Labour's Western Voice [195-?]—[1959?]. Manchester; m
    B   3d. Workers' Northern Publishing Society.
    L(Col) ns I, 1 (April/May 1957)—23 (Dec. 1959); LabP† ns I, 19, 22, 23

1801 Lamp 1929. Seaham; w
    B   Communist. Minority Movement. Editor: George Burdess.
    Joe Dawson, Windsor Rd., Seaham, Co. Durham

1802 Lamp [1949?]−?; m

    A   Clerical and Administrative Workers Union, National Coal Board HQ Central Branch. Reproduced from typewriting.

    TUC† 32 (Sept. 1951), 109 (Dec. 1961), 110, 111

Lamp. 1960 see **Your Magazine**

1803 Lanarkshire Clarion [194-?]−? Shotts; m?

    B   2d. Printed for the Lanarkshire Labour Publications Company by the SCWS, Ltd. (Printing Dept.), Glasgow. Editor: James Inglis. Mainly local Labour Party events, but some national comment. No. 47 contains article by Clement Attlee.

    GU, Broady Coll. 47 (April 1952)

Lancashire and Cheshire News see **Lancashire News**

Lancashire and Yorkshire Co-operator, or, Useful Classes' Advocate see **Lancashire Co-operator**

1804 Lancashire Beacon 1, [1849]−[21, 1849?] Manchester; w

    B   1d. Numbers not dated. 1849 added in manuscript in Bodley's copy. Published by A. Heywood and George Smith (No. 1) then by J. R. Cooper and George Smith (No. 13). Edited by Charles Southwell. 'The projectors of this periodical have two great objects in view − one is, to show the causes which lie at the root of bad government; the other, how they may be removed.' 'We are resolved to expose the enormous frauds practiced upon the working people of this country . . . ' Support for Ten-Hours' Bill (No. 1). No. 13 says 'to be continued' and the **Museum Book Shop Catalogue** says there were 21 numbers.

    O 1−13

1805 Lancashire Co-operator 1 (11 June 1831)−6 (20 Aug. 1831); then **Lancashire and Yorkshire Co-operator, or, Useful Classes' Advocate**: 1 (3 Sept. 1831)−12 (4 Feb. 1832); ns 1 (March 1832)−(Oct. 1832). Manchester; fortn

    B   1d. Published by the Manchester and Salford Co-operative Council. Printed by Hignett and Jackson, then by W. Jackson. Editors: E. T. Craig; Thomas Hirst. 'A working-class miscellany that is devoted to disseminating co-operative ideas.' (Wiener).

    Co-op. Union ns; Eu 1−6, 1−12; L; Lu; ONC 6, ns 4; Greenwood reprint and microfiche: microfiche distributed in Britain and Europe by the Harvester Press Ltd.

1806 Lancashire News I, 1 [1941?]−VI, 40, 9 Oct. 1943; then **Lancashire and Cheshire News**: VI, 41 (16 Oct. 1943)−X, 22 (28 June 1947); then **Bulletin**: X, 23 (5 July 1947)−XV, 16 (May 1954). Manchester; m; w (1942−51); fortn; irreg

    B   1d. etc. Published by the Lancashire (then Lancashire and Cheshire) DPC of the Communist Party of Great Britain, for members only.

    CPGB† V, 4 (May 1942)−XV, 16 (w occ. nos); WCML† occ. nos

1807 Lancaster and District Co-operative Record [March 1890]−?
Lancaster;; m
     A   Gratis. Lancaster and District Co-operative Society, (sometimes
Lancaster and Skerton Equitable Industrial Co-operative Society?). (Fifty
years of co-operation in Lancaster, 1910.)
     L 248 (1914)−

1808 Lancaster Forward I, 1 (Jan. 1930)−? Lancaster; m
     B   2d. Official organ of the Lancaster Divisional Labour Party.
Both January and February 1930 were numbered I, 1 and the March
number is I, 3.
     Lancaster PL I, 1−I, 6 (June 1930)

1809 Lancaster Labour News [194-?]. [Preston?] ; m
     B   2d. Published by Preston Labour Party. (Labour Party. **Your
own Journal**, 1948.)

1810 Land and Labour: the Organ of the Land Nationalisation Society I, 1
(Nov. 1889)−XXIII, 12 (Dec. 1912). Derby; then **Land Nationaliser**:
XXIV, 1 (Jan. 1913)−XXIX, 6 (March 1921). London etc.; m
     C   1d. Printed for the Society by Frederick Shaw and Company.
Edited by the Secretary, Joseph Hyder. To further the cause of land
nationalisation. Object: 'to restore the land to the people and the people
to the land'. A 'theoretical' and propagandist journal urging State
ownership of land for redistribution. Records activities of the Society in
the regions. Two later numbers (No. 1, July 1935, No. 2, February 1936)
were published on the occasion of a parliamentary Bill proposing land
nationalisation. No. 2 is concerned with nationalisation of the mines.
     L(Col)† 1889−1914, 1916−21; LE*; O V−XXVI, 5; ONC occ. nos;
Warwick UL (microfilm)

Land and Liberty see **Single Tax**

1811 Land and People: the Organ of the Allotments and Small Holdings
Association I, 1 (3 April 1886)−X, 8 (1 Aug. 1894). Birmingham; m
     C   1d. Published by F. Spooner Neville. Motto: '3 acres and a cow'.
Seeks to check the depopulation of country districts by giving the people a
direct connection with, and interest in, the land. Sees a plot of land, fair
rent and secure tenure as the right of every mechanic, labourer and
tradesman. Urges State purchase of land for allotments and small holdings.
'We claim the help of the working classes, and we trust to have the aid of
all who desire to improve the condition of the labouring poor.' President
of the Association: Jesse Collings. Ceased with the passing of a Local
Government Act by which labourers could secure land through the Parish
Councils, thus fufilling the policy of the Association.
     L(Col)†

Land Nationaliser see **Land and Labour**

Land Values see Single Tax

1812 Land Worker I, 1 (15 May 1919)–; m
    A   1d. etc. Official organ of the National Agricultural Labourers'
and Rural Workers' Union, later the National Union of Agricultural
Workers. 'With which is incorporated **The Labourer**".
    L(Col)†; LE I, 9– ; NU XXXII (1952)– ; TUC*; Warwick UL
1933–41*; 1942–

1813 Lansbury's Labour Weekly I, 1 (28 Feb. 1925)–III, 123 (16 July
1927); w
    B   2d. printed by Odhams Press for The Palace Publications, Ltd.
Editor: George Lansbury. Organ of the Left wing of the Labour Party.
Stands for the emancipation of the working class, Socialism by peaceful
means. Contributors: Raymond Postgate (Assistant Editor), Ellen
Wilkinson, G. D. H. Cole, George Hicks. Succeeded by **The New Leader**.
    L(Col)†; LdU; ONC*; TUC

1814 Lanterne (The Lantern). 1 (18 July 1874)–29 (1875). London; w
    B   6d. Printed and published by Simpson and Company. Editor:
Henri Rochefort. Nos 1–3 in French and English. The main edition was
published, 1868–76, in Paris and Brussels. An 'underground' journal,
intended for circulation in France. Easily concealed because of its small
size.
    L

1815 Last 1 (25 Oct. 1844)–14 (24 Jan. 1845); w
    A   Issued by the Committee of Management of the Cordwainers'
General Mutual Assistance Association. 'Union, Justice, Benevolence,
Humanity.' Printed (?) by J. Cleave.
    MP† Original (restricted use) and microfilm

1816 Laughing Philosopher I, 1 (28 July 1832)–5 (25 Aug. 1832); w
    B   1d. Published and editied by James H. B. Lorymer. 'A radical
satirical miscellany that denounces in extreme terms the aristocracy,
royalty, the organized churches, the tax on newspapers, and restrictions on
the suffrage' (Wiener).
    LU2; O 1, 3; O(JJ) 1

1817 Laughter Grim and Gay 1, 1 (26 Feb. 1910)–I, 24 (6 Aug. 1910).
Manchester; w
    B   1d. Published by H. J. Pearce, printed by the Co-operative
Newspaper Society. A satirical weekly journal, containing anti-capitalist
cartoons, and cartoons favouring social reform and Socialism.
    L(Col)†; MP

1818 Leader I, 1 (30 March 1850)—XI, 536 (30 June 1860); then **Saturday Analyst and Leader**: XI, 537 (7 July 1860)—557 (24 Nov. 1860); w

B   6d. Published by Joseph Clayton, junior, then by Thornton Hunt. Editors: G. H. Lewes, T. Leigh Hunt. Appeal is to 'The People'. Supports working-class co-operative schemes, and the political objective of universal suffrage, and secular education; also European national liberation movements. Social and literary review, miscellaneous items, correspondence.

BP I—IX; C 1—4, 16, 19—24; GU I—IX; L(Col)†; MP; ONC II, 41—92

1819 Leader: For the Social, Political and Industrial Advancement of the Masses. 1, [June 1890?]—69 (Oct. 1891). Bolton; Manchester; w

B   1d. Editor: T. R. Threlfall. Upholds the cause of Labour, shorter working hours, political representation etc. With No. 67 (19 September 1891) it became **The Leader and Workers Advocate** when it incorporated **Worker's Cry**.

L(Col) 23 (15 Nov. 1890)—69; LU† 2 (June 1890); ONC† 67 (19 Sept. 1891), 69

Leader and Workers' Advocate see **Leader**, [June 1890?]—1891

1820 Leaflet Newspapers . 1 (4 Feb. 1888)—22 (23 June 1888); then b **Socialist**: I, 1 (7 July 1888)—II, 14 (April 1889); w; m (1889)

B   1d. for 25 (1—22); ½d. Printed and edited by Thomas Bolas, member of the Fabian Society and the Socialist League. The **Leaflet Newspaper** was in the form of a 'socialistic handbill' intended as a ready propagandist weapon. Was enlarged to four pages with the change of title. Chiefly Fabian, but also publicises other Labour and socialist tendencies.

L(Col)†; LE b; LU b; O(JJ)† 1—22; ONC b

1821 League Against Imperialism and for National Independence. Press Service [1927?]—? Berlin; fortn

B   Reproduced from typewriting. Issued to newspapers and to British readers. James Maxton, Chairman of the British Section. Links struggles of the British working class with those of colonial peoples.

TUC† 5 (1 July 1927)—15/16 (7 July 1930)

1822 League Leaflet, Being a Paper to Interest and to Help Members of the Women's Labour League and Other Friends of the Labour Party 1 (Jan. 1911)—28 (April 1913); then b **Labour Women**: I, 1 (May 1913)—LXI, 8 (Sept. 1971); m

B   ½d. etc. National Women's Labour League; Labour Party. Expanded from a four-page leaflet to the fully fledged journal, **Labour Woman**. In early years contained district news on the work of the League organising women workers on questions of wages and conditions, also on suffrage. Contributors: Margaret Bondfield, K. Glasier, Marion Phillips (one-time editor). Superseded by **Labour Weekly**.

(L(Col)); LE a 5—   ; LabP b; O b 7—   ; ONC 1950—71

1823 Leaguer: the Organ of the Pioneer Socialist League. 1 (Jan. 1907)–13 (Jan. 1908); m

A   ½d. Printed by the Twentieth Century Press. The Pioneer Socialist League 'has for its object the propagation of the principles of Socialism, its field being primarily, but not exclusively, the personnel of the various Postal Services, from which the membership is drawn'. No. 13 says the Pioneer Socialist League merged with the Civil Service Socialist Society.

L 1–12; O(JJ)† 12, 13

1824 Leaguer: a Monthly Record of Daily Herald **League Work** 1 (Jan. 1914)–3 (March 1914); m

B   1d. Published by the London Committee **Daily Herald** League. MML†

1825 Leamington Bulletin [194-?]. Leamington Spa; m

B   2d. Labour Party. Reproduced from typewriting. (Labour Party. **Your own Journal**, 1948.)

1826 Leamington Worker [193-?]. Leamington Spa; m

B   Labour Party. (Labour and Socialist International. **The Socialist Press**, 1933.)

Leeds and District Teachers' Journal see National Union of Teachers. Leeds and District Association. **Monthly Notes**

1827 Leeds and District Weekly Citizen 1 (21 Oct. 1911)–213 (5 Nov. 1915); then **Leeds Weekly Citizen**: 214 (12 Nov. 1915)–2814 (20 June 1966); then **Citizen**: 2815 (17 June 1966)–   . Leeds; w

B   1d. etc. Leeds Labour Publishing Society, Ltd. Editor for more than twelve years: Solly Pearce. Probably the longest serving local Labour and socialist paper still being published.

L(Col)† 1–24, 61–   ; LE 1917–19; LdP

Leeds Co-operative News see **Leeds Co-operative Record**

1828 Leeds Co-operative Pioneer March 1935–May 1942. Leeds; m

B   Printed and published by the Co-operative Press. One of the 'Citizen' series.

L(Col)†

1829 Leeds Co-operative Record I (1878)–LXXXVIII (1965); then **Leeds Co-operative News**: June 1965–May 1967. then **Co-operative Newsletter**: I. 1 (Dec. 1967)–I, 27 (April 1970); then **Leeds Society News**: II, 1 (July 1970)–II, 22 (1973); then **Co-operator.** 1 (Jan. 1974)–   . Leeds; m

A   Gratis. Leeds Industrial Co-operative Society. Reports, features, opinion, correspondence. Inside title sometimes: Leeds Industrial Co-operative Society, Limited, **Monthly Record.**

Co-op. Union 1897–8; L XXXV–   ; LE XIX, XX*; XLII–XLIII; LdP† XV, 1892–   (w 32; 1965–7*)

1830 Leeds Co-operator Jan. 1935. Leeds; m

    B   Published by the Leeds Voluntary Co-operative Party, which was trying to win the Leeds Co-operative Society 'back to its allegiance to the official policy of the Movement' and back to support for Co-operative politics.

    L(Col)†

1831 Leeds Gazette 1964– . Leeds

    A   National and Local Government Officers' Association, Leeds and District Gas Branch. Reproduced from typewriting. First number does not bear series title.

    L

Leeds Industrial Co-operative Society. Monthly Record see **Leeds Co-operative Record**

1832 Leeds Monthly, Issued by the Promoters of the 'British Workman' Public Houses 1870–[1872?]. Leeds; London (21 [Dec. 1871]–); then **'BW' Review**: ns 1 (Oct. 1873)–12 (Sept. 1874?) Manchester; London; m

    C   ½d.; 1d. Promotes free reading rooms for working-men as 'a public house without the drink'. Temperance, daily, weekly, newspapers, periodicals, useful books, religious welfare, clubs to organise socials for men and their wives, and summer excursions into the country. Says that after September 1874 will be published quarterly or half-yearly, but it is not known if this was done.

    LdP† 13 (April 1871)–21 (Dec. 1871) ns 1–12

1833 Leeds Patriot and Yorkshire Advertiser 1, [1824?]–467 (16 Feb. 1833). Leeds; w

    B   By 1829 supported parliamentary reform, and later triennial parliaments and vote by ballot.

    L(Col)† 94 (14 Jan. 1826), 250 (13 Jan. 1829)–467

Leeds Society News see **Leeds Co-operative Record**

1834 Leeds Teacher: the Organ of the Leeds and District Teachers' Association 1 [1908?]–92 (June 1939?) Leeds; m, q

    A   Free. From earliest days tries to enrol teachers as members of the National Union of Teachers. By September 1912 is 'official organ of the Leeds Branch of the NUT'. Numbering is in several series.

    LdP† 7 (April 1909)–29*, 1930–9

1835 Leeds Typographical Circular [18--?]–? Leeds; m

    A

    LSF 22 (Aug. 1893) 24 (Feb. 1894)

1836 Leeds Vanguard [193-?]. Leeds; m?

    B   Communist Party, Leeds Branch.

    LdP July, Aug. 1937 (not available)

Leeds Weekly Citizen see **Leeds and District Weekly Citizen**

Left. 1939—1950 see **Controversy. 1936—1939**

1837 Left: Journal of the Labour Party Young Socialists 1 (Oct. 1968)— ; m
 B   6d. Printed by Brewster Printing Company for LPY Socialists' National Committee. News, features, correspondence.
 LE†

1838 Left Book News 1 (May 1936)—7 (Nov. 1936); then **Left News**: 8 (Dec. 1939)—128 (March 1947); m
 B   For the Left Book Club, published by V. Gollancz. Reviews and articles on politics and literature. Contributor: John Strachey. From No. 60, June 1941, has supplement, **International Socialist Forum**, edited by Julius Braunthal.
 C 124—8; L; LabP 5—128; ONC 5—128*; Warwick UL 1940—7*

Left Forum see **Controversy. 1936—1939**

Left News see **Left Book News**

1839 Left Review I, 1 (Oct. 1934)—III, 16 (May 1938); m
 B   Published by T. Wintringham for the Writers' International, British Section. Organ of the Left intelligentsia influenced by Marxism in the 1930s. Early editors: Montagu Slater, A. Williams-Ellis, T. H. Wintringham. Contributors: John Strachey, Ralph Fox. Incorporated **Viewpoint**.
 BP; L; MP; ONC*; Warwick UL

1840 Left Wing [1924?]—?; w
 B?
 TUC Oct. 1924—Dec. 1924* (missing)

1841 Left Wing [196-?]—? Leeds; irreg?
 B   6d. (May 1968.) Reproduced from typewriting. University of Leeds, Labour Society; Leeds University Union Socialist Society.
 L II, 4 (Jan. 1962)— ; LdU† May 1968

1842 Leicester Co-operative Citizen 1 (Nov. 1932)—? Leicester; irreg
 B   Printed by the National Co-operative Publishing Society for the Leicester Co-operative Society. 'Citizen' series
 L(Col)† occ. nos

Leicester Co-operative Magazine see **Leicester Co-operative Record**

1843 Leicester Co-operative Record [1873?] −590, 1922; then **Leicester Co-operative Magazine**: 1 (Jan. 1923)−? Leicester; m

    A   Gratis. Leicester Co-operative Society. Editors: H. Harrott; Henry Clark

    L a 465−

1844 Leicester County Teachers' Gazette 1 (Summer 1928)−[3?] (31 Dec. 1929). Leicester; s-a

    A   National Union of Teachers, Leicestershire Associations. Reports and news.

    L

1845 Leicester District Co-operative Record [c1897] −? [Leicester?]; m?

    A   Organ of communication for the Leicester District Association, comprising as its members many enterprising village societies. Printed by the Leicester Co-operative Printing Society (**Ideas and Facts: a short History of the Leicester Co-operative Printing Society Ltd**, Leicester 1901.) Editor: J. H. Woolley (**Labour Annual**, 1897).

1846 Leicester Independent Labour Party. Monthly Notes [19--]]. [Leicester?] ; m

    B

    ILP Jan. 1916

Leicester Pioneer see **Pioneer** [19--?] −**1913**

1847 Leicestershire Movement; or, Voices from the Frame and the Factory, the Field and the Rail 1 (9 Feb. 1850)−19 ([26 May?] 1850). Leicester; w

    B   1d. Printed and published by Joseph Ayer. To give expression to working-class rights. For a more equal distribution of wealth etc. Attacks 'let alone' political economy. Favours co-operation, national free education, political franchise. Latter-day Chartist.

    L

1848 Leigh Friendly Co-operative Society's Monthly Record [1896] −570 (May 1954?) Leigh; m

    A   Gratis. Issued by the Educational Department. Reports of meetings and social activities.

    L 223 (Jan. 1915)−570

1849 Leigh Monthly Magazine of Instruction and Amusement 1 (1 Nov. 1844)−12 (1 Oct. 1845). Wigan; Leigh

    C   2d. 'Conducted by a Committee of the Leigh Mechanics' Institution.' Published by J. Ramsdale. Fiction, poetry etc.

    L; MP 1, 7

1850 Leith Labour Party. News [c1950]. [Leith?]

    B   (**Edinburgh and Lothians Clarion**, September 1950)

1851 Lenton Co-operative Society. [**Magazine**] [c1901]. [Lenton?] ; m
    A   (**Reformers' Year Book**, 1901, states that a local monthly co-operative magazine was produced by Lenton, but gives no further details.)

1852 Let's Look I (1957)– . South Shields
    A   National and Local Government Officers' Association, South Shields Branch
    L

Letters to the Human Race on the Coming Universal Revolution see **Robert Owen's Weekly Letter to the Human Race**

1853 Levenax I (1955)– . Dumbarton
    A   National and Local Government Officers' Association, Dumbartonshire Branch.
    L

Lewes Divisional Labour Party's Monthly Bulletin see **Southdown Press Monthly Bulletin**

1854 Lewisham Labour News 1 (June 1921)–6 (Dec. 1921). Lewisham; m
    B   1d. Organ of Lewisham Labour Party. Published by A. Elliman.
    L(Col)† ; Lewisham PL (microfilm)

1855 Leyton and Leytonstone Pioneer [1924?] –?; m
    B   Labour Party.
    Leyton PL 5 (Jan. 1925)–29 (April 1930) (w 9, 11, 14)

1856 Liberal 1 (17 Nov. 1832). Sheffield; w?
    C   1d. Printed by Anthony Whitaker. 'A local miscellany that features radical analyses of local politics' (Wiener). Addressed to 'those whose means are yet comparatively insignificant'. Advocates civic improvements. Pro-Mechanics Institutes. Anti-Church of England.
    SP†

1857 Liberal Labour Journal: the Organ of the Liberal Labour League 1 (15 Jan. 1904)–2 (15 Feb. 1904); m
    B   1d. Published by A. L. Cox at the offices of the League. Printed by The Twentieth Century Press. Organ of 'Lib-Labism'. G. J. Holyoake was President of the League. 'To secure a fair representation of Labour in Parliament'.
    L(Col)† ; O(JJ)† 1

1858 Liberator Nov. 1832–[Oct. 1836?] ; then **New Liberator**: 13 Nov. 1836–1838. Glasgow; w

    B   4d. (No. 213, [26 Oct. 1836]). Editors: John Tait; Dr John Taylor (November 1836?–). No. 213 mourns the death of editor John Tait, and says the paper is to be taken over by John Taylor and to be continued as 'the organ of the working classes'. Format that of a general newspaper, with radical/trade union representation.

    L(Col)† 213

1859 Libertarian: a Common Wealth Publication 1 (Summer 1966)–13 (1972)

    B   1s. Edited by W. J. Taylor with an editorial Board of Members of the National Committee of Common Wealth. Reproduced from typewriting. Incorporated in **Resurgence**.

    E 2– ; LE† 1–2; ONC 3–

1860 Libertarian Teacher: Journal of the Libertarian Teachers' Association [196-?] – . London; Leicester; irreg; termly

    A   No. 7 (Autumn 1971), published by Libertarian Education Group, Leicester

1861 Liberty: a Weekly Democratic Organ. 1 (28 April 1883)–3 (12 May 1883); w

    B   1d. Published by E. Belfort Bax, and conducted by him to emancipate the 'toiling millions' from aristocratic and class privilege. Sympathetic to Socialism. Advocates land nationalisation. Reviews Marx's **Das Kapital**. Contribution by the veteran Democrat J. Sketchley.

    L(Col)†

1862 Liberty: a Journal of Anarchist Communism I, 1 (Jan. 1894)–III, 12 (Dec. 1896); m

    B   1d. Editor: J. Tochatti. Contributors: E. Malatesta, L. S. Bevington, Henry Seymour, Joe Clayton (Leeds Independent Labour Party)

    L(Col)† ; LE†

1863 Liberty: Official Organ of IT and GWU I (1949)– . Dublin; m

    A   Irish Transport and General Workers' Union.

    CoU; D XXVI, 10 (1971/2)– ; University College, Dublin XXII (1967/86)–

1864 Liberty I, 1 (Jan. 1969)–I, 3 (March 1969). Selby; m

    B   6d. Published by the Yorkshire Anarchist Federation, a network of Anarchists and Syndicalists, federated with the Anarchist Federation of Great Britain. For workers' control and federal administration of society. Reproduced from typewriting

    LE† ; LdP† 1

1865 Licensed Vehicle Trades Record: a Journal Devoted to the Interests of the Cab, 'Bus and Tram Services I, 1 (16 July 1913)–VI, 155 (9 July 1919); then **Record**: ns I, 1 (23 July 1919)–II, 52 (6 July 1921); fortn

    A   1d.; 2d. Published by the London and Provincial Union of Licensed Vehicle Workers. Later 'The Official Organ of the United Vehicle Workers and the Official Organ of the Owner-Drivers Branch of the UVW. Editor: J. Gill.

    L(Col)†; Transport and General Workers' Union 1913–17, 1919; TUC 1916–18*

1866 Life Assurance Agents' Journal: the Official Organ of the National Union of Life Assurance Agents I, 1 (16 Nov. 1885)–ns 134 (1 Feb. 1890); then **Agents' Journal and Official Gazette**: ns 1 (8 Feb. 1890)–LXIV, 2986 (30 Aug. 1947). Manchester; London; m; w

    A   1d. After 1892 its interest is marginal. Until then it contains union branch news, discussion of conditions, grievances. Afterwards becomes increasingly devoted to discussion of insurance schemes, and provision of professional information.

    L(Col)† 4 (16 Feb. 1886)–1947 (w 1889); LCI LII–LXIV, 2985*

1867 Light and Liberty: Libertarian Review and Miscellany 1944–?
Inchinnan

    B   Libertarian League.

    L 3–(missing)

1868 Light of Labour: a Paper Devoted Entirely to the Interests of Labour 1 (May 1895)–[Sept. 1896?]. Bury; m

    B   ½d. Bury and Eldon Independent Labour Party. 'District Notes', news of local Labour movement, short signed articles and extracts on Socialism etc., reviews, general local news (No. 12).

    AbU 11–13 (microfilm); O(JJ)† 11 (April 1896)–13 (June 1896)

1869 Linacre Ward Bulletin [194-?]. Bootle; fortn

    B   Free. Labour Party. (Labour Party. **Your own Journal**, 1948.)

1870 Lincoln Co-operative Citizen 1 (June 1935)–?; m?

    B

    L(Col) 1; [ns], 1 (Sept. 1936)

1871 Lincoln Co-operative Society Record c1886] –? Lincoln; q

    A   Free. Lincoln Equitable Co-operative Industrial Society. Editor: William Turner (**International Directory of the Co-operative Press**, 1909). 'By 1886 a quarterly **Record** had been established' (D. McInnes, **History of Co-operation in Lincoln 1861–1911**, Manchester 1911).

1872 Lindfield Standard and Workman's Friend 1 (Jan. 1861)–6 (June 1861). Lindfield; m

    C   1d. Printed by Owen Breads, later Paine, Worthing. Moral improvement from Christian viewpoint.

    L(Col)†

1873 Link: a Journal for the Servants of Man. 1 (4 Feb. 1888)–44 (1 Dec. 1888); w

B   ½d. Printed and published for the proprietor by A. Bonner (1–20), by Annie Besant (21–44). Editors: Annie Besant, William T. Stead. 'Founded as link of communication between circles of Law and Liberty League; devoted chiefly to free speech struggle; claimed to seek temporal salvation of world and dispossessed' (Brophy). News, articles, reports on working conditions, union news etc.

L(Col); LE (w 44); ONC† (w 44); TUC, John Burns Lib., Tower Hamlets PL (w 44)

1874 Link [19--?]–? Stirling

A   Union of Post Office Workers, Stirling Branch. (W. Dunlop, 'Local Journals' **Belpost**, IV, 5 [May 1965].)

1875 Link I, 1 (Sept. 1911)–II, 17 (Feb. 1913); m

B   1d. Printed and published for the proprietor by the Twentieth Century Press. From Vol. II, No. 13, Oct. 1912 sub-titled: 'The Organ of the Women's Socialist Movement'. To educate the working class in socialist theory. Notes on trade unions, Young Socialist League, Church Socialist League. Contributors: J. T. Brownlie, G. Lansbury, Litchfield Woods, Zelda Kahan. Later editor: Norman Young.

L(Col)† (w 9)

1876 Link: the Journal of the Hertfordshire County Teachers' Association 1 (Nov. 1921)–41 (Nov. 1934). Watford; q

A   3d. The Association was a federation of all the Local Associations of the National Union of Teachers in Hertfordshire. For unity and co-operation of teachers and 'expression of collective opinion upon matters affecting the interests of Education and the Teaching Profession'. Reports, correspondence.

L

1877 Link 1933–? Manchester

A   Co-operative Wholesale Society.

LE*

1878 Link I (1955)–? Gillingham; m

A   National and Local Government Officers' Association, Gillingham Branch. Reproduced from typewriting.

L I–Feb. 1956

1879 Link 1 (June 1958)–? Swindon

A   Issued by the Shop Stewards of the Industrial Hydraulics Division, Cheyney Manor, Amalgamated Engineering Union. Single typewritten sheet. Minutes and report of meeting.

L 1

1880 Link: County Borough of Derby Branch Magazine [1961?] –Derby
  A   National and Local Government Officers' Association.
Reproduced from typewriting
  L 1961–

1881 Link I (1963)– . Hawarden
  A   National and Local Government Officers' Association,
Hawarden Branch. Reproduced from typewriting. I, 1, does not bear title.
  L

1882 Link [1964?] –
  A   National and Local Government Officers' Association,
Hounslow Branch. Reproduced from typewriting.
  L 1964–

1883 Link: the Voice of Bootle NALGO [1965?] – . Bootle
  A   National and Local Government Officers' Association, Bootle
Branch. Reproduced from typewriting.
  L 13 (May 1966)–

1884 Link [1969?] – ; bi-m
  A   Civil and Public Services Association, Post and
Telecommunications Group
  Warwick U(MRC) 1 undated issue, 2 issues for 1973

Links see **NALGO Bulletin** (Lindsey County Officers Branch)

1885 Links Reflector: Organ of the Prestonlinks Communist Cell.
[1930?] –? Edinburgh; fortn
  A   1d. Reproduced from typewriting. United Mine-workers of
Scotland pit paper.
  E 6 Sept. 1930

1886 Link-Up Doncaster
  A   Doncaster rank and file miners' paper.
  Information from Doncaster Trades Council

1887 Lion I, 1 (4 Jan. 1828)–IV, 36 (25 Dec. 1829); m
  B   6d. Printed, published and edited by Richard Carlile. Carlile's
tour of the country serialised. Only road to 'radical or useful reform' is a
'breaking up of the Church and other religious establishments and reform
of the House of Commons'.
  C; GM; L; LE; LY; MP; O I; ONC (w III); WCML†; Warwick UL
(microfilm)

Literary Pioneer see **Penny Satirist**

1888 Literature of the World Revolution 1 (June 1931)–5 (Oct. 1931); then b **International Literature**: [1] (1931)–[xv] (1945); then c **Soviet Literature**: I, 1 (Jan. 1946)–   ; Moscow; m
    B   1s. (1955).
    BU c I, 4–(w II, 1–2, 8); C b III–VIII, XI–XV, c; DnP b III–IX, XII–XIV; L b III, 5–XV, 11*, c; LSL 1942–4, 1946–   ; LU c; LUC b, c IV–X; LdU 1945–   ; LvP c V–   ; SwU b XII–XIV

1889 Lithographer: the Journal of the Amalgamated Society of Lithographic Printers of Great Britain and Ireland I, 1 (March 1949)– Manchester; m
    A   Internal news, articles, correspondence.
    E X, 10 (Oct. 1958)–   ; GM†

1890 Littlehampton Labour News [194-?]. Littlehampton; m
    B   2d. Duplicated. Labour Party. (Labour Patry. **Your own Journal**, 1948.)

1891 Live Rail: the Paper of the London Tramway and Electric Supply Workers. [1925?]–?; fortn
    A   1d. Printed, except No. 27, (23 June 1926), which was a special number, free, commenting on the General Strike. Published by the Tramways Committee, London District Committee of the Communist Party. Policy statements and information.
    O(JJ)† 26 (29 April 1926)–33 (2 Sept. 1926) (w 32)

1892 'Live-Wire': the Official Organ of the National Ex-Service Men's Union of Temporary Civil Servants I, 1 (June 1920)–XXIX, 334 (Nov. 1953); m
    A   2d. etc. Name of union changed in 1920 to National Ex-Services Men's Union of Civil Servants, and in 1921 to Association of Ex-Service Civil Servants. In 1954 the Association was incorporated in the National Guild of Civil Servants. Reflects the struggle of ex-service civil service employees for permanent post in government offices, and for better wages and conditions
    L

1893 Live Wire: the Magazine of the Brighton, Hove, Worthing and District Electricity Branch of NALGO [1951?]–   . Brighton
    A   National Association of Local Government Officers; National and Local Government Officers' Association. Reproduced from typewriting.
    L III, 1 (Spring 1953)–

1894 Liverpool Co-operative Citizen I, 1 (Sept. 1932)–(Sept. 1939); Sept. 1946; ns 1 (Aug. 1949)–21 (June 1951). Liverpool; m
    B   Printed and published by the Co-operative Press. Issued by the Liverpool Co-operative Society.
    L(Col)†

1895 Liverpool Forward 1 (4 May 1912)–127 (2 Oct. 1914?) Liverpool; w

    B   1d. Printed and published by the Liverpool Independent Labour Party. Newspaper for the Labour Movement in Liverpool. No. 127 states 'our next issue will be a monthly **Forward** and come out on Friday, November 13'.

    L(Col)†

Liverpool Institute Magazine see **Mechanics' School of Arts**

Liverpool Labour Chronicle see **Labour Chronicle. 1894–1899**

Liverpool NALGO Journal see National Association of Local Government Officers. Liverpool Branch. Journal

1896 Liverpool Pioneer: the Official Organ of the Liverpool Labour Movement 1 (Aug. 1919)–? Liverpool; m

    B   Labour Party.

    LvP 4 (Nov. 1919)

1897 Liverpool Teachers' Association. **Newsletter** 1920–   . Liverpool; 3-yr

    A   (Willing's, 1970.)

1898 Liverpool Typographical Society. **Quarterly Report**

    A

    TUC March 1921

1899 Liversey's Progressionist, or Advocate of Temperance and Physical, Moral, Social and Religious Reform I, 1 (1852–I, 24 (1853); then **Progressionist and Magazine for the People**: ns I, 1 (Jan. 1854)–12 (Dec. 1854). Preston; London; m

    C   1d. Printed and published by Joseph Livesey, then by William Horsell and Shirrefs, when Livesey dropped control. To advocate the teetotal cause and enforce its claims upon the public. Also takes up questions where 'the world's progressive movement is involved'. The new series is explicitly addressed to working people and for their improvement. From No. 4 the first series is entitled **Livesey's Teetotal Progressionist**.

    L; LU i; MP; O; ONC 1854

1900 Llais Llafur. [Labour Voice] 1898–889 (2 Jan. 1915); then **Labour Voice: [Llais Llafur]** 890 (9 Jan. 1915)–2165 (25 June 1927); then **South Wales Voice:** 2166 (2 July 1927)–4540 (12 March 1964); then **South Wales and Swansea Voice:** 4541 (19 March 1964)–4592 (11 March 1965); then **South Wales Voice:** 4593 (18 March 1965)–4943 (2 Dec. 1971); Ystalyfera; w

    B   1d. etc. First editor or publisher: Ebenezer Rees. In Welsh and English. Became increasingly anglicised. Ended as a Moral Rearmament paper.

    AbN 1909–15; L(Col) 410 (25 Nov. 1905)–

1901 Llanelly Labour News Oct. 1924—April 1926. Llanelly
     B   Edited by James Griffiths, and pp. 1 and 4 were local news, pp. 2—3 syndicated national Labour news.
     Llanelly PL

1902 Lleufer: Cylchgrawn Cymdeithas Addysg y Gweithwyr yng Nghymru I (1944)—?. Bala; q
     C   6d. Workers' Educational Association, Welsh Branch. Originally a supplement to **Highway**. In Welsh.
     AbU; BnU; CrU; O IX (1953)—XXV, 2 (1971); SwU

1903 Lloyds Bank Magazine. [c1905]. Hastings; q?
     A   6d. Published by Herbert Cave Willmott, Lloyds Bank, Hastings. 'Written and illustrated by bank staff.' (Mitchell, 1905.)

1904 Local Government News. I, 1 (Jan. 1924)—VIII, 10 (Dec. 1931); m
     B   1d. Issued by the Fabian Society in conjunction with the Labour Party. Published by F. Galton. Edited by William A. Robson. To promote, in the sphere of local government, the aims and principles of the Labour Movement in general and the Fabian Society in particular.
     L(Col)†; LE; LabP†; LvU V—VIII; TUC

Local Government Officer see **LGO, Local Government Officer**

Local Government Service see **LGO, Local Government Officer**

1905 Local Notes: the Journal of the Southampton Branch of the National and Local Government Officers' Association I (1953)— Southampton
     A
     L

1906 Locomotive Engineers' and Firemen's Monthly Journal I (1888)—XVI, 12 (Dec. 1903); then **Locomotive Journal**: Official Organ of the Associated Society of Locomotive Engineers and Firemen: XVII, 1 (Jan. 1904)— ; m
     A   2d. etc. Includes articles on social, cultural and political matters.
     L† VII, 7 (July 1894)— ; LE IX—X, 12; LdP† 1913—22; NU 1955— ; ONC 1948— ; the Society

Locomotive Journal see **Locomotive Engineers' and Firemen's Monthly Journal**

Log see **Middlesex County Teachers' Journal**

1907 London Alfred, or People's Recorder 1 (25 Aug. 1819)–12 (17 Nov. 1819); w

    B   1½d. Printed and published by and for T. Davison. First issue expresses indignation at Manchester Massacre. Reports radical/reform meetings in London, also in Norwich and Yorkshire, declaring against military opposition, as at Peterloo, and advocating 'Rights of Man'.

    LU†

1908 London and Counties' Labour Record [189-?]–?; m

    A?   1d. Publisher?: Charles Beale, 'Trade Union Organ.' (Mitchell, 1895; **Labour Annual**, 1897.)

1909 London Building Trades Federation. Quarterly Report 1 (30 Sept. 1892)–4 (30 June 1893); q

    A   Printed by F. Worthy. No. 1 consists of editorial and financial statement, then enlarged from 4pp. to 16pp. Addresses and reports illustrating growth of the Federation.

    LE†

1910 London Calling: Bulletin Issued by the London Area Council, Clerical and Administrative Workers Union [1946?]–?; irreg

    A

    TUC† 2 (Sept. 1946), 4 (May 1947), 5 (July 1947)

1911 London Chartist Monthly Magazine 1 (June 1843)–?; m

    B   Editor: John Watkins? (H. S. Foxwell, 'Bibliography of the English Socialist School' in A. Menger, **The Right to the whole Produce of Labour**, 1899, Appendix II.)

1912 London Citizen. East Ham Edition 1 (June 1921)–53 (April 1926); then **East Ham South Citizen**: 54 (June 1926)–288 (Sept. 1939); ns 1 (Jan. 1947)–[1962?]; m

    B   Gratis. Published by London Co-operative Society.

    L(Col); LabP occ. nos 1960–2; Stratford PL 1931–8

1913 London Citizen. Tottenham Edition 1 (June 1921)–17 (Oct. 1922); 18 (May 1923)–60 (Oct. 1926); then **North Tottenham Citizen** 61 (Nov. 1926)–213 (Sept. 1939); ns 1 (Jan. 1947)–26 (Feb. 1949); then **Wood Green Citizen**: 27 (March 1949)–67 (Dec. 1952); then **Wood Green and North Tottenham Citizen**: 68 (Jan. 1953)–158 (Nov./Dec. 1962); then **Wood Green Citizen**: 159 (Feb./March 1963)–160 (June/July 1963); m; irreg

    B   Published by London Co-operative Society. See also **Tottenham Citizen; South Tottenham Citizen**.

    Haringey PL 1921–49*; L(Col)† (w 15 [Aug. 1922])

London Citizen. 1940–1942 see **London Co-operative Citizen**

1914 London Class Teacher: Organ of the London Certificated Teachers' Association I, 1 (Oct. 1910)—IV, 1 (July 1914); m
A   1d. The Association was affiliated to the National Federation of Assistant Teachers, and urged support for the National Union of Teachers. Concerned with wages, working conditions, promotion.
L(Col)† (w Nov., Dec. 1911, Jan., March, April, May 1912, Jan.—April 1914)

1915 London Co-operative Citizen 1 (Oct. 1939)—3 (Dec. 1939); then **London Citizen**: ns 4 (Jan. 1940)—34 (Dec. 1942); m
B   Free. Printed and published by the Co-operative Press. Organ of the London Co-operative Society's Political Committee (a branch of the Co-operative Party).
L(Col)†

London Co-operative Magazine see **Co-operative Magazine and Monthly Herald**

London Co-operative Monthly Magazine see **Stratford Co-operator**

London County Chronicle see National Association of Local Government Officers. London County Council Branch. **Branch Notes**

1916 London Dairy Worker [c1936] ; irreg?
A   Issued by the Transport and General Workers' Union.
TUC 1 issue for 1936

1917 London Democrat 1 (April 1839)—9 (8 June 1839); w
B   1d. Printed, published and edited by G. Julian Harney and J. C. Coombe. Organ of the London Democratic Association, a militant physical force Chartist organisation.
L†

1918 London Dispatch, and People's Political and Social Reformer 1 (17 Sept. 1836)—160 (6 Oct. 1839); w
B   1½d.; 4d.; 5d. Printed and published by Henry Hetherington. From its inception, a democratic and universal suffrage organ, and against the 'profit-mongering middle classes'. From mid-1836, articulated the anti-physical force Chartist viewpoint of the London Working Men's Association. Reports of Chartist meetings, correspondence, and other working-class intelligence. Absorbed **Cleave's Weekly Police Gazette**, and **The Operative**.
L(Col)†; ONC 1

1919 London Federation of Anarchists. **Internal Bulletin** I, 1 [Jan. 1969] –?; irreg

B   Published by the Federation. 'The purpose of this Bulletin is to give information which is of importance to the London groups.' Dealt with Anarchist organisation, and includes items from and/or on Socialist Current Group, Scottish Anarchist Federation, Anarchist Federation of Britain, Black Cross, as well as from other countries. Reproduced from typewriting.

LE† I, 1

London Head Teacher see London Head Teachers' Association. **Pamphlet**

1920 London Head Teachers' Association. **Pamphlet** April [1919] –July [1926]; then **London Head Teacher**: ns 1 (June 1927)–98 (July 1939); then **LHTA Bulletin**: 1 (Nov. 1939)–?; m

A

L*†

1921 London Hotel and Restaurant Employé's Gazette. 1 (31 May 1890)–43 (21 March 1891); w

A   2d. Printed for the proprietors by M. Fischer. Organ of the London Hotel and Restaurant Employés Society. In German.

L(Col)†

London-Information of the Austrian Socialists in Great Britain see **Austrian Socialist News: London Information**

1922 London Investigator: a Monthly Journal of Secularism I, 1 (April 1854)–III, 36 (March 1857); then **Investigator**: IV, 37 (April 1857)–VI, 81 (Aug. 1859);

B   1d. Published by Holyoake and Company, then by E. Trulove. Editors Robert Cooper (I–III), 'Anthony Collins' (ie W. H. Johnston) (IV), 'Iconoclast' (ie Charles Bradlaugh) (V–VI). Review and reports of secularist propagation in the regions, including Scotland, involving working-men. Also discussion of social questions, and latter-day Owenism etc. 'The working classes need something more than that refinement of eclecticism which leads the people into a maze of ambiguity and incertitude . . . Their want now is sound instruction and organisation . . .'

Co-op. Coll. April 1856–Aug. 1859; L†; LU; ONC† I, 1–III, 35

London Journal and Pioneer Newspaper see **Pioneer Newspaper and Oddfellows' Journal**

London Labour Chronicle see **London Labour Party Circular**

1923 London Labour Party Circular 1 (Nov. 1915)–34 (Aug. 1918); then **London Labour Chronicle**: 35 (Sept. 1918)–108 (Oct. 1924); m

B 1d. Published by Herbert Morrison for the London Labour Party (during the years 1918 to 1921 for the London Labour Party and the London Trades Council). Review of local government affairs. Incorporated **The Councillor**.

Greater London Labour Party (w 1); L 19–108 (not traced); LabP† 19 (May 1917)–34*, 36 (Oct. 1918)–108

1924 London Lines: the Organ of the London Passenger Transport Staff Association I, 1 (Oct. 1933)–I, 7 (April 1934); ns 1 (May 1934)–XVII, 4 (Spring 1954); m

A Issued for members. First seven numbers are little more than circulars; thereafter a magazine. Saw its duty as disseminating information of importance, and forging a common purpose and close contact among members. Concerned with status, salaries, conditions, prospects. Wound up when the Association joined the Transport Salaried Staffs' Association.

L†

London Literary Pioneer see **Penny Satirist**

1925 London Mechanics' Register I, 1 (6 Nov. 1824)–IV, 112 (4. Nov. 1826); then **New London Mechanics' Register and Magazine of Science and the Useful Arts**: I (1827)–II (1828); w; irreg?

A 3d. Published by Cowie and Strange. Reproduces the lectures delivered to members of the London Mechanics Institution. Later series was not numbered, dated or priced.

C ii; EU I*, ii; GM ii; HU ii; L†; LGU; LU I, 1–3, 5–27, 45; MP II, 14; SaU ii

1926 London Mercury 1 (18 Sept. 1836)–53 (17 Sept. 1837); w

B 4½d.; 3½d. Printed and published by Samuel Finch. Editor: John Bell. Contributor: Bronterre O'Brien. Later printed for the proprietor, James B. Bernard, of King's College, Cambridge, by Samuel Finch. Agitates for shorter factory hours, against Poor Law, for universal suffrage, and in defence of rights of Labour. Reports activities of working-men's radical associations.

L(Col)†

1927 London News 1 (8 May 1858)–28 (13 Nov. 1858); w

B 1d.; 2d. Printed and published by the proprietor, Ernest Charles Jones. Editors: Ernest Jones; J. Baxter Langley (4 July 1858–   ). 'We are Reformers . . . we desire comprehensive and just Reform by constitutional and legitimate means . . . Politically, we demand Manhood Suffrage . . .' Reported the proceedings of the Northern Political Union and of the Political Reform League. Also reports on Working Men's Colleges, and Free Sunday Men.

L(Col)†

1928 London News 1 (Nov. 1924)–272 (Dec. 1949); ns 1 (Jan. 1950)–158 (Sept. 1964); m

    B   1d., etc. Published by Herbert Morrison for the London Labour Party, then by London Labour Publications. A newspaper to appeal to a wider circle than its predecessor, **London Labour Chronicle**. Emphasis on local government matters but also national coverage.

    L(Col)†; LabP*

1929 London Phalanx, Established for the Purpose of Calling Public Attention to the Practical Importance of Universal Principles, and More Particularly to the Science of Attractive Industry, Propounded by the Late Charles Fourier, as a Component Part of the Law of Universal Unity and Harmony, by Him Discovered I, 1 (3 April 1841)–69 (May 1843); w; m (June 1842–

    B   Published by the proprietor Hugh Doherty. To propound the laws of society as discovered by the late Charles Fourier and the Phalansterian School. Promotes co-operative collectives, communities, association and social harmony, also home colonisation. Also general news.

    L(Col); LE+; LU; Warwick UL (microfiche); Greenwood reprint and microfiche: microfiche distributed in Britain and Europe by the Harvester Press Ltd

London Pioneer see **Penny Satirist**

1930 London Post: the Official Organ of the London District Council of the Union of Post Office Workers 1920–   ; m

    A   1d.

    L† ns XI, 5 (May 1948)–XIV, 8 (Aug. 1951) (w XI, 12–XII, 2)

London Press Journal and General Trades Advocate see **Typographical Circular**

London Printer's Circular and Vigilance Gazette see **Vigilance Gazette**

1931 London Schoolmaster: the Organ of the London Schoolmasters' Association I (1922)–XVII, 158 (July 1939); m

    A   2d. Published by F. A. Gibbs. The Association was organised for the defence and furthering of professional standards, salaries and conditions.

    L† V, 37 (June 1927)–XVII, 158; LU 107, 109–58

1932 London Social Refromer 1 (2 May 1840)–2 (May 1840)

    (H. S. Foxwell. 'Bibliography of the English Socialist School' in A. Menger, **The Right to the whole Produce of Labour**, 1899, Appendix II.)

1933 London Socialist Medical Association. **Bulletin** [1938?] –?; m

    B

    HU 28 (Jan. 1941)–43 (April 1942)

1934 London Star: the Star of England's Redemption, or Gazette of News, Police and Politics 1 (20 April 1834); w

B 3d. Published and printed by James Reeve. 'A Radical political Newspaper' (Wiener). Article on Tolpuddle, much news of trade union meetings, police new, foreign news.

ONC†

London Teacher and London Schools Review see **Board Teacher**

1935 London Trades and Labour Gazette 1 (March 1901)−38 (April 1904); then/**Trades and Labour Gazette**: 39 (May 1904)−149 (June 1913); m

A 1d. Printed by the Twentieth Century Press. Edited by James MacDonald, Secretary of the London Trades Council, and published by him until taken over in 1903 as the official organ of the Council. Founded to publicise the work of the London and provincial Trades Councils. Addressed, in particular, to trade unionists. Reports of labour struggles, strikes etc.

L(Col)*†

1936 London Typographical Journal: the Official Organ of the London Society of Compositors I, 1 (Jan. 1906)− LVIII, 689 (Dec. 1963); m

A Published by the Society. Consistent support for the Labour Party. In 1955 the London Society of Compositirs was incorporated into the London Typographical Society. Then the LTS and the Typographical Association amalgamated in January 1964 for form the National Graphical Association, whose journal was **Graphical Journal**.

L†; LE*; LSF; ONC Nov. 1949−Dec. 1963

1937 London University. University of London Labour Party. Broadsheet [193-?]−?

B Issued for private circulation.

LU 11 (1939)

1938 London Voice: the Paper for London Chartists Spring 1968−   ; m

B 9d. 'A Labour Party publication' (British Museum).

L(Col)†

1939 London WEA Bulletin [192-?]−?

C Workers' Educational Association.

TUC occ. nos July/Aug. 1927−34

1940 London Worker: Bulletin of the London Industrial Council 1 (June 1929)−4, [1929?]; m

A 1d. National Minority Movement. No. 1 contains full report of the inaugural meeting of the Council. Reproduced from typewriting.

ONC†, Tanner Coll. 1−2 (July/Aug. 1929); WCML† 1 (photocopy)

Londoner. (Edition of St Pancras) see **(St Pancras) Londoner**

1941 Londoner. (North Islington Edition) 1 (22 Sept. 1894)–74 (7 Feb. 1896) then **(Islington) Londoner**: 75 (14 Feb. 1896)–122 (8 Jan. 1897); then **(Islington) Londoner**: 75 (14 Feb. 1896)–122 (8 Jan. 1897); then **Londoner, Edition for Islington,** etc): 123 (15 Jan. 1897)–147 (2 July 1897); w

    B   1d. Printed and published for the proprietors by S. C. Slade. Radical, Progressive and Labour. See also other editions: **St Pancras Londoner, Pioneer.**

    L(Col)†

1942 Londoner Arbeiter-Zeitung (London Workers' Newspaper). I, 1 (27 Nov. 1886)–II, 45 (1 Oct. 1887); then **Londoner Freie Presser** II, 46 (8 Oct. 1887)–V, 26 (28 June 1890); w

    B   1½d.; 2d. Printed and published for the proprietor by Detloff Bros. **Londoner Freie Presse** issued by Londoner Verlags-Genossenschaft. 'Herausgageben vom Communistischer Arbeiter-Bildungs-Verein.' A Social-Democratic (ie Marxist) paper. In German.

    L(Col)†

Londoner Freie Presse see **Londoner Arbeiter-Zeitung**

Londoner Kommunistische Zeitschrift see **Kommunistische Zeitschrift**

1943 Long Eaton Co-operative Citizen [193-?]. London
    B   Issued by the Long Eaton and District Co-operative Party.
    L(Col) March 1939

1944 Long Eaton Co-operative Home Magazine I, 1 (June 1899)–[May 1900?]. Long Eaton; m

    A   1d. Issued by the Educational Committee of the Long Eaton Working Men's Co-operative Society. Occasional articles on the Society or co-operation in general, with fiction, fashion, gardening, cooking, correspondence, reviews, children's page, notes, announcements.

    Long Eaton PL June 1899–May 1900; O(JJ)† 2–4

1945 Long Eaton Co-operative Record June 1901–20. Long Eaton; m

    A   'The monthly publication of the **Long Eaton Co-operative Record** was commenced in 1901 and continued for over 19 years, mainly under the able editorship of Mr T. H. Edinborough. It was printed in the town by the then recently formed Co-operative Productive Society ... Distributed free, the **Record**'s circulation had risen from 4,000 at the commencement to 7,000 in 1920, when, owing to financial reasons, it was decided to discontinue it.' During the first two years the editorship was shared by Edinborough and C. L. Denchar. The **Record** was replaced by the local **Wheatsheaf.** (Gertrude R. Lane and Robert Bowley, **Through six Decades: the Story of Co-operation in Long Eaton and District, 1868–1928,** Manchester 1929. pp. 148–58.)

    Derbyshire Record Office 1913–20; Long Eaton PL 1901–10

1946 Long Eaton Co-operative Society. **Co-operative Record** 1879– ?
Long Eaton; q

A 'The issue of a quarterly **Co-operative Record**, with a circulation
of a thousand copies, was commenced in 1879. . . .' (Gertrude R. Lane and
Robert Bowley, **Through six Decades: the Story of Co-operation in Long
Eaton and District, 1868–1928,** Manchester 1929.) 'Early in 1879 it was
resolved to issue a quarterly **Co-operative Record,** the numbers to be
issued one week prior to the termination of each quarter. The secretary
[of the Education Department, George Wallace] edited the magazine,
receiving a salary of 10s. per number, and it was determined to commence
with a thousand copies of the first issue.' (Samuel Clegg, sb,Co-operation
in Long Eaton, 1901, p. 220).

1947 Look-Out [c1928]; m
A Minority Movement. (**Red International of Labour Unions,** Oct.
1928.)

1948 Lorry Driver's Special: News and Views of Interest to All Motor
Lorry Drivers I, 1 (Feb. 1934)–2 (Aug./Sept. 1935); 3 (Nov. 1938); irreg
A Gratis. Editorial offices: Transport and General Workers' Union.
'A journal devoted to the interests of all commercial road transport
workers' (No. 2). Urging lorrymen to organise in a trade union, preferably
TGWU. Issued by the latter for distribution. Addresses by Ernest Bevin,
General Secretary.
L(Col)† (w 3); TUC

1949 Loughborough Labour News [194-?]. Loughborough; m
B 2d. Labour Party. (Labour Party. **Your own journal.** 1948).

**1950 Louis Blanc's Monthly Review: the New World of Politics, Art,
Literature, and Sciences.** 1 (July 1849)–4 (Nov. 1849)
B 1s. Published by T. C. Newby. 'Published under Louis Blanc's
immediate inspection, and edited [and translated into English] by F. R.
Trehounsis.' Louis Blanc's reflections in exile on the developing political
situation in France, and analysis of events of 1848. To vindicate socialist
and republican principles against their opponents and misrepresenters.
C; D; L†

1951 Loyal Reformers' Gazette. I, 1 (7 May 1831)–II, 53 (5 May 1832);
then Reformers' Gazette: II, 54 (12 May 1832)–242, (4 Dec. 1841).
Glasgow; w; m. (1833–)
B 2d. Published by W. R. M'Phun, then printed and published by
Muir, Gowans & Co., then printed, published and edited by the owner,
Peter Mackenzie. Started as the organ of Glasgow radicalism, and reports
Glasgow Political Union agitation and news of the trades. After 1832
advocates gradual reformist measures, yet claims to represent working
class interest; in opposition to Chartism, sponsors working class self-help,
savings banks, Mechanics' Institutes and national education.
Dumbarton PL May 1831–May 1834; E I–III†; GM; GU I–III†;
L I–III, 90; LU I–III, 90; MP I; O I–III; ONC I–VI, 180.

1952 Ludd 1 (15 May 1966)–4 (22 June 1966); fortn

    A   2d. Printed and published by CCR Publications. By the team running **Cuddon's Cosmopolitan Review**? 'A news review with an anarchist bias.' 'Produced by workers who feel that the seamen's struggle is also theirs' – at the time of seamen's strike. 'Break bureaucracies, not machines.'

    LE†

1953 Luton Citizen ns 1 (June 1958)–10 (Dec. 1959); irreg

    B   Issued by Luton Borough Labour Party.

    L(Col) ns

1954 Lympet. Lymington

    A   National and Local Government Officers' Association, Lymington Branch. Reproduced from typewriting.

    L [1959] –

1955 MARC: Organ of the Marconi Shop Stewards, AUEW [194-?] –? [London?] ; m?

    A   2d. Amalgamated Union of Engineering Workers.

    TUC† 19 (July 1949)–(June 1951)

1956 'M. & S.' Co-operative Citizen 1 (Oct. 1931)–2 (Dec. 1931); then **Manchester and Salford Co-operative Citizen**: 3 (Jan. 1932)–10 (Sept. 1932); then **'M. & S.' Co-operative Citizen**: ns 1 (March 1940). Manchester; m

    L(Col)

1957 M.H.A.A. Gazette 1 (30 Aug. 1886)–42 (15 June 1887); w

    A   Published by the Music Hall Artistes' Association. Runs and publicises an employment agency for bona fide artistes. For maintenance of professional standards etc.

    L(Col)†

M.H.I.W. Journal [Mental Hospital and Institutional Workers' Union] see **NA-WU Magazine**

1958 'M.R.' View: the Monthly Journal of the Manchester Branch of the Union of Post Office Workers. I, 1 (Feb. 1921). Manchester

    A   2d. Printed by the William Morris Press, Manchester.

    L†

1959 Macclesfield Labour Monthly 1 (Nov. 1896)–[Dec. 1896?] . Macclesfield; m

    B   ½d. Independent Labour Party. Localised edition of a newspaper launched in 1896 by Allen Clarke.

    AbU microfilm of O(JJ) holding; O(JJ) I, 2 [sic] , (2 Nov. 1896)–2 (Dec. 1896)

1960 McDouall's Chartist and Republican Journal 1 (3 April 1841)—27 (2 Oct. 1841). Manchester; w

B   1d. Published by Abel Heywood, printed by John Williamson, Ashton-under-Lyne. Editor: Peter McDouall. Contributors: Harney, O'Brien. Urges the trades to take up the fight for the People's Charter since they can never have protection until the working class gains political power. Articles denouncing the factory system; poetry. Sometime title: **McDouall's Chartist Journal and Trades Advocate.**

LE; LU; MP; NpP; ONC; Greenwood reprint and microfiche: microfiche distributed in Britain and Europe by the Harvester Press Ltd

McDouall's Chartist Journal and Trades Advocate see **McDouall's Chartist and Republican Journal**

1961 Magazine of Useful Knowledge, and Co-operative Miscellany 1 (1 Oct. 1830)—4 (13 Nov. 1830); fortn

B   2d. Published by William Strange. Printed by W. Hill. 'The organ of the British Association for Promoting Co-operative Knowledge. A radical miscellany that fuses an advocacy of co-operative principles with a "useful knowledge" format. Prints accounts of the meetings of the above Association' (Wiener).

L; LU

1962 Maidstone Telephone and Monthly Thought Exchange [April 1896—Dec. 1900?]. Maidstone; m

B   Gratis. Editor: Jesse Hawkes. 'Socialist critic of local affairs' (**Labour Annual**, 1897; **Reformers' Year Book**, 1901). Possible changes of title: **Maidstone and Kent Telephone; Telephone**

Mail Drivers' Despatch see **GPO Mail Drivers' Despatch**

1963 Mail Train: Commercial Travellers' Advocate and Post Office and Railway Services' Guardian 1 (23 April 1884)—111 (1 May 1887; w; fortn; m

A;C   Issued by E. Harford to kill **The Train** of F. W. Evans. The first number was issued a day before **The Railway Review** and was that paper, with small exceptions. The Executive Committee of the Amalgamated Society of Railway Servants paid Harford £40 for his losses. (See G. W. Alcock, **Fifty years of Railway Trade Unionism**, London 1922, p. 265.) Later becomes a commercial travellers' paper and changes content.

L(Col)† (w 1); O 2—106

1964 Mainstream Nov. 1963—Oct. 1965; termly

B   6d. Published by the Communist Party National Student Committee. Articles on a range of political topics. 'Little Brother' of **Marxism Today.**

L; MML

1965 Majority: the Organ of All Who Work for Wage or Salary 1
[Registration issue] (14 May 1906); 1 (10 July 1906)–?; d

    B   ½d. Content of registration issue not relevant. No. 1 10 July
published for Majority, Limited, by Sydney H. E. Foxwell. Printed by the
Clements Printing Works. Newspaper format. Editorial under the main
heading 'The Voice of Labour' introducing the paper, by 'S.M.H'.
[Servetus Mortimer Holden], begins: 'You are reading the first number of
the first British Labour daily newspaper.' 'Bound to no party, to no
league, to no association. It is animated by a genuine desire to promote the
welfare and the prosperity of the working classes in this country.' Support
for parliamentary representation. 'Attack measures, not men. This is the
course I shall continue to pursue in my daily notes in these columns.' Says
he will be printing an article by Ben Tillett in next day's number. Usual
newspaper contents, serial. Contribution: 'In Parliament', by John Ward,
MP. Supported by Tillett, Havelock Wilson, John Ward, and William Bruce,
with the profits to go into a' Labour parliamentary fund.

    O(JJ)† 1 10 July (poor condition); ONC† registration issue

Malden and Kingston Clarion see **Malden Workers' Monthly**

Malden Clarion see **Malden Workers' Monthly**

1966 Malden Workers' Monthly 1937; then **Malden Clarion**: 1938–272
(mid-Dec. 1964); then **Malden and Kingston Clarion**: 1 (Jan. 1965)–36
(Dec. 1967); then **Kingston Borough Clarion** : 37 (Jan. 1968)– ; m; q; m

    B   Local Labour Parties. Latterly title varies: **Clarion: Kingston,
Surbiton, New Malden** [etc.]; **Kingston and Surbiton Clarion.**

    L(Col) 209 (mid-Aug. 1959)– ; LabP† 1960–70*., the Editor
later nos

1967 Malden Commonwealth 1 (April 1929)–?

    B   Gratis. Newspaper format. Printed an; published by the National
Labour Press. Urges support for the Prospective Labour Candidate for
Malden Division, Major Herbert Evans. Looks at Tories' record and puts
forward Labour's programme (No. 1).

    O(JJ)† 1

1968 Male Nurses' Journal [194-?] –?; q

    A   4d. Society of Registered Male Nurses.

    LMH 52 (1955)–

1969 Maltby Flatsheet Guide [1927?] –? Maltby

    A   1d. Published by the Maltby Pit Group of the Communist Party.
Reproduced from typewriting.

    WCML† 2 (17 June 1927)

1970 Man: a Rational Advocate for Universal Liberty, Free Discussion and Equality of Conditions I, 1 (7 July 1833)–II, 30 (10 Aug. 1834); w
B   1d.; 2d. Published, printed and edited by Richard E. Lee. 'One of the best known radical newspapers of the decade. Advocates universal suffrage, the nationalization of land, the forming of trades unions, and a 'rational' approach to religion. Contains many articles by the Spencean propagandists Allan Davenport and George Petrie' (Wiener).
GM I, 20–1, 27; HO 64/15 II, 17, 30; HO 64/19 I, 20, II, 15, 20; L I; LE II, 1, 2, 8–10, 15; O I, 1, 21, 23

1971 Man! the Measure of All Things: an Anglo-American Anarchist Publication. 1933–40; ns I, 1 (May 1955)–6 (March/April 1957). [USA]; London (ns); s-a
B   4d. 'From 1933 to 1940 under the editorships of Marcus Graham and the late Hippolyte Havel, represented the voice of uncompromising Anarchism in the English language movement of North America.' New series issued in Britain. Published by S. E. Parker. Issued by the Man! Group (London) in association with the Man! Group (Los Angeles). Discusses the relevance of Anarchism and Marxism, but not associated with Syndicalism, or with the workers' movement.
L

Man and Metal see Iron and Steel Trades Confederation. **Journal**

1972 Manchester: a Monthly Journal of the Manchester and Salford Independent Labour Party 1 (May 1899)–25 (May 1901); then **Social Reformer**: 26 (June 1901)–29 (Sept. 1901). Manchester; m
B   Gratis. Published and printed by A. C. Lindley. Editor: J. Taylor Kay
Bolton Trades Council Feb. 1901; Salford PL 2, 21; Swinton and Pendlebury PL 22

1973 Manchester Alliance of Operative House Painters. **Half-yearly report**
A   Postgate stated the above for the years 1866–70 (not necessarily all those published) were in the office of the National Amalgamated Society of Operative House and Ship Painters and Decorators. Not traced. From 1870 the body was called the General Alliance.

1974 Manchester Unity Operative Bricklayers. **Monthly Report** 1870–(1884?). From 1870 the body was called The General Union of Operative House Painters.
Warwick U (MRC) 1, 1870 (no number), 1884

1975 Manchester and Salford Advertiser 1 (17 Oct. 1828)–32 (23 May 1829); then **Manchester Times and Gazette**: 33 (30 May 1829)–1035 (26 Aug. 1848); then **Manchester Times and Manchester and Salford Advertiser and Chronicle**: 1036 (2 Sept. 1848)–1044 (28 Oct. 1848); then **Manchester Examiner and Times**: 1 (4 Nov. 1848)–691 (16 June 1855); then **Manchester Weekly Examiner and Times**: 692 (23 June 1855)–818 (5 Dec. 1857); then **Manchester Weekly Times and Examiner**; 819 (12 Dec. 1857)–3407 (22 July 1922). Manchester; w

    B   Staunch supporter of radical parliamentary reform in 1831. Held Cobbett and Paine in high regard. After dispute about editorship in 1833 the new editor affirmed his continued support for reform and the rights of the labouring classes.

    L(Col)†

Manchester and Salford Co-operative Citizen see 'M. and S.' Co-operative Citizen

1976 Manchester and Salford Co-operative Herald I, [1888?] –Manchester; m

    A   Manchester and Salford Equitable Co-operative Society. Title varies slightly.

    Co-op. Union 1896–1960*; L XXIV, 283 (1912)–   ; MP LXVI, 5 (May 1954)–

1977 Manchester City Labour Party Bulletin [1969?]– . Manchester; irreg

    B

Manchester Examiner and Times see **Manchester and Salford Advertiser**

1978 Manchester Herald 1, (31 March 1792)–52 (23 March 1793). Manchester; w

    B   3½d. Printed by M. Falkner and Company. Claimed to be 'the Paper of the People'. Jacobin in tone, published London Corresponding Society manifestos; about January 1793 Jacobin emphasis faded and the paper became more moderate in tone.

    L(Col)†; MP

1979 Manchester Observer, or **Literary, Commercial and Political Register**
I, 1 (3 Jan. 1818)–II, 22 (29 May 1819); then **Wardle's Manchester
Observer**: I, 1 (5 June 1819)–5, (3 July 1819); [ns] 1 (10 July 1819)–   ;
ns 2 17 July 1819; then **Manchester Observer**: II, 28 (24 July 1819)–III,
157 (30 Dec. 1820); ns 1 (25 Aug. 1821)–52 (14 Sept 1822). Manchester;
w

    B   7d.; 3½d., unstamped (**Wardle's Manchester Observer**). First
printed and published by Thomas Rogerson, then by James Wroe. Begins
as moderate radical then becomes more advanced. For 'the freedom of the
Press, the Palladium of all our rights'. Appeals to the 'artisans and
mechanics of Manchester'. From 5 June to 17 July 1819 editor and
proprietor was Mark Wardle, previous editor and part-owner of the
Manchester Observer. The new series of the latter had as an alternative title
Wooler's British Gazette, was printed by T. J. Wooler, published by J. T
Saxton, and under the guidance of Wooler and friends. 'The Union of the
Reformers of the North is our first object.' To revive the 'People's Press'
and campaign to restore the Rights of Man. Organ of the Great Northern
Radical Union.
    Chetham's Lib. 5 June 1819; L(Col)†; MP*

1980 Manchester Political Register, or **Reformers' Repository** I, 1 (4 Jan.
1817)–I, 8 (1 March 1817). Manchester; w
    B   Printed by W. Wardle. Edited by John Knight. Radical outcry
about Peterloo.
    MP†; ONC 1

1981 Manchester Spectator 1818. [Manchester? w?]
    B   Edited by John Knight. (J. Foster, **Class Struggle and the
Industrial Revolution; early industrial capitalism in 3 English towns,**
London 1974).
    HO (18 Nov. 1818) (no. 42/182)

1982 Manchester Teacher: the Journal of the Manchester Teachers'
Association 1 (Spring 1961)–15 (Spring 1966). Manchester; 3-yr
    A   National Union of Teachers.
    MP†

1983 Manchester Teachers' Association. **Newsletter and Journal** 1960–   .
Manchester; 5-yr
    A   National Union of Teachers.
    MP; WCML† Jan. 1969–

Manchester Times and Gazette see **Manchester and Salford Advertiser**

Manchester Times and Manchester and Salford Advertiser and Chronicle
see **Manchester and Salford Advertiser**

1984 Manchester Unity Operative Bricklayers **Monthly Report** 1868–86
    Warwick U (MRC) 1868–86

1985 Manchester Unity Operative Bricklayers **Quarterly Report**
1886−1918
    Warwick U (MRC) 1886−86

1986 Manchester Weekly Citizen 1 (7 Oct. 1911)−57 (1 Nov. 1912).
Manchester; w
    B   1d. Printed and published by the National Labour Press. First
object to be 'the mouthpiece of the overwhelming body of industrial
workers' in Manchester, then to deal with the affairs of workers'
representative on public bodies. Contributor: James Leatham. Features in
common with **Leeds and District Weekly Citizen**, eg, the serial story.
Absorbed by its 'younger brother' the **Daily Citizen**.
    L(Col)†

Manchester Weekly Examiner and Times see **Manchester and Salford
Advertiser**

Manchester Weekly Times and Examiner see **Manchester and Salford
Advertiser**

1987 Manx Star 1 (11 Jan. 1928)−(31 Dec. 1930). Douglas; w
    B   1d.; free (after 5 Dec. 1928). Printed and published by William
James Ramsbottom. 'Born of a great hope, this issue presents itself as the
accredited organ of the Manx Labour Movement. We imply by that, that
the paper will emphasise the Labour ideals in political and social life.' (No.
1.) Editor: W. J. Ramsbottom, Assistant Editor: T. N. Hinton.
    Manx Museum and National Trust, Douglas

1988 Margate Mirror: News Sheet of the Margate Borough Branch NALGO
[1], (1961)−7 [1962]; [ns 1] (Nov. 1965)−[2] (Dec. 1965); then
Clanger: 3 (Jan. 1966)−   . Margate
    A   National and Local Government Officers' Association.
    L

Marine Caterer see **Union Magazine**

Marine Engineer Officers' Magazine see **Marine Engineers' Association.
Journal**

1989 Marine Engineers' Association. Journal I, 1 (Jan. 1909)−XI, 110
(Nov. 1919); then b **Marine Engineer Officers' Magazine**: I, 1 (Jan.
1920)−XXXV (Summer 1953). London; Glasgow; m
    A   Free; 1s. Covers wages and conditions; also much technical
information.
    C b I−XVII, 3; L

Marine Worker see **Union Magazine**

Mariner, 1941−? see ΝΑΥΤΕΡΓΑΤΗΕ

1990 Marx Memorial Library. **Quarterly Bulletin** 1 Jan.–March 1957–   ;
q
  B
  MML; ONC 40 (Oct.–Dec. 1966)–*

1991 Marxism Today: Theoretical and Discussion Journal of the
Communist Party. I, 1 (Oct. 1957)–   ; m
  B   1s. 6d. etc. Published by the Communist Party. Editor: John
Gollan.
  AU; E; L; O; ONC† 1961 (Aug. 1963)–

1992 Marxist: a Discussion Journal I, 1 (Nov./Dec. 1966)–I, 4 (May/June
1967); bi-m
  B   2s. 6d. Published by Oasis Publishing Company.
Marxist–Lenisnist/Maoist comment and discussion on British and world
politics.
  E; LE

1993 Marxist League. **Information Bulletin** [193-?] –?
  B
  Warwick UL, Maitland/Sara papers July 1937

Marxist Quarterly see **Modern Quarterly**

1994 Marxist Review: a Journal of International Socialism I, 1 (July/Aug.
1950)–?; bi-m?
  B   6d. Published by G. Gray. Reproduced from typewriting.
Theoretical journal. 'The contents are directed towards Trotskyists and
friends of our Movement'.
  ONC† 1

Marxist Studies see **Bulletin of Marxist Studies**

1995 Marxist Studies. Newsletter 1 (April 1970)–? m
  B   Published by BMS Publications. Reproduced from typewriting.
Contributors: John Walters, Carol Day. Aims: 'to allow an exchange of
ideas and experiences among comrades who subscribe to **Marxist Studies**
[ie **Bulletin of Marxist Studies**]'. 'The main activities in which
comrades . . . are engaged are four areas of work: 1 Workers' Control . . . 2
Women's liberation . . . 3 Youth . . . 4 Work in the Labour Party and other
traditional organisations of the working class . . .' Reports of meetings,
activities, news from abroad.
  O 1

1996 Maryhill Clarion: Monthly Journal of the Constituency Labour Party
[1949?] –? Glasgow; m
  B   1d. Published by Maryhill Constituency Labour Party.
Newspaper format. Local and national news and comment.
  LabP† XII, 2 (Feb. 1960)–XV, 6 (June 1963*)

Masons' and Granitecutters' Journal see Operative Masons' and
Granitecutters' Journal

1997 Mason's Journal [c1838]. Glasgow
    A   'Periodical conducted with very great ability by a working man.'
(**Monthly Liberator**, 13 June 1838, p. 10).

1998 Masses I, 1 (Feb. 1919)–I, 5 (20 Aug. 1919)
    B?
    L (not traced)

1999 May Day Manifesto Bulletin [Jan. 1968?]–? [London? m?]
    B
    ILP 3 (March 1968)

2000 Mazdoor: the Monthly Bulletin of the Indian Workers Association
(Great Britain) 1 (Jan. 1950)–4 (April 1950); m
    B   For an independent socialist republic for India. Brief notices,
news of political events from different parts of India in struggle for
independence and workers' rights. A journal of this title is listed in DeWitt
John's **Indian Workers' Associations**, 1969, as being published in 1964–5.
Not traced.
    L

2001 Mechanics' Magazine, Museum, Register, Journal and Gazette I, 1
(30 Aug. 1823)–ns XXVIII, 2517 (1872); w
    C   3d. Published by Knight and Lacey. Edited by J. C. Robertson,
1823–52. Promoted the ideals and work of mechanics' institutions. In the
early years discussed means of education and social improvement, but
predominantly technical in content thereafter. In 1824 articles and
correspondence supported repeal of the Combination Acts.
    L; ONC 1823–5, 1836

Mechanics' Newspaper see **Journeyman and Artizan's London and
Provincial Circular**

2002 Mechanic's Organ, or Journal for Young Men and Women I, 1 (1 Oct.
1847)–III, 29 (1 Feb. 1850); m
    C   1d. Publisher: B. L. Green. Addressed to working men and
women with a view to their moral and mental improvement. Extols virtues
of temperance, self-reliance; also advocates 'early rising and early closing'
on the question of working hours. Plea for peaceful means of change in
response to the upheavals of 1848.
    L

2003 Mechanic's Weekly Journal; or, Artisans' Miscellany of Inventions, Experiments, Projects and Improvements in the Useful Arts 1 (15 Nov. 1823)–26 (8 May 1824); w

    C   3d. Published by Westley and Parrish. 'devoted exclusively to subjects of practical utility,' for artisans.

    C; L; SaU

Medical Association of Eire. **Journal** see Irish Free State Medical Union. **Journal**

Medical News and Views see Socialist Medical Association. **Bulletin**

2004 Medical Record : Official Journal of the Association of Medical Record Officers I (1949)– ; q

    A   1s. (1955).

    LMH

Medical Student Opinion see **Hospital**

2005 Medical Superintendents' Society. **Quarterly Bulletin** June 1946–Jan. 1950; q

    A

    L

2006 Medical World: Official Organ of the State Medical Service Association I, 1 (7 Aug. 1913)– ; w

    A   1d. etc. Latest sub-title: **Journal of the Medical Practitioners' Union, a Section of the ASTMS** [Association of Scientific, Technical and Managerial Staffs]. Put forward the idea that 'the Medical Profession should be organised as one of the Civil Services of the country'. 'The services of the State Doctors to be free to every man, woman and child, rich or poor.'

    BU LXIV, 3–(w LXIV, 20); C XXXIX (1934)– ; CPA I–IX; GU LXXXII– ; L; LCH LXXXII– ; LMA VI–; LMD I–VI, XXXII–(LXIV*); LMH XLIX– ; LUH LXXXII– ; LS I–XII, XLVI– : LdU LXXVIII– ; LvP LXXXIV– ; MP XLIX–

2007 Medical World Newsletter ?–1968

    A   Absorbed by **Medical World**.

    L Jan. 1950– ; LMH 1955– ; TUC 1954–68*

2008 Medecine Today and Tomorrow : the Official Organ of the Socialist Medical Association I, 1 (Oct. 1937)–XVIII, Nov./Dec. 1966; then b **Socialism & Health**: I, 1 (Jan./Feb. 1967)– ; m; bi-m

    B

    BP b IV, 4 (1970)– ; BrU; L; LE b; LMD; ONC occ. nos; SwU b II, 2 (1968)– ; TUC; the Association

2009 Medley [1967?] –   ; Newark
A   National and Local Government Officers' Association, Newark
Branch. Reproduced from typewriting.
L 1967–

2010 Medusa, or, Penny Politician I, 1 (20 Feb. 1819)–II, 1 (28 Jan.
1820); w
B   1d. Printed and published by and for Thomas Davison.
Unstamped. ultra-radical. For universal suffrage, annual parliaments.
Richard Carlile was associated with it.
L I, 1–I, 47 (7 Jan. 1820); LU I, 1–47; MP I, 29–32, 34; NP I, 29,
31–2; ONC I, 27

2011 Medway Monitor: the Official Journal of the City of Rochester
branch of NALGO [1963?]–. Rochester
A   National and Local Government Officers' Association.
Reproduced from typewriting.
L 1963–

2012 Meeting Point [1962?]–
A   Published jointly by the Paddington, St Marylebone and
Westminster Branches of the National and Local Governemnt Officers'
Association. Reproduced from typewriting.
L 1962–

2013 Member: Official Journal of the Sheffield NALGO Branch
[19--?]–   ; Sheffield
A   National and Local Government Officers' Association.
SP XLIII, 1 (May 1969)–XLIII, 3, XLIV, 1, XLV, 1

Mental Health Services Journal see **NA-WU Magazine**

Mental Hospital and Institutional Workers' Journal see **NA-WU Magazine**

2014 Mental Notes [192-?]–?
A   Irish Mental Hospital Workers' Union
TUC Dec. 1923, Nov. 1925

2015 Mercantile Marine Service Association Reporter I, [1876?]–XLVII,
569 (Dec. 1922); then **Salt Spray: a Journal for the Master, Navigating and
Engineer Officers of the British Navy**: XLVIII, 570 (Jan. 1923)–LXVII,
723 (July 1942). Liverpool; m; q (1933–9); s-a
A   1s. (1940). Merged with **Merchant Navy Journal**.
L XXIX (1904)–   ; LvP VI-XLVII, LXVI–LXVII; the Association
1886–94, 1896–1915, 1917–42

2016 Merchant Navy Journal: the Official Organ of the Navigators and Engineer Officers' Union I, 1 (Jan. 1937)–XXXI, 2 (June 1969); q

    A   6d. etc. Published by the Union

    LvP 1942–   ; L; Mercantile Marine Service Association; Merchant Navy and Airline Officers' Association; TUC.

2017 Mercia News [196-?]–? Birmingham

    B   Printed and published by West Midlands Labour Party Young Socialists. Reproduced from typewriting.

    Warwick U.(MRC)† 7 undated numbers 1970–2

2018 Mercury [19--?]–?

    A   Union of Post Office Workers, Overseas Telegraph Operators, Branch. (W. Dunlop, 'Local journals', **Belpost**, IV, 5 [May 1965].)

2019 Mercury [19--?]–? Wolverhampton

    A   Union of Post Office Workers, Wolverhampton Amalgamated Branch. (W. Dunlop, 'Local journals'. **Belpost** IV, 5 [May 1965].

2020 Mercury: the Organ of the Leeds T. and T. and Leeds Postal Branches of the Union of PO Workers I, 1 (Sept. 1922)–(Sept./Oct. 1948); m

    A   1d. To articulate grievances, comment on policy etc. For strong Trade Unionism.

    L; LdP

2021 Mercury [195-?]–

    A   Civil Service Union.

    L

2022 Merlin: Carmarthenshire Branch Magazine I, 1 (Spring 1953)–II, 3 (Spring 1954). Carmarthen; m

    A   National and Local Government Officers' Association. Reproduced from typewriting.

    L

2023 Mersey Docker: the Paper of the Dockers of Merseyside 1 (June 1934)–? Liverpool

    A   Communist Party paper. Reproduced from typewriting.

    WCML† 1

2024 Mersey Magazine 1909–10. [Liverpool?]

    A   'Issued for about a year. The editor who wrote more or less all of it was George Milligan, a docker and member of the National Union of Dock Labourers. It never became the official journal of the union and collapsed after a few months. It contained articles and poems written by Milligan, devoted to propagating the virtues of trade unionism; and general material on life at the docks. The articles contain a strong religious fervour as Milligan was a devout Catholic. Fortunately Milligan published a selection of material from the magazine in a book **Life Through Labour's Eyes**, 1911, my only source of information' (E. Taplin, letter).

2025 Merseyside Building Trade Worker 1 (June 1932)–2 (July 1932).
Liverpool; m
    A   1d. Editor?: Leo McGree. 'Not for publication.' 'Incorporating
Furnishing Trade Worker.' Liverpool Building Workers Forward
Movement.
    WCML† 1

2026 Merseyside Labour's Voice [195-? 196-?] –?
    B

2027 Merseyside Militant I (1947)–? [Liverpool]
    (BUCOP)
    L (not traced)

2028 Merseyside 'New Leader' Bulletin [192-?]
    B?
    ILP No. 37

Merthyr Borough Labour Pioneer see **Pioneer, 1911–1922**

Merthyr Pioneer see **Pioneer**, 1911–1922

2029 Merton and Morden Citizen ns 1 (Oct. 1949)–27 (Aug. 1952)
    B   Issued by the Political Purposes Committee of the Royal
Arsenal Co-operative Society.
    L(Col) ns

2030 Merton and Morden Labour Party. **Weekly Bulletin** [1956–70?] ; w
    B
    Merton and Morden Labour Party 1956–70

**2031 Messenger; Being the Chronicle of the War Office Boy Messengers'
Friendly Society.** A (July 1907)–4 (Dec. 1909); irreg
    A
    L

2032 Messenger: the Weekly News Letter of the Isle of Ely Labour Party
June 1966–? March; w
    B   Duplicated and published by Eric Parsloe, Labour Agent. Short
comments, notes, diary of meetings.
    LabP† I, 26 (2 Dec. 1966)–33 (18 Aug. 1967*)

2033 Metal Worker: the Official Organ of the Metal Trades Federation I, 1
(Jan. 1907)–II, 17 (May 1908); [ns] I, 1 (June 1908)–I, 7 (8 Dec. 1908);
III, 8 (Jan. 1909)–IV, 42 (June 1910) Sheffield; m
    A   1d. Published and edited at the office of the Federation by
Charles Hobson, the Secretary. In 1908 becomes also the official organ of
the National Federation of Blastfurnacemen. Articles and comment on
Unionism and workers' movements in the metal trades here and abroad,
also on working-class living standards. Supports Labour representation.
    BP† ; LE I–III; SP; TUC Dec. 1908–June 1910

2034 Metal Worker: the Official Organ of the National Society of Amalgamated Brass Workers and Metal Mechanics I (1907)–III, (1909); Birmingham
    A
    LE

2035 Metal Worker 1 (Sept. 1930)–?; m
    A   Printed and published by the National Minority Movement. Reproduced from typewriting. A successor to **The Working Engineer** which ceased to appear 'a year ago . . . after a run of 2 years'. Notes, news at home and abroad on conditions and developments in the industry.
    ONC† 1, 2 (Oct. 1930)

Metal Worker, 1946–1963 see **New Propellor**

2036 Metal worker (27 Dec. 1924); (21 Feb. 1925). Glasgow
    A   A supplement in **The Worker** (qv).

2037 Metropolitan Co-operator [1897?] –?; m
    A   ½d. Co-operative Printing Society.
    O(JJ)† Oct. 1897

2038 Mets Journal: Organ of the Metropolitan Districts Branch, Union of Post Office Workers I, 1 [1931?] –? m
    A
    TUC† 11 occ. issues between VIII, 5 (May 1938) and 1950

2039 Middlesbrough Co-operative Record 1 (1908)–? Middlesbrough; bi-m
    A   Gratis. Middlesbrough Co-operative Society. Editor: George Bedford (1909).
    L V, 10 (1912)–

2040 Middlesex County Teachers' **Journal**. 1 (March 1926); then **Log**: Middlesex County Teachers' Journal: 2 (June 1926)–53 (June 1939); then **Middlesex Log**: Journal of the Middlesex County Teachers' Association: ns 1 (Feb. 1951)–17 (Autumn 1956). Teddington; q
    A   2d. etc. National Union of Teachers.
    L (w i 43)

Middlesex Log see **Middlesex County Teachers' Journal**

2041 Middleton Herald [c1909]; m
    B   Gratis. Independent Labour Party. Editor?: W. J. Blackmur, Forest Gate, Essex (**Reformers' Year Book**, 1909).

2042 Mid-Essex Leader. [193-?]. Chelmsford; m
    B   Labour Party. (Labour and Socialist International. **The Socialist Press**, 1933.)

2043 Midgie [1926?] –? Blyth
    A   Issued by the Communist Group at New Hartley Pit.
Reproduced from typewriting.
    NwP† 2 ([22 May 1926] [Xerox])

2044 Midland Chronicle, and Beacon for the Working Man I, 1 (July
1833)–I, 5 (Oct. 1833). Birmingham; m
    C   2d. Printed and published by B. Hudson. 'This periodical is
conducted by some philanthropic individuals whose sole aim is to point
out the way by which the moral respectability and domestic comforts of
the industrious classes may be increased.' Miscellany addressed to the
labouring classes, urging temperance and thrift.
    BP† ; L 1–3

Midland Chronicle, 1951– see **Venture, 1920**

2045 Midland Counties Illuminator 1 (13 Feb. 1841)–16 (29 May 1841).
Leicester; w
    B   1½d. Published by John Seal. Edited by Thomas Cooper.
Largely preoccupied with the education of the working class for the
exercise of their political rights. Chronicles dispute between the rival
tendencies in Leicester Chartism.
    L(Col)†

2046 Midland Medical Journal: the Official Organ of the Birmingham and
District General Medical Practitioners' Union I, 1 (Nov. 1901)–XXIV, 7
(Oct./Nov. 1925). Birmingham; m
    A   4d. To advance the professional interests of its members and
defend standards and status. Much of the content on medical matters.
Merged in **Birmingham Medical Review**.
    BP† ; BU I–XVII, XXLLL–XXIV (XVI–XXIV*); C; L

2047 Midland Progressionist: a Periodical for the People, Devoted to
Popular Enfranchisement and Progress. I (1848). then **Progressionist**: 1
(1849)–48 (1849). Buckingham; London; m; w
    B   Edited by John Small, Joseph Barker, then Gammage when it
'changed hands' (C. R. Gammage, **History of the Chartist Movement
1837–1854**. [1894], p. 346) Advocates the 'rights of the people'. Opposed
to the aristocracy and class legislation. Advocates taxation of landed
property.
    L 1848

2048 Midland Representative, and Birmingham Herald I, 1 (23 April 1831)–I, 59 (2 June 1832). Birmingham; w

    B   7d. Printed and published by Charles Watson, then by James Powell. Editor: Bronterre O'Brien. A general newspaper 'founded by the People and for the People'. Strenuously advocates a full, free, and fair representation of the People in Parliament, by General Suffrage, annual parliaments, and ballot vote. Against 'Taxes on Knowledge'. Reports of reform meetings in Midlands area, and Political Union agitation. Incorporated into the **Birmingham Journal**.

    L(Col)†

Midland Venture see **Venture. 1920**

2049 Midland Workman, and General Advertiser 1 (12 Oct. 1861)–17 (1 Feb. 1862). Leicester; w

    B   1d. Printed and published by James Thoburn Brown. 'edited by a son of Toil.' To answer 'the great need of a provincial journal, advocating the cause of the Sons of Toil, the Repeal of the Paper Duties'. Claims to advocate franchise extension, ballot vote, abolition of church rates, intellectual and moral advancement of the People, army and navy retrenchment, temperance, reading rooms, libraries, trade unions, co-operative societies, Oddfellow and Benefit societies. Moderate. Chiefly general news and police court gossip, but correspondence includes contributions from working men. Contributor: J. Sketchley.

    L(Col)†

2050 Midlander

    B   A 'Voice' paper.

Midwives Chronicle see **Nursing Notes**

Midwives Chronicle and Nursing Notes see **Nursing Notes**

2051 Milestones: the Official Magazine of the St Mark's Tramway Brotherhood of the United Kingdom I (1908)–?; q; s-a

    C   1d., free to members of the Brotherhood. In later years entitled **Traffic Workers' Brotherhood**, and issue for February 1948 announces change of title to **Transport Workers Christian Fellowship**. Founder President: Rev. John Darlington, St Mark's Temporary Church, Tramway Hall, Kennington Oval. Aims of Fellowship (1947–8): 'To unite all Transport Workers, both men and women, who profess the Christian faith, in a fellowship of work and witness to proclaim and establish the laws of Christ as the supreme authority of our individual and communal life, and to minister to all engaged in the industry.' News of meetings, branches etc.

    L II (1909)–; O IV (1911)–XLII, 1 (1948*)

Militant, 1937–1946 see **Youth Militant**

2052 Militant: Organ of the Socialist Left of the Labour Party. ns 1 (Sept. 1941)—11 9c. 1942); then **Militant Scottish Miner Edition**: 12 (Feb. 1943)—20 (Nov. 1943); then **Militant Miner Edition**: 21 (Dec. 1943)—30 (Nov. 1944). Glasgow; m

    B; A   (1943—4). 2d. Published by the Pioneer Publishing Association. Printed by voluntary labour. Propagandist paper campaigning for revolutionary socialist policy within the Labour Party. Pro-Trotskyist, anti-Stalinist. From February 1943 concentrates on the fight for socialist policies within the Scottish Miners' Union, and against the official Right-wing bureaucracy. Written by comrades in Lanarkshire, with an editorial board of workers.

    L(Col)†

2053 Militant, For Youth and Labour 1 (Oct. 1964)—; m; w

    B   Labour Party Young Socialists. For last few years sub-titled: 'The Marxist Paper for Labour and Youth'.

    LE†

Militant Miner Edition see **Militant. 1941—1942**

Militant Scottish Miner Edition see **Militant. 1941—1942**

2054 Militant Socialist I, 1 (May 1933)—? [Nottingham?; m?]

    B   Independent Labour Party, Nottingham.

    ILP May, June 1933

2055 Militant Trade Unionist 1 (1 May 1933); fortn

    A   2d. Published by the Trade Union Co-operative Publishing Society. Edited by Tom Mann. Details of the proposed paper were given by Mann in a letter in **Busman's Punch**, March 1933: it was to be an 'essentially popular, illustrated journal . . . '. Review of events in the Labour Movement. Numerous photographs.

    O(JJ)† 1; WCML† 1

Milk Worker see **Dairy Workers' Journal**

Mill and Factory Herald see **Dundee Mill and Factory Operatives' Herald**

Millenial Gazette see **Robert Owen's Millenial Gazette**

Millgate and Playgoer see **Millgate Monthly**

2056 Millgate Monthly: a Popular Magazine Devoted to Association, Education, Literature and General Advancement. I, 1 (Oct. 1905)—XL, 458 (May/June 1945); then **Playgoer and Millgate**: XL, 459 (July/Aug. 1945)—XLVI, 503 (Feb. 1951); then **Millgate and Playgoer**: Magazine of the New Age: ns I, 1 (April 1951)—II (Spring 1953). Manchester; m; q (1952—)

    A   3d. etc. Printed and Published by the Co-operative Press. Stated in its first number that its object was to deal 'with social, historical, literary, and biographical subjects in a popular manner . . . ' Later emphasis on the stage, television and films. Early title varied: sometimes **Millgate; Millgate and Playgoer**.

    Co-op. Coll.; Co-op. Union 1905—38; D; L; MP; O 1905—37

2057 Million: New Left Writing. First Collection [194-?] —**Third Collection 1946** Glasgow

    B   2s.; 2s. 6d. Published by William McLellan and Company. Edited by John Singer. A magazine of creative writing. 'a Left synthesis', poems, stories, articles, reviews. Contributor: H. McDiarmid.

    E; MP 1—2

2058 Millworker: One Union for the Textile Industry [Jan. 1937?] —? Bradford; bi-m?

    A   Published by the West Riding Group, Militant Woolen Textile Trade Unionists.

    MRC, Warwick U2 (March/April 1937)

2059 Milnrow and Newhey Echo. [193-?]. Rochdale; w

    B   Labour Party. (Labour and Socialist International. **The Socialist Press**, 1933.)

Miner. 1875—1878 see **Labour Press and Miner's and Workman's Examiner**

2060 Miner 1 [Oct. 1879?] —? Glasgow; m

    A   1d. Printed for the proprietors by McLaren and Sons. Articles and news from the Scottish coalfields on conditions and struggles of the miners, darg, sliding scale etc. Reports and correspondence.

    GM† 3 (Dec. 1879)

2061 Miner: a Journal for Underground Workers [I], 1 (Jan. 1887—9). Cumnock, Ayrshire; m

    A   Printed by Arthur Guthrie at the **Herald** Office, Ardrossan (I, 1—11) then by William Robertson and Company at the Office of the **Ayrshire Post**, Ayr. Edited by Keir Hardie. 'Claimed its aim was to be a leader, not merely a chronicler of events; advocated State-owned railroad, eight-hours day, national insurance for miners, reform of land laws, payment of election expenses and of MPs, free education, and that these would be brought about through organization of workers. Title changed to **Labour Leader** in February 1889' (Brophy). Vol. II sub-titled: 'an Advanced Political Journal'.

    ONC† I (w 3, 5, 8); TUC, John Burns. Lib. I, (1887)—II, (1888)

2062 Miner: Organ of the Rank and File 1 (30 Sept. 1922)–106 (23 Oct. 1926). Dunfermline; fortn

    A   1d. Published by Philip Hodge. Rank-and-file syndicalist paper of Fife, Kinross, Clackmannan Miners' Association, Emergency Committee, formed to fight for socialist policies and against officialdom. By December 1923 organ of breakaway union, Mineworkers' Reform Union of Fife, Kinross and Clackmannan. Struggled against 'autocracy' of William Adamson, MP, General Secretary of the FKCMA.

    L(Col)†

2063 Miner 1 (4 June 1926)–231 (1 Nov. 1930); w

    A   1d. Printed for the publishers, The New Leader, Ltd., later published by the Miners' Federation. Organ of the Miners' Federation of Great Britain. The 'purpose of this new paper is to place before the miners and the public generally, the case for the miner in the present great lock-out.' Established with the help of Brailsford's **New Leader**. Editor (1926): John Strachey. Wound up because of 'small circulation and financial loss'.

    L(Col)†; LE 1927–29*; LdU 1–137; O(JJ)† 13. ONC 3; TUC

2064 Miner: Official Organ of the South Wales Miners I, 1 (Oct. 1944)–IV, 1/2 (Nov./Dec. 1947?). Cardiff; m

    A   Free to members. Published by the South Wales Miners' Federation.

    South Wales Miners' Library*

2065 Miner: the Magazine of the South Wales Area of the NUM I, 1 (Jan./Feb. 1953)–[ns], 18 (Nov./Dec. 1968). Cardiff?; bi-m

    A   Free to members. National Union of Mineworkers, South Wales Area.

    South Wales Miners' Library*; TUC IX, 1 (Jan./Feb. 1961)–[ns], 18 (Nov./Dec. 1968)

2066 Miner: Voice of the National Union of Mineworkers 1 (Jan. 1969)–; m

    A   Free (No. 1); ed. etc. News of the union, the industry, and related topics.

    L(Col)†: ONC 13 (Feb. 1970)–

Miner and Workman's Advocate see **British Miner and General Newsman**

Miners' Advocate. 1843–1847 see **Miner's Journal. 1843**

2067 Miner's Advocate and Record I, 1 (17 Jan. 1873)–II, 88 (31 Oct. 1874). Middlesbrough; w

   A   1d. Printed and published by Joseph Gould. 'Proprietors and editor are working miners.' Organ of militant coal and ironstone miners in Northumberland and Durham. For emancipation of the working class from the tyranny of capital, Criminal Law Amendment Act, Masters and Servants Act etc. Support for universal suffrage and working men as MPs. Proletarian Republicanism frequently expressed in the correspondence of working men.

   L(Col)†

2068 Miners Campaign Special 1 (Sept. 1935)–? irreg.

   A   Issued by the Mineworkers' Federation of Great Britain. Propaganda newspaper to further the campaign for higher wages, and for re-organisation and modernisation of the industry.

   O(JJ)† 1–5 (Dec. 1935) (w 4); TUC

2069 Miners' International News Sept. 1956–July 1967; irreg

   A   Published by WFTU Publications for the World Federation of Trade Unions. Reports activities of the Miners' Trade Unions International, a Trade Department of WFTU. Numbering varies.

   C; E; L; O†

2070 Miner's Journal 1 (21 Oct. 1843)–3 (18 Nov. 1843); then **Miners' Advocate**: [I], 1 2 Dec. 1843)–II, 25 (Feb. 1845); ns 1 (May 1845)–? Newscastle-upon-Tyne (1843–5); Preston (1845); Douglas; fortn; m (May 1845–)

   A   1d.; 1½d. Miners' Association of Great Britain and Ireland. Editors: William Beesley; William Daniells. Not published May 1846–Jan. 1847. With new series, No. 13 changed title to **Miners' Advocate and Manx Intelligencer**. May have been published as late as 1850 but copies have not been traced.

   NwP† 1843–Oct. 1847 (w ns 17, 18) (original and microfilm); ONC occ. nos 1844–5; WiP 1843–Feb. 1845

2071 Miners' Monthly I, 1 (Jan. 1934)–(Sept. 1939). Cardiff; m

   A   Printed and published for the South Wales Miners' Federation by the Cymric Federation.

   CrP; South Wales Miners' Library; TUC 2 (April), 3 (May) 1934

2072 Miner's Monthly Magazine 1 (March 1944)–5 (July 1844). [Newcastle-upon-Tyne?] ; m

   C   Editor and owner: William Prowting Roberts, Miners' Attorney General. Assisted in publication by William Beesley, former editor of **Miner's Journal,** then acting as clerk to Roberts. Ceased publication in middle of Durham lock-out 1844.

   WiP

2073 Miner's National Gazette: the Organ of the Miners of Great Britain and Ireland 1 (14 April 1883)—17 (4 Aug. 1883). Exeter; w

    A   1d. Printed and published for the proprietors by H. Leduc. Founded to supply a weekly newspaper, 'an educational medium', for the 1¼ million miners of Britain. Conference and district reports, 'official' news. Supported Thomas Burt, miners' MP, representation of Labour in Parliament, and adult suffrage. Contributor: E. A. Rymer, Miners' Agent.

    L(Col)†

2074 Miners' Watchman and Labour Sentinel I, 1 (5 Jan. 1878)—I, 18 (4 May 1878); w

    B   1d. Printed and published for the proprietors by the London Co-operative Printing and Stationery Company. Edited by Lloyd Jones.

    LE†

2075 Miners' Weekly News 1 (16 Aug 1873)—23 (17 Jan 1874). Coventry; w

    C   1d. Published by H. J. Hodson. Printed by the proprietors Edward Goode and Ebenezer Price. Addressed to Midlands mine workers. Supports Trade Unionism, but adopts motto: 'Defence not Defiance'. Reports trade-union affairs. Seeks moral and social improvement of the mining community.

    L(Col)†

2076 Mineworker: the Official Organ of the National Miners' Minority Movement I, 1 (16 Feb. 1924)—III, 18 (4 Dec. 1926); fortn.

    A   ½d.; 1d. Published by Nat Watkins, National Secretary. Vigorous militant paper of the miners' section of the National Minority Movement. Contributors: Arthur Horner, A. J. Cook, Jack Williams. Then issued as a supplement in **The Worker** (qv).

    L(Col)† (w 1)

2077 Mineworker : Organ of the National Miners' Minority Movement. (17 Dec. 1926)—(11 Oct. 1929); w

    A   Issued as one page in **The Worker** (qv). See previous entry.

2078 1 [early 1967]—8 [early 1972]. Doncaster; 2/3-yr

    A   Mineworkers Internationale. Edited by David Douglass. Trotskyist, theoretical and agitational rank-and-file journal. Distributed in Yorkshire, Wales, Nottinghamshire, Derbyshire, County Durham.

    L? (not traced)

2079 Mine-Workers' Journal I, 1 (March 1923)—III, 2 (1926). [Barnsley?] ; q

    A   'For the use of the Local Officials and Members of the Yorkshire Mine-Workers' Association.' Title changes (in 1924?) to **Yorkshire Mine-Workers' Quarterly Journal**.

    Barnsley PL March—Dec. 1923; March—Dec. 1925; LdU I, 2—4, II, 4, III, 2

2080 Minus One: an Individual Anarchist Review 1964–?; bi-m

B   6d. etc. Published and edited by S. E. Parker. Libertarian. Not connected with the working-class movement. Reproduced from typewriting.

LE 10 (1965)–25 (Dec. 1969); LUC 2 (1964)–

2081 Mirror for Magistrates, a Strictly Legal Publication 1 (16 April 1836); w

B   2d. Published and printed by G. Burton. Edited by John Bell, as successor to the suppressed **New Weekly True Sun**. 'A radical political and "useful knowledge" miscellany that attacks the Poor Law Amendment Act and repeatedly stresses the debilitating effects of the "free trade" system' (Wiener).

O†

2082 Mirror of Truth 1 (10 Oct. 1817)–2 (7 Nov. 1817)

B   1s. Exposition and discussion of Robert Owen's **New View of Society**, and schemes for relief of the poor.

LU†

2083 Miscellany: Journal of the Hackney Branch of NALGO I (1959)–

A   National and Local Government Officers' Association.

L

2084 Mitcham Citizen: a Journal of Labour Politics, Circulating in Mitcham, Tooting, Merton, Carshalton, Beddington and Wallington 1 (Jan. 1921)–? m?

B   1½d. Newspaper, printed for the proprietors by Twentieth Century Press. 'Local medium for the expression of working-class aspirations and ideals . . .' News of local Labour and Co-operative Movement, and general local news, with an occasional article on national politics. Gardening column, home hints, correspondence. *See also* following two entries.

O(JJ)† 1

2085 Mitcham, Beddington and Wallington Citizen ns 1 (Nov. 1958)–?

B   Issued by the Mitcham Constituency Labour Party.

L(Col) Nov. 1958–; Mitcham PL Nov. 1958

2086 Mitcham Citizen [1934?] –? ns 1 (Sept. 1950–34 (July 1953)

B   New series issued by the Political Purposes Committee of the Royal Arsenal Co-operative Society.

L(Col) ns; Mitcham PL 2 (Dec. 1934)–13 (June 1936)

2087 Mitcham Labour's Voice I, 1 (Sept. 1946)–?; irreg?

B

Mitcham PL I, 1–4 (Feb. 1947)

2088 Mitcham Observer 1 (July 1936)—?; irreg?
B   Labour
Mitcham PL 1—3 (Oct. 1936)

2089 Mitcham Voice [194-?] ; m
B   2d. Published by 'Voice'. (Labour Party. **Your own Journal**, 1948.)

2090 Model Republic: a Monthly Journal of Politics, Literature and Theology. 1 (1 Jan. 1843)—7 (1 July 1843); m
B   2d. Published by the Society for the Encouragement of Socialist and Democratic Literature. Publisher: J. Watson. Edited and printed by James Napier Bailey. Advocates a union of Socialism with Chartism under the title of Republican Socialism. Opposes O'Connor. Demands a united and organised movement under responsible leadership, eg. Joseph Sturge, Robert Owen.
LE†; LU 1—2, 6

2091 Modern Education I, 1 (July 1946)—IV, 1 (July/Aug. 1950); m
A   6d. National Association of Labour Teachers (affiliated to the Labour Party). 'The only official educational organisation on the Left.' Articles, letters, reviews. Absorbed **The New Ploughshare**.
L†; LIE

2092 Modern Quarterly I, 1 (Jan. 1938)—II, 2 (July 1939); ns I, 1 (Dec. 1945)—VIII, 4 (Autumn 1953); then b **Marxist Quarterly**: I, 1 (Jan. 1954)—IV, 1 (Jan. 1957); q
B   2s.6d. etc. Published by Gollancz, and Lawrence and Wishart, then by the latter alone. Communist academic and theoretical journal. Aim: to put the advances of science and learning at the disposal of the struggle for Socialism. Contributors: Bernal, Needham, Haldane, Dobb etc.
BP a i, ii I, III—VIII, b; BU a i—ii VII, 2; C; CME a ii; E a i—ii II; L†; LE a i, ii I, 3—VIII, b; LU a ii I, 3—VIII, b; LdP a i II—ii VIII, b; ONC 1939, 1945—9; WCML†; Warwick UL*

2093 Modern Times, or Age of Folly I, 1 (24 March 1832); w
B   1d. Printed by V. Slater. 'Edited by the author of the Modern Law List.' 'A working-class miscellany that strongly attacks the Church of England, the aristocracy, the national debt, and the Napoleonic wars' (Wiener).
O†

Monitor; or, Framework-Knitters Magazine, 1818—? see **Stocking Makers' Monitor, and Commercial Magazine**

2094 Monitor [19--?] —; m
A   3d. (1970). Journal of the Association of Government Supervisors and Radio Officers. (Association unable to provide information as records were destroyed in a burglary.)
The Association: last two or three years only

2095 Monkey Wrench: For Members' Rights and Democracy Within the Union. I, 1 (July 1932)–?; m

    A   1d. Published for Members' Rights Movement, by T. Smith. Rank-and-file paper initiated by Minority Movement members among militants in the Amalgamated Engineering Union.

    CPGB† 1, 2, 4, 5; ONC† 1, 2, 4; WCML† 3, 4, 5

2096 Monmouthshire Labour News [19--?]–[1906?]

    A   Preceded **Western Valleys Labour Journal**. Produced by an unofficial miners' group.

2097 Monotype Casters' and Typefounders' Society. **Quarterly Report** ?–Feb. 1969; q

    A

    TUC† 1959–Feb. 1969*

2098 Monthly Democrat: [Y Gwerinwr:] a Monthly Magazine of Social, Political and Religious Progress 1 (Jan. 1912)–11 (Nov. 1912). Cardiff; London; m

    C   2d. Published for the proprietors by E. Rees. London publishers (No. 2–   ): Simpkin, Marshall and Company. Edited by W. F. Phillips. Liberal, anti-socialist. Claims to represent the interests of Labour; makes distinction between Labour and Socialism, and states that the latter is not the true friend of Labour. Articles opposing Keir Hardie, Labour Party; extracts, short notes, union accounts etc. to illustrate views on Socialism and Trade Unionism. Attacks **Rhondda Socialist**. Motto: 'Wales for the Friends of Wales'. In English, with occasional articles in Welsh.

    BnU; L(Col); O†

2099 Monthly Herald (South Ward) [19--?]–? m

    B   Mitcham Labour Party?

    Mitcham PL ns 30 (Oct.)–31 (Nov.) 1935

2100 Monthly Institutional Journal 1 (March 1857)–? Newcastle; m

    C   1d. Published by the Northern Union of Literary and Mechanics Institutions of Durham, Northumberland, Westmoreland and Cumberland.

    South Shields PL† 1

Monthly Labour Journal see **Hull Trades Council. Labour Journal**

2101 Monthly Liberator 1 (13 June 1838)–11 (13 April 1839). Glasgow; m

    B   2d. Printed and published by W. and W. Miller, later published by John Cumming. Editor: John Taylor, late editor of the **Glasgow Liberator**. No. 1 regrets the fall of the **Liberator**. Leads campaign for National Petition and Charter in Scotland. Discussion on radical politics, correspondence.

    GM† 11; LU 1–3, 6

2102 Monthly Messenger: a Repository of Information Comprising Original Articles on Various Subjects, and Select and Elegant Extracts from the Writings of Both Ancient and Modern Authors, Interpreted with Remarks Critical and Explanatory, by J. N. Bailey, Social Missionary 1840; m

    B   Edited by James Napier Bailey. Individual parts not numbered or dated. Propounds Owenite system of Socialism and National Education on materialist principles, and related philosophical topics.

    L†; LU

2103 Monthly Miners Gazette and Public Advertiser 1 (Oct. 1918)–15 (Dec. 1919); then **Whitehaven Miners Monthly Gazette**: 16 (Jan. 1920)–57 (June (1923). Whitehaven; m

    C   Gratis. Editor?: Wilson Graham, 'W.C.' A patriotic sheet for miners urging hard work and better production for the war effort. 500 copies distributed; two of the four pages are advertisements. Urges co-operation between employer and workman. Consistently Right-wing.

    L(Col)†

2104 Monthly Notes: Official Organ of the Poor Law Workers' Trade Union [1920?]–? m

    A   2d.

    TUC† III, 11 (Nov. 1922)

Monthly Political Register see **New Political Register**

2105 Monthly Review of Friendly Societies 1 (Sept. 1863)–20 (May 1865); m

    A   1d. Printed and published by Diprose and Bateman. In the interests of self-respect and independence among artisans. Reports and proceedings of mutual benefit societies, Orders, Lodges. Some features on recreation, co-operation etc.

    L†

2106 Moral and Political Magazine of the London Corresponding Society June 1796–Dec. 1796

    C

    MUC (w 1); Warwick UL (microfilm)

Moral World see **New Moral World**

2107 Moralist I, 1 (26 Sept. 1823–[1824?]

B   2d. Published and printed by Richard Carlile. Individual numbers are not dated. Moral and social strictures from Carlile's pen; a series of lectures, discourses, snippets on the formation of character and the exposure of vices. 'At this period Carlile could no longer be regarded as a Radical Reformer in the ordinary sense of the term. The fight for free speech, he had decided, was all in all: political reform would be useless without intellectual enlightenment. So the **Moralist**, in which he appealed to reformers to observe a high standard of personal conduct, expressing sentiments to most of which not even his most inveterate opponents could have taken any exception.' (G. D. H. Cole, **Richard Carlile**, 1943).

L†; LDW; LU

2108 Morecambe Labour News [194-?]. Morecambe; m

B   2d. Published by Preston Labour Party (Labour Party. **Your own Journal**, 1948.)

Morning Star see **Daily Worker**

2109 Morning Star, or Herald of Progression I, 1 (Dec. 1844)–ns 42 (27 Jan. 1847); fortn; w

B   1d. Published by Henry Hetherington, James Watson, Cleave. Editor: James Emslie Duncan. Advocate of the Tropical Emigration Society, formed to facilitate working-class emigration to republican Venezuela and the setting up of a community. Later title: **Morning Star, or Herald of Progression and People's Economist**. Later sub-title: 'A Weekly Journal of Industrial Organization, Moral Improvement and Educational Reform'. Advocated 'schemes' such as trade unions, 'plans of social reform', as well as emigration for the emancipation of the working class. Closed down when the settlement scheme failed.

L*†

2110 Morning Star, or Phalansterian Gazette: a Weekly Herald of Universal Principles and Progressive Association, Industry, Science, Morality, Religion and Liberty 1 (21 Oct. 1840); w

B   1d. Printed and published by B. D. Cousins. Edited by Hugh Doherty. 'Introduced to the British Public as an instrument for promulgating those principles of universal association which have been discovered by the late Charles Fourier in France. Makes distinction between itself and "infidel" socialism.'

L†

Morskoi Listok see **Seamen's News**

Mosaic see **Bath NALGO Branch Magazine**

2111 Moss Side Mercury 1 (Aug. 1922). Manchester

    B   Published by T. Anderson on behalf of the Manchester Co-operative Party. Purpose of the paper stated as being 'to spread co-operative ideas, to disseminate knowledge of co-operative aims and principles, to champion the workers' cause, and to speak on behalf of women consumers'.

    L†

2112 Moss Side News [193-?]. Manchester; m

    B   Labour Party. (Labour and Socialist International. **The Socialist Press**, 1933

2113 Motorman: a Weekly Journal for Public Service and Commercial Drivers; Official Organ of the National Union of Vehicle Workers I, 1 (27 Dec. 1913)–I, 11 (14 March 1914); w

    A   1d. Printed by Odhams Ltd. Editor: Sam Marsh, General Secretary.

    L(Col)†

2114 Mount Review I, 1 (Dec. 1925)–(March 1947); [ns], I, 1 (April 1947)–VIII, 12 (Dec. 1959); ns I, 1 (Jan. 1960)–IV, 12 (Dec. 1964); ns I, 1 (March 1965)– ; q; m

    A   1d. etc. Issued by the Inland Section Branch of the Union of Post Office Workers.

    L†

2115 Movement, and Anti-Persecution Gazette [I], 1 ([16 Dec.] 1843)–II, 68 (2 April 1845) w

    B   1½d.; 2d. (68). Printed and published by G. J. Holyoake. Edited by Holyoake, assisted by M. Q. Ryall. Motto: 'Maximize morals, minimize religion' – Bentham. Used as an organ of the Anti-Persecution Union. Articles and correspondence. Title on title-page of volume: **The Movement, Anti-Persecution Gazette, and Register of Progress: a Weekly Journal of Republican Politics, Anti-Theology, and Utilitarian Morals.** Succeeded by the **Circular** of the Anti-Persecution Union.

    Co-op. Coll. I; GM; L; LE I; LU; MP 1844–5; O; ONC†; Warwick UL (microfilm)

2116 Mr View [19--?] –? Manchester

    A   Union of Post Office Workers, Manchester Amalgamated Branch. (W. Dunlop. 'Local journals' **Belpost**†, IV, 5 [May 1965].)

2117 Múinteoir Nàisiunta : Official Journal of the Irish National Teachers' Organisation I (1956)– . Dublin; m; 10-yr

    A   Formerly **Irish Teachers' Journal** etc.

    C V, 1960–*; D I, 2 (1956)– ; University College, Dublin

2118 Municipal Employés Monthly: the Organ of the Birmingham and District Municipal Employés Association I, 1 (July 1913)–II, 24 (June 1915). Birmingham; m

    A   Gratis. To unite corporation employees into 'one great industrial trade union'. Includes a serial story: 'The Red Judgement: a Striking Story of the Great Labour Revolt of 1920'. Merged in the **Monthly Journal** of the Amalgamated Society of Gas, Municipal and General Workers.

    BP†

2119 Municipal Free Lance: a Weekly Journal Devoted to the Interests of the Ratepayers and Trade Unionists of Darlington 1 (7 Nov. 1903)–63 (14 Jan. 1905). Darlington; w

    B   1d. Printed for the publishers by the Oliver Bros. Printing and Publishing Company. In opposition to 'capitalist controlled papers'. Suggests that the time has arrived when the tradesman, the trades unionists, and the working classes in general should possess an organ through which to ventilate any grievance they might have. Reports activities of the Town Council, Board of Guardians, trade unions and other working-men's societies, and the local Labour Representation Committee.

    L(Col)†

Municipal Murmurs see National Association of Local Government Officers. Evesham Borough banch. **News Sheet**

2120 Municipal Officer I (1899)–VI, 11 (Feb. 1904); m?

    A   London Municipal Officers' Association.

    L; LE 1899–1902*

Municipal Officer. 1911–1920 see **LGO, Local Government Officer**

Municipal Reformer and Land Reform Advocate see **Municipal Reformer and Local Government News**

2121 Municipal Reformer and Local Government News, 1 (Oct. 1898)–VI, 74 (Nov. 1904). Bolton; Manchester (Feb. 1899)–   ; m

    B   2d.; 1d. Printed and published for the proprietors by Pendlebury and Sons, then by John Heywood. Editors: H. Bodell Smith; W. P. Price-Heywood. 'Advocated municipal reform in all possible branches, municipal ownership; claimed much improvement in life and environment of working classes could be accomplished by persistent plodding' (Brophy). Encourages its readers to use their vote to change the workers' life. The journal will 'try to teach . . . what you want' especially in the conducting of municipal affairs. Motto in some numbers: 'United effort for the collective whole; and public needs by collective control'. Includes a column 'Special to workingmen'. No. 1 has 'photo and sketch of Mr Sidney Webb and his work' in a series on Municipal Reformers. Title changed in January 1904 to **The Municipal Reformer and Land Reform Advocate**.

    LE (w Aug., Oct. 1904); O Oct. 1898–Dec. 1899 (w 2–4)

Municipal Workers' Journal see **General Workers' Journal**.

2122 Music and Life 1 (1958)–   ; q.
B   1s. (1961) etc. Published by the Music Group of the Communist Party. Edited by Alfred Corum, then by an editorial board. Reproduced from typewriting. Articles and correspondence on music and society.
O 13 (1961)–

2123 Musician: Voice of the Musicians' Union 1 (July 1950)–
A
The Union; the Union, Glasgow Branch Office (w 30, 33)

Musicians' Journal see **Musicians' Report and Journal**

2124 Musicians' Report and Journal: the Official Organ of the Amalgamated Musicians' Union. 1 (Jan. 1895)–314 (July 1921); then b **Musicians' Journal**: 1 (Aug. 1921)–ns 16 (Jan. 1933). Manchester; London; m; q
A   1d. Amalgamated Musicians' Union (1895–1921); Musicians' Union, (1921)–   .
GM 1904–16, 1929–32; LE 1911, 8–1912*, 1913–18, 1919–21*; MP a 67–314, b i 7–18; the Union; the Union, Glasgow Branch Office 1895–1916 (w 1905–10)

2125 Musicians' Union Monthly Report [19–?]–? Birmingham; m
A   'Strictly private, for the use of members only.' 1930–2 covered the campaign against the exclusion of musicians from 'Cinema Talkies and Soundies'.
GM† ns 1 (Jan. 1930)–(1932)

2126 Musselburgh Herald [194–?]. Musselburgh, Midlothian; m
B   Labour Party. (Labour Party. **Your own Journal**, 1948.)

Musselburgh Monthly Reporter see **Musselburgh Reporter**

2127 Musselburgh Reporter [1896?97–1900?]. Musselburgh; m
B   Free; 1d. Published by M. Hogg. Edited by Robert Hogg. Not an official Independent Labour Party paper but followed the activities of members of the ILP, especially of R. Hogg on the town council and school board. Sometimes entitled **Musselburgh Monthly Reporter: an Organ of Democratic Socialism**. There was no No. 32 due to mis-numbering.
LE† II, 21 (Dec. 1898)–III, 37 (March 1900) (w 24); ONC Jan. 1899

2128 Muthill ILP [194–?]. Muthill, Perthshire; irreg
B   Independent Labour Party. Duplicated. (Labour Party. **Your own Journal**, 1948.)

2129 Mutual Education Society Record [c1898]; m
A?C?   1d. Edited by C. Benson. (**Labour Annual**, 1898.)

NAFTO Record see Furnishing Trades Association. **Monthly Report**

2130 NALGO: St Helens and District Health Services Branch Magazine I
(1953)–   . St Helens; m
A   National and Local Government Officers' Association.
L II, 7 (July 1954)–

NALGO Branch Magazine (Stafford Branch) see **Branch Brevities**

2131 NALGO Branch News [1961?]–   . Gravesend
A   National and Local Government Officers' Association,
Gravesend Branch. Reproduced from typewriting.
L 1961–

2132 NALGO Branch News, Eastbourne Branch 1961–   . Eastbourne
A   National and Local Government Officers' Association.
Reproduced from typewriting.
L (W 5, 6, 8)

2133 NALGO Bulletin. Taunton
A   National and Local Government Officers' Association. Taunton
and West Somerset Hospitals Branch. Reproduced from typewriting.
L 1954–

2134 NALGO Bulletin ?–Dec. 1960; then **Links.** I, 1 (Jan. 1961)–III, 6
(Autumn 1964?)
A   National and Local Government Officers' Association, Lindsey
County Officers Branch. Reproduced from typewriting.
L Dec. 1960–Autumn 1964

2135 NALGO Forum 1966?–   . Harlow
A   National and Local Government Officers' Association, Harlow
Development Corporation Branch. Reproduced from typewriting.
L 1966–

NALGO Herefordia see **County Nalgo**

2136 NALGO Magazine
A   National and Local Government Officers' Association, East
Barnet Branch. Reproduced from typewriting.
L 1959–

2137 NALGO Magazine 1962?–   . Swansea
A   National and Local Government Officers' Association, Swansea
and District Health Services Branch. Reproduced from typewriting.
L 1962–

2138 NALGO Matters. Southampton
   A   National and Local Government Officers' Association,
Southampton Branch, Public Relations Sub-Committee. Reproduced from
typewriting.
   L 1959—

2139 NALGO News
   A   National and Local Government Officers' Association, Irlam
Branch. Incorporated by **Review**.

2140 NALGO News I, 1 (March 1949)—I, 18 (Oct. 1953); then **Taurus**: I,
1 (Feb. 1954)—7 (April 1956); then **NALGO News**: I, 8 (Sept. 1956)—   .
Southsea; Portsmouth; irreg
   A   National Association of Local Government Officers, later
National and Local Government Officers' Association, Portsmouth Branch.
   L

2141 NALGO News I (1953—). Scunthorpe
   A   National and Local Government Officers' Association,
Scunthorpe Branch.
   L

2142 NALGO News I, 1 (Spring 1953)—
   A   National and Local Government Officers' Association, Willesden
Branch. Reproduced from typewriting.
   L

2143 NALGO News 1960?—   . Shrewsbury
   A   National and Local Government Officers' Association, Salop
County Branch. Reproduced from typewriting.
   L 1960—

2144 NALGO News 1961?—   . High Wycombe
   A   National and Local Government Officers' Association, High
Wycombe and District Health Services Branch. Reproduced from
typewriting.
   L 1961—

2145 NALGO News 1961?—   . Hounslow
   A   National and Local Government Officers' Association, No. 1,
Sub-Area Branch. Reproduced from typewriting.
   L 1961—

2146 NALGO News 1961?—. Manchester
   A   National and Local Government Officers' Association, North
Western Electricity Division Branch. Single sheet.
   L 1961—

2147 NALGO News 1964?–   . Dingwall
   A   National and Local Government Officers' Association, Ross and Cromarty Branch. Reproduced from typewriting.
   L 1964–

2148 NALGO News 1964?–
   A   National and Local Government Officers' Association, Hammersmith London Borough Branch. Reproduced from typewriting.
   L 1964–

2149 NALGO News [Torquay], 1964– see National Association of Local Government Officers. Torquay (Local Government Branch). **Social Committee News Sheet**

2150 NALGO News 1966?–   . Exeter
   A   National and Local Government Officers' Association, Exeter Branch. Reproduced from typewriting.
   L 1966–

2151 NALGO News and Views. Clacton
   A   National and Local Government Officers' Association, Clacton and District Branch. Reproduced from typewriting.
   L 1956–

2152 NALGO News Bulletin [1950?] –
   A   National Association of Local Government Officers, later National and Local Government Officers' Association, London (Southern) Electricity Branch. Reproduced from typewriting.
   L 42 (June 1953)–

2153 NALGO News Bulletin [195-?] –   . Manchester
   A   National and Local Government Officers' Association, North Western Gas Board Headquarters Branch.
   L 29 (Nov./Dec. 1958)–

2154 NALGO News Bulletin: the Official Magazine of the Worcestershire Branch 1959?–? Worcester
   A   National and Local Government Officers' Association. Reproduced from typewriting.
   L 1959–

NALGO News, Fulham Branch see **NALGO News Sheet, Fulham Branch**

2155 NALGO News Letter; then **News and Local Goings On**: (Aug. 1966)–   . Chelmsford
   A   National and Local Government Officers' Association, Chelmsford Hospitals Branch. Reproduced from typewriting.
   L Feb./May 1966–

2156 NALGO News Sheet 1 (Feb. 1951); then **Contact**: 2 (March 1951)–   . Southend-on-Sea; m
     A   National Association of Local gvernment Officers, later National and Local Government Officers' Association, Southend-on-Sea Branch.
     L

2157 NALGO News Sheet 1 [1952?]–   . Rochdale
     A   National Association of Local Government Officers, later National and Local Government Officers' Association, Rochdale Branch. Reproduced from typewriting.
     L 12 (May 1953)–   .

NALGO News Sheet. **1958–1961** see National Association of Local Government Officers. Paddington Branch. **News Sheet**

2158 NALGO News Sheet 1961?–   . Rushden
     A   National and Local Government Officers' Association, Rushden and District Branch. Reproduced from typewriting.
     L 1961–

2159 NALGO News Sheet, **Fulham Branch** 1 (Dec. 1959)-34 (22 Sept. 1961); then **NALGO News, Fulham Branch**: 35 (11 Oct. 1961)–
     A   National and Local Government Officers' Association. Single sheet, reproduced from typewriting.
     L

2160 NALGO Newscaster 1961?–   . Darlington
     A   National and Local Government Officers' Association, Darlington and District Branch. Reproduced from typewriting.
     L 1961–

2161 NALGO Newssheet. I (1955)–   . Chester
     A   National and Local Government Officers' Association, Chester City Branch. Reproduced from typewriting.
     L

2162 NALGO Newssheet 1965?–   . Sutton
     A   National and Local Government Officers' Association, Surrey Electricity Branch. Reproduced from typewriting.
     L 1965–

2163 NALGO Newsletter I (1948)–   . Manchester
     A   National Association of Local Government Officers, later National and Local Government Officers' Association, No. 1 Sub-Area, North-Western Electricity Board. Reproduced from typewriting.
     L

2164 NALGO Newsletter I (1954)– . Liverpool
    A   National and Local Government Officers' Association, No. 3 Merseyside and North Wales Electricity Branch. Single sheet.
    L

2165 NALGO Newsletter [1961?] –
    A   National and Local Government Officers' Association, Electricity Council Branch. Reproduced from typewriting.
    L IV, 4 (May 1964)–

2166 NALGO Newsletter 1 (Feb. 1961); then **Be and Cee**: [2] (Easter 1961)– . Brentford
    A   National and Local Government Officers' Association, Brentford and Chiswick Branch. Reproduced from typewriting.
    L

2167 NALGO Newsletter 1963?– . Dunfermline
    A   National and Local Government Officers' Association, Fife Electricity Branch. Reproduced from tyepwriting.
    L (Nov. 1963)–

2168 NALGO Newsletter [1966?] – . Barking
    A   National and Local Government Officers' Association, Barking Branch. Reproduced from typewriting.
    L 2 (March 1966)–

2169 NALGO News-Sheet Nov. 1953– . Edinburgh
    A   National and Local Government Officers' Association, Edinburgh Branch. From Nov. 1954 issued as a supplement to **NALGO News**, 1952–.
    L

2170 NALGO Norfolk News Norwich
    A   National and Local Government Officers' Association, Norfolk Branch. Reproduced from typewriting.
    L 1956–

2171 NALGO Notes I (1956)– . Eton
    A   National and Local Government Officers' Association, Eton and District Branch. Reproduced from typewriting.
    L

2172 NALGO Outlook [1961?]– . Harrogate
    A   National and Local Government Officers' Association, Leeds Regional Hospital Board Branch. Reproduced from typewriting.
    L [1961]–

NALGO Quarterly Review see **Nalgo Local Gazette**

2173 NALGO St Helens and District Health Services Branch Magazine
[1953?] — . St Helens
    A   National and Local Government Officers' Association. II, 7 does
not bear title.
    L II, 7 (July 1954)—

2174 NALGO Wiltshire Journal: Official Publication of the Wiltshire
County Branch. [1942?] — . Trowbridge; m?
    A   National Association of Local Government Officers, later
National and Local Government Officers' Association.
    L XVI, 6 (June 1957)—

2175 NAPO Newsletter 1965— ; m
    A   National Association of Probation Officers.
    (Willing's Press Guide, 1970.)

2176 NASD Mersey Broadsheet [195-?] —?
    A   National Amalgamated Union of Stevedores and Dockers.
    TUC 21 (May 1955)

2177 NATE Journal I, 1 (Jan. 1921)—I, 12 (Dec. 1921). Letchworth; then
Amusement Workers' News: I, 1 (Jan. 1922)—III, 8 (June 1928). London;
m; irreg (1924—)
    A   Free to members; 2d.; 1d. to non-members. National
Association of Theatrical Employees.
    L; TUC Jan. 1921—Aug. 1925

2178 NATNews: Official Journal of the National Association of Theatre
Nurses [1964?] — . Windsor; Matlock; bi-m
    A   1s. 6d. (1970).
    Royal College of Nursing 1964—(w occ. nos)

2179 NA-WU Magazine I, 1 (Jan. 1912)—XIX, 12 (Dec. 1930); then **MHIW
Journal**: XX, 1 (Jan. 1931)—XXIV, 3 (March 1935); then **Mental Hospital
and Institutional Workers' Journal**: XXIV, 4 (April 1935)—XXVIII, 5
(May 1939); then **Mental Health Services Journal**. XXVIII, 6 (June
1939)—XXXIV, 12 (Dec. 1945); then b **Health Services Journal**: Official
Organ of the Confederation of Health Service Employees: I (1946)— .
Manchester; m
    A   National Asylum-Workers' Union; Mental Hospital and
Institutional Workers' Union; Confederation of Health Service Employees.
Absorbed **County Officers' Gazette** and **Guild of Nurses' Quarterly
Review**.
    L 1955— ; ONC II, 10, 1949— ; the Confederation

2180 NCF News March 1918
    B   No-Conscription Fellowship.
    L

NCW News see National Union of Women Workers. **Occasional Paper**

NFRB Quarterly see New Fabian Research Bureau. **Quarterly Journal**

2181 NOYNA: News of Your NALGO Area 1967?– . Colne
      A   National and Local Government Officers' Association, Colne,
Nelson and District Branch. Reproduced from typewriting.
      L 1967–

NUBE News see **Bank Officer**

2182 NUCO, London Area, **Quarterly Recorder** 1 (March 1941)–   ; q
      A   National Union of County Officers.
      TUC† 1

2183 NUCO Review: Official Organ of the Northern Provincial Council of
the National Union of County Officers [193-?]. Gateshead
      A
      TUC† May/June 1935

NUFTO Record see Furnishing Trades Association. **Monthly Report**

NUG and MW Journal see **General Workers' Journal**

NUT Birmingham Association News Sheet see **NUT Journal**

2184 NUT Journal: the Organ of the Birmingham Association of the
National Union of Teachers 1 (May 1925)–28 (March 1939); then b **NUT
Birmingham Association News Sheet**: 1 (Oct. 1939)–15 (June 1945); then
c **Birmingham Teachers' Journal**: the Organ of the Birmingham
Association of the NUT: I, 1 (Oct. 1949)–   . Birmingham; s-a
      A   Vehicle for current news and views of professional and
educational interest to members.
      BP†; O† c

2185 NUT Magazine [192-?] –? Newcastle-upon-Tyne
      A   Newcastle-upon-Tyne Teachers' Association, National Union of
Teachers.
      NwA 19 (1927)–50 (1935) (w 20, 21, 25, 26, 29, 31–48). (not
traced in catalogue)

2186 NUT News I, 1 (Spring Term, 1957)–(1964); then **NUT Newsletter**:
(Feb. 1965)–VII, 1 (Jan. 1969); irreg
      A   National Union of Teachers. To keep members informed of
Union's activities, plans and policies. Newspaper format.
      L(Col)† 1957–63; O† 1961–9

2187 NUT News [1, 1969], 2 (April 1969)–[1971?]. 10–12-yr
    A   National Union of Teachers. Single foolscap sheets, printed on one side only 'for notice board display'.
    O†

NUT Newsletter see **NUT News. 1957–1964**

2188 NUVB Headlight: Monthly News-Sheet of the London District Committee of the National Union of Vehicle Builders [19–?]–? m
    A   (World Federation of Trade Unions. **International Bulletin of the Trade Union and Working Class Press**, Index, Nov. 1959–Dec. 1960.)

2189 Naie Tsait: a Sotsial-Demokratisher Vochenblat. [**New Times**: a Social-Democratic Weekly] I, 1 (4 March 1904)–III, 4 (18 May 1906). London; w; s-m
    B   ½d.; 1d. Published by the League of the Jewish Social-Democratic Assocations in England. Yiddish.
    L(Col)†

2190 Nalgazette [1955?]– . Brighton
    A   National and Local Government Officers' Association, Brighton Health Service Branch.
    L III, 5 (April 1957)–

2191 Nalgazette 1963?–
    A   National and Local Government Officers' Association, Hackney and Queen Elizabeth Group of Hospitals Branch. Reproduced from typewriting.
    L 1963–

2192 NALGO Branch News Jan. 1953– . Croydon
    A   National and Local Government Officers' Association, Croydon Branch. Single sheet, reproduced from typewriting.
    L

2193 NALGO Bury Branch Magazine [I] 1962; then **Bury-Go-Round**: 2 (Dec. 1962)– . Bury
    A   National and Local Government Officers' Association. Reproduced from typewriting.
    L

2194 NALGO Local Gazette I, 1 (Aug. 1953)–(June 1954); then **NALGO Quarterly Review**: March 1955–March 1957; then **Coulsdon and Purley Review**: June 1957–March 1964. Coulsdon
    A   National and Local Government Officers' Association, Coulsdon and Purley Branch. Reproduced from typewriting.
    L (w Sept. 1955)

2195 NALGO Matters: News Sheet of the East Riding County Branch of NALGO 1961?— . Beverley
A   National and Local Government Officers' Association.
Reproduced from typewriting.
L 1961—

2196 NALGO News [19--?—195-?]. Widnes; m?
A   National Association of Local Government Officers, Widnes
Branch. Preceded **Forward** 1954—[1958?].

2197 NALGO News: Magazine of the Edinburgh Branch of the National and Local Government Officers' Association I, 1 (May 1952)— .
Edinburgh
A   Reproduced from typewriting
L

2198 NALGO News 1 (Feb. 1963); then **Fifeline**: 2 (March 1963)— .
Glenrothes; m
A   National and Local Government Officers' Association,
Glenrothes Branch. Reproduced from typewriting.
L

2199 NALGO Newssheet 1 (March 1957)—14 (Dec. 1959). [Swinton?]
A   National and Local Government Officers' Association, Swinton
and Pendlebury Branch.
Bolton Trades Council Library

2200 NALGO Review 1962?— . Eastbourne
A   National and Local Government Officers' Association,
Eastbourne Branch. Reproduced from typewriting.
L 1962—

2201 Nalgonian: Journal of the Warrington Branch 1960?— . Warrington
A   National and Local Government Officers' Association,
Reproduced from typewriting.
L 1960—

2202 Nalgopinion I, 1 (April 1954)— . Shrewsbury
A   National and Local Government Officers' Association,
Shropshire Branch.
L

2203 Nalgopinion News Bulletin I (1955)— . Shrewsbury
A   National and Local Government Officers' Association,
Shropshire Branch.
L

2204 Nalgosportian: the Official Journal of the Gosport Branch of the National and Local Government Officers' Association 1 (Autumn 1953). Gosport

    A   Reproduced from typewriting.

    L

2205 Nalgossip: Bolton Hospitals Health Service Branch Magazine 1961?– . Bolton

    A   National and Local Government Officers' Association. Reproduced from typewriting.

    L 1961–

2206 Nation: a Weekly Journal of Literature, Politics and the Arts I, 1 (15 Oct. 1842)–VI, 303 (22 July 1848); ns [VII], 1 (1 Sept. 1849)–XLIX, 28 (11 July 1891); L, 1 (13 June 1896)–LI, 23 (5 June 1897). Dublin; w

    B   Founded by Charles Gavan Duffy, John Dillon and Thomas Davis. Radical organ of the Repeal Association. Strong democratic tendencies, seeking alliance with English Chartism. A leading contributor was John Mitchel until he left to found his own **United Irishman**.

    D 1–6; L(Col)

2207 National: a Library for the People 1 (5 Jan. 1839)–26 (29 June 1839); w

    B   Printed by James Watson. A magazine edited by W. J. Linton, conveying popular information designed to 'assist the struggles of the unmonied in their pursuit of knowledge'. Original contributions in prose and verse, democratic in opinion, and snippets from the 'best authors, past and present', including extracts from Owen, Godwin, Paine, Hodgskin, Volney, Cobbett, Shelley, Frank Wright, Rousseau, Milton etc. In a section 'Notes of the Month' Linton demonstrates his support for the Chartist movement.

    Bishopsgate Institute; L†; LU; LE; MP; Warwick UL (microfilm); Greenwood reprint and microfiche: microfiche distributed in Britain and Europe by the Harvester Press Ltd

National Agricultural Labourers' Chronicle and Industrial Pioneer see **Labourers' Union Chronicle**

National and Local Government Officers' Association see National Association of Local Government Officers

2208 National Association Gazette: the Rights of Man and the Rights of Woman. 1 (1 Jan. 1842)–31 (30 July 1842); w

    B   1½d. Unstamped. Printed and published by H. Hetherington. Chartist. Organ of the National Association for Promoting the Political and Social Improvement of the People. Addresses, correspondence, poetry. Discusses relations with middle-class Radicalism, national education, rights and duties of women.

    L† 1–28; LabP Archives, Minikin/Vincent MSS 1–2, 21–2, 24–7

2209 National Association of Card, Blowing Room and Ring Frame Operatives. **Quarterly Report** ?–May 1968. Manchester; Oldham; q
    A   Printed at 'Cotton Factory Times' Office, Ashton-under-Lyne.
TUC† April 1921–May 1968*

2210 National Association of Local Government Officers (from 1952, National and Local Government Officers' Association). **Andover Branch. Magazine** [1959?]–   . Andover
    A   Reproduced from typewriting.
    L   July 1959–

2211 Ashford and District Branch. **Branch Newsletter** 1 (Feb. 1961); then **Compass**: (2 [April 1961])–   . Ashford, Kent
    A   Reproduced from typewriting.
    L

2212 Bedford County Branch. **News Letter**. 1 (1951)–   . Bedford
    A   Reproduced from typewriting.
    L 2 (Aug. 1951–)

2213 Bexley Branch. **Newsletter** 1964–   . Bexley Heath
    A   Reproduced from typewriting.
    L

2214 Billericay Branch. **Billericay Branch Circular** 1959–
    A   Reproduced from typewriting.
    L

2215 Brighton, Hove, Worthing and District Electricity Branch. **News Sheet** 1963?–   . Hove
    A   Single sheet, reproduced from typewriting.
    L [1963]–

2216 Bristol Branch. **Bristol and District Quarterly** Bristol
    A
    BrP (1949)–

2217 Bristol Electricity Branch. **News Letter** I, 1 (April 1953)–   . Bristol
    A   Reproduced from typewriting.
    L

2218 Bucks County Branch. **Branch News Sheet** [195-?]–   . Aylesbury
    A
    L 27 (May 1953)–

2219 Bucks County Branch. **Bucks Branch Bulletin** 1964?– Aylesbury
    A   Reproduced from typewriting.
    L 1964–

2220 Caernarvon and Anglesey Hospital Management Committee Branch.
Branch Newsletter 1967?–   Llandudno
    A   Reproduced from typewriting.
    L 1967–

2221 Caernarvon and District Branch. **Newsletter** I, 1 (Jan. 1955)–[II].
20 (Aug. 1956); then **Cronicel** NALGO: II, 21 (Sept. 1956)– Caernarvon
    A
    L

2222 Cardiff and District Electricity Branch. **Bulletin** I, 1 (April
1953)–   . Cardiff
    A   Reproduced from typewriting.
    L

2223 Carshalton Branch. **Journal** 1 (Jan. 1953)–7 (July 1953); then
Ponder: 8 (Aug. 1953)–   . Carshalton
    A   Reproduced from typewriting.
    L

2224 Christchurch Branch. **News Letter** 1966?–   . Christchurch
    A   Reproduced from typewriting.
    L   1966–

2225 City of Oxford Branch. **Bulletin** 1 (Jan. 1953)–   . Oxford
    A   Reproduced from typewriting.
    L

2226 Colne, Nelson and District Branch. **Official Branch Journal** 1 (March
1958)–   . Nelson
    A
    L 1

2227 Coventry and District Health Services Branch. **News Sheet**
1967?–   . Coventry
    A   Reproduced from typewriting.
    L 1967–

2228 Derbyshire Branch. **Bulletin** [195-?]. [Derby?]
    A   Preceded **Derwent** (qv).

2229 Dumbartonshire Branch. **News Sheet** 1966?–   . Dumbartonshire
    A   Reproduced from typewriting.
    L 1966–

2230 East Dorset Water Branch. **News Sheet** 1964?–   . Poole
    A   Reproduced from typewriting.
    L 1964–

2231 Essex County Branch. **Newsletter** [194-?] –   . Chelmsford
    A
    L 64 (Sept. 1953)–

2232 Evesham Borough Branch. **News Sheet** 1962?–   . Evesham
    A   Reproduced from typewriting. Alternative title: **Municipal Murmurs.**
    L 1962–

2233 Folkestone Branch. **Newsletter** 1 (1952)–   . Folkestone
    A   Reproduced from typewriting.
    L (w 3, 5–6, 9)

2234 Hampstead Branch. **Official Magazine** [1] (April 1963); then **Hampstead Heathen**: 2 (July 1963)–
    A
    L [1]–5 (April 1964)

2235 Hastings Area. Health Services Branch. **News Sheet** Jan. 1953–Oct. 1953; Dec. 1958–April/May 1963; then **1066 and All That**: June 1963–   . Hastings
    A   Reproduced from typewriting.
    L

2236 Hendon Branch. **News Sheet** I (1958)–   . Hendon
    A
    L

2237 Hereford City Branch. **Newsletter** [April 1964?] –Aug. 1964; then **Branch Lines**: Sept. 1964–   . Hereford
    A   Reproduced from typewriting.
    L April 1964–

2238 Hertfordshire County Branch. **News Letter** Hertford
    A   Reproduced from typewriting.
    L XIX, 1 (Dec. 1952/Jan. 1953)–XX, 6 (Oct. 1954)

2239 Herts and Essex Border Branch. **News Sheet** 1961?–   . Saffron Walden
    A   Reproduced from typewriting.
    L 1961–

2240 High Wycombe and Beaconsfield Branch. **News Sheet** [1964]?; then **Wycombe Beacon**: News Sheet of the High Wycombe and Beaconsfield Branch of NALGO: [1964]–   . High Wycombe
    A
    L

2241 Hillingdon Branch. **News-Letter** 1965?—   . West Drayton
    A   Reproduced from typewriting. Incorporated in **Spot-on**.
    L 1965—

2242 Hinckley Branch. **Newsletter** ns 1 (Sept. 1962); then **Castle Guardian**: (Dec. 1962)—   . Hinckley
    A   Reproduced from typewriting.
    L

2243 Inverness and District Branch. **News and Views**. 1966?—   . Inverness
    A   Reproduced from typewriting.
    L 1966—

2244 Kingston Group Hospitals Branch. **Magazine** I, 1 (Nov. 1961); then **Prescription**: I, 2 (Dec. 1961/Jan. 1962)—   . Kingston-on-Thames
    L

2245 Kingston-upon-Thames Branch. **Journal** 1965?—   . Kingston-upon-Thames
    A   Reproduced from typewriting.
    L 1965—

2246 Leeds and District Electricity Branch. **News-Sheet** [195-?]—   . Leeds
    A   Reproduced from typewriting.
    L 17 (Jan. 1953)—

2247 Leeds Regional Hospital Board Branch. **News-letter** 1966?—   . Harrogate
    A   Reproduced from typewriting.
    L 1966—

2248 Leicester and District Health Service Branch. **News-Sheet** 1967?—   . Leicester
    A   Reproduced from typewriting. Alternative title: **Focus**.
    L 1967—

2249 Leyton Branch. **News and Views** [194-?]—39 (Christmas 1954?). Leyton
    A   Reproduced from typewriting.
    L 32 (Dec. 1952)—39 (Christmas 1954)

2250 Lincoln Branch. **Branch Bulletin** 195-?]—   . Lincoln
    A   Reproduced from typewriting.
    L 26 (Feb. 1959)—

2251 Liverpool and District Electricity Branch. **Newsletter** [[1] 1949?]—VII, 4 (Sept. 1955?). Liverpool
    A   Single sheet. Alternative title: **News and Notes**.
    L V, 1 (Feb. 1953)—VII, 4 (Sept. 1955)

2252 Liverpool Branch. **Journal** I, 1 (May 1924)–VI, 8 (Dec. 1946); then **Liverpool NALGO Journal**. VII, 1 (Feb. 1948)–? Liverpool

    A   Not published in 1947.

    L I–VII, 2 (w I, 11–14)

2253 Liverpool Branch. **Service Conditions Bulletin** I (1948)– . Liverpool

    A

    LvP*

Liverpool Guild. **Gazette** see **Guild Gazetee, 1898–1920**

2254 National Association of Local Government Officers. London County Council Branch. **Branch Notes** I (1930)–VI, 10 (Oct. 1935); then London County Chronicle: I, 1 (Nov. 1935)–? m

    A

    L V, 9 (Nov. 1934)–

2255 Manchester Branch. **News Letter** 1 (5 Dec. 1967)– . Manchester

    A   Reproduced from typewriting.

    MP†

2256 Manchester Gas Branch. **Bulletin** [1949?]– . Manchester

    A

    L 6 (Nov. 1949), 17 (Dec. 1950), 38 (May 1953)–

2257 Manchester Sub-Area Electricity Branch. **Newsletter** [1948?] – Manchester

    A   Nos. 1–24 reproduced from typewriting.

    L 3 (March 1949)–(w 4, 12, 13, 25)

2258 Medway Gas Branch. **Monthly Newssheet** 1965?– . Rochester; m

    A

    L 1965–

2259 Merseyside (No. 2 Sub-Area) Electricity Branch. **Newsletter** [195-?] – . Eversley

    A

    L II, 9 (March 1953)–

2260 New Forest Branch. **Quarterly News Sheet** 1 (Jan. 1966); then **New Forest Notes**: 2 (April 1966)– . Lyndhurst; q

    A   Reproduced from typewriting.

    L

2261 Newport Branch. **Branch Bulletin** I (1953)– . Newport, Mon

    A   Reproduced from typewriting.

    L

2262 Newport Branch. **Newsletter** 1 (Nov. 1942)–11 (Dec. 1945). Newport, Mon.

    A

    NpP

2263 North Western and North Wales District Committee. **District News Sheet** I, 1 (March 1950)–I, 4 (Nov. 1951); then **Public Relations**: I, 5 (May 1952)–I, 7 (Dec. 1953). Manchester

    A

    L

2264 North Western Gas Board Headquarters Branch. **News Bulletin** [195-?]– . Manchester

    A

    L 29 (Nov./Dec. 1958)–

2265 Norwich Branch. Branch. **Bulletin** 1 (1952)– . Norwich.

    A

    NrP

2266 Nottinghamshire County Council Branch. **Branch News** 1 (1948)–74 (June/July 1956); then **County Comment**: 1 (Sept. 1956)– Nottingham

    A

    L 2 (June 1948)–(w 33, 40–)

2267 Oxford Branch. **Bulletin** I (1953)–   Oxford

    A Reproduced from typewriting.

    L

2268 Paddington Branch. **News Sheet** April 1958–Dec. 1961

    A Reproduced from typewriting. Alternative title: **NALGO News Sheet**.

    L

2269 Paddington Group Hospitals Branch. **News Review** 1963?–

    A Reproduced from typewriting. Alternative title: Journal.

2270 Port of London Authority Branch. **Journal** [194-?] –

    A

    L 64 (Jan. 1953)–

2271 Ramsgate Branch. **Review** 1 (1956)–3 (1956); then **Spotlight**: 4 (Jan./Feb. 1957)– . Ramsgate

    A

    L 2, 4–

2272 St Pancras Branch. [**Branch Magazine**] [1954?]–1958; then **St Pancras Miscellany**: Spring 1960–Christmas 1961; then **Saint**: Quarterly Journal of the St Pancras Branch of NALGO: (1 [Sept. 1962])–7 (March 1964)

    A   Reproduced from typewriting. Not published in 1959.

    L

2273 Salford Branch. **Official Magazine** 1963?– . Salford

    A   Reproduced from typewriting.

    L 1963–

2274 Somerset County Branch. **News Sheet**; then **Scoop**: Somerset County Officers' Own Paper: Jan. 1964– . Taunton

    A   Reproduced from typewriting.

    L Nov. 1963; Jan. 1964–

2275 South West Essex Health Services Branch. **Newsletter** 1960?–

    A

    L Jan. 1960–

2276 Stâines Branch. **Magazine** 1954; then **Bridge**: (July 1954)– . Staines

    A

    L

2277 Sunderland Branch. **Newsletter** 1 (Feb. 1960)–3 (June 1960); then **Intercom**: News and Views of the Sunderland Branch of NALGO: 1 (Aug. 1960)– . Sunderland

    A   Reproduced from typewriting.

    L

2278 Tonbridge and District Branch. **News Letter** 1 (Feb. 1961)–2 (April 1961); ns 1 (Dec. 1961)– . Southborough

    A   Single sheet, reproduced from typewriting.

    L

Torquay (Local Government) Branch. **News Sheet** see Torquay (Local Government) Branch. **Social Committee News Sheet**

2279 Torquay (Local Government) Branch. Social Committee **News Sheet** [1] (1 Aug. 1963)–4 (1 Feb. 1964); then News Sheet: 5 (1 April 1964)–6 (June 1964); then **NALGO News**: 7 (Aug. 1964)– . Torquay

    A   Reproduced from typewriting. Alternative title: **Branch News Sheet**.

    L

Wandsworth Branch. **Gazette** see **Wendelsworth Gazette**

Wandsworth Branch. **News and Views** see **Wendelsworth Gazette**

2280 Warwickshire County Council Branch. **Bulletin** [194-?] –
Warwick
  A   Reproduced from typewriting.
  L 55 (Jan. 1953)–

2281 West Midlands Gas Board, Solihull HQ Branch. **Newssheet.**
1965?–   . Solihull?
  A
  Solihull PL 1965–

2282 Westhoughton Branch. **Newsletter** 1967?–   . Westhoughton
  A   Reproduced from typewriting.
  L 1967–

2283 National Association of Operative Plasterers. **Monthly Report**
[1860?–1931?] ; m
  A   Name of union changed in 1860 to National Association of
Plasterers, Granolithic and Cement Workers. From 1901 reflects a keener
interest in political matters. (**'Hitherto: the story of an Association, by
Onlooker** [ie Mrs A. H. Telling] , 1930.)

2284 National Association of Plasterers, Granolithic and Cement Workers.
Quarterly Report [1932?–1967?] ; q
  A
  NU 22 (1954–); TUC July 1932–Dec. 1967*

2285 National Association of Schoolmasters. **Bulletin** 1 (Oct. 1939)–36
(June 1944); q; m
  A   Free to members. Published during the period when **The New
Schoolmaster** was suspended.
  L; Warwick U (MRC)†

2286 National Association of United Trades for the Protection of
Industry. **Monthly Report** I, 1 (Dec. 1847)–I, 4 (March 1848); then
National United Trades' Association Report and Labour's **Advocate**: I, 5
(1 April 1848)–I, 10 (15 July 1848). London; Douglas, Isle of Man; m
  A   1d. Printed by W. Congreve; later (from No. 5) printed and
published by William Shirrefs and Andrew Russell. Details of the
programme and progress of the Association. Succeeded by **Labour League,
or Journal of the National Association of United Trades.**
  Bishopsgate Institute† (w 2, 9, 10); ONC

National Building Trades' Gazette see **Building Trades' News**

2287 National Charter Association. **Executive Journal** I, 1 (16 Oct. 1841)–I, 4 (6 Nov. 1841). Bath; w

    B   1d. Printed and published for the Executive by Philp and H. Vincent. Edited by the Executive, P. McDouall, J. Leech, R. K. Philp, M. Williams, and J. Campbell, Secretary. Addressed to the regions, plan for re-organisation, to organise campaign for second National Petition and a National Chartist Convention at start of 1842. Correspondence. J. Campbell answers queries.

    L (Place Coll. Set 56, p. 195–)

2288 National Co-operative Leader 1 (16 Nov. 1860)–27 (17 May 1861); then **Co-operative Newspaper**: 28 (24 May 1861)–29 (31 May 1861); w

    A   1d. Organ of the National Industrial and Provident Society, blending the principles of co-operation and mutual assurance. Suggests that working men, by putting their resources into co-operative schemes, can become their own employers, and remove the necessity for 'strikes' etc. Sympathetic to the 'Nine-Hours Movement' in the building trades.

    L; LU 1–27

2289 National Co-oerative Men's Guild. **Monthly Letter to Branches** ns 1 (July 1919)–(Feb. 1925?). Manchester; m

    A   Usually a single address, signed or unsigned, eg March 1921 – 'International co-operation: its present position and future development', by H. J. May. Alternative title; **Letter to the Branches**.

    Co-op. Coll.† July 1919–Feb. 1925*

2290 National Federation of Claimants Unions. **Federation Bulletin** [1970?]– . [Birmingham?]

    B   Mentioned in the Federation's **Journal**.

2291 National Federation of Claimants Unions. **Journal** 1 (Aug. 1970)– . Birmingham; irreg

    B   5s. (No. 1), special price to Claimants Union members fixed by local unions. Reproduced from typewriting. 'As many editions shall appear as there is material, but hopefully not less than three monthly.' 'Aim of the Journal to broaden and push forward the horizons of the Claimant movement, to provide a theoretical forum for the whole movement, so that it may be united in a common understanding.' 'Editorial Control: the editor shall publish in full all matter sent to the Journal by Unions of the Federation' [ie not edited centrally]. Intention was to publish articles of a theoretical, descriptive and historical nature on the politics and organisation of Social Security, the Claimant Movement and all related matters. 'The approach will be outward looking rather than inward in order to establish the position of the Claimant Movement in working-class politics.' News and day-to-day material would be published in other NFCU or Claimants Union publications.

    BP; LE; O; ONC† 1–3 [Nov. 1972]

National Federation of Discharged and Demobilised Sailors and Soldiers. **Bulletin** see **Bulletin, 1919–1921**

2292 National Federation of Shipworkers. **Report Sheet** [c1898].
    A   Gratis. (**Labour Annual**, 1898.)

2293 National Glass Workers Trade Protection Association. **Official Monthly Journal** I, 1 (Jan. 1924)–? Castleford; m
    A
    TUC† I, 1–II, 3 (March 1925)

2294 National Guardian 1–2 [cJuly 1932]; w?
    B   Edited by Henry Berthold. 'A radical periodical that agitates for an economy based not upon gold or silver but solely upon "the productiveness of labouring classes" ' (Wiener). In **The Regenerator** Berthold says the latter is a continuation of the **National Guardian**, with a change of title.
    HO 64/17 1

2295 National Home-Reading Union. Artizan's Section. **Monthly Journal** 1 (Oct. 1889)–8 (May 1890); m
    C   Editor and Secretary of Section until No. 6 was George Howell. Instruction, courses in proper reading and appreciation using texts like Carlyle's **Past and present**, and biographies of working men.
    L

2296 National Instructor I, 1 (25 May 1850)–I, 32 (28 Dec. 1850); ns 1 (4 Jan. 1851)–18 (3 May 1851); w
    B   1d. Printed and published by W. Rider. Conducted by Feargus O'Connor and others. With the Charter, it promotes peasant proprietorship home colonisation, national education and the organisation of Labour. Also letters, and autobiography, 'Life and adventures of Feargus O'Connor'. Contributors: Samuel Kydd, Josiah Merriman.
    BP; L(destroyed); LE (w I, 1); LU 1850; MP 1850; ONC†

2297 National Insurance Clerks' Journal: the Official Organ of the Association of National Insurance Clerks 1 (June 1915)–12 (May 1916); m
    A   1d. Trade-union journal established as a medium by which 'the members and the executive would be enabled to keep in closer touch' and as a forum for all shades of opinion within the Association.
    L(Col)†

2298 National League Journal: a Monthly Record of the Working Men's National League for the Repeal of the Contagious Diseases Act [Aug. 1875?]–?; m

A   1d. Printed and published by Dyer Bros. Edmund Jones, a working man, was President of the League which opposed the 'state regulation of vice' and saw the danger to the freedom of the individual involved in the working of the Act which gave power to 'spy police' to seek out prostitutes for medical examination. "The Acts are enforced to provide clean prostitutes for wealthy scoundrels, mostly military men.' Records agitation throughout the country in trade unions, workmen's clubs etc. Nearly all Labour and trade union leaders were connected with it.

L(Col)† 23 (June 1877)–32 (March 1878), 42 (Jan. 1879)–101 (Dec. 1883) (w 96)

2299 National Liberator 1842. Glasgow

B   Published by W. and W. Miller, publishers of the **Chartist Circular**, and previously of the **Monthly Liberator**. 'Final flicker of Chartist journalism in Glasgow' (R. M. W. Cowan, **The Newspaper in Scotland: a Study of its first Expansion, 1815–1860**, Glasgow 1946, p. 145).

2300 National Reformer 1 (Nov. 1844)–75 (April 1846); then **National Reformer, and Manx Weekly Review of Home and Foreign Affairs**: ns 1 (3 Oct. 1846) (29 May 1847). Douglas, Isle of Man; w

B   2½d. Editor: Bronterre O'Brien. Chartist, with main emphasis on the land question: O'Brien, against O'Connor's advocacy of small peasant proprietorship, agitates for public ownership of the land and a popular system of tenure as the salvation of the country. Much interest in American Radical movements. No. 1 of the new series is No. 76 of the old series.

L ns; LU ns; LE ns (reprint); Warwick UL (microfiche); Greenwood reprint and microfiche; microfiche distributed in Britain and Europe by the Harvester Press Ltd.; Mrs D. Thompson, Department of History, University of Birmingham

2301 National Reformer I, 1 (14 April 1860)–ns LXII, 14 (1 Oct. 1893); w

B   2d. Published by Messrs Holyoake, then printed and published by Bradlaugh, published by Watts. Editors: Joseph Barker and 'Iconoclast' [ie Bradlaugh]; in 1880s for a time, Charles Bradlaugh and Annie Besant; John M. Robertson. Radical, progressive, secularist and republican. In the 1870s an organ of Republican Clubs, and the Land and Labour League. Supported Co-operative activities. Contributors: Charles Watts, William Macall, Edward Aveling.

GM 1864–93*; L(Col)†; MP; NP LVII–LIX; ToP; XXIX*–XXXVIII; ONC XIX, 1–25

National Reformer, and Manx Weekly Review of Home and Foreign
Affairs see National Reformer. 1844—1846

2302 National Socialist and Labour Journal [c1905]. Liverpool
     B   (Historical Manuscripts Commission. **List of Labour
Representation Committee material in Labour Party archives.** Contains a
reference to the above.)

2303 National Society of Amalgamated Brassworkers and Metal
Mechanics. **Quarterly Report** [1] (Oct. 1918); then **Quarterly Journal**: 2
(Jan. 1919)—11 (Sept. 1921). Birmingham; q
     A   1d. No. 1 consists mainly of the proceedings of the recent
Annual Conference, then enlarged to include editorial, district reports,
comment on Labour and trade union issues.
     BP†; O(JJ)† 2, 3; TUC 1919—

2304 National Society of Drillers and Holecutters. **Quarterly Report**
[18--?]—?
     A
Amalgamated Society of Boilermakers, Shipwrights, Blacksmiths and
Structural Workers, Newcastle 1893—1900.

2305 National Society of Metal Mechanics. **London Newsletter**
     A
TUC Feb. 1953

2306 National Society of Painters. **Monthly Journal** I, 1 (Sept. 1921)—XL,
9 (May 1961); then Amalgamated Society of Painters and Decorators.
Journal: XL, 10 (June 1961)—XLIX, 6 (Feb. 1970). Manchester; m
     A   Originally full name of union was: National Amalgamated
Society of Operative House and Ship Painters and Decorators. Journal 'to
be of live interest and of some educational value'. Superseded the
Quarterly Report. Ceased publication when the Society became a branch
of the Woodworkers' Union, and superseded by that Union's **Viewpoint.**
     L; NU XLII—   ; ONC Dec. 1956—   ; TUC; Warwick U (MRC)

2307 National Society of Painters. **Quarterly Report** [19—?]—[1921?].
[Manchester?]; q
     A   Superseded by **Monthly Journal** (qv).

**2308 National Sunday League Record, Established to Promote the
Opening of the Public Museums, Galleries, Libraries and Gardens, on
Sunday, in London and in the Towns of England, Ireland and Scotland,
for the Instruction, Recreation, and Innocent Amusement of the Working
Classes** 1 (May 1856)—35 (March 1859); m
     C   1d. Published by the League (President, Sir Joshua Walmsley,
Liberal). Record of its activities, and articles on the general question.
     EU 3—6; L

2309 National Union: a Political and Social Record 1 (May 1858)—9 (11 Dec. 1858); m; w (8—9)

    B   ½d. Published by Wilkes and Company. Printed by J. B. Leno. Organ of 'the National Political Union for the Obtainment of the People's Charter, a small group of London Chartists and O'Brienites, with Charles Murray, J. B. Leno, and Thomas Martin Wheeler among its most active members' (A. Plummer, **Bronterre: a Political Biography of Bronterre O'Brien, 1804—1864**, 1971, p. 240). The journal was conducted by members of the executive Committee, including O'Brien, for the reorganisation of the Chartist movement.

    L

2310 National Union Journal Nov. 1908—April 1917; then **Journalist**: (May 1917)— . London etc.; q; bi-m;m

    A   National Union of Journalists. Started under the editorship of a founder member of the union, H. M. Richardson.

    L 1917—(March 1920); ONC 1949—*; Warwick UL 1967— ; the Union

2311 National Union of Bookbinders' and Machine Rulers' Trade Circular 1 (March 1911)—? Sheffield; q

    A   Issued to members only. No. 1 is the first quarterly circular of the new amalgamation, namely that of the Bookbinders' and Machine Rulers' Consolidated Union, the London Consolidated, Vellum Binders', and Day Workers' Societies.

    L 1—2 (June 1911)

National Union of Boot and Shoe Operatives. **Monthly Report** see National Union of Boot and Shoe Rivetters. **Quarterly Report**

2312 National Union of Boot and Shoe Rivetters. Quarterly Report 1874—6; then **Monthly Report**: 1877—90; then National Union of Boot and Shoe Operatives. **Monthly Report**: 1890— . London etc. q;m

    A   1d. Then National Union of the Footwear, Leather and Allied Trades.

    L Dec. 1894— ; LE, Webb Coll. 1889—?; NU ns, I (1962)— ; ONC 1946— ; TUC 1950— ; Warwick UL 1967— ; the Union

2313 National Union of Corporation Workers. Journal I, 1 (July 1923)—11 (May 1928); s-a?

    A   Agitates for one union for public employees from asylum workers to gas workers. London and provincial reports.

    TUC*†

National Union of General (then General and Municipal) Workers. **Journal** see **General Workers' Journal**

2314 National Union of Gold, Silver and Allied Trades. Quarterly Report 1903—24; q

    A

    TUC

National Union of Horticultural Workers. **Journal** see British Gardeners'
Association. **Journal**

National Union of Insurance Workers, Royal London Section. **Gazette** see
Royal London Mutual Assurance Society Staff Association. **Gazette**

2315 National Union of Mineworkers. **Information Bulletin** I, 1 (Jan.
1946)–XIX, 7/8 (July/Aug. 1964); m; bi-m
    A   Information on the coal industry, economic notes, book reviews
etc. Indexes published for a time.
      L 1946–63; ONC† 1950–64; TUC*

2316 National Union of Mineworkers. Colliery Officials and Staffs Area.
Area News Service 1 [1951?]–10 (June 1952); then **COSA News Bulletin**:
11 (July 1952)–57 (July 1963); then **COSA Bulletin**: 58 (Dec. 1963)–   ;
irreg
    A
    L 3 (Dec. 1951)–(w 12)

2317 National Union of Packing Case Makers (Wood and Tin), Box
Makers, Sawyers, and Mill Workers. **Monthly Report** [1916?]–?; m
    A
    TUC† 44 (Nov. 1919), 47 (Feb. 1920)

2318 National Union of Printing, Bookbinding and Paper Workers. Oxford
Branch. **Quarterly Bulletin** I, 1 [Jan. 1928?]–? Oxford; q
    A   For circulation among members only. Editorial, local news and
notes, report for quarter, balance sheet.
    ONC† I, 2 (April 1928), [April?] 1942)

2319 National Union of Scalemakers. [**Newsletter.**] Oct. 1928–   ; q; m;
bi-m; q
    A   Single printed sheet.
    L Nov./Dec. 1962–   ; the Union

2320 National Union of Sheet Metal Workers. **Quarterly Journal**. ?–1969;
then National Union of Sheet Metal Workers, Coppersmiths, Heating and
Domestic Engineers. **Journal**: 1 (Feb. 1970)–   ; q
    A   National Union of Sheet Metal Workers, then National Union of
Sheet Metal Workers and Braziers. Amalgamated in 1959 with the National
Society of Coppersmiths, Braziers and Metalworkers to form the National
Union of Sheet Metal Workers and Coppersmiths. Amalgamated in 1967
with the Heating and Domestic Engineers' union to form the National
Union of Sheet Metal Workers and Coppersmiths. Amalgamated in 1967
Engineers.
    E 1970–   ; L Jan. 1957–*

2321 National Union of Teachers. **Bulletin** 1 (Oct. 1939)–9 (June 1940). Toddington; m

    A   Information bulletin consisting of material reprinted from **Schoolmaster and Woman Teacher's Chronicle**.

    L

2322 National Union of Teachers. Cumberland County Association. **Magazine** 1 (May 1936)–9 (May 1939). Penrith; 3-yr

    A   Published by Stanley Allason on behalf of the Association. To keep members in touch with local and national activities concerning the welfare of teachers.

    L

2323 National Union of Teachers. Leeds and District Association. **Monthly Notes**. 1 (Nov. 1892)–(June 1898); then **Leeds and District Teachers Journal**: [1899?]–Dec. 1906? Leeds; m

    A   Reference to **Monthly Notes** appears in issue of the **Journal** for Dec. 1906.

    LdP† Jan. 1905 Dec. 1906

2324 National Union of Teachers. Portsmouth Association. **Journal** ?–Nov. 1964? Portsmouth

    A

    PmP Dec. 1922–Nov. 1964

National Union of Textile Workers. **Monthly Record** see **Textile Record**

National Union of Textile Workers. **Quarterly Record** see **Textile Record**

National Union of the Footwear, Leather and Allied Trades. **Monthly Journal and Report**. see National Union of Boot and Shoe Operatives. **Monthly Report**

2325 National Union of Vehicle Builders. **Quarterly Report and Journal** 1 (July 1919)–225 (April 1972). Manchester; q

    A   1d. Issued to members only. The first issue was a joint publication of the United Kingdom Society of Coachmakers, the London and Provincial Coachmakers' Trade Union, the Operative Coachmakers' Federal Union, and the Coachsmiths and Vicemen's Trade Society, which amalgamated to become the National Union of Vehicle Builders. This number was called **Joint Quarterly Report and Journal**. Later entitled **Quarterly Journal**. Ceased publication on the amalgamation of the Union with the Transport and General Workers' Union, when it became the Vehicle Building and Automotive Group of the TGWU. During 1919 and 1920 published a serialised history of the United Kingdom Society of Coachmakers, by Charles Kingsgate, former General Secretary.

    GM† 1–(Oct. 1922), (Feb. 1923)–(April 1932)*, (Oct. 1933)–(April 1953)*; L 168 (Jan. 1958)–(w 176); ONC† 215 (Oct. 1969)–225; TUC Jan. 1921–April 1972

2326 National Union of Women Workers. **Occasional Paper** 1 (Jan. 1896)–112 (Nov. 1922); then **NCW News**: 113 (Jan. 1923)–185 (Dec. 1930); then b **Women in Council**: I, 1 (Jan. 1931)–XVII, 6 (July 1939); then c **Women in Council News Letter**: I, 1 (Oct. 1939)–? q;?

A   1d. Central Conference of Women Workers, 1892–3; National Union of Women Workers; National Council of Women of Great Britain.

BS a 72–6, 78–9; L a 66–183, 185–   ; LE a 11–85*; O a 54, 59–61, 63–72; OW 1923–30, b I–

National United Trades' Association Report and Labour's Advocate see **National Association of United Trades for the Protection of Industry**

2327 National Vindicator 1840–April 1842; w

B   Proprietor: Henry Vincent. See also **Western Vindicator**

NpP (18 Sept 1841), (12 Feb. 1842); (LabP) (13 Nov. 1841)–(8 Jan. 1842), ([22 Jan., 29 Jan.], 1842); L 23 April 1842; L Place Newspaper Coll. Set 56. 115

2328 Nationalization News: the Journal of the Nationalization of Labour Society I, 1 (4 Oct. 1890)–III, 31 (April 1983); m

B   1d. Editors: Walter Godbold (until mid-1892); John Orme. 'Founded by the Nationalization of Labour Society which aimed at promoting the system in Edward Bellamy's **Looking backward**. Advocated lawful and peaceful social reformation. Supported co-operative distributive agencies as forerunner of productive co-operatives. Supported collective colonies' (Brophy). Later sub-titled: 'A Labour Paper'.

L(Col)†; O

2329 Natproban: the Official Organ of the National Provincial and Union Bank Staff Association I, 1 [March 1920?]–L, 196 (Spring 1969); q

A   6d. Later dropped 'and Union' from the sub-title. Merged with **National Westminster** when the two banks amalgamated.

L I, 2 (June 1920)–L, 196

2330 Natsopa Journal: Official Organ of the National Society of Operative Printers and Assistants I, 1 (May 1917)–XLIX, 578 (Aug. 1965); then **Journal** (Society of Graphical and Allied Trades. Division I. Natsopa): XLIX, 579 Sept. 1965)–LI, 595 (Jan. 1967); ns I, 1 (Nov. 1970)–   ; m

A   Superseded 1967–70 by **SOGAT Journal** (qv). New series published by Natsopa. Present title: **Journal and Graphic Review**.

HU Sept. 1965–   ; L Sept. 1965–   ; LE Sept. 1965–   ; LSF; NU IX, 1924–   ; ONC Dec. 1949–   ; the Union

2331 Ναυτεργατης 1 (25 March 1948)–164 (April/May 1959). Cardiff

A   Published by the Federation of Greek Maritime Unions.

L(Col)

Navvy's and General Laborer's Guide see **Navvy's Guide, and General Laborer's Own Paper.**

Navvy's and Laborer's Guide see Navvy's Guide, and General Laborer's
Own Paper.

2332 Navvy's Guide, and General Laborer's Own Paper 1 (1 Jan. 1891);
then Navvy's and Laborer's Guide: 2 (Feb. 1891)–4 (April 1891); then
Navvy's and General Laborer's Guide: 5 (1 May 1891)–8 (July 1891).
Eccles; m; fortn
    A   1d. Printed and published by Leonard Hall. Organ of the
Navvies', Bricklayers' Laborers', and General Laborers' Union, an example
of 'new unionism'. Had London branches and Northern District. Contains
news of where work could be obtained, in opposition to the employers'
scab paper, Labour News. Ultimate aim: the co-operative common wealth.
Mainly snippets of news.
    L(Col)†. 1–7; WCML† 8 (poor condition)

2333 ΝΑΥΤΕΡΓΑΤΗΣ [Mariner]: Organ of the Union of Greek Seamen
in Britain I (1941)–? Cardiff irreg;
    A   At first, reproduced from typewriting.
    L 1941–2

2334 Nelson Gazette [194-?]. Nelson; w
    B   1d. Labour Party. (Labour Party. Your own Journal, 1948.)

2335 Nelson Socialist [c1900]. [Nelson?]
    B   (Labour Annual, 1900.)

2336 Nelson Socialist Journal 1901. [Nelson?]
    B   (Labour Leader 9 Nov. 1901.)

2337 Nelson Workers' Guide Nov. 1902–Jan. 1903; then Workers' Guide:
[1903?]–? Nelson; m
    B   Free. Published by Nelson Independent Labour Party
Newspaper Committee. Edited by 'Penman', ILP Club, Nelson. (Labour
Leader, 10 Jan., 24 Jan. 1903; Reformers' Year Book, 1903.)
    ILP Nov. 1902, April 1904

2338 Neston Socialist Bulletin [194-?]. Neston, Wirral; m
    B   Duplicated. Labour Party. (Labour Party. Your own Journal,
1948.)

2339 Netley Monthly Review [194-?]. Netley Abbey, Hampshire; m
    B   Duplicated. Labour Party. (Labour Party. Your own Journal,
1948.)

2340 Neue Zeit: Organ der Demokratie 1 (1858)–42 (16 April 1859).
London; w
    B
    L(Col) 2–42

2341 New Advance: Journal of the Young Socialists I, 1 (Nov. 1960)–V, 23 (mid-Feb. 1966); m

    B   3d. Published by the Labour Party, Press and Publicity Department. Illustrated magazine.

    O (w 1); LE IV, 1964–

2342 New Age: a Weekly Record of Christian Culture, Social Service, and Literary Life I, 1 (4 Oct. 1894)–ns, LXII, 22 (7 April 1938); w

    B   1d.; 3d. Less relevant in earlier years, but in 1907 a new series was started under the editorship of A. R. Orage and Holbrook Jackson. By the end of the year Jackson had dropped out leaving Orage in charge until 1922. The new series began discussion of Socialism, and culture, and from 1912 to 1918 advocated Guild Socialism. Latterly, again outside our categories, as became an advocate of Social Credit. Incorporated **Labour Record and Review** in May 1907 with new series.

    BP ii XIII–LXII; C i I–II, 32, XII, 322–XIX; ii I–LVIII, LX–LXII; E ii L–LXII; EP ii VII–XV, XIX, XXII–XXIX; L(Col)†; LdP ii I–XXV; LvP ii I–XXIII; LE*; MP ii I–XXIX; ONC 1907–15*

2343 New Age and Concordium Gazette: a Journal of Human Physiology, Education, and Association I, 1 (6 May 1843)–I, 6 (10 June 1843); then **New Age, Concordium Gazette, and Temperance Advocate**: a Monthly Journal of Human Physiology, Education, and Association: I, 7 (1 July 1843)–I, 24 (1 Dec. 1844); w (1–6); m

    B   1d.; 2d. Organ of the 'Concordium' Community, or Harmonious Industrial College, devoted to Communism, co-operation etc. Published by R. Buchanan (1–2), J. Cleave. Printed by Concordium Press (1–19), V. Torras. Articles on education, physiology, association etc., with tales and sketches. Communications from America and the Continent. The 'Pater' of Concordium was William Oldham. Address to Vol. I states 'This volume of the **New Age** . . . records the second phase of one progress in Spirit culture (the **Healthian** representing the first) . . . '

    LU; MP; OR†

New Albion, for British Renaissance and Western Alliance see **New Atlantis, for Western Renaissance and World Socialism**

2344 New Atlantis, for Western Renaissance and World Socialism 1 (Oct. 1933)–2 (Jan. 1934); then b **New Albion, for British Renaissance and Western Alliance**: I, 1 (April 1934); then c **New Europe**: a Monthly Journal for Federation and Disarmament: I, 1 (Sept. 1934); q; m

    B   2s. 6d.; 3s. 6d.; 2s. 6d.; 1s. Editors: Watson Thomson; Lilian Slade and David Davies; W. Gordon Fraser. A. R. Orage associated with **New Albion**. Favoured Workers' Control. Resembled **New Britain** by which it was absorbed.

    E a; L b; L(Col)† a, c

2345 New Attack. [1932]

B   London and Southern Independent Labour Party Guild of
Youth.

ILP July 1932

2346 New Books for Workers: Monthly Bulletin of the Workers' Bookshop
1 [Feb. 1935?] –? m

B   Free. Single sheet printed on both sides, giving details of new
publications. Workers' Bookshop, 38 Clerkenwell Green, London EC1.

O(JJ)† 2 (March 1935)

2347 New Britain: Quarterly Organ of the 11th Hour Group I, 1 (Oct.
1932)–III, 64 (Autumn 1934); (29 Jan. 1936); ns I, 1 (5 Feb. 1936)–I, 8
(25 March 1936); q; w; q; w

B   2s. 6d.; 2d. (1936.) Published by The Search Publishing
Company for the XIth Hour Group. Editors: Watson Thomson and David
Davies (1932); C. B. Purdom (1934); Leslie Lohan and Watson Thomson
(1936). Sub-title: 'A Weekly Organ of National Renaissance' (1933–4);
'For National Renaissance and the Social State' (29 Jan. 1936). Stood for
'New Empire and New Socialism' but did not support any political party.
Started as a propagandist for Social Credit, acquired a religious tone.
Sought flexibility in institutions, favoured Guilds rather than trade unions.
Critical of capitalist system. Final issue stated 'Guild Socialism, Social
Credit and Regional Devolution . . . such is our Constructive Revolution,
wholly constructive. No bloodshed.' Absorbed **New Atlantis.**

C (29 Jan. 1936); E; L(Col)†; LE

2348 New Broom: Bromley NALGO News 1967?–

A   National and Local Government Officers' Association.

L 1967–

2349 New Builders' Leader [I], 1 (Oct. 1935)–XXV, 3 (March 1960); m

A   1d. etc. Published by the New Builders' Leader Editorial
Committee; F. Pendred for the Committee; New Builders Leader, Ltd. 'A
militant trade journal for the building industry.' With this as the objective
the New Builders' Leader was created out of the movement towards unity
and fighting strength that ran through the entire trade as a result of the
wages claim put forward by the NFBTO on 20 September 1934' (No. 1).
Initiated by members of the Minority Movement. Title during the 1940s:
New Builders' Leader and Electricians' Journal.

CPGB; L(Col)† (w 19 [April 1937]); MML IV; WCML†*

New Builders' Leader and Electricians' Journal see **New Builders' Leader**

New Charter see **Out of Work**

2350 New Citizen 1, [193-?] –? Aberdeen

B   1d. Socialist. First editor was William Diack.

AU(MSS Coll.) 15 (Feb. 1940)

2351 New Citizen 1 (Dec. 1949)–? Worcester

    B   Issued by the Worcester Co-operative Party in association with the Worcester Constituency Labour Party.

    L(Col)† 1

New Clarion see **Clarion, 1891–1932**

New Commonwealth see **Christian Commonwealth**

2352 New Crusader: a Journal of Enquiry into the Foundation of War I, 1 (25 March 1916)–I, 53 (3 Jan. 1919); then **Crusader**: ns I, 1 (10 Jan. 1919)–X, 8 (Sept. 1928); then b **Socialist Christian**: I, 1 (Oct. 1928)–(Jan. 1960); then **CSM News**: Bulletin of the Christian Socialist Movement: 1 (July 1960)–14 (April 1963); then **Christian Socialist**: 15 (June 1963)–. London etc.; w; m; bi-m

    B   2d. etc. Committee for the Promotion of Pacifism; Society of Socialist Christians; Christian Socialist Movement. Early editors included John Corner Spokes, Fred Hughes.

    C*; L 1960–; L(Col)† 1916–60; LE*; O*; ONC 1927–9

2353 New Dawn: the Official Organ of the National Union of Distributive and Allied Workers I, 1 (Jan. 1921)–XXVI, 26 (28 Dec. 1946); ns 1, 1 (11 Jan. 1947)–. Manchester; fortn; m (1967–)

    A   2d. etc. In 1947 became the official organ of the Union of Shop, Distributive and Allied Workers, formed by the amalgamation of the National Union of Distributive and Allied Workers with the National Amalgamated Union of Shop Assistants, Warehousemen and Clerks.

    AU 1921–51*; BP; L(Col)†; LE*; MP i XXVI, ii I–; NU ii IV, 7, 1950–; ONC 1924–37, 1940–1, 1950–; TUC; the Union

2354 New Epoch I, 1 (March 1926)–?

    B   University Labour Federation

    TUC 1

2355 New Era: Newsletter and Magazine 1966–. Tamworth

    A   National and Local Government Officers' Association. Reproduced from typewriting. First issue does not bear title.

    L

New Europe see **New Atlantis, for Western Renaissance and World Socialism**

2356 New Fabian Research Bureau. **Quarterly Journal** 1 (March 1934)–10 (June 1936); then **NFRB Quarterly**: 11 (Autumn 1936)–20 (Winter 1938–9); then **Fabian Quarterly**: 21 (Spring 1939)–58 (Summer 1948); q

   B   1s.; 6d. From No. 21 issued by the Fabian Society. To supply the worker/socialist with ready facts and figures on trade, employment, wages etc., and to publish research articles on domestic and international issues. Vehicle for detailed information on the work of the Bureau. Contributors: R. W. B. Clarke, Colin Clark, G. D. H. Cole, H. Gaitskell, H. N. Brailsford. Merged in **Fabian News.**

   BP 24–58; BS 3–58; DrU 19–49*; ExU 40–58; GM 1939–48; L; LU 22–58; LabP; MML; MP 12–52; ONC 11–58

New Focus see **Focus. 1950–1967**

New Forest Notes see National Association of Local Government Officers. New Forest Branch. **Quarterly News Sheet**

2357 New Forward I, 1 (Dec. 1958); then **Ayrshire Forward**: I, 2 (Jan. 1959)–? Manchester; m

   B   A 'Labour's Voice' newspaper. Published by Workers' Northern Publishing Society.

   L(Col) I, 1–I, 25 (Feb. 1961); LE I, 3; TUC I, 1

2358 New Free Press 1 (27 May 1899)–? Grimsby; w

   B   ½d. Printed and published by the proprietor, Abel Hinchcliffe, editor of the **Grimsby Observer.** 'All classes of the community, but especially the workers, should read **The New Free Press** . . . [On] Labour Questions, it stands alone and distinct from that section of the capitalist press which sometimes throws "a sop to Cerberus" whilst blinding the worker to his own interests. It is well informed and always up to date. Its contributions include the best thought from local and national leaders of labour. It is everywhere, in its wide district of circulation, the official organ of the Labour Party . . . '(Advertisement). Circulated in Yorkshire and Lincolnshire.

   Grimsby PL 1–46 (7 April 1900)

2359 New Future 1954–   ; m

   C   10s. pa Published by the Economic League. For apprentices and young workers in industry.

   Economic League 1961–

2360 New Generation: the Paper with a Progressive Outlook 1 (3 Dec. 1960)–? Leeds

   B   3d. Paper of the Young Socialist League of the Independent Labour Party. Editor: E. Preston. For a United Revolutionary Socialist Youth Movement.

   TUC† 1

2361 New Harmony Gazette I, 1 (1 Oct. 1825)–III, 52 (22 Oct. 1828); then **Free Enquirer**: ns I, 1 (29 Oct. 1828)–V, (19 Oct. 1833); ns I, 1 (27 Oct. 1833)–II (28 June 1835). New Harmony, Indiana; New York

     B   Editors: Frances Wright (afterwards D'Arusmont), R. D. Owen, R. L. Jennings.

       Co-op. Coll. i I–II; GM April 9–(14 May 1831); L i; LU i I, 1–48, ii II–III; Greenwood reprint and microfiche: Microfiche distributed in Britain and Europe by the Harvester Press Ltd

2362 New Horizon: Journal for Rubber and Plastic Workers [196-?] – Manchester; q?

     A   United Rubber Workers of Great Britain.

     TUC† IV, 1 (Spring 1972)

2363 New John Bull and Penny Satirist 1 (10 Jan. 1835?)–21 (30 May 1835); w

     B   1d. Printed by Richard E. Lee. 'A radical satirical political miscellany. It features accounts of radical activities, descriptions of crimes, and anecdotes' (Wiener).

     O(JJ) 21

New Leader see **Labour Leader. 1893–1922**

2364 New Leader Supplement and Norwich ILP Local Notes [c1943]

     B   Independent Labour Party.

     ILP (15 May 1943)

2365 New Left Review 1 (Jan./Feb. 1960)–; bi-m

     B   3s. 6d. etc. Editors: Stuart Hall, Perry Anderson etc. 'A development of "**New Reasoner**, and **Universities and Left Review**" '

     BP; BU 7– ; BnU 35– ; E; EU 23– ; HU; LE; LdP; MP; O; ONC†; SP; SwU 1–22; YU 29–

2366 New Legal Observer 1 (26 April 1834); w

     B   2d. Published and printed by C. Penny. 'An illustrated radical newspaper that features extensive accounts of trades union meetings and police intelligence' (Wiener).

     O(JJ)

2367 New Loaf, or Food-for-the-Mind 1 [1831]–12 [1831]. Edinburgh

     C   ½d. Published by A. W. Maclean. 'Adapted to all, but especially prepared for artisans, their wives and their children; in other words, a magazine of such instructive, useful, and entertaining knowledge as may tend to excite to action our best faculties, that is to say, our moral and religious feelings.' A miscellany of literary extracts and anecdotal snippets. Special interest in contemporary school events; suggests 'infant schools for the labouring classes'.

     EP†

New London Mechanics' Register and Magazine of Science and the Useful Arts see London Mechanics' Register

2368 New Man: a Bi-monthly Publication Devoted to Socialist Culture and World Outlook I, 1 (Jan./Feb. 1947)—I, 2 (May/June 1947); bi-m
    B   1s. Published by the British Society for the Creation of the New Man. Editor: P. N. Harker. Stands for world Socialism, 'emancipation of subject peoples', 'true and purposive culture'. Opposes atomic bomb, Racialism, Imperialism, Fascism, Philistinism etc.
    L

2369 New Mills Labour Party Bulletin [194-?]. Strines, nr. Stockport; irreg

    B   Free. (Labour Party. **Your own Journal**, 1948.)

2370 New Moral World: a London Weekly Publication, Developing the Principles of the Rational System of Society I, 1 (1 Nov. 1834)—XIII (3rd ser. VI), 64 (13 Sept. 1845); then b **Moral World**: 1 (30 Aug. 1845)—11 (8 Nov. 1845). London; Manchester; Birmingham; Leeds; London; w
    B   Conducted by Robert Owen and his followers. The sub-title varies.
    BP a I, 1—3, V—IX, 26; BnU a L—IV; Co-op. Coll.*; GU a VII, 68—b; L(Col)*; LE a I—XI; LU; LdP occ. vols.; MP a I; ONC a I—VIII; Warwick UL (microfiche); Greenwood reprint and microfiche: microfiche distributed in Britain and Europe by the Harvester Press Ltd.

2371 New Moral World, and Official Gazette of the National Association of Industry, Humanity, and Knowledge 1 (30 Aug. 1834) w
    B   1½d. Published and printed by Benjamin D. Cousins. A successor to **The Crisis**. 'An Owenite co-operative miscellany that features accounts of lectures by Robert Owen as well as correspondence from John Finch, a Liverpool co-operator' (Wiener).
    O

2372 New Nation I, 1 (Jan. 1933)—IV, 7 (July 1936); m
    B   1½d. Published by the Labour Party. The official organ of the Labour Party League of Youth. Will 'seek to make our primary task the propagation of socialist principles'. Records activities and progress of League branches. Urged joint membership of a trade union and the Labour Party. Articles by prominent members of the Labour Party. Contributors: Maurice Webb, full time organiser, A. L. Rowse, W. Arthur Peacock, Stafford Cripps, Anthony Greenwood.
    C; L

New Order see **Croydon Brotherhood Intelligence**

New Outlook. 1934—see **Federation Outlook**: Organ of the National Federation of Pearl Officials

2373 New Outlook: the Organ of the Taxes Left Wing Group I, 1 (Oct. 1935)–II, 2 (Summer 1938); q

    A   3d. Printed for the publishers, the Taxes Left Wing Group, by George Mitton and Company. Editor: S. E. Raymond. Led by a group within the Civil Service Clercial Association. For a new outlook in Civil Service Trades Unionism. To put progressive opinion in touch with ordinary members. Demands abolition of grades, of paid and unpaid overtime, increased wages, political liberties for civil servants. Later name of group: Civil Service Progressive Group.

    L

2374 New Oxford 1 (Dec. 1919)–21 (1 June 1923). Oxford irreg?

    B   The first and only long-lived of Labour journals in post-war Oxford. Founded by D. F. Brundritt, then Secretary of the Labour Club, as a purely personal venture representing progressive views in general and those of the Labour Party in particular. Among first contributors were Henri Barbusse, Ernest Barker and Arthur Greenwood. After two numbers became the official organ of the Labour Club. Edited February 1921 (for two numbers?) by Arthur Reade. He followed too a revolutionary policy and was substituted by an editorial board. Became 'a sane and sober university paper'. Edited to the end of the summer term 1922 by S. S. Smith, and the next term by Richard Pares. (M. P. Ashley and C. T. Saunders, **Red Oxford**, 2nd ed. Oxford 1933, pp. 16, 32, 34, 35.)

    C; L(Col) 13–21; O 3

2375 New Penny Chap-Book I 1 (Feb. 1900)–? Glasgow; m

    B   Published by Frederick W. Wilson and Company. Articles on culture and literary figures by a wide range of socialist contributors. No. 1 mentions a projected 12 numbers.

    ILP 1; O(JJ)† 1, 4 (May 1900)

2376 New Penny Magazine, or Weekly Miscellany of Literature, Science, and Art 1 (22 Sept. 1832); w

    B   1d. Published by William Strange. Printed by G. Eccles. 'A "useful knowledge" miscellany that is popular in format and similar to **The Penny Magazine**, except that it contains radical political comment. It attacks the system of taxation, tithes, and the aristocracy' (Wiener).

    O; O(JJ)

New Pioneer see **Pioneer of the Folk**

2377 New Ploughshare: the Teachers' Peace Paper I, 1 (April 1938)–I, 14 (July/Aug. 1939); m

    B   Published by the Teachers' Committee of the British National Committee of the International Peace Campaign. 'Its sole object is to help in the struggle for peace, without which no great forward movement for education is possible.' Claimed to be non-political, but was welcomed by Lansbury and Norman Angell.

    L

2378 New Political Dictionary 1 [May 1832]—2 [cJune 1832?]. Glasgow; w?

1d? Published and printed by Muir, Gowans and Company together with **The Reformers' Pocket Companion**. 'A working-class political journal that employs a lexicographical format to make radical comments' (Wiener).

GM(missing)

2379 New Political Register 1 (17 Oct. 1835)—?; then: (2 April 1836); w

B 2d. Published by Ashton Yates. Printed by Richard E. Lee. Owned and edited by John Bell. 'A radical political miscellany that advocated universal suffrage, annual Parliaments, the ballot, and a system of economic protection' (Wiener).

LU 1, 4

2380 New Propellor: Organ of the Aircraft Shop Stewards National Council I, 1 (Sept. 1935)—XI, 14 (March 1946); then **Metal Worker**: XI, 15 (April 1946)—XXVI, 2 (1963); m

A By 1940 organ of the Engineering and Allied Trades Shop Stewards' National Council. Editors: Peter Zinkin, Dave Michaelson.

MML 1936—40*; 1942—9; TUC 1941—63*; WCML†*

2381 New Reasoner : a Quarterly Journal of Socialist Humanism I, 1 (Summer 1957)—I, 10 (Autumn 1959). Halifax; q

B 4s. Published by E. P. Thompson, 'The New Reasoner', Halifax. Editors: John Saville, E. P. Thompson. '**The New Reasoner** will carry material of three kinds. First, theoretical and analytical articles of some length (as well as briefer review articles and commentary). Second, documents, translations and commentary on the international socialist and communist scene. Third, a wide range of creative writing . . . ' Incorporated in **New Left Review**.

C; E; L; LdP; O

New Red Stage see **Red Stage**

2382 New Schoolmaster: the Organ of the London Schoolmasters' Association ns [I, 1] (May 1921)—; m

A 2d. etc. From February 1922: **Organ of the National Association of Schoolmasters**. May 1921 is Vol. III, No. 21 of an earlier series. States that the new series is 'under a new president and new editorial control'. Not published Sept. 1939—Sept. 1944. For this period see: National Association of Schoolmasters, **Bulletin**.

L; LdU XIX, 187— ; Warwick UL May 1921—

2383 NEW SPUR, BECAUSE THE WORKERS NEED A SPUR MORE THAN EVER, IF THEY ARE TO CONQUER BREAD, FREEDOM AND ROSES I, 1 (Dec. 1933)–I, 5 (April 1934). Glasgow; m

    B   Voluntary subscription. Anarchist. 'Edited and printed by Guy Aldred at his office, 145 Queen Street, Glasgow. Printed in France by the editor's Anti-Parliamentary comrades at their own press, because the Bakunin Press no longer exists, and because no printing press in Britain would undertake the risk of printing.' Main contents are character sketches of leading anarchists, eg, Bakunin, Malatesta.

    L(Col)† (w 1)

2384 New Standard [c1921]. Ipswich

    B   Local Labour Party paper. (**Labour Organiser**, July 1921.)

New Standards see **Guildsman. 1916–1921**

2385 New Statesman I, 1 (12 April 1913)–XXXVI, 930 (21 Feb. 1931); then **New Statesman and Nation**: ns I, 1 (28 Feb. 1931)–   ; w

    B   Latterly, **New Statesman**.

    BP; BdP; BrP; C; L(Col); LE; MP; NwP; O; for further, incomplete, runs see BUCOP

2386 New Times [c1905]. [Leeds?]

    B   East Leeds Labour Representation Committee.

    ILP (1 Nov. 1905)

2387 New Times: the Eastern Counties Labour Paper 1 (Sept. 1913)–8 (May 1914). Colchester; m

    B   ½d. Published by the New Times Committee at the Headquarters of the Colchester Independent Labour Party. 'To preach the Labour and Socialist gospel to the working class of the Eastern Counties, East Anglia region. Emphasis on municipal Socialism.'

    L(Col)†

2388 New Times I, 1 (Feb. 1921)–? Chelmsford; m

    B   2d. An Essex Labour paper, newspaper format. Published by P. F. Pollard. Hopes to extend circulation to every village. Union and Labour Party news and articles, and shorter items. Contributors: J. E. Mills, MP, Kelvin Bankes.

    O(JJ)† 1

2389 New Unionist: Newspaper of the National Union of General and Municipal Workers 1 (Nov. 1963)–5 (April 1966), irreg

    A   No. 2 was 'Education issue', No. 3 '75th birthday issue', No. 4 'Local government issue', No. 5 'Engineering issue'.

    E; L(Col); NU; ONC†

2390 New Way: a Pioneer Journal for Modern Methods. I, 1 (March 1917)–III, 7 (Aug. 1919); then **Irish Railway Review**: III, 8 (Sept. 1919)–III, 9 (Oct. 1919). Dublin; m

    A   2d. Printed for the F. W. Crossley publishing Company. For railway workers. Champions railway trade unions, and advocates State ownership of the railways. Supports Labour Party. Articles, union branch reports, jokes, short stories, poems.

    L(Col)†; LE I, 1–9

2391 New Weekly True Sun 1 (16 Jan. 1836)–12 (2 April 1836); w

    B   2d. Published and printed by Ashton Yates. Edited by John Bell. 'A full-sized working-class newspaper that advocates universal suffrage, reform in Ireland, and repeal of the Poor Law Amendment Act of 1834. After repeated Stamp Office seizures, it ceased publication and was then succeeded by the **Mirror for Magistrates**' (Wiener).

    L(Col) 12; O 1

New White Rose see **County Service Journal**

2392 New World: a Monthly Magazine of Justice and Equity I, 1 (Dec. 1908)–IV, 40 (March 1913); m

    B   1d.; ½d. Published and printed by Eastern Chronicle Co-operative Printing and Publishing Society; North West Ham Branch of the Social Democratic Party; (1910); from January 1912 published by the North West Ham Branch of the British Socialist Party and printed by Walter Godbold. Editors: W. J. Blackmur; H. Kirby; George Finch; E. Farrell. Initially supported the Independent Labour Party. Later sub-title: 'A Journal of Social Revolution'.

    L(Col)† 1 (Dec. 1908)–5 (April 1909); LE† I, 11 (Aug. 1910)–IV, 40*

2393 New World: Sailors' and Soldiers' Own Paper 1 [1919?] –? Glasgow; m

    A   2d. Printed by Robert Thompson for the publisher New World Publishing Company. An organ of the militant National Union of Ex-Servicemen 'fighting shoulder to shoulder with organized labour'.

    TUC† 11 (Jan. 1920), 12 (Feb. 1920)

2394 New World I, 1 (May 1930)–III, 9 (May 1933); m

    B   2d. Printed for the No More War Movement by the Blackfriars Press, Leicester and London. From No. 8 sub-titled: 'Journal of the No More War Movement'. Editors: Lucy A. Cox; J. Allen Skinner. Contents resemble those of **No More War** (qv). See also **Points for Pacifists**.

    L(Col); O*†

2395 Newcastle Citizen [193-?] –? Newcastle-upon-Tyne

    B   Free. Published by Newcastle Voluntary Co-operative Party. Printed by the Co-operative Press.

    L(Col)† Oct. 1936

2396 Newcastle Co-operative Record June 1879—? Newcastle-on-Tyne;m
    A   Free. (Mitchell, 1895; **Presenting Newcastle Co-operative**
Services, 1951, p. 3.)

Newcastle Daily News see **Newcastle Evening News**

2397 Newcastle Elector, and LRC Herald [1905?]—? Newcastle-on-Tyne
    B   Published by A. Wilson Hildreth. Newspaper with local Labour
news etc.
        ONC† 2 (April 1905)

2398 Newcastle Evening News (2 Oct. 1893)—(27 April 1899?) Newcastle;
d
    B   ½d. Prospectus of Newcastle Evening News Company
announced 'This Company has been formed for the purpose of establishing
an Evening Newspaper for the great Industrial Community of the North of
England. The need for a journal which shall fully recognise and advocate
the wants of the workers, while placing in the hands of the general public a
thoroughly efficient Newspaper, is clearly apparent.' 'The provisional
Directors were to include the President, the Secretary and the Assistant
Secretary of the Newcastle Typographical Society, and another member of
that body, W. F. Toynbee, was to be the secretary of the new company.
Several officials of other trade unions were to be on the Board.' Arthur
Henderson was also on the Board. (M. Milne, **The Newspapers of
Northumberland and Durham,** 1971.) 'The lack of sympathetic
treatment — indeed, the almost constant misrepresentation of the workers'
aims by the ordinary press of the country, has emphasised the want of an
outspoken mouthpiece as a vital necessity to the existence and well being
of the cause of Labour Organization Prospectus). 115,000 copies of the
first issue. In 1894 the paper was transferred to new proprietors, and
became more moderate in tone, Lib.—Lab. rather than Labour, but in
1897 it became again more distinctly Labour. In 1896 the title was
changed to **Newcastle Daily News,** but resumed its original title in October
1898. By 1899 another change had taken place: the paper was smaller, had
a London address (the same address as the **Morning Mail** syndicate), had
less local news and a 'stereotyped' appearance.
        L(Col)

2399 Newcastle-upon-Tyne Muncipal Officer: the Organ of the
Newcastle-upon-Tyne Municipal Officers' Association I, 1 (June
1908)—VI, 10 (Dec. 1914); ns 1 (Nov. 1925)—9 (Sept./Oct. 1926).
Newcastle; m
    A   No price; 2d.; 6d. In affiliation with the National Association of
Local Government Officers.
        NwP†

2400 Newcomer : the Official Organ of the Maldon Divisional Labour Party 1 (1 June 1925)–? [Maldon?]

    B   1d. Published by the Maldon Divisional Labour Party and printed for them in Chelmsford. A newspaper covering local and national affairs, news of local Labour activities, correspondence.

    O(JJ)† 1

2401 Newcomer [193-?]. Braintree; m

    B   Labour Party. (Labour and Socialist International. **The Socialist Press**, 1933.)

2402 Newgate Monthly Magazine or Calendar of Men, Things and Opinions I, 1 (1 Sept. 1824)–II, 12 (1 Aug. 1826); m

    B   1s. Printed and published by R. Carlile for Messrs Perry, Hassell and Campion, Chapel Yard, Newgate. 'Edited by Mr. Carlile's late shopmen now confined in Chapel Yard, Newgate.'

    L (missing); LE; LGU I, 2–12, II, 1–2, 5, 7–8; MP†; WCML† I

2403 Newport Citizen May 1938–? Newport

    B   Newport Labour Party.

    NpP

2404 Newport Labour Searchlight 1 (9 Jan. 1925)–33 (21 Aug. 1925). Newport; w

    B   Newport Labour Party

    NpP

News and Local Goings On (Chelmsford Hospitals Branch, NALGO) see **NALGO News Letter**

2405 News and Notions 1 (July 1932)–39 (Sept. 1935). Birmingham; m

    B   Organ of the West Birmingham Divisional Labour Party. Printed and published by Wilfred Whiteley, the Agent. Editor: O. George Willey, 'prospective candidate'. League of Youth section, Women's Section, 'Victory for Socialism' campaign. Reproduced from typewriting.

    BP†

2406 News Box: the Journal of the Staff of Leatherhead UD Council I, 1 (Sept. 1952)–(March 1956). Leatherhead; q

    A   3d. Editor: R. F. Richards. Reproduced from typewriting.

    L† I, 2 (Christmas 1952); the Editor (w I, 1, II, 2)

News from Nowhere see **Socialist Round Table**

2407 News from Spain I, 1 (1 May 1937). Glasgow

    B   1d. Edited and published for the United Socialist Movement in support of the CNT, FAI and Youth Movement (Anarchist and POUM) by Guy Aldred, at Bakunin Hall. Statements, speeches by various leaders, denounces role of Stalinism from standpoint of Anarcho-Syndicalism.

    L(Col)†

2408 News from the British Council Staff Association 1 (Oct. 1962)–20 (March 1973); s-a
    A   Includes discussion of policy, history (serialised) of the Association, news etc.
    ONC† 2, 4–6; Warwick UL† 1, 3, 7–20

2409 News-Letter: the National Labour Fortnightly. I, 1 (2 April 1932)–ns X, 2 (April/July 1947); fortn
    B   2d. Organ of the those in the Labour Party, headed by MacDonald, who supported the National Government. Published by the National Labour Committee. Articles by leading 'Labourites' on current political issues and problems. Editorials by MacDonald in the early years. Contributors: Lord Allen of Hurtwood, J. H. Thomas, Viscount Sankey.
    E i, ii I–VII; L†; LE

2410 News Letter: Thurrock Branch Magazine, NALGO I, 1 (Jan. 1953)– . Thurrock
    A   National and Local Government Officers' Association. Reproduced from typewriting.
    L

2411 News Letter: Organ of the Sign and Display Trades Union I, 1 (Jan. 1947)–; m; bi-m
    A   The Union was amalgamated with the National Society of Operative Printers, Graphical and Media Personnel in 1972 and became the Sign and Display Trades Section of that Union. No. 1 says that the News Letter was preceded by a duplicated sheet.
    L Nov./Dec. 1963– ; TUC†; the Union

2412 News Letter: Official Organ of the Faversham Constituency Labour Party [1957?]– . Sittingbourne; m
    B   For members only. Published by W. H. Gray (1962). Short signed articles, notes, notices of meetings, gardening column.
    LabP† occ nos 1962–5; Faversham Constituency Labour Party

2413 News Look: Magazine of the South Shields Branch of NALGO 1961?– . South Shields
    A   National and Local Government Officers' Association. Reproduced from typewriting.
    L 1961–

2414 News Sheet 1 (4 Feb. 1917)–17 (1917). Prince Town etc., Devon; w
    B   Printed for private circulation, issued by conscientious objectors. 1–4 were handwritten and typewritten. No. 17 was suppressed. 'To present a true statement of fact re the position and conditions of COs at the many Camps and Work Centres throughout the country.' Camp reports show refusal to work for private employers, fight for eight-hour day, and that many 'prisoners' were committed socialists and trade unionists.
    L† 5–16

2415 Newsdesk [19--?] –?

    A   Union of Post Office Workers, TPO Branch. (W. Dunlop, 'Local Journals'. **Belpost**, IV, 5 [May 1965].)

2416 Newsletter: a Service to Socialists I, 1 (10 May 1957)–XIII, 687 (23 Sept. 1969). then **Workers Press** 1 (27 Sept. 1969)– ; w; s-w; d

    B   Organ of the Socialist Labour League Central Committee; from November 1973 of the Central Committee of the Workers Revolutionary Party. Trotskyist.

    E I, 12– ; HU 1969– ; L(Col); LE 1969– ; O 1969– ; ONC† Dec. 1958– ; TUC Nov. 1958–

2417 Newsletter for Labour Groups [195-?] –22 (Aug. 1962); irreg.

    B   'Produced by the Local Government Section of the Labour Party Research Department.' 'Confidential.' Published by the Labour Party.

    LabP 7 (June 1954)–22; ONC† 10 (Dec. 1955); TUC (June 1954)–22

2418 News-Litter: Magazine of the Merioneth Branch of NALGO 1 (Feb. 1967)–2 (May 1967); then **Y Gadwyn**: 3 (Sept. 1967)– . Dolgellau

    A   National and Local Government Officers' Association. Reproduced from typewriting.

    L

2419 Newsreel Kingston-upon-Thames

    A   National and Local Government Officers' Association, Surrey County Officers' Branch.

    L ns IV, 1 (Jan. 1956)– ; TUC June 1957–Nov. 1968*

2420 Nibs and Quills: the Official Organ of the General Railway Clerks Association, and Other Clerks' Associations I, 1 (Dec. 1898)

    A   Claims to cater for a wide range of clerks in financial houses, the Law, and offices in general, 'with a view to the enlightenment and encouragement of improvement of those of both sexes engaged in clerical pursuits', but No. 1 contains material only on technicalities and professional etiquette.

    L†

2421 Nigerian Journal, Being the Official Organ of the Association of European Civil Servants [1919?] –? Lagos; q

    A   (Mitchell, 1935)

    L II, 1 (Aug. 1920)–

2422 Ninety-Two: the Official Journal of the St Cuthbert's Co-operative Association I, 1 (July 1950)– . Edinburgh; m

    A   3d. etc. For both members and employees; named after the street number of the Association's headquarters.

    E

2423 No More War: the Monthly Organ of the No More War International Movement I, 1 (10 Feb. 1922)–X [i.e. IX], 2 (April 1930). London; ns I, 1 (Jan. 1935)–II, 9 (Oct. 1936). Guildford (I, 1–9); Tongham; m

    B   1d. First series printed by the Blackfriars Press for No More War International Movement, then No More War Movement (the British Section of the War Resisters' International). Editors: A. Fenner Brockway; W. J. Chamberlain; J. Allen Skinner. The 'Explorer' pages, for children, which were incorporated, were prepared by Theodora Wilson Wilson; these were dropped after April 1922 and replaced by a children's column. Left-wing sympathies; articles by Independent Labour Party members. Second series, I, 1–9, published by the Southern Counties Workers' Publications, Ltd. for the Movement, then printed and published by Lucking and Son. Editor: J. Allen Skinner. The leadership and the journal were socialist (see July and August 1935 where a complaint from a member that the assumption is made that all members are socialists is dealt with). No. 1 states 'In accordance with the decision of the Annual Conference of the No More War Movement, with this issue **No More War** becomes again the national organ of the Movement. The Midlands Council, who have been responsible for the production of the journal throughout the past year, have given every assistance in transfering its control to the National Executive.' Minnie Pallister, who edited the journal for the Midlands Council, agreed to serve on the new Editorial Board. **See also New World; Points for Pacifists.**

    L(Col); O*; TUC 1923–36*

2424 No More War 1934

    B   Published by the Midlands Council of the No More War Movement. Taken over and became the national organ as ns I, 1 (Jan. 1935)–   (see separate entry).

2425 No Name: the Magazine of the Holborn Branch of the National Association of Local Government Officers [I], 1 (May 1947)–3 (Nov. 1947); then **Holborn Inn Brief**: 4 (Feb. 1948)–II, 7 (June 1958)

    A   Later National and Local Government Officers' Association, Holborn Branch. Alternative title: **The Understudy**.

    L

2426 Non-Partisan Leader: the Paper with a Kick. Official Organ of the National Non-Partisan League for Socialism [192-?]–? w

    B   1d. Reproduced from typewriting. Published and printed by the editor, Nathan Birch, then by John Syme. Mottos: 'For neither Right nor Left Wing but for Socialism; Ballot Box and not Bullets; Every Day an Election Day; Education by Propaganda'. Much space devoted to the claim of 'Ex-Inspector John Syme' for justice from the Home Office. Refers to an episode in 1909 when he called attention to maladministration in B Division of the Metropolitan Police Force, and was dismissed. This is a constant theme throughout. Also comment on current political issues.

    LabP† VII, 15 (9 Nov. 1929)–XI, 16 (15 Aug. 1931*)

2427 Norfolk Socialist Review 1 (Jan. 1901)–? Norwich; m

    B   Social Democratic Federation. (**Reformers' Year Book**, 1901.)

2428 Norfolk Yeoman's Gazette and Eastern Advertiser 1 (8 Feb. 1823)–13 (3 May 1823); w

    B   7d. Printed and published by J. M. Cobbett. Upholds the interests of the independent tenant freeholders against aristocratic landlords, jobbers, and speculators of the metropolis. Norfolk Petition was moved in the House of Commons by William Cobbett, who contributed to the paper. For parliamentary reform, tax reduction, and equalisation of taxes; for sound currency, and removal of rural distress. Reports of other rural provincial meetings for parliamentary reform etc., eg, Suffolk.

    C 4; L(Col)†; NrP

2429 North and East London Star 1 (30 March 1889)–7 (11 May 1889); then **North London Press and Star**: ns 513 (18 May 1889)–516 (8 June 1889); then **North London Press**: 517 (15 June 1889)–547 (25 Jan. 1890); w

    B   ½d. Relevant from No. 513 when it takes up the numbering of the earlier **North London Press** (1978–). Radical with Labour notes. 'In the class warfare of today, ours is the cause of the worker.' Local trade union news. Contributor: 'A Worker'. Editor, proprietor, publisher: Edward O. Adams. Resumed in March 1890 as **People's Press** (Brophy).

    L(Col)†

2430 North Battersea Citizen 1 (Sept. 1931)–70 (Sept. 1939); m

    B   Free. Published by the London Co-operative Society's Political Committee, except the last number which was printed and published by he Co-operative Press. One of the 'Citizen series'.

    L(Col)†

2431 North British Weekly Express 1845–8. Edinburgh; w

    B   'The paper became the property of the leading Edinburgh Chartists at the end of 1847' (A. Wilson, **The Chartist Movement in Scotland**, 1970). Advocate of Chartism, Repeal, Rights of Labour etc, and claimed to be 'the only democratic newspaper in Scotland'. Editor: Rev. William Hill, Sub-editor: Henry Rankine, Committee of Management: Robert Cranston, John Adair, John Eckings, Alexander Elder, John Grant, Robert Hamilton. Published by Archibald Walker. First printed by John Harthill, then by Robert Tofts. Premises raided on 27 July 1848. (**Scottish Notes and Queries**, Sept. 1901, p. 41.) Later editors: James Bertram, John Blair, and at later date Henry Rankine, until his imprisonment as a Chartist, when the management fell into the hands of Robert Cranston (W. Norrie, **Edinburgh Newspapers, Past and Present**, 1891).

2432 North Briton 1 (2 May 1855)–2218 (18 Oct. 1879). Edinburgh; s-w; w

    B   1d. Relevant at certain periods only. Printed and published by James Williamson; James Bell; John Wilson. Editor: George Bertram. In middle years discusses democratic reform, working-class social improvement. Forum for letters by working-men. Later a more general popular paper with less discussion. Coverage of Trade Unions, Reform Movement etc.

    E 682, (30 Nov. 1861); L(Col)† (16 June 1855), Jan. 1857–18 Oct. 1879

2433 North Bucks Atom [194-?]. Stoke Hammond; m

    B   2d. Labour Party. (Labour Party. **Your own Journal**, 1948.)

2434 North Camberwell Citizen 1 (Feb. 1933)–79 (Sept. 1939)

    B   Published by the 'London and Royal Arsenal Co-operative Societies' Political Purposes Committee.

    L(Col)

2435 North Derbyshire Labour Clarion [194-?]. Chesterfield; m

    B   2d. Labour Party. (Labour Party. **Your own Journal**, 1948.)

2436 North East Kent Chronicle 1 (Oct. 1931)–45 (Oct. 1935). Sittingbourne; m; ns 1 (March 1936)–13 (July 1939). London; q

    B   Free. First series published by A. E. Castle, an official of the local Labour Party. Printed by the National Co-operative Publishing Society. Second series printed and published by the Co-operative Press. Editor: R. J. Davie, Secretary of Faversham Divisional Labour Party (first series); H. L. Wise (second series). In both series is one of the 'Citizen series' of papers.

    L(Col)†

2437 North-East Bethnal Green Citizen 1 (June 1931)–99 (Sept. 1939); m

    B   Gratis. Published by the London Co-operative Society's Political Committee, except the last number, which was printed and published by the Co-operative Press. One of the 'Citizen' series.

    L(Col)†

2438 North Hackney Citizen 1 (May 1930)–12 (April 1931); m

    B   Published by the London Co-operative Society, Political Committee.

    L(Col)†

2439 North Hammersmith Citizen 1 (Jan. 1934)–67 (Sept. 1939); ns 1 (Oct. 1958)– ; m; irreg

    B   Gratis. First series published by the London Co-operative Society's Political Committee. 'Citizen series'. Second series issued by the North Hammersmith Labour Party, printed and published by the Co-operative Press.

    HsP 24, 43–4, 51, 53; L(Col)†

2440 North Hammersmith Sentinel 1 (Dec. 1927)—48 (Dec. 1931); ns
[194-?] —?; m; irreg?
    B   1d. Published and edited by H. Riley, then published by the
North Hammersmith Labour Party. Local and national news, comment,
notes, support for the Labour Party.
    HsP 1—48; ns 11 (Jan.), 13 (May), 17 (Nov.) 1947; L(Col)† 1—48

2441 North Hendon Citizen: Official Organ of the North Hendon
Constituency Labour Party. [1] (Oct. 1957)—   ; irreg
    B
    L(Col); LabP 36 (Dec. 1961), 37 (March 1962), 40 (Nov. 1962)

2442 North Ilford Citizen ns 1 (Jan. 1947)—80 (April 1954); m
    B   Gratis. Issued by the Political Committee of the London
Co-operative Society.
    L(Col) ns

2443 North Islington Citizen 1 (May 1930)—37 (May 1933); m
    B   Published by the London Co-operative Society, Political
Committee.
    L(Col)

2444 North Kensington Citizen 1 (Sept. 1931)—95 (Sept. 1939); m
    B   Gratis. Published by the London Co-operative Society's Political
Committee, then later in 1939 printed and published by the Co-operative
Press. 'Citizen series'.
    L(Col)

2445 North Lambeth Citizen 1 (Feb. 1934)—64 (Sept. 1939); m
    B   Published by the Royal Arsenal Co-operative Society's Political
Committee.
    L(Col)

2446 North Lancashire and Teetotal Letter-Bag. 1804—?
    B   Chartist. Editor: William Beesley.

2447 North London Citizen ns 1 (Jan. 1947)—60 (May 1952); m
    B   Gratis. Issued by the Political Committee of the London
Co-operative Society.
    L(Col) ns

North London Press see **North and East London Star**

North London Press and Star see **North and East London Star**

2448 North Mitcham Review I, 1 (Jan. 1938)—?; bi-m
    B   Labour Party?
    Mitcham PL I, 1—II, 1 (Jan. 1939)

2449 North of England's People's Paper: a Journal of Social, Industrial and Political Progress 1 (2 Dec. 1871)—5 (30 Dec. 1871). Middlesbrough; w

    B   1d. Published by H. G. Reid. Advocates the rights of Labour, free Trade Unionism. Special columns report wage and short-hours movements. In politics, democratic. For universal suffrage, and Ballot Act, then pending discussion in Parliament.

    L(Col)†

2450 North Paddington Citizen [1962?]—?

    B   Printed and published by the Co-operative Press.

    LabP† 5 (Dec. 1962).

2451 North Shields and District Co-operative Record 1885—? [North Shields?]; m

    A   North Shields Co-operative Society. 'In the year 1885, **The North Shields and District Co-operative Record**, a four-page leaflet, was distributed monthly, thus paving the way for the more ambitious **Wheatsheaf** . . .' (E. F. Morton, **An Adventure in Co-operation among the Working Classes of North Shields**, Pelaw-on-Tyne 1925, p. 77.)

2452 North Southwark Citizen 1 (June 1934)—63 (Sept. 1939); m

    B   Published by Royal Arsenal Co-operative Society's Political Committee.

    L(Col)

2453 North Staffordshire Labour News: the Official Organ of the Stoke-on-Trent Labour Party and North Staffs. Trades and Labour Council I, 1 (Jan. 1939)—? Stoke-on-Trent; m

    B   1d. Published by G. H. Meir for Stoke-on-Trent Labour Party.

    StP I, 1—II, 17 (May 1940) (w 4, 10), II, 27 (March 1941)

2454 North Star. Swindon

    B   Issued by the Swindon Communist Party. For railwaymen.

    Warwick U (MRC).

North Tottenham Citizen see **London Citizen. Tottenham Edition**

2455 North Wales Labour Searchlight 1 (Dec. 1931)—9 (Sept. 1932). Wrexham; m

    B

    L(Col)

2456 North West Democrat: the Voice of Labour. [19--?]—? [Belfast?]; m?

    B   1d. Published by the North West Labour Party of Northern Ireland. Edited by Samuel Pollock, Portrush. Duplicated by EGA, Duplicators and Printers, London.

    LabP† Sept. 1939

2457 Northampton Pioneer 1 (Aug. 1900)–? Northampton; m
    B   Organ of the local Social Democratic Federation. Published by
C. J. Scott. Succeeded **Northampton Socialist**
    NoP 1–104 (16 July 1910)

2458 Northampton Socialist 1 (17 July 1897)–[1899?1900].
Northampton
    B   Published by C. J. Scott. Succeeded by **Northampton Pioneer**
    NoP 1–18 (April 1899)

2459 Northampton Town Crier [194-?]. [Northampton] ; m
    B   Labour Party. Duplicated. (Labour Party. **Your own Journal**,
1948.)

2460 Northern Beacon 1 (27 March 1919)–22 (21 Aug. 1919). Barrow-in
Furness; w
    B   1d. Published for the Barrow Labour Press Committee by W. B.
Ward. A local Labour weekly for workers of the North West. Militant.
Reports on Barrow Labour Party and Trades Council. Later sub-titled:
'The Paper of the Workers, for the Workers, by the Workers'.
    Barrow PL; L(Col) 1, 22

2461 Northern Clerk: Journal of the Clerical and Administrative Workers'
Union, Northern Ireland Area [19--?] –? Belfast; bi-m
    A
    TUC† occ. nos between XLIV, 2 (June/July 1944) and XLVIII,
(Sept. 1948)

2462 Northern Democrat 1 (Aug. 1906)–68 (June 1912). Newcastle; m
    B   1d. To promote the Independent Labour Party and Socialism in
Durham and Northumberland. Serves the North-East Federation of the
ILP Editor: M. T. Simm. Contributor: F. J. Shaw. Inspired by the memory
of Joseph Cowen's **Northern Tribune**, fifty years earlier.
    L(Col)†

2463 Northern Democrat: the Organ of the No. 2 Divisional Council of
the ILP ns I, 1 (Sept. 1927)–II, 2 (Oct. 1928). Gateshead; m
    B   1d. Independent Labour Party. Editor: Fred Tait. Contributors:
Harry Crook, W. T. Symons. Covers Northumberland, Durham, Cleveland
and Cumberland. North East counterpart of the North West **Northern
Voice**. Articles, branch news.
    L(Col)†

2464 Northern Ireland Labour Bulletin I, 1 (July 1941)–I, 2 [1941] ; then
Labour Progress: I, 3 (Oct. 1941)–? Belfast; m
    B   1d.; 2d. Northern Ireland Labour Party. Nos. 1–2 reproduced
from typewriting. News, policy etc. Absorbed **The Torch**.
    B1U 1941–3*; LabP† I, 1–V, 3 (Oct. 1945*)

2465 Northern Liberator 1 (21 Oct. 1837)–165 (19 Dec. 1840). Newcastle-upon-Tyne; w

    B   4½d. Founded, printed and published by Robert Blakey, a local businessman of liberal opinions, in collaboration with Augustus Beaumont and Thomas Doubleday. First editor: Augustus H. Beaumont until his death on 28 Jan. 1838. Later printed by Arthur James Cobbett. 'Established expressly to advocate the cause of the working classes' (No. 15). For universal suffrage, vote by ballot and annual parliaments. In July 1838 became an organ of the Chartist Movement. No. 14 boasts circulation of 4,000. Absorbed **The Champion and Weekly Herald** and changed title to **Northern Liberator and Champion**.

    L(Col)†; MP; NwP; Warwick UL (microfilm)

Northern Liberator and Champion see **Northern Liberator**

2466 Northern Light 1 (15 March 1946)–? Aberdeen; irreg?

    B   2d. Published and printed by the Communist Party, North East Scotland Area. Reproduced from typewriting.

    AU, MSS Coll. 1, 2 (May 1946)

2467 Northern Lights; or, Political Whims, Oddities and Digressions of the Northern Liberator for AD 1838 [1839, 1840]. I, 1 (20 Jan. 1838)–III 49 (19 Dec. 1840). Newcastle-upon-Tyne; w

    B   Printed by John Bell, **Liberator** Office. Dedicatory preface by 'The Writers of **The Northern Liberator**'. Articles by them. Political satire, sketches, addresses, poetry. Democratic, attacking the Whigs.

    BP†; LE 1838, 1839

2468 Northern Lights [19--?] –?

    A   Union of Post Office Workers, Northern Post Office. (W. Dunlop, 'Local Journals'. **Belpost**, IV, 5 [May 1965].)

2469 Northern News [196-?] –   ; Newcastle

    A   National Association of Theatrical and Kine Employees. Duplicated

    TUC† 66 (June 1967)–*

2470 Northern News-Letter [c1950]

    A   Union of Post Office Workers. (**Mets Journal** [May 1950]).

2471 'Northern Projection' 1961?–   ; Manchester

    A   National and Local Government Officers' Association, Northern Project Group Branch. Reproduced from typewriting.

    L 1961–

2472 Northern Reformer's Monthly Magazine and Political Register for Northumberland, Durham, Yorkshire, Lancashire, Westmoreland and Cumberland. I, 1 (Jan. 1823)–I, 4 (April 1823). Newcastle-upon-Tyne; m

     B   6d. Printed and sold by J. Marshall. Radical reform magazine which supported Henry Hunt. For universal suffrage, annual parliaments, secret ballot.

     LE; LU†; NwP 1

2473 Northern Seamen's Friend I, 1 (June 1849)–I, 4 (Sept. 1849); m

     C   2d.; 3d. Published by Partridge and Oakey. Edited by Thomas George Bell, General Secretary of the Newcastle-on-Tyne Sailors Society 'to promote the Moral and Religious Improvement of Seamen, in the Port of Newcastle, on the Coast of Northumberland and on the East Coast of Scotland.' Chiefly to promote spiritual welfare and temperance, but also 'to plead on behalf of the sailor with his fellow-men and fellow countrymen to demand some return for all the advantage he brings to the country', its trade and its wealth

     L

2474 Northern Sectional Record [c1910]. Manchester; m

     A   Free. Co-operative Notes. (Mitchell, 1910.)

Northern Star. [1837]–1852 see **Northern Star, and Leeds General Advertiser**

2475 Northern Star 1 (April 1951)–37 (July 1954). Newcastle; m

     B   2d. Published by the **Northern Star** Editorial Board. Printed by the CWS Printing Works, Pelaw. Local Labour Party, trade union and co-operative organ for the North East area. News, opinion, correspondence.

     NwP†

2476 Northern Star: Journal of the Banbury (North Oxfordshire) Constituency Labour Party 1 (March 1967)–[1969?]. Kidlington (1); Banbury; irreg

     B   Reproduced from typewriting. Published by J. Candey (1–2), J. Hodgkins, Terry Stoton (6), Labour Party, Banbury (7). Local news and comment on national affairs.

     LabP† 1–7 (Spring 1969); Oxfordshire County Record Office 7 nos: March 1967–Christmas 1969

2477 Northern Star, and Leeds General Advertiser I, 1 [18 Nov. 1837]–VIII, 367 (23 Nov. 1844). Leeds; then **Northern Star, and National Trades' Journal**: VIII, 368 (30 Nov. 1844)–XV, 749 (13 March 1852); then **Star and National Trades' Journal**: XV, 750 (20 March 1852)–XV, 755 (1 May 1852); then b **Star of Freedom**: I, 1 (8 May 1852)–I, 14 (7 Aug. 1852); ns 1 (14 Aug. 1842)–16 (27 Nov. 1852). London; w

    B   4½d.; 5d.; 4½d. First printed in Leeds for the proprietor, Feargus O'Connor, by Joshua Hobson, then with No. 368 published in London by William Hewitt, printed by Dougal M'Gowan, edited by Joshua Hobson. Title changed 'so that that which has hitherto been only a class newspaper may be accepted by all parties . . .'. Later published by Pavey, printed by William Godfrey; printed and published by John Bezer; printed and published by George Julian Harney. Last issue entitled **The Star of Freedom: Journal of Political Progress, Trades' Record, and Co-operative Chronicle**. The leading newspaper of Chartism as a national movement, and organ of the National Charter Association.

    HO 73/52 3 (2 Dec. 1837), 5 (16 Dec. 1837); HP (14 June 1842); L a I, 8–b (originals and microfilm); LU a 209–313*, 532–687*; LdP (4 Jan. 1840)–Dec. 1850* (originals); (6 Jan. 1838)–(1 May 1852), (8 June–11 Nov., 1852) (microfilm); ONC Jan. 1838–Nov. 1852 (microfilm): Warwick UL 1838–52 (microfilm)

2478 Northern Teacher April 1854– . Belfast; q
    A   Journal of the Northern Committee of the Irish National Teachers' Organisation.
    D X, 4 (1972)–

2479 Northern Tribune I 1 (Jan. 1854)–II, 9 (3 March 1855). Newcastle-upon-Tyne; London; m; w (Jan. 1855–)
    B   5d., stamped. Publishers: W. J. Linton, Joseph Barlow, and Holyoake and Company, London. Proprietor and chief editor: Joseph Cowen; second editor: G. J. Harney. A local democratic newspaper, dedicated to the self-improvement of the people of Tyneside. Advocates a national agitation for Manhood Suffrage, unattended by other details, but also supports a national system of education, shorter working hours, public amenities etc. Support for European national liberation struggles eg, Poland, Hungary. The experience of 1848 proved that universal suffrage could not be gained without the aid of the enlightened middle class. Contributors: Thomas Cooper, Gerald Massey, Samuel Kydd, Frank Grant, W. J. Linton (engravings).

    Co-op. Coll. I; L; LE; LU I: MP I; NwA 1, 1–5, 11–12; NwP; Warwick UL (microfiche); Greenwood reprint and microfiche: microfiche distributed in Britain and Europe by The Harvester Press Ltd.

2480 Northern Typographical Union. Monthly Circular [183-?] –? m

A   'The General Secretary issued a "monthly Circular" giving details of strikes, the names of "unfair" houses, non-members, and "rats", information about tramps etc. There are references to this Circular in the minutes of the Manchester Society as early as 1834, but no copy appears to have survived. It was the forerunner of the **Typographical Societies' Monthly Circular,. . . .**' (A. E. Musson, **The Typographical Association**, Oxford University Press, 1954).

2481 Northern Vindicator 1 ([June?], 1839)–([3] [Aug. 1839?]). Aberdeen; m

A   Printed and published by the proprietor, John Legge, Chairman of the Aberdeen Working Men's Association (**True Scotsman**, 7 Sept. 1839). Chartist.

2482 Northern Voice I, 1 (1 May 1925)–I, 30 (20 Nov. 1925); then **Labour's Northern Voice**: I, 31 (27 Nov. 1925–(April 1964). Manchester; w

B   1d. etc. First published by the Independent Labour Party, then by the Workers' Northern Publishing Society. **See also Labour's Northern Voice. Stockport Edition.**

L(Col); LabP*; MP

Northern Weekly and Teddy Ashton's Journal see Teddy Ashton's Journal

2483 Northfield Labour Messenger 1 [1938?] –10 (Nov. 1940). Birmingham; q

B   Northfield Ward Labour Party.
BP† 5 (April 1939)–10

2484 Northfleet News Letter [194-?]. Northfleet, Kent m;

B   Labour Party. Duplicated. (Labour Party. **Your own Journal**, 1948)

2485 Northumberland Miners' Mutual Confident Association. **Monthly Circular** [19--?] –July 1935. Newcastle; m

A   Edited and written by W. Straker, General Secretary for 22 years. News of industry, personalities, wages, conditions. Some issues are biographical: portraits or obituaries, often with photograph.

NwU Aug. 1913–Feb. 1917; ONC† Oct. 1915–Jan. 1934*; TUC June 1915–July 1935*

2486 Northumberland NALGO Branch Magazine I, 1 (May 1965)–?; then **Northumbrian**: II, 1 (Feb. 1966)–   . Newcastle-upon-Tyne

A   National and Local Government Officers' Association. Reproduced from typewriting.

L I, 1–2 (Aug. 1965), II, 1–

Northumbrian see Northumberland NALGO Branch Magazine

2487 Norwich Co-operative Monthly Herald [1889]—525 (March 1933); then **Norwich Co-operative Herald and Wheatsheaf**: XXXVII, 442 (April 1933)—L, 600 (July 1946). Norwich; m

    A   Gratis. Norwich Co-operative Society. Preceded by **Norwich Co-operator.**

    L 298 (April 1914)—   ; NrP May 1896—Dec. 1926

2488 Norwich Co-operator [July 1876—1888?89]. Norwich; m?

    A   Four-page pamphlet brought out by the Educational Sub-Committee of Norwich Co-operative Society. Enlarged June 1887. 'Pioneer of the **Herald**' (W. Patrick, **The Rise and Progress of the Norwich Co-operative Society Ltd., from 1875—1925**, Norwich 1925, pp. 32—3.)

2489 Norwich Labor Elector. [Norwich?] ; m

    B   Independent Labour Party.

    ILP May 1906

2490 Norwood Labour News [194-?] ; m

    B   2d. Labour Party. Duplicated. (Labour Party. **Your own Journal**, 1948.)

2491 Norwood Pioneer 1 (May 1920)—8 (Dec. 1920); m

    B   1d. Published by the Norwood Labour Club. Left-wing Labour. Outlines policies for Labour in parliament, programme of full nationalisation. Editorial advocacy of Guild Socialism. Articles relating to the history of the Norwood Labour Party.

    L(Col)†

2492 Notes: the Organ of the Association of Head Postmasters. I, 1 [192-?]—? Doncaster (printed); bi-m

    A   'For private circulation only.' Printed by the Chronicle Company, Doncaster. Editors: H. C. A. White; T. Dalby

    ONC† XV, 1 (April 1938)—XVII, 2 (June 1940)

Notes for Speakers (Labour Party and Trades Union Congress) see Labour Party and Trades Union Congress. **Notes for Speakers**

2493 Notes to the People (May 1851)—(May 1852); w

    B   Publisher: J. Pavey. Printers: Jackson and Cooper. Owned and edited by Ernest Jones, it represented the extreme Left of Chartism; an organ of Labour and social democracy. Contributors: Marx and Engels, with whom Jones was in close contact. In two volumes.

    LE†; LU: MP: ONC† (reprint); Merlin reprint

2494 Nottingham Citizen 1 (Nov. 1960)—9 (May 1963); irreg

    B   Published by the Co-operative Press. Issued by Nottingham Labour Party.

    L(Col); LabP 2, 5, 6; NP 7, 9

2495 Nottingham Co-operative Herald 1 (April 1932)–112 (May 1953). Nottingham; London; m; irreg

B   First published by Douglas Morgan, Nottingham Co-operative Society, then printed and published by the Co-operative Press, later published by Roland Elson Green. Co-operation and politics. 'Citizen series'. Discontinued for a time in May 1942.

L(Col)†; NP occ. nos 1944–53

2496 Nottingham District Co-operative Record 1885–LX, 12 (Dec. 1948). Nottingham; m

A   Gratis. Issued by the District Conference Association, later by the Nottingham District Council. 'Supplied to nineteen societies belonging to the Nottingham District' (**International Directory of the Co-operative Press**, 1909). Latterly, localised edition of **Wheatsheaf**.

Co-op. Union 301 (Jan. 1914)–324 (Dec. 1915); L 283 (1912–48); O(JJ)† 100 (April 1897)

2497 Nottingham Forward 1 [1928]–? Nottingham; m?

B   Published by Nottingham Co-operative and Labour Party Joint Committee. Editor: Douglas Morgan.

NP† 8 (March 1929), 23 (Oct. 1930), 59 (April 1934)

Nottingham Labour Echo see **Labour Echo. 1896–?**

2498 Nottingham Labour Journal 1 [190-?]–? Nottingham; m

B   Gratis. Published by S. Higenbottam at the Independent Labour Party Rooms.

ILP Feb. 1911; NP† 45 (July 1912)

2499 Nottingham NALGO News 1965?–   . Nottingham

A   National and Local Government Officers' Association, Nottingham Branch. Reproduced from typewriting.

L 1965–

2500 Nottingham Tribune: a Weekly Journal Devoted to the Interests of the Worker by Hand or Brain. 1 (1 Oct. 1920)–? Nottingham; w

B   Publisher: Nottingham Tribune Company. 'Published . . . from the Labour Party Office . . .'

NU† 1–2 (8 Oct. 1920)

2501 Nottingham Voice I, 1 [Aug. 1964?]–? London; Manchester; m

B   4d. etc. Published by 'Voice of the Unions', then by the Workers' Northern Publishing Society. One of the group of 'Labour's Voice' newspapers.

NP† occ. nos 1964–7

2502 Nova 1960–   . Birkenhead

A   National and Local Government Officers' Association, Birkenhead Branch. Reproduced from typewriting

L

2503 Now: a Journal of Good Writing 1 (Easter 1940)–7 (1941); ns 1 (1943)–9 (July/Aug. 1947). Maidenhead (1); London; bi-m

    B   1s. 6d. (1943). Anarchist. No. 1 reproduced from typewriting. Edited by George Woodcock. Second series in collaboration with the Freedom Press, and published by them. Poetry, fiction, essays, reviews. Contributors: Woodcock, Julian Symons, Roy Fuller, Herbert Read, Victor Serge.

    E ii 1–7; L; ONC† ii 1

2504 Now: LCS News Magazine I, 1 (Dec. 1963)– ; irreg

    A   Published by the London Co-operative Public Relations Department. Newspaper for employees of London Co-operative Society. Superseded **Beehive**.

    L; WhP*†

2505 Nucise: the Official Organ of the National Union of Co-operative Insurance Society Employees I, 1 [1931?]–? Derby; m

    A   6d.

    TUC† II, 6 (Oct. 1932)–III, 7 (Nov. 1933)

2506 Nucleus 1 [1956]–? (Jan. 1971); m

    C   Workers' Educational Association, London District.

    TUC† 38 (Sept. 1959), 52 (Jan. 1961–Jan. 1971)

2507 Nursing Notes 1 (1887)–52 (Dec. 1907); then **Nursing Notes and Midwives Chronicle**: Jan. 1908–39; then **Midwives Chronicle and Nursing Notes**: 625 (Jan. 1940)–847 (July 1958); then **Midwives Chronicle**: Official Organ of the Royal College of Midwives: 848 (Aug. 1958)– ; m

    A   The Royal College of Midwives is now an official negotiating body. Nos. 1–6 were issued as supplements to **Woman**, 1887.

    L(Col); LMD 42–51*, 53– ; LNU 11–14, 16–24, 27– ; Royal College of Midwives Library

2508 Nut and Bolt Journal [187-?]

    A   Nut and Bolt Makers' Association, then National Association of Nut and Bolt Makers (1877). Union built up by Richard Jiggins. (J. Bellamy and J. Saville eds., **Dictionary of Labour Biography**, Vol. I, 1972, p. 207.)

2509 Obrero: (The Worker: Illustrated magazine for the Working Classes). Periodico Ilustrado para las Clases Trabajadoras 1 [1868]–17 [1875]

    C   In Spanish

    L(Col)†

2510 Observanda 1966?– . Winchester

    A   National and Local Government Officers' Association, Winchester and District Health Services Branch. Reproduced from typewriting.

    L 1966–

2511 Occasional Papers of the Working Men's Club and Institute Union, on the Formation, Progress, and Results of Working-Men's Clubs, Halls and Institutes 1 (March 1863)–24 (1876); irreg

    C   1d. Issued by the Council of the Working-Men's Club and Institute Union. Facts and figures, statement of objectives, addresses and reports. Prescribes orderly Trade Unionism, co-operation, arbitration machinery, self-improvement, education, temperance. Council members include Henry Solly, Rev. Robertson etc.

    L (w 8, 22)

2512 Odd Fellow 1 (5 Jan. 1839)–205 (10 Dec. 1842); w

    B   1d. Published and printed by H. Hetherington. Editors: J. Cooke, W. J. Linton. Consistent editorial support for the People's Charter. An organ of moral force Chartism emphasising the importance of total abstinence and national education. Supported Lovett's National Association 'New Move' in 1841 against the attacks of O'Connor.

    L(Col)†

2513 Oddfellows Recorder, and Friendly Societies Journal I, 1 (March 1892)–?; then **Friendly Societies' Recorder, for Oddfellows, Foresters, Gardeners, Shepherds, Druids etc.**: ?–199 (July 1899); then **Wage-Earners' Weekly and Friendly Societies' Recorder**: 200 (8 July 1899)–216 (Nov. 1899); then **Recorder**: 217 (4 Nov. 1899)–287 (9 March 1901). London; Manchester; m; w

    A   1d. Printed by the Co-operative Printing Society. Illustrates the activities of the Friendly Societies and Orders. Some trade union news.

    L(Col)† II, 5 (Jan. 1893)–? 287

2514 Odger's Monthly Pamphlets on Current Events 1 (1872)–2 (1872); m?

    B   2d. Pamphlets on individual subjects: 1 **Monarchy and republicanism**; 2 **Crimes of English monarchs.**

    L

2515 Odyssey 1 [1970?]– . Glasgow; bi-m

    A   Civil and Public Services Association, Scotland West Area, Post and Telegraph Group. Reproduced from typewriting. Illustrated.

    Warwick U (MRP)† 13 nos

2516 Off Duty: a Magazine of Recreation for the Service I, 1 (Jan. 1899)–II, 14 (May 1900); m

    C   1d. Printed for the proprietors by Smith's Printing and Publishing Agency. Edited by 'Oval'. As a contribution to the recreation of civil servants 'off duty'. Articles on a range of social activities, eg, football, cycling.

    L I, 1–11, II, 14

2517 Office News: Bulletin of Aberdeen Branch of the Clerical and Administrative Workers Union [194-?]−?

    A   Single sheet, reproduced from typewriting.

    TUC† 55 (Nov. 1951)

2518 Office Worker: Bulletin of the London and Home Counties Area Council 1 (Feb. 1954)−?; bi-m

    A   Clerical and Administrative Workers' Union.

    TUC† 1−7 (Dec. 1955)

2519 Official Gazette of the Trades' Unions 1 (7 June 1834)−4 (28 June 1834); w

    A   1½d. Publisher: William Strange. Printer: George Cowie. 'The organ of the Grand National Consolidated Trades Union. A working-class miscellany that strongly supports the co-operative and trades union movements, and advocates a general appropriation of profits.' Regular contributor: Rowland Detrosier (Wiener).

    HO 64/19 1, 3−4; ONC 1

2520 Official Peterborian 1 (July 1920)−2 (Dec. 1920). Peterborough; s-a

    A   1d. Issued to members free of charge. Union of Post Office Workers, Peterborough and District Branch. Published by Peterborough Branch of the Postmen's Federation. Printed by the Worker Newspaper Society, Huddersfield. Brief editorial and submission of half-yearly report.

    L

Old Age Pensioner see **Pensioner**

2521 Old Oak Star: the Paper of the Old Oak Railwaymen of All Grades; Organ of the Communist Cell 1 [1930?]−?

    A   Reproduced from typewriting.

    Warwick U (MRP)† 17 (Jan. 1932)

2522 Oldbury and Halesowen Citizen 1 (Nov. 1963)−4 (June 1964). Warley, Worcestershire

    B   Issued by the Oldbury and Halesowen Labour Party.

    L(Col); LabP 4

2523 Oldham Co-operative Record I, 1 (May 1894)−XV, 5 (May 1920). Oldham; m

    A   Gratis. Oldham Industrial Co-operative Society. Superseded by **Wheatsheaf**.

    Co-op. Union I, 1−II, 12 (April 1896); L XI, 9 (Sept. 1912)− ; the Society

2524 Oldham Industrial Co-operative Citizen 1 (May 1936)−6 (Aug. 1937)

    B   Issued by Oldham Industrial Co-operative Society.

    L(Col)

2525 Oldham Labour Gazette [193-?]. Oldham; m

    B   Labour Party. (Labour and Socialist International. **The Socialist Press**, 1933.)

2526 Oldham NALGO News I, (1954)– . Oldham

    A   National and Local Government Officers' Association, Oldham Branch.

    L

2527 Oldham Operative 1 (14 Nov. 1884)–12 (30 Jan. 1885). Oldham; w

    C   1d. Published and conducted by Joseph Burgess. Intended as 'the Working Class Organ for Oldham and District'. A miscellany, uncommitted to any political party, 'Whig, Tory or Radical'. Directed at working-class readership. Main emphasis on local politics; supports right of working-men to political representation nationally and locally. In form of snippets, gossip etc.

    L(Col)†; Oldham PL

2528 Oldham Operative Cotton Spinners' etc. Provincial Association. Monthly Report [18--?]–? Oldham; m

    A   Branch financial accounts; extensive notes of dispute cases between employees and managers. All confidential to members.

    Bishopsgate Institute June 1889–Feb. 1920; L ns 274 (Nov. 1894)–287 (Dec. 1895)

2529 Oldham Standard 1 (6 Aug. 1859)–5618 (19 July 1947). Oldham; w

    B   One-time editor: J. R. Stephens. Contributor: William Marcroft, co-operator. It became a conventional Tory paper after the first five or six years.

    L(Col) (w 1911); (microfilm 1897)

2530 Oldham Voice [194-?]. Oldham; m

    B   Labour Party. Published by **Voice**. (Labour Party. **Your own Journal**, 1948.)

2531 Oldham Worker, and District Advertiser 1 (20 Aug. 1904)–2 (10 Sept. 1904). Oldham; w

    B Gratis. Printed and published by the proprietors, G. H. Lees and Company. Circulating in Oldham, Middleton, Chadderton, Shaw, Royton, Lees and Saddleworth, in working-class homes. Primarily an advertising sheet. Advocated direct Labour Representation in Parliament.

    L(Col)†

2532 On the Line: the Journal of the United Kingdom Railway Temperance Union [188-?]–(July–Sept. 1963); m

    C   ½d. etc. Published at the Head Office of the Union. Reports branch meetings; combines religious instruction with temperance and self-help, among railwaymen. Serial story, poems, correspondence; 'in the interest of traffic safety'.

    L(Col)† XIV, 166 (Jan. 1897)–1917, 1920–1, 1923–7, 1931–63

2533 On the MAP: News Letter 1 [Aug? 1941]–[4] (Dec. 1941); m

    A   Civil Service Clerical Association, Ministry of Aircraft
Production, London Branch. Reproduced from typewriting. To make good
the deficiency of local news in **Contact**, the monthly organ of the Air
Ministry and MAP and to keep members in communication with the
Committee, and inform them of wage increases and bonuses etc. Editor:
Mrs W. McGuire.

    L

2534 On-Call June 1967–   ; bi-m; m

    A   Junior Hospital Doctors' Association.
The Association

2535 One and All [c1969]. [Camborne]; m

    B   6d. 'Sells well in factory and mine, town and village, because it
tells things more like they are than the local unfree press. It is a scurrilous
and anarchist magazine for Cornwall peoples.' (**Resurgence**, II, 8/9,
July–Oct. 1969).

2536 One Pennyworth of Pig's Meat, or Lessons for the Swinish Multitude
I (1793)–III (1795); w

    B   1d. Published and written by Thomas Spence. Republican and
democratic. Champion of the labouring classes. Second and third editions
entitled **Pig's Meat** . . .

    L (I missing); LU II–III; Second edition DrU; L; LU; O; Third
edition O I, 1–24; WCML† I–II

2537 Onward [c1922]; m

    B   League of Young Socialists.
ILP Oct. 1922.

2538 Open Door: Organ of the Open Door International for the Economic
Emancipation of the Woman Worker I, 1 (Sept. 1929)–24 (Nov. 1939); q;
irreg

    B   4d.; 1d. Printed for the Open Door International by the Rydel
Press, Keightley. The organisation was founded on 16 June 1929 to
campaign for equal rights and equal pay for women workers. The President
was Chrystal Macmillan, a former suffragette. Journal includes reports
from all countries.

    L

2539 Open Forum I, 1 (26 Aug. 1929)–I, 14 (Feb. 1931); m

    A   Published by the Superannuation Rights Association. Agitates
on the question of the right of public servants to proper superannuation
on retirement. Intended to provide publicity for these claims, 'publicity
which they have failed to obtain from the majority of the Civil Service
Staff journals'. Non-political, with no party ties. Opposed by the Treasury.

    L

2540 Operative: Established by the Working Classes for the Defence of the Rights of Labour I, 1 (4 Nov. 1838)–II, 35 (30 June 1839); w

B   6d.; 4d. Publisher: Henry George Warren. Printer: John Gathercole. Editor: Bronterre O'Brien. A militant Chartist and anti-capitalist newspaper managed by a committee of working-men. Reports of radical and Chartist public meetings and trade-union struggles in the metropolis and the provinces. Strategy: 'Peaceably if we may, forcibly if we must'. Portraits of delegates to the Chartist National Convention, contributed by Dr John Taylor. One of the best of the Chartist newspapers. Absorbed by **London Dispatch**.

L(Col)†; Warwick UL (microfilm)

2541 Operative I, 1 (4 Jan. 1851)–80 (10 July 1852); w

B   1½d.; 1d. Publisher: G. Berger (1–29); George Vickers. Printer J. Stanton. Founded to advance the rights of Labour. 'The special consideration which has prompted the commencement of the **Operative** is the amalgamation into one Association of the various trades societies of the iron-workers', ie Amalgamated Society of Engineers, Machinists, Millwrights, Smiths, and Pattern Makers. Promotes the new engineering union, but is an advocate of Trade Unionism in general. Ambitiously hopes to become newspaper organ of a 'central committee' of all Labour in the Empire. Gives brief sketch of origins and formation of ASE, details of new membership, chronicles disputes. Hopes to attract the whole family as readers, including tales, sketches, poetry etc.

L; LU 3–5, 13

2542 Operative: Devoted to the Classes Connected with the Constructive and Decorative Arts I, 1 (July 1862). Dublin

B   1d. Printed by Peter Roe. Proprietor: c/o T. J. Smythe. Intended as an 'independent periodical for the operatives of Ireland. Issued as an experiment, bidding for mass support. For the elevation of working men, practical and overall improvement. Intended to cover Trade Societies, eg, a report of the operative house-painters'.

L(Col)†

2543 Operative Bricklayers' Society. **Quarterly Report** 1862–1920; q
A
Warwick U (MRC)

2544 Operative Bricklayers' Society's Trade Circular and General Reporter I, 1 (1 Sept. 1861)–1920; m

A   1d. Conducted by George Howell, assisted by C. Shearman and H. Noble, then Nos. 2–4 by Howell, Shearman, Noble and Coulson, 5–11 under management of the Council and General Secretary, E. Coulson. Mottos: 'Union is Strength'; 'Knowledge is Power'. Discusses principles and practice of trades unions, reports meetings, state of trade, includes information to branches, and a section, 'The Workman's Library', with reviews of books on Labour questions and hints for reading. Sometimes **Monthly Circular**.

L 1–11 (1862); LU 1; 371 (1892); Warwick U (MRC) 1947–62

2545 Operative Builder I, 1 (Dec. 1921)–(1932); ns 1947–XV, 6 (Nov./Dec. 1962); q; bi-m

    A   3d. etc. National Federation of Construction Unions; National Federation of Building Trades Operatives. Replaced by **Builders' Standard**.

    L (not traced in cat.); ONC† ns II, 6 (Nov./Dec. 1949)–XV, 6; TUC

2546 Operative Dyers Magazine: Official Organ of the Amalgamated Society of Dyers, Bleachers, Finishers and Kindred Trades. I [1923?] –XIV (May 1936). Bradford; m

    A

    TUC† VII, 4 (April 1929)–XIV, (May 1936)

2547 Operative Masons' and Granitecutters' Journal I, 1 (May 1901)–(Aug. 1917?). Aberdeen; m

    A   1d. Organ of the United Operative Masons' and Granitecutters' Union. Reports from branches in Aberdeen and area, building and monumental workers' trade reports, correspondence, occasional features, news from granitecutters' union in America. Sometimes 'Granite-Workers' instead of 'Granitecutters' in title.

    AP† 1903–9; Au 1901–10; E I–VIII (1909); LE† 1911–Aug. 1917*; L., Vols. 1–10, 1911–20

2548 Operative Tailors' National Appeal 1866–?

    A   Scottish Amalgamated Society. Editor: John Williamson. Preceded **The Tailor**, 1866–   . (M. Stewart and L. Hunter, **The needle is threaded**, 1964.)

2549 Operatives Free Press: a Monthly Journal of Labour, Politics and Education, Conducted by Working Men 1 (Sept. 1849)–4 (Dec. 1849); ns (Jan. 1850)–? Cambridge; London; Newcastle-on-Tyne; m

    C   1d. Published in Cambridge by J. Mouel (1–4), then by J. Nichols, in London by J. Watson, in Newcastle by J. Barlow. Editorial in ns 1 states 'Having enlarged and improved . . . the mechanical part of the O.F.P. . . . we desire to enlarge our sphere of action and extend our circulation beyond the localities of Cambridge and London . . . '.

    Cambridge PL 1–4, ns 1

2550 Opportunity: the Organ of the Federation of Women Civil Servants. I, 1 (Jan. 1921)–XX, 7 (15 July 1940); m

    A   2d. Published by the Federation. Later the organ of the National Association of Women Civil Servants. Association news and features on wages and conditions negotiations under the Whitley Council. Preceded by **Association Notes**.

    L(Col)†; OW

2551 Optimist: a Review Dealing with Practical Theology, Literature, and Social Questions in a Christian Spirit I, 1 (Jan. 1906)—III, 4 (Oct. 1908); then **Church Socialist Quarterly, or Optimist**: IV, 1 (Jan. 1909)—VI, 2 (April 1911); then **Optimist: a Review Dealing with Practical Theology, Literature, and Social Questions**: VI, 3 (Oct. 1911)—XL, 4 (Feb. 1917); q

    B   6d. Printed by the New Age Press (1909); Frank Palmer (1910—12); Robert Scott (1913—14); A. Brown and Sons (1915—17). Taken over by the Church Socialist League in 1909. Editor: Rev. Samuel Proudfoot. Contributors: H. M. Hyndman, Conrad Noel, Egerton Swan. Retained radical flavour up to 1912, when reverts to **The Optimist**, but continued to advocate Socialism. Contributors: Stuart Headlam, Philip Snowden. The Church Socialist League distinguished between 'Church Socialism' and 'Christian Socialism' (P. d'A. Jones, **The Christian Socialist Revival, 1877—1914**, Princeton 1968).

    C; L; LdU (w I, 2); O; O(JJ) 1

2552 Oracle: the Post Office Magazine ns I, 1 (July 1908)—I, 6 (Dec. 1908). Cardiff; m

    A   1d. Printed and published by Evans and Williams, Ltd. for the proprietors.

    L

2553 Oracle of Reason; or, Philosophy Vindicated I, 1 (6 Nov. 1841]—II, 103 (2 Dec. 1843). Bristol (1—7); London; w

    B   1d. Printed and published in Bristol by Field, Southwell and Company, later printed and published by Thomas Paterson; William Chilton. Editors: Charles Southwell (1—7); G. J. Holyoake (8—36); Thomas Paterson (37—85); William Chilton (86—103). 'The only exclusively atheistical print that has appeared in any age or country' (Preface to Vol. I). Articles and controversy on religion, atheism, utopian Socialism etc. and the fight for the right of free expression. Correspondence pages an important feature.

    L; LU (w I, 2); MP (w I, 2); NwA; ONC

Orbiston Register see **Register for the First Society of Adherents to Divine Revelation at Orbiston**

Orpington Labour News see **Your Business**

2554 Oscar [196-? 1970?71]. Southampton

    A   **Civil and Public Services Association, Ordnance Survey Branch,** Southampton.

    Warwick U(MRC)† Dec. 1971

2555 Other Paper: 'A Socialist News Service' 1 (10 Oct. 1969)—11 (13 March 1970). Leeds; fortn

    B   Illustrated, lively production, concentrating on local community issues in Leeds.

    LdP†

2556 Our Circle: a Magazine for Young People I, 1 (Oct. 1907)–(July 1960). Manchester; m

    A   1d. etc. Printed and published by the Co-operative Newspaper Society, then by the Co-operative Press. For young Co-operators. In early issues put forward the ideal of social service and formed the Social Service League for children. Latterly contents were for entertainment only. Later title: **Our Circle and Pathfinders' Monthly** (from Sept. 1956).

    L

Our Circle and Pathfinders' Monthly see **Our Circle**

2557 Our Corner I, 1 (Jan. 1883)–XII, 12 (Dec. 1888); m

    B   6d. London Freethought Company. Editor: Annie Besant. She declares herself a socialist in 1885. Latterly, chief contributors were prominent Fabians, including Wallas, Bland, Carpenter etc.

    L; LE*; O

2558 Our Fight; [Nuesto Combate] Journal of the XVth International Brigade [193-?]–? Published in Spain; m?

    B   Edited and published by and for the soldiers of the XVth International Brigade under the direction of the Brigade Commissariat. In Spanish and English.

    WCML† 35 (Dec. 1937/Jan. 1938)

2559 Our History 1 (Spring 1956)– ; q

    B   1s. etc. Published by the Historians' Group of the Communist Party of Great Britain. Nos 1–51 reproduced from typewriting.

    E 11– ; L; O 11–

2560 Our Land I, 1 (Feb. 1908)–IV, 49 (Feb. 1912); m

    C   Published by Cassell. Edited by George Radford. Advocates agricultural co-operation, rural collectivism with local government supervision and State aid. 'Land for the people', and decent standards, eg, in housing, for labourers and smallholders. Publicises the work of the Agricultural Organisation Society, though it is not the organ of the Society, also work of the Land Club Movement. Illustrated.

    L; LE†

2561 Our Magazine: Subjects for Thought and Discussion in Social and Political Clubs 1 (Jan. 1891)–12 (Dec. 1891); m

    C   2d. Published by Co-operative Printing Society (1–4); Simpkin, Marshall, Hamilton, Kent and Company. Editor: Henry Solly. A journal edited by one of the most ardent promoters of Working Men's Clubs. From an advanced Liberal, and deeply individualist viewpoint, it is addressed to the respectable 'skilled' working-man of the 'New Model' craft union type. Some discussion of social and political questions relating to the 'improvement' of the working man.

    L; LE; LU 1; O

2562 Our Opinion [19--?] –? [Miles Platting?] ; m?
    B   Miles Platting Labour Party.
    ILP (Jan. 1913), (Feb. 1919)

2563 Our Opinion [194--?]. Southend-on-Sea
    B   2d. Labour Party. Duplicated. (Labour Party. **Your own Journal**, 1948.)

Our Record see **Textile Record**

2564 Our Time I, 1 (Feb. 1941)–VIII, 7 (July/Aug. 1949); m
    B   6d. Publishers: Newport Publications; Our Time Publications.
Editors included: Edgell Rickword, Frank Jellinek, Randall Swingler,
Beatrice Lehmann, John Banting, Birkin Haward, Ben Frankel, Ted Willis.
Incorporates **Poetry and the People.** First issue states 'The people who
write here want to restore these essentials [cultural pursuits] to human
living. To show that the power and the plan exists, is the purpose of the
magazine'. For the production and control of 'culture', anti-status quo,
anti-Establishment. Articles on theatre, art, music, literature, films,
architecture etc.
    C; E I–III; L; MML† (w VIII, 7)

2565 Our Youth: Discussion Magazine of the Young Communist League 1
(April 1938)– ?; then **Club News**: [194-?] –?; m
    B   2d. Deals with political education, analysis of perspectives and
practice, how to build a mass YCL, how to fight for the Youth Charter,
the basic rights of youth to jobs, good living standards, entertainments,
etc., to improve and expand **Challenge**.
    MML 1–II, 8 (Sept. 1939), (March 1940); WCML† 2, 8; (Jan. 1947)

2566 Ourselves: CWS Employees Magazine [19–?] –? ns I, 1 (Dec.
1946)–(1967?). London; Manchester; m
    A   1d.; 2d. etc. Co-operative Wholesale Society. Several local
editions published.
    Co-op. Union ns II, 1 (Jan. 1948)–XXI, 2 (April 1967); Lns; O III,
6 (March 1949)–XXI, 3 (1967)

2567 Out of Bounds, Against Reaction in the Public Schools I, 1
(March-April 1934)–I, 4 (June 1935); irreg
    B   1s. 'The Editors of **Out of Bounds** make no attempt to disclaim
their political convictions. They believe that modern society, based on
class-exploitation, is vicious and unstable . . . ' (No. 1.) Written for the
Public Schools by schoolboys. Most of the contributors in No. 1 are from
Wellington College, and include Esmond Romilly, Giles Romilly.
Anti-Fascism, anti-OTC. Includes news of socialist feeling in schools and of
anti-socialism among the authorities. News, articles, fiction, reviews,
advertisements for Marxist literature.
    L; O(JJ)† I, 1

2568 Out of the Hat: the Annual Miscellany Published by the Luton
Branch of NALGO 1963?—   . Luton; a
    A   National and Local Government Officers' Association.
Reproduced from typewriting.
    L 1963—

2569 Out of Work 1 (19 March 1921)—60 (8 June 1923); then **New
Charter**: 1 (22 June 1923)—4 (3 Aug. 1923); fortn
    B   1d. Published by the London District Council of Unemployed,
then by the National Administrative Council of Unemployed. Organiser
and editor: Wal Hannington. For unemployed workers. Publicises the
Workers' Committee Movement. Under the direction of the Communist
Party.
    CPGBI—53; L(Col)†; ONC† 19

2570 Out on Strike 1872—?; then **Craftsman**.?—Feb. 1873. Edinburgh; w
    A   1d. Printed for the proprietors, the Edinburgh Typographical
Society (No. 5). 'In the end of the year 1872, a strike occurred among the
printers of Edinburgh, and lasted about three months. When the strike
commenced, the men brought out weekly a small paper, which at first
took the title of **Out on Strike**, but was subsequently altered to the more
comprehensive one of the **Craftsman**. While professing to take up the cry
of no political party, its principles were thoroughly democratic, and it
aimed at giving news affecting all trades in Scotland, England, Ireland and
the Principality. With the resumption of work by the strikers, in Feb.
1873, the career of the **Craftsman** came to an end.' (W. Norrie, **Edinburgh
Newspapers, Past and Present**, Earlston, 1891).
    E 5 (4 Jan. 1873)

2571 Outlook: the Organ of the Leeds Postmen's Federation. 1 (Nov.
1915)—51 (Dec. 1920). Leeds; m
    A   Gratis. Published by the Leeds Branch of the Postmen's
Federation. Printed by the Leeds Labour Publishing Society. Ardent
Labour Party supporter. Discussion on Whitleyism, and wages and
conditions of all grades. In 1920 becomes the organ of the Union of Post
Office Workers, Leeds No. 1 Branch.
    L(Col)† 2—51 (w 3); LdP

2572 Outlook: the Organ of the Rochdale Teachers' Association. 1 (May
1938)—57 (Nov. 1950). Rochdale; bi-m
    A   Reports and features on union activities and members' interests.
    L

2573 Outlook: Journal of the National Youth Committee of the Civil
Service Clerical Association 1 [1942?]—114 (June 1952); m
    A   Published by the Educational Committee of the Association.
Provides educational facilities and promotes principles of collective action
and Trade Unionism, and the role of young trade-union members in the
Association. Correspondence. Later sub-title: 'Journal of the Youth
Organization of the Civil Service Clerical Association'.
    L 94 (Aug./Sept. 1949)—   (w 95, 98, 101—2)

2574 Outlook 1 (Lent 1948)–? q
   B   National Union of Labour Students.
   TUC 1–4 (Autumn 1949)

2575 Outlook: the Magazine of the Heywood Labour Party League of
Youth I, 1 (Feb. 1951)–I, 3 (April 1951). Heywood; m
   B   Published for the Heywood Labour Party League of Youth by
CPS, Ltd., Manchester. Edited by Jack Connell.
   J. Smethurst

2576 Outpost 1923–? [Belfast?]
   A   Union of Post Office Workers, Northern Ireland District
Council. Occasional breaks in publication. (W. Dunlop, 'Local journals'.
Belpost, IV, 5 [May 1965].)
   D Feb. 1932

2577 Outpost: the Official Organ of the Northern Ireland District Council,
Union of Post Office Workers [1930?]–? Belfast; m
   A
   L XXXIII, 6 (Sept. 1962)–XXXVII, 6 (June/July 1966); TUC
1924–62*

2578 Oxford Citizen Feb. 1938–? Oxford
   A   Issued by the Oxford Co-operative and Industrial Society.
   L(Col) Feb. 1938

2579 Oxford Citizen: Organ of the Oxford City Labour Party 1 (Oct.
1947)–? Oxford; m
   B   2d. 'The aim of **The Citizen** is to provide a means by which
members of our City in general, and of the Labour Movement in
particular, can be informed of matters, both national and local, which are
important to them.' Sometimes subtitled: 'Journal of the Oxford City
Labour Party'.
   ONC† 1–26 (Nov. 1949) (w 16, 24, 25)

2580 Oxford City Labour Party. **Gazette** [pre-1939–45 war]. Oxford
   B   Preceded the **Oxford Citizen** and ceased when war prevented
publication. (**Oxford Citizen**, No. 1.)

Oxford Clarion see **Clarion. 1947–[1950?]**

2581 Oxford Co-operative Citizen 1 (Feb. 1937)–?
   B
   L(Col) 1

2582 Oxford Co-operative Quarterly Circular (1 May 1889)–[1890?].
Oxford; q
   A   Oxford Co-operative and Industrial Society. Editor: Walter
Neale. (Oxford Co-operative and Industrial Society.**A Historical Sketch
from 1872–1909**, Manchester 1909, p. 51.)

2583 Oxford Forward I, 1 (1935); then **Forward**: I, 2 (March 1935); then **University Forward**: I, 3 (Summer 1935)–[1940?]; [ns], I, 1 (Oct. 1940)–IX, 5 (May 1944); then **Student Forward**: X, 1 (Oct. 1944)–XIII, 1 (Winter 1947). Oxford; Cambridge; London

    B   University Labour Federation; Student Labour Federation. Latterly, contributions from leading Communist Party academics.

    C VII– ; E VII (1941)–XIII, 1; L I, 2–*; MML† occ. nos 1940–4; O VII–XIII; TUC occ. nos 1935–7

2584 Oxford Forward: the University Progressive Weekly ns 1 (23 April 1938)–? ns 1 (14 Jan. 1939)–? Oxford; w

    B   3d. etc. 23 April 1938 states that it is 'for the first time in a new format as a regular weekly paper'; 'a progressive and representative undergraduate paper'. 'An OU Labour Club publication' appears on several numbers. Articles, notes, book reviews, film and theatre reviews, stories, poems, correspondence. Articles on politics and current affairs. See also **Oxford University Elector**.

    O 1–14 (2 June 1939); TUC† (23 April 1938)–May 1938

2585 Oxford Leader: Labour and Socialist News. 1 [May 1909?]–? Oxford; m

    B   ½d. Newspaper with News, announcements, short articles on conditions of work etc. Printed and published for the proprietors by W. T. Brayne at the Oxonian Press. Editor: Theodore Chaundy, member of the Independent Labour Party and some time Treasurer of the Oxford Fabian Society, a mathematical student at Christ Church. 'A short-lived Labour paper.' (M. P. Ashley and C. T. Saunders, **Red Oxford**, Oxford 1933, p. 14.)

    O (2 [June], 3 [July] 1909)

2586 Oxford Left: Official Journal of the University Socialist Club. I, 1 [1949?1950]–I, 6 [1950?1951]; ns 1 (Michaelmas Term 1951)–? Oxford; termly?

    B   Ns 1 was also Vol. I, No. 7 of the first series. Format, size, printing etc. vary enormously from year to year, some reproduced from typewriting, some printed. Editors include: Alan Brownjohn, Asher Cashdan, Stanley Mitchell, Ralph Samuel, Phyllis Kline, Gabriel Pearson. Articles of all kinds, reviews, notes, poetry.

    O Michaelmas Term 1951, Hilary Term 1952, Trinity Term 1953, Trinity 1954, Michaelmas 1954, Hilary 1954, I, 1 (Michaelmas Term 1956)

2587 Oxford Left: the Socialist Group [of the Oxford University Labour Club] Magazine [1, Oct. 1965]–? Oxford; m; during term

    B   Reproduced from typescript. Editors: John Chartres; George Myers; Stan Gray. Articles on a variety of topics. Reflects the internal struggles within the Labour Club and the Left generally in the University.

    L; LE; O 1–5 (Trinity 1966)

2588 Oxford Left [1967?1968] –? Oxford; irreg

B   At first the organ of the ORSS [Oxford Revolutionary Socialist Students], then of 'the Revolutionary Left in Oxford'. Reproduced from typewriting. Numbering varies.

O 4 occ. nos 1968–9

2589 Oxford Left: Voice of the Oxford City Labour Party Young Socialists [1970?] –   . Oxford

B   2d. Printed and published by the Oxford City Labour Party Young Socialists. Reproduced from typewriting.

O Winter 1970

Oxford Reformer see **Oxford Socialist**

2590 Oxford Socialist 1 (Michaelmas Term 1908)–3 (Summer Term, 1909); then **Oxford Reformer**: Nov. 1909–Nov. 1910. Oxford; termly

B   3d. 'Earliest undergraduate socialist magazine'. 'Backed by **The Iris**, whose editor was a friendly Fabian, the paper acquired some notoriety.' '. . . contained a number of serious as well as amusing articles on Socialism, together with a certain amount of bad poetry: one of the most interesting articles was by Tawney on "Lord Curzon's message to socialists" showing how university reform was tending and might tend towards the democratisation of education.' (M. P. Ashley and C. T. Saunders, **Red Oxford**, Oxford 1933.) Editors: F. K. Griffith, G. D. H. Cole. In the course of a year the **Oxford Reformer** contained an article by Sidney Webb on the Poor Law, two epigrams by L. B. Namier, and a symposium on the Osborne Judgement.

ONC† 1–3

2591 Oxford Syndicalist June 1912–? Oxford

B   1d. Probably only one number published. Published by the Oxford Fabians 'partly by way of a "rag" ' according to G. D. H. Cole. Articles entirely anonymous; the first one laid emphasis on the revolutionary character of Syndicalism, another urged co-operation between State and Unions. (M. P. Ashley and C. T. Saunders, **Red Oxford**, Oxford 1933, p. 19.)

2592 Oxford University Elector [1938?] –? Oxford; s-a

B   3s. per year; free to members. **Oxford Forward**, ns No. 7 (25 Feb. 1939) contains as a supplement **Oxford University Elector**, No. 3 (Feb. 1939). A note says 'This broadsheet is the publication of the Oxford University Labour Party, and is published at least twice a year – in February and September.'

O 3

2593 Oxford Worker [193-?] Oxford; m

B   Labour Party. (Labour and Socialist International. **The Socialist Press**, 1933.)

2594 Oxford Worker 1 (May Day, [1969])– . Oxford; irreg
    B   Single sheet reproduced from typewriting. Numbered not dated.
'Maoist'. No further information given.
    O 1–7

2595 Oxted Searchlight 1 (March 1897)–2 (April 1897); then **Village
Search Light**: 3 (May 1897)–18 (Aug. 1898); ns 1 (April 1901)–5 (Aug.
1901); m
    B   ½d.; 1d. Printed and published by W. B. Maclean, London.
Issued by F. E. Green, Oxted, Surrey – 'to induce folks to take more
interest in their local affairs'. Defends the right of the rural population and
rural poor (agricultural labourers) to decent cottages and adequate living
standards, and a check upon landlord tyranny etc. Urges the fight against
the iniquities of the Poor Law; and the democratisation of District and
County Councils.
    L(Col)†

2596 Oyez : Local Branch Magazine 1960?– . Mansfield
    A   National and Local Government Officers' Association,
Mansfield and District Branch. Reproduced from typewriting.
    L 1960–

2597 PEN News 1963?– . Plymouth
    A   National and Local Government Officers' Association,
Plymouth Electricity Branch. Executive Committee. Reproduced from
typewriting.
    L 1963–

PIMCO Co-operative Citizen see **Portsmouth Co-operative Citizen**

PO Controlling Officers' Journal see **Controlling Officers' Journal**

POEU Journal see **Journal: the Official Organ of the Post Office
Engineering Union,** [1915?]–1957

PROfile see **PROgress**

2598 PROgress: a Bulletin of Public Relations. I, 1 (Summer 1948)–?
then **PROfile** [195-?]–? q;
    A   1s. (1955). A public relations bulletin published by the National
Association of Local Government Officers, 'to encourage the revival of
branch activity'. (A. Spoor, **'White-collar union: sixty years of Nalgo'**
London 1967, pp. 440, 447).
    L 1–11, Winter 1952/53; LE

2599 P and TO [19--?] –?; m
    A   2d. National Association of Postal and Telegraph Officers.
(Mitchell, 1955.)

2600 PTU: Journal of the Plumbing Trades Union I, 1 (June 1947)—VII, 8 (Dec. 1968); q

A   2d. etc. Ceased when the union amalgamated with the Electrical Trades Union.

L (w I, 1); NU† (w I, 1); TUC; the Union

2601 Padd Notes 1 (Aug.—Oct. 1957)—?

A   Union of Post Office Workers, Paddington No. 1 Branch. (W. Dunlop, 'Local journals'. **Belpost**, IV, 5 [May 1965].)

TUC 1

Paddington Canal Boatman's Magazine see **Canal Boatman's Magazine**

2602 Paddington Echo [193-?] ; m

B   Labour Party. (Labour and Socialist International. **The Socialist Press**, 1933.)

2603 Paddington Echo. March 1948—June 1949; m

B   3d. (No. 1); 2d. Published by the Paddington Echo Management Board. A local Labour Party publication, supported by local Labour Parties and affiliated organisations. Newspaper format, local news, Labour policy. Unnumbered.

L(Col)† (w Feb. 1949)

2604 Paddington Green: Official Journal of the Paddington Branch of NALGO. 1962?—

A   National and Local Government Officers' Association. Reproduced from typewriting.

L 1962—

2605 Paddington Socialist Pioneer [c1932] ; m

B   Independent Labour Party.

ILP April 1932

2606 Paddington Star: the Paper of the Paddington and Old Oak Common Railwaymen of All Grades. [1926?]—?; fortn

A   Reproduced from typewriting. Produced by the 'Communist Group of Railwaymen'. Agitational, for Communist Party and Minority Movement. No. 20: 'the Paper of the Paddington, Westbourne Park and Old Oak Common Railwaymen of All Grades. The forerunner of the Great Western Star'.

O(JJ)† 5 (June 1926), 6, 8, 20 (Jan. 1927)

2607 Padiham Advertiser 1884– . Padiham; w

B   Gratis; ½d. etc. Supports Labour Movement. In 1919 consists mainly of advertisements, but an occasional column of notes indicates its political attitude eg, 4 Feb. 1919 advocates trade unions' place in politics; 1 July 1919 supports rank and file in textile union in fight for improved union executive. Printed and published by John Howarth. By 1925 much more text, larger. Published by the proprietor H. Howarth. Contains serial story, 'Trade union topics', 'Labour sayings', series on the cotton industry with contribution by Charles Roden Buxton, and usual features of a newspaper. Continues commitment to Labour movement. By 1935 printed and published for the proprietor by 'The Padiham Advertiser', Ltd. Title extended to **Padiham Advertiser, and West End (Burnley) Observer**. Leader, 12 Jan. 1945, states 'We belong to that rather large minority of rank and file Labour men who would like to see the Communists, "Common Wealth", and any and every other "left" organisation incorporated in the Labour Party with full freedom to express their own particular views as to the best way to attain the Socialism we are all supposed to be striving for.' Less political comment in the 1960s, and latterly simply a local newspaper with no overt commitment to Labour. Published by C. L. Hargreaves (1970).

L(Col)† 1139 (7 Jan. 1919)–

2608 Paisley Observer 1 (4 July 1905)–41 (6 April 1906); then **Scottish Observer**: 42 (13 April 1906)–64 (7 Sept 1906). Paisley; w

B   ½d. Printed and published by Thomas Collinge at The Progressive Press, the proprietors. At first declared independent, free-lance, non-political party organ. General local news. No particular coverage of Labour Movement. Change occurs with No. 32, 26 Jan. 1906, when shows support for Robert Smillie, and Labour. [On] 16 Feb. states that the 'scope of the **Observer** is now extended; it is recognised as the only weekly paper issued in the interests of Labour in Scotland.' News of local Labour organisations, discussion on Socialism, correspondence. Contributor: David Lowe, with column, 'Glasgow affairs'.

L(Col)†

2609 Paisley Pioneer 1 (Feb. 1934)–22 (Nov. 1935). Paisley; m

B   Published by the Paisley Branch of the Co-operative Party. Editor: E. E. Andrews.

L(Col)†

2610 Palmeira Telephone and Stores Medium [c1890]. Brighton; m

A   1d. Organ of the Brighton and Hove Co-operative Supply Association. (Mitchell, 1890.)

2611 Pamphlet, or Northern Scourge I, 1 [1817]. Durham
    B   Printed by R. Brockett, for the author. A pamphlet 'containing political disquisitions, prominent historical narrations, and just expositions of all public affairs'. Radical. Defends the right of the People against the system of aristocratic corruption, its spies, and its despotic laws, eg, the suspension of Habeus Corpus in 1817.
    L

2612 Pan Bolt: Organ of the (Communist) Peeweep Pit Cell [1930?]–? Lumphinnans
    A   News for publication to be sent to Abe Moffat.
    E (29 Aug. 1930 [Xerox])

2613 Paperworker: Official Organ of the National Union of Printing, Bookbinding and Paper Workers I, 1 (May 1940)–XXVIII, 1 (Jan. 1967); m
    A   1d. etc. Information, articles on general Labour topics, on historical subjects of interest to Union members, General Secretary's monthly survey, letters, book reviews, short stories, gardening column, knitting patterns. Previously, for some years the Union had been responsible for four pages in the **Bulletin** of the Printing and Kindred Trades Federation. From March 1966 was **The Paperworker, Society of Graphical and Allied Trades, Division A**. Superseded by **SOGAT Journal**
    GM (–X; L I, 11 (March 1941)–*; O XXV, 1 (1964–); ONC† I–V, X, 9–   ; TUC; the Union

2614 Parcel Section Post [19--?]–?
    A   Union of Post Office Workers, LPS Amalgamated Branch. (W. Dunlop, 'Local Journals'. **Belpost**, IV, 5 [May 1965])

2615 Park and Heeley Gazette [192?]–48 (July 1939). Sheffield; m?
    B   Gratis. Published by Park Divisional Labour Party. Leading contributor: George Latham, MP.
    L(Col)† 17 (Jan. 1930)–48

2616 Parti Socialiste Polonais. **Bulletin Officiel** (Polish Socialist Party-Official Bulletin). I, 1 (June 1895)–III, 27 (July 1899). London; irreg
    B   Printed and published by Aleksander Debski. The journal 'reflète le mouvement socialiste dans des trois partis de Pologne'. Published for **'L'Union des Socialistes à l'Etranger'**; Social-Democratic programme, for Socialisation of all means of production and of exchange. In French.
    L(Col)

2617 Partick ILP Monthly Bulletin [c1920]. [Glasgow?]; m
    B   Independent Labour Party.
    ILP April 1920

2618 Partnership: a Newsletter for Labour Councillors I, 1 (April 1965)–IX, 8 (Aug. 1973); then **Labour Councillor**: (Oct. 1973)–; m

B   Published by the Labour Party. Reproduced from typewriting. Information and policy statements on all aspects of local government.

E; LabP; O; ONC† III (1968)–; SwU III (1968)–   ; Warwick UL 1967–70

2619 Party Life I, 1 (Oct. 1962)–I, 7 (Oct./Nov. 1963); bi-m

B   Organising bulletin of the Communist Party of Great Britain. Reports of Party Executive Committee meetings, experiences of branches, electoral work, education, work of Young Communist League, women in conference, literature sales.

E; LE; O; ONC 6–7; WCML†

2620 Party Organiser 1 (March 1932)–8 (Dec. 1932?); m or bi-m

B   3d. Communist Party of Great Britain. Contributions by leading members on the problems of the working-class movement, building the Party etc.

WCML† 1, 2, 7, 8

2621 Party Organiser: a Monthly Publication I, 1 (July 1938)–II, [10] (June 1940); m

B Communist Party of Great Britain, Central Committee. July 1938 states 'Starting with this issue the **Party Organiser** will in future appear regularly as a monthly publication.'

E; L; O; ONC*†; WCML*†

2622 Party Organiser: Internal Bulletin of the Revolutionary Communist Party [1945?]–?; irreg

B   Reproduced from typewriting.

ONC† II, (2 [Feb.] 3, [April] 1946), 4 (July 1947), (Oct., Nov., 1947), (Jan., April 1948)

2623 Passed to You! [1951?]–? Northwood; m?

A   National and Local Government Officers' Association, Ruislip-Northwood Branch. Reproduced from typewriting.

L 18 (Feb. 1953)–34 (Christmas 1956); [ns] 1 (Dec. 1961)–

2624 Pateley Bridge Progressive [194-?]. Pateley Bridge; bi-m

B   Duplicated. Labour Party. (Labour Party. **Your own Journal**, 1948.)

2625 Patriot; or, Political, Moral and Philosophical Repository, Consisting of Original Pieces and Selections from Writers of Merit; a Work Calculated to Disseminate These Branches of Knowledge Among All Ranks of People, at a Small Expense. By a Society of Gentleman I, 1 (3 April 1792)—III, 10 [1793]; fortn

B   Printed for G.G.J. and J. Robinson. Includes proto-democratic materials, and articles on political reform, suffrage etc. and attacks on abuses. The editors in the introduction to Vol. I say they are to enlighten the People 'and stand up for equal representation of the People'.

C I; L; LDW III, 1—3; O; SP

2626 Patriot: a Periodical Publication Intended to Arrest the Progress of Seditious and Blasphemous Opinions, Too Prevalent in the Year 1819 1 (28 Aug. 1819)—19 (1 Jan. 1820). Manchester; w

C   2d. Printed and published by J. Aston. As indicated by the sub-title, it opposed radical extremism, and stood for moderate constitutional reform. Includes articles with 'a tendency to ameliorate the conditions of those who compose the great bulk of society, by pointing out the means of adding to their comforts, or assisting them in personal economy'. But upheld Constitution, King, Law and Religion against the 'universal suffrage or death' extremists and promotors of 'Anarchy'

L; MP

2627 Patriot 1 (9 Oct. 1819)—7 (20 Nov. 1819). Edinburgh; w

B   2d. Published and edited by John C. Denovan. Thoroughly democratic. For universal suffrage, exposure of corruption etc.

GM†

2628 Patriot 6 Nov. 1819—? Dudley; w?

B   2d. Printed and published for J. Wallace by George Walters. 'It is not known how many numbers of this publication appeared' . . . 'the only local radical paper known to have been published in the Black Country' (G. Barnsby, **The Dudley Working-Class Movement**, Part 1, Dudley 1966, pp. 11—12).

Dudley PL 1 (photocopy); HO 42. 198: 6 Nov., 13 Nov., 17 Nov.; HO 42. 199: 26 Nov.

2629 Patriot 1 (27 Aug. 1831)—2 (3 Sept. 1831?); w

B   2d. Published by William Strange. Printed by G. Cowie. 'A radical political miscellany that attacks wars, taxation, and factory conditions and advocates a "moral revolution" to reconstruct society' (Wiener).

O 1

2630 Patriot 1 [Registration No.] Jan. 1922; I, 1 (9 Feb. 1922)—1950?; w

C   6d.; 3d. Published by the Boswell Printing and Publishing Co. Anti-socialist.

C; L: LWL I—XLVII*; O I—XLVIII (1950); ONC† III, VII, IX

Patternmaker see United Patternmakers Association **Monthly Report**

2631 Peacemaker: an Occasional Bulletin Issued by the Canterbury Branch of the British Movement Against War and Fascism. 1 (March 1935)–11 (Nov./Dec. 1937). Canterbury; q

    B   1d. Editor: Stephen Coltham. A united-front paper against War and Militarism. Principle activities of the Canterbury Club were research, education, propaganda; social education against 'militarism, imperialism and other oppression'. Later numbers appeal to the working class to defeat the menace. Policy of non-co-operation and passive resistance. Last number boasted a circulation of 2,000 among the working class of East Kent.

    L(Col)†

2632 Pearl Agents' Gazette [1926?]–1967; then **Gazette**: Official Organ of the Pearl Section, National Union of Insurance Workers: [1968?]–   ; m

    A   National Union of Pearl Agents; National Union of Insurance Workers, Pearl Section.

    LCI, XX, 3– ; The Union?

2633 Peckham Citizen ns 1 (May 1949)–24 (Sept. 1951); m

    B   Issued by the Political Purposes Committee of the Royal Arsenal Co-operative Society.

    L(Col)†

Pendleton Co-operative Monthly Review see **Pendleton Co-operative Record**

2634 Pendleton Co-operative Record 1 (Sept. 1897)–454 (June 1935); then b **Pendleton Co-operative Monthly Review**: 1 (July 1935)–119 (Dec. 1955). Pendleton; m

    A   Gratis. Pendleton Co-operative Industrial Society. Editors included James Lyons (1897–1903); Alexander Caldwell. Alternative title of b: **Pendleton Co-operative Review**. Superseded by **Co-operative Home Magazine**.

    L a 179 (July 1912)–

Pendleton Co-operative Review see **Pendleton Co-operative Record**

2635 Penge Disucssion 1 (May 1938); then **Beckenham and Penge Discussion**: 2 (June 1938)–3 (July 1938); then **Beckenham and Penge Discussion and Labour News**: 4 (Sept. 1938). Penge; m

    B   1d. Published by the Penge Communist Party. To fulfil the need for a monthly paper in the branch, as an open forum for 'thrashing out difficulties' at a critical period in the class struggle, at home and internationally. Serious, self-critical. Reproduced from typewriting.

    L

2636 Pennine Ranger 1961?– . Sowerby Bridge

A National and Local Government Officers' Association, Sowerby Bridge Branch. Reproduced from typewriting.

L Oct. 1961–

Penny Bee Hive see **Bee Hive**

Penny Magazine of the Society for the Diffusion of Useful Knowledge see **Knight's Penny Magazine**

2637 Penny Monthly Sermons : Plain Preaching to Poor People [1869–72]; m

C Sermons published at a low price intended for parochial distribution especially among poor parishioners. Published in five series.

L (w occ. nos)

Penny Paper by a Poor Man's Advocate see **Poor Man's Advocate, and People's Library**

2638 Penny Papers for the People, Published by the Poor Man's Guardian 1 (1 Oct. 1830)–ns 28 (2 July 1831); irreg

B 1d. Printer and publisher: Henry Hetherington. Editor: Thomas Mayhew. 'A radical working-class newspaper designed as a "pamphlet". It principally agitated for universal suffrage and repeal of the "taxes on knowledge". It was suppppressed by the Stamp Office in July 1831 and succeeded by **The Poor Man's Guardian**' (Wiener). Publicised the National Union of the Working Classes of which Hetherington was a leading member. Earlier numbers sometimes referred to as 'To the People of England'.

BP (25 Dec. 1830)–(2 July 1831); HO 64/11 9 occ. nos; HO 64/16 (4 June 1831); HO 64/17 35 occ. nos; L; LU; LUC; MP (1 Oct. 1830)

2639 Penny Red 1 (11 May 1966)– . Leeds; irreg; w

B Published by Leeds University Union, Communist Society. Reproduced from typewriting. Not confined to student politics. In 1973 title changed to **Red Star**.

LdU† *

2640 Penny Satirist I 1 (22 April 1837)–X, 471 (25 April 1846); then b **Penny Satirist and London Pioneer**: I, 1 (30 April 1846); then **London Pioneer**: I, 2 (7 May 1846)–II, 104 (13 April 1848); then **London Literary Pioneer**: III, 105 (15 April 1848)–III, 135 (11 Nov. 1848). then **Literary Pioneer**: III, 136 (18 Nov. 1848)–III, 138 (2 Dec. 1848); w

C 1d. Printed and published by B. D. Counsins. A miscellany addressed to working-class audience, really to distract them from serious politics, eg in Chartism, to which there are a number of hostile satirical references. Highly amusing, with excellent cartoons.

C a II, 63, b; L(Col)† a, b I, 2–III; LU b I, 1; MP a I–VIII; NpP a III, 135; O b

402

2641 Penny Times 1 (22 Feb. 1860)–2 (3 March 1860)
    B   1d. Proprietor and editor: Ernest Jones. For manhood suffrage.
General parliamentary and foreign news, and literary miscellany. Several
editions published. Distributed with **The Weekly Telegraph.**
    L(Col)†

Pennyworth of Politics by the Poor Man's Advocate see **Poor Man's
Advocate, and People's Library**

2642 Penpusher: Quarterly Review of the Wandsworth and SW Branch of
the Clerical and Administrative Workers' Union I, 1 (Sept. 1941)–? q
    A   Reproduced from typewriting.
    L (mislaid)

2643 Pensioner I, 1 (Jan. 1939)–[1950?]; then **Old Age Pensioner**:
Official Publication of the National Federation of Old Age Pensions'
Associations: June 1950–[196-?]; then **Pensioner's Voice** [196–?] –.
Blackburn; m
    A   Later National Association of Old Age Pensioners.
    ONC April 1940–38 (March 1943), 127 (March)–133 (Sept. 1951
[missing]; TUC Jan., Nov. 1939, May 1964–

Pensioner's Voice see **Pensioner**

2644 Pensions and Progress: a Quarterly Magazine of Help and Old Age
Pension Record. I, 1 (April 1899)–II, 7 (Dec. 1900); q
    C   1d. Organ of a non-political party crusade to bring about old age
pensions. Founded at a time when legislative enactment of old age
pensions had been proposed.
    L; LE I; O I, 1

2645 People 1 (19 April 1817)–15 (26 July 1817); w
    B   Published by William Butler. Printed by Hay and Turner.
Nos. 6–15 printed and published by William Wilks. Well-conducted,
thorough-going radical reform weekly. Demands universal suffrage, secret
ballot, annual parliaments as the key to problems of the labouring
population as 'the majority' and 'the staff of life of the community'
Lengthy articles in defence of democratic rights; campaigns against
despotic suspension of Habeus Corpus etc. Supports all radical popular
movements, including insurrectionary ones. Contains an early reference to
Robert Owen.
    L; Lu; MP; ONC 3, 7

2646 People: Their Rights and Liberties, Their Duties and Their Interests
I, 1 (27 May 1848)–III, 157 (1851); ns [I], 1 (15 March 1851)–II, 42 (27
Dec. 1851); II, ns 1 (3 Jan. 1852)–40 (2 Oct. 1852). Wortley, Leeds;
London; w

    B   1d. Printed and published by Joseph Barker, Wortley, then
published by J. Watson, London. Barker, a Unitarian and advanced Liberal
reformer, advocated abolition of class legislation. Personal addresses and
contributions on land questions, hereditary and class legislation, the need
for popular political representation. In 1848 welcomes working-class
support for Chartist principles, though not members of Chartist
associations. Moral force standpoint. Correspondence with local grass-roots
Radicalism. In 1850 and 1851 more on religion and democratic literature.
Letters from America, and letters on emigration societies, eg Bradford
Co-operative Emigration Society.

    GM†; L i I, 1–52; LU† i, ii I; LdP ii I–II; MU i, ii*; MUC i I–II;
ONC† *; Warwick UL (microfilm)

2647 People 1 (18 April, 1857)–55 (1 May 1858); w
    B   2d. Published by William Field. Printed by William John
Johnson. A popular radical general newspaper 'to elevate the condition of
the masses, physically, socially and morally'. Concerned with the relations
between Labour and Capital; stands with the labourer, though does not
denounce the capitalist class as a whole. Favours co-operative production,
warmly endorses the Short-Hours' Movement, universal suffrage and full
political representation for the working class, including working-class MPs
without financial qualification. For a secret ballot, popular education etc.
Designed as a medium of communication through which 'intelligent men
(from the ranks of the people) can speak to their brethren'. Contains a
series, beginning 3 Oct. 1857 by Thomas Cooper, entitled 'Pictures of the
people', which consists of lengthy sketches of the trades in several areas,
eg, ribbon weavers of Coventry, potters of Staffordshire. Sub-title varies.

    L(Col)†

2648 People and Politics: the Workshops Journal of Correspondence
[1965?]–?; q [ie irreg]
    B   2s. 6d. etc. Printed by AA Publishing Company. 'The
Workshops are a vehicle for social action and a forum for study and
debate. It is an association of people with radical ideas who have a vision
of society which enables the individual to realise his potential in active
co-operation with his fellow man.' Editors: Dick Booth, George Clark,
Roy Haddon, Peter Moule, Stuart Hall, Michael Rustin. Succeeds **Journal
of Correspondence**.

    LE† Nov./Dec. 1965, Spring 1966, Summer 1966, Easter 1967

2649 People of Ireland: a National and Democratic Journal I, 1 (18 Sept. 1869)–? Dublin; w

    B   2d. Printed and published for the proprietors by Charles P. O'Connor. Editor: T. F. MacCarthie. Aims were Irish unity and 'The Elevation of the Working Classes of Ireland, and the attainment of their Rights, by an equitable adjustment of the relations between Labour and Capital'. News, literary articles, patriotic poems etc.

    L(Col)† I, 1

2650 People's Abstinence Standard, and True Social Reformer: the Organ of the Metropolitan Working Men's Union I, 1 (28 July 1849)–II, 53 (27 July 1850); w

    A   1d. Printed by Shirrefs and Russell for the Executive Committee of the London Total Abstinence Union, and published by W. Horsell, then W. Tweedie. Edited by P. W. perfitt. A 'publication devoted to the advocacy of entire abstinence from alcohol'. The journal was started with the patronage of 15 societies, based on the principle of mutual aid, principally composed of working-men. Saw abstinence as the panacea for the removal of all vice from the world. Contained reports on meetings and demonstrations of the Union, articles on the evils of drink, facts and figures, book reviews. Editorials have a religious tone.

    LU†

2651 People's Advocate, and National Vindicator of Right and Wrong 1 (19 June 1875)–16 (2 Oct. 1875); ns 1 (15 April 1876)–5 (13 May 1876); w

    B   1d. Printed for the proprietor by the National Press Agency, Ltd. Published by the People's Newspaper and General Publishing Company Ltd. Editor of new series: Maltman Barry. A general democratic newspaper espousing the People's Rights, ie for universal suffrage, law, land and parliamentary reform, payment of members, right of working-men to send their own representatives to parliaments, shorter parliaments, protection of the rights of working-men from the tyranny of Capital and class legislation. Considerable Labour news, eg, supports the Labour Protection League (1875), and publishes correspondence from working-men.

    L(Col)†

People's and Howitt's Journal see **People's Journal. 1846–1849**

2652 People's Cause: Organ of the New 'People's Party' 1 (June 1888). Manchester; w

    B   Edited by F. A. Binney, a Manchester solicitor. Main object to found a new political party to secure the more equal distribution of wealth. Populist rather then Labour.

    MP†

2653 People's College Journal: a Monthly Periodical Chiefly Devoted to the Cause of Popular Education 1 (Nov. 1846)–7 (May 1847). Sheffield. m

    C   2d. Printed and published at the People's College, Sheffield' Edited by Rev. R. S. Bayley. Concentrates on the theme of popular education, for the elevation of the working classes to a postion of political and social responsibility. Mildly radical, ie against the aristocracy and privilege.

    L; SP

People's Conservative see **'Destructive'** and **Poor Man's Conservative**

People's Courier see **Spade and Whip**

2654 People's Guardian 1 (21 June 1862)–24 (29 Nov. 1862). Dundee; w

    B   1d. 'The People – their Rights, Privileges, and Progress.' Printed and published for the proprietors by Bowes Brothers. 'Published every Saturday to advocate the Interests of the Working Classes, advanced Liberals and the Trades in general.' Special features were a column devoted to 'Men of the People', and one to 'The People's Literary Column'. (A. C. Lamb, 'Bibliography of Dundee periodical literature.' **Scottish Notes and Queries**, III.)

2655 People's Hue and Cry, or **Weekly Police Register** 1 (22 March 1834)–19 (10 Aug. 1834); w

    B   1d. Published, printed and edited by Richard E. Lee. No. 15 was published by a committee headed by George Petrie while Lee was in gaol. 'A radical political and trades union newspaper that focuses upon police news and accounts of criminals. It copies most of its news stories from **The Man** which is simultaneously published by Lee' (Wiener).

    HO 64/15 No. 19; L(Col)† 15; O(JJ) 1

2656 People's Journal I (3 Jan. 1846)–VII (June 1849); then **People's and Howitt's Journal**: VIII, (July 1849)–XI, (June 1851); w

    C   1½d. Printed and published by F. Newton, then by John Bennett. Editor (and co-owner from April 1846): John Saunders. A well-produced miscellany concerned with improving the welfare of 'the people', interpreted as the mass of the working class. Emphasis on education and collective self-improvement. Contains William Howitt's series of 'Letters on Labour, to the Working Men of England'. Occasional contributors: W. J. Linton (articles and engravings), Ebenezer Elliot (poetry), Harriet Martineau, Barnby, Cooper. Has a supplement entitled **Annals of Industry**, which contains brief notes on strikes and worker's organisations. Vols. VIII–XI are also numbered New Series, I–IV.

    BP I–VIII; BrP I–VI; C I–VIII; Co-op. Coll.*; EP 1846–7; EU I–III; HU I–VII; L I–III, VII, ns IV; LU I–VI; MP I–IV, VIII–XI; O I–X; O(JJ) 1–26, 61 (w 18, 21); ONC† 1–26; RU I–IX

2657 People's Magazine: a Monthly Journal of Politics etc. 1841–2. Leeds; m

    B   Editor?: J. R. Stephens. (**Museum Book Shop Catalogue,** 1913–14; **Stephens Monthly Magazine,** 1840.)

2658 People's Messenger, Producers' and Ratepayers' Friend 1 (Aug. 1894); Bolton

    B   Printed for the proprietor, James Bleakley, by the **Echo.** Edited by James Bleakley. 'Populist.' Advocates a parliament of producers and ratepayers. Against party government. Sees the key issue as the need for legislation to promote productive employment of the labouring poor. Sees Tory and Radical politicians as being self-interested. 'Idle capital and labour is the fruit of partisan leaders' misgovernment.' 'The only paper to champion the cause of the Poor against all their enemies in Church and State.' Contains an address by Bleakley to Keir Hardie 'in the labour cause', and correspondence with F. Brocklehurst.

    L(Col)†

2659 People's Miscellany: a Monthly Journal for the Workshop and the Fireside 1 (1853); m

    C   1d. Published by Houlston and Stoneman. Printed by Mr Bowden. A curious 30-page miscellany written by one 'Randle Treadwell', weaver, wanderer and scribe. Suggests useful hints on self-improvement. Advertises friendly and mutual benefit associations.

    L

2660 People's Newspaper 1 (30 May 1847)–16 (11 Sept. 1847); w

    A   3d. Published by Eneas Mackenzie. Printed for the proprietors by William Lake, then by William George Graeme Ross. Published every Sunday. Home and foreign news, discussion of matters of concern to the Labour movement, details of meetings of Labour organisations in a column 'The people's societies', lectures, law notes, correspondence, reviews. For the furtherance of the popular cause. 'The efforts at co-operative production in 1820–1 and 1834 had not been supported by the typographical societies. In 1846, however, when the NTA [National Typographical Association] was collapsing amid widespread unemployment and strikes, many similar schemes were advocated in the **Typographical Gazette,** as a means of "employing the unemployed", and an alternative to useless expenditure on strikes and out-of-work benefit. The outcome of these various proposals for "co-operative printing offices", journeymen joint-stock "typographical companies", a "National Printing Office", or "National Press", was the establishment in London of the **People's Newspaper,** a weekly newspaper, the first number of which appeared on 30 May 1847. About twenty strike hands and fifteen out-of-work members were employed on this paper. Unfortunately, however, "the discontinuance of the London trade subscriptions, which were absolutely necessary for the continuance of the paper, rendered it impossible to proceed beyond the fifth number, and it was most reluctantly abandoned," after incurring a net loss of about £100. It was

taken over by a typographical joint-stock company, which, however, was
only able to survive by receiving "the loan of the strike hands of the
Association upon credit". The Delegate Meeting in August therefore
decided to drop it. It had never received much support from the provinces,
where many members objected to thy appropriation of Association funds,
intended solely for trade-union purposes, to the establishment of a
newspaper, "thereby bringing the employed into competition with the
employer".' (A. E. Musson, **The Typographical Association**, Oxford
University Press 1954, pp. 79–80.) There were several editions of each
number.

    L(Col)†

People's Newspaper. 1902 see **Gazeta Ludowa**

2661 People's Outlook (Northants and North Bucks.) 1 (22 Oct. 1920)–?;
w

    B?
    ILP 1

2662 People's Paper: the Champion of Political Justice and Universal
Right 1 (8 May 1852)–331 (4 Sept. 1858); w

    B   3d.; 4d. Printed and published for the proprietor, Ernest Charles
Jones, by Alexander Grant, then printed and published by E. Jones, then
for E. Jones by John Watts. Editor: Ernest Jones; on 26 June 1858 handed
over to J. Baxter Langley, of the Political Reform League, and democratic
editor of the **Morning Star**, to whom he had mortgaged the **People's Paper**
and **The London News**. Organ of the National Charter Association. For
reorganisation of the Chartist movement. Coverage of, and support for,
international liberation and democratic movements. Reports of trade
union activities, correspondence on Labour questions. In later years has
more extensive coverage of general political news.

    L(Col)†; LE (microfilm); Warwick UL (microfilm)

2663 People's Party 1 (2 May 1885)

    B   1d. Registation issue. Published for the proprietors by Edward
Frederic Bullen. 'Started at the instance of various working men's
committees, formed in several of the most important manufacturing
districts', the 'people's party' advocates a programme of political
democracy, working-class MPs and payment of members, in opposition to
the Tories and Radicals who do not represent the working-men. Also for
free State education, technical schools, a national insurance scheme for the
unemployed and needy, in place of the poor-house and Guardians, and
proposed a thorough-going collectivist programme.

    L(Col)†

2664 People's Pictorial 1 (Summer 1952)–3 [1953?] ; irreg

    B   3d. Published by the Labour Party. Illustrated magazine putting
forward Labour Party criticisms of Tory government policy and pointing
to alternatives.

    L; ONC 1, 3

2665 People's Police Gazette 1 (27 Nov. 1841)–4 (19 Dec. 1841); w
     B   3½d. Printed and published by Joseph William Last. Advocated
manhood suffrage and a secret ballot.
     L(Col)†

2666 People's Police Gazette, and Tradesmen's Advertiser 1 [c Aug.
1833?]–38 (3 May 1834); w
     B   2d. Published and printed by Charles Penny. 'Contains extensive
accounts of trades union and police activities. It was suppressed by the
Stamp Office. It claims a weekly circulation of 15,000 (Wiener).
     HO 64/19 No. 38

2667 People's Press 1 (11 Dec. 1830)–[6?] (17 Dec. 1830); d
     B   4d. Published, printed and editied by C. M. Riley. 'A radical
newspaper disguised as a "pamphlet". It denounces the Church of England
and calls for appropriation of all church property. It reprints extensive
news accounts that have already appeared in other journals.' (Wiener).
     HO 64/18 (17 Dec. 1830)

2668 People's Press 1 (8 March 1890)–52 (28 Feb. 1891); w
     A   1d. The official organ of the General Railway Workers' Union,
the Gas Workers' and General Labourers' Union, the Potter's Labourers'
Union, the Coach, Bus, Cab and Van Trades' Union, and subsequently of
several other of the 'new unions'. Directors: W. S. de Mattos, Rev. W. A.
Morris, Will Thorne, C. Watson. Editor from August 1890: Shaw Maxwell.
Contributors: Edward Aveling, Eleanor Marx Aveling, Cunningham
Grahame.
     L(Col)†; LE; MML 1890; TUC, John Burns Lib

2669 People's Press and Cork Weekly Register I, 1 (20 Sept. 1834)–II, 73
(10 Feb. 1836). Cork; w
     B   6d. Printed for the proprietors by John Hennessey. 'This
publication will be of that class usually termed – the Movement' and
sought to provide the 'uncompromising advocacy of the interests and
feelings of the great body of the people.' Favoured reform.
     L(Col)†; MR

2670 People's Press and Monthly Historical Newspaper I, 1 (1847)–III, 33
(25 Dec. 1848). Douglas, Isle of Man; m
     B   2d. Printed and published by William Shirrefs. 'Letters to the
working class, and on the rights of women, claims of labour etc.'
Contributors: Goodwyn Barmby, Elihu Burrit, G. J. Holyoake etc.
     L I; MP II–III

2671 People's Review 'of Literature and Politics, Edited by Friends of "Order and Progress" ' 1 (Feb. 1850)–3 (April 1850); m

    B   The above title is that of the title page of the volume of collected numbers; the title at the head of each number is simply: **The People's Review**. Published by C. Mitchell. Edited by G. J. Holyoake and others. 'We believe it is true . . . that no organ has been set up by members of the Working Classes, to which the writers of this Review personally belong, in which political, social and other revolutions were sought in the same temper – ie so anxiously regarding the interests of opponents and invariably conceding their good intentions . . . We wrote neither for fame nor pastime, but to create another power on the side of the people . . . ' (Preface); Review articles of works of politics, economics, literature, art etc.

    L; LU; MP; O

2672 People's Tribune I, 1 (14 Dec. 1895)–V, 286 (20 Aug. 1898) Nuneaton; w

    B   ½d. Printed and published by H. Fieldhouse. Editor: William Johnson. Primarily an advertiser for the district. Sympathetic to workmen's organisation and sane Trade Unionism, and to miners in the area. Against poverty and the degradation of the slums. Changes title after No. 286 to **Tribune**, and is no longer relevant.

    L(Col)†

2673 People's Weekly I, 1 (6 Oct. 1928)–IV, 104 (27 Sept. 1930); ns I, 1 (4 Oct. 1930)–I, 18 (31 Jan. 1931). Manchester; w

    B   1d. Co-operative. Information on the Labour and Co-operative movements, educational articles, family pages.

    Co-op. Coll.; Co-op. Union; L(Col); O(JJ)† I, 11; TUC

2674 People's Weekly Dispatch 1 (4 Oct. 1835?)–33? (14 May 1836); w

    B   2d. 'A radical miscellany that describes itself as the "Largest, cheapest, and best newspaper in the Kingdom". It repeatedly agitates against the stamp duty on newspapers and advocates revolution, if necessary, to redress grievances' (Wiener).

    HO 40/33, Part 2 No. 9; L, Place Newspaper Coll. Set 70, pp. 500–1 (23 April 1836); Set 70, p. 519 (14 May 1836)

2675 People's Weekly Police Gazette I [c1834?]–II, 28 (7 May 1836); w

    B   2d.; 2½d. Published and printed by T. Wilson. 'An illustrated newpaper that features comprehensive news summaries as well as readical political comment. It attacks the aristocracy, the Poor Laws, and the Church of England, and advocates the common ownership of land' (Wiener).

    L(Col) II, 9 (27 Dec. 1835), II, 28 (7 May 1836)

People's Year Book and Annual of the English and Scottish Wholesale Societies see Co-operative Wholesale Societies, Ltd. **Almanack and Diary**

2676 Performer: Official Organ of the Variety Artistes' Federation, the Music Hall Artistes' Railway Association, the English Section of the International Artistes' Lodge and Various Music Hall Societies I, 1 (29 March 1906)—CV, 2674 (26 Sept. 1957); w

    A   1d. etc. Paper was founded by Frederick Russell.

    L(Col)†; O 1912—14, 1926—   ; TUC 1922—30*

2677 Performer Annual 1907—32; a

    A   Variety Artistes' Federation etc. See **Performer**.

    L(Col); O 1911—13, 1920—1

2678 Periscope 1945. Liverpool

    A   Shop stewards' paper, Cammell Lairds. (**New Propellor**.)

2679 Perkin Gazette [1955?]— . Perth; m?

    A   National and Local Government Officers' Association, Perth and Kinross County Branch. Reproduced from typewriting.

    L VII, 1 (Jan. 1961)—

2680 Perth Chronicle 1836—42. Perth; w

    B   4½d. (1839). Printed for the proprietors, David Wood and Company by William Belford. Primarily a local commercial paper, but with a commitment to Chartism.

    E 163 (28 Nov. 1839); L(Col) 158 (24 Oct. 1839)

2681 Perth Herald 1 (Autumn 1936). Perth

    A   Gratis. Published by Perth Trades and Industrial Council. Resists the new unemployment regulations and Means Test as part of the Labour and Co-operative struggle against government policy.

    L(Col)

2682 Peterborough Co-operative Citizen 1 (Nov. 1939); then **Peterborough Co-operator**: 2 (Dec. 1939)—33 (July 1942); m

    A   Edited by the Educational Committee, Peterborough and District Co-operative Society.

    L(Col)

Peterborough Co-operator see **Peterborough Co-operative Citizen**

2683 Peterborough Leader I, 1 [Jan. 1940?]—V, 1 (June 1944). Peterborough; m

    B   2d. Published by the Peterborough Branch of the Communist Party of Great Britain. Last number reproduced from typewriting.

    WCML† III, 10 (Oct. 1942)—IV, 3) V, 1

2684 Petersfield Branch NALGO Magazine 1963?—. Petersfield

    A   National and Local Government Officers' Association. Reproduced from typewriting.

    L 1963—

Phalanx see **London Phalanx**

2685 Pheon [May 1956] –   . Reading; m
    A   Institution of Professional Civil Servants, War Department Branch.
    L 46 (Feb. 1960)–

2686 Philanthropist; or, Benefit and Trades' Societies' Magazine 1 (19 July 1834); w
    B   1d. Published by J. Rees. Printed by G. H. Davidson. No. 1 concerns legislation affecting Benefit Societies. 'Our next will contain a monthly report of the "doings and sayings" of Societies, and a particular account of the Tailors' Strike, with a lucid expose of the Great Masters oppressiveness . . . Our Periodical will be open to the use of all the Members of Friendly Societies, (in which we, of course, include Trades Unions) . . .'
    ONC†

2687 Philanthropist: a Monthly Journal Devoted to Social, Political, and Moral Reforms 1 (July 1843)–13 (July 1844); m
    C   6d. Published by William Brittain. Middle-class radical-reformist. Against hereditary aristocracy and monopoly. Supports the Complete Suffrage Movement, believes in the right of every man to elective franchise. Advocates free trade, national education, and the Short-Hours' Movement. The last number promises 'In order that the principles we advocate may be more generally promulgated, the **Philanthropist** will in future be supplied at half-price to News Rooms, Mechanics' Institutes, all institutions of a similar kind, and to the working classes in general'
    L(Col)†

Philistine see **Cheltenham Working Men's College Magazine**

2688 'Phoblacht (na h-Eireann). Republic (of Ireland). I, 1 (3 Jan. 1922)–ns VII, 4 (21 Nov. 1931). then b **Republican** file. I, 1 (28 Nov. 1931)–I, 14 (27 Feb. 1932). then a **Phoblacht. Republic.** VII, 5 (12 March 1932)–X, 17 (25 May 1935). then c **Republic.** (29 June 1935)–(24 Aug. 1935). then a **Phoblacht. Republic.** ns XI, (14 March 1936)–XL, 15 (20 June 1936). Dublin; w
    B   2d. Proprietors: Republic Press Organ of Irish republicanism.
    E a ii VII, 5–VIII, 7, b; L(Col)*

2689 Phoenix; or, the Christian Advocate of Equal Knowledge I, 1 (5 Feb. 1837)—I, 5 (5 March 1837); w

B   4d. Published by Alfred Carlile. Printed by John Cunningham. Edited by Richard Carlile. For the abolition of the House of Lords, the increase of the knowledge of the people, reform of the Church, and reliance on Christianity as based on physical and moral science. 'The scientific teacher is the necessary Christian minister.' Disclaims allegiance with any party. At first rejected by the Stamp Office, the paper was finally allowed after Carlile had written a long letter explaining its aims. This letter is reproduced in full in No. 1.

L(Col)†

2690 Phoenix. Souvenir first edition (21 Nov. 1960)

A   3d. Published by the Action Committee of the **News Chronicle**. The Action Committee was formed by a group of the staff after the folding of the **News Chronicle**, to cushion the blow on employees (a Hardship Fund was established), and to plan how to replace the paper. Declared its intention to found a genuinely independent morning newspaper 'to provide a bold platform for all shades of radical, and in particular, left-of-centre opinion'. The paper was to be called **The Phoenix** like this first edition, which has four pages of which only pages 1 and 4 are printed. Main headline: 'Out of the ashes of Fleet Street a new radical newspaper rises'.

L(Col)†

2691 Physic [1965?]—   . Worthing; m?

A   National and Local Government Officers' Association, HMC Branch, Worthing Group. Reproduced from typewriting.

L 13 (June 1966)—

2692 Piano Tuner [19--?] —?; m

A   For members of the Pianoforte Tuners' Association. (Mitchell, 1930.)

2693 Piano Worker [192-?] —?

A   Issued by the Communist Piano Workers. Number for 14 July 1926 urged readers to resist the bosses' terms as the miners did. Reproduced from typewriting.

O(JJ)† Special strike edition (14 July [1926])

Pig's Meat see **One Pennyworth of Pig's Meat**

Pilgrim see Bedford and District **NALGO Branch Magazine**

2694 Pillar-Box: a Fiction Magazine by Members of the Union of Post-Office Workers 1923

A
L

2695 Pilot, Being a Record of the Transactions of the British and Foreign Sailors' Society I (1820)–X, [18--?]; then **Sailors' Magazine (and Nautical Intelligencer)**: ns I [18--?]–[3rd ser.] XVIII (1970); then **Chart and Compass: Sailor's Magazine**: [4th ser.], I (1879)–; m

    C   Religious addresses, temperance fiction, nautical intelligence, poetry, Society's agents' reports.

    C 1843–50; L 1842– ; MP 1933–(1936–7*); 0 1835–1920*

2696 Pioneer; or, Trades' Union Magazine 1 (7 Sept 1833)–44 (5 July 1834). Birmingham; London; w

    A   1d. and 2d. Owned and edited by James Morrison. Printed by Dewson and Son; B. D. Cousins (12–44). Initially the organ of the Builders' Union, then moved to London, becoming the organ of the Grand National Consolidated Trades' Union. Sub-title changes with No. 25 to become: . . . 'or, Grand National Consolidated Trades' Union Magazine'. Contributor: Rev. J. E. 'Shepherd' Smith. Articles, news, correspondence, verse, women's page. Estimated weekly circulation of 20,000 (**Tait's Edinburgh Magazine**, Oct. 1834, p. 622).

    L; LE; LU; MP; ONC† (Nos 1–2 are 2nd edition); Greenwood reprint and microfiche: microfiche distributed in Britain and Europe by the Harvester Press Ltd

2697 Pioneer: a Record of Social Progress and Friendly and Industrial Association 1 (15 Dec. 1883)–8 (2 Feb. 1884); w

    C   1d. Published by Frederick Tallis. A substantial publication which essentially expresses the ideology of self-help for working-men. A medium for the interchange of views on pressing social problems, i.e. those confronting the masses. Records the progress of working-class organisations, ie trade unions (includes strike news), co-operative bodies, short-hours movements, friendly societies, building societies. Columns on work and wages, state of trade in the regions. Correspondence. Contributors: Smiles, Holyoake, G. Howell.

    L(Col)†

2698 Pioneer: Weekly Radical Journal I, 1 (21 Jan. 1887)–15 (29 April 1887). Glasgow; w

    B   1d. Printed for 'The Pioneer' Publishing Company. Democratic, for the removal of class legislation and the establishment of popular control home rule, the 'country should be governed by the people for the people', and agitates on the land question, taxation, better conditions for labour and the carrying over of the Chartist programme.

    GM†

Pioneer. 1894–1895 see **York Pioneer**

Pioneer, 1894–? see **Bolton and District Independent Labour Party Pioneer**

2699 Pioneer 1 (March 1895); then **Hunslet Pioneer**: 2 (April 1895)–?
Hunslet; m
    B   Gratis. Printed for the East Hunslet Independent Labour Party
by Emmett and Davy, Leeds. Short items and notes. First page consists of
advertisements.
    AbU 1–2 (microfilm); O(JJ) 1–2; ONC† 2, 3 (May 1895)

2700 Pioneer: Being the Edition of The Londoner for Tottenham, Wood
Green, Edmonton and Enfield Lock 1 (Oct. 1895)–92 (2 July 1897); w
    B   Radical, Progressive and Labour. **See also The Londoner, North
Islington Edition; The (St Pancras) Londoner**
    L(Col)

2701 Pioneer I, 1 (Jan. 1896)–? [Glasgow?] ; m
    B?   For Glasgow and District.
    ILP 1

2702 Pioneer: the Organ of the Burnley Branch of the Social Democratic
Federation 1, 1896–255 (July 1917). Burnley; m
    B   Gratis. Later printed and published for the British Socialist
Party. Editor: Dan Irving. Local news and notes, verse, suggestions for
reading, notices of meetings, correspondence. Sub-title varies; later 'The
Organ of the Labour and Socialist Movement in Burnley'.
    Burnley PL 72, 75, 154, 196; L(Col)† 213 (Jan. 1914)–255 (July
1917); ONC† 42 (Oct. 1899)

2703 Pioneer: the Local Organ of the Independent Labour Party; a
Journal of Labour and Progress for Pendlebury and Swinton I, 1 (Nov.
1898)–(Feb. 1908?). Pendlebury; m
    B   Gratis. Pendlebury and Swinton Independent Labour Party.
Editors: 'Neonomian', ie Peter Lindley; John Halliday. Editorial Board;
A. C. Lindley, P. Lindley, W. S. Mycock, W. S. Heywood, and others.
Numbering dropped sometime in 1902 or 1903.
    AbU 34 (Aug. 1901 [microfilm]); Bolton Trades Council 34 nos.
mainly in the early years; O(JJ) 34; ONC 32; Smethurst Coll. 1; Swinton
Branch of Salford Metropolitan Libraries. 1–3, 5–8, 13–15, 17–20, 27,
29, 30, 32–7, 39, Oct. 1903, Nov. 1903, May 1905, Jan. 1908, Feb. 1908

2704 Pioneer: a Monthly Journal of Working-Class Politics 1 (Jan.
1899)–? Portsmouth; m
    B   Free. Printed and published for the proprietors by G. Humby.
'Properietors not mentioned by name but Portsmouth ILP advertised as
"the only Socialist organisation in Portsmouth" '. (D. Hopkin, 'Local
Newspapers of the Independent Labour Party, 1893–1906'. Society for
the Study of Labour History, **Bulletin**, 28 [Spring 1974].)
    AbU 1 (microfilm); O(JJ) 1

2705 Pioneer 1 (June 1899)–20 (Feb. 1902). Birmingham; m; q (Oct. 1900–Jan. 1901); irreg

    B   1d.; gratis. Edited by J. Arthur Fallows. To disseminate socialist principles in the Midlands. News and notes, book reviews, editorial, notices of meetings, verse. Later signed articles appear. Contributors: Rebecca Wicksteed, Rev. Charles H. Vail. Later subtitled: 'a (Quarterly) Magazine for Midland socialists'.

    BP; O (w 15)

2706 Pioneer 1, [1901?]–6146 (28 Nov. 1913); then **Leicester Pioneer**: 7146 (5 Dec. 1913)–7389 (30 Aug. 1918); then **Pioneer**: ns 1 (6 Sept. 1918)–(June 1928). Leicester; w

    B   1d. Published for the Labour Representation Committee until 1906. Thereafter, a popular paper, supporting Labour in national and municipal politics. Numbering is irregular

    L(Col)† 231 (11 Nov. 1905)–(June 1928)

2707 Pioneer [c1904–5]. [Preston]; m

    B   Preston Independent Labour Party.

    ILP Nov. 1904, Feb. 1905

2708 Pioneer 1 (8 Feb. 1905)–? [Leeds?]; m

    B   Armley and Wortley Labour Representation Committee.

    ILP 1

2709 Pioneer 1 (Dec. 1905)–1907? Manchester; m

    B   Issued by Eccles Division Representation Committee. Edited by P. Lindley, Will Hughes. Published by the Co-operative Printing Society.

    Eccles PL 1, Election special, 3 (Jan. 1910); Swinton PL 2 (Jan. 1906).

2710 Pioneer: the Organ of the Eccles Divisional Branch, Independent Labour Party 1 (Feb. 1906)–1908? Manchester, Pendlebury; m

    B   Free. Printed and published by Pioneer Press

    Swinton PL II, 2 (March 1907)

2711 Pioneer: the Organ of the Eccles Branch of the Independent Labour Party 1 (Feb. 1907)–1908? Manchester, Pendlebury; m

    B   Published by Peter Lindley, Pioneer Press.

    Swinton PL I, 3 (April 1907)

2712 Pioneer 1 (1911)–568 (6 May 1922). Merthyr Tydfil; w

    B   Sometimes **Merthyr Pioneer; Merthyr Borough Labour Pioneer**?

    L(Col) 116 (31 May 1913)–568

2713 Pioneer [c1913]; m

    B?   For Carlton, Netherfield and District.

    ILP July 1913

Pioneer. 1922–1926 see Woolwich and District Labour Notes

2714 Pioneer: the Monthly Newsletter of the Irish Labour Party and Trade Union Congress 1 (Feb. 1924)–? Dublin; m

    B   Single sheets, reproduced from typewriting. Preceded by the Irish Labour Party and Trade Union Congress's **Weekly Labour Notes**

        LabP† 1–8, (March 1925)

Pioneer. 1937–1938 see **Co-operative Party Citizen**

2715 Pioneer: the Magazine of the London Co-operative Party [c1954]; m

    B   2d. Published by the Political Committee of the London Co-operative Society. Editor: Hardy Brown. News, short stories, illustrated.

        ONC† Feb. 1954

Pioneer and Labour Journal see **Woolwich and District Labour Notes**

2716 Pioneer and Weekly Record of Movements 1 (19 April 1851)–11 (28 June 1851); w

    C   3d. Published and printed by William Horsell. A quality self-improvement journal which promotes teetotalism, working-class co-operation and association, mutual instruction societies. Advocates national education, early closing, parliamentary reform, free trade. Short notice, trade-union snippets, series of 'Letters on labour reform' by James Benny, extensive correspondence.

        L(Col)†

2717 Pioneer News [192-?]

    B   1d. For young Communists; 'to organize the young socialist army'. 'The **Drum** used to come out, it was a big paper with news of troops all over the country, Scotland, Wales, London, all the news of school strikes, protests, sports, and so on. We want **Drum** to come out again, bigger and better. Depends on you!' To organise and fight against victimisation and oppression of children and unemployed children. Reproduced from typewriting.

        MML† one undated no. [192-?]

2718 Pioneer News: Organ of the Young Comrades' League of Great Britain [Jan. 1929?]–? m?

    B   ½d. Reproduced from typewriting. News, reports, short items.

        O(JJ) I, 8 (Aug. 1929)

2719 Pioneer Newspaper, and Oddfellows' Journal ? (19 Jan. 1845)–(2 March 1845); then **London Journal and Pioneer Newspaper**: 1 (15 March 1845)–68 (6 June 1846); w

    C   6d. Published G. H. Lovegrove. 'To exalt and improve the working classes will be the ruling object of its conductors.' Advocate of the Manchester Unity of the Independent Order of Oddfellows. General newspaper with news of Oddfellows. Superseded by **The Journal**, 1846–7.

        L(Col)†

2720 Pioneer of the Folk I, 1 (May 1932)–III, 12 (July 1936); then **New Pioneer**: I, 1 (Aug. 1936)–VI, 10 (Aug. 1939). Nottingham; m

A 'The monthly for children of the Woodcraft Folk.' The movement developed in the early years of this century, was similar to the Boy Scouts, but without the nationalistic emphasis, more working class, close to the Co-operative Movement. Woodcraft Folk (Federation of Co-operative Woodcraft Fellowships) established at the end of 1925. An auxiliary organisation of the Co-operative Union.

L 1 (mislaid); Woodcraft Folk?

2721 Pioneers' Record: a Quarterly Record for Rochdale Co-operators 1 (1908)–? Rochdale; q

A Gratis. Issued by the Educational Committee of the Rochdale Equitable Pioneers' Society. Editorial, local Co-operative news, reports of meetings.

L 23 (Oct. 1913)–33 (1916)

2722 Pivot: Organ of the Telephone Contract Officers' Association [193-?194-?]– . Manchester.

L XXVII, 7 (Aug. 1963)– ; TUC† XXI, 8 (Dec. 1959)

2723 Plain Speaker; or, Politics for the People 1 (2 Dec. 1837)–2 (9 Dec. 1837); w

B 2d. Published by William Strange. Printed by James Anderson. Attacks the monopoly of political power held by the rich. Radical and entertainment miscellany. Advocates the ballot and political representation for the working class, by moral force means.

L

2724 Plain Speaker I, 1 (20 Jan. 1849)–50 (29 Dec. 1849); w

B 1d. Published by Benjamin Steill. Editors: Thomas Cooper; Thomas Wooler. Preceded **Cooper's Journal**. Chartist. Outlines Cooper's plans on popular reading and education, and on social questions, eg 'organisation of labour', a form of co-partnership.

LE†; LU 1–49; MP; O 1–40; Warwick UL (microfilm)

2725 Plan 1 [Michaelmas Term, 1931]–1932. Oxford; 'about twice a term in 1932'

B 6d. Started by several members of the Labour Club of the University of Oxford. First editor: H. Smith. Contributors (No. 1): G. D. H. Cole, E. A. Radice, Richard Goodman. '**Plan** is a journal of constructive Socialism . . . Recognising that socialist thought which is isolated from the organised working classes tends to become academic and sterile, it will associate itself with every phase of the workers' struggle for freedom' (No. 1). '. . . admirable articles on industrial and economic problems and their solutions. The third number contained a special supplement on the cotton industry.' (M. P. Ashley and C. T. Saunders, **Red Oxford**, Oxford 1933, pp. 16, 36).

O(JJ)† 1

Plan, 1942– see **Plan for World Order and Progress**

Plan Bulletin see **Plan for World Order and Progress**

Plan for Freedom and Progress see **Plan for World Order and Progress**

2726 Plan for World Order and Progress: a Constructive Monthly Review I, 1 (April 1934)–VI, 9 (Sept. 1939); then b **Plan Bulletin**: I, 1 (Oct. 1939)–II, 11 (Dec. 1941); then **Plan** : IX, 1 (Jan. 1942)–?; m
    B   3d. (1936). Later subtitled: 'The Monthly Journal of the Federation of Progressive Societies and Individuals'. Issued by the Progressive League. Editors (May 1936): Leslie Paul and John Dudding. The FPSI stands for 'Regional and world planning with a view to the progressive replacement of production for profit by production for use . . .'. Articles, correspondence, reviews. Later title: **Plan for Freedom and Progress**. Latterly reproduced from typewriting.
    L (mislaid); ONC† a III, 5 (May 1936)

2727 Planet: the Official Journal of the Slough Branch of the National and Local Government Officers' Association I, 1952–   . Slough
    A   Reproduced from typewriting.
    L

2728 Platform 1 (6 July 1901)–3 (20 July 1901). then **Independent Labour Party Platform**: 4 (27 July 1901)–168 (10 Sept 1904); w
    B   20 for 1d. Published by the Independent Labour Party, then by John Penny, later by Francis Johnson. A small leaflet issued as propaganda material explaining the socialist programme of the ILP. Each number has one concise article.
    L

2729 Platform: a Paper for All Passenger Transport Workers 1 (Nov. 1949)–200 (Dec. 1966); m
    A   3d. Published for **The Platform** by G. Moore. Militant rank-and-file, trade-union journal founded to fight for better wages, conditions and rights against the wage freeze policy of the Labour government, and the 'collusion', in this policy, of the trade-union leadership. For London Passenger Transport workers, members of the Transport and General Workers Union. Campaigns for trade-union democracy, ie for the removal of the ban against Communists' holding union positions. Main contributor: Bill Jones
    L (w 41); ONC; WCML† 81–3, 92; Warwick U (MRC)

2730 Platform: the Paper of the Co-operative Party 1 (Sept. 1965)–46 (Nov. 1969); [ns], I, 1 (Jan. 1970)–   ; m; bi-m; m
    B   4d. Published by the Co-operative Union. Newspaper format. From 1970 printed as a supplement to the **Co-operative News** and the **Scottish Co-operator**.
    E; LE; O

Playgoer and Millgate see **Millgate Monthly**

Plebs see **'Plebs' Magazine**

2731 'Plebs' Magazine I, 1 (Feb. 1909)—XI, 6 (July 1919); then **Plebs**: XI, 7 (Aug. 1919). Oxford; London; m
    B   2d. etc. Published by the 'Plebs' League to further the interests of the Central Labour College in London and the formation of similar bodies elsewhere to be controlled by organised labour. Later 'Organ of the National Council of Labour Colleges'.
    BdP. I—XXXVIII, CXVI— ; E*; GM 1935— ; HU X, 12—(w XII, 10); L; LE 1912—27*; LabP 1955— ; MML; NULV, 3 (March 1963)— ; O XVI— ; ONC 1910—68*; TUC 1920—*

2732 Plough: a Monthly Magazine for Scottish Ploughmen, Small Holders, and Crofters 1 (15 April 1893)—III, 25 (15 Nov. 1895). Edinburgh; m; w (April 1895—)
    B   1d. Published by the Plough Publishing Company. Devoted to the interests of farm servants and small holders in Scotland. Organ of the Scottish Ploughmen's Federal Union, and of the Scottish Small Holdings and Allotments Association. Committed to State legislation to improve the conditions of rural workers, small holders, and crofters. Outlook in politics is Liberal. Agitates on wages, hours, rural housing, land reform. Union notes by county. Letters.
    E (microfilm); L(Col)†

2733 Ploughshare: a Journal of Radical Religion and Morality I, 1 (Oct. 1885)—ns 16 [1888?] ; m; irreg
    B   1d.
    AP*†; AU*†

2734 Ploughshare: Organ of the Socialist Quaker Society I, 1 (Nov. 1912)—12 (Nov. 1915); ns I, 1 (Jan. 1916)—V, 5 (June 1920); q; m(ns)
    B   3d. Printed and published by Newnham, Cowell and Gripper. Editors: William Loftus Hare, Hugh William Peet. Founded in order to bring the message of Socialism to the members of the Society of Friends. Proclaimed as an economic gospel, but opposed to violent revolution, although against "capitalist tyranny".' Articles on economic problems, religion, war, responsible morality from the Christian Socialist point of view
    C ii; L; LE i; LFS i—ii, 4; o ii

2735 Ploughshare: Organ of the Teachers' Anti-War Movement I, 1 (Jan. 1934)—21 (Jan./Feb. 1938); bi-m
    A   2d. Published by Teachers' Peace Publications. To consolidate the position of the Movement, to express and record opinion against 'War, Economies, and Tyranny'. 'Aimed at winning the active interest of the teaching profession in the prevention of war.' Popular Front. Secretary: Neil Hunter. Member of Editorial Board: Edward Upward.
    L

2736 Plymouth and District Labour Gazette [c1921]. [Plymouth?] ; w
  B   1d. Local Labour Party paper (**Labour Organiser**, July 1921.)

2737 Plymouth Citizen 1 (March 1961)—10 (Feb. 1963). Plymouth; irreg
  B   Issued by the Plymouth Labour Party.
  L(Col); LabP† 6 (Oct. 1961), 9 (Oct. 1962)

Plymouth Co-operative Journal see **Plymouth Co-operative Record**

2738 Plymouth Co-operative Record Dec. 1889—April 1938; then
Plymouth Co-operative Journal: [May 1938?]—Sept. 1947. Plymouth; m
  A   Gratis. Plymouth Co-operative Society. Editors included E. C.
Burton; T. W. Mercer. Title sometimes **Monthly Record**. Superseded by
local pages in the **Co-operative Home Magazine**.
  Co-op. Union 217, 314—25 (1916), 369; P1P occ. nos

2739 Plymouth Co-operator 1917—? Plymouth; w
  A   'Early in 1917, there appeared a very stimulating weekly
publication, **The Plymouth Co-operator**. Its object was to keep members
more informed as to the activities of their Society, and, further, to supply
Co-operators with "information from sources without a capitalist taint".
The issue of the paper ended with the return to power of committee
members of the "Blue Ticket" persuasion, who terminated its publication
on the grounds of unnecessary expense' (R. Briscoe, **Centenary History: a
hundred Years of the Plymouth Co-operative Society**, Manchester 1960,
p. 73).

2740 Poetry and the People I, 1 (July 1938)—I, 20 (Sept. 1940); irreg
  B   3d.; 6d. Printed and published by Progressive Publications for
Poetry and the People. Issued by the Left Book Club, Poetry Group. Then
merged in **Our Time**.
  C*; L 11, 16—20; MML

2471 Poilisher Yidl. [Polish Yidel] 1 (25 July 1884)—15 (31 Oct. 1884).
London; w
  B   1d. A general Jewish paper, with interest in Jewish workers'
affairs. Socialist leanings. Yiddish.
  L(Col)

2742 Pointer: Bi-monthly of the Chislehurst and Sidcup Branch
1960?—   . Orpington; bi-m
  A   National and Local Government Officers' Association.
Reproduced from typewriting.
  L 1960—

2743 Points for Pacifists: a Quarterly Bulletin of Anti-Militarist Information 1 (Sept. 1933)–5 (Nov. 1934); q

B   4d. per dozen (4–5). Printed for the No More War Movement by the Freegard Press, Sittingbourne, then by Watford Printers, Watford. '. . . supplied . . . not as reading material, but as an instrument to assist you in your work for Pacifism'. Material for use in speeches, conversations, and communications to the local press See also **No More War; New World**.

O

2744 Points West [194-?] –?

A   National Association of Local Government Officers, later National and Local Government Officers' Association, London Electricity (Western) Branch.

L IV, 5 (Dec. 1952)–VI, 3 (Autumn 1954)

Police see **Police Federation News-Letter**

2745 Police and Prison Officers' Journal. Organ of the National Union of Police and Prison Officers I, 1 (30 Jan. 1914)–III, 66 (30 April 1915); then **Police and Prison Officers' Magazine**: I, 1 (19 Dec. 1918)–I, 39 (19 Nov. 1919). Bristol; London

A   1d.

L; TUC Aug. 1915, 1919

Police and Prison Officers' Magazine see **Police and Prison Officers' Journal**

2746 Police Federation News–Letter I, 1 (March 1957)–VI, 16 (1968); then **Police**: the Monthly Journal of the Police Federation. I (1968)–   ; m

A

E 1968–   ; L; O 1968–   ; TUC*†

2747 Police Review and Parade Gossip: Organ of the British Constabulary I, 1 (2 Jan. 1893)–2164 (29 June 1934); then **Police Review** 2165 (6 July 1934)–; w

A   (until 1919) For a time the organ of the Police Union (ie National Union of Police and Prison Officers, founded 1913, re-organised 1917), a collective negotiating body on pay, service and pension issues. After the police strike of 1919, was succeeded by the Police Federation, which was started by the authorities, and the journal ceases to be relevant, being primarily a recruiting and information publication.

L(Col)†; MP 1893–1919

2748 Polish Labour Fights, for Freedom, Equality, Independence 1 (1944)–5 (1944). London

B   Published by Liberty Publications. Reproduced from typewriting. Supports solidarity between British and Polish labour. Started while the Battle for Warsaw was being engaged.

L(Col)†

Political and Historical Essays see **Carpenter's Political and Historical Essays**

2749 Political Anecdotist and Popular Instructor 1 (18 June 1831)–4 (9 July 1831); w

    B   2d. Published by William Strange (1), then by William Carpenter. Printed and edited by W. Carpenter, recently imprisoned for publishing **Political Letters and Pamphlets**. 'A radical political miscellany that attacks the aristocracy, the Church of England, the Corn Laws, and the "taxes on knowledge" ' (Wiener).

    LU

2750 Political Economist and Universal Philanthropist 1 (11 Jan. 1823)–?; fortn

    B   6d. Editor: George Mudie. Printer: Hetherington. The prospectus demonstrates a plan whereby the working classes, the sole producers, can have an eight-fold increase in wages, and urges the right to work for all. Only one number?

    O Prospectus

2751 Political Equity, for the Payment of Wages Without Stoppages: a Labour Advocate and Ratepayers' Journal 1 [1855?]–2 (1856). Derby

    B   Edited by Jeremiah Briggs, General Manager of the National Labour Alliance. No. 1 consists of a reprint of the motion put in the House of Commons on 11 May 1853, by Sir Henry Halford, MP for Leicestershire, for the Payment of Wages without Stoppages, in the Hosiery Manufacture, concerning guarantees for payment of net wages and upkeep of contracts, and is opposed to the conduct of middlemen in deducting framerent charges from the weavers' pay. No. 2 contains the manifesto of the National Labour Alliance, for the removal of legislation prohibiting the freedom of labour and the enjoying of the fruits of one's labour.

    LU†

2752 Political Examiner 1 (8 Sept. 1832)–2 (15 Sept. 1832). Glasgow; w

    B   1½d. Published by W. R. M'Phun. Printed by MacLure. 'A radical political miscellany that advocates the ballot, universal suffrage, repeal of the Corn Laws, and the establishment of a republican form of government' (Wiener).

    GM†

2753 Political Examiner: a Weekly Democratic Journal 1 (2 March 1853)–47 (14 Jan. 1854); w

    B   1d. Published by James Watson, then by Holyoake and Company (46–7). 'An endeavour will be made to record co-operative progress, educational movements, and the advocacy of temperance will not be forgotten. A space will be kept for the purpose of noting the progress of the agitation for the removal of "taxes on knowledge" ' (Vol. II). Reviews, correspondence, information on trade-union affairs, demands for higher wages etc. Supports universal suffrage. Information on foreign national liberation movements. Contributor: William Newton.

    LU† I; MP I; ONC† II

2754 Political Investigator 1 (9 June 1832)—4 ([July 7] 1832); w

    C   2d. Printed for the proprietors by Isaac Bass. Object 'to instruct the industrious and productive classes' in the responsibility of struggling for political reform. Against the aristocracy. Advocates free trade. Theoretical articles.

    L; LU 1—2; ONC 1

2755 Political Letter 1 (4 June 1831)—11 (13 Aug. 1831); w

    B   1d. Edited by William Carpenter. Aimed at diffusing 'sound and useful knowledge amongst a numerous class of his fellow countrymen, from which they were in a great measure previously debarred, by the monopoly — price of the regular journals.' Incorporated with **Ballot** (qv).

    L(Col)†

2756 [Political Letters and Pamphlets] 1 (9 Oct. 1830)—34 (14 May 1831); w

    B   2d. etc. Printed, published and edited by William Carpenter. Unstamped. Each number is in newspaper format, prefaced by a letter. Each has a separate title, eg, 'A Political Letter', 'A Political Observer', 'A Political Omnibus', 'A Political Repertory', and Carpenter claimed that each was a separate paper, and liable only to pamphlet duty. Deals with radical political reform.

    L; LU; O*; Greenwood reprint and microfiche: microfiche distributed in Britain and Europe by the Harvester Press Ltd

2757 Political Penny Magazine 1 (3 Sept. 1836)—9 (29 Oct. 1836); w

    B   1d. Published and printed by S. Whaley (1—7), then by Edward Morris. 'An illustrated pro-Catholic radical miscellany that vigorously advocates repeal of the Poor Law Amendment Act (1834), and attacks the institution of property. It asserts that it is not discussing "news", but only historical events that have an influence on the present' (Wiener). Asserts that labour is the sole source of value.

    Columbia UL, New York 5—9; O 1, 3; ONC 1

2758 Political Register: Late the London Police Gazette 1 (12 July 1834?)—62 (12 Sept. 1835); w

    B   2d. Published by 'Benjamin Franklin', ie James H. B. Lorymer. Printed by S. Wilson. 'A working-class radical miscellany that denounces Tories and Whigs, the House of Commons, and the Church of England. It agitates vigorously for an untaxed press. Many of its articles are written by George Edmonds' (Wiener).

    HO 40/33, Part 2 58—9; LU a clipping from No. 62 is in Oastler's **Letters and Cuttings—White Slavery 1835—36**

2759 Political Soldier 1 (7 Dec. 1833)—5 (4 Jan. 1834); w

B   1½d Published and printed by George Pilgrim. First number edited by A. Somerville who resigned after a dispute with Richard Carlile who then edited the succeeding numbers. 'A radical miscellany that seeks to disseminate sound republican principles amongst the soldiers. It advocates abolition of flogging and other forms of military torture' (Wiener). Later subtitle: 'A Paper for the Army and People'.

Co-op Union 1—4; GM 2; HO 64/19 1—2; NwP; ONC 1

2760 Political Stage 1 (19 Sept. 1835?)—11 (28 Nov. 1835); w

B   1d. Published by George Johnson. 'A radical political miscellany' (Wiener).

L Dept. of Prints and Drawings 9—11

2761 Political Union Register 1 (March 1832)—3 (May 1832).
Birmingham; m

B   Records the proceedings of the Birmingham Political Union, and describes its role and achievement during the Reform crisis. Also deals with the amelioration of the conditions of the working class, eg with tax reduction, home colonisation. Correspondence.

BP 1; LU†

2762 Political Unionist 1 (30 June 1832)—2 (July 1832); w

B   2d. Published by William Strange. Edited by William Carpenter. Reports of meetings of the National Union of the Working Classes. Intended to become the organ of Political Unions as permanent bodies, continuing after the enactment of the Reform Bill of 1832.

L; LU

2763 Politician 1 (13 Dec. 1794)—?; w

B   1d. Published by the London Corresponding Society. Edited by William Townly. For annual parliaments and universal suffrage. 'The labours of the various Societies instituted for the purposes of promoting political Knowledge, lessening the abuses of Government, and supporting the Rights of the People, shall find in this work a faithful register.' No. 3 contains letter, address and poem by J. Thelwall.

ONC† 1, 3 (Dec. 27)

Politics for the People. 1793—1795 see **Hog's Wash**

2764 Politics for the People 1 (6 May 1848)—17 (29 July 1848); w

B   There are monthly supplements which are numbered in the same sequence, eg, No. 15 is 29 July 1848, Nos. 16 and 17 are supplements for July 1848. 1d.; monthly parts with a supplement, 6d. Published by John W. Parker. Editors: F. D. Maurice, J. M. Ludlow etc. Christian Socialist. Articles on history, politics, social questions, religion, verse, aphorisms etc.

C; L; LK; LU; O; ONC†

2765 Politics for the Poor and the Rich: Addresses to the People, by a British Officer Banished from France in 1834 for His Political Opinions. 1 (1836)–3 (1836)

    B   Published by Mr Murison. 'Universal suffrage, nationalization of land and mines, founding of a commonwealth' (**Museum Book Shop Catalogue**, 1922, p. 12).

Ponder see National Association of Local Government Officers. Carshalton Branch. **Journal**

2766 Poor Man's Advocate, and People's library; or, a Full and Fearless Exposure of the Horrors and Abominations of the Factory System in England, in the Year 1832 1 (21 Jan. 1832)–50 (5 Jan. 1833); then **Poor Man's Advocate, and Scourge of Tyranny**: 51 (11 Oct. 1834)–55 (6 Dec. 1834). Manchester; w

    B   1d. Published and printed by A. Wilkinson (1–5), John Doherty (6–34), Joshua Hobson (35–50), and James Turner (51–55). Edited by John Doherty (1–50), then James Turner (51–55). 'A working-class political miscellany that principally agitates for factory legislation by means of leaders, accounts of meetings, and repeated exposures of abuses by the "cotton lords"' (Wiener). A successor to **The Workman's Expositor**. The titles of Nos. 34–50 are varied, eg 'A Pennyworth of Politics by the Poor Man's Advocate' (8 Sept. 1832), 'A Penny Paper by a Poor Man's Advocate' (15 Sept. 1832). Columbia UL, New York 1–50, 55; L 1–18, 25–30; L Place Coll. Add. MSS. 35, 149 pp. 322–5. 51; LE† 1–50 (reprint); LU 34–50; MP 1–35; ONC† 1–50 (microfilm); Warwick UL 1–50 (microfilm); Greenwood reprint 1–50 and microfiche: microfiche distributed in Britain and Europe by the Harvester Press Ltd.

2767 Poor Man's Guardian: a Weekly Newspaper for the People Established Contrary to the Law to Try the Power of 'Might' Against 'Right' 1 (9 July 1831)–238 (26 Dec. 1835); w

    B   ½d. Printed and published by H. Hetherington. Editors: Bronterre O'Brien, Thomas Mayhew. 'The best known and most important illegal newspaper of the decade with an estimated peak circulation of 15,000 (according to Secret Service Report of Oct. 30, 1832, HO 64/12)' (Wiener). Champions universal suffrage; a working-class newspaper which prosecutes class war against the profit managers etc.

    BP; L(Col); LE 1–186; and reprint; LU; Mp 1–223; NwP 1831–4; ONC 73–107, 109–51, 194–5; Greenwood reprint and microfiche: microfiche distributed in Britain and Europe by the Harvester Press Ltd.

2768 Poor Man's Guardian 1 (6 Nov. 1847)–8 (25 Dec. 1847); w

    C   1d. Organ of the Poor Man's Guardian Society, a philanthropic institution established to secure a better deal for the destitute among the labouring poor of the metropolis.

    L; LU 1–7; O

2769 Poor Man's Guardian and Repealer's Friend: a Weekly Journal of Politics, Literature and Moral Science 1 (3 June 1843)–14 (26 Aug. 1843); w

    B   1d. Published and edited by Bronterre O'Brien. Chartist. Opposes anti-Corn Law agitation, espouses cause of Irish Repeal, discusses the land question.

    LU†; O 1–13

2770 Poor Man's Paper 1 [c March 1832?] –? Birmingham; w?

    B   Printed by Joseph Russell. See A. Briggs, 'Background of the Parliamentary Reform Movement in three English cities, 1830–32; **Cambridge Historical Journal**, 1952, pp. 293–317, p. 299n. (Wiener).

    HO 52/20

2771 Poor Richard's Journal for Poor People 1 (24 Nov. 1832)–3 (8 Dec. 1832); w

    C   2d. Published by W. Howden. Printed by Mills, Jowett and Mills. 'Seeks to inculcate morality and industriousness among the poor by advising them on legal, medical and related practical subjects' (Wiener).

    L: O(JJ) 1

2772 Poplar Labour League Gazette March 1900–? m

    B   1d. (Reformers' Year Book, 1901.)

2773 Port Watch. 1961?–   Gosport

    A   National and Local Government Officers' Association, Gosport Branch.

    L 1961–

2774 Portcullis Post: a Monthly Publication of the Customs and Excise A and CG's. (Southend) Branch. [19--?] –. [Southend?] ; m

    A   Civil and Public Services Association. Confidential to members. Reproduced from typewriting.

    Warwick U(MRC)† LIV (Jan. 1971)

2775 Portland Pages [1951?] –

    A   National Association of Local Government Officers, later National and Local Government Officers' Association, Metropolitan Regional Hospital Boards' Branch. Reproduced from typewriting.

    L II (Feb. 1952)–(w II, 2–3)

2776 Portlight I, 1 (May 1934)–1935; m

    A   2d. Issued by the Joint Members' Committee, Clerical and Supervisory Section, Transport and General Workers' Union. Editorial Board of five. Rank-and-file paper for clerical workers in the Port of London, initiated by Minority Movement members.

    WCML† 1 (Xerox)

2777 Portsmouth (Cent.) Courier [194-?]. Portsmouth; fortn
    B   2d. Labour Party. (Labour Party. **Your own Journal**, 1948.)

2778 Portsmouth Co-operative Citizen 1 (Feb. 1935)—2 (March 1935); then **PIMCO Co-operative Citizen**: 3 (April 1935)—9 (Oct. 1935). Portsmouth; m
    B
    L(Col)

2779 Portworkers' Bulletin 1 (Oct. 1965)—? Grays, Essex; m
    A   Published by the National Union of Portworkers. Edited by Sydney Senior, General Secretary. Agitates for full workers' control in the docks. Reproduced from typewriting.
    L 1—2 (Nov. 1965)

2780 Portworkers' Clarion: organ of the Birkenhead Portworkers' Committee. [Nov. 1951?]—? Birkenhead; m
    B   2d. Published and edited by D. Brandon. Trotskyist.
    ONC† 5 (March 1952)

2781 Post: a Fortnightly Postal Journal, the Organ of the Fawcett Association I, 1 (8 Feb. 1890)—XXX, 796 (26 Dec. 1919). fortn
    A   1d. Published by W. B. Cheesman, Secretary of the Association. Started by W. E. Clery for Post Office workers; he 'was not only editor, but almost the sole contributor, as few dared to join in the risk of "writing for the press".' No. 1 was 'an unpretentious pamphlet . . . for a considerable period it was allowed to be sold and circulated within the precincts of the Post Office.' (H. G. Swift, **A History of Postal Agitation from eighty Years ago till the Present Day**, New edition, **Book 1**, Manchester, London 1929, pp. 184—5.) 'The Fawcett Association is a federation of all classes of the Sorting Force of the Postal Service, its objects being 1 The Promotion and protection of their Civil Service interests; 2 The provision of mutual help in sickness; 3 Life Insurance at the lowest cost consistent with security.' Later editor: Thomas Edward Morris. Ceased when the Association was merged into the Union of Post Office Workers.
    L(Col)† V, 122 (7 July 1894)—796; Union of Post Office Workers*

2782 Post: the Organ of the Union of Post-Office Workers I, 1 (3 Jan. 1920)— . Manchester (3 Jan. 1920—23 April 1921); London; w (to 1939); fortn
    A   1d. Publishers: George Middleton; Francis Andrews; Norman Stagg etc. Union matters, branch notes; later enlarged to include articles, correspondence, reviews, crossword etc. Later subtitle: 'Journal of the Union of Post Office Workers'.
    L(Col); LE III—XI; NU LIX, 1954— ; ONC occ. nos 1948, 1949, 1953, LXXII, 1967— ; TUC*; the Union

2783 Post-Office Engineer. 1 (July 1959)–   ; m

    A   Society of Post Office Engineers.

    L 18 (Jan. 1961)–

2784 Post Office Engineering Inspector [19–?] –? m

    A   Society of Post Office Engineering Inspectors.

    TUC III (1921)–(Jan. 1923*)

2785 Post Office Gazette 1 (16 Nov. 1889)–?

    C   1d. One number only? Printed and published for the proprietors by Bowers Brothers. Condensed news, leisure reading. Absorbed **The Telegraphist**; **The Postal Gazette**; **The Postal and Telegraph Service Gazette**.

    L

2786 Post-Office Journal (20 June 1892)–?; then **Postal Journal**: (March 1893)–(Nov. 1894). Liverpool; m

    A   2d. Postal Clerks' Association. (H. G. Swift, **A History of Postal Agitation from eighty Years ago till the Present Day**, New edition, **Book 1**, Manchester, London 1929, p. 260.)

    L June 1894–Nov. 1894 (w Aug. 1894). (not traced in catalogue)

2787 Postal Advocate: Official Organ of the LPPA [1905?] –XIV, 172 (18 Dec. 1919); m

    A   1d. London Postal Porters' Association. Branch reports, correspondence, enquiries. The Association was amalgamated in 1920 with the Union of Post Office Workers.

    L(Col)† III, 35 (18 July 1908)–XIV, 172

Postal and Telegraph Record see **Postal Clerk's Herald**

2788 Postal and Telegraph Service Gazette [188-?] –?; then **Postal Service Gazette**: [188-?]

    A   An 'outlet for the pent-up discontent of years.' (H. G. Swift, **A History of Postal Agitation from eighty Years ago till the present day**, New edition, **Book 1**, Manchester, London, 1929, p. 162.)

2789 Postal Clerk's Herald I, 1 (Sept. 1898)–XVI, 310 (May 1914); then b **Postal and Telegraph Record**, the Official Organ of the Postal and Telegraph Clerks' Association: I, 1 (14 May 1914)–XI, 294 (25 Dec. 1919). Huddersfield; Manchester; m; fortn?; w

    A   1d. First official organ of the United Kingdom Postal Clerks' Association. Publishers include R. C. Adamson, George Middleton.

    L(Col)†; LE a*, b; ONC occ. nos

2790 Postal Forward 1934; m

    A   1d. Reproduced from typewriting. Forward Movement. Rank-and-file paper initiated by Minority Movement workers. CPGB

2791 Postal Free-Lance: a Medium of Free Expression I, 1 (Dec. 1920)–VIII, 11 (July/Aug. 1929); m

    A   2d. Published and edited by J. V. Wallace, then edited by J. Naughton. Conducted and managed by members of the Union of Post Office Workers, but not the organ of any one association. Later subtitle: 'A Medium of Free Expression and a Review of Trade Unionism, Sport, Literature and Art, Conducted by the Staff, GPO, Mount Pleasant'.

    L(Col)†

2792 Postal Gazette [188-?]

    C?   Absorbed by **The Post Office Gazette** (qv)

2793 Postal Inspector: the Official Journal of the Postal Inspectors' Association, Comprising Postal Inspectorate and Head Post Men, Outer London and Provinces I, 1 (15 Jan. 1952)–VIII, 7 (30 June 1959). Lincoln; m

    A   4s. 6d. per year. Printed and published by the **Lincolnshire Chronicle**. Subtitle not on No. 1. Union affairs. Ceased publication on the amalgamation of the Association with the Association of Post Office Controlling Officers.

    C; O

Postal Journal see **Post-Office Journal**

2794 Postal Review 1890–? Birmingham; m

    A? C?   For circulation among sorting clerks. (H. G. Swift, **A History of Postal Agitation from eighty Years ago till the Present Day**, New edition, **Book 1**, Manchester, London 1929, pp. 238–9.)

Postal Service Gazette see **Postal and Telegraph Service Gazette**

2795 Postal Telegraph: the Official Organ of the National Federation of Postal and Telegraph Clerks I, 1 (March 1921)–XVI, 3 (July 1948); m; fortn

    A   Later, official organ of the Guild of Postal Sorters. Published by the Federation then by the Guild. The Federation was formed by members leaving the Union of Post Office Workers to further their particular interests. Union and inter-union news, reviews, occasional articles etc. Ceased publication when the Guild was wound up.

    L(Col)†

Postal Worker see **An Dion**

2796 Postman: a Journal Devoted to the Interests of Money Order and Savings Bank Clerks, Sorters, Messengers, Register Clerks, Letter Carriers, Mail Drivers, Mail Guards, Change Takers, Auxiliaries, Supernumaries etc. 1 (1 Aug. 1867)–?; m?

A   2d. Printed by John Hall and William Henry Foster; 'to all interested in the great question of post office reform', employees in the lower grades 'of official life at Post Offices of the Metropolis and the provinces'. To redress grievances. Interesting correspondence including contributions by postmen.

L(Col)† 1

2797 Postman's Gazette I, 1 (4 May 1892)–XXVIII, 26 (20 Dec. 1919). London; Glasgow; fortn

A   1d. Official journal of the Postmen's Federation. Published in the interests of all grades of postmen. Superseded by **The Post**. There are references to a journal of this title beginning in October 1889. Was this an earlier series?

L(Col)†; LE XV–XXVIII (XX*); ONC XXVII, 12–14, 17; TUC 1906–19*; the Union

2798 Postmaster: the Organ of the Head Postmasters' Association I, 1 (May 1907)–I, 9 (Aug. 1909). Chorley; q

A   3d. Started at the time of a Select Committee decision on postmasters' wages and prospects. Articles and reports.

L (w I, 8)

2799 Postmen's Alarm: the Organ of the Postmen's Association I, 1 (Sept. 1930)–III, 12 (Aug. 1933); then **Postmen's Journal**: IV, 1 (Sept. 1933)–IX, 16 (May/June 1944); m

A   Published by the Editorial Committee of the Postmen's Association. London Postmen's Association, then National Association of Postmen. Rival of the Union of Post Office Workers.

L

Postmen's Journal see **Postmen's Alarm**

2800 Postmen's Knock [19--?] –?

A Union of Post Office Workers, ECDO No. 1 Branch. (W. Dunlop. 'Local journals'. **Belpost**, IV, 5 [May 1965].)

2801 Potteries Examiner [1864?]–838 ([5 June?], 839 [12 June?] 1880); then **Staffordshire Potteries Examiner**: (839 [12 June?], 840 [19 June?] 1880)–891 ([11 June 1881) Hanley, Stoke-on-Trent? w

B   1d.; 1½d. Printed and published by William Owen. 'devoted to the interests of labour'. For labour representation. One of the Examiner series.

L(Col)† 348 (18 March 1871)–1881 (w 1872; No. 839) (1874 on microfilm)

Potteries Free Press and Staffordshire Knot see **Staffordshire Knot**
[Weekly edition]

2802 Potteries Free Press and Weekly Narrative of Current Events 1 (12
Feb. 1853)–10 (26 April 1853). Stoke-on-Trent; w
    B   1d. Printed and published by the proprietor, Collet Dobson
Collet. Issued to defy the Stamp Office. An organ of working-class
interests, 'and of those in the Potteries especially'. Advocates manhood
suffrage and national secular education. Comment and news on current
events.
    L(Col)†; Warwick UL (microfilm)

2803 Potteries Mechanic's Institute Magazine I, 1 (Feb. 1860)– (Jan.
1861); II (Feb. 1861)–12 (Jan. 1862). Hanley; m
    C   Printed and published by William Timmis.
    William Salt Library, Stafford; StP

2804 Potteries Republican: a Monthly Journal, Advocating the Interests of
All Classes, With a View to the Equality of All. [Dec. 1872?]–? Hanley; m
    B   1d. Printed by H. Adams for Henry Wedgwood. Antimonarchist.
Contents of No. 3 include: 'Have hereditary monarchies conduced to the
social, political and religious order of nations? Chapter 1. France',
correspondence on local council affairs, a letter: 'An atheist in the witness
box' by D. Lowndes, review of Bradlaugh's 'The impeachment of the
House of Brunswick'.
    O(JJ)† I, 3 (1 Feb. 1873)

2805 Potters' Examiner and Workman's Advocate I, 1 (2 Dec.
1843]–[1848?]; then **Potters' Examiner and Emigrants' Advocate**: July
1848–[1851?]. Shelton; w
    A   1d. Published by William Evans. Printed for the Executive of
the United Branches of Operative Potters. Organ of the Operative Potters'
Union. To further 'the Rights and Interests of the Working Classes'. A
medium for discussion of trade-union and labour problems in the district.
Contributions by Working-men. Trade-union news and correspondence.
    L I–II; StP I, 1–III, 26 (24 May 1845 [originals]); I–VII, IX–X*
(microfilm)

2806 Potter's Union. News Letter [Jan. 1963?]–[1969?]; then Ceramic
and Allied Trades Union. **Newsletter**: [1969?]– . Hanley,
Stoke-on-Trent; q
    A   National Society of Pottery Workers, then Ceramic and Allied
Trades Union.
    TUC 4 (Oct. 1963)–1969*, 1970–

2807 Power [1926?]–?; m
    A   ½d. 'Published by the Communists in the ETU', ie the ETU
[Electrical Trades Union] Communist Group. Reproduced from typewriting
    O(JJ)† ns 1 (March 1927)

2808 Power of the Pence I, 1 (11 Nov. 1848)–I, 24 (21 April 1849); w

B   1d. Published at the **Power of the Pence** and 'People's Press Office'. Printed by Sheriffs and Russell (11); printed and published by W. Winn (24). Edited by Bronterre O'Brien. Chartist weekly. O'Brien carried on, for six months, a genuine attempt at adult education by means of well-written, full-length articles on many aspects of current affairs, such as universal suffrage, nationalization of land and minerals, banks for the people, church disestablishment' (A. Plummer, **Bronterre**, London 1971). Also news and correspondence.

Columbia UL New York; LU*; O 2–11, 13–24; ONC† I, 11, 24; Toronto UL; Yale UL

2809 Power Worker: Organ of the Combined Works Committees of the Electrical Supply Industry(ies) I, 1 (Oct. 1947)–?; m

A   2d. First printed and published by E. Brewer. Originated in a mass meeting at Holborn Hall, 19 May 1947 to discuss the Charter for immediate application of a 40-hour week. No. 1 reproduced from typewriting.

R. Harrison I, 1–V, 5 (Feb. 1952), occ. nos to VI, 6 (March 1953)

2810 Practical Socialist: a Monthly Review of Evolutionary or Non-Revolutionary Socialism. I, 1 (Jan. 1886)–II, 18 (June 1887); m

B   1d. Printed and published by W. Reeves. Edited by Thomas Bolas, a member of the Fabian Society and the Socialist League. Publicises the proceedings of the Fabian Society, and most of contributions by members of the Society

L; LE; O

2811 Prayer Leaflet Jan.–March 1951–? Northwood; q

C   Glynn Vivian Miners' Mission

L

2812 Precursor of Unity: a Monthly Magazine for the Many I, 1 (Jan. 1844)–8 (Aug. 1844); m

C   6d. 'Illustrative of the System of Association Upon Christian Principles, for the Protection and Distribution of Wealth, and the Physical, Mental and Spiritual Improvement of Mankind.' Makes proposals for a solution to the dangerous 'condition of England question'. In the interests of 'Capital Talent and Labour', each to be given remuneration for his contribution to the wealth of the community, with a decent standard of living for all. Contains reviews of social theories for the improvement of society, eg St Simonism, Fourierism. Reviews current publications on the 'condition of England question' and related matters. Not specifically addressed to the working-man but has concern for his condition. Seeks to dissolve class antagonisms and create a harmony of interests.

L

Prescription see National Association of Local Government Officers. Kingston Group Hospitals Branch. **Magazine**

2813 Present Day: a Journal Discussing Agitated Questions Without Agitation I, 1 (June 1883)–III, 40 (Oct. 1886); m

    B   2d. Publishers: R. H. Squire; Crown Publishing Company; John Heywood. Editors: G. J. Holyoake; T. S. Barrett. For progress, fewest laws possible compatible with order and equal rights for all, freedom of the press, the platform and the ballot-box, secular and co-operative efforts, duty as citizens. Short articles, extracts of secularist propaganda, biographies, literary articles, poems, politics, accounts of meetings.

    Co-op. Union I–III, 36; E; L; MP; O I–III, 36. [Another edition of III, 37–40] 1–4. 1887. E; L

2814 Press Telegraphist: the Quarterly Journal of the National Union of Press Telegraphists [194-?] –; q

    A

    L VI, 5 (March 1955)–(w VII, 10, VIII, 3)

2815 Preston Co-operative Record I, 1 (1894)–XXVI, 12 (Dec. 1920). Preston; m

    A   Gratis. Issued by the Educational Committee of the Preston Industrial Co-operative Society. Reports of local Co-operative organisations. Replaced by **Wheatsheaf**.

    L XVIII, 1912–XXVI; PrH 1905, 1907, 1912, 1918.

2816 Preston Labour News 1 (July 1936)–363 (June 1965). Preston; m

    B   Free. Labour Party.

    L(Col) 292 (July 1959)–363; LabP 299, 300; Lancashire County Library*

2817 Print: a Journal for Printing-House Employés, of All Grades and Departments. I, 1 (May 1896)–6 (15 Oct. 1896); m

    A   1d. Printed by Thomas Hibberd. 'Recent events have certainly proved the necessity for such a journal , in which may be voiced the opinions, of different sections of the trade, from the wage-earners' point of view.' '. . . to be genuinely representative of printing-house employés, whose interests it will be its chief duty to defend'. News, reports of some meetings of the London Society of Compositors, Trades Council jottings, occasional longer article, eg, H. J. Tozer, 'The economic theory of Trades Unionism' (No. 5).

    L(Col)†; LSF; O 1–5

Print. 1968– see Graphical Journal

2818 Printer 1 (1 Nov. 1843)–19 (1 June 1845); m

    A   2d. Published by R. Thompson at the office of 'The Printer'. A trade-union organ of London and provincial compositors. Correspondence on wages, conditions, disputes.

    LSF

2819 Printer's Assistant: a Monthly Magazine for the Printing and Allied Trades as a Whole and for Printers' Assistants in Particular I (Nov. 1908)–5 (March 1909); m

    A   1d. Organ of the National Society of Operative Printers' Assistants. Extensive union journal, with news, views, fiction etc. For strong Trade Unionism. Editor: Edwin S. R. Smith, General Secretary. Ceased because of financial difficulties.

2820 Printers' Watchword I, (1921)–?; m

    A   2d. London Society of Compositors, Right-to-Work Committee. For rank-and-file interests. Printed by the Printers' Watchword Propaganda Society.

    L (mislaid); TUC† II (14 [May], 15 [June] 1922)

2821 Printers' Pilot: a Journal Catering for All Sections of the Trade I, 1 (June 1926)–II, 10 (March 1928); m

    A   1d.; 2d. Printing Trades Minority Movement.

    L; O(JJ)† I, 10 (March 1927)

2822 Printing Federation Bulletin I, 1 (Jan. 1923)–V, 20 (Jan./Feb. 1942); then **Bulletin**: the Official Journal of the Printing and Kindred Trades Federation: VI, 1 (March/April 1942)–VIII, 10 (Oct./Dec. 1949); then **Federation Bulletin**: I, 1 (Feb. 1950)–II, 27 (Dec. 1958); q

    A   1d. Records activities of the Joint Industrial Councils associated with the printing and paper-making unions. Announcements, explanations of policy to members. District notes. Discussion of general issues of interest to members. Title varies slightly. First title is sometimes: **Printing Federation Bulletin and Supplement of the National Union of Printing, Bookbinding and Paper Workers**.

    EP i I–III, 12; L (w occ. nos); LSF i VI, 15–   ; O 1950–8; ONC 1925–*; TUC*; the Federation

2823 Printing Machine Managers' Political Quarterly: the Official Organ of the Political Section I, 1 (Aug. 1926)–III, 2 (April 1935?); q

    A   Machine Managers' Trade Society? 'We shall strive to put the Labour view-point clearly and lucidly . . . It is no exaggeration to claim for Mr. Ramsay MacDonald and Mr Arthur Henderson that in 1924 they not only created an entirely new atmosphere in international politics, and [sic] brought the world a long way towards the ideal of a permanent peace.'

    L

2824 Printing News: a Monthly Journal for the Workers I, 1 (Aug. 1892)–II, 11 (15 June 1894); m

    A   1d. Printed and published by Feilden, McMillan and Company. 'Officially recognised by the London Society of Compositors, and the Printers' Labourers' Union'. '. . . its one aim will be to serve the interests of the working fraternity, and its policy will be moulded on their needs and aspirations.' Deals with Unionism, eight-hour day, boy labour, systematic overtime etc.

    L(Col)†; LSF

2825 Print-Worker I, 1 (July 1932)—I, 4 (Nov. 1932); m

A   1d. Published by the Printing Trades Section of the National Minority Movement. To organise a 'Revolutionary Trade-Union Opposition' to the official leadership. For workers in all section of the printing and paper industry.

L(Col)†

2826 Priory View I, 1 (June 1957)—. Tunbridge Wells

A   National and Local Government Officers' Association, Tunbridge Wells Branch, and the Tunbridge Wells and District Joint Electricity Branch.

L

2827 Prison Officers' Magazine: the Representative Organ of His Majesty's Prison Service. 1910—   . Bristol; London; m

A   Prison Officers' Association. Before 1920 an individual officer published the magazine under a pseudonym, to safeguard his employment, as the Home Office would not accept the claims for a representative association for prison officers.

L IV, 6 (June 1914); the Association 1920—

2828 Prisoner: the Organ of the ICWPA 1 (Feb. 1926)—?

B   1d. Published by the International Class War Prisoners' Aid, to build a strong British Section. Agitates for legal aid and defendants' maintenance for imprisoned South Wales miners and Communist Party leaders.

TUC† 1

2829 Probe: Journal of the General Dental Practitioners' Association ns 1 (Aug. 1959)—   ; m

A   Free to members. Registered trade union.

E 2—

2830 Process Journal: Organ of Newspaper Process Workers [1928]—ns 59 (Spring 1967); then **SLADE Journal**: 60 (Summer 1967)—   ; m; q

A   2d. etc. Society of Lithographic Artists, Designers, Engravers and Process Workers.

LSF ns 1 (Spring 1952)—   ; TUC† Dec. 1930—Oct. 1935*, Sept. 1941—March 1967*, Summer 1967—

2831 Producer I, 1 (Nov. 1916)—XLVI, 271 (Dec. 1966). Manchester: m

A   2d., 3d. Trade and business journal for the Co-operative movement. Printed for the CWS Publicity Department by the Co-operative Wholesale Society. Editor: James Haslam. Last issue states: 'For fifty years it has done its job as a means of communication between the two wings of the movement, wholesale and retail.' Absorbed **The Consumer**. 1966 subtitled: 'The Co-operative Trade Journal'. Discontinued between December 1939 and May 1944.

Co-op. Coll. 1917/8, 1922/3—1939, 1946—66 (w 1948); Co-op. Union; L(Col) Jan. 1917—Dec. 1939, May—Dec. 1944, Jan. 1946—Dec. 1966; LE; O

2832 Professional Chauffeurs' Club Journal I, 1 (May 1914)—I, 3 (July 1914); m

    A   Edited by Joseph J. Copestrake. For members to air views and grievances, urges organisation. Not a trade union, but acting for the advantage of its members and the profession. Managed by 'practical men who have been through the profession'.

    L

2833 Profit-Sharing and Co-partnership I, 1 (June 1912)—II, 6 (Nov. 1913); m

    C   2d. Published by Co-partnership Publishers, Ltd. Issued by the Labour Co-partnership Association. 'Organ of the Movement that seeks the Transformation of Capitalism through Co-partnership, Profit-Sharing and kindred means, for the reconciliation of the interests of Capital and Labour.' Publicises co-partnership schemes eg Port Sunlight, Gas, Light and Coke Company. Illustrated. Merged in **Labour Co-partnership**

    L(Col)†; O I—II, 3

2834 Progress: a Monthly Magazine for the Working Classes I, 1 (Jan. 1878)—I, 6 (June 1878); m

    C   2d. Published for the proprietors by Robert Banks (1—3), then by W. H. Guest (4—6). Edited by William Knighton. '**Progress** owes its origin to a committee of working-men, who have determined to endeavour to place before the public a first-class magazine at so low a price that it may be within the reach of all. It is for all classes of readers and workers — whether they work by hand or head — from the crossing-sweeper to the cabinet minister. Its object is to find out the truth, and to describe it without fear or favour.' To assist understanding between capital and labour, to give help in social and economic science for the improvement of the homes and habits of the working classes; also, discussion, accounts of foreign lands, and lighter articles to enliven and amuse.

    O

2835 Progress: a Monthly Magazine of Advanced Thought I, 1 (Jan. 1883)—VII, 12 (Dec. 1887); m

    B   3d. Published by the Progressive Publishing Company. Editors: G. William Foote (Jan.—April 1883); Edward Aveling (April 1883—April 1884); Foote and Aveling (April—Oct. 1884); Foote. Concentrates upon radical critique of literature, freethought reviews. Occasional article on Socialism, eg, by Aveling, Joynes, Belfort Bax. Contributors: J, L. Joynes, Belfort Bax, A. J. Robertson, J. M. Wheeler, James Thomson.

    L; LE*; LU I—V; O I—II

2836 Progress: Organ of the Gloucester Independent Labour Party 1 (Feb. 1898)—6(July 1898). Gloucester; m

    B   Free. Edited by J. H. Alpass. News of local affairs, meetings etc. and general articles on Socialism.

    AbU (microfilm); O(JJ)

2837 Progress 1960?–. Atherton
    A   National and Local Government Officers' Association, LUT Branch.
    L 1960–

2838 Progress 1967–. Bedford
    A   National and Local Government Officers' Association, Bedford and District Branch.
    L

Progress and the Scientific Worker see **Scientific Worker**

Progressionist. 1849 see **Midland Progressionist**

Progressionist. 1854 see **Livesey's Progressionist**

2839 Progressive Books [c1931]
    B   Preceded **Forge: Journal of the Progressive Book Society** (qv).

2840 Progressive Front: Bulletin of the Cambridge University Progressive Front (1 March 1938). Cambridge:
    C

2841 Progressive Review: a Monthly Review of Progressive Thought in Politics, Economics, Literature, Science and Art I, 1 (Oct. 1896)–II, 12 (Sept. 1897); m
    B   1s. Published by Horace Marshall and Son. Editors: William Clarke and J. A. Hobson, assisted by J. R. Macdonald. Essays on social and labour questions. An organ of the 'New Liberalism' it holds that the Liberal Party is an anachronism unable to solve the pressing social problems of the day. A few contributions by socialists, eg, Edward Carpenter.
    C; EP; L (also a registration issue dated 1895); LE I; LdU; O; ONC June 1897

2842 Projectionist [19--?] –?
    A   Kinema Projectionists' and Engineers' Association.
    TUC Jan. 1945–May 1950*

2843 Prolegomena 1962?–. Banstead
    A   National and Local Government Officers' Association, Banstead Branch. Reproduced from typewriting.
    L 1962–

2844 Proletareets: Politikas un Sinatnes Laikraksts; Latviešu Socialdemokratu Savienibas Organs. [**Proletarian**: Political and Scientific Journal, Organ of the Union of Latvian Social-Democrats] I (1903)—II (1904). London; m

    B   Latvian. Succeeded by **Revoluziunara Baltija** [**Revolutionary Baltic**]

    L I, 7—II, 6

2845 Proletcult: a Magazine for Girls and Boys I, 1 (March 1922)—? Glasgow; m

    B   Printed and published by the Proletarian Press. Official organ of the Proletarian Schools and Colleges. Communist education for children and young workers, maxims, stories, songs. Led by Tom Anderson.

    L I, 1—III, 5 (July 1924); MML† ns II, 9 (Dec. 1932); 11 (Feb. 1933)

2846 Promethean, or Communitarian Apostle: a Magazine of Societarian Science 1 (Jan. 1842)—4 (June 1842); m

    B   6d. Printed and published by B. D. Cousins. Edited by Goodwyn Barmby. Organ of the Communitarian School of Societarian Reformers (Utopian Communist). Supports universal suffrage for men and women over 21. 'It is on the broad principles of Communism, it is on the grand principles of community of sentiment and of communization of property, that we enter into the editorial field.' Points out that the **New Moral World** is 'exclusively Owenian', the **London Phalanx** 'exclusively Fourierist'.

    L; MP

2847 Prompter I, 1 (13 Nov. 1830)—53 (12 Nov. 1831); w

    B   3d. Published, printed and edited by Richard Carlile with probable financial assistance from Julian Hibbert. 'A political miscellany that strongly reflects the republican and free-thought views of Carlile. Features extensive accounts of working-class meetings at the Rotunda' (Wiener).

    GM; L; LY; MP; NpP

2848 Prophet: a Monthly Magazine of Personal and Social Life I, 1 (March 1894). London: Manchester; m

    B   1d. Edited by John Trevor. 'Our Altered Form. For some time I have wished that the **Labour Prophet** (qv) could be published in the form of an illustrated Magazine, in which, while the quantity would be more limited, the quality should be of the best. Since the issue of our last number an arrangement has been made with Keir Hardie by which this change has become possible. He has generously placed a corner of his weekly **Labour Leader** at my disposal for Labour Church matter, and I am also to write for his paper . . . With this magazine and the space in the **Labour Leader**, our movement will be better represented in future than by the **Labour Prophet** only.' Contributors: Rev. Stopford Brooke, James Sexton, J. C. Kenworthy etc. Short story. Information on Labour Church.

    L; O(JJ)†

2849 Prophetic Messenger

'J. Eagles, **The Bristol Riots, their Causes, Progress, and Consequences, By A Citizen** (1832), pp. 18—20 is the only authority for the existence of this "monthly horoscope" of an inflammatory, radical tendency. It is supposed to have existed Jan. 1831.' (A. Hart, **A Catalogue of Periodicals printed in Bristol, 1820—1840,** University of Leicester Victorian Studies Centre, 1972).

2850 Prospect: the Bulletin of the Southern District Public Relations Committee of NALGO 1 (Jan. 1963)—30 (May 1968); irreg?

A   National and Local Government Officers' Association. Reproduced from typewriting.

L

2851 Protector and Herald of the Productive Classes

No copies located. All information from Prospectus in Bristol Public Libraries. To be 2pp., 2d., unstamped, 'printed on a large sheet'. edited by J. C. Fitzgerald, and printed and published by him. 'Open to all parties and influenced by none' (A. Hart, **A Catologue of Periodicals printed in Bristol, 1820—1840,** University of Leicester Victorian Studies Centre, 1972).

2852 Protestant: the Organ of the Working Men's Evangelistic Association 1 (2 Dec. 1873)—18 (31 March 1874). Glasgow; w

C   1d. Published for the proprietors by William Love. Edited by H. A. Long. In defence of the Protestant Establishment, against Popery and secularist agitation, eg, campaigns by Bradlaugh and Holyoake. Published for, not by, working-men.

GM†

2853 Protoplasm [early 1890s]. Edinburgh

B   A small Socialist sheet issued by Fred Hamilton, compositor, John Leslie etc. (**Labour Standard**, Edinburgh, 5 Oct. 1929).

2854 Provident [18--?] —? Wigan; w? m?

C?   3d. Published by Wall. 'For employés and employed' (Mitchell, 1885).

2855 Provident Philanthropist, Published for Promoting the Union for Benevolence 1 (6 Jan. 1844)—8 (24 Feb. 1844); w

C   Printed and published by Luke James Hansard, and edited by him. Established to promote the Society for the Union for Benevolence, an organisation of all classes, and principally to promote the knowledge and advantage of Charitable Institutions. Dedicated to the relief of metropolitan distress and destitution. Non-political.

L(Col)†

Provincial Typographical Circular see **Typographical Societies' Monthly Circular**

Prudential Section Gazette see **Prudential Staff Gazette**

440

2856 Prudential Staff Gazette Oct. 1910—June 1945; then **Prudential Staff Union Gazette**: July 1945—March 1966; then **Prudential Section Gazette** April 1966—; 13-yr

A   Published first by the Prudential Staff Mutual Aid Federation (PSMAF), which was founded in 1909, and renamed the Prudential Staff Federation (PSF) in 1913. In 1921 the PSF merged with the National Association of Prudential Assurance Agents to form the Prudential Staff Union (PSU). The National Union of Insurance Workers (NUIW) was formed in October 1964 and the PSU became the Prudential Section of that union. Commonly known as **The Gazette**.

LCI XXVIII—*; NU 1953—   ; NUIW, Prudential Section

Prudential Staff Union Gazette see **Prudential Staff Gazette**

2857 Prune, Being the New Journal of the Dagenham Branch of NALGO 1961?— . Dagenham

A   National and Local Government Officers' Association. Reproduced from typewriting.

L 1961—

Public Employees see **Public Employees' Journal**

2858 Public Employees' Journal: the Official Organ of the National Union of Public Employees. I, 1 Sept. 1931)—(Dec. 1967). then **Public Employees**: Journal of the National Union of Public Employees: Jan. 1968— ; q

A   1d. Official business, union news, articles.

L; ONC† March 1934—*; the union

2859 Public Eye: the News Sheet of the Preston and District Branch of NALGO 1963?— . Preston

A   National and Local Government Officers' Association. Reproduced from typewriting.

L 1963—

2860 Public Eye 1965?— . Newcastle-upon-Tyne

A   National and Local Government Officers' Association, Newcastle-upon-Tyne Branch.

L 1965—

2861 Public Eye 1967?—. High Wycombe

A   National and Local Government Officers' Association, Wycombe Rural District Council Branch. Reproduced from typewriting.

L 1967—

2862 Public Officer: the Magazine of the Nottingham and District Local Government Officers' Association I, 1 [Oct. 1911?]—? [Nottingham?] m;

A   Editors: John Potter Briscoe and Arthur Rhodes.

NP† II, 1 (Oct. 1912)—IV, 3 (Dec. 1914*)

2863 Public Officer: Journal of the Ulster Public Officers' Association [1959?] –   . Belfast; q?

    A

    ONC† I, 2 (Spring 1960)

2864 Public Pharmacist: the Official Organ of the Guild of Public Pharmacists [I], 1 (Jan. 1934)–1962; then **Journal of Hospital Pharmacy**: XX, 1 (Feb. 1963)–   . Nottingham etc.; London; q

    A   To improve status and conditions.

    E 1964–   ; L; LPH 1936–   ; LSC 1945–

Public Relations, 1952– see National Association of Local Government Officers. North Western and North Wales District Committee. **District News Sheet**

Public Service see **Local Government Officer**

Pudsey Labour Herald see **Labour Herald, 1897**–?

2865 Punch: Manchester Corporation Transport Dept. Employees 1 (May 1937)–? Manchester; m

    A   1d. Published by the 'Punch' Campaign Committee (6/5 Branch, Transport and General Workers' Union).

    WCML† 1

2866 Putney Citizen ns 1 (Sept. 1950)–57 (Dec. 1955); m

    B   Issued by the Political Committee of the London Co-operative Society.

    L(Col)

2867 Putney, Southfields and Roehampton Citizen 1 (Sept. 1932)–21 (June 1934)? m

    B   Published by the London Co-operative Society's Political Committee

    L(Col)

2868 Pylon I, 1 (June/July 1953)–(Dec. 1954). Newbury; irreg?

    A   National and Local Government Officers' Association, Newbury Area, Southern Electricity Board Branch. Reproduced from typewriting.

    L

2869 Pyramid: Staff Journal of the Co-operative Permanent Building Society I, 1 (Spring 1948)–; q

    A   Editor: H. V. Bailey.

    L (w I, 3)

2870 Q: Organ of the NUWM (SE Area) [1933?] –?

    A   ½d. National Unemployed Workers Movement. Issued by the Southwark Unemployed Council. Reproduced from typewriting.

    MML† 9 (10 May 1933)

2871 Quarterly Letter to Men on Public Works [c1910]; q
    C   Gratis. Navvy Mission Society. Religious tract. (Mitchell, 1910.)

2872 Quarterly Letter to Navvies [c1910]. Leeds; q
    C   Free. Petty and Sons, Ltd. Religious. (Mitchell, 1910.)

2873 Quarterly Mail I, 1 (July 1887)–?; q
    C   2d. Issued by the Christian Post Office Association, later Postal, Telegraph and Telephone Christian Association, then Post Office Christian Association. Religious publication of Post Office employees.
    L I, 1–98 (April 1912*)

Quarterly Report and Review see **Women' Union Journal**

2874 Quartern Loaf 1 (1 March 1834)–?
    C   1d. Published by Benjamin Steill. Anti-Corn Laws. Presents arguments against them, and gives account of their history and debate in Parliament. Gives quotation of prices abroad and at home 'as showing the disadvantages under which the British labourer is placed, in competing with the foreign workman'.
    ONC† 1

2875 Quarto 1966– . Hemel Hempstead
    A   National and Local Government Officers' Association, Hemel Hempstead and District Branch.
    L 1966–

2876 Quayside and Office: a Monthly Organ of the National Union of Docks, Wharves, and Shipping Staffs [19–?]–? ns I, 1 (Aug. 1919)–III, 1 (Jan. 1922); m
    A   1d.; 2d. Not a 'rival' but a 'complement' to the **Docks' Gazette.** Edited by Charles G. Ammon, then A. Creech-Jones. Extensive union news. With Vol II, No. 10, after amalgamation becomes: **Monthly Organ of the Administrative, Clerical and Supervisory Group of the Transport and General Workers' Union.** Superseded by **The Record.**
    L ii; Transport and General Workers' Union 1919–20

2877 Quest: the Monthly Journal of the Postmasters' Association [c1940?]– Stirling; m
    A   (Notes, Association of Head Postmaster, June 1940, p. 46.)
    L Jan./Feb. 1964–

2878 Qui Vive. Journal Quotidien: Organe de la Démocratie Universelle 1 (3 Oct. 1871)–60 (11 Dec. 1871). London; d
    A   1d. Founded by the Société Co-operative Typographique. Editors are printing workers. Chief editor: Eugène Vermersch. Democratic, for exiled Communards. A daily review of international working-class events, with correspondence from the rest of England, France, Germany, Belgium etc. In French.
    L(Col)†

Quill. 1890 see **Clerks' Journal**

2879 Quill, Being the Monthly Report of the Society of Civil Servants I, 1 (Jan. 1923)–VIII, 87 (April 1930); m
    A   2d (in later years). Published by the Society. 'For private circulation to members only.' Main purpose to keep members informed of matters discussed and determined by the Council and the Executive Committee, but extended to cover other issues, including promotion, prospects etc. Later subtitled: 'the Official Organ of the Society of Civil Servants'.
    L

RBA Circular see **Retail Book, Stationery and Allied Trades Employees' Association Circular**

2880 RFSA Journal. 1 (Jan. 1921)–2 (April 1921); then **Refuge Staff Journal**: 3 (July 1921)–   . Aberdare etc.; q; m
    A   Refuge Field Staff Association; National Union of Insurance Workers, Refuge Section. Latterly **The Journal**.
    L

RILU Magazine see **Red International of Labour Unions**

RILU Monthly Magazine see **Red International of Labour Unions**

2881 RPU News and Views: Bi-monthly Bulletin of the Registered Pharmacists' Union [19--?]–[196-?]; bi-m
    A   Reproduced from typewriting. The RPU amalgamated with the National Association of Salaried Pharmacists to form the Salaried Pharmacists' Union. See also **SPU News and Views**.
    ONC† (White Collar Coll.) 1 undated issue [196-?]

2882 Radcliffe and Pilkington Co-operative Review 1 [July 1895?]-228 (June 1952). [Radcliffe?]; q
    A   Gratis. Issued by the Educational Department of Radcliffe and Pilkington Co-operative Society. Title sometimes ... **Quarterly** instead of ... **Review**.
    L 69 (4 June 1912)–228

Radical see **Wales Radical Cymru**

2883 Radical 1 (20 Aug. 1831)–8 (8 Oct. 1831); then **Radical Reformer**: 9 (15 Oct. 1831)–24 (26 Jan. 1832); w
    B   1d.; 2d. Publisher and printer: H. Hetherington. Editor: James B. Lorymer. 'A working-class journal that repeatedly agitates for universal suffrage and for the convening of a National Convention' (Wiener). All radicals are urged to join both the National Political Union and the National Union of the Working Classes. Also carries support for Doherty's National Association for the Protection of Labour (Manchester based) and published addresses and details of its meetings.
    L 1–6, 9–22; O 1

2884 Radical 1 (13 March 1836)–19 (17 July 1836); w

B   7d. Stamped. Printed and published by George John Morgan. Edited by Augustus Beaumont, democrat. Radical reformist. Agitates for untaxed press. Much space given to parliamentary and police news. Series of editorial addresses: 'Common Sense to the Working Classes'. In the number of 17 July promotes the Association of Working Men to Procure a Cheap and Honest Press (forerunner of the London Working Men's Association).

     L(Col)†; Warwick UL (microfilm)

2885 Radical I, 1 (4 Dec. 1880)–II, 27 (8 July 1882); w

B   1d. Printed and published for the proprietors by Samuel Bennett, later by the Bennett Brothers. Editors: Samuel Bennett; F. W. Souter. Radical democratic. Reports from radical and democratic clubs and associations in the metropolis. Social democratic opinion, working-class Radicalism, land nationalisation, Republicanism etc. Contributors: Herbert Burrows, William Webster, Hyndman, James Hooper, A. R. Winks, John Sketchley.

     L(Col)†; TUC, John Burns Lib. (4 Dec. 1880)–(21 Jan. 1882)

Radical. 1886–1889 see **Republican Chronicle**

2886 Radical Leader 1 (4 Aug. 1888)–16 (17 Nov. 1888); w

B   1d. Printed and published by R. Forder. Radical democratic, sympathetic to the claims of working-men, scornful of socialists. Organ of London radicalism and radical working mens' clubs. 'Circulating largely among the Radical Clubs in London and the elite of the working classes'. Column of 'Labor Notes'. Includes useful account of history and proceedings of some of London's radical workmen's clubs.

     L(Col)†

Radical Reformer see **Radical, 1831**

Radical Reformer and Hertford and Ware Patriot see **Ware Patriot**

2887 Radical Reformer's Gazette 1 (17 Nov. 1832)–14 (16 Feb. 1833). Glasgow; w

B   1d.; 2d. Published by Francis Reid (1–12); George Murray (13–14). Printed by W. and W. Miller (1–5, 12); J. H. Cowan (6–11); G. Murray (13–14). Editor: A. Dallas. 'A radical political miscellany that strongly advocates factory reform, universal suffrage, the abolition of paper money, and a forcible division of land. It was suppressed by the Stamp Office in Feb. 1833' (Wiener).

     E 1; Gm; GU

2888 Radical Reformer, or People's Advocate I, 1 (15 Sept. 1819)–I, 10 (17 Nov. 1819); w

B   1d. Printed and published by W. Mason.

     MP† (w I, 3); ONC† 1

2889 Radical Register, and Liberal Gazette 1 (20 Feb. 1835). Liverpool; w
     B   1d. Printed by Riddick and Kerr. 'A radical political miscellany
that favours universal suffrage, the ballot, and repeal of the Poor Law
Amendment Act of 1834' (Wiener).
     L

2890 Radical Times 1 (19 Feb. 1887)–8 (9 April 1887). Paisley; w
     B   ½d.; 1d. Printed and published by J. T. Melvin. Radical
democratic. Supports Home rule for Ireland, and Scotland. Advocates the
establishment of a democratic society by physical force means if
necessary, 'through the application of the principles of Liberalism'.
Contains a serial history of the Radical Rising of 1817–20, and a
three-part review of Laurence Gronlund's **Co-operative Commonwealth**.
     L(Col)†

2891 Radlett and District Labour News [194–?]. Radlett, Hertfordshire;
m
     B   Labour Party. Duplicated. (Labour Party. **Your own Journal**,
1948.)

2892 Rag 1 (9 Sept. 1882)–89 (17 May 1884); then **Rorty Review**: 90
(24 May 1884)–95 (28 June 1884); then **Rag**: 96 (5 July 1884)–97 (12
July 1884); w
     C   One of several papers which in the 1880s 'pretended to have
espoused the cause of the men [in the Post Office]'. '. . . an appropriately
named print . . . sold at a halfpenny, and with which for the brief period
of its existence there was a lately-resigned sorter, who, from a knowledge
of his own cruel experiences in the General Post Office, either wrote or
inspired the bitter and vulgar paragraphs which with pointed personality
were aimed for most part at the minor supervisors, who were represented
as acting the part of bullies and petty tyrants towards their helpless
underlings.' (H. G. Swift, **A History of Postal Agitation from Eighty Years
ago till the Present Day**, New ed. **Book 1**, Manchester, London 1929,
p. 161.) See also **Toby** and **Town Talk** for similar papers.
     L(Col)

2893 Railway Advocate: an Independent Fortnightly Journal Devoted to
the Interests of All Employed on Railways 1 (23 Sept. 1881)–3 (21 Oct.
1881); fortn
     B   2d. Published by Davis and Helmer. 'To advocate the interests
of the railway employees generally.' Covers railway matters and conditions
of work of railway servants. Some union news. In favour of the
Nine-Hours' Movement for railwaymen and schemes of social
improvement.
     L(Col)†

Railway Chariot see **Railway Servants' Chariot, and Companion**.

2894 Railway Clerk: the Official Organ of the Railway Clerks' Association I, 1 (1 Jan. 1904)–XVI, 181 (15 Jan. 1919); then **Railway Service Journal**: XVI, 182 (15 Feb. 1919)–XLVII, 566 (April 1951); then **Transport Salaried Staff Journal**: XLVIII, 567 (May 1951)–   ; m

   A   1d. etc. 'To champion the cause, voice the needs, and register the progress of the railway clerk.' The name of the Association was later changed to Transport Salaried Staffs' Association.

   L(Col)† I–X, XI–XII*, XXL–   ; MP IV–V; NU 1912–63*; ONC 1945–   ; TUC Feb. 1910–; Warwick U(MRC) 1904, 1908–23, 1926, 1937, 1939–41, 1944

2895 Railway Express [1883?]
   A   'The General Railway Workers' Union . . . started the **Railway Express**, an eight-page quarto sheet, price ½d., at the time of the Scotch strike, which had a short existence. The first and succeeding issues are in my possession. It was not a very vigorous organ' (G. W. Alcock, **Fifty Years of Railway Trade Unionism**, London 1922).

2896 Railway Herald I, 1 (7 Sept. 1887)–XXIX, 851 (26 Dec. 1903); w
   A   2d.; 1d. At first the contents consisted of general transport engineering matters, but from 1897 contains correspondence on wages and conditions, and accounts of meetings of the Railway Clerks' Association. Later advertised as the 'official organ of the Railway Clerks' Association'. Also contains notes of the activities of the General Railway Workers' Union.

   L(Col)†

2897 Railway Pioneer: the Official Organ of the South Wales and Monmouthshire District Council of the National Union of Railwaymen I, 1 (July 1925)–I, 12 (June/July 1926). Cardiff; m
   A   1d. Published by the Council. Covers activities of the 'Grade Committees, Sub-Councils, District Council and Organiser' and includes 'Speakers' Notes, General Trade Union Notes, and Political Notes', also correspondence. Launched at a time when employers were raising questions of redundancy and wage-cutting. Advocates industrial Unionism based on the National Union of Railwaymen.

   L(Col)†

2898 Railway Review: a Weekly newspaper for the Railway Service 1 (16 July 1880)–   ; w
   A   1d. etc. From 1881 the organ of the Amalgamated Society of Railway Servants, later National Union of Railwaymen.

   L(Col)†; LE 1911–   ; ONC 3714 (11 Nov. 1949)–   ; the Union

2899 Railway Servants' Chariot, and Companion 1 (July 1880)–46 (April 1884); then **Chariot**: 47 (May 1884)–50 (Aug. 1884); then **Railway Chariot**: 50 (Sept. 1884)–ns II, 4 (15 Nov. 1886). Liverpool; m

    C   ½d. Editor: Charles Irlam. 'A Monthly Record of Christian and Temperance Life and Work Among our Railway Servants and Their Families at Home and Abroad.' 'Edited by a Railway Engine Driver, author of the Railway Servants' Tracts. Aim and object to promote and extend Christianity and Temperance among railway servants.' Incorporated with **Railway Signal.**

    L (w Jan.–May 1885)

2900 Railway Service Gazette, and Weekly Observer of Our Railways and Their Interests 1 (3 Feb. 1872)–484 (10 June 1881); w

    A   1d. Published by Marshall and Son. Puts before the public 'the just claims' of railway servants. The organ of the Amalgamated Society of Railway Servants. 'New Model' outlook, emphasis on benefit funds etc. Includes Branch reports and correspondence.

    L(Col)†

Railway Service Journal see **Railway Clerk**

2901 Railway Signal, or Lights along the Line: a Monthly Journal Advocating Christian Life and Christian work on the Railways of Great Britain 1 (Aug. 1882)–1930?; m; Later,' official organ of the Railway Mission'. For temperance etc.

    C   1d. Absorbed **Railway Chariot.**

    C XII–XIII, XLV–XLVIII, 9; L 6 (Jan. 1883)–   ; O 1894–1930

2902 Railway Signalman [19–?]– . Cardiff; London?; m

    A   2d (1930). Official organ of the Union of Railway Signalmen. (Mitchell, 1930.)

2903 Railway Telegraph: a Paper Devoted to Railway men in Liverpool, Yorkshire and Cheshire 1 (Nov. 1889)–14 (Jan. 1891). Liverpool; m

    C   1d. Organ of the Liverpool Evangelistic and Temperance Mission to Railway Men. Published by William Tharme at the offices of the Mission. For the spiritual, moral and social good of all grades of railwaymen and their families. Contents cover evangelism, temperance, and benefit societies.

    L(Col)†

2904 Railway Vigilant: Official paper of the Railwaymen's Vigilance Movement Jan. 1932–Dec. 1932; ns 1 (Jan. 1933)–12 (Dec. 1933); m;

    A   1d. Published by the All Grades Railwaymen's Vigilance Movement. Communist Party rank-and-file paper. 1932 reproduced from typewriting.

    CPGB; L(Col)† ns; ONC ns 3*; Mrs Winnie Renshaw, 26 Chaucer Road, London E11 2RE; Warwick U(MRC) 1933–5 (m)

2905 Railway Women's Annual 1949; a

    C   2s. 6d. 'Designed to attract and interest that vast army of women in the employment of British Railways and London Transport.' Published with approval from government, official and trade union circles. Edited by Thomas Ashcroft, editor of **Railway Review**. Articles on all aspects of women's work on railways and London Transport, with additional material, eg, 'Home Hints', 'Use and Care of Garden Produce'. Illustrated with photos. Then merged in **Railwaymen's Year Book**.

    E; O

2906 Railway Worker Oct. 1909–[1910?]. Leeds; m

    A   Run by members of the General Railway Workers' Union. Unofficial. 'Well-edited', short-lived, at least seven issues (G. W. Alcock, **Fifty Years of Railway Trade Unionism**, London 1922).

2907 Railway Worker, Published by St Margaret's Council of Action I, 1 (27 Feb. 1932)–10 (2 Dec. 1932). Edinburgh; irreg

    A   1d. St Margaret's Depot (Edinburgh) Council of Action. Reproduced from typewriting. A Communist Party rank-and-file-paper for all grades.

    E 1, 4, 10

2908 Railwaymen's Year Book 1946–?; a

    C   'A book of information and reference for railwaymen and women of all grades'. Absorbed **Railway Woman's Annual** (qv).

    BP; GrP; L; MP; NP.

2909 Rally [194-?]–? Birkenhead etc.; m

    B   Issued by the Labour League of Youth. Edited at Birkenhead Central Branch for some months. Title varies: **Rally for a Youth Charter; Rally for Socialism**. Trotskyist.

    ONC† II, 1 (July 1950)–III, 1 (May 1952) (w II, 6)

2910 Ramparts 1968–9. [Derry?]

    B   Published by Derry Labour Party. (P. Howard, 'The paper war: Communism and Socialism'. **Fortnight**, 78 [22 Feb. 1974].)

2911 Ranelagh Worker, Published by the Communist Group at Glovers 1 (1925)–?; w?

    A   Supports policy of one union for metal workers, and Industrial Alliance. Reproduced from typewriting

    TUC† (15 [3 Nov.], 20 [17 Dec.], 1925).

2912 Rank and File: a Journal for Active Trade Unionists I, 1 (Oct. 1921); m

    A   2d. Published by the Rank and File League. 'We think we represent the un-co-ordinated opinion of the thinking rank and file within the trade unions, who are suffering from officials who refuse to follow the wish of the majority.' 'At present we are the unofficial journal of the unofficial movement — free lances — but we are prepared to be absorbed or controlled by any unofficial rank-and-file organisation that will continue the work we are setting out to do.' Short articles, reports, news. Contributors: C. L. Everard ('Gadfly' of the **Daily Herald**); Jack Tanner; George Hicks.

    L(Col); ONC†

2913 Rank and File [196-?] –

    A   'Produced by left-wing teachers within the NUT'.

2914 Rank and File: Organ of the Militant Building Worker 1 (March 1966)–15 (Feb./March 1969?). Middleton, nr. Manchester; irreg

    A   4d.; 6d. Published by Jack Gateley. Printed by 'Rochdale Times, Ltd.,' then by Socialist Review Publishing Company. Newspaper format. Subtitle varies: 'Organ of the Militant Building and Construction Worker' (12–13); 'Paper of the Militant Building and Construction Workers' (14–15).

    ONC† 1–15 (w 2–3)

2915 Rank and File Engineer 1 (Spring issue, 1968)–? Hazel Grove, Cheshire; q?

    A   4d. Published by D. Langley. Printed by 'Rochdale Times Ltd'.
    ONC† 1

2916 Ratepayer: the Organ of the Oppressed 1 (1 May 1890 [Registration issue])

    B?   Contents of registration issue irrelevant and miscellaneous.
    L(Col)†

Rational Quarterly Review see **Robert Owen's Rational Quarterly Review and Journal**

2917 Rational Reformer; or, Illustrations and Testimonies in Favour of the Rational Social System I, 1 (Oct. 1832); m?

    B   Printed by Guthrie. 'Reprint extracts from a wide variety of sources that support the doctrines of Robert Owen' (Wiener).
    LU

2918 Rational Religionist, and Independent Enquirer into Social and Political Economy, Religion, Science, and Literature I–3, [c1841?]; Manchester

    B   Edited by R. Buchanan, Owenite propagandist. (BUCOP; J. F. C. Harrison, **Robert Owen and the Owenites in Britain and America**, London 1969).

2919 Rationalist 1 [cAug. 1833]—11 [cNov. 1833?]; w
    B   1d. Published and edited by Samuel Cornish.
        'It features essays which reject the supernatural element in religion' (Wiener). Individual numbers are not dated. There is information about the periodical in: Samuel Cornish, 2 Sept. 1833, **Letter to Robert Owen** (Owen Papers, Co-operative Union Library).
    L 11

2920 Rawtenstall Socialist [c1907]; Rawtenstall.
    B   Gratis. (**Reformers' Year Book**, 1907)

2921 RCN Nursing Standard March 1968—   ; bi-m
    A   Free to members. Royal College of Nursing and National Council of Nurses of the United Kingdom.
    Royal College of Nursing.

2922 Reading Citizen 1 (Jan. 1924)—? Reading; m
    B   Labour Party.
    L(Col) 1—2 (Feb. 1924); RP 8 (Feb. 1925)—340 (Nov. 1952) (w 1—7, 17—18, 159, 209, 231, 339)

2923 Reading Co-operative Record 1894—? Reading; m
    A   Free. Reading Industrial Co-operative Society. Replaced by **Wheatsheaf**. (Mitchell, 1910.)

2924 Reading Co-operator 1 (Feb. 1932)—40 (June 1935). Reading; m
    B
    L(Col)

2925 Reading Labour's Voice I, 1 (Feb. 1960)—I, 26 (May 1962); then **Labour's Reading Voice**: 27 (June 1962)—30 (Nov. 1962). Reading; m
    B   3d. Published for the Reading Labour Party.
    L(Col) (w 30); LabP 1, 2, 4, 9, 13—16, 26; RP (w 19, 27)

Reasoner, 1846—1861 see **Reasoner and 'Herald of Progress'**

Reasoner, 1865—1872 see **Reasoner and 'Herald of Progress'**

2926 Reasoner: a Journal of Discussion I (July 1956)—3 (Nov. 1956). Hull; bi-m
    B   2s. Reproduced from typewriting. Printed and published by John Saville. Editors: John Saville, E. P. Thompson. A discussion journal 'in the main, written by and addressed to members of the Communist Party'. Second aim to provide copies and translations of documents published in the Communist and Socialist press of other countries and not readily available in Britain. The final number disassociates itself from Soviet intervention in Hungary.
    E; L; ONC† (No. 3 incomplete)

2927 Reasoner and 'Herald of Progress' I, 1 (3 June 1846)–XXVI, 788 (23 June 1861); then **Secular World** (sometimes **Secular World and Social Economist**): I, 1 [ie 789] (Jan. 1863)–II, 14 [ie 826] (1 Dec. 1864); then **Reasoner and Secular World** (sometimes **Reasoner**): XXVII, 827 (1865)–XXX, 910 (1872); w

    B   2d. Published by James Watson, then printed and published by Holyoake. Edited by G. G. Holyoake. Organ of the Rational Society. 'Communistic in Social Economy, Utilitarian in Morals, Republican in Politics' (No. 1), and Secularist. Preceded by **Herald of Progress**. Absorbed **Northern Tribune**. See also **Counsellor on Secular, Co-operative and Political Questions**, published in 1861.

    Bishopsgate Institute I–XXXI; C a 1–XVII; Co-op. Coll.*; GM I–XXIII, XXX; L a, b (w 789–816, 839–910); LE a XVI–XVIII; LU a I, 1–3, III, XX, 506, XXV*; MP a I–XV, XVII–XVIII, XXV–XXVI, b I–II, XXX; ONC June 1846–Dec. 1855

Reasoner and Secular World see **Reasoner and 'Herald of Progress'**

2928 Rebel, Published by the North London Branch Herald League I, 1 (Oct. 1916)–11 (Oct. 1917); ns I, 1 (June 1919)–II, 7 (Dec. 1920); m

    B   1d. News sheet of the North London 'Herald' League. Printed and published by the Rebel Press. 'Chief aim to disseminate news concerning the many activities of the League in North London, and in a lesser degree give information concerning the larger movement outside our area.' Editor: Percy W. Howard. No set programme or rigid constitution but propagandising and working for the establishment of Socialism. Supported socialist sunday schools. Members included Newbold, Pollitt, R. M. Fox. Early series reproduced from typewriting.

    L 1919–20; MML†

2929 Rebel [196-?] –; m

    B?   6d. Edited by Fred Milson. (Mitchell, 1970.)

2930 Rebel: the Official Organ of the Gloucester Young Socialists [1962?] –4 [Feb. 1964]. Gloucester; irreg

    B   Labour Party Young Socialists.

    L 2 (Sept. 1962)–4

2931 Rebel Student [192-?] –? Edinburgh; m

    B   Edinburgh University Labour Club Vol. III, 1–2 (Oct.–Nov. 1929) in possession of Mr J. K. Annand, Edinburgh (I. McDougall, **An interim bibliography of the Scottish Working-Class Movement**, Edinburgh 1965)

2932 Rebel Worker [1965?] –1966

    A   Anglo-American edition, published in London. Industrial Workers of the World. Succeeded by **Heatwave** (qv).

2933 Record: Organ of the Halifax ILP. 1 (March 1897)–1899. Halifax; m

B   Independent Labour Party. Editor: Mont Blatchford. (**Labour Annual**, 1899, 1900.)

2934 Record [1897?]–?; m

B   Later subtitled: 'The Monthly Journal of the ME and C Society'. Reproduced from manuscript, duplicated foolscap sheets folded to quarto. Edited by C. Benson, then F. G. Hull. 'The Objects of the society are to promote the interest of its members in order to provide them with the means of education in social and economic subjects.' No indication of the full name of the society, which established a co-operative section '18 mths. ago,' (July 1897 issue). News and accounts of the stores. Also had a library. Advocates Socialism. News of Co-operative and Labour world. The unnumbered issue says 'The Record is published at 19 Albion Buildings, Aldersgate Street, EC.' Discusses dangers for British workers of cheap labour in Asia. Motto: **Dum spiro spero.**

O(JJ)† I, 4 (June 1897, July 1897, Sept., Oct. (no year or number), one number undated and unnumbered

2935 Record [19--?]–? Liverpool

A   Union of Post Office Workers, Liverpool Amalgamated Branch. (W. Dunlop, 'Local journals.' **Belpost**, IV, 5 [May 1965].)

Record, 1913 see **Garden City Co-operator's Record**

Record, 1925 see **Hammersmith Record. 1923–?**

2936 Record: Official Organ of the Transport and General Workers' Union I, 1 (Aug. 1921)–XVIII, 212 (May 1939); then **Transport and General Workers' Record**: XIX, 213 (June 1939)–XLI, 6 (June 1961); then **TGWU Record**: XLI, 7 (July 1961)–? (June 1971); then **Record**: July 1971–   ; m

A   Gratis to members. 'Our immediate ancestors were the **Dockers' Record**, the journal of the Dockers' Union; **Quayside and Office**, of the Docks, Wharves and Shipping Staffs: **The Record** of the United Vehicle Workers; and **The Vehicle Worker**, of the National Union of Vehicle Workers.'

L(Col); LE; NU XXXII, 1953–   ; O; ONC† XXIX, 336 (Nov. 1949)–

Recorder, 1899–1901 see **Oddfellows Recorder and Friendly Societies Journal**

2937 red blob [196-?]–? Nottingham

B   University of Nottingham Socialist Society. '. . . the editorial board of the Red Blob is made up of all the members of Soc-Soc.' Title entirely in lower case.

NU 3 nos received 1969, 1970

2938 Red Challenger [1927?28]. Merthyr; fortn

    B   1d. Issued by the Merthyr Local of the Communist Party.
Printed and published by W. D. Hindmarsh. Reproduced from typewriting.

    O(JJ)† 3 (undated), (4 [13 Dec.], 5 [28 Dec.], 1927?28)

2939 Red Commune: Official Organ of the Glasgow Communist Group
and Affiliated Bodies I, 1 (Feb. 1921). Glasgow; m

    B   2d. Published by the Bakunin Press for the Group. Issued by the
Guy Aldred anarcho-communist Glasgow Communist Group.
Anti-parliamentarian, for the goal of a British Soviet Republic. Designed as
a Party paper, alongside the **Spur**.

    L(Col)†

2940 Red Dawn: a Magazine for Young Workers; Official Organ of the
Proletarian Schools and Colleges I, 1 (March 1919)–III, 7 (Sept. 1921).
Glasgow; m

    B   1d. Published by the Proletarian School. For Communist work
amongst youth. Proletarian schools and colleges started in Glasgow by
Tom Anderson and spread to other towns in the British Isles. Connection
with youth section of the Third Communist International.

    E 1–12 (20 Feb. 1920 [microfilm]); L; Warwick U (MRC) 1919–20

2941 Red Flag: an Unofficial Organ of International Democracy 1 (3 Jan.
1891)–2 (10 Jan. 1891); w

    B   1d. Published by Lena Wardle. Organ of the United Democratic
Club, which includes among its members John Hobson, J. Shaw Maxwell,
Bennet Burleigh. To campaign for democracy. Written in the form of
'snippets', often like a radical 'squib'. 'Platform built on three
foundations: Socialist, Republican, Democratic. Without the third, the
second means tyranny; without the first, the other two are frauds.'

    L(Col)

2942 Red Flag: Organ of the Young Socialist League 1 (May 1920); then
Young Worker, with which is incorporated The Red Flag: I, 1 (May
1921)–I, 5 (Sept. 1921); then **Young Communist: the Organ of the Young
Communist League, with which is incorporated The Young Worker and
The Red Dawn**: 1 (Dec. 1921)–ns II, 8 (July 1923); then **Young Worker**:
1 (Aug. 1923)–[1926?]; ns 1 (1 May 1926); then **Weekly Young Worker**:
1 (22 May 1926)–51 (21 May 1927); then **Young Worker**: ns 1 (28 May
1927)–114 (7 Sept. 1929); ns 1 (12 Oct. 1929)–7 (23 Nov. 1929); [ns],
1 (Feb. 1930)–?; m; w

    B   2d.; 1d. Communist paper for youth.

    Buckhaven and Methil PL, Proudfoot Papers Jan. 1925; L(Col–†
1920–9*; MML† Dec. 1921–31*; O(JJ)† Feb. 1930; WCML† May 1921,
July 1923–Jan. 1924

2943 Red Flag: a Monthly Magazine Devoted to Communism, for Edinburgh and the Lothians I, 1 (Feb. 1927)–   ? Edinburgh; m

    B   2d. Published by the Edinburgh Local of the Communist Party. Reproduced from typewriting.

    E 1

2944 Red Flag: Monthly Organ of the British Section, International Left Opposition I, 1 (May 1933)–II, 1 (Nov. 1934); m; bi-m; then **Red Flag**: Organ of the Marxist League: ns 1 (May 1936)–8 (May/June 1937); irreg

    B   Subtitle varies: 'Monthly Organ of the Communist League' (Oct./Nov. 1933–   ) 'Organ of Revolutionary Marxism' (Nov. 1934–   ). Published by Hugo Dewar (I–II, 1); A Boyd [Hilary Sumner-Boyd]. Editor: Reg Groves.

    L(Col); Warwick UL 1933–4

2945 Red Flag: Organ of the Revolutionary Workers' Party (Trotskyist), British Section, IVth International I, 1 [July/Aug.?] 1963–   ; m

    B   6d. Published by the Revolutionary Workers' Party.

    E (w 1) (The Left in Britain – microfilm – Harvester Press Ltd)

2946 Red Front, for Working Class Power, for a Socialist Britain: Organ of the Marxist-Leninist Organisation of Britain. I, 1 (Oct. 1967)–(May/June 1972); ns 1 (Jan./Feb. 1973–); m; bi-m

    B   Later subtitle: 'Bulletin of the Red Front Movement'. Superseded **Hammer or Anvil**.

    LE†

2947 Red International of Labour Unions: Official Organ of the RILU I, 1 (Oct. 1928)–II, 7/8 (Nov./Dec. 1930); then **RILU**: Organ of the Red International of Labour Unions: ns I, 1 (Feb. 1931)–II, 24 (Jan. 1933); then **Red International of Labour Unions Monthly Magazine**: III, 1 (Feb. 1933)–III, 4 (May 1933); m

    A   6d.; 3d.; 2d. Not so much a magazine of the British Section of the RILU as a central RILU journal in English. Published for the RILU by the National Minority Movement, then by RILU Publications. Contributors: John Mahon, G. Hardy, A. Losovsky etc.

    L i–ii III, 1, 3, 4; LE Aug. 1929–Nov. 1932*; MML†; ONC† I, 1 (Oct. 1928)–I, 5 (Feb. 1929), I, 10 (Nov. 1929), Feb. 1931–Jan. 1933; Warwick UL 1928–30

2948 Red International of Labour Unions Agitprop Department. Press Service 1 (May 1930)–?

    A   Reproduced from typewriting. Place of publication doubtful. 'For the Factory Papers', how they should be run, for training political fighters in trade unions and among the unemployed.

    MML† 1

Red International of Labour Unions Monthly Magazine see **Red International of Labour Unions**

2949 Red Labour Union International: Bulletin of the Executive Bureau 1 (30 Aug. 1921)—12 (Feb. 1922). Moscow; fortn?

    A   In English. To describe all activities and developments of the Red International of Labour Unions. Articles reflecting the views of the Executive Bureau on vital questions of international Labour. Communist work in trade unions and the Labour Movement. Some news from Great Britain.

    MML†; ONC† 3 (17 Sept. 1921); WCML† 12

2950 Red Letter: the Paper of the Rank and File Postal Workers [1931]—?; m

    A   1d. Published by the Postal Workers Communist Group.

    WCML† 4 (Dec. 1931)

2951 Red Mole 1 (March 1970)—65 (14 April 1973); then **Red Weekly**: 1 (May 1973)— ; fortn

    B   International Marxist Group

    O; Warwick UL; (The Left in Britain — microfilm — Harvester Press Ltd)

2952 Red Needle: an International Organ of Left-wing Needle Workers I, 1 (Feb. 1929)—I, 4 (15 June 1929); m

    A   1d. Issued by the British Section of the International Needle Workers' Propaganda Committee. Published by D. Gershon. Spoke for the breakaway union, United Clothing Workers' Union of Great Britain. Minority Movement and Red International of Labour Unions influence. Against the official trade union leadership, for a mass industrial union. News from London and the provinces.

    L(Col)†

2953 Red Patriot 1969— ; Dublin; irreg

    B   Published by the Irish Revolutionary Youth.

    D

2954 Red Republican; Equality, Liberty, Fraternity 1 (22 June 1850)—24 (30 Nov. 1850); then **Friend of the People**: 1 (14 Dec. 1850)—33 (26 July 1851); ns 1 (7 Feb. 1852)—12 (24 April 1852); w

    B   1d. Editor and proprietor: G. Julian Harney. Social democratic leanings. The last four numbers of the **Red Republican** printed the 'Communist Manifesto' in the first English translation. Mottoes of the **Friend of the People**: 'The Charter and Something More'; 'Abolition of Classes and Sovereignty of Labour'.

    L a*; LE† a; LU 1852; Merlin Reprint (without 1852)

2955 Red Rose: the Organ of NALGO, Lancashire County Branch ns I, 1 (July 1963)— . Preston

    A   National and Local Government Officers' Association.

    L

2956 Red Stage: Organ of the Workers' Theatre Movement I, 1 (Nov. 1931)–I, 5 (April/May 1932); then **New Red Stage**: 6 (June/July 1932)–7 (Sept. 1932); m

    B   1d.; 2d. Published by the Workers' Theatre Movement. 'Movement' dropped from subtitle after No. 1. Motto: 'Art is the weapon of the Revolution'. Communist. Later editor: Charles B. Mann. Occasional signed articles. Contributors: Ivor Montagu, Tom Thomas. News of groups, reviews, short articles, advertisements for performers, sketches. Illustrated.

    E 1–2; L (destroyed); O; WCML† 3–5

Red Star see **Penny Red**

2957 Red Tape: a Civil Service Magazine. I, 1 (Oct. 1911)–   ; m

    A   1d. etc. Organ of the Assistant Clerks' Association, then the Civil Service Clerical Association, then the Civil and Public Services' Association. Absorbed **The Scribe**.

    E 1955–(w occ. nos); L(Col)†; LDS; LE I–VII; NU 1925–*; ONC XXXIV, 1944/5–; SwU XLIV, 54 (1955)–   ; TUC*

2958 Red Tape Newsletter 1 (June 1954)

    A   Civil Service Clerical Association. A single sheet 'to enable Red Tape agents to keep in touch with the Editor'. Reproduced from typewriting.

    L

2959 Red Vanguard: a Journal of the Theory and Practice of Marxism-Leninism. 1 (Spring 1970)–?; q

    B   6s. Marxist-Leninist Organisation of Britain. Printed and published by M. Scott (2–3). No. 1 contains 'The Thought of Mao Tse-Tung'. Numbers 2 and 3 are undated.

    E; O 1–3

Red Weekly see **Red Mole**

2960 Redcar Herald [194-?]. Redcar; m

    B   3d. Labour Party. (Labour Party. **Your own Journal**, 1948.)

2961 Reform News [1888?]; [ns] 1 (April 1890)–5 (Aug. 1890); m

    B   Printed and published by the proprietors, Catlin and Kerwood. The 1890 series refers (in No. 1) to an earlier appearance 'some 2 years ago' of the **Reform News**, which ran for a few months. Revived on Democratic lines as before. '5000 distributed gratis monthly.' Hopeful of readers from the numerous radical clubs in london. Liberal/Radical.

    L(Col)† 1890

2962 Reformer 1 (3 Nov. 1819)—5 (1 Dec. 1819). Glasgow; w
 C 2d. Printed by Young, Gallie and Company. Published strictures by a 'radical reformer' who attacks the objectives of radical political reform, infidelism, demagoguery etc. of the reformers, Cobbett, Hunt, Carlile, Sherwin etc. Advocates self-betterment through education in the home, ie the reading of certain journals, the Bible etc. and a 'moral reformation' beginning in the heart.
 GM†

2963 Reformer 1 (12 May 1833)—33 (5 June 1834); w
 B 4d.; 3½d.; 2d. Published, printed and edited by James H. B. Lorymer. '(On several occasions Lorymer used "Dummy publishers", such as W. Simmens and J. G. Smith, to reduce the risk of prosecution.) A working-class radical newspaper that attacks the aristocracy, the Church of England, and the "tax-gorgers", and advocates universal suffrage and non-payment of taxes' (Wiener). Merged with **The People's Conservative**.
 HO 64/15 No. 33, HO 64/19 No. 1

Reformer. 1835—1911 see **Diwygiwr**

2964 Reformer 1, 1 (6 Aug. 1836)—4 (27 Aug. 1836). Liverpool; w
 B 2d. Published and printed by J, Donbavand. 'A political miscellany that advocates an extension of the suffrage, short Parliaments, a reduction of taxation, the disestablishment of the Church of England, and poor laws for Ireland' (Wiener). Support for London engineers' strike, trade union organisation, and 'Rights of Industry'.
 L 1; LU† 1—4

2965 Reformer 1 (13 Sept 1861)—2 (20 Sept. 1861); then **Reformer and South Wales Times**: 3 (27 Sept. 1861)—32 (25 April 1862). Newport, Mon.; w
 C 1d. Printed and published by Henry Evans. Object: 'elevation of the working men of this populous district'. Campaigns aganst the Truck System, for social improvement via temperance, and promotion of popular religious revivalism against the Establishment, the upper class and the masters.
 L(Col)†

2966 Reformer 1 (15 Aug. 1868)—341 (27 Feb. 1875). Edinburgh; w
 B 1d. Editor: Councillor David Lewis, well-known advocate 'of Liberal measures and the rights of the Working Classes for the last 20 years'. In politics, advanced Liberal, or radical, including the ballot and land question, but especially addressed to the working class and advocating the rights of Labour, Trade Unionism, the removal of class legislation, eg, repeal of the Criminal Law Amendment Act. A special feature is the detailed reporting of trade-union matters from correspondents in various parts of Scotland and the United Kingdom. Contributors: Ernest Jones, George Potter. Then incorporated with **Edinburgh Weekly Review**.
 E (microfilm); EP 1—(7 Oct 1871); L(Col)†

Reformer and South Wales Times see **Reformer, 1861**

2967 Reformer's Almanac 1848–50. Wortley, Leeds; a
    B   Printed and published by Joseph Barker. Bound with
Reformer's Companion to the Almanacs, with common title page:
Reformer's Almanac and Companion to the Almanacs.
    L 1848–9 (missing); LDW; ONC†

2968 Reformer's Companion to the Almanacs I, 1 (Jan. 1848)–II, 14
(Feb. 1849). Wortley, Leeds; m
    B   1d. Printed and sold by Joseph Barker. Supports the principles
of the Charter. For full employment and fair remuneration for work done.
For peaceful constitutional agitation. In No. 8 support for Lovett's
People's League, to win the Charter. Also published complete and bound
with **Reformer's Almanac** (qv).
    LDW 1–9, 12–14; LE†; LU 1–6; ONC†

Reformers' Gazette see **Loyal Reformers' Gazette**

2969 Reformers' Pocket Companion 1 (2 June 1832)–2 (9 June 1832).
Glasgow; w
    B   Published and printed Muir, Gowans and Company together
with **The New Political Dictionary**. 'Features radical extracts, many of
which emphasize the evils of the factory system' (Wiener).
    GM 2 (missing)

Reformers' Year Book see **Labour Annual**

2970 Reformists' Register 1 (28 Sept. 1811)–18 (25 Jan. 1812); w
    B   1s. Printed and published by and for John Hunt. Well-written
essays and reviews advocating political reform. Against
borough-mongering, the evils of a depreciated paper currency, the vices of
the aristocracy; supports civil and religious liberties. Airs Major
Cartwright's plans for reform. Exposes prison abuses, principally in
Ireland.
    LU†

Reformists' Register and Weekly Commentary see **Hone's Reformists'
Register and Weekly Commentary**

Refuge Staff Journal see **RFSA Journal**

2971 Regeneration [sometimes **Regeneracion**] 1 (29 July 1936)–19 (7
Oct. 1936); ns 1 (21 Feb. 1937)–4 (14 March 1937). Glasgow; irreg?; w
    B   Gratis (voluntary subscription); 1d. Issued by Guy Aldred on
behalf of the United Socialist Movement (Anarchist). For solidarity with
the Spanish workers.
    E ns 1–3; L(Col)† (w 4–7, 9, 13, ns 3); ONC ns 1–2

2972 Regenerator 1 (1 June 1844)—5 (29 June 1844); w

B 2d.; 1d. Published by Henry Hetherington. Purpose: 'the independent and philosophical discussion of all the questions now before society relating to man as an intellectual, social and moral being'. Opposes superstition and the supernatural explanation of human and material phenomena, and supports exposition, rationalism, naturalism. Deals wih questions of social economy. Reports of the annual conference of the Rational Society held at Harmony Hall in Hampshire.

LU†

2973 Regenerator, and Advocate for the Unrepresented: a Legal Substitute for a Stamped Paper I, 1 ([Oct. 19?], 1839)—? then **Regenerator, and Chartist Circular**: ns 1 (1840)—2 (1840). Manchester; w

B 1½d. Published by T. P. Carlile. Editor?: R. J. Richardson. Chartist viewpoint, militant, physical force centred on Manchester. A forum for various types of radical views, Chartist, Owenite, Carlile's.

LU† I, (2 [26 Oct]. 3 [2 Nov].) 1839

Regenerator, and Chartist Circular see **Regenerator, and Advocate for the Unrepresented**

2974 Regenerator, or Guide to Happiness 1 (1 Aug. 1832); w?

B 1d.; Published, printed, edited and written by Henry Berthold. ' . . . a continuation of my **National Guardian** . . . ' 'Political essays written by Berthold who repeatedly urges the need for a more equitable system of distribution as well as for a currency proportionate to productive needs' (Wiener). Directs his remarks to the 'labouring and producing millions'.

L; LU†; O

2975 Register for the First Society of Adherents to Divine Revelation at Orbiston 1 (10 Nov. 1825)—34 (19 Sept. 1827). Edinburgh; w; m

B 2d. Published by W. R. McPhun. Printed by J. and J. Gray, then by the Orbiston Press, Edited by Abram Combe. Record of the Owenite communitarian experiment at Orbiston, Lanarkshire. Sometimes referred to as **Orbiston Register**.

Co-op. Coll.; LU†; Motherwell PL 1—25

2976 Reid's Glasgow Magazine 1 (1 June 1834). [Glasgow?].

B Radical. Expresses a 'sense of betrayal' at the hands of the Whigs; includes a treatise in defense of Trade Unionism, condemning 'Nobs', ie blacklegs.

GM†

2977 Reporter 1834 Glasgow

B 'ultra-radical'. (R. M. W. Cowan, **The Newspaper in Scotland**, Glasgow 1946, p. 145.)

Republic. 1935 see **Phoblacht**

2978 Republican: a Weekly Historical Magazine. 1 (6 Jan. 1813)–22 (23 May 1813); w

    B   M. M. Mortimer. 22 numbers complete with letter to the readers; 'Terminated through the stamp duties' (**Museum Book Shop Catalogue**, 1922).

2979 Republican 1 (1817)–5 (29 March 1817): then b **Sherwin's (Weekly) Political Register**: I, 1 (1817)–V, 16 (21 Aug. 1819); then c **Republican**: I, 1 27 (Aug. 1819)–XIV, 25 (29 Dec. 1826); w

    B   2d. etc. Printed and published by W. T. Sherwin, then by R. Carlile, and Julian Augustus St John. Radical reformist, for a democratic republic with annual parliaments. Against organised religion and State churches.

    BP b II–III, 25, c; GM c; L a 1, b I–III, IV, 2, V, 8, c; LE b I–II*, c*; LU a 5–b III, IV, 3, V, 3, 16, c I–VI; MP b I–III, V, 16, c; MU c; O c; ONC†*; NwP a, b

Republican, 1819–1826 see Republican, 1817

Republican, 1833 see Bonnet Rouge

2980 Republican: a Magazine Advocating the Sovereignty of the People I (1848)

    B   Published by James Watson. Edited by C. G. Harding. Proclaims the principles of republican democracy. Advocates Chartist principles to be realised by peaceful means. Many articles on this theme and on international republicanism, by W. J. Linton. The 'people' are the labouring classes, 'the wealth creators and tax-payers'. Linton's articles originally appeared in the contemporary **Cause of the People**.

    Bishopsgate Institute; L; LE†; LU; O

2981 Republican: a Monthly Advocate and Record of Republican and Democratic Principles and Movements 1 (1 Sept. [1870])–26 (1 Feb. [1872]); m

    B   1d. Organ of the Land and Labour League, committed to a programme of land nationalisation, national free and secular education, reduction of the hours of labour, universal suffrage, and payment of MPs.

    L; O 1–11

Republican, 1879–1886 see Republican Chronicle

2982 Republican; or, Voice of the People I, 1 (26 March 1831)–(II, 47 [28 July 1832?])); then **Republican and Radical Reformer**: III, 1 (4 Aug. 1832)–(III, 19 [15 Dec. 1832?])); then **Republican.** IV, 1 [23 March 1834?]–IV, 6 (27 April 1834); w; m; w

    B   ½d.; 1d.; 3d.; 1d.; 1½d. Printed and published by Henry Hetherington (I–III), then 'Benjamin Franklin' ie James H. B. Lorymer (IV). Edited by Lorymer. 'One of the best-known working-class newspapers of the decade. It advocates universal suffrage, the appropriation of church property, the "common use" of land, the convening of a national convention to reconstruct society. It rejects Owenite co-operative ideas as utopian" (Wiener). Merged with **The Radical Reformer** in Aug. 1832. During 1833 a separate version of this periodical was published as **Le Bonnet Rouge.**

    HO 64/11 I, 1, 16, 19; HO 64/16 I, 20; HO 64/17 I, 2, 11–14, 17–18, 24, 26; HO 64/19 IV, 3–4, 6; L II, 1–7, 11, III, 7, 10–11, 13–15; LU I, 1–4, 6–32; ONC* (microfilm)

Republican and Radical Reformer see **Republican.** 1831–1832

2983 Republican Chronicle: a Monthly Journal Advocating Democratic Principles, and Recording Republican Work and Progress 1 (April 1875)–[1878?]; then b **Republican**: I, 1 (Jan. 1879)–XII, 6 (Aug. 1886); then c **Radical**: I, 1 (Sept. 1886)–IV, 1 (Sept. 1889); Feb. 1897; m

    B   1d. Published by E. Truelove. Printed and edited by George Standring. Advocated radical republicanism. Promotes republican clubs 'to obtain political power for the good of all'. In the 1880s publicised the Republican League and the Democratic Federation. Discussion on Republicanism in relation to social democracy. In February 1897 Standring published an additional issue to ascertain whether a new journal of free thought would win support, but it was not continued.

    L a 1–3 (June 1875), b, c; LE c I

Republican File see **Phoblacht**

Republican Herald see **International Herald**

2984 Republican Record: a Series of Tracts to be Issued Occasionally by the Republican Brotherhood of Newcastle-upon-Tyne 1 (Jan. 1855)–? Newcastle-upon-Tyne; irreg

    B   ½d.; 1d. Printed and published by the Republican Brotherhood (Treasurer: Joseph Cowen, Secretary: G. J. Harney). Editor: Harney . Periodical in format and content. Militant democratic republican. 'government of the people by and for the people.' No. 2 announced that the next number would appear in April, with articles by Harney, Linton, Holyoake etc.

    NwP† 1–2 (March 1855)

2985 République Exilée: Revue Démocratique 1 (11 Oct. 1856)–2 (1 Nov. 1856)

    B

    L(Col)

2986 Resistance: Action for Peace. Committee of 100 Bulletin [1963?] –?

    B   Reproduced from typewriting. Produced by the London Committee of 100.

    L II, 1 (22 Jan. 1964)–

2987 Retail Book, Stationery and Allied Trades Employees' Association. Circular 1921–; q

    A   For members only. Current title on cover: **RBA Circular: Official Journal of the Retail Book, Stationery and Allied Trades Association**. Inside title: **The Circular**.

    The Association

2988 Retained Fireman [c1955]; m

    A   Gratis. Official retained firemen's journal of the Fire Brigades Union. (Mitchell, 1955.)

2989 Retort: the Official Organ of the Gas Sales Staff Association, the Gas Light and Coke Company I, 1 (April 1934)–3 (Oct. 1934); q

    A   1d. Published by the Association. Seeks the welfare of its members in job security and good wages, in a year of unemployment and of competition to the gas industry.

    L

2990 Reveille: a Monthly Organ of the Workers 1 (Oct. 1894)–?; m

    B   1d. Published by the South East District Independent Labour Party, circulating in Deptford, Greenwich and Woolwich. Edited by Jim Connell. (**Labour Leader**, 20 Oct. 1894; **Labour Annual**, 1895.)

2991 Reveillé : Organ of the Salford Unemployed Workers' Committee I, 1 (4 March 1922). Salford; m

    A   1d. Only one number. The National Headquarters of the National Unemployed Workers' Movement induced the Salford Committee to discontinue publication in favour of **Out of Work**.

    WCML†

2992 Reveille I, 1 [May 1940?] –?; fortn

    B   2d. Founded, edited and published by W. R. Hepwell. 'The Services Newspaper'. Agitates for better wages and conditions in the forces. Later official organ of the Allied Ex-Service Association.

    TUC† occ. nos between I, 8 (31 Aug. 1940) and 87 (13 Sept. 1943)

2993 Reveillé: WOYAC Magazine. 1 (May [1940])–Jan. 1942; q

    A   2d. A 'recruitment' Magazine published by the Civil Service Clerical Association, War Office Youth Advisory Committee. Reproduced from typewriting.

    L

2994 Revelry I (1954)–. Reading

    A   National and Local Government Officers' Association, Berks. County Officers Guild.

    L

2995 Review: the Staff Magazine of the CIS [19--?] –. Manchester

    A   Co-operative Insurance Society, Ltd.

    Co-op Union 1962–; L XXV, 4 (April 1957)–

2996 Review: the Organ of the Sorter Tracers' Association 1 (June 1905)–154 (Jan. 1926); bi-m

    A   1d. First published for the Association by F. C. Parkinson, then from March 1910 by G. C. Holyoake. Edited by Parkinson, then by Holyoake. For telegram and mail sorters in the Inland Telegraph Branch and Accountant General's Department. Agitates for better wages and more secure conditions of employment. Reports; no general articles.

    L; TUC Dec. 1922–Feb. 1924*

Review, 1947– see **SPOEI Review**

2997 'Review' 1960?–. Manchester

    A   National and Local Government Officers' Association, Irlam Branch. Incorporates **NALGO News**. Reproduced from typewriting.

    L 960–

Review of International Co-operation see **International Co-operative Bulletin**

Revolt see **Spain and the World**

2998 Revolt: the London and South of England Workers' Paper 1 (1933)–? fortn; m

    B   1d. Published by the Independent Labour Party, London and Southern Counties Division. Contributors: Pat Sloan, Hilda Vernon. (See also the entry under 'Branson' in Bellamy, J. and Saville, J. **Dictionary of Labour Biography**, Vol. II, for further information.)

    ILP 1932–3*; ONC† 4 (June 1933)

2999 Revolution: Official Organ of the Socialist School I, 1 (June/July 1917)–12 (June 1918). Glasgow; m

B   1d.; 2d. 'A magazine for young workers' published by the Socialist School. Printed by the Socialist Labour Press. Marxist education and culture. Contributors: A. E. Cook, J. Main, A. Henry, John S. Clark, W. Paul, Tom Anderson.

E 3 (original), 1–12 (microfilm); WCML†

3000 Revolutionary Communist Party. **Internal Bulletin** [194-?]–[195-?]; irreg?

B   Price and size vary. For Party members only. Reproduced from typewriting.

ONC† No. 3 (undated), (19 Oct. 1945)–(Aug. 1950*)

3001 Revolutionary Communist Party. **Speakers' Information Service** [1946?]–?; irreg

B   Edited by G. Noseda. Reproduced from typewriting.

ONC† 2 (Jan. 1947)–12 (Dec. 1948/Jan. 1949) (w 4)

3002 Revolutionary Review I, 1 (Jan. 1889)–I, 9 (Sept. 1889); m

B   3d. Published and edited by H. Seymour. The revolutionist 'is a prophet, not a warrior'. 'Our programme, then, is simply the education of the workers in sound economic doctrine.' Against physical force. Contributor: Lothrop Withington.

L

3003 Revolutionary Youth Federation. **Monthly Bulletin I**, 1 (1 Feb. 1938); then **Struggle**: I, 2 (March/April 1938)–I, 3 (June 1938); m

B   1½d.; 1d. Bulletin of the anarchist Revolutionary Youth Federation and the syndicalist Committee for Workers' Control. Promotes Anarcho-Syndicalism as the means of workers' emancipation. Reproduced from typewriting.

L

3004 Revoluziunara Baltija. [**Revolutionary Baltic**] 1 (1905)–3 (1905)

B   Succeeded **Proletareets** (qv)

L

3005 Revue: International Organ for the Interests of All Employees in Hotels, Restaurants, Boarding Houses etc. I, 1 (Oct. 1905)–V, 11 (1 June 1909); m

A   ½d.; 1d. In English, French and German. Published by A. Baumeister, later by H. Fisher. Official organ of the Caterers' Employees' Union. Promotes international federation of Trade Unionism in the catering trades. Militant fight against abuses eg, against bogus and exorbitant registry employment offices; for better pay and shorter hours. Socialist. Widespread continental coverage. Boasted that it had the 'largest circulation of any Hotel Employees' Paper in the United Kingdom'.

L(Col)†; ONC I, 8–10

3006 Reynard 1 (Autumn 1956)–? Nottingham; q

    A   National and Local Government Officers' Association, Leicestershire Branch.

    L 1–7 (Autumn 1958)

Reynolds News see **Reynolds's Weekly Newspaper**

Reynolds News and Sunday Citizen see **Reynolds's Weekly Newspaper**

Reynolds's Illustrated News see **Reynolds's Weekly Newspaper**

Reynolds's News see **Reynolds's Weekly Newspaper**

Reynolds's Newspaper see **Reynolds's Weekly Newspaper**

3007 Reynolds's Political Instructor 1 (10 Nov. 1849)–27 (11 May 1850); w

    B   Editor: G. W. M. Reynolds. An organ of the Chartist movement. Merged with **Reynolds's Weekly Newspaper**.

    BP; L(Col)†; LE† (reprint); LU; MP

3008 Reynolds's Weekly Newspaper 1 (5 May 1850)–26 (9 Feb. 1851);
    Reynolds's Newspaper: 27 (16 Feb. 1851)–3784 (25 Feb. 1923)
then **Reynolds's News**: 3785 (4 March 1923)–3865 (14 Sept. 1924); then
Reynolds's Illustrated News: 3866 (21 Sept. 1924)–4460 (23 Feb. 1936);
then **Reynolds News**: 4461 (1 March 1936)–4902 (13 Aug. 1944); then
Reynolds News and Sunday Citizen: 4903 (20 Aug. 1944)–5841 (16 Sept.
1962). then **Sunday Citizen**: [5842] (23 Sept. 1962)–6087 (18 Jan.
1967); w

    B   Editors: until 1879 G. W. M. Reynolds; until 1894 Edward
Reynolds; until 1907 W. M. Thompson. Started as a Chartist organ; by
1880 pro-radical Liberal, devoting much attention to foreign news with
special attention to mistreatment of colonies. In 1889 favoured the
formation of a new political party. By 1907 sympathetic to socialists as
reformers but not in favour of State control; full of news of stage
personalities and murder trials; carried Labour news and had progressive
democratic political line (Brophy). Later became a newspaper of the
Co-operative movement. There was also a Scottish edition: **Reynolds's
Newspaper** (Special Scottish edition). 3140, (Oct. 16, 1910)–3142 (30 Oct
1910) then **Scottish Reynolds's**. 3143 (6 Nov. 1910)–3181 (30 July
1911).

    L(Col)

3009 Rhondda Clarion: the Official Organ of the Rhondda Borough
Labour Party 1 (Sept. 1935)–14 (Jan. 1937). Penygraig, Rhondda; m

    B   1d. Published by the Editorial Board at the Labour Hall,
Penygraig. Includes articles on education, and on peace and war. Labour
League of Youth section. Contributor: W. H. Mainwaring, MP.

    L(Col)†

3010 Rhondda Socialist Newspaper, Being the Bomb of the Rhondda Workers 1 (19 Aug. 1911)–39 (10 May 1913). Pontypridd; m; fortn (March 1912–)

B ½d. Published by the Rhondda Socialist Newspaper Committee. Printed by the Welsh Democracy Printing Company; 'issued under the control of a committee of the Rhondda ILP branches'. Aims at 'consolidating the Trades' Union and Socialist forces of the Rhondda, together with spreading the light of knowledge in the interest of the workers'. Prominence given to the work of Trades' Councils, of the socialists on Rhondda Urban District Council, to the local branches of socialist organisations, the Social Democratic Federation, and the British Socialist Party, as well as the Independent Labour Party, and to trade union news. Latterly, sympathetic towards Syndicalism. Succeeded by the enlarged paper, the **South Wales Worker** (qv).

L(Col)†; South Wales Miners' Library

3011 Rich and Poor: a Weekly Journal, Being an Inquiry into the Trades Unions of the Privileged Classes 1(30 Nov. 1867) –8 (18 Jan. 1868); w

A 1d. A fictional clever and witty exposure of the 'combination' of the sections of the ruling class against the working class, ie of the aristocracy, the capitalists, the Law. An obvious parody of the Royal Commission which was at that time investigating the principles of Trade Unionism as part of the general attack on union rights in the 1860s. Conducted by working-men, who remain anonymous for fear of proscription.

L

3012 Richmond and Barnes Clarion. Edition of the Surrey and Middlesex Clarion. [194-?] –April 1970; then **Richmond Clarion**: May 1970–April 1973. m

B Issued by the Richmond and Barnes Labour Party. Intended for sale in the wards to members and supporters. Stopped because it was felt that something was needed that could be delivered to every house and not sold. Replaced by several editions of **Labour Voice**.

L(Col) 166 (Dec. 1956)– ; LabP† 1964–70*

Richmond Clarion see Richmond and Barnes Clarion

3013 Riding Around: Journal of the West Riding County Officers' Association. I, 1 (Spring 1953)–? Wakefield

A National and Local Government Officers' Association. Reproduced from typewriting.

L I, 1–2, II, 1–13, III, 1–6, 1956

Right Angle see Association of Civil Service Designers and Draughtsman. Monthly Circular

3014 Rights of Industry 1 (1848)–2 (1848); m

    C   3d. Unstamped. Published with **Voice of the People**, by Charles Knight.

    L

Ringer see **Rossington Ringer**

Ripley Gazette see **Heanor and Ripley Gazette**

3015 Rising Tide [c1921]. Hastings; m

    B   2d. Local Labour Party paper. (**Labour Organiser**, July 1921.)

3016 Rising Tide: Official Organ of the Northern Ireland Labour Party [1949?]–? Belfast; m

    B   2d. etc. Signed articles, news and information.

    LabP† II, 5 (Aug. 1950)–7 (Oct. 1950), 9 (Dec. 1950); Linen Hall Library, Belfast I, 4 (1949)–III, 4 (1951), Special issue, May 1952 (xerox copies)

3017 River: Journal of the Thames Conservancy Staff Association 1 [1952?]–

    A   National and Local Government Officers' Association. Reproduced from typewriting.

    L 10 (Jan. 1953)–

3018 Rivoluzione Sociale (Social Revolution). 1(4 Oct. 1902)–9 (5 April 1903); fortn

    B   In Italian. Published by A. Galassini on behalf of the Libertarian Group 'La Rivoluzione Sociale'. Theoretical analysis and reports on anarchist movements in Italy and elsewhere.

    L(Col)†

3019 Road Haulage News Letter, By Drivers, For Drivers March [1946]–July [1946]; then **Headlight**: Journal of the Road Transport Worker: I, 1 (Sept. 1946)– ; m

    A   3d. etc. For nationalisation of the road transport industry. Also to air grievances and support the Transport and General Workers' Union.

    L June 1946– ; TUC

3020 Road Journal 1 (27 April 1889)–9 (17 Aug. 1889); fortn

    A   ½d. Printed and published for the proprietors by William George King. An organ in which vehicle drivers of the metropolis can 'ventilate grievances'. Advocates shorter working hours, special courts in cases of trivial driving misdemeanours and power to detain persons who refuse fares, by Act of Parliament. Reports of the Cabdrivers Mutual Aid and Protection Society.

    L(Col)†

3021 Robert Owen's Journal, Explanatory of the Means to Well-Place, Well-Employ, and Well-Educate the Population of the World I, 1 (2 Nov. 1850)–IV, 104 (23 Oct. 1852); w

B   1d. Published by James Watson. Edited by Henry Travis. Addresses and contributions by Robert Owen on Utopian socialist doctrines and schemes, and a full explanation of his **New Views of Society**, an outline of which was first published in 1812–13. Correspondence with other social reformers.

CrU I; L; LE; LU; MP

3022 Robert Owen's Millenial Gazette, Explanatory of the Principles and Practices by which, in Peace, with Truth, Honesty, and Simplicity the New Existence of Man Upon the Earth May Be Easily and Speedily Commenced 1 (1 March 1856)–16 (21 June 1858); irreg

B   6d. Published by Owen, who expounds his principles and plans for a federated co-operative commonwealth of nations, in the interests of universal peace, enlightenment and prosperity. Also contains his addresses to members of the ruling class. No. 11 reports the proceedings of the Congress of the Advanced Minds of the World convened by Owen in May 1857.

Co-op. Coll.† 5–10, 12, 16, 2nd ed. 11; L 1–12; LE 3; LU 14–15, 2nd ed. 11; o 8–11; ONC; 2nd ed. 11

3023 Robert Owen's Rational Quarterly Review and Journal I, 1 (Feb. 1853)–4 (Nov. 1853). London, Manchester; q

B   1s. Publishers: J. Clayton; J. Watson; Truelove; Cooper; Heywood, Manchester. Edited by Robert Owen, who continues to campaign for acceptance of his view for social change. Letter appealing to members of the ruling class. In last number concerned with spirit mediums etc. Running title: **Rational Quarterly Review**. Succeeded **Robert Owen's Journal**.

L (w 2); LU

3024 Robert Owen's Weekly Letter to the Human Race 1 (1850)–18 (May 1850); w

B   Also a second edition entitled **Letters to the Human Race on the Coming Universal Revolution**, London, 1850. Need for 'an entire change of system, in principle and practice'.

LU 16 (April 1850)–18 (May 1850)

3025 Robotnik: Organ Polskiej Partji Socjalistycznej (**The Worker**: Organ of the Polish Socialist Party). 1 (June 1894)–   . Warsaw; London; m; bi-m

B   Latterly, a socialist, democratic, anti-communist paper for Polish socialists in exile. The later part is supposed to be a continuation of the earlier paper.

L 1–237 (Feb. 1914); L(Col) 8131 (Jan. 1950)–

3026 Robotnik Polski w Wielkiej Brytanji: Pisnio Socjalist ow Polskich, Czlonkow PPS [**Polish Worker in Great Britain**: Organ of the Polish Socialists, Members of PPS] I, 1 (25 Aug. 1940)–X, 12 (Dec. 1949) fortn; m

B 2d.; 3d.
L(Col)

3027 Rochdale Citizen 1 (July 1905)–? Rochdale; m
B Rochdale Socialist Party. Published by James Clegg, Aldine Press.
Rochdale PL 1 (July 1905)–(June 1907*)

3028 Rochdale Labour News: an Organ of Socialism for Rochdale and District 1 (June 1896)–[Sept. 1900?]; ns 1 (21 Oct. 1922)–13 (10, Feb. 1923); ns 14 (1) (23 March 1923)–332 (Jan. 1941). Rochdale; m; w (1922–Feb. 1923); m
B 1d. etc. First published by J. W. Scott. Started by Rochdale Independent Labour Party. Later published by the Rochdale Trades and Labour Council. Local Labour and trade union news, and coverage of municipal politics.
Abu* (microfilm); L(Col)† III, 7 (Jan. 1899)–1941; Rochdale PL June 1896–Feb. 1937 (w occ. nos)

Romford and Brentford Citizen see **Romford and Hornchurch Citizen**

3029 Romford and Hornchurch Citizen 1 (Feb. 1932)–ns 24 (Sept. 1939); then **Romford and Brentwood Citizen**: ?–ns 24 (Feb. 1955); then **Romford Citizen**: 25 (July 1955)–86 (Feb. 1963); m; irreg
B Gratis. Published by the London Co-operative Society's Political Committee.
L(Col) 1 (Feb. 1932)–ns 24 (Sept. 1939), ns 5 (June 1953)–86

Romford Citizen see **Romford and Hornchurch Citizen**

3030 Romford Labour Review [194-?] Romford; m
B 2d. Labour Party. (Labour Party. **Your own Journal**, 1948.)

Rorty Review see **Rag**

3031 Rossington Ringer
A Issued by the Rossington Communist Pit Group. Title sometimes **The Ringer** (R. G. Neville).

3032 Rostra: Newport, Mon., NALGO Branch Magazine I, 1 (Jan. 1954)–? Newport, Mon. q
A National and Local Government Officers' Association. Reproduced from typewriting.
L 1–April 1954

3033 Rother Valley Labour Journal [c1921]. Thurcroft, nr. Rotherham; m

    B   2d. Local Labour Party paper. (**Labour Organiser**, July 1921.)

3034 Rotherhithe Citizen 1 (July 1938)–15 (Sept. 1939); m
    B   Published by the Co-operative Press.
    L(Col)

3035 Rotherhithe Labour Magazine I (1934)–III (1936); IV, 1 (Jan. 1948)–IV, 6 (June 1948); m?
    B?
    BeP

3036 Rothwell Labour Monthly 1 (Oct. 1896)–3 (Dec. 1896). Rothwell; m

    B   ½d. Published by Wright Stead for the Rothwell Independent Labour Party. Localised edition of a paper launched in 1896 by Allen Clarke.
    AbU 2–3 (microfilm); O(JJ) 2–3

3037 Roundabout Nov. 1963?– . Mitcham
    A   National and Local Government Officers' Association, Mitcham Branch. Reproduced from typewriting.
    L Nov. 1963–

3038 Roundabout July 1966?–. Merton
    A   National and Local Government Officers' Association, Merton Branch. Reproduced from typewriting.
    L July 1966–

3039 Royal Liver Workers' Journal 1919–71; then **Journal** 1971– ; bi-m
    A   Royal Liver Employees' Union, then National Union of Insurance Workers, Royal Liver Section.
    L LII, 7 (Feb. 1963)–; TUC May 1936–

3040 Royal London Mutual Assurance Society Staff Association. Gazette [19--?] –
    A   Then the **Gazette** of the National Union of Insurance Workers, Royal London Section.
    L 532, June 1965–

3041 Royal London Staff Gazette: the Official Organ of the Royal London Staff Association 1921– ; m
    A   Royal London Staff Association, later Royal London Section of the National Union of Insurance Workers. Preceded by **The Sentinel**. Latterly entitled **The Gazette**.
    L 431 (Jan. 1957)– ; the Union

3042 Rubery Beacon [194-?]. Rubery; irreg
    B   Reproduced from typewriting. Labour Party. (Labour Party.
Your own Journal, 1948.)

3043 Rugby Co-operative Citizen 1 (Feb. 1936); then **Rugby Co-operator**:
2 (July 1936); irreg
    B   Issued by the Rugby Industrial and Provident Co-operative
Society.
    L(Col)

3044 Rugby Co-operative Citizen 1 (Nov. 1939) .
    B
    L(Col)

Rugby Co-operator see **Rugby Co-operative Citizen. 1936**

3045 Ruislip-Northwood Citizen ns 1 (Dec. 1950)—15 (March 1952); m
    B   Edited by the Political Committee of the London Co-operative
Society.
    L(Col)

3046 Running Buff-et: a News Supplement to the Buff 1963?—
Orpington
    A   National and Local Government Officers' Association,
Orpington Branch. See also **The Buff.**
    L 1963—

Rurabanian see **Rurabanian News-Sheet**

3047 Rurabanian News-Sheet ?—June 1966; then **Rurabanian**: July
1966—   . St Albans; m
    A   National and Local Government Officers' Association, St
Albans Rural Branch. Reproduced from typewriting.
    L March—June 1966; Conference edition, July 1966—

3048 Rural Crusader 1 (June 1946)—38 (June 1949); then **Rural Crusader
and Country Standard**: 39 (Aug. 1949)—(April 1951). Braintree;
London (Aug. 1949—.   ); m
    B   3d. Edited and published by William Savage, then published by
Jack Dunman (40—   ). A local agitator on questions such as tied housing
and low pay of farm workers. 'To voice the needs and desires of the
ordinary village folk.' Supports Labour Party, then under Dunman's
editorship apparently moves nearer to the Communist Party.
    L (w 39); MML 1—38

Rural Crusader and Country Standard see **Rural Crusader**

3049 Rural World: a Journal Advocating the Interests of Rural Labourers, Artisans, Cottagers, Farmers, and the Country Population Generally 1 (22 Dec. 1888)–824 (Dec. 1915). Birmingham; London; w; m

    C   1d. Organ of the Rural Labourers' League, President, Jesse Collings; 'to improve the material and social condition of the rural labouring class', and a 'channel for the expression of the views of the rural classes'. To promote peasant holdings, Allotments Acts, rural education, culture and improvement. Unionist Liberal in politics. In later years promotes village industries and is a more general agricultural journal.

    BP; BU V–X, XIII–XIX, XXVII; L(Col)† (w April 6, Aug. 3, 17, 24, 1894); LAM I–XII

3050 Rushlight 1841. Leicester

    B   ½d. Editor and proprietor: Thomas Cooper. Succeeded **Midland Counties Illuminator**. In **Northern Star**, 9 July, Cooper says the **Extinguisher** and the **Rushlight** were 'merely ½d substitutes for a little periodical'.

3051 Rusholme Contact [194-?]. Manchester; m

    B   Free. Labour Party. (Labour Party. **Your own Journal**, 1948.)

3052 Ruskin Collegian: the Magazine of Ruskin College, Oxford I, 1 (Jan. 1911)–V, 8 (1918). Oxford

    B
    L

3053 Ruskin Hall News [18--?]–[1899?]. Manchester; m

    A   Edited by James Rowbottom. Then incorporated with **Young Oxford**. (**Reformers' Year Book**, 1901.)

3054 Russia Today: Official Organ of the Friends of Soviet Russia I, 1 (Feb. 1930)–(Special issue, Jan./Feb. 1956); m

    B   2d. etc. Illustrated magazine lauding the Soviet achievement. Later journal of the British Soviet Friendship Society. Carries political advice and messages to the British working class on the international obligations towards the working class and Socialism.

    L(Col)†; ONC† 1–3

3055 Russia Today Newsletter [193-?]–446 (29 Dec. 1956); then British Soviet Newsletter: 447 (12 Jan. 1957)–660 (25 May 1968); fortn?

    B   Issued by the magazine **Russia Today** (qv), the British Soviet Friendship Society.

    L(Col) 110 (28 Aug. 1943)–660; O 447–660

3056 Russian Co-operator: a Journal of Co-operative Unity I, 1 (Dec. 1916)–V, 1 (April 1921); m

A   2d. Published by J. V. Burnoff and A. N. Balakshin, later by the Joint Committee of Russian Co-operative Organizations in London. To reach the consumer and producer in Russia. For promotion, internationally, and particularly with the Russian Co-operative Movement, of co-operative ideas and exchange of materials, 'business Entente between English and Russian co-operators'. Ceased after the signing of the Anglo-Russian trade treaty of March 1921.

L(Col)†; LE 1916–20

3057 Rutherglen Pioneer 1 (March 1906)–? Rutherglen; m

B   Published by Rutherglen Independent Labour Party. (**Labour Leader**, 31 March 1906, p. 108.)

3058 Rutherglen Searchlight [c1913–1918]. [Rutherglen?] ; m

B?

ILP July 1913, March 1918

3059 SACA: a Weekly Journal Published in the Interests of Salesmen, Assistants, Clerks, and Apprentices in Every Trade and Profession. Preliminary number, 1 April 1896; I, 1 (29 April 1896)–6 (4 June 1896); w

C   1d. Published by SACA [Salesmen, Assistants, Clerks, Apprentices] Publishing Company. Organ of Employees of both sexes in retail houses. Declares its opposition to Socialism and Trade Unionism, and not 'opposed to our employers', but encourages combination in mutual help schemes, including provident societies, and advocates profit-sharing. Supports shorter hours, early closing, literary and debating societies, athletic clubs, music-societies. The editor hoped workers would subscribe as shareholders of the magazine.

L(Col)†

3060 SC and T [c1935]. Liverpool; m

A   1d. Guild of Sorting Clerks and Telegraphists. (Mitchell, 1935.)

3061 SDP News: the Monthly Journal of Internal Affairs for Members of the SDP I, 1 (Aug. 1910)–II, 13 (Aug. 1911); m

B   ½d. Social Democratic Party. News and reports for branches.

L(Col) 1–13

S. Ken. Labour Party Clarion see **South Kensington Citizen**

SLADE Journal see **Process Journal**

SMA Bulletin see Socialist Medical Association. **Bulletin**

3062 SPOEI Review: the Official Organ of the Society of Post Office Engineering Inspectors I, 1 (Oct. 1938)–IX, 5 (May 1947); then **Review**: the Monthly Journal of the Society of Telecommunication Engineers: IX, 6 (June 1947)–XXXIX, 12 (Dec. 1968); m

    A   6d. etc. 'To safeguard and improve conditions of service.'

    L

3063 SPU News and Views: Bulletin of the Salaried Pharmacists Union [196-?]–?

    A   Reproduced from typewriting. The Union was formed by the amalgamation of the Registered Pharmacists' Union and the National Association of Salaried Pharmacists. See also **RPU News and Views**. The Union is in the process of merging with the Association of Professional Scientists and Technologists, and will become the Pharmaceutical Group of APST.

    ONC† (white collar coll.) March 1965

3064 SSTA Magazine I, 1 (Oct. 1946)–? (Dec. 1968). Edinburgh; 3-yr

    A   Official journal of the Scottish Secondary Teachers' Association.

    GU I, 1–XVI, 3 (1962)

3065 Sailors' Friend and Coastguard Gazette I ? (1893)–IV, 12 (Dec. 1896); m

    C   1d. Published by John Heywood. Edited by R. M. Thompson. Mission among seamen, precepts for daily life, temperance page, didactic sketches and anecdotes.

    L IV (1896)

Sailors' Magazine see **Pilot**

Saint see National Association of Local Government Officers. St Pancras Branch. [**Branch Magazine**]

3066 St Albans' City Members Bulletin [194-?]. [St Albans?] ; irreg

    B   Duplicated. Labour Party. (Labour Party. **Your own Journal**, 1948.)

3067 St Crispin: a Weekly Journal Devoted to the Interest of Boot and Shoe Makers and All Engaged in the Leather Trades. I, 1 (2 Jan. 1869)–XII, 317 (23 Jan. 1875); w

    A   1½d. Printed for the proprietors by the Westminster Printing Company, order to J. B. Leno. Starts as a means of communication between masters and journeymen, favours Courts of Arbitration for settling disputes. Articles, correspondence on Labour questions. The journal continued in a new Series after January 1875, and then changed title several times but changed in character and contained only trade and technical matter.

    L (w 228–39); LP; LU

3068 St Cuthbert's Co-operative Association. Record [1877?] Edinburgh; m

    A   'In the early years educational work was arranged by the board of management. Their work was restricted to occasional lectures. When the members decided, in 1877, that the time had come for the work to be done by a separate committee the board were none too pleased. That first educational committee was appointed with the specific task of publishing a monthly journal for the information of members. With a direct mandate from the members – and given £10 to spend for an experimental period of six months – they showed an independence which the board of management did not appreciate. The **Record**, as the monthly journal was called, contained criticisms which the management considered reflected upon their ability and were not in the best interests of the Association. A series of clashes resulted in the matter being placed before the quarterly meeting. There by a majority vote it was decided to cease publication of the **Record** (W. E. Lawson, **One hundred Years of Co-operation: the History of St Cuthbert's Co-operative Association Ltd., 1859–1959,** Manchester 1959, p. 65).

3069 St George's Co-operative Society. [Monthly Journal] [18–? 19–?]. Glasgow; m

    A   The Welfare Council 'issues a monthly journal, which is edited by Mr Norval, the accountant of the Society, and which takes a high place amongst journals of that character' (W. Reid, **Fifty years of the St George's Co-operative Society Ltd., 1870–1920,** Glasgow 1923, p. 143).

3070 St Helen's Social Reformer 1899–1901. [St Helen's?] ; m

    B   Free. Secretary: J. H. Standring. (**Labour Annual,** 1900; **Reformers' Year Book,** 1901.)

    O(JJ) 6 (March 1900)

3071 St Marylebone Labour Life [194-?] ; m

    B   2d. Labour Party. (Labour Party. **Your own Journal,** 1948.)

3072 St Mungo 1 [1922?] –? Glasgow; m

    A   Union of Post Office Workers, Glasgow Amalgamated Branch.

    E 36 (Oct. 1925)–197 (March 1939); TUC April 1926–Sept. 1957*

3073 St Nicholas Labour News. [194-?]. Southampton; irreg

    B   Duplicated. Labour Party. (Labour Party. **Your own Journal,** 1948.)

3074 St Pancras Bulletin 1 (4 May 1926)–14 (15 May 1926); d [ns] 1 (May 1926)–?; w

    A   The first series was a strike bulletin, ½d; the second a general Labour bulletin, 1d. Issued by the St Pancras Labour and Trades Council. Reproduced from typewriting. Subtitles of second series vary: 'The Paper of the Organised Workers of St Pancras'; 'The Organ of Organised Labour'.

    O(JJ)† i, ii (3 [5 June], [9], [17 July] 1926)

3075 St Pancras Citizen 1 (Aug. 1930)–32 (May 1933); m

    B   Published by the London Co-operative Society, Political Committee.

3076 St Pancras Labour Whip: Official Organ of the Trade Union and Labour Movement in St Pancras. I, 1 (Dec. 1924)–I, 2 (Jan./Feb. 1925); m

    B   1d. Published by the St Pancras Labour Party and Trades Council. Organ of North St Pancras Labour Party, and Independent Labour Party. Urges more socialist propaganda to prepare working-class electors for the next Election, to unseat the Tories.

    L(Col)†

St Pancras Local CPGB Bulletin see **Bulletin**: the Organ of the St Pancras LPC, 1925–?

3077 (St Pancras) Londoner: a Paper for the People of Camden Town, Kentish Town, Euston, Hampstead etc. 1 (14 Feb. 1896)–48 (8 Jan. 1897); then **Londoner. Edition of St Pancras**. 49 (15 Jan. 1897)–73 (2 July 1897); w

    B   1d. Printed and published by H. G. Chancellor at the office. Progressive and radical. Concentration on local municipal politics and social issues. Has separate columns on Labour questions and socialist and trade union news. Correspondence. **See also Londoner. North Islington Edition; Pioneer**, 1895–7.

    L(Col)†

St Pancras Miscellany see National Association of Local Government Officers. St Pancras Branch. [**Branch Magazine**]

3078 St Pancras (SE) Herald [194-?]; m

    B   1d. Labour Party. (Labour Party. **Your own Journal**, 1948.)

3079 St Pancras Woman Worker 1 [1925?]–?

    B   ½d. Printed and published by the Communist Party of Great Britain. Reproduced from typewriting.

    O(JJ)† 2 (Dec. 1925)

3080 St Pancras Worker [c1929?]

    B   'Produced by the St Pancras Local of the Communist Party.'

    O(JJ)† 1 copy undated and unnumbered [1929?]

3081 Salford Docker: the Paper of the Workers in the Port of Manchester 1 [11 Aug. 1932?]–52 (20 Sept. 1934). Salford; fortn

    A   Communist Party industrial paper. News items from the docks with trade union and general dockers' affairs, with political items. Reproduced from typewriting.

    WCML† 43, 47–9, 51 51A, 52

Salford Labour's Voice see **Labour's Salford Voice**

3082 Salford Patriot, Published by a Society for the Diffusion of Useful Knowledge, Including Morals and Politics 1 (16 Feb. 1833)–6? (16 March 1833?). Salford; w
    B   1d. Published and printed by B. Hackett. 'A working-class political miscellany that champions "Equal Rights" and "Equal Laws" for the poor, denounces the factory system, and provides an account of radical activities in the Manchester area' (Wiener).
    MP 1–2; ONC 1–2 (photocopy)

3083 Salisbury Citizen 1 (June 1960)–11 (Feb. 1962); irreg
    B   Published by the Co-operative Press.
    L(Col); LabP 10 (Nov. 1961)

3084 Salisbury Labour Bulletin [194-?]. Salisbury; irreg
    B   1d. Duplicated. Labour Party. (Labour Party. **Your own Journal**, 1948.)

Salt Spray see **Mercantile Marine Service Association Reporter**

3085 Saltaire Searchlight 1 [1926?] –? Shipley
    A   1d. Issued by Salts Communist Group, Shipley (weaving and textile mills). To press for the setting up of a Factory Committee. Information on militant activities in the factory. Cartoons. Reproduced from typewriting.
    O(JJ)† 3 (13 March 1926)

3086 Sam: the Standard Apprentice Association Magazine I (1958)–? Coventry
    A?   Standard Motor Company.
    L

3087 Sanitary Inspector I, 1 (Aug. 1898)–VI 7 (Feb./March 1904). Liverpool; bi-m (to Dec. 1899); m
    A   North Western and Midland Sanitary Inspectors' Association, then from Vol. III, No. 1, July 1900, National Union of Sanitary Inspectors. Founder and editor for the six years of its existence: H. H. Spears.
    LvP†; LvU (I–III*)

3088 Sanitary Inspectors' Magazine: the Organ of the Sanitary Inspectors' Association of Scotland i [1953?54] –? [Glasgow?] ; 3-yr?
    A   Content largely on technical, professional matters, but also on conditions of service. The Association worked with the National and Local Government Officers Association for national salary scales.
    ONC† 3 (June 1954)–32 (May 1964*)

3089 Sanity: Monthly Peace Paper Oct. 1961–?; m

B   Campaign for Nuclear Disarmament.

E; O; LE; (The Left in Britain – microfilm – The Harvester Press Ltd)

3090 Saoghal Gaedhealach. [Irish World and Industrial Advocate] I (1917)–[1918?]; ns I, 1 (7 Sept. 1918)–III, 2 (20 Sept. 1919). Dublin; w

B   2d. Sinn Fein paper, pro-Labour. Published for the proprietors at 13 Fleet Street, Dublin. Short articles, notes on current events, reviews, literary notes. Occasional article in Gaelic. Suppressed by military authority.

D I, 2, 4–7, 9, ii; L(Col)† ii (w 28 Dec. 1918, 12 July 1919)

3091 Satire: a Paper of Social Criticism. I, 1 (Dec. 1916)–II, 17 (April 1918); m

B   1d. Address is that of the Freedom Press. Printed by the Blackfriars Press. Edited by L. A. Motler (14–17). Manager: G. Scates. 'All comrades in the rebel [later "Labour"] Movement are invited to send contributions to the Editor – prose, verse, sketches, cuttings with reference etc. **Satire** is a workers' paper, run by workers.' Many cartoons, jokes, epigrams etc. No. 1 states: '**Satire** is one of those upstart proletarian rags published by crafty agitators to mislead the ignorant working-man, and is, of course, paid for by German gold.' Raided December 1917. Intended to publish at a new price from May 1918.

L(Col); MP; ONC†

Saturday Analyst and Leader see **Leader, 1850–1860**

3092 Sawdust, Published by Aberdeen Communist Party and Young Communist League 1925. Aberdeen

B   Organising woodworkers at Fiddes and Sons etc. Reproduced from typewriting.

MML† (Hutt papers) 8 (Oct. 1925)

School Attendance Gazette see **School Attendance Officers' Gazette**

3093 School Attendance Officers' Gazette: a Monthly Journal Devoted to the Improvement of School Attendance I, 1 (April 1900); then **School Attendance Officers' Gazette**: the Official Organ of the National Association of School Attendance Officers: I, 2 (May 1900)–I, 7 (Oct. 1900); then **School Attendance Gazette**: I, 8 (Nov. 1900)–IV, 44 (March 1904); m

A   2d.; 1d. Objects of the Association include improving status, obtaining superannuation.

L(Col); O (w IV, 44)

3094 Schoolmaster: an Educational Newspaper and Review 1 (6 Jan. 1872)—ns 815 (9 Jan. 1925); then **Schoolmaster and Woman Teacher's Chronicle**: 816 (16 Jan 1925)—2787 (28 Dec. 1962); then **Teacher**: Journal of the National Union of Teachers: I, 1 (4 Jan. 1963)—   ;w
    A   1d. Earlier, organ of the National Union of Elementary Teachers. News of teachers' associations, reviews, correspondence, articles on education, conditions of employment, job vacancies.
    C; L(Col); O; the Union; (for further, incomplete, holdings, see BUCOP

3095 Schoolmaster and Edinburgh Weekly Magazine, Conducted by John Johnstone. I, 1 (4 Aug. 1832)—II, 48 (29 June 1833). Edinburgh; w
    C   1½d. Printed by and for John Johnstone. Published by John Anderson, Jun. Not as title might suggest an educational journal. Purpose to be as political as laws would allow. Intended for the mass of the people. No. 1 contained 'Hints to the operative classes', by George Combe, anti-flogging articles. Includes excerpts from books, serials, passages from contemporary writers, condensed stories. The chief contributor of original matter seems to have been the editor's wife. (**Scottish Notes and Queries**, Jan. 1893.) Cheap and universal diffusion of useful information of every kind, intended for 'the many', with sympathetic sketches of working-class life. Besides appearing in weekly numbers was also issued in monthly parts 'stitched in a neat cover'. The latter contained in addition to the ordinary weekly numbers a digest of the main occurrences of the month, entitled **Johnstone's Monthly Register**. Succeeded by **Johnstone's Edinburgh Magazine**, a more literary publication, and not within our categories.
    EP; L

Schoolmaster and Woman Teacher's Chronicle see **Schoolmaster**

3096 Schoolmasters' Review: the Organ of the National Association of Men Teachers I, 1 (Sept. 1919)—II, 3 (June 1921); ns 1 (Dec. 1921); q
    A   2d.; 3d. Printed and published by Buck Bros. and Harding, Ltd. On salary increases, raising of status, professionalism etc. Reports, news.
    L

3097 Schoolmistress: a Weekly Paper Specially Devoted to the Interests of Those Engaged in Female Education I, 1 (1 Dec. 1881)—CVIII, 2802 (4 Sept. 1935); w
    A   1d. Published by Howard Barnes for the Schoolmistress Newspaper Printing Company. Counterpart of **The Schoolmaster**. Absorbed **The Teacher's Aid**. Merged in **Woman Teacher's World**. Devoted to the furtherance of female education. Professional matters, status and salaries.
    L(Col)†

Scientific Worker and the BAC Bulletin see **Scientific Worker**

3098 Scientific Worker: the Official Organ of the National Union of Scientific Workers I, 1 (Feb. 1920)–V, 23 (March 1924); then Scientific Worker and the BAC Bulletin: Official Organ of the National Union of Scientific Workers and of the British Association of Chemists: ns I, 1 (May 1924)–I, 10 (Dec. 1925); then **Scientific Worker**: II, 1 (Feb. 1926)–XIII, 11 (Dec. 1945); ns I, 1 (Feb. 1946)–IX, 6 (Nov. 1954); then **A Sc W Journal**: I, 1 (Jan. 1955)–XIV, 1 (Jan. 1968); bi-m

    A   Later, organ of the Association of Scientific Workers. Superseded by **ASTMS Journal**. There was also a separate publication, **Progress and the Scientific Worker**, (July/Aug. 1932)–(Aug./Sept. 1935), the result of an association between **Scientific Worker** and **Progress**: **Civic, Social, Industrial**.

      C 1935–54; EP iii II, 4–   ; L i I, 3–ii V, 5, IX–iii; LAP iii I–*; LC ii I–VI (w III, 2); LSC ii IX–(1944*); ONC 1949–   ; TUC; Walthamstow PL 1955–

Scoop see National Association of Local Government Officers. Somerset County Branch. **News Sheet**

3099 Scots New Leader ns I, 1 (4 Oct. 1935)–? Glasgow; w

    B   Independent Labour Party, Scottish Divisional Council.

      L(Col) ns I, 1–II, 61 (27 Nov. 1936); GU (Broady Coll.) XXXI, ns 271 (24 March 1939)

3100 Scots Socialist 1 [1940?]–? Glasgow; m; bi-m

    B   2d. Published by J. H. Miller, then by the Scottish Socialist Party. Edited by Oliver Brown. For a Scottish socialist republic 'and the full development of world Socialism'. 'We are inspired by the work of Fletcher, Muir, Keir Hardie, Connolly, and John Maclean.' Contains serialised life of Maclean by Hugh MacDiarmid. At first reproduced from typewriting.

      E occ. nos between 4 (Sept. 1940) and 53 ('First issue', 1949)

3101 Scots Theatre 1 (Sept. 1946)–6 (May 1947). Glasgow; m

    B   3d. Published by the Glasgow Unity Theatre, which was 'established as the most vital native cultural influence in Scotland. Its actors, playwrights and technicians have been drawn from the ranks of ordinary working people whose background and everyday life is identical with the masses who form its audiences.' Stages plays on working-class life, eg, **The Gorbals Story,** by Robert McLeish, but not formally connected with any working-class organisations.

      E; EP; L

3102 Scots Times 1, I (16 July 1825)–XVI, 1379 (26 May 1841). Glasgow; s-w; w (1841)

    B   4½d.; 6d. Printed and edited by Robert Malcolm. Radical, later Chartist of the moral force type, newspaper.

      Baillie's Institution, Glasgow 1830–5; GM 1825–32, 1835–8, 1840–1; GU 1, 1825–337 (1831); L(Col) 486 (2 June 1832)–589 (28 May 1833) [microfilm]), 1167 (12 Dec. 1838), 1257 (23 Oct. 1839 [originals])

Scottish Baker see Scottish Union of Bakers and Confectioners. **Journal**

Scottish Class Teacher see **Class Teachers' Pamphlet**

3103 Scottish Congress Bulletin 1 (Sept. 1926)—319 (Feb. 1958); then **Scottish TUC Bulletin**: 320 (March 1958)—   . Glasgow; m
  A   Published by the Scottish Trades Union Congress General Council.
      E; NU 1962—   ; ONC† 106 (March 1937)—115 (Feb. 1938); 241 (May 1950)—   ; TUC

3104 Scottish Co-operative Citizen 1 (Feb. 1935)—4 (June 1935). Glasgow; irreg
  B
  L(Col)

3105 Scottish Co-operator 1863—71
  A   Merged in **Co-operative News** (A. Bonner, **British Co-operation**, Revised ed., Manchester 1970.)

3106 Scottish Co-operator: a Journal of Progress and Economy I, 1 (May 1893)—   . Glasgow; m; w
  A   1d. etc. Published by the Scottish Co-operative Wholesale Society. To educate in matters relating to the Co-operative Movement and social questions generally. Gradually more attention given to politics. Became the 'official journal of the Co-operative Movement in Scotland'.
      Co-op. Union 1908, 1920, 1946—   ; E 1937—   ; GM†; L(Col) 1904—   ; LE 1898—1930

Scottish Daily Worker see **Daily Worker**

3107 Scottish Farm Servant: the Official Organ of the Scottish Farm Servants' Union I, 1 (April 1913)—XIX, 225 (Dec. 1931). Aberdeen (1913—19); Stirling (1919—27); Caldercruise (1927—31); Dalmacoulter, Airdrie (1931); m
  A   1d.; 2d. Printed and published for the Scottish Farm Servants' Union by John Bell and Company. Joseph Duncan, the Vice-President of the Union, started the journal and was the mainspring throughout. Agitates against long hours and low pay. Closed down because of financial difficulties occasioned by the depression, and unemployment among members.
      L(Col)†; LE I—XI*; OAC XVII, 193—XIX

3108 Scottish Farm Servants' Union. Notes and News 1 [Dec. 1931?]—? [Scotland]; m
  A   Monthly bulletin consisting of a leader by Joseph Duncan, the Secretary, until June 1945, then by his successor, Alex Ewen.
      GM† 131 (Jan. 1943)—334 (Dec. 1959)

3109 Scottish Free Press I, 1 (May 1933)–? Glasgow; m
    B   Later 1d. Organ of the Scottish Socialist Party.
    E 1, 26 (Nov. 1935); ILP July, Sept., Nov. 1933

3110 Scottish Friendly Societies' Journal I, 1 (11 Sept. 1896)–II, 39 (25 Feb. 1898). Glasgow; fortn
    A   1d. Published by Robert McKirdy. 'The first public organ of a national character' for the more than one million Friendly Society members in Scotland. 'to voice their sentiments and give expression to their wants'. Contains branch reports, notices of meetings, social gatherings, conferences, and short topical features, eg, on the issue of old age pensions. Illustrated. Portraits of area officials, with account of their history in the movement.
    GM; L(Col)†

3111 Scottish Miner 1 (Feb. 1954)–   . Edinburgh; m
    A   2d; Published by the Scottish Area of the National Union of Mineworkers.
    E; TUC

3112 Scottish Mineworker 1 [1929?]–? Glasgow; w?
    A   1d. Newspaper published by The Mineworker Publications Committee. To obtain support for the United Mineworkers of Scotland, and thus for the establishment of Committees in every colliery in every Scottish coalfield. Opposes the Miners' Federation of great Britain. News of activities of the UMS.
    O(JJ)† 23 (28 Sept. 1929)

3113 Scottish Mineworker 1 [1931?]–? Glasgow; m?
    A   1d. Published by the United Mineworkers of Scotland. Dealt with miners' rights and grievances and gave information on incidents occurring in the mining fraternity all over Scotland.
    Buckhaven and Methil PL 2 ([6 June], 3 [July] 4 [July (special strike edition)], 1931)

3114 Scottish NALGO: the Organ of the Scottish Council of the National Association of Local Government Officers I,1 (Oct. 1925)–II, 9 (Oct. 1929); ns XIII [ie III], 1 (June 1930)–XIV [ie III], 4 (Dec. 1931). Glasgow; q
    A   2d (ns). Includes articles on local government reform, education etc., women's page. The errors in numbering were due to a printer's mistake.
    GM†

3115 Scottish National Operative Plasterers' Federal Union. Monthly **Report** [18--?]–July 1966. Dundee; Glasgow; m
    A   For the use of members only.
    GM† Aug. 1900–July 1966*; L Jan.–April 1895

Scottish Observer see Paisley Observer

3116 Scottish Painters Society. **Monthly Journal?**–1963; m
    A   Internal business and short articles on wider trade union issues.
GM† 1927, 1929–51, 1953–8, 1961; TUC ns (Feb. 1911)–XXVII,
3 (Nov./Dec. 1963*)

3117 Scottish Patriot I, 1 (6 July 1839)–[184-?]. Glasgow; w
    B   4½d. Printed and published by Robert Malcolm. Chartist organ
for Scotland. Opening address on behalf of the Committee of Trades'
Delegates and Directors of the Universal Suffrage Association.
E I (July 1839)–IV (April 1841); GM 1839–40

3118 Scottish Radical 1840. Glasgow; m
    B   Unstamped. Produced by W. and W. Miller, 90 Bell Street,
Glasgow, the publishers of the **Chartist Circular**. 'One surviving issue' 5
December 1840. (R. M. W. Cowan, **The Newspaper in Scotland**, Glasgow
1946, p. 145).

Scottish Reynolds's see Reynolds's Weekly Newspaper

3119 Scottish Schoolmaster: Official Organ of the Scottish Schoolmasters'
Association. I, 1 (March 1935)–? Arbroath; s-a; q
    A   3d. Covers job security, salary negotiation, reports and general
articles on the profession.
L I, 1–XL, 6 (1953) (w XI, 5–6)

3120 Scottish Secondary Teachers' Association. **Bulletin** 1 [195-?]–170
(Dec. 1971?). Edinburgh; m
    A   Sent to all members. Information on salaries, conditions,
negotiations, training.
O 134 (Jan. 1968)–170

Scottish TUC Bulletin see Scottish Congress Bulletin

3121 Scottish Trades' Union Gazette 1 (14 Sept. 1833)–14 (14 Dec.
1833). Glasgow; w
    A   Published by W. W. Miller. Edited by Alexander Campbell. 'A
trades union miscellany that ceased publication in Dec. 1833 after a Stamp
Office information was laid against it.' (See A. Campbell, **Trial and Self
Defence of A. Campbell, Operative, before the Exchequer Court,
Edinburgh, for printing and publishing** 'The Tradesman' **contrary to the
infamous Gagging Act**, W. W. Miller, Glasgow 1835, p. 26.) Succeeded by
The Tradesman (Wiener). Also referred to as **Trades Advocate or Scottish
Trade Union Gazette**.
    Harvard UL

3122 Scottish Typographical Circular 1 (Sept. 1857)—6 (Feb. 1858); ns 1 (March 1858)—568 (Dec. 1908); then **Scottish Typographical Journal**: 569 (Jan. 1909)—   . Edinburgh; m

    A   1d. etc. Official organ of the Scottish Typographical Association, after being issued by the Edinburgh Branch on behalf of the Association. Contains much material of general interest, as well as trade-union reports.

    E Sept. 1857—Feb. 1872 (w 10 nos.), 1879, 1895, 1904, 1905, 1935—   ; GM 569—   ; L(Col) 373, Sept. 1892—   ; LE; LSF 1861—*

Scottish Typographical Journal see **Scottish Typographical Circular**

3123 Scottish Union of Bakers and Confectioners. **Journal** I, 1 (1928—[1949?]); then **Scottish Baker**: May 1950—June 1959. Glasgow; q

    A   In earlier years articles on wider trade-union and political issues. Title sometimes **Quarterly Journal**.

    GM† 4 (Feb. 1929)—1949*; TUC† 1947—59*

3124 Scottish United Operative Masons. **Monthly Journal**

    A   Postgate says 1911—21 were in the office of the Building and Monumental Workers' Association of Scotland.

3125 Scottish Vanguard: Journal of the Workers' Party of Scotland (Marxist-Leninist) I, 1 (1967—   ). Glasgow (1); Edinburgh; bi-m [ie irreg]

    B   Printed and published by D. Livingstone Smith, then by C. Lawson; later published by the Party, and printed by 'Vanguard' Books (Scotland). Reproduced from typewriting.

    E; LE; GM; ONC†; (The Left in Britain — microfilm — Harvester Press Ltd)

3126 Scottish Vindicator [1838?—1839?]. Paisley

    B   Local Chartist paper. Published by John Cumming. (R. M. W. Cowan, **The Newspaper in Scotland**, Glasgow 1946, p. 145; A. Wilson, **The Chartist Movement in Scotland**, Manchester 1970, p. 183.)

3127 Scottish Worker: Official Organ of the Scottish Trades' Union Congress 1 (10 May 1926)—6 (15 May 1926). Glasgow; d

    A   1d.

    E; GM; GU; Dept. of Economic History, Herbert Highton Coll.

3128 Scottish Workers' Republic: Official Organ of the Scottish Workers Republican Party [192-?]—? Glasgow; m?

    B   1d. Printed and published by The Liberty Press. Campaigns on a revolutionary Communist platform.

    TUC† 36 (Oct. 1930).

3129 Scottish Workman and Social Reformer. A prospectus was issued in February 1865, but the periodical was not published 'Prospectus was issued of a joint stock company, the object of which was to establish a bi-weekly to advocate and defend the rights of labour . . . it was proposed to raise the capital in 6000 shares at 5s. each. The provisional committee was composed of the members of the Trades Council, and a considerable number of the trades in and around Edinburgh promised to support them in their attempt to establish an organ of working-class opinion. The requisite number of shares were not taken up, however, and the project collapsed (W. Norrie, **Edinburgh Newspapers, Past and Present**, Earlston, 1891).

3130 Scourge for the Littleness of 'Great' Men, By Richard Carlile. 1 (4 Oct. 1834)—16 (21 Feb. 1835); irreg
    B   1d. Printed by Cunningham and Salmon. Used by Carlile to denounce Hetherington and Cleave (P. Hollis, **The Pauper Press**, 1970). Replaced **The Gauntlet** (G.D.H. Cole, **Richard Carlile**, 1943).
    BP 1835; MP; ONC (w 4, 8, 11)

3131 Scout: a Journal for Socialist Workers. I, 1 (30 March 1895)—II, 4 (April 1896); m
    B   1d.; 2d. Printed and published by Clarion Newspaper Company. Edited by Montague Blatchford. 'Not launched as a paper for general readers but as an organiser and co-ordinator of the energies of Scouting groups.' Extensive reports of the work of the Clarion Scouts in centres like Birmingham, Glasgow, Dewsbury. Aim was to disseminate socialist ideas and 'make socialists'. Much space devoted to cycling clubs, glee clubs etc.
    L(Col); LE; LU (w I, 4, II, 4); LdP; MP I—II, 1; O(JJ) 1; ONC July, Sept. 1895

3132 Scribe I [1912?]—X, 12 (Dec. 1921); m
    A   2d. Official organ of the Civil Service Union. Aims to build a union among all grades of civil service workers, and to break down sectional prejudices. Ceased when the union amalgamated with the Clerical Officers' Association. Superseded by **Red Tape**.
    L(Col) VII, 11 (Nov. 1918)—VII, 12, VIII, 3—X, 12.

3133 Scribe: Organ of the Midland Area Council, Clerical and Administrative Workers' Union 1 [194-?]—? Birmingham; bi-m?
    A
    TUC† 11 (Sept. 1946), 12 (Nov. 1946), 15 (Sept. 1947)

3134 Scribe I [194-?]—?
    A   Published by the London South East Industrial Branch of the Clerical and Administrative Workers' Union, Peckham. Reproduced from typewriting.
    TUC† IV, 6 (Oct. 1951), VI, 8 (Dec. 1953)

3135 Script: Newsletter Published by the Derby Health Services Branch of NALGO 1 [1964?] –. Derby; bi-m?

    A   National and Local Government Officers' Association. Reproduced from typewriting.

    L 2 (Sept./Oct. 1964)–

3136 Scunthorpe Co-operative Citizen I, 1 (Jan. 1934)–(1939); 1946–54. Scunthorpe

    B   Published by Scunthorpe Co-operative Society.

    L(Col)

3137 Seafarers' Record 1 (21 Nov. 1928)–5 (11 May 1929); m

    A   Published by the Transport and General Workers' Union. Urges membership of the Marine Section of the TGWU. Opposes the National Union of Seamen under Havelock Wilson. Editorials by Ernest Bevin, articles by James Henson.

    L(Col)†; LE (w 3); TUC (w 2, 5)

3138 Seafaring: the Organ of the Seafaring Class I, 1 (7 July 1888)–I, 23 (8 Dec. 1888); II, 1 (30 March 1889)–VIII, 175 (5 March 1892); w

    C   1d. Published by Victor G. Plarr. Later editor and proprietor: A. Cowie ' . . . to furnish a fair and fearless organ in the Press for that hitherto inarticulate class . . .' To advocate the interests of the seafaring class. News, fiction, historical accounts, verse, notes, notices, information. At first sympathetic to but later broke with the Sailors' and Firemen's Union. Latterly includes the 'Fishermen of Great Britain' in its intended audience.

    GM*; L(Col)†; O

3139 Seaham Harbour Labour News [193-?]. Seaham Harbour; m

    B   Labour Party. Edited by Blackwell, local councillor, Chairman of the local Labour Party.

    Some copies held by Olive Blackwell (Richard McKay)

3140 Seaman: the Official Organ of the International Seafarers, and of the National Sailors' and Firemen's Union 1 (Nov. 1907)– ; m; etc.

    A   1d. etc. Published later by the National Union of Seamen. Not published continuously in the early years.

    HU 1921; L 1943– ; L(Col)†; LE 1941– ; NU 1961– ; TUC 1914–22*, 1923–39; Aug. 1941– ; the Union Feb.–Aug. 1908, ns 1 (April 1911)–2 (May 1911), 1912–

Seaman's and Fisherman's Friendly Visitor see **Fisherman's Friendly Visitor and Mariner's Companion**

3141 Seamen's Charter Dec. 1970– . Liverpool; irreg

    A   Published by Jack Coward (1–5), then by Dave McGrath. Communist seafaring journal.

    National Union of Seamen 1–6, 9–

3142 Seamen's Chronicle: a Weekly Journal Devoted to the Interests of the Seafaring Community and Kindred Industries 1 (20 Jan. 1894)–197 (4 Dec. 1897); w

A   1d. Editor: Leslie M. Johnson. 'Founded as public medium to make known grievances of seamen. Official organ of the National Amalgamated Sailors and Firemen's Union' (Brophy). President of the Union: J. Havelock Wilson. Large, well-produced with extensive contents and correspondence.

International Transport Workers' Federation, London III, 103–IV, 196; L(Col) 21–47; TUC† John Burns Lib†

3143 Seamen's News 1 (5 Aug. 1915)–2 (25 Aug. 1915). London

A   Also entitled **Morskoi Listok**. In Russian. Published by the Central Council of Russian Seamen's Union. Editor: D. Amitchkin.

L(Col)†

3144 Seamen's Record: Official Organ of the International Seafarer ns 1 (June 1906)–?; m

A   National Sailors' and Firemen's Union. Editor?; Edmund Cathery, General Secretary. (Research Officer, National Union of Seamen.)

3145 Searchlight [19--?] –? Ipswich

B   Ipswich Trades Council and Labour Party.

Ipswich and East Suffolk Record Office, Ratcliffe Coll., Ipswich Municipal Elections Oct. 1926; Ipswich Labour Party?

3146 Searchlight I, 1 (May 1932)–9 (Jan. 1933); m

B   1d. The paper of the British Section of the Workers' International Relief, and published by the National Secretary. 'Founded to throw the light of truth upon the many problems facing the working class.' Campaigns against the means test and declining living standards at home, against war, and in defence of the Soviet Union. Organises aid for workers in their struggle at home and abroad, eg, distribution of food to strikers. Includes appeal to working-class women.

L(Col)†; WCML† 3

3147 Searchlight 1 (May 1935)–? Sheffield

A   Printed and published for the Carcroft National Unemployed Workers' Movement.

MML† 1

Searchlight. 1936– see **Voice. 1936**

3148 Searchlight 1 (7 Oct. 1938)–? Hanley, Staffordshire

A   1d. Published by Hanley Branch, National Unemployed Workers' Movement. Reproduced from typewriting.

MML† 1

3149 Searchlight 1 (Jan. 1960)–4 (April 1960). Leeds; m
     B   Edited by J. Roche. A New Left industrial bulletin. 'Contains short pieces by such New Left founders as John Saville, Lawrence Daly and Ken Alexander. "William Brown" is a joint pseudonym for William Hampton and Michael Barratt Brown' (W. A. Hampton).

3150 Searchlight: Official Magazine of the Huddersfield Branch of NALGO 1964–   . Huddersfield
     A   National and Local Government Officers' Association. Reproduced from typewriting. The first issue does not bear a title.
     L

3151 'Seax': the Journal of the Staff of the Essex County Council I, 1 (Nov. 1934)–I, 3 (July 1935). Chelmsford; 3-yr
     A   1s. per year. Records the activities of the staff and those of their association, the National Association of Local Government Officers.
     L

3152 Secondary School Journal I, 1 (Jan. 1908)–X, 2 (Sept. 1917). Edinburgh; 3-yr
     A   6d. Published and printed by H. and J. Pillans and Wilson for the Association of Teachers in the Secondary Schools of Scotland. Later subtitled: 'The Organ of the Secondary Education Association of Scotland'. 'The Secondary School Journal, although published primarily in the interests of the Association of Teachers in the Secondary Schools of Scotland will, we venture to hope, be found to be of some service to those who are interested in the development of these schools and in Secondary Education generally. The principal aims of the Association as set forth in its constitution are the furtherance of the interests of Higher Education in Scotland, the promotion of union and intercourse among the teachers in Secondary Schools, and the better co-ordination of these schools with the Universities.' Primarily concerned with professional and educational matters, but does cover conditions of employment like superannuation and salary agreement. In later numbers reflects the working of the Association towards union with other teachers' associations to form the [new] Educational Institute of Scotland. Amalgamated with the **Educational News** and the **Scottish Class Teacher**.
     L(Wx2); O; SaU

3153 Secondary Teacher: Journal of the Association of Secondary Teachers I (1966–). Dublin; m (except July and Aug.)
     A   Association of Secondary Teachers, Ireland.
     DUC

Secular World see **Reasoner and 'Herald of Progress'**

3154 Seed 1 [192-?] —? Watford
    B   Printed and published for the local Women's Committee of the Communist Party of Great Britain, Watford, by P. A. Neal. Reproduced from typewriting.
    O(JJ)† 9 (April 1926)

Seed-Time see **Sower**

3155 Selly Oak Clarion 1 [1936?] —41 (Oct. 1947). Birmingham; q
    B   Issued by Selly Oak Ward Labour Party.
    BP† 6 (Dec. 1937)—34, 37—41

3156 Sempstress 1 (Oct. 1855)
    C   1d. Published by W. H. Dalton. Reflects philanthropic concern at the plight of distressed needlewomen.
    L

3157 Sentinel; in the Interest of the Ex-Naval and Military Civil Servants' Association [190-?] —108 (Oct. 1913); m
    A   1d. Printed and published by Elliott Bros. Edited by W. J. Renshaw; D. A. Gray. On pensions, conditions of employment, news of branches, and activities of the Association. Support for the Labour Party. The Association amalgamated with the Imperial Colour Service to Count Association in 1913 to form the United Association of Ex-Naval and Military Civil Servants with the organ **The Campaigner**. The first 39 numbers may have been published in a different form.
    L(Col) 40—98 (Dec. 1912); O 40—108

3158 Sentinel Feb. 1908—1920; m
    A   Royal London Staff Association.
    National Union of Insurance Workers, Royal London Section 1908

Sentinel. 1912 see **South Wales Sentinel and Labour News**

3159 Sentinel [193-?] ; w
    B   Labour Party, Wood Green. (Labour and Socialist International. **The Socialist Press**, 1933.)

3160 Servants' Magazine I, (1838)—XXXII, [1869]
    C   1d. 'Under the superintendence of the Committee of the London Female Mission.' Information, improvement, instruction, fiction. Profits to go to benefit female servants. Illustrated. From Vol. IV title is: **Servants' Magazine, or Female Domestic's Instructor**. Vols. XXVI—XXIX are new series I—IV; XXX—XXXII are new series I—III. A second edition of Vol. I was published in 1841.
    C II—XXIX, XX—XXXII*; I (2nd ed.); L (mislaid); O V—XXXII; O(JJ)† I—V

3161 Servants' Own Paper 1 (18 July 1893); I, 1 (19 Aug. 1893)—I, 16 (2 Dec. 1893); w

    C   1d. Published for the proprietors by W. J. Sinkins. A journal for domestic servants, 'an independent paper, founded to help amuse, and instruct servants'. Includes an 'Enquiry Service' where servants can air their problems and be answered by any one of a 'large staff' engaged for this purpose, eg, a physician to reply to medical questions,and a barrister to reply on legal points bearing upon the position of servants in cases of dispute between them and the mistresses. Also 'serial stories by well known authors'.

    L(Col)†

3162 Service: Official Organ of the Union of Temporary Civil Servants 1 (Sept. 1924)—(Sept. 1926); m

    A

    TUC†

3163 Service: a Monthly Magazine for the Modern Maid I, 1 (Nov. 1931)—I, 5 (March/April 1932); m

    C?

    L(destroyed)

3164 Service: the Monthly Journal of the Sheffield and Eccleshall Co-operative Society I, 1 (Sept. 1946)—(Autumn 1957). Sheffield; m; q

    A

    L

3165 Service Dec. 1964?—. Barnstable

    A   National and Local Government Officers' Association, North Devon Branch. Reproduced from typewriting.

    L Dec. 1964—

3166 Service Conditions Bulletin 1 ([Nov.?] 1948)—1952. Liverpool

    A   National Association of Local Government Officers, Liverpool Branch.

    L; LvP*

Service Man see **Ex-Service Man**

3167 Settmaker's and Stoneworker's Journal I, 1 (June 1891)—XLIII, 7 (Dec. 1933). Aberdeen (1891—1906); Glasgow (1906—14); Leicester (1914—33); m

    A   1d.; 2d. Official organ of the Settmakers' Union, later of the Amalgamated Union of Quarryworkers and Settmakers Editors: A. Beattie; William Lawrie; John Adan.

    L(Col)†; LE XXI—XLIII, 7

3168 Sevenoaks Monthly Herald [194-?]. [Sevenoaks?] ; m

    B   2d. Labour Party. (Labour Party.**Your own Journal**, 1948)

3169 'Sez Us': the Co-operative College Students' Magazine, Holyoake House, Manchester [193-?]–? Manchester

    A   The number for June 1932 states that this is the first time the magazine appears in 'real print'. Short articles, humorous pieces.

    Co-op. Coll. June 1932

3170 Shadgett's Weekly Review of Cobbett, Wooler, Sherwin and Other Democratical and Infidel Writers, Designed as an Antidote to Their Dangerous and Destructive Doctrines and to Desseminate [sic] Just and Sound Principles on All Popular Subjects I, 1 (1 Feb. 1818)–II, 78 (26 July 1819); w

    C   4d.

    L

3171 Shafts I, 1 (3 Nov. 1892)–VII, 3 (Oct./Dec. 1899); m

    C   1d. etc. Edited by Margaret Shurmer Sibthorp. 'For women and workers', later 'for women and the working classes'. A magazine dealing with a variety of social matters, concerned about the 'Labour question' and franchise for women.

    L(Col)†; O I–VII, 2; ONC II, 4–5, 9–11, 16; OW

3172 Sheerness Co-operative District Record [18--?]–? [Sheerness?] district.

    (W. H. Brown, **A Century of Co-operation at Sheerness, being a Chronicle of the oldest Co-operative Society in Existence in the United Kingdom, 1816–1916**, Manchester 1920, p. 67).

3173 Sheffield Anarchist 1 (28 June 1891)–8 (4 Oct. 1891?). Sheffield; fortn

    B   'Pay what you like.' Published and printed by J. Creaghe. Issued by the Sheffield Anarchist Group.

    SP† (3 [19 July], 7 [20 Sept.], 8 [4 Oct.], 1891)

3174 Sheffield Co-operator 1 (May 1922)–170 (July 1939?) Sheffield; m

    B   Organ of the Sheffield Co-operative Party. Printed by the National Co-operative Publishing Society, Manchester.

    SP† 1–170

3175 Sheffield Forward I (1920–). Sheffield; m; bi-m

    A   Sheffield Trades and Labour Council. Not published continuously.

    SP; Sheffield Trades and Labour Council

3176 Sheffield Guardian 1 (Jan. 1906)–532 (3 March 1916). Sheffield; w

    B   ½d. Published by John Penny for the Sheffield Independent Labour Party, later by Richard Hawkin, who was also editor. Main contributor was John Penny, General Secretary of the Party. Later subtitle: 'A Weekly Journal for the Assertion of the Rights of Labour and the Promotion of Socialism'.

    L(Col)† (w 1)

Sheffield Iris see Sheffield Register

3177 Sheffield Municipal Officers' Journal [1919?]—XVI, 10 (1940); then
Guild Journal: XVI, 11 (Jan. 1941)—; Sheffield; m; bi-m
    A   Sheffield Municipal Officers' Guild. Latterly Branch Lines?
National and Local Government Officers' Association.
    L Aug. 1951—; SP† VII, 12 (Dec. 1926)—*

3178 Sheffield Radical 1 (21 Dec. 1872)—3 (4 Jan. 1873?). Sheffield; w
    B   1d. Publisher: Joseph Brown. 'Anti-vaccinators, trade unionists,
co-operators, teetotallers, the advocates of the repeal of the Contagious
Diseases Acts, and others may . . . rely on getting fairplay' (No. 1).
    SP† 1—3

3179 Sheffield Register, or Yorkshire, Derbyshire and Nottinghamshire
Universal Advertiser 9 June 1787—27 June 1794; then Iris, or the Sheffield
Advertiser: 1 [1794?]—[18-?]; then Sheffield Iris [18-?]—3341 (31 Dec.
1856). Sheffield; w
    B   Produced by Joseph Gales, then publishers included J.
Montgomery, J. Blackwell. Pro-reform.
    L(Col)† 1807—56*, SP 1787—94 (also 1787—9 [microfilm])

3180 Sheffield Transportman: Organ of the Employees of the Sheffield
Transport Department I ? (1938)—VII, 1 (Aug. 1945). Sheffield; m
    A   1d. Issued by Sheffield Transport Department Employees.
Edited by the Sheffield Transport Esperanto Group. Motto: 'Let us
remove the barriers of distance and language'. Esperanto lessons and
employees' news.
    SP† I—III, IV, 5—12, V—VI, 1—8, 10—12, VII, 1

3181 Sheffield Worker Dec. 1917—1918. Sheffield
    A   Published by Sheffield Workers' Committee. Suppressed after
two issues. See also the Firth worker

3182 Sheffield Workers' Gazette I, 1 (mid-Jan. 1949)—6 (17 Sept 1949?).
Sheffield; irreg
    B   Sheffield Communist Party.
    SP† 1—6

3183 Sheffield Working Man's Advocate 1 (6 March 1841—5 (3 April
1841). Sheffield; w; irreg
    B   1d. Published by James Pashley. Pro-Chartist and women's
rights. Profits to go to a fund to build a hall for working-men.
    SP†

3184 Shepherd: a London Weekly Periodical Illustrating the Principles of Universal Science I, 1 (30 Aug. 1834)–III, 40 (31 March 1838); w

B   1d.(I); 3d.(II, 1–4); 2d.(II, 5–8); 1½d.(III). Published and printed by Benjamin D. Cousins. Editor: Rev. J. E. 'Shepherd' Smith. 'Features essays by Smith in which he expounds the theme of a perfect natural harmony in the universe' (Wiener).

BP; L; LU; MP (w III, 8–17); NwP; O I, 1–28; Warwick UL 1–52

Sherwin's (Weekly) Political Register see **Republican, 1817**

3185 Shetlander, for Shetland Workers 1 (Oct. 1922)–6 (Dec. 1923). Lerwick; bi-m

B   1½d. Printed for the Economics Club, Lerwick, by Kirkwood and Company, Glasgow. Written 'by workers for workers'. For an independent working-class education, education for socialist change. Simple articles on the elementary principles of Marxist economics, and on history from the standpoint of historical materialism. Also poetry.

L; MML (w 1)

Shield of the Workers see **Workmen's National Protection Association Magazine**

Shilling Magazine see **Cobbett's Magazine**

Ship Repairer see **Siren**

3186 Shipconstructors' and Shipwrights' Association. Monthly Report [19--?]–? [Newcastle?]; m

A

Amalgamated Society of Boilermakers, Shipwrights, Blacksmiths and Structural Workers, Newcastle*

3187 Shipconstructors' and Shipwrights' Association.Quarterly Report [19--?]–? Newcastle; q

A

Amalgamated Society of Boilermakers, Shipwrights, Blacksmiths and Structural Workers, Newcastle*; TUC 1908–16*

3188 Ships' Telegraph I, (1958)–XII, 4 (May/June 1969); m

A   Merchant Navy and Airline Officers' Association. Merged with **Merchant Navy Journal**

L; TUC† VIII (1965)–XII*

3189 Shipwrights' Journal: a Periodical of General Literature, and Useful Information on the Social Condition of the Working Classes, and a Record of the Progress of Trades' Unions, Co-operation, and Association 1 (April 1858)–4 (July 1858). Sunderland; m

    A   1d. Printed by William and Henry Pickering. Edited by John Hopper. Advocates shorter hours, co-operation, legislation for working-men's halls, libraries and schools. 'Not a journal exclusively devoted to the interests of the Shipwrights,' pages open to all classes of workmen. Some correspondence. The journal was first announced in a pamphlet by Hopper, **A defence of trades' unions.**

    LU†

3190 Shoe Worker [1920s]

    A?   (National Minority Movement Conference reports)

3191 Shop Assistant: a Monthly Journal of Shop Life, Social Advancement and Reform I, 1 (1 July 1896)–ns 1976, 28 May 1938; then **Distributive Trades Journal**: Jan. 1939–Jan. 1947. Cardiff; London; m; w; m

    A   1d. Organ of the National Union of Shop Assistants, Warehousemen and Clerks. Then incorporated in **New Dawn.**

    GM 1925–26; L(Col)† (w 1905–7); LE XXVII–XXXVI; Union of Shop, Distributive and Allied Workers.

3192 Shop Assistant's Gazette [c1897]

    A?C?   Editor? publisher?: Will Johnson. (**Labour Annual**, 1897.)

3193 Shop Life Reform: the Recognised Organ of the National Shop Assistants' Union 1 (18 Feb. 1891)–21 (8 July 1891). Manchester; w

    A   1d. Started by William Johnson, Secretary, later President, of the Union, in conjunction with F. J. Rowe. 'Promoted by shop assistants . . . and for the special purpose of urging the promotion of a national union' (**Shop Assistant**, 2 [Aug. 1896]). Reports from the regions, especially London, Manchester, Leeds; 'had a wide circulation among 37 various associations.' Ceased because of lack of financial resources.

    L(Col)†

3194 Shop-Life Year Book 1899. Manchester: a

    A   1d. Published for the Manchester Branch of the National Union of Shop Assistants, Warehousemen and Clerks by Manchester Labour Press. Editor: W. P. Redfern.

    MP†

3195 Shop Steward 1 (April 1942)–? [London?] ; m

    A

    ILP April, Aug., Oct. 1942

3196 Shop Stewards Report: Issued by the Shop Stewards of Messrs
Crossley Bros., Manchester 11. [194-?]–? Manchester
    A   Engineering factory.
    WCML† 5 (March 1945)

3197 Shoreditch and Finsbury Citizen: Official Organ of the Shoreditch
and Finsbury Labour Party ns 1 (Sept. 1955)–
    B
    L(Col) ns

3198 Shoreditch Citizen 1 (March 1930)–114 (Sept. 1939); m
    B   Gratis. Published by the London Co-operative Society, Political
Committee.
    L(Col); ShP*

3199 Shoreditch Echo I, 1 (Jan. 1927)–III, 18 (Oct. 1929); irreg
    B   1d. Published by The Labour Press Committee. Shoreditch local
Labour Party paper.
    L(Col)†; ShP 2–17 (w 15)

3200 Shoreditch Monthly Bulletin [194-?]; m
    B   Labour Party. Duplicated. (Labour Party. **Your own Journal**,
1948.)

3201 Shrewsbury Progress [194-?]. Shrewsbury; m
    B   1d. Labour Party. (Labour Party. **Your own Journal**, 1948.)

3202 Shropshire Examiner and All Round the Wrekin Advertiser: a
Journal of Local and General Intelligence; the Official Organ of the Mining
and Other Industrial Interests 1 (1873)–214 (5 Oct. 1877). Madeley;
Oakengates; w
    B   1d. Published by John Randall, then by Owen, Jeffrey and
Spencer. Chronicles miners' movements, primarily in the Staffordshire
area. Some coverage of other trade union news, eg, agricultural labourers.
Then incorporated in the **Midland Examiner and Times**.
    L(Col)† 37 (2 May 1874)–214

3203 Shropshire Labour News 1 (March 1909)–? [Shrewsbury?] m
    B
    ILP 1

3204 Shropshire Teacher: the Organ of the County Teachers' Association
I, 1 (June 1936)–12 (June 1940). Wellington; 3-yr
    A   National Union of Teachers, Shropshire Teachers' Association.
Object: 'to foster professional comradeship, to keep members informed of
educational activities in the county, to act as a channel for the expression
of the Association's views, and to secure a 100% membership of the
National Union of Teachers in Shropshire'.
    L

3205 Siemens Shop Stewards Committee. **Journal** 1 (Sept. 1931)–35 (1939); irreg

    A   1d. Editor: Charles Wellard. Printed by J. A. Mann.

    ONC† 27 (undated); TUC 20, 31; WCML† 28, 32, 35

3206 Signal: the Official Organ of the Association of Wireless and Cable Telegraphists i (July 1921)– . London; Upminster; m; bi-m

    A   1s. 'Our aim and endeavour will be to obtain an equitable settlement of all conditions of service and employment for all those whose interests are in our charge.' Later, organ of the Radio (and Electronic) Officers' Union.

    L; Warwick UL (missing vols 45(1), 47(3), 48(1), 49(4,5), 51(3)

3207 Signal: the Organ of the Civil Service Clerical Association, Admiralty Branch No. 1 1 (May 1925)–13 (June 1926); m

    A   1d. Terminated because of 'circulation difficulties'.

    L: O 1–11

3208 Signal: Organ of Methil Branch, NUR 1 ([Aug.?], 1925)–19 (6 May 1926). Methil, Fife; fortn

    A   1d. National Union of Railwaymen. Reproduced from typewriting.

    MML† (Hutt Papers) 3 (24 Sept. 1925)–19

3209 Signal 1 [1931?] –? Manchester

    A   1d. 'Issued by the Action Group at Ducie St,' ie Railmen's Minority Movement. Reproduced from typewriting.

    ONC† 4 (15 May 1931)

3210 Signal Box [19--?] –? Cardiff; m

    A   2d. Official organ of the Union of Railway Signalmen. (Mitchell, 1940)

3211 Signpost 1 (July 1962)–12 (Sept. 1964). [Hornchurch?] ; irreg?

    B   Horchurch Constituency Labour Party.

    London County Record Office (Ref. A/HHL/18)

3212 Single Tax: the Organ of the Scottish Land Restoration Union I, 1 (June 1894)–VII, 96 (May 1902); then **Land Values**: IX, 97 (June 1903)–XIX, 300 (May 1919); then **Land and Liberty**: XX, 301 (June 1919)– . Glasgow; London; m

    C   1d. etc. 'Devoted to the cause of taxing land values' for public purposes, claiming that, by 'relieving industry of the burdens of taxation it would solve the problem of unemployment and low wages'. Later, organ of the Scottish Single Tax league, then United Committee for the Taxation of Land Values.

    L(Col)†; LAP LII– ; LE XIII– ; LY VIII– ; ONC Nov. 1899, Sept. 1901, June 1902, Feb. 1903

3213 Sir I, (1967)— . Belfast; 3-yr
  A   Gratis. National Association of Schoolmasters, Northern Ireland Federation.
  Belfast PL II (1968)—

3214 Siren 1 (July 1936)—3 (Sept. 1936); then **Ship Repairer**: 4—7 (Feb./March 1937); m
  A   1d. Published by the Ship Repairers' AEU [Amalgamated Engineering Union] Rank and File Committee. Editor: Bob Lovell. Published in London and sold in London and other ports during the ship-repair ban on overtime arising from a wage claim. Reproduced from typewriting. Title changed when it was discovered that the journal of one of the shipping firms was named **The Siren**.
  WCML† 1, 3—7 (Xerox); Bob Lovell

3215 Sitrep [19--?] — . Ipswich; q?
  A   National and Local Government Officers' Association, Ipswich Branch. Reproduced from typewriting.
  L 54/1 (March 1954)—

3216 Skipton Monthly Bulletin [194-?]. Skipton; m
  B   ½d. Labour Party. (Labour Party. **Your own Journal**, 1948.)

3217 Slap at the Church 1 (21 Jan. 1832)—17 (12 May 1832); w
  B   1d. Published by William Strange. Printed by W. Johnston. Editors: John Cleave and William Carpenter. 'Illustrated radical miscellany that advocates reform of the Church of England, attacks tithes, and asserts that church possessions are the property of the State' (Wiener). Succeeded by **Church Examiner and Ecclesiastical Record**.
  BP; Gm 1, 9; HO 64/18 1—8, 11—17; L(destroyed); MU; O; O(JJ)

3218 Sleeper Awake 1 (May 1922)—3 (Oct. 1922). Glasgow; irreg
  B   Printed and published by Glasgow University Labour Club. Sponsors H. G. Wells as Labour candidate at the Rectorial Election.
  GM†

3219 Small Chat: Official News Sheet of the Dorset County Branch of NALGO 1966?— . Dorchester
  A   National and Local Government Officers' Association. Reproduced from typewriting.
  L 1966—

3220 Snap: RCN Student Nurses' Paper 1970— ; fortn
  A   Circulated free of charge to hospitals. Published by Brandshare, Ltd. for the Student Section of the Royal College of Nursing. The views expressed in **Snap** are not necessarily those of the College.
  Royal College of Nursing

3221 Sniprets 1966?— . Urmston
    A   National and Local Government Officers' Association, Urmston
Branch.
    L 1966—

3222 Social and Family Companion 1 (25 Nov. 1882)—3 (9 Dec. 1882);
then **Social Reformer and Family Companion**: 4 (16 Dec. 1882)—6 (30
Dec. 1882); w
    C   1d. 'The official organ of the League for Shortening the Hours
of Unnecessary Labour.' The Shop Hours Labour League, a philanthropic
body founded in 1881, President, Thomas Sutherst, Vice-President, Lord
Randolph Churchill, was concerned with campaigning for shorter hours
and better working conditions for both shopkeepers and assistants, but not
by trade union means. The journal was not intended exclusively for
working-class readers, but for all who were interested in the regulation of
shop labour. Contents also include some literary and household matters.
    L (w 2)

Social Democrat see **Justice**

3223 Social-Democrat: a Monthly Socialist Review I, 1 (Jan. 1897)—XV,
12 (Dec. 1911); then b **British Socialist**: I, 1 (Jan. 1912)—II, 12 (Dec.
1913); m
    B   2d.; 3d. Published by Twentieth Century Press. 'While the
principles we set ourselves to serve and promulgate will be those of
scientific revolutionary Social-Democracy as set forth in the writings of its
best known writers, Marx, Engels, Hyndman, and others, we shall gladly
welcome contributions from representatives of other schools of
thought . . .' 'The main object of our magazine . . . is to present to
Socialists . . . in a condensed form, the various articles and criticisms on
Socialism which appear each month in different magazines, books, and
newspapers.' Contributors: Edward and Eleanor Marx Aveling, G.
Lansbury, R. B. Cunninghame Graham.
    C a VII—   b; Co-op. Coll. b; E; GM; L; LdP A VII—XV; LE*; O;
ONC 1897—1910*; SP b

Social-Democrat, 1907 see **Sotsial-Demokrat, 1907**

3224 Social-Democrat: a Monthly Bulletin of SDF News and Views 1
(July 1934)—?; m
    B   1d. Social Democratic Federation. Editor: E. Archbold.
Reproduced from typewriting.
    LabP† 1934—9

3225 Social-Economic Labour Review: Bulletin of the RILU Labour Research Department. [1926?] –? [Moscow?] ; m

A   Red International of Labour Unions. In English. Includes information on Great Britain. Reproduced from typewriting. Analyses the economic situation. Facts, figures, prospects for international working class, the trade union situation, wages struggles.

MML† Third year, 4(19), July, 8 (23), Nov., 9 (24), Dec. 1928, Fifth year, 1 (57), Jan., 2 (58), Feb. 1930; ONC† Third year, 1 (16), Jan.-March, 2 (17), April-May, 1928

Social Economist, Industrial Partnerships' Record and Co-operative Review see **Industrial Partnerships' Record**

3226 Social Institutes Union Magazine: the Official Organ of the Social Institutes Union, with which is amalgamated the Federation of Working Men's Social Clubs I, 1 (Jan. 1908)–III, 12 (Dec. 1910?); m

C   1d. A means of communication between members of Institutes and Clubs providing healthy recreation and education in leisure hours. Record of lectures, outings, and social activities generally, in London and the provinces.

L I, 1–III, 12 (w I, 8, 9)

3227 Social Notes Concerning Social Reforms, Social Requirements, Social Progress I, 1 (9 March 1878)–V, 126 (31 July 1880); then **Social Notes: an Illustrated Weekly Journal of Social Progress**: VI, 1 (7 Aug. 1880)–VII, 174 (30 June 1881); then **Social Notes and Club News**: 175 (9 July 1881)–193 (12 Nov. 1881); w

C   1d. Philanthropic concern with all social questions. Editors: S. C. Hall; A. A. Hill. Reports proceedings of working-men's clubs. Incorporated with **Labour News**. Vol. VI–VII, 174 are new series I–II, 48; Nos. 175–93 are new series 1–19.

BP i–ii; L; O i–ii

3228 Social Outlook: an Occasional Magazine 1 (Sept. 1889)–? Kendal (1); Kendal; London; irreg

C   2d. No. 1 published by William Birkett, Kendal; later published also by William Reeves, London. Edited by Herbert V. Mills, 'on behalf of the Home Colonisation Society' (No. 3). Articles and notes. Contributors: Rev. H. R. Haweis, on strikes; Charles Booth, on the Poor Law; Elizabeth Blackwell on home colonisation. Information on the Home Colonisation Society, and other articles on home colonisation for unemployed labour. In No. 3 is an article by the editor on 'The beginning of the first experiment', ie Starnthwaite Mills.

LU 1; O(JJ)† 1, 2 (Dec. 1889), 3 (Autumn 1892)

3229 Social Pioneer; or, Record of the Progress of Socialism 1 (9 March 1839)–10 (11 May 1839). Manchester etc.; w

    B   1d. Publishers: A. Heywood, Manchester; Hetherington, London; Cleave, London; J. Hobson, Leeds; J. Guest, Birmingham. Editor: 'Epicurus'. Owenite reformist. Records the proceedings of the Cambridge Colony, an Hodsonian community (following the principles of W. Hodson). For the Association of All Classes.

    LU†

3230 Social Reformer 1 (20 Oct. 1839)–10 (22 Dec. 1839); w

    B   3d. Published by James Parry, the younger. Printed by George Davidson. Advocates the general establishment of Home Colonies which will provide a comprehensive national education and 'permanent beneficial employment' as a solution to distress and political party divisions. Purpose to unite leaders of all parties to adopt measures to educate and employ the people, 'and thus put an end to Chartism, and all other isms'. Owenite Rationalist.

    L(Col)†

3231 Social Reformer I, 1 (11 Aug. 1849)–11 (20 Oct. 1849); w

    B   1d. Published by G. Vickers. Printed by Archibald Syme. Edited by Bronterre O'Brien, and Friends. Organ of the Eclectic Club. Lengthy editorials by O'Brien on Chartism. To prepare the public for those reforms which would 'emancipate the labouring classes'. The last numbers record the foundation of the National Reform League.

    LU†

Social Reformer, 1882 see **Social and Family Companion**

Social Reformer, 1901 see **Manchester**

3232 Social Review: a Monthly Record of Industrial, Sanitary and Social Progress I, 1 (Jan. 1875)–III, 6 (June 1877); m

    C   2d. Published for the proprietors by Joseph Snell. Medium of communication for shareholders and friends of The Artizans', Labourers' and General Dwellings Company, which aims to provide cheaper and better housing for labourers. Also includes discussion of such topics as public health, recreation grounds for the people, preservation of the countryside, articles on labour markets of the world to enable British workmen to form correct opinions on the wisdom or otherwise of emigration, all working towards improving the social conditions of working-men. Also correspondence, book reviews, notices of meetings and movements for social reform.

    L(Col); O

3233 Social Service News I, 1 (June 1940)–[VIII], 76 (Dec. 1946); ns IX, 1 (Jan. 1947)–[1949?1950?]; m

    B   Published by the Labour Research Department. First series reproduced from typewriting. Absorbed by **Labour Research**. Deals with housing, education, working conditions, local government finance etc. Comments on government policy.

    L I, 3–*; ONC† 13 (June 1941)–X, 23 (Nov. 1949)

3234 Socialism and Education: Journal of the Socialist Educational Association 1 (1963)–4 (1963); irreg?

    B   9d. Published and edited for the Association by John Dixon (2–3), Robert Thornbury (4). The Association arose out of the National Association of Labour Teachers, and was affiliated to the Labour Party. Articles, reviews, notes. No. 3 is dated May 1963; no month is given on the other numbers. No. 1 does not bear the subtitle. Preceded by **The Labour Teacher**

    E; L 1–2; O

Socialism and Health see **Medicine Today and Tomorrow**

3235 Socialist [187-?]. Sheffield

    B   Editor?: W. Harrison Riley. (A. Plummer, **Bronterre**, 1971, p. 271)

3236 Socialist I, 1 (July 1886)–I, 6 (Dec. 1886); m

    B   1d. Organ of the Socialist Union. Managing and editing committee: A. Campbell, C. L. Fitzgerald, J. R. Macdonald. For the emancipation of the working class from capitalism by the capture of political power of the State. Mainly short snippets on international labour, including notes from Scotland, Ireland and America.

    L; O

Socialist, 1888–1889 see **Leaflet Newspaper**

3237 Socialist: the Organ of the Sunderland Independent Labour Party 1 (12 June 1894)–6 (Jan. 1895). Sunderland; m

    B   1d. Printed for the proprietors by Summerbell and Johnson. Advocates Labour representation, local and national. 'Ethical' socialist. 'ILP Notes' by Tom Mann.

    AbU (microfilm); L(Col)†

3238 Socialist I, 1 (July [1895])–3 (Sept. 1895?). Plymouth; m

    B   1d. Printed and published for the proprietor by George F. Jackson and Company. Sponsored by the United Democratic Club (a member of the Working Men's Club and Institute Union), and the Plymouth Branch of the Independent Labour Party. 'Issued by a few pioneers – members of various Socialistic and Industrial Organizations – for the purpose of diffusing knowledge on Political Economy, Industry, Science, Art, and Social Problems, by the exchange of individual ideas.'

    AbU 1–3 (microfilm); L 1; O(JJ) 1–3

3239 Socialist 1896. Chatham. (Hopkin)

Socialist: the Organ of the Nelson Branch of the British Socialist Party, [1896?]—1914 see **Socialist and North-East Lancashire Labour News**

3240 Socialist: Official Organ of the Socialist Labour Party I, 1 (Aug. 1902)—ns II, 4 (Feb. 1924); [ns] I, 1 (Jan. 1939)—XII, 1/2 (Jan./Feb. 1950); [ns] I, 1 (Aug. 1952)—   . Edinburgh; Glasgow (July 1912—Feb. 1924); Edinburgh; Cheltenham; m; q

    B   1d. etc. Initiated by a pressure group within the Social Democratic Federation in Scotland, which broke off in 1903 to form the Socialist Labour Party. As the organ of the SLP, it propagated the De Leonist perspectives of revolutionary political action and industrial Unionism. Concentrated on Marxist theory, but reported progress of the Movement in the regions. Editors: George Yates, Neil Maclean, George Harvey, J. W. Muir, A. McManus. Lately reproduced from typewriting.

    E 1902—24, 1939—50, 1952—   (w 1955—7); GM 2 Jan. 1919—Oct. 1923; L 1952—   (w 1953—7); L(Col)† 1902—24, 1939—50; LE 1904—11*; O*

3241 Socialist: Organ of the World Order of Socialism 1 (Feb. 1915)—3 (April 1915); then **World Socialist**: 4 (May 1915)—36 (July 1919); m

    B   1d. Issued by the Executive of the World Order for Socialism, Hon. Secretary, Keighley Snowden. For 'world fraternity and socialist unity'. World Order is 'not an active political body but a Freemasonry for Democrats'. 'Its work is to save the soul of Socialism and to make Socialists.' The Order was organised in Lodges in London and the provinces. Emphasis on education of youth in the principles of Socialism.

    L(Col)†

Socialist, 1935—1937 see **Socialist Leaguer**

3242 Socialist [1937?]—[194-?]. Birmingham; m?

    B   Published by Birmingham University Socialist Club. Popular Front, Labour Party/Communist Party perspective.

    BP† 5 (March 1938)

3243 Socialist: Official Organ of the Labour Party League of Youth 1 (Jan. 1940)—?; m

    B

    LabP 1—7 (July 1940)

3244 Socialist [1947]. Birmingham; fortn; m

    B   Published by K. Tarbuck. Edited by J. R. Guest. Reproduced from typewriting. Trotskyist.

    ONC† 3—13, and 4 unnumbered issues

3245 Socialist: Magazine of the Eastbourne Labour Party 1962?— Eastbourne

    B   Reproduced from typewriting.

    L 1962—

Socialist Advance see **Young Socialist, 1946—1948**

Socialist Affairs see **Comisco Information Service, International Socialist Conference**

3246 Socialist and Labour Journal [c1907]. [Bootle?] ; m
  B   ½d. Editor?: Grayson, Bootle. (**Reformers' Year Book**, 1907)

3247 Socialist and North-East Lancashire Labour News 1 (7 Oct. 1893)—[1896?]. then **Socialist**: the Organ of the Nelson Branch of the British Socialist party: ns 1 [1896?] —144 (Sept. 1914). Burnley; w; m
  B   1d. First published by Ernest Charles Johnson, and owned by the Burnley, Nelson, Colne, Barrowford and Padiham branches of the Social Democratic Federation. Contributor: Henry Hyndman. Sometimes **Burnley Socialist**?
     Burnley PL (23 [9 March], 35 [1 June], 45 [10 Aug.] 1894), Jan. 1910; L(Col)† 1—11 (22 Dec. 1893); 136 (Jan. 1914)—144

3248 Socialist Annual 1906—14; a
  B   3d. (1914). Printed and published by Twentieth Century Press. Sponsored by the Social Democratic Federation, then the Social Democratic Party. Editor: Theodore Rothstein..
     E 1910—14; L (not traced on shelf); LE 1906, 1908, 1913; MP 1906, 1910—12; O 1910—14; ONC† 1914

3249 Socialist Annual 1925; a
  B   2s. 6d. Prepared for the Independent Labour Party by the ILP Information Committee. Facts and figures, and contributions from leading Party members.
     BP; C; E; EP; LE; MP; O; ONC†

Socialist Appeal see **Youth for Socialism**

3250 Socialist Broadsheet: Organ of the Socialist League Feb. 1937?—April 1937; m?
  B   1d. Published by the League.
     L(Col) Feb., April 1937; ONC† Feb. 1937

Socialist Christian see **New Crusader**

Socialist Commentary see **Vanguard, 1934—1936**

Socialist Commentary and Forward see **Vanguard, 1934—1936**

3251 Socialist Critic. March 1900—? Walthamstow; m
  B   Gratis. Local Social Democratic Federation. (**Reformers' Year Book**, 1901.)

3252 Socialist Current: a Journal of Labour Opinion I, 1 (May 1956)– ;
m; bi-m

B   4d. etc. Published by Socialist Current Publications. Organ of
the tendency calling itself the 'Marxist Wing in the Labour Party'. Editor:
Sam Levy. Editorial board members: Frank Rowe, Morry Sollof.
Discussion on the philosophy and practice of transforming the Labour
Party from within for the adoption of revolutionary socialist policies.
Reproduced from typewriting.

   L

3253 Socialist Dialogue I, 1 (Oct. 1964)–3 (Summer Term, 1965). Leeds;
termly

B   Published in the University 'to express and to foster socialist
commitment in a Socratic spirit'. A forum for non-partisan socialist
opinion.

   LdU†

3254 Socialist Digest Jan. 1957–Dec. 1958; m

B   1s. Published by the Labour Party Press and Publicity
Department, then by the Labour Party. A 'pocket-size digest magazine'.
'We shall reprint – in full or condensed – articles from many different
magazines and reviews, British and foreign. We shall reproduce cartoons
showing world reactions to current events. Some features will appear
monthly: a parliamentary digest, an international section, commonwealth
affairs, books, statistical data. The section headed "The Party Machine"
makes **Socialist Digest** – besides being something much wider as well – the
"house magazine" of the Labour Party.' Absorbed **Fact**. Suspended 'in
order that the whole resources of the Labour Party can be used for the
"Into Action Campaign".'

   L; LabP; ONC†

3255 Socialist Doctor: Official Organ of the Socialist Medical Association
I, [1932?]–? irreg

B   3d. The Association was affiliated to the Labour Party.
Campaigns for a free State medical service.

   TUC† II, (1 [Aug.], 2 [Nov.], 1933), 3 (May 1934)

3256 Socialist Echo: Quarterly News Sheet of Moseley and King's Heath
Ward Labour Party 1 (April 1947)–7 (Oct. 1947). Birmingham; m

   B
   BP†

Socialist International Information see **Comisco Information Service**

Socialist Leader see **Labour Leader. 1893–1922**

3257 Socialist Leaguer I, 1 (June/July 1934)–I, 13 (July/Aug. 1935); then **Socialist**: ns 1 (Sept. 1935)–13 (Dec. 1936/Jan. 1937); m
    B   2d. Published by the Socialist League, which was led by Stafford Cripps, Brailsford, J. T. Murphy etc.
    L(Col)†; Warwick UL (microfilm)

3258 Socialist Medical Association. **Branch Bulletin** [1] (April 1946)–23 (April 1950); m
    B   News bulletin, reproduced from typewriting. From No. 9 called **Bulletin to Branches.**
    HU†

3259 Socialist Medical Association. **Bulletin** 1 [1938?]–34 (July 1941); then **Medical News and Views**: 35 (Aug. 1941)–?; then **SMA Bulletin**; m
    B   1d.
    TUC† (30 [March], 33 [June], 34 [July], 35 [Aug.] 1941); June–July 1951

3260 Socialist Monthly 1970. [Belfast]
    B   'The Northern Ireland Labour Party Left published several issues of **Socialist Monthly** in 1970 . . .' (P. Howard, 'The paper war: official organs'. **Fortnight**, 75 [11 Jan. 1974])

3261 Socialist Opinion [c1940]. [Southampton?] ; m
    B   Monthly Bulletin of Southampton Independent Labour Party. (Issue for April 1940 noted in **The Word**, Oct. 1940, p. 33)

3262 Socialist Outlook I, 1 (Dec. 1948)–149 (8 Oct. 1954); m; w
    B   2d. Started as the paper of the Trotskyist and Socialist Left in the Labour Party, then organ of the Socialist Fellowship (founded 1949). Banned by the Labour Party Right Wing at the 1954 Conference at Scarborough. Published by the Labour Publishing Society (1951–2).
    L; ONC† III, 4 (April 1951)–45 (27 June 1952*)

3263 Socialist Record: a Monthly Journal fo Internal Affairs for Members of the British Socialist Party I, 1 (July 1912)–ns 12 (April 1916); m (July 1912–May 1913); q
    B   ½d.; 1d. Published by the Editorial Committee of the British Socialist Party. Printed by Utopia Press, later by Twentieth Century Press. Launched after a decision taken at the First Annual Conference of the BSP. Record of the Movement includes branch news and directory, and reports of the Executive Committee.
    L(Col)†

3264 Socialist Register 1964–   ; a
    B   30s. etc. Published by Merlin Press. Edited by Ralph Miliband and John Saville. 'A series of annual volumes of socialist analysis and discussion.' Signed essays on socialist theory and practice.
    AU; BU; StrU; HU; LE; ONC†; Ru; SU; SoU; SwU

3265 Socialist Review: a Monthly Magazine of Modern Thought I, 1 (March 1908)—ns [3rd ser.] VI, 2 (May 1934); m; q

    B   Independent Labour Party.

    BP; BS i I–XIII, 76*; C i X, 59–iii VI, 2; E; GM; L; LE; LabP 1908–1929; LdP i V–XXIV; LdU i I–VII; MP (w i XIII–XVIII); O*; ONC I–ns VI, 1 (April 1934); SP i XII–iii VI

Socialist Review, 1940, 1945–1948? see **Youth Review**

3266 Socialist Review: Live Writing on World Politics I, 1 (Nov. 1950)–9th Year, 14 (Nov. 1959); m; fortn (1958–)

    B   6d. Published by Socialist Review Publishing Company. Editor (1959): Mike Kidron. Anti-Stalinist Left, from the perspective of international Socialism. Articles on shop-floor problems and struggles by industrial militants, theoretical articles and reviews, a forum for discussion. To return a Labour Government pledged to a socialist programme of nationalisation and workers' control of industry. Contributors: Eric Heffer, Stan Newens, P. Sedgewick, Tony Cliff etc. Vol. I reproduced from typewriting.

    BP; L; ONC I, 1–IV, 10/11 (June/July 1955); Warwick U (MRC) 1, 1 Nov.–6 1, Oct. 1956

3267 Socialist Round Table. **Journal** I, 1 (Oct. 1923); then **News from Nowhere**: I, 2 (Nov. 1923)–II, 11 (April 1926); m; q; (1926)

    B   4d.; 6d. Published by the Executive Committee of the Socialist Round Table, which was 'born 1923', 'a national association for young Socialists of all schools of thought and of all sects. All Socialists who consider themselves young – spiritually or physically – are cordially invited to join the Round Table', to develop as socialists, and make Socialism a 'philosophy of life'. Working towards 'Culture, Beauty, Truth, Fellowship'. Its main activity is the publication of the magazine. Short articles on aspects of socialist theory and individual practice, and reports of local activities.

    L

3268 Socialist Standard: the Official Organ of the Socialist Party of Great Britain I, 1 (Sept. 1904)–   ; m

    B   1d. etc.

    GM XXIX, 1933–   ; L(Col); LE*; MP XXV–XLII; ONC Sept. 1954, 1968–   ; TUC, John Burns Lib.† 1904–15; the Party

3269 Socialist Star I, 1 (3 May 1933)–I, 7 (14 June 1933). Glasgow; w

    B   1d. Published by Glasgow Independent Labour Party Federation. 'Organ of the ILP in Glasgow and the West of Scotland.' Contributors: J. Middleton Murry, Maxton, J. McLure.

    L(Col)†

3270 Socialist Torch [c1908]. Glasgow; irreg?

    B

    ILP 19 March, 4 June, 20 Oct., 23 Oct., 1908

Socialist Vanguard see **Vanguard, 1934—1936**

Socialist Vanguard Newsletter Service. Bulletin see **Vanguard, 1934—1936**

3271 Socialist Voice 1 (1949)–? Luton
   B   Labour Party League of Youth, Luton Branch. Duplicated.
(Mentioned in **Socialist Advance**, Oct. 1949, as 'a new publication'.)

3272 Socialist Voice: an International Socialist Forum I, 1 (Summer 1969)
   B   1s. 6d. Printed and published by J. Plant. Reproduced from typewriting. Editors: Jim and Nasrin Plant, who resigned from the Socialist Party of Great Britain on 9 Feb. 1969. Started publication of **Socialist Voice** to provide a forum for discussion 'around the objective of building a new — genuinely scientific and genuinely democratic — Party'. 'Initially we will be concentrating on the publication of documents and statements directly relevant to the internal situation, and programmatic problems, of the Socialist Labour Parties.' Only one number published. A large part of this number taken up by 'Bruce Cameron's letter of resignation from Section New York, Socialist Labor Party of America', 4 July 1967.
   E; O; ONC†

Socialist Worker see **Labour Worker**

3273 Socialist Workers' Group. Internal Bulletin 1 (April 1952)?
   B   6d. Not for sale to the public. Published by the SWG. Reproduced from typewriting. Trotskyist.
   ONC† 1

3274 Socialist World: an International Socialist Quarterly I, 1 (June/Aug. 1947)–I, 7 (Dec. 1948–Feb. 1949); q
   B   1s. 3d. Published by the Socialist Information and Liaison Office. Official organ of the International Socialist Conference, 'an informal organisation which has taken the place of the former Second International'. The journal 'aims at presenting socialist thought and theory of international interest'. Articles contributed by Labour party members of various countries.
   L; LabP; ONC

Socialist Year Book see **ILP Year Book**

3275 Socialist Youth [c1929–31] ; m
   B   Independent Labour Party Guild of Youth
   ILP April 1929, Feb. 1931

3276 Socialist Youth: Official Organ of the Scottish Socialist Party Youth and the Socialist Youth Committee I, 1 (Sept. 1936)–2 (Oct. 1936). Glasgow; m

     B   1d. Published by the Scottish Socialist Party Youth Movement, in place of the hitherto separate publications, **Youth** and **Socialist Youth**. Under Socialist League auspices, after the Labour Party had suspended the League of Youth. Promotes a front of democratic socialist youth. Scottish and English branch news. Declaration on Spain.

     L(Col)†

Society for the Diffusion of Useful Knowledge. **Year Book, or, Pocket Library and Encyclopaedia of General Information** see **Working Man's Year-Book**

3277 Society of Civil Servants. **Society News Bulletin** 1 (July 1949)–22 (Jan. 1952); irreg

     A   For members only. 'Intended to bridge the gap between issues of **Civil Service Opinion**, to provide "the quick Dissemination of information on matters of major general interest" '. Deals with pay, conditions, civil rights.

     L

3278 Society of Civil Servants. Ministry of Supply Branch. **Society Bulletin** ns 1 (Feb. 1946)–13 (March 1947); [ns] 1 (Aug. 1947)–28 (Dec. 1949); [ns] 1 (Jan./Feb. 1950)–44 (Dec. 1955); m

     A   The Ministry of Supply Branch amalgamated in 1946 with the Ministry of Aircraft Production Branch, to form the Ministry of Supply and Aircraft Production Branch, and in June 1946 was renamed Ministry of Supply Branch. From 1950 was called Ministry of Supply Section. On wages, hours, conditions etc.

     L

3279 Society of Civil Servants. Post Office Section. **News Bulletin** 1 (Aug. 1950)–3 (Dec. 1950); then **Society Post**: 4 (April 1951)–III (Oct. 1970?). Manchester; q

     A   News sheet issued to members, on wages, conditions etc.

     L 1–111 (w 8)

3280 Society of Friends of Italy. **Monthly Record** 1853–5; m

     B?   (J. Bellamy and J. Saville eds., **Dictionary of Labour Biography** Vol. I, 1972, p. 95.)

3281 Society of Post Office Engineers. **Monthly Circular to Members** 1 [191-?]–?; m

     A

     TUC† 109 (Nov. 1923)–116 (June 1924)

3282 Society of Women Journalists. **Bureau Circular** May 1910–July 1910; then **Woman Journalist**: 1 (Dec. 1910)–50 (Jan. 1920); [ns] 1 (Jan. 1923)–   ; bi-m; q

    A   Later Society of Women Writers and Journalists.

    L; O 1923–

Society Post see Society of Civil Servants. Post Office Section. **News Bulletin**

Sogat Bulletin† see **Sogat Journal**

3283 Sogat Journal: Monthly Journal of the Society of Graphical and Allied Trades Feb. 1967–   ; m

    A   6d. etc. Union news, trade information, general political and economic articles, revues, correspondence, women's pages, illustrations. Superseded the earlier **Journal**, and also **The Paperworker**.

    L; ONC; O

3284 (Soho) Forward [Aug. 1913?]–? [Birmingham?] ; m

    B   Published by Handsworth Labour and Socialist Party.

    BP I, 5 (Dec. 1913 [temporarily unavailable])

3285 Soldiers' Voice 1 (Sept. 1929)–?; m

    B   ½d. Published by the Communist Party of Great Britain. A Communist paper for soldiers. Only one number published?

    ILP 1; TUC† 1

3286 Solidarity: Monthly Organ of Garden City Press, Ltd. [I], 1 (March 1907)–II, 4 (Dec. 1908). Letchworth; m

    B?   2s. 6d. 'Represents the interests of the inhabitants of First Garden City, Letchworth. Deals with Co-operation, Town-Planning, Housing Question etc.' (**International Directory of the Co-operative Press**, 1909.)

    L I, 3–12, II, 1–4

3287 Solidarity: a Monthly Journal of Militant Trade Unionism 1 (Sept. 1913)–7 (April 1914); ns I (1915)–[1916?] ; ns I, 1 (Dec. 1916)–V, 17 (13 May 1921); m; s-m; w

    A   Publishers: Industrial Democracy League, (Secretary: J. V. Wills); Building Workers' Industrial Union; Solidarity Press; S. A. Wakeling. Editors included J. V. Wills, Jack Tanner.

    L(Col) March–April 1914, Feb. 1914–May 13, 1921; LE 1913–14*; ONC† 1–4,6, ns I, 5 (20 Nov. 1915)–*, 13 (May/June 1916) (w 7), ns I, 1 (Dec. 1916)–III, 12 (Dec. 1919) (w II, 7); Warwick UL 1914–21 (microfilm)

3288 Solidarity: Advocate of the Workers' Revolutionary Unity. 1938–[1939?] ; m?

    B

    WCML† 9/10, March/April 1939

Solidarity for Workers Power see Agitator for Workers Power

3289 Sons of Vulcan [c1832] –? m
    A   Probable editor: John Kane, president of the ironworkers'
union. 'No record exists of those early days . . . ' (A. Pugh, **Men of steel,
by one of them**. Iron and Steel Trades Confederation, 1951; p. 33.)

3290 Sorting Assistant: Organ of the Association of Sorting Assistants and
the Supervisors of Same 1 [1926?] –? irreg?
    A   Free to members.
TUC† 3 (Nov. 1926), 4 (March 1927)

3291 Sotsial-Demokrat (Social Democrat). I (1888)–[ns] IV (1892)
    B   Also entitled **Le Démocrate-Socialiste**. Russian
L; LE ii

3292 Sotsial-Demokrat: Literarno-Politiczeskii Obzor 1888–92. q
    B   Editor: G. V. Plekhanov?
L

3293 Sotsial-Demokrat. [Social-Democrat] I, 1 (Nov. 1907). m
    B   2d. 'Party organ of the Jewish Social-Democratic Union.'
Yiddish.
    L(Col)†

3294 South Battersea Citizen 1, (Sept. 1931)–96, (Sept. 1939); ns 1 (Jan.
1947)–59 (Feb. 1952); ns 1 (Sept. 1959)–?; m
    B   Gratis. Published by the London Co-operative Society's Political
Committee.
    L(Col)

3295 South Bucks Clarion: Organ of the South Bucks Divisional Labour
Party 1 (April 1937). High Wycombe
    B
    L(Col)

3296 South Bucks Socialist: Journal of the South-Bucks Constituency
Labour Party I [1950?] –? Jordans, Buckinghamshire; bi-m
    B   2d. (1960–4). Published for the South Bucks Labour Party by
Russell Everett, the editor. Short notes and comment.
    LabP† occ. nos between XI, 3 (May–June 1960) and XV, 3
(May–June 1964); TUC XII, 3 (May–June 1961)

3297 South East Ham Worker [1897?] –? m
    B   Free
    O(JJ) 3 (Oct. 1897)

3298 South Eastern Progressive and Labour News 1 (1 July 1893)–4 (22 July 1893); w

B ½d. Printed and published for the proprietors by W. H. Thomas and J. P. Denman. Edited by O. N. Ward. 'Published in Deptford, Greenwich and surrounding districts.' Newspaper, advocating Labour representation, reporting trade union and Labour news in the area, with one special article each week, and advertising and reporting local trade union meetings. Contributors: E. Pease, F. E. Gree, Sidney Webb.

L(Col)†

3299 South Gloucestershire Labour News 1 (July/Aug. 1965)–[May 1966?]. Hanham, Bristol; bi-m

B Published by the South Gloucestershire Labour Party. Newspaper containing foreign, national and local news, and comment.

GrP 1–4 (Feb./March 1966); LE† 1; LabP† 1–4

3300 South Hackney Citizen 1 (July 1930)–112 (Sept. 1939); m

B Gratis. Published by the London Co-operative Society's Political Committee.

L(Col)†

3301 South Hammersmith Citizen 1 (Oct. 1927)–52 (Feb. 1932); [ns] 1 (June 1937)–27 (Sept. 1939); ns 1 (Jan. 1945)–4 (May 1945); [ns] 1 (Jan. 1947)–91 (Jan. 1955); then b **Barons Court Citizen**: ns 1 (Feb. 1955)–65 (May/June 1963); m; irreg

B Gratis. Published by the London Co-operative Society.

HsP*; L(Col) (w 1945); LabP† b 40–65*

3302 South Hammersmith Labour News I, 1 (Nov. 1946)–? m

B

HsP 1–4 (Feb. 1947)

3303 South Ilford Citizen ns 1 (May 1947)–48 (June 1951); [ns] 1 (March 1964)–? m

B Issued by the Political Committee of the London Co-operative Society.

L(Col)

3304 South Islington Citizen 1 (Dec. 1929)–118 (Sept. 1939); m

B Gratis. Published by the London Co-operative Society.

L(Col)†

3305 South Kensington Clarion Dec. 1967; then **S. Ken. Labour Party Clarion**: Jan. 1968–March 1968; m

B 6d. Published by Thames Valley Publishing Society. Newspaper, with news and discussion. Running title is **The Clarion**.

L(Col)†; ONC†

3306 South Lewisham Citizen ns 1 (May 1949)–?
    B   Issued by the Political Purposes Committee of the Royal
Arsenal Co-operative Society.
    L(Col)

3307 South Lewisham Labour Party Digest I [195-?]–? bi-m
    B   Edited and published by Mrs M. Raison, then by C. J. Hillam.
'For members of the South Lewisham Labour Party with the compliments
of the General Council.' Short signed articles, notes etc.
    LabP† II, 5 (Jan./Feb. 1960)–III, 9 (Jan./Feb. 1963)*

3308 South Norfolk Clarion 1 (Feb./March 1961)–(July 1964).
Wymondham; m
    B   Published for the South Norfolk Labour Party.
    L(Col); LabP† 8 (Nov. 1961)–28 (Dec. 1963*)

3309 South Nottingham Herald 1 (May 1955)–? Nottingham
    B   Published by R. E. Green, for South Nottingham Constituency
Labour Party. A lavishly illustrated 'people's' paper, circulated to electors.
    L 1

3310 South Notts NALGO Branch News and Views 1960?–Nottingham
    A   National and Local Government Officers' Association.
Reproduced from typewriting.
    L 1960–

3311 South Oxfordshire Democrat [194-?]. Chinnor, Oxfordshire; m
    B   2d. Labour Party. (Labour Party. **Your own Journal,** 1948.)

3312 South Shropshire Pioneer [c1930]. Ludlow; m
    B   1d. Ludlow Divisional Labour Party. (Mitchell, 1930.)

3313 South Side Standard I, 1 (13 Dec. 1924)–III, 121 (14 April 1928).
Glasgow; w
    B   1d. Printed and published by A. H. Barnett. A news medium for
the working-class districts of Glasgow South, pro-Labour. Contributors:
Campbell Stephen, M.P., Steekie MacWhirr.
    GM; L(Col)†

3314 South Staffordshire Examiner: a Journal of General Intelligence,
Devoted to the Interests of Labour 1 [1873?]–49 (21 Nov. 1874).
Wednesbury; w
    B   1d.; 1½d. Published by William Owen. Printed for the proprietor
by the Co-operative Newspaper and General Steam Printing Society. For
miners and ironworkers of the South Staffs area. Includes correspondence
from working men on Labour and trade union matters.
    L(Col)† 20 (2 May 1874)–49

3315 South Suburban Co-operative Citizen 1 (July 1938)–7 (March 1939); irreg
    B   Published by the South Suburban Co-operative Society.
    L(Col)

3316 South Tottenham Citizen 1 [1929?]–123 (Sept. 1939); m
    B   Gratis. Published by the London Co-operative Society.
    L(Col) 9 (Jan. 1930)–123 (Sept. 1939)

South Wales and Swansea Voice see **Llais Llafur**

3317 South Wales Co-op Courier [1970?]–? Cardiff
    A   Minimum of news, mainly advertising.
    L(Col) 3 (Jan. 1971)

3318 South Wales Democrat. [Gwerinwr] 1 (1951)–10 (1951); then **Cymric Democrat.** [Gwerinwr]: 11 (1951)–75 (1958). Ystrad, Rhondda; m
    B   3d. (1956). Published by Cymric Democrat Publishing Society. 'All Wales Socialist monthly.' Editors: Ann Ward; Reg. Ley. Supports the Labour Party. Articles, news, comment and other newspaper features.
    LabP† I, 54 (Sept. 1956)–65, Aug. 1957*;SwP

3319 South Wales Labour Times 1 (4 March 1893). Cardiff
    B
    L(Col)

3320 South Wales Miner: a Fortnightly Journal to Advocate Militant Trade Union Policy Throughout the South Wales Coalfield 1 (22 June 1933)–42 (10 July 1935). Rhondda; fortn
    A   1d. Published by the South Wales Miners' Rank-and-File Movement Editorial Board. 'The official organ of the Rank-and-File Movement of the South Wales Miners.' Demands guaranteed minimum wage, seven-hour day without wage cuts, abolition of overtime etc. Contributors: Arthur Horner, D. J. Williams, Edgar Lewis. Discontinued because of lack of financial support.
    CPGB; L(Col)†; South Wales Miners' Library*

3321 South Wales Sentinel and Labour News 1 (29 Sept. 1911)–22 (23 Feb. 1912); then **Sentinel**: 23 (1 March 1912)–40 (28 June 1912). Llanelly; w
    B   ½d. Published by N. S. H. Gascoigne. A working-class newspaper which advocates Trade Unionism, industrial federation. Cautious of political action via the Independent Labour Party, but supports the candidature of Frank Vivian early in 1912. Supports the strikes struggles in Wales, 1911–12. Claimed circulation of 8,000 at peak.
    L(Col)†

South Wales Voice see **Llais Llafur**

South Wales Worker see **Rhondda Socialist Newspaper**

3322 South Wales Worker 1 (15 Feb. 1902)–?; 40 (May 24 1913)–70 (25 July 1914). Swansea; Merthyr Tydfil; m; fortn
    B   1d. First published by South Wales Labour Press Association. Started by members of Swansea Independent Labour Party. New series continues numbering of **Rhondda Socialist Newspaper** (qv). 'Outgrowth of **Rhondda Socialist**, aimed at wider area. Advocated world-wide social revolution as solution to working-class problems, and saw education toward that end as the primary need; violently opposed to Workers' Educational Association and in favour of Central Labour College' (Brophy).
    AbU 1–4; L(Col) 40–70; O(JJ) 1–4 (17 May 1902)

3323 South-West Bethnal Green Citizen 1 (March 1931)–8 (Nov. 1931); ns 1 (March 1934)–21 (Jan. 1936); ns 1 (Oct. 1937)–24 (Sept. 1939); m
    B   Gratis. Published by the London Co-operative Society, Political Committee.
    L(Col)

3324 South West Ham Worker 1 (Aug. 1897)–[1901?] ; m
    B   Free. Published by South West Ham Independent Labour Party. Editor: Harry Davis.
    AbU 3 (Oct. 1897 [microfilm]); ILP Jan. 1899, Feb. 1900; O(JJ) 3 (Oct. 1897)

3325 South-West St Pancras Citizen 1 (March 1935)–4 (July 1935); irreg
    B   Published by S. W. St Pancras Labour Party.
    L(Col)

3326 South Western Chronicle: the Progressive Organ for Battersea, Clapham, Kennington and Wandsworth 1 (5 Oct. 1894)–20 (16 Feb. 1895); w
    B   ½d. Printed and published for the proprietors by Kent and Matthews. Issued 'uninvited by any political party or sect, it will doubtless be welcomed by all who are striving to uplift and sweeten the daily life of the masses.' An advocate of progress and democracy as against 'old-fashioned and crusted Toryism on one hand and capitalistic Liberalism on the other'. Wish to make it the paper of the people. Labour column and notices on trade unions. In 1894 attention to John Burns as councillor, Battersea. Also articles on other social reform organisations, temperance, free education, municipal affairs.
    L(Col)†

3327 Southampton Co-operative Citizen 1 (1935)–2 (Nov. 1935)
    B
    L(Col) 2

3328 Southampton Labour Voice: Organ of the Southampton Trade and Labour Council I, 1 (April 1947)–? Southampton; m

B   2d. Sub-title from I, 2 (May 1947): 'Organ of Southampton Labour Party'; from II, 4 (July 1948); 'Organ of Labour Party; Labour, Trade Unionism, Co-operation'. A local edition of **Labour's Northern Voice**.

SoP I 1–June 1951

3329 Southdown Press Monthly Bulletin: for Peacehaven, Rottingdean and Newhaven. 1 (Aug. 1932)–9 (May 1933). Peacehaven; m

B   1d. From No. 8 an edition is published with the cover title: **The Lewes Divisional Labour Party's Monthly Bulletin**.

L

3330 Southend-on-Sea and District Citizen 1 (May 1930)–33 (Feb. 1933). Leigh-on-Sea; m

B   Published by the London Co-operative Society, Political Committee.

L(Col)

3331 Southern Co-operative Education Association Record [c1920]. London

A   Free. (Mitchell, 1920.)

3332 Southern Democrat and Irish Notes and Industrial News I, 1 (12, Oct. 1917)–III, 94 (29 Aug. 1919). Newcastle West, Co. Limerick; w

B   1d. At first had similar aims to its predecessor, **Irish Notes and Industrial News**, ie the promotion of 'the Irish language and Industrial Revival movements', but in 1919 gives increasingly more coverage and support to the Labour Movement. On 21 March 1919 is started a column called 'The workers' forum' intended to be 'a series of sound, stimulative articles on Labour Organisation, and other matters of interest to the members of the Labour Movement'. More comment on trade unions, strikes etc. Letters on Socialism; contributions by workers and socialists. Its main support was for trade unions and co-operative enterprises. Towards the end, however, there is less 'Labour' content, and there is disapproval of the less than active support for temperance from the Labour Movement.

L(Col)†*

3333 Southern Star, and London and Brighton Patriot 1 (19 Jan. 1840)–(12 July 1840); w

B   6d. etc. Published and printed by George Cowie. Proprietors: O'Brien and William Carpenter. Editor: Bronterre O'Brien, until his arrest in February 1840; Thomas Smith. An extensive newspaper of Chartist news from London and the provinces, and general news. Promoted to parallel **Northern Star**. Sponsoring body: Radical Registration and Patriotic Association Brighton.

Bishopsgate Institute† 1–11 (29 March 1840); L(Col)†

Southern Worker see **Worker. 1912–1914**

3334 'Southerner': Official Publication of London, Southern, Electricity
Branch NALGO 1961?–
    A   National and Local Government Officers' Association, London
(Southern) Electricity Branch. Reproduced from typewriting.
    L 1961–

3335 Southgate Intercomm [194-?] ; m
    B   Duplicated. Labour Party. (Labour Party. **Your own Journal,**
1948.)

3336 Southwark Citizen ns 1 (May 1949)–?
    B   Issued by the Political Purposes Committee of the Royal
Arsenal Co-operative Society.
    L(Col)

3337 Southwark Labour News: the Organ of the Central Southwark
Labour Party 1 (March 1921)–7 (Nov./Dec. 1921); m
    B   1d. Published by the Editor.
    L(Col)†

3338 Southwark Sun [195-?] –?
    A   National and Local Government Officers' Association,
Southwark Branch. Reproduced from typewriting.
    L 28 (Dec. 1958)

Soviet Literature see **Literature of the World Revolution**

3339 Soviet Russia Pictorial 1 (May 1923)–10 (April 1924); m
    B   1d.; 2d. Organ of the Workers' International Russian Relief,
British edition. Succeeded by **Workers' International Pictorial.**
    L(Col)†; LE 3–10

3340 Sower: the Organ of the New Fellowship 1 (July 1889); then
Seed-time: 2 (Oct. 1889)–34 (Feb. 1898). Kingston-on-Thames; q
    B   1d.; 2d. Published by the Fellowship of the New Life. Editor:
Maurice Adams. Promotes ethical and Christian Socialism and moral and
social regeneration. Influenced by Thoreau and Emerson.
    L; LE; MP 3–18; O 1–4; ONC 28

3341 Sowerby Herald 1 (June 1964)–? Hebden Bridge; irreg
    B   Published by Sowerby Division Labour Party. News and
comment.
    LabP† 1–3 (Sept. 1964), 6 (Feb. 1968)

3342 Sozialdemokrat: Organ der Sozialdemokratie Deutscher Zunge.
1 (1 Jan. 1888)–39 (27 Sept. 1890). Zurich; London (Oct. 1888–); w
    B   Published in London from the German Co-operative Publishing
Company. German social democratic organ; Marxist. Includes foreign
coverage. In German.
    L(Col)

3343 Sozialdemokrat: Halbmonatsschrift der Sudetendeutschen Sozialdemokratie (Social Democrat: Bimonthly of the Sudeten—German Social Democracy) I, 1 (2 April 1940)—XII, (1951); fortn

    B Published by Lincolns-Prager. Publication of the Sudeten-German Social Democracy. Principal editor: Wenzel Jaksch. In German.

    LE†*

3344 Sozialistische Mitteilungen: [News for German Socialists in England] 1 (6 Jan. 1940)—81 (Dec. 1945). London; fortn

    B Issued by the London Representative of the German Social Democratic Party. 'News letter published for the information of Social Democratic refugees from Germany who are opposing dictatorship of any kind.' Includes information on conditions and on the working-class movement in Germany. In German. Reproduced from typewriting.

    L* (Col) 25 (April 1941)—52 (Aug. 1943)

3345 Sozialistische Nachrichten: Organ der Deutschen Sozialdemokratischen Arbeiter-Partei in der Tschechoslowakischen Republik, Auslandsgruppe (Socialist News: Organ of the German Social-Democratic Workers' Party in the Czechoslovak Republic, the Group Abroad). I, 1 (6 Nov. 1940)—V, 16 (Aug. 1945); fortn

    B Issued by the Executive Committee of the German Social Democratic Party in the Czechoslovakian Republic. Reproduced from typewriting. In German.

    L

3346 Spade and Whip and Bucks. Weekly Times 1 (28 Feb. 1874)—12 (16 May 1874); then **People's Courier**: 13 (23 May 1874)—17 (20 June 1874). Aylesbury; w

    B 1d. Publisher, editor and sole proprietor: Edward Richardson. 'This journal proclaims itself an Independent Organ on the side of the weak and poor; and all classes of working men are invited to peruse its columns and to promote its interests . . . The writer [Richardson] is known to many of the labourers of Bucks. and the adjoining counties, as having publicly proposed himself anxious to see the labourers better housed, better fed, better clothed, better educated, and better men. The motto of **The Spade and Whip** is "Reform".' Supports the agricultural labourers' movement, and 'the labour movement'. News and comment, and correspondence on the farmers' lock-out of 1874. No. 11 states that Richardson, 'who has long been known in this neighbourhood as the founder of the Labourers' Unions in Buckinghamshire', opened the meeting at the second anniversary of the formation of 'Local Unions', attended by members of Aylesbury district of the National Agricultural Labourers' Union. Promotes the enfranchisement of the agricultural labourer, and the exposure of grievances, whose corrective is 'The Labourers' Union, Temperance principles and Self-Reliance'.

    L(Col)†

3347 Spain and the World I, 1 (11 Dec. 1936)–II, 47 (23 Dec. 1938); then **Revolt**: III, 1 (11 Feb. 1939)–III, 6 (3 June 1939). Stroud (11 Dec. 1936)–(24 June 1938); London; irreg; fortn

    B   2d. Published by Thomas H. Keell, then by Narod Press, later by S. Clements; S. Edelman. Anarchist and anarcho-syndicalist. A lot of space in early numbers given to the economic organisation and government of Catalonia by the Spanish anarchists. Newspaper format. Contributors: E. Goldman, R. Rocker etc. Enlarges coverage when changes title; **Revolt** 'will bring to the workers the ideas and ideals of Anarchism and Anarcho-Syndicalism.' Vol. III, Nos. 1–6 are also numbered 48–53.

    L(Col)

Spain Today and Volunteer for Liberty see **Volunteer for Liberty**

3348 Spangle: the Quarterly Magazine of the Royal Leamington Spa Branch. [1958?]–. Leamington Spa; q

    A   National and Local Government Officers' Association.

    L 4 (Spring 1959)–.

3349 Spanish News: the Organ of the Friends of the Spanish Republic. I, 1 (8 Jan. 1937)–I, 13 (1 May 1937); w

    B   2d. Published by The Friends of the Spanish Republic. Edited by Viscount Churchill. 'Organised in support of the people of Spain in the fight for a free democracy and against Fascism.' Members of the National Council were Chairman: Jack Tanner; Teasurer: John Jagger; Secretary: Dick Beech; and other prominent members of the Communist Party, Socialist Leagues, Fabian Society.

    L(Col)†; ONC; WCML† I, 8

3350 Spanish Relief: Bulletin of the National Committee 1 [1937?]–19 (June 1939); irreg?

    B

    L(Col) 13 (June 1938)–19

3351 Spark I, 1 (Jan. 1925)–? Manchester; m

    B   1d. Official organ of the Manchester District Committee of the Communist Party. Editor: Arthur McManus.

    TUC I, 1; WCML† I, 2 (Feb. 1925)

3352 Spark [1925?]–?; irreg?

    A   ½d. Paper of 'the Nine Elms Communist Railwaymen'; 'Nine Elms and Battersea Railwaymen'; ' "Spark" Communist Railway Group'. Reproduced from typewriting.

    O(JJ)† 19 2–9 Oct. 1925; 34 (16 April 1926), 35 (30 April 1926); 2 unnumbered issues for 25 and 30 June 1926

3353 Spark: the Organ of the Bishopsgate and Broad St Rail Workers [1926?] –?

    A   Issued by The Communist Group, Bishopsgate and Broad Street. 'Printed and published for the CP Group by XYZ.' Reproduced from typewriting. Cartoons, militant policy.

    O(JJ)† 12 (25 June 1926); unnumbered and undated issue, [1926]

3354 Spark: Organ of the Methil Communist Pit Group I, 1 [1926] –?; II, 1 (11 Feb. 1927)–(14 July 1928); III, 1 (19 July 1930)–7A, (25 Dec. 1931). Fife; fortn

    A   'Organ of the Methil Local Communist Party', and from 11 October 1930 'Organ of the Militant Section, Wellesley (Colliery) Workers'.

    E*; Buckhaven and Methil PL, Proudfoot Papers II, 1–*

3355 Spark [c1932]

    A   Issued at Crookbolton Textile Works. (**Daily Worker**, 20 May 1932)

3356 Spark Organ of the Bardykes Militant Group 1 (1933)–? [Scotland]; m

    A   Appeals to miners to become organised in the United Mineworkers of Scotland, because of the failure of the Miners' Federation of Great Britain to fight for better conditions. Demands seven-hour day, with no wage cuts, a National Agreement with National Guaranteed Minimum Wage based on 5% increase for all miners, increased safety precautions, abolition of overtime. Reproduced from typewriting.

    MML† (3 [June], 5 [Aug.] 1933)

3357 Spark [1937?] –? Derby; q

    A   Published by the National Union of Co-operative Insurance Society Employees (NUCISE), section of the National Society of Clerical and Supervisory Staffs.

    TUC† 8 (April 1939), 10 (July/Oct. 1939)

3358 Spark 1 (19 May 1970)–20 (March 1971?) Leeds; w

    B   1d. Leeds University Union, Socialist Society broadsheet. Reproduced from typewriting.

    LdU† 1–20

3359 Sparks: the Newsletter of the North-East London Electricity Branch of NALGO 1 (March 1949)–30 (Aug. 1955). Ilford; irreg

    A   National Association of Local Government Officers, later National and Local Government Officers' Association.

    L

3360 Spectabo: the Official Journal of the Lambeth Municipal Officers' Guild 1959– .

    A   National and Local Government Officers' Association. Reproduced from typewriting.

    L 1959–

3361 Spectrum: Magazine of the Co-operative College [195-?] –?
Loughborough; a
    A   Students' magazine.
    Co-op. Coll.† 1956/7–1960/1, 1964/5–1969

3362 Spelthorne Clarion [194-?] –Feb. 1970. [Staines?] ; m
    B   Labour Party newspaper.
    L(Col) 170 (April 1957)–(Feb. 1970); LabP† 260 (Nov.
1964)–(Nov. 1969)–(Jan. 1970*)

3363 Spen Valley Citizen Jan. 1938. Spenborough
    B   Issued by the Spen Valley Co-operative Societies.
    L(Col)

3364 Spen Valley Pioneer 1 [1930?] –108 (Oct. 1939). Dewsbury; m
    B   Gratis. Published by the Spen Valley Divisional Labour Party.
Local Labour information and outlook, local and national news, sport etc.
    L(Col)† 52 (Jan. 1935)–108

3365 Spirit of Freedom? –1849. Uxbridge
    B   Editors: J. B. Leno and Gerald Massey. 'It was full of fire and
breathed the spirit of republicanism' (R. G. Gammage, **History of the
Chartist Movement**, reprint, Merlin Press, 1969, p. 346).

3366 Spirit of the Age: Journal of Political, Industrial and Educational
Progress I, 1 (1 July 1848)–II, 32 (3 March 1849); w
    B   4½d. Editors: Alexander Campbell; G. J. Holyoake (from Nov.
1848). Stands for the political and social emancipation of Labour.
Supports all the principles of the People's Charter. Collectivist ideals.
Reports all progressive movements seeking to organise industry in the
interests of the producers, eg, Fourierist, Icarian, Communist. Reports on
international Labour. Contributor: Robert Owen. Succeeded by **The Spirit
of the Times**.
    L(Col); LU; LE† ; Warwick UL (microfilm)

3367 Spirit of the Times, or Social Reformer: a Journal of Education,
Colonisation, Politics and Social Progress 1 (10 March 1849)–30 (29 Sept.
1849); then **Weekly Tribune**: 3·1 (6 Oct. 1849)–72 (6 July 1850); w
    B   2d. Unstamped. Publisher: George Vickers. Printers: Archibald
Campbell, then D. Aird. Organ of the Committee of the League of Social
Progress. Principal members: Alexander Campbell, Lloyd Jones, James
Rigby (Secretary), G. J. Holyoake, Hetherington, Walter Cooper.
Advocated 'principle of industrial co-operation on the land as the only
effectual social remedy for pauperism and destitution'. For universal
suffrage, national secular education, collectivism in production and
distribution of wealth. Contributors: Robert Owen; Louis Blanc, with
'Letter on social reform'. Succeeded **The Spirit of the Age**.
    BP 6 Oct. 1849–9 Feb. 1850; L(Col)† ; LE† 1–29

3368 Spirit of the Tyne and Wear, or, the Masters' and Workmen's Guardian 1 (Dec. 1832). Hetton-le-Hole; m?

  C?   Published by Johnston and Carr. Printed by E. Mackenzie. Durham County Library

3369 Spirit of the Union i 1 (30 Oct. 1819)—11 (8 Jan. 1820). Glasgow; w

  B   3d. Printed by G. Macleod and Company for the editor. Unitarian. Organ of the radical reformers of the West of Scotland, who advocated annual parliaments and universal suffrage.

  GM† (w 4—5)

3370 Spitalfields Weavers' Journal 1 (1 Aug. 1837)—5 (Dec. 1837); m

  A   1d. Printed by J. S. Forsaith for the United Operative Weavers of London. It is 'devoted solely to the advocacy of the interests of the Operative Weavers.' Published by Charles Cole, Secretary. States that a cheap and honest press is required to remedy social evils, including the distress of the weavers. Reports all that is of interest to weavers, public meetings, parliamentary proceedings, arbitration proposals, correspondence.

  LU†

3371 Splash [c1950]

  B   Issued by Labour Party Young Socialists, Friern Barnet branch. Duplicated. (**Socialist Advance**, Aug. 1950.)

3372 Spotlight [194-?]—? [Folkestone?]

  A   Union of Post Office Workers, Folkestone and Hythe Branch. TUC X, 9 (Nov. 1955)—10 (Dec. 1955)

Spotlight. 1957— see National Association of Local Government Officers. Ramsgate Branch. **Review**

3373 Spotlight 1960?— . Leicester

  A   National and Local Government Officers' Association, Leicester County Branch. Reproduced from typewriting.

  L 1960—

3374 Spotlight I, 1 [1969?]— ; bi-m?

  A   Printed and published by the Civil and Public Services Association, Department of Health and Social Security Branch. Reproduced from typewriting.

  Warwick U(MRC)† II, 3 (Nov./Dec. 1970)—*

3375 Spotlight and Backstage [19-?]—Sept. 1970. Glasgow; q?

  A   Published by the National Association of Theatrical and Kine Employees, Scottish District. Reproduced from typewriting.

  TUC† Sept. 1970

3376 Spot-On [1942?–44?]. Liverpool
    A   Shop stewards' paper, Napiers. (E. Frow)

3377 Spot-on 1966– . West Drayton
    A   National and Local Government Officers' Association, Hillingdon Branch. Reproduced from typewriting.
    L

3378 Sprag: Organ of the Militant Miners of Shotts 1 [1930?] –? irreg?
    A   Organ of the United Mineworkers of Scotland, and of the Shotts Communist Party. Reproduced from typewriting.
    E 2 (25 April 1930), 17 (5 Sept. 1930 [xerox])

3379 Spring-70, for Better Conditions: the Paper of the Spring and Axle Workers 1 [1932?] –? Manchester
    A   Issued by W. E. Carey's Red Bank, now Jonas Woodhead's, Manchester. Reproduced from typewriting.
    WCML† 2 (26 Feb. 1932)

3380 Spur; Because the Workers Need a Spur I, 1 (June 1914)–III, 8 (April 1921); m
    B   1d.; 2d. Printed and published by The Bakunin Press. Edited by Guy Aldred, later Rose Witcop. A journal of anarchist Socialism, successor to **The Herald of Revolt** 'to goad the workers' into action and understanding of the need for social revolution. Ceased when the premises in London and Glasgow were raided by the police. The issue for April 1921 was published in Glasgow.
    L(Col)†; LE 1914–May 1919

3381 Spur [1926]. Fife; irreg?
    A   1d. Produced by Fife rank-and-file railway workers. Reproduced from typewriting. Undated.
    MML† (Hutt papers) 3 numbers

3382 Spur 1 (Feb. 1957)–? Tottenham; q
    A   National and Local Government Officers' Association, Tottenham Branch.
    L 1–3 (Sept. 1957)

3383 Spur: Official Magazine of the Harrogate and District Branch of NALGO 1964?– . Harrogate
    A   National and Local Government Officers' Association. Reproduced from typewriting.
    L 1964–

3384 Spy, or Political Inspector I, 1 (15 June 1795)–I, 16 (28 Sept. 1795). Sheffield; w
    B   1d. Printed by J. Crome. Articles include 'Essay on Libel', 'Advantages of Trial by Jury', 'On Slavery and Oppression'.
    SP

3385 Squatter [1946]. Aberdeen
  B   2d. Printed and published by Aberdeen Communist Party.
  AU (MSS Coll.) 1 undated number issued sometime after 27 Aug.
1946

3386 Staff: Journal of the Bedford County Branch, NALGO 1 (Autumn
1951)–19 (April 1956). Bedford; q
  A   Free. National Association of Local Government Officers, later
National and Local Government Officers' Association.
  L

3387 Staff Mag 1 (March 1946)–100 (Nov. 1957). Boston. Lincolnshire;
m
  A   National Association of Local Government Officers, later
National and Local Government Officers' Association, Holland County
Officers' Branch. Reproduced from typewriting.
  L (w 12, 32–3, 46–7, 64)

3388 Staff News Bulletin [19--?] –? [Manchester?]
  A   Union of Shop, Distributive and Allied Workers.
  TUC Jan. 1947–Feb. 1951

3389 Stafford and District Monthly News [193-?] –? Stafford; m
  B   Stafford Divisional Labour Party. (Labour and Socialist
International. **The Socialist Press**, 1933.)
  WCML† ns (9 [June], 12 [Oct.], 14, 15 [Nov.] 1935)

3390 Stafford and District Record [18--?] –   ? [Stafford?]
  A   'In February, 1896, the Committee [ie the Education
Committee of the Walsall and District Co-operative Society] decided to
continue taking the **Stafford and District Record**, which, no doubt,
fulfilled many of the purposes of the modern **Wheatsheaf**' (F. Hall, **From
Acorn to Oak, being the History of the Walsall and District Co-operative
Society, Ltd., 1886–1936**, Birmingham 1936, p. 153).

3391 Stafford Citizen [194-?]. Stafford; m
  B   2d. Labour Party. (Labour Party. **Your own Journal**, 1948.)

3392 Stafford Co-operative Citizen 1 (Oct. 1935)–?
  B
  L(Col) 1

3393 Staffordshire Knot [Daily edition] I, 1 (4 May 1885)–20 (29 May 1885). then **Staffordshire Morning Knot**: 1 (1 June 1885)–(882 [14 Oct. 1887?], 883 [Oct. 1887?]; then **Staffordshire Knot**: (883 [Oct. 1887?], 884 [17 Oct. 1887?])–1017 (16 March 1888). Hanley; d

 B ½d.; 1d. Printed and published by William Owen and Company, later with Ebenezer Gould. Like the weekly edition it bases itself upon working-class support, and claims that it 'consistently advocates the progress and well-being of the working classes'. Radical, advanced Liberal. Deals with local life and public questions. Supports working men's candidates for Parliament, eg, Broadhurst, the new member for the Potteries. Also, serial story, sports coverage etc.

 L(Col)† (w 883)

3394 Staffordshire Knot [Weekly edition]. 1 (13 May 1882)–1202 (31 Oct. 1891); then **Potteries Free Press and Staffordshire Knot**: 1203, (7 Nov. 1891)–1210 (26 Dec. 1891). Hanley; w

 B 1d. Printed and published for the proprietors by William Owen, and edited by him. (Owen was accepted in July 1886 as the Liberal candidate in the Ecclesall division, Sheffield.) 'Besides the potters, the miners, and the ironworkers, this paper will also represent the workmen of all classes in Staffordshire.' Says it will expose grievances, support trade combination, but also conciliation and arbitration, and friendly feelings between operative and employer. Includes trade union news, special articles on the pottery trade etc., serial story, home hints. By 1886 it is a Liberal weekly family paper with little in the way of Labour news, but in 1891 it claims to be the representative of the working-man. Succeeds **The Potteries Examiner**.

 L(Col)†

Staffordshire Morning Knot see **Staffordshire Knot**. [Daily edition]

3395 Stage Staff Journal I, 1 (Dec. 1901)–II, 17 (March 1904); m

 A 1d. Published by C. Thorogood. Organ of the National Union of Theatrical Stage Employees. 'To serve the stage employee and his craft'; to fight for higher rates of pay. Union membership was open to 'Theatrical Carpenters, Stage and Cellarmen, Flymen, Propertymen, Gasmen, Electricians, and Limelight men over 18 years, who have not had less than 6 months' experience in a theatre or music hall or theatrical workshop.'

 L(Col)†

Star.1858 see **Edinburgh Star**

3396 Star 1 (17 Jan. 1888)—22509 (17 Oct. 1960); d

C ½d. Relevant from 1888 to 1894 only. Editors: T. P . O'Connor (until 1892); James Stuart. States that since the rich and privileged need no advocate, it will judge policies 'from the standpoint of the workers of the nation, and of the poorest and most helpless among them', and will be for their elevation. Vilified by papers like **Commonweal** and **Freedom** for its truckling to the Liberals. Claims that 'it is not for or against socialism, but that it takes individual policies on their own merits'. Support for moderate Trade Unionism.

L(Col)†; ONC occ. nos 1888—90; Warwick UL 1888—92 (microfilm)

3397 Star of the West 1 (15 Jan. 1876)—6 (19 Feb. 1876) Merthyr Tydfil; w

B Published by The Labour Press and Industrial Co-operative Society, Managing Editor: J. T. Morgan, Secretary of Merthyr and Dowlais Trades Council. Promotors included Merthyr District Miners' Agent, Treasurer and Secretary, Glamorgan Ironworkers' Agent, President of the Independent Association of Tin-Plate Workers, General Secretary of the National United Association of Enginemen, Firemen and Fitters, General Secretary of Bristol, West of England and South Wales Labourers' Union etc. 'The object of the Co-operative Society is to publish a good family newspaper . . . in the direct interests of the working classes, which it is believed can be secured for their mutual advantage and protection. As it will be the unflinching Advocate of the Rights of Labour, it is hoped every Collier and Artizan, and all Working Men's Unions or Lodges will aid the project by taking up shares.' Succeeded the **Workman's Advocate**, 1873—6 (qv).

L(Col)†

3398 Standard: Tyneside's Labour Weekly [c1926]. [Newcastle?]; w
B? (**British Worker**, 5 (15 May 1926,)

3399 'Standaw' [19--?] —? Ellesmere Port
A Union of Shop, Distributive and Allied Workers, Stanlow Laboratory Branch.
TUC May 1949

3400 Stanmore Labour News: Official Organ of the North and South Stanmore Wards of the Harrow Local Labour Party I, 1 (June 1936)—III, 15 (Aug. 1939). Stanmore; m
B Gratis. Published by the North and South Stanmore Wards Labour Party. 'To keep in touch with our supporters and inform them what their representatives are doing on their behalf.' Editor: C. H. Ballard. Articles, comment, record of activities.
L

Star and National Trades' Journal see **Northern Star and Leeds General Advertiser**

Star of Freedom see Northern Star, and Leeds General Advertiser

3401 State Railways: Organ of the Railway Nationalisation Society I, 1 (April 1917)–? 40 (April 1931); q
  B 1d. Published for the Society by F. W. Galton, Secretary.
  TUC†

State Service see State Technology

3402 State Student: the Monthly Journal of the Civil Service University and Professional Association I, 1 (March [1930])–I, 18 (Feb./March 1932); m
  A For graduates of those professionally employed by any government department or local government body. To promote study [ie higher education] to serve the State, and to secure fair financial recompense for these services. Motto: 'We study to Serve the State: Education increases Efficiency'.
  L

3403 State Technology : the Journal of the Institution of Professional Civil Servants I, 1 (April 1921)–V, 12 (March 1926); then **State Service**: VI, 1 (April 1926)– ; m
  A 6d. etc. Published by the Institution. Illustrated journal with much technical news, but serves as a medium for the expression of points of view by members of the Institution on all matters affecting the efficiency of the Civil Service and their own prospects. Reports the work of the Institution, and its representation before Whitley Councils and Civil Service Committees. The Institution is a staff association not a professional institution.
  L(Col); LMA IX–XIII; ONC XLI, 1961–

3404 Staveley and District Spark [192-?]. [Staveley?]
  B 1d. Printed and published by the Staveley Tenants Defence Committee. Fights the means test, unemployment and bad housing. For a workers' front against capitalism. Asks readers to join the National Unemployed Workers' Committee Movement. Reproduced from typewriting.
  MML† 19 (24 Aug.), 20 (13 Sept.)

3405 Steam Engine Makers' Society. **Monthly Report** 1 [1907?]–162 (12 June 1920). Manchester; m
  A 1d.
  Bishopsgate Institute 1907–20; L 161 (12 May 1920)–162

3406 Steel Smelters' Journal [c1915]
  A Steel Smelters' Association. Was being published in 1915 (A. Pugh, **Men of steel, by one of them.** Iron and Steel Trades Confederation, 1951).

3407 Steel Workers Voice: a Socialist Voice for Peace and Prosperity 1 (1964)–?
    A
    LE

3408 Stephens' Monthly Magazine of Useful Information for the People 1 (Jan. 1840)–10 (Oct. 1840). Manchester; m
    B   Edited by Rev. J. R. Stephens. A pastoral letter sent from gaol, containing a mixture of politics and religion. From February the title is simply **Stephens' Monthly Magazine**
    Ashton PL†; LU† 1

3409 Stepney Citizen 1 (Dec. 1929)–116 (Sept. 1939); ns 1 (April 1949)–10 (Jan. 1950); m
    B   Gratis. Published by the London Co-operative Society.
    L(Col)

3410 Stepney Labour Times 1928; m?
    B
    SyP Oct. 1928

3411 Stepney Workers' Standard 1934; m
    B   Independent Labour Party.
    ILP Nov. 1934

3412 Stepping-Stone: the Organ of the Secular Reformers Society I, 1 (April 1862)–12 (March 1863); m
    B   1d. Published by Farrah and Dunbar. Organ of the General Secular Reformers' Society, the re-established London Secular Society. To explain its principles and objects. Defends free speech and action, promotes co-operation in production and distribution of wealth, for secular education. Takes up questions affecting the working class, eg, wages, is anti-Malthusianism, and for manhood suffrage.
    L

3413 Stereotyper: Official Organ of the National Society of Electrotypers and Stereotypers I, 1 (Oct. 1955)–XIII, 8 (Aug. 1967); m
    A   3d. Editorials by the General Secretary, A. J. Buckle. Illustrated trade-union journal, dealing with questions of wages and conditions, and some technical matters.
    L; TUC

3414 Stimulus 1965?–. St Helen's
    A   National and Local Government Officers' Association, St Helen's Branch. Reproduced from typewriting.
    L 1965–

Stirlingshire Echo see Stirlingshire NALGO Bulletin

3415 Stirlingshire NALGO Bulletin Jan. 1962?–March 1962; then **Stirlingshire Echo** April 1962–. Stirling; m
    A   National and Local Government Officers' Association, Stirlingshire Branch. Reproduced from typewriting.
    L

3416 Stocking Makers' Monitor, and Commercial Magazine 1 (18 Oct. 1817)–? (24 Dec. 1817); then **Monitor, or Framework-Knitters' Magazine**: (1 Jan. 1818)–? Nottingham (printed); w
    A   Edited by C. Wright and J. Turvey (8 Nov. 1817–24 Dec. 1817). 'Edited by a Company of Framework Knitters' (1 Jan.–12 May 1818). Printed by Sutton and Son, who published the newspaper the **Nottingham Review**.
    NP† 2 (25 ot. 1817)–([3 Dec.], [24 Dec.], 1817); ([1 Jan.–15 Jan.], [12 Feb.])–ns 10 (March 1818)

3417 Stockport Herald [1904?]–? Stockport; m?
    B   Stockport Labour Representation Committee.
    Stockport PL 41 (July 1907 [pp. 1–2 only])

3418 Stockport Labour Journal 1 (April 1898)–(Jan. 1900?). Stockport; m
    B   Gratis. Independent Labour Party. Editors: F. W. Plant and G. Clithero.
    Stockport PL 6 (1898)

Stockport Labour Times see **Stockport Times**

3419 Stockport Sentinel I, 1 [1935?]–? Stockport; m
    B   Stockport Labour Party.
    Stockport PL II, 10 (Oct. 1936)

3420 Stockport Standard [19--?]–? Stockport
    A   Union of Post Office Workers, Stockport Amalgamated Branch. (W. Dunlop, 'Local journals'. **Belpost**, IV, 5 [May 1965])

3421 Stockport Times: a Labour and Trades Union Journal 1 (6 Oct. 1893)–20 (16 Feb. 1894); then **Stockport Labour Times**: 21 (23 Feb. 1894)–32 (11 May 1894). Stockport; w
    B   1d. Printed and published for the proprietors by G. Mansell; The Stockport Times Newspaper and Printing Company Ltd. A paper 'whose mission it will be to champion the cause of the workers in the mills, factories, hat shops, iron foundries, bleach workers, and of the assistants in the shops of sweating grocers, tailors, drapers'. Popular Labour paper, socialist, supporting the Independent Labour Party, with local trade union and municipal notes, fiction, women's column, column for boys and girls. 'The working classes have called for an independent organ of their own for years, and now they have one.' Contributor: 'Autolycus' (1894).
    L(Col)†

Stockport Voice see **Labour's Northern Voice** Stockport edition

3422 Stockton Co-operative Citizen 1 (July 1933)–43 (Feb. 1937); m
B
L(Col)

3423 Stockton Labour Monthly [1896]. Stockton-on-Tees; m
B   'In view of the date of the only known issue,it is reasonable to
suppose that it was another localization of the **Labour Monthly**' (launched
by Allen Clarke) (D. Hopkin, 'Local Newspapers of the Independent
Labour Party, 1893–1906'. Society for the Study of Labour History,
Bulletin, 28 [Spring 1974], p. 37).

3424 Stoke, Fenton and Longton Clarion [194-?]. Stoke-on-Trent; m
B   2d. Labour Party. (Labour Party. **Your own Journal**, 1948.)

3425 Stoke Newington Citizen 1 (May 1930)–111 (Sept. 1939); m
B   Gratis. Published by the London Co-operative Society, Political
Committee.
L(Col)

3426 Stokehole Xmas 1925–44. Manchester; irreg; a
A   Produced by students of the Co-operative College. Reproduced
from typewriting. The title on the cover of the first issue was **Stokehold**,
changed to **Stokehole** with the second issue. Succeeded by **Co-operative
College Magazine.**
Co-op. Coll.†; MP 1930–44*

3427 Store : a Trade Journal for Co-operative Societies, and the Official
Organ of the Federated Productive Societies of the United Kingdom I, 1
(July 1883)–III, 12 (April 1886); q
A   6d. Published by Edward W. Greening. A substantial trade
journal for the management and practical working of the distributive
stores, and provides a link between the distributive and productive
societies. Regards itself as a business complement to **Co-operative News**.
Includes leaders on Co-operation in general.
L; LU I–II, III, 9–10

3428 Storm: Stories of the Struggle I, 1 (Feb. 1933)–3 (1933); irreg
B   6d. Published by G. Douglas Jefferies. Stories, sketches, poems,
depicting the class struggle. Aspired to be the 'cultural magazine of the
revolutionary movement in Britain'.
C 1–2; E 1–2; L; ONC 2

3429 Stormy Petrel: a Week-End Magazine for Thinking Men and Women
I, 1 (29 Feb. 1908)–(30 May 1908); w
B   1d. Editor, proprietor, publisher: John Shaw. Christian Socialist.
Criticises 'unfairness' in the judicial system; for women's suffrage;
anti-vivisection; against private ownership of land. Some humour, fiction.
L; ONC† 1

3430 Straight Left: Official Monthly Organ of the Bethnal Green Trades Council and Labour Party 1 (Feb. 1928)–2 (March 1928); m

B 1d. Published by A. H. Gillison. Supports the policy of the Left Wing Movement, militant Left Labour and Communist Party. Stands 'for a militant workers' policy and . . . [has] nothing in common with the Lib–Labour policy of the reformist "Right" Labour leaders'. Strikes a "blow against Capitalism and Labour Fakers". For a united Left front with youth and Trade Union involvement.

L(Col)†

Stratford Co-operative Monthly Magazine see **Stratford Co-operator**

3431 Stratford Co-operator I, 1 (July 1896)–XIV, 3 (Sept. 1909); then b **Stratford Co-operative Monthly Magazine**: I, 1 (Oct. 1909)–XI, 12 (Sept. 1920); then **London Co-operative Monthly Magazine**: XII, 1 (Oct. 1920)– ?; m

A Gratis. Organ of the Stratford Co-operative and Industrial Society, then, when London societies were amalgamated in 1920, of London Co-operative Society. Extensive and varied contents. Became **London Co-operative Magazine and Wheatsheaf**.

Co-op. Coll. July 1896–June 1898; Oct. 1909–Sept. 1910; L a IX, 104, 109, X–XIII, 9, 11–XIV, 2; b (not traced); WhP† July 1896–Oct. 1927

3432 Streatham Leader 1 (July 1924)–4 (Jan. 1925); irreg

B 1d. Published by the Executive Committee of the Streatham Labour Party. Home and foreign affairs, women's column, youth column etc.

L(Col)

3433 Streatham Pioneer 1 (May 1920)–2 (Oct. 1920); irreg

B ½d. Published for the Streatham Labour Party by A. J. York. Small paper which advocates nationalisation, municipalisation and working-class internationalism as against the 'fraudulent' League of Nations, and urges the readiness of the Labour Party to govern nationally.

L(Col)†

3434 Streatley and Warden Hill Chanticleer [194-?]. Streatley, Bedfordshire; m

B Labour Party. Duplicated. (Labour Party. **Your own Journal**, 1948.)

3435 'Street' Newsvendor: Official Organ of the National Union of Newsvendors I, 1 (July 1930)–?; m

A Printed and published by the Union. Edited by Nathan Birch, National Organising Secretary. Account of branch news and union activities. Is listed in Mitchell, 1940.

O(JJ)† 1

3436 Stretford Searchlight I, 1 (Oct. 1955)–III, 3 (June/July 1957).
Stretford; bi-m
    A   4d. National and Local Government Officers' Association,
Stretford Branch. Reproduced from typewriting.
    L

3437 Struggle: Devoted to the Advocacy of Free Trade and the Repeal of
the Corn Laws 1 [1842]–235 [1846]. Preston; w
    C   ½d. Written and printed by Joseph Livesey. Addressed chiefly
to working-men with the aim of enlisting their support for agitation for
cheap bread. Anti-Chartist, preaches the unity of capital and labour against
aristocratic monopoly. Supports the Anti-Corn Law League.
    Co-op. Coll. 1–53; L; LE; LU (w 105–56); MP; MU 21, 54, 64, 66,
68–197, 205, 211; ONC*

Struggle, 1938 see **Revolutionary Youth Federation; Monthly Bulletin**

3438 Stub: Magazine of Bacup NALGO 1967?– . Bacup
    A   National and Local Government Officers' Association.
Reproduced from typewriting.
    L 1967–

3439 Stud Easter 1964?– . Stevenage
    A   National and Local Government Officers' Association,
Stevenage Branch.
    L Easter 1964–

3440 Student: a Magazine of Theology, Literature and Science I, (1844);
then **Student and Young Men's Advocate**: ns, [I], 1 (Jan. 1845)–[II, 26]
(Dec. 1846); m
    C   Published by Aylott and Jones. In 1845 'Under the
superintendence of the Metropolitan Drapers' Association', and reported
meetings of the Association whose aim was to shorten hours of work of
drapers' assistants. General articles towards self-improvement and
education.
    C ii II; L; O (pp. 81–96 of I [1844] missing)

Student and Young Men's Advocate see **Student**

Student Forward see **Oxford Forward**

3441 Student Front, Against War and Fascism Nov. 1934–Summer 1936?; irreg

      B   1d. Published by Students' Anti-War Council; Student Movement for Peace, Freedom and Cultural Progress. Working through universities, societies, and clubs 'carrying on the struggle against the OTC with its militarist implications, against every attempt of Fascism to gain a foothold in our college; and for the fullest freedom for students to express their opinions fearlessly, whether these be orthodox or not' (Nov. 1935). Superseded by **Student Forum**, which reduced the political content, and does not fall within our categories.

      L(Col)†; O(JJ)† Nov. 1935

3442 Student Leader: the Official Organ of Glasgow University Labour Club [I], 1 (June 1925)–II, 2 (Oct. 1928). Glasgow; irreg

      b   Supported the candidature of Sydney Webb for Rector in 1925.

      E II, 1 (May 1928); L

3443 Student Observer: Journal of the Labour Society of the London School of Economics and Political Science I, 1 (Michaelmas 1947)–II, 1 (Michaelmas Term, 1948); 3-yr

      B   6d. Editor: Sydney Irving.

      L; LE

3444 Student Vanguard I, 1 (Nov. 1932)–? m

      B   3d. Reflects student political participation, mainly in London, in hunger marches and anti-war meetings. Urges unity with working class against war and ruling-class oppression, Communist Party front. Contributors: F. D. Klingender, F. Jackson, John Cornford.

      L I, 1–II, 6 (March 1934); MML 1 (Nov. 1932)–6 (July 1933), 1934; ONC I, 1–III, 2 (Nov./Dec. 1934*)

3445 Student Voice [c1954]

      B   Published by the 'SLF' (**Oxford Left**, Hilary 1954, sends fraternal greetings.)

3446 Students' Bulletin I, 1 (Nov. 1924)–I, 5 (April 1925); bi-m

      C   1d. Issued by the Workers' Educational Association and the Workers' Educational Trade Union Committee. Addressed to existing members, to encourage them to propagate the work of the WEA among their workmates and persuade them to join classes. Directly opposed to the National Council of Labour Colleges 'which exists for Marxian propaganda', whereas the WEA exists for a broader purpose, a wider all-round education within the organised working-class movement. The **Bulletin** merged with **The Highway**.

      L

3447 Sub-Postmaster: Official Organ of the National Federation of Sub-Postmasters I, 1 (Sept. 1899)–   . Manchester etc.; m

      A   2d. etc.

      L(Col); LE IX–XIII, XVIII–

3448 Success: the Magazine of Progressive Management I, 1 (June 1949)–II, 1 (Oct. 1950); bi-m; irreg

A   The professional journal of the Association of Supervisory Staffs, Executives and Technicians. Also intended to record trade union reactions to modern management and to assist trade unionists in their increased activity in management.

GM; L; ONC†

3449 Sudbury and Woodbridge Signpost 1 [1961?] –? Ipswich; m

B   A local Labour Party organ, published by Jack Roberts. National and international news and comment, readers' letters, Labour Party policy, meetings.

LabP† 19, (Feb.)–22 (June), 24 (Sept.) 1963

3450 Sudbury Suffolk News Sheet [194-?]. Hadleigh, Suffolk; m

B   1d. Labour Party. (Labour Party. **Your own Journal**, 1948.)

3451 Suffolk Citizen April 1953–Dec. 1955. Ipswich

B   Published for the Labour Party.

L(Col)

3452 Suffolk Punch: Journal of the East Suffolk Branch, NALGO I, [195-?] –IV, 3 (April 1961?). Ipswich

A   National and Local Government Officers' Association.

L III, 3 (Autumn 1958)–IV, 3

3453 Sun I, 1 (21 April 1889)–II, 49 (23 March 1890); w

B   1d. A Sunday newspaper published by the Radical wing of the Liberal Party. Sympathetic to the claims of Labour. Later commitment to Labour and trade unions. Reports of London Radical Political Clubs. From Sept. 1889 is the organ of the Labour Union and of new Unionism and socialist agitation. Motto: **Vox populi**.

L(Col)†

Sunday Citizen see **Reynolds's Weekly Newspaper**

3454 Sunday Worker: the Only Labour Sunday Newspaper 1 (15 March 1925)–247 (1 Dec. 1929); w

B   2d. Published by Workers' Publications Ltd. Organ of Left Wing of the Labour movement. A class-war paper declaring a 'united front of labour' against the capitalist offensive. Late in 1929 it became a Communist Party organ, before the launching of the **Daily Worker** in 1930.

L(Col)†

Sunday World see **Labour World**

3455 Sunderland Co-operative Record: a Chronicle of Social, Industrial and Educational Progress [c1897?] –? Sunderland; m

A   Gratis. (**Labour Annual**, 1897; Mitchell, 1910.)

3456 Sunderland Pilot 1 (13 July 1832)–? Sunderland; w

B   1½d. Printed at the office by T. Wright. '. . . will plead the cause of the people' and 'support the poor man against the grasping, avaricious spirit of the aristocracy'. Supports Political Union agitation.

NwP 1; Sunderland PL† 1, 5 (10 Aug. 1832)

3457 Sunderland Wearsider [194-?]. Sunderland; m

B   2d. Labour Party. (Labour Party. **Your own Journal**, 1948.)

3458 Supervising I, 1 (Oct. 1911)–I, 99 (Dec. 1919); ns I, 1 (1 Jan. 1920)–V, 23 (Dec. 1967). London; Lincoln; Bracknell; m; fortn

A   2d. etc. Issued by the Association of London Postal Superintending Officers; then the Federation of Post Office Supervising Officers; then the Association of Post Office Controlling Officers. Later sub-titled: 'The Accredited Organ of the Postal, Telegraph and Telephone Supervising Forces'. Extensive contents.

L; LE ii I–II; NU XI, 12 (1962)–

3459 Suppressed United Ireland 1 (15 Dec.)–2 (16 Dec.) 1890; then **'Insuppressible': William O'Brien's Paper**: 3 (17 Dec. 1890)–34 (24 Jan. 1891). Dublin; d

B   ½d. Printed and published by William O'Brien. Continued after the government suppression of **Suppressed United Ireland**. Anti-Parnellite wing of the Irish nationalist movement, Irish National League. Coverage given to the Irish Democratic Labour Federation.

L(Col)†

3460 Surbiton Clarion. Edition of the Surrey and Middlesex Clarion 1 [194-?]–(Dec. 1967); m

B   Issued by Surbiton Labour Party.

L(Col) 166 (Dec. 1956)–(Dec. 1967); LabP† occ. nos between 251 (Feb. 1964) and 285 (Dec. 1966)

3461 Surrey and Middlesex Clarion [194-?]–   . Richmond; m

B   Published for Kingston Labour Party etc.

L(Col) (Dec. 1944)–*; LabP† 1961–70*

3462 Surrey County Clarion [194-?]. New Malden; m

B   2d. Labour Party. (Labour Party. **Your own Journal**, 1948.)

Surrey Teacher see **Surrey Teachers' Quarterly and Educational Gazette**

3463 Surrey Teachers' Quarterly and Educational Gazette 1, [Jan. 1920]–111, (Sept. 1938); then **Surrey Teacher**: ns 112 (Jan. 1939)–167 (Nov. 1952). Guildford; q; bi-m

A   2d. etc. Surrey County Teachers' Association. Review of happenings in the profession, features on status and remuneration. According to No. 1 of **Surrey Teacher** it is stated that **Surrey Teachers' Quarterly** was revived in January 1920 after an interval of five years, but this series has not been traced.

L 57 (March 1925)–167

3464 Surrey Worker I, 1 (May 1925)–I, 6 (Oct. 1925); m

    B   2d. Printed and published by the Victoria House Printing Company, Ltd. for the proprietors, the Kingston Hall Committee. 'Started by the Kingston Hall Committee, consisting of delegates from Kingston, New Malden, Thames Ditton and Esher, Surbiton and East Moseley Labour Parties, the Kingston ILP and the Kingston and district Workers International Relief. Delegates from Wimbleton and Mitcham Labour Parties, and from the Surrey Federation of Labour Parties and Trades Councils have since jointed the Editorial Board.' Further additions to the Board were made. Reports the activities of the local working-class movement.

    L(Col)†

3465 Sussex Post [19--?]–?

    A   Union of Post Office Workers, Sussex District Council. (W. Dunlop, 'Local Journals'. **Belpost**, IV, 5 [May 1965])

3466 Sutton and Cheam Citizen 1 (Oct. 1961)–27 (March 1964); m

    B   Published by the Co-operative Press.

    L(Col); LabP† 1–24 (Dec. 1963*); Sutton PL (w 5, 13, 18, 24, 26)

3467 Sutton Division Magazine [194-?]. Plymouth; irreg

    B   Free. Labour Party. (Labour Party. **Your own Journal**, 1948.)

3468 Swansea and District Workers' Journal: the Official Journal of the Trades' and Labour Council 1 (Aug. 1899)–29 (Dec. 1901). Swansea; m

    A   Free. Published by the Swansea Trades Council. Editor: 'A Socialist'.

    O(JJ) 1–2; SwP

3469 Swansea and District Workers' Journal 1 (Jan. 1910)–51 (April 1914). Swansea; m

    B   Swansea Socialist Party.

    SwP (w 21, 40, 47–50)

3470 Swansea Labour News: Official Organ of the Swansea Labour Party 1 (23 Sept. 1921)–247 (26 June 1926). Swansea; w

    B   Published by the South Wales Labour Press Association

    SwP.

3471 Swiatlo Czasopsimo Popularmo-Mankowe [Light Popular-Scientific Journal]1898–1904; q

    B   Organ of the Union of Polish Socialists Abroad, (later known as Polish Socialist Party). Publisher: J. Kaniowski. In Polish.

    L

3472 Swindon Broadsheet I 1 (Oct. 1968)–III, 6 (June/July 1970); ns I, 1 (Oct. 1970)–4 (June 1971). Swindon; m; bi-m

    B   Published by Swindon Communist Party. Articles and local news on industrial and political events and campaigns.

    'Edith Stevens House', 1 Bridge Street, Swindon

3473 Sword and Shield: a Journal for Labour in the Factory and the Field
1 (31 May 1890)–6 (5 July 1890). Norwich; w
    B   1d. Printed and published by Edward Harvey. 'We specially aim
at being the genuine champion of honest working men and working
women.' Reports workers' meetings, trade union matters, and supports the
Norwich shoemakers on strike. Radical. Correspondence, gossip.
    L(Col)

3474 Sylvester Rebel
    A   Organ of the Stainforth Pit Group (near Hatfield). Communist
Party pit paper. (R. G. Neville.)

3475 Syndicalist I, 1 (Jan. 1912)–11 (Dec. 1912); then **Syndicalist and
Amalgamated News**: II, 1 (Jan. 1913)–III, 5 (Aug. 1914); m
    A   1d. 'Edited under the auspices of the Industrial Syndicalist
Education League, with purpose of popularizing syndicalist principles
among trade unionists, advocating industrial solidarity and direct action.
Aimed at strengthening trade unions, rather than the use of Parliament, to
fight class war and bring about Socialism by general strike of international
proportions.' Edited by Guy Bowman. Tom Mann was President and
Bowman, Secretary of the Industrial Syndicalist League (Brophy).
Superseded Tom Mann's **Industrial Syndicalist**.
    L(Col)

3476 Syndicalist; for Workers' Control I, 1 (1 May 1952)–I, 12 (April
1953); m
    B   2d. Published by the Anarcho-Syndicalist Committee. Printed
by Philip Sansom. Discussion on trade union politics. Criticism of the
official political parties of the Labour Movement.
    L

Syndicalist and Amalgamated News see **Syndicalist, 1912**

**3477 Syndicalist Railwayman, Advocating Syndicalism Among
Railwaymen** I, 1 (Sept. 1911)–4 (Dec. 1911); m
    A   Published by Guy Bowman. Unofficial railwaymen's journal, in
opposition to Railway Review.
    ONC (photocopy)

3478 Szociáldemokrata Népszava. [Social Democratic People's Voice] :
Official Paper of the Social Democratic Party of Hungary in Exile; s-m
    B   Reproduced from typewriting. In Hungarian.
    L(Col) 3/4 (March/April 1951), 7/8 (July/Aug. 1951)

TASS Journal see **Draughtsman**

TASS News see **Association of Engineering and Shipbuilding Draughtsmen.**
Vacancy List

3479 T-Break 1964?–. Hatfield

    A   National and Local Government Officers' Association, Hatfield
Branch.

    L 1974–

TGWU Record see **Record, 1921–1939**

3480 TSA Gazette: the Monthly Journal of the Temporary Sorters'
Association 1 (22 Nov. 1915)–6 (27 April 1916); then **Temporary Postal
Workers' Gazette**: 7 (8 June 1916)–V, 4 (Sept. 1920); m

    A   1d. Temporary Sorters' Association, then Temporary Postal
Workers' Association, later National Association of Temporary Postal
Employees. At first open to all in the London area, then extended to the
provinces. Agitates for higher wages, accident claims; open to female
workers where ' "equal pay for equal work" will be the first business'.

    L(Col)†

TUC in War-Time see **What the TUC is Doing**

3481 TUC Times 1 [1938?]–?

    A   1d. Newspaper published by the Trades Union Congress to
encourage workers to join a union. News and information on organisation
among workers and the benefits resulting therefrom. Women's page.

    O(JJ)† 1

3482 Tailor: a Weekly Trades Journal and Advertiser I, 1 (6 Oct.
1866)–(6 April 1867); then **Tailor and Cutter**: 27 (13 April 1867)–; w

    A   1d. etc. Editor: John Williamson. 'Aimed at a national
circulation among all tailors in the kingdom, and had offices in London,
Manchester, Birmingham, Glasgow and Edinburgh. Both the Amalgamated
Society and the London Association gave it their blessing and helped in its
distribution. So too did unions in Scotland and Ireland. From its inception
The Tailor played a vital part in the struggle for steady, progressive
reform.' (M. Stewart and L. Hunter, **The Needle is threaded**, Heinemann
and Newman Neame for the National Union of Tailors and Garment
Workers, 1964). In earlier years news and correspondence on strikes,
disputes, Labour issues, with political content, but later became chiefly
concerned with practical, technical matters, with occasional items of
Labour news.

    BP XXIII; L(Col†; LdP XLIV–   ; LvP LXXV–   ; MP 1871–*; ShP
LXXXIV–

Tailor and Cutter see **Tailor**

Tailor and Garment Worker, 1932– see Amalgamated Society of Tailors.
Journal

3483 Tailors' Advocate [c1845–1846]

A   Noted by **The Tailor and Cutter**, 3 Oct. 1868, that 'The Tailors' Advocate was the organ of the United Tailors Protection Society of Great Britain', Secretary and Editor: J. W. Parker. A notice in **The Apprentice and Trades Weekly Newspaper**, Dec. 1845, p. 246, states that a 'portion of the good sense of the National Association [of United Trades] was sown there, but the correspondent studiously avoided any mention of the name'; mentions land plot schemes of Leeds tailors.

3484 Tailors' Gazette: the Official Organ of the National Federation of Foremen Tailors' Societies I, 1 (Jan. 1897)–II, 12 (Dec. 1898); m

A   Gratis. A record of the proceedings of the various trade associations, mutual improvement and benefit. Edited and published by J. P. Thornton, Executive member of the Federation.

L(Col)†

3485 Tailors' Magazine: a Social and Religious Journal Conducted by an Honorary Staff of Tailors; the Organ of a Movement Begun by Miss Angelica Fraser in 1856 for the Welfare of Tailors I, 1 (1892)–? 265 (Feb. 1915). Edinburgh; London; m

C   1d. Published by the Management Committee. Editor (1892–1909): Rev. R. D. Shanks. The founder, Miss Angelica Patience Fraser (1823–1910), was moved by a reading of **Alton Locke** to engage in philanthropic work among Edinburgh tailors. Was connected with **The National Appeal**, a trade journal which developed into the **Tailor and Cutter**. Religious welfare and improvement.

L(Col)† XVIII, 205, (Jan./Feb. 1910)–265

3486 Tailor's Measure, for Unity and Action: the Paper of the Militant Rank and File Clothing Workers 1 (Jan. 1932); Leeds

A   1d. Reproduced from typewriting.

Warwick U(MRC)

3487 Tailors' Record: a Journal Devoted to the Interests of the Organised Workers in the Clothing Industry I, 1 (May 1907)–6 (Sept. 1907); m

A   1d. Published by H. Beck, Tailors' Publishing Association. A trade-union journal 'not published in opposition to the official journal of the AST but rather to assist and to amend where the other is wanting. There is sufficient room for two papers to advance the cause of the journeyman tailor.' Militant, socialist and internationalist. London based; the London Jewish branches are prominent. Exposes and campaigns against sweating, gives trade notes and international news of tailors' unions. Main contributor is M. Daly, Organising Secretary, AST, urging 100% trade union membership and the return of socialist MPs to Parliament.

L(Col)†

3488 Talking Points 9 Jan. 1948–23 July 1971; fortn

   B   Published by the Labour Party. Each number gives facts, policy statements etc. on any political points at issue.

   E; L (mislaid); LabP; O; ONC†

Tamworth Examiner see **Tamworth Miners' Examiner and Workingmen's Journal**

3489 Tamworth Miners' Examiner and Workingmen's Journal 1 (13 Sept. 1873)–19 (27 Dec. 1873); then **Tamworth Examiner and Workingmen's Journal:** 20 (Jan. 1874)–124 (15 Jan. 1876). Tamworth; w

   B   1d. Editor and publisher: William Owen, member of the Trades Union Congress Parliamentary Committee. Later published by J. P. Elliott. Published at the Co-operative Newspaper and General Steam Printing Society's Works, Hanley. Official organ of the Tamworth district of the Miners' Association, with nearly 2000 members, 'and organ of all the other recognised trade societies'. An extensive source of information on miners' Trade Unionism locally (in Staffordshire and Derbyshire) and in other areas. General Labour news, including material on iron workers, information on anti-Labour legislation. Advocated independent Labour representation.

   L(Col)†

3490 Tamworth News 1 (Oct. 1957)–? Tamworth; q?

   B   Labour Party.

   Mitcham PL 1–2 (Jan. 1958).

3491 Target: Journal of the Rank and File Busmen I, 1 (July 1967)–V, 4 (Oct. 1971); varies

   A   6d. Published for **Target** by A. D. Roberts. Edited by J. Roberts. Aims 'to carry forward the traditions and principles of **Platform**', but also to be a paper of busmen, not just for them. From Jan. 1970 sub-titled: 'The Busman's Newsletter'.

   E; ONC†

3492 Target: the Tubeman's Newsletter I, 1 (Feb. 1970)–I, 2 (April 1970); bi-m

   A

   E; LE

3493 Tarian y Gweithiwr: Cofnodydd Gwladol a Gweithfarol 1 (1875)–2062 (9 July 1914); then **Darian**: 2063 (16 July 1914)–3081 (25 Sept. 1934). Aberdare; w

   B   1d. Lib.-Lab.

   L (Col) 480 (10 April 1884)–(25 Sept. 1934*); SwU 1887, 1905, 1913

3494 Taunton Labour Monthly [194-?]. Taunton; m

   B   1d. Labour Party. (Labour Party. **Your own Journal**, 1948.)

Taurus see **NALGO News. 1949–1953**

3495 Tawe: the Quarterly Journal of the Swansea Branch of NALGO 1 (1949)–19 (1953). Swansea; q
    A   National Association of Local Government Officers, later National and Local Government Officers' Association.
    L 17 (Summer 1953)–19 (Winter 1953); SwP

3496 Tax Clerks' Journal: Organ of the Association of Tax Clerks I, 1 (Sept. 1912)–IV, 12 (Dec. 1922); then **Taxes**: the Journal of the Association of Officers of Taxes; V, 1 (Jan. 1922)–; m
    A   Later publication of the Inland Revenue Staff Federation.
    L   IV, 1921– ; NU XXXVI, 1953–XLVI, 1963; XLVIII, 1965– ; O IV, 9 (Sept. 1921)–V, 9 (Sept. 1922); ONC† Dec. 1949– ; the Federation

Taxes see **Tax Clerks' Journal**

3497 Taxette: the Organ of the Association of Temporary Women Tax Clerks I, 1 (Feb. 1920)–(June 1923); m
    A   2d. A medium of communication and expression among members. Central and area news, and some literary efforts. Editor (May 1922–Jan. 1923): Rose J. Florence.
    L(Col)†

Taxi Trader see **Green Badge Journal**

3498 Tayport Bulletin [194-?]. Tayport, Fifeshire; m
    B   2d. Labour Party. (Labour Party. **Your own Journal**, 1948.)

3499 Teacher 1 (21 June 1879)–93 (25 March 1881); w
    A   1d. Published for the proprietors by G. B. Clough. To 'plead the teacher's cause' and uphold the 'whole profession'. An educational journal not intended to compete with others already in the field. Contains lengthy School Board reports, and many advertisements. Some focus on teachers' problems, incidentally on salaries. Reports on teachers' associations, eg, National Union of Elementary Teachers, in 1879, with correspondence.
    L(Col)†

3500 Teacher: a Paper Conducted in the Interests of Schoolmasters and Schoolmistresses 1 (7 Nov. 1903)–335 (Oct. 1911); w
    A   1d. On educational and professional matters, but in June 1908 became the organ of the National Association of Head Teachers. Absorbed **The Head-Teacher**, then merged in **Woman Teacher's World**.
    AU I*–IV, VI–VII; L(Col)†; O I–IV

Teacher. 1963– see **Schoolmaster**

3501 Teachers' International: Official Organ of the Educational Workers' International [19--?] –1932. Paris
    A   English edition.
    MML† June/July/Aug. 1932 (special conference number)

3502 Teachers' International Review I, 1 (July 1935)–III, 8 (Oct. 1938). London; 5-yr
    A   6d. Editor: G. Coquist, General Secretary of the Educational Workers' International. To organise the teaching profession in a united movement 'against Economism, Fascism, and War'. Also discusses the immediate questions of the protection of salaries and standards, and ideas on educational reform.
    MML†*

3503 Teachers of the World: Bi-monthly Journal of the World Federation of Teachers' Unions (FISE), Trade Dept. of the WFTU 1 (Jan. 1952)–22/23 (Dec. 1958); bi-m; q
    A   1s. Published by WFTU Publications. News of teachers' 'struggle', and of education throughout the world. 'For the defence and progress of education, international friendship among teachers, co-operation with industrial workers, and world peace.' Thereafter published in Prague.
    E; L(Col); O; TUC

Technical Journal see Association of Teachers in Technical Institutions. **Journal**

Teddy Ashton's Christmas Annual see Bolton Trotter

3504 Teddy Ashton's Journal: a Gradely Paper for Gradely Folk 1 (22 May 1896)–(5 March 1898); then **Northern Weekly and Teddy Ashton's Journal**: 12 March 1898–13 May 1899; then **Teddy Ashton's Northern Weekly**: 20 May 1899–13 April 1907; then **Teddy Ashton's Weekly Fellowship**: 20 April 1907–1 Nov. 1907; then **Teddy Ashton's Weekly**: 8 Nov. 1907–615 29 Feb. 1908; then **Teddy Ashton's Lancashire War Journal**: ns 1 (616) (23 Oct. 1914)–16 (631) (1 May 1915). Bolton; Manchester (20 April 1907–4 Jan. 1908); Blackpool (11 Jan. 1908–29 Feb. 1908); Manchester; w
    C   ½d.; 1d. Owned and edited by C. Allen Clarke. Conscious intention not to set up the paper as an overtly political paper in opposition to existing Labour papers. Designed for amusement, 'to entertain and to teach the people'. Aimed at a working-class audience; sympathy with the 'poor, oppressed and miserable'. In favour of all movements that will remove suffering. In 1908 Clarke was calling himself an evolutionary socialist, seeing the goal in the distant future. Articles, including sketches of working conditions in Manchester industries, serial stories, children's corner, letters from readers, editorial chat.
    L(Col)† 1896–1908; MP† 1914–15

Teddy Ashton's Lancashire War Journal see Teddy Ashton's Journal

Teddy Ashton's Northern Weekly see Teddy Ashton's Journal

Teddy Ashton's Weekly see Teddy Ashton's Journal

Teddy Ashton's Weekly Fellowship see Teddy Ashton's Journal

3505 Tees and Cleveland Pioneer [19--?] —? Stockton-on-Tees; m
    B   Labour Party. (Labour and Socialist International. **The Socialist Press**, 1933.)
    Middlesbrough PL Aug. 1923

3506 Teesside and Cleveland Voice 1 (June 1969)—(Feb. 1970). Redcar; m
    B   9d. A local edition of **Voice**, published at Redcar Labour Club. For a socialist united front within the Labour Party in opposition to the Right wing. Articles by local activists as well as the features provided by **Voice**.
    L(Col)†

3507 Telecommunications Sales Superintendents' Association. Report I [1954?] —? Sheffield; m?
    A   Published for the Association.
    TUC† VIII, 1 (Jan. 1961)

3508 Telecommunications Sales Superintendents Association. Report [19--?] — . St Albans
    A
    L IX, 1 (May/June 1961)—

3509 Telegraph 1 (Sept. 1969)— ; m
    A   Created from the merger of the **Merchant Navy Journal** (Navigators and Engineer Officers' Union) and **Ships' Telegraph** (Merchant Navy and Airline Officers' Association).
    L; TUC

3510 Telegraph Chronicle and Civil Service Recorder I, 1 (17 March 1893)—564 (8 March 1914); fortn
    A   2d. Official organ of the Postal Telegraph Clerks' Association. Editor: John Gennings. News on postal and telegraphic topics for Association members and civil servants generally.
    L(Col)†; ONC 562 (10 April 1914)

3511 Telegraph Journal: a Monthly Journal for Disseminating Information Through the Postal and Telegraph Services I, 1 (1 Nov. 1889)—IV, 81 (19 April 1893); m
    A   2d.; 1d. Official organ of the Postal Telegraph Clerks' Association.
    L

3512 Telegraphist: a Monthly Journal for Postal, Telephone, and Railway Telegraph Clerks I, 1 (1 Dec. 1883)–V, 54 (1 May 1888); m

    A   2d. Printed and published for the proprietors by Charles Wyman. Edited by William Lynd. 'An organ devoted exclusively to the interests' of postal and telegraph workers and officials. Combines amusement and items of practical interest. Correspondence on grievances, eg, Sunday labour. News of the Postal Telegraph Clerks' Association. Merged in **Postal Office Gazette**.

    L(Col)

Telephone see **Maidstone Telephone and Monthly Thought Exchange**

3513 Telephone Review: Official Organ of the National Society of Telephone Employés I, 1 (March 1906)–IV, 10 (March 1910); m

    A   1d. Printed and published by The Twentieth Century Press for the Society. Conducted by V. E. Moir, General Secretary. To unite and inform telephone employees. Branch reports, practical information, correspondence.

    L(Col)†

3514 Telephonist: Official Journal of the National Guild of Telephonists 1 [c1930?]–504 (Dec. 1970). London; Croydon; m

    A   1d. etc. There was opposition to the Guild from the Union of Post Office Workers.

    L 415 (July 1963)–

3515 Temporary Clerk: an Organ for Government Temporary Clerks I, 1 (Jan. 1920); ns I, 1 (April 1920)–2 (May 1920); m

    A   3d.; 2d. Printed and published for the proprietors by C. D. Flint. Official organ of the Public Services Temporary and Unestablished Clerks' Association, membership drawn from temporary male and female clerks employed in the Foreign Office and the Passport Office. Recognised as a representative body by the Treasury and the Civil Service Arbitration Board.

    L(Col)†

Temporary Postal Workers' Gazette see **TSA Gazette**

Ten Acres and Stirchley Citizen see **Ten Acres and Stirchley Co-operative Citizen**

3516 Ten Acres and Stirchley Co-operative Citizen 1 (Nov. 1939)–31 (June 1942); then **Ten Acres and Stirchley Citizen**: ns 1 (Aug. 1947)–84 (Dec. 1954); m

    B   First series published by the Co-operative Press; second series issued by the Birmingham and District Co-operative Party.

    L(Col)

3517 Ten Hours Advocate and Journal of Literature and Art 1 (26 Sept. 1846)–38 (12 June 1847). Manchester; w

A   1d. Printed and published for Joseph Mulleneaux, Secretary to the Lancashire Central Short Time Committee, by Grant and Company. Edited by Philip Grant. Agitates for a ten-hour working day in factory employment, by peaceful persuasion. Also instructs the operative classes in the use of their leisure hours. Details the progress of the Ten-Hours' Movement.

LU†; NwP

1066 and All That see National Association of Local Government Officers. Hastings Area. Health Services Branch. **News Sheet**

3518 Test 1 (May 1927)–4 (Aug. 1927). Southampton; m

B   Southampton Independent Labour Party.

SoP 1, 4

3519 Textile Machinery Worker: Bulletin of the TMM [Textile Machinery Makers] Central Shop Stewards' Committee I, 1 (June 1951)–(March 1956). Salford; irreg?

A   1½d. Edited by Harry Ratner, a shop steward at the Barton works, and an editorial committee. Ceased when Platt's of Barton closed down in 1956.

WCML† I, 6 (Dec. 1951); Feb., Sept., Oct., 1952; Nov. 1955; March 1956

3520 Textile Picker: Organ of Dundee Textile Communist Group I, 1 (June 1925)–[1926?]. Dundee; irreg

A   ½d. Advocates one union for textile workers. Reproduced from typewriting.

MML† (Hutt papers) (2 [20 June], 3 [12 July], 1925), II, 1 (10 June 1926)

3521 Textile Record [1911?–1921?]; then General Union of Textile Workers. **Monthly Record**: [Oct. 1921?] –7 (April 1922); then National Union of Textile Workers. **Monthly Record**: 1 (June 1922)–7 (Jan. 1923); then National Union of Textile Workers. **Quarterly Record**: 1 (March 1923)–47 (March 1936); then **Our Record**: Official Organ of the National Union of Dyers, Bleachers and Textile Workers: 1 (Nov. 1936)–16 (Aug. 1940). Bradford; q; m; q

A   First printed at the Yorkshire Factory Times Office, Huddersfield, then by Worker Press, Huddersfield. First editor: Ben Turner. Sometimes entitled **Textile Workers' Record**. Early title has been quoted as: **HWD [Heavy Woollen District] Textile Record**.

LE† 1923–*, 1935–6; TUC† 16 (May 1915); Nov. 1921–Aug. 1940 (w occ. nos)

Textile Workers' Record see **Textile Record**

3522 Theatrical Employees' Journal: the Official Organ of the National Association of the Theatrical Employees I, 1 Oct. 1904–12 (Sept. 1905); m

    A   1d. Printed by The Twentieth Century Press. Published by William Johnson, General Secretary, and conducted by him. For stage-working staff: heads of departments, carpenters, daymen and nightmen, cellarmen, flymen, gasmen, electricians, of over 18 years and with no less than six months of theatre, music hall or theatrical workshop experience. To raise status and living standards. Association and stage news, fiction, features, illustrated.

    L(Col)†

Theological and Political Comet, or Free-Thinking Englishman see **Theological Comet or Free-Thinking Englishman**

3523 Theological Comet, or Free-Thinking Englishman 1 (24 July 1819)–5 (21 Aug. 1819); then **Theological and Political Comet, or Free-Thinking Englishman**: 6 (28 Aug. 1819)–17 (13 Nov. 1819); w

    B   1½d. Printed and published by Robert Shorter. First editor: Sir John Falstaff, 'infidel', radical, Paineite, anti-priestcraft. Extracts Paines's work on religion etc. Motto: 'It is shame to trust our souls in the hands of those we should be afraid to trust with our money. Come, come, venture to think for yourselves'. Changed title after Peterloo; new motto: 'The cause for which the blood of the people of Manchester hath been accidentally shed'.

    L

3524 Thermfare 1 (Dec. 1946)–146 (Dec. 1962); m

    A   Free to members. Official journal of the British Gas Staff Association, which was subsequently amalgamated with the National and Local Government Officers' Association.

    Warwick U(MRC)

3525 Theydon Bois News Letter [194-?]. Theydon Bois, Essex; m

    B   Duplicated. Labour Party. (Labour Party. **Your own Journal,** 1948.)

3526 Things: Trade Union, Labour, Co-operative–Democratic History Society 1 (April–June 1968)– . Reigate; q

    B   6d. etc. On the history of the Labour Movement, and the need and methods to collect and preserve objects of interest.

    LabP†

Third World see **Empire**

3527 This Week 1 (27 Nov. 1958)–25 (30 July 1971); w

    B   Published by the Press and Publicity Department of the Labour Party. Current comment. Latterly reproduced from typewriting.

    LabP†*; ONC IV, 32 (11 Oct. 1962)

3528 This Week: a New Left Bulletin [196-?] –? w?

    B   Published by the **New Left Review**. Reproduced from typewriting.

    ONC† Labour Party Conference issue [3 Oct. 1962?]

3529 Thorne Butty Squasher: Organ of the Thorne Pit Group (CPGB). [1930?] –? Thorne; w

    A   1d. Reproduced from typewriting. Communist

    R. Harrison, Centre for the study of Social History, University of Warwick 36, 43, 44, 52, 56

3530 Thornhill Lees Social Reformer 1 (Nov. 1899)–? Thornhill Lees, Yorkshire

    B   Published by Thornhill Lees Independent Labour Party. (**ILP News**, Dec. 1899.)

3531 Thought in and about Watford: a Quarterly Review of Local Affairs 1 (Aug./Sept. 1947)–? Watford; q

    B   Prepared for Watford Fabian Society by an Editorial Board.

    Watford PL 1

3532 3871 1964?–   . Loughton

    A   National and Local Government Officers' Association, Chigwell Branch. Reproduced from typewriting.

    L 1964–

3533 Throckley Co-operative Record [190-?] –? Manchester; m

    A   Gratis. Issued by the Educational Association, Northern Section, for Throckley District Co-operative Society. Contributed articles, eg, by Percy Redfern, sketches, reviews, and comment.

    L 137 (May 1914)–155 (Nov. 1915)

3534 Throstle [1900?–1901?]. [West Bromwich?]; m

    B   Organ of the Labour Church and Socialist Party. Editor?: Fred Hughes, West Bromwich. (**Reformers' Year Book**, 1901.)

3535 Tichborne News, and Anti-Oppression Journal: a Weekly Newspaper Advocating Fair Play for Every Man 1 (15 June 1872)–13 (7 Sept. 1872); w

    C   1d. Printed for George Gilbert by Booth and Tyson. Started, on the anniversary of the signing of Magna Carta, to support the claim of the Tichborne Claimant, but contains important coverage of Labour disputes and strikes, and shows sympathy to Labour.

    L(Col)†

3536 Tidings I, 1 (May 1950)–II, 7 (Jan. 1952). Southport

    A   National Association of Local Government Officers, Southport Branch. I, 1–4 have no title, but 'Nalgo branch magazine' appears on the cover.

    SptP (w I, 1)

3537 Tilehurst Times [193-?]. Tilehurst; m

    B   Labour Party. (Labour and Socialist International. **The Socialist Press**, 1933.)

3538 Tilehurst Times 1 (Dec. 1959)–2 (Jan. 1960). Reading; m

    B   Duplicated news sheet published by Tilehurst Ward Labour Party.

    RP

3539 Time and Space: the Workers' Chess League's Monthly 1 (Aug. 1938)–(May 1940); m

    A   2d. etc. Edited and produced by W. Quinnell and E. Potter for the Workers' Chess League. Later edited by W. Winter, then by E. Klein. 'To propagate the art of chess among the working class of Britain who, up to the present, have been excluded from any worthwhile standard of life', and therefore from chess (No. 8).

    L; O

3540 Tobacco Worker: the Official Organ of the Tobacco Workers' Union. I, 1 (April 1947)–   ; bi-m

    A   2d. etc. For all workers employed directly or indirectly in the tobacco industry. The first journal of the Union, it was originally militant and political. Articles and union news. Currently an illustrated newspaper.

    L

To the People of England see **Penny Papers for the People, Published by the Poor Man's Guardian**

3541 Toby: the East London Watch-Dog I, 1 (27 March 1886)–IV, 194 (12 Oct. 1889); w

    C   1d. Printed and published by Francis Henry Parsons, Thomas Burrell and John Thomas O'Callaghan, at their printing works. Later published by F. H. Parsons, alone, then by M. Parsons for the proprietor. '. . . of somewhat better tone and character' than **Town Talk** and **The Rag**. 'An East-End local organ . . . which, during 1886, dealt week after week with Post Office abuses. **Toby** was supposed to have some additional claim on the patronage of postal servants by its being edited by a man who had once been behind the scenes in the Post Office.' Included caricatures, and 'it was principally while the caricatures lasted to afford the amusement and excitement of guessing competitions among the sorters and letter-carriers of the General Post Office' that the paper flourished. (H. G. Swift, **A History of Postal Agitation from eighty Years ago till the Present Day**, New ed. **Book 1**, Manchester, London 1929, pp. 161–2.) No. 1 criticises the Poor Laws and those who administer them and similar officials in authority over the poor and powerless. Attacks by satire. For outdoor relief, reduction of poor rate by cutting salaries of those administering it, non-interference of Charity Organisation Society. Defends Post Office employees, 'the working classes of Government' and asks for better rewards and redress of wrongs. Reports proposals for reform of elementary education. Later in 1886 largely devoted to 'Can't think why', a series of scurrilous notes on unnamed individuals. By 1889 still in this vein, but editorials etc. are still attacking sweating, and conditions of Post Office Employees. Approbation for dockers in dock strike.

L(Col)†

3542 Tocsin: Organe Hebdomadaire 1 (6 Jan. 1893)—8 (23 Sept 1894). London; w

    B   Social Revolutionary, anarchist. Printed by International Printer, London. In French.

L(Col)† 1, 2, 8

3543 Tocsin: an Illustrated Labour and Socialist Journal 1 (April 1909)—7 (Oct. 1909). Dundee; m

    B   1d. 'Joint creation of various representatives of Labour, socialist, trade union, co-operative and kindred movements in Dundee and district . . . [and with the help of the] Women's Freedom League.' Editor: Joseph Lee. Contributors: Alex Wilkie, local Labour MP, Agnes Husband, Joseph Sime, Secretary of the Dundee and District Union of Jute and Flax Workers. News, articles, character sketches of local personalities, serial story, letters. No. 6 contains a four-page article by Sidney Webb on 'Practical remedy for unemployment'.

DnP; LE† 1, 5, 6

3544 To-Day: a Monthly Gathering of Bold Thoughts I, 1 (14 April 1883)—5 (Sept. 1883); ns I, 1 (Jan. 1884)—XI, 67 (June 1889); then b **International Review**: 1 (July 1889)—3 (Sept. 1889); m

    B   The first series does not fall strictly within our categories. Printed by the Modern Press, then by William Reeves. Editors: Ernest Belfort Bax, J, L. Joynes, Hubert Bland (from Feb. 1887), H. M. Hyndman (July—September 1889). Later sub-titled: 'The Monthly Magazine of Scientific Socialism'. No. 1 sub-titled: 'A Mid-monthly Gathering of Bold Thoughts'.

BlU a i—ii*; Co-op. Coll. 1884—8; D a i—ii IX, X—XI*; L; LE May 1883—9; LU a ii VII, 43; LabP a ii; LdP a ii II, V, IX; MP a ii I—II; O (a ii II*)

3545 Today 1 (19 Sept. 1959)—16 (7 Oct. 1959); 1 [ns] (25 Sept. 1964)—17 (14 Oct. 1964); 1 [ns] (12 March 1966)—16 (30 March 1966); 1 [ns] (1 June 1970)—15 (17 June 1970). d.

    B   Campaign publication, duplicated and published by the Labour Party, with indexes. Quick guides to facts and figures, notes on policy etc.

LabP†; Warwick UL 1959—66

3546 Together, Being the Staff Magazine of the Royal Arsenal Co-operative Society Limited 1938—?

    A   Business news.

L (w 1938)

3547 Tommy Wrott's Journal: Being Witless Efforts . . . By . . . Juvenile Journalists of the National Trade Union Club 1–2. [1932]

    A   Editors: W. Arthur Peacock and W. L. Dixon. An unofficial publication, literary, flippant. Reproduced from typewriting.

    L

3548 Tomorrow's Teacher: Student Newsletter of the National Union of Teachers 1955–   ; s-a

    A   Published by the National Union of Teachers for students in Colleges of Education. Numbering in error No. 21 follows No. 18.

    L (w 2–4, 6–8, 10); O 17–

3549 Tong Pioneer of Social Reform 1 [1901?]–? Bradford; q

    B   Free; ½d. Published by C. A. Glyde, Tong Ward, Bradford, on behalf of the Independent Labour Party. 'The journal was launched in 1901 and each issue cost the owner £2. A special election issue was published in 1904 when Glyde won the Tong Ward for the ILP against the incumbent Liberal.' (D. Hopkin, 'Local newspapers of the Independent Labour Party, 1893–1906.' Society for the Study of Labour History, **Bulletin**, 28 (Spring 1974.) Later, organ of Tong and Dudley Hill Socialist Party?

    ILP Jan., April, July 1905; Oct., Dec. 1906

3550 Top Dog 1 (1953)–? Barking

    A   National and Local Government Officers' Association, Barking Branch. Reproduced from typewriting.

    L 3 (Aug. 1953)

3551 Torch 1 (1842)–?

    B?   Editor: James Napier Bailey.

    LdP 1–4

3552 Torch: a Revolutionary Journal of Anarchist-Communism 1 ([June?] 1894)–II, 4 (18 Sept. 1895); then **Torch of Anarchy**: II, 5 (18 Oct. 1895)–II, 12 (1 June 1896). m

    B   1d. Printed and published by F. Macdonald. Lively organ of London anarchists. Contributors: Louise Michel, Malatesta, Carl Quinn, Ernest Young, A. Agresti etc. Succeeded **Commonweal**.

    L(Col)† (w 1–2); ONC 3 (Aug. 1894); Warwick UL (microfilm). [missing Vol. 1, Nos. 1–2, 4, Vol. II No. 1]

3553 Torch I, 1 (July 1912)–I, 5 (Jan. 1913). Birmingham; m

    B   1d. British Socialist Party, King's Heath Branch. 'Each of the 9 branches of the BSP in the Birmingham Federation is invited to have its own column for reports, articles, ads.' Articles, reports, correspondence.

    BP†

3554 Torch 1 (1913)–4 (1914)

    B   Anarchist Education League.

    LE (not traced in catalogue)

3555 Torch [1919] –?

    B   Local Labour Party paper for North East Kent. ('has battled on now for 2 years' **Labour Organiser**, April 1921.)

3556 Torch [1926?] –?

    A   ½d. 'Issued by the Communists in Talbots', engineering firm. Editorial signed 'The CP Group'. Militant. Cartoons. Reproduced from typewriting.

    O(JJ)† 9 (1 July 1926)

3557 Torch: Organ of the Militant Section, Frances [Colliery] Workers 1 (18 Oct. 1930)–? Buckhaven; fortn

    A   1d. Printed and published by John McArthur. Reproduced from typewriting.

    Buckhaven and Methil PL, Proudfoot Papers 4 (29 Nov. 1930)–6 (10 Jan. 1931); E 1, 3 (15 Nov. 1930 [Xerox])

3558 Torch [1939?] –VI, 18 (29 April 1944). Dublin; w

    B?

    D III, 18 (3 May 1941)–VI, 18 (29 April 1944); ILP occ. nos 1941

3559 Torch: Magazine of University Labour Club and College of Technology Labour Society, Manchester 1 (May Day 1950)–II, 2 [ie No. 3] (March 1951). Manchester; termly

    B   Published by the Labour Club. Articles on theory and analysis of the prospects facing the Labour Party. Intention also to make some contribution to undergraduate thinking 'within the community'.

    L.

Torch of Anarchy see **Torch, 1894–1895**

3560 Torpedo 1 (Jan. 1899)–? Newport, Mon. m

    B   Ceased in 1899. Editor?: T. B. Bevan. 'Treats local social questions' (**Labour Annual**, 1899, 1900).

    LE (not traced)

3561 Tote Bulletin [19--?] – ; w

    B   Merton and Morden Labour Party.

    Morden PL (23 Oct. 1967)–(18 March 1974*)

3562 Tottenham Citizen ns 1 (May 1949)–?; m

    B   Gratis. Issued by the Political Committee of the London Co-operative Society. **See also London Citizen. Tottenham Edition.**

    Haringey PL 29 (Nov. 1951)–71 (Dec. 1955*); L(Col)

3563 Tottenham Clarion 1 (Sept. 1965)–

    B   Published by Tottenham Labour Party.

    L(Col)†

3564 Totton Party News Letter [194-?]. Totton; m
    B   Labour Party. Duplicated. (Labour Party. **Your own Journal,**
1948.)

3565 Towards: a Magazine of Interest and Information for Members and
Friends 1 (March 1930)–5 (March 1932); s-a
    A   Co-operative Permanent Building Society. Illustrated business
journal and advertiser.
    L

3566 Town and Country Post 1 (Oct. 1950)–[48], [Oct.? 1961]; irreg
    B   Published by the Labour Party. Newspaper format.
    L(Col); LabP; O; ONC 14–46

3567 Town and Country Review: the Journal of Common Wealth I, 1
(Sept. 1943)–?; m
    B   6d. Published by Common Wealth. Editor: Tom Wintringham.
    L 1–4 (Dec. 1943)

3568 Town Call 1 (July 1959)–[11] (Feb. 1961). Eastbourne
    A   National and Local Government Officers' Association,
Eastbourne Branch. Reproduced from typewriting.
    L (w 4)

3569 Town Crier: Birmingham's Labour Weekly I, 1 (3 Oct. 1919)–?
1673 (27 Oct. 1951). Birmingham; w
    B   1d. etc. Organ of the Birmingham Labour Party.
    BP†; L(Col); LabP 1928–51

3570 Town Crier: the Official Organ of the Carters' Association; a Journal
Devoted to Labour and General Matters I, 1 [May?] 1903–I, 2 (June
1903). Leith; m
    A   1d. Printed for the Carters' Association by Waterston and
Johnston. Supports Labour representation. Correspondence on local trade
union and Labour matters.
    EP† 2

3571 Town Crier I, 1 [Dec. 1935?] –? Saltcoats; w
    B   Free. Printed and published by Saltcoats Independent Labour
Party.
    ILP 19 June, 3 July, 4 Sept., 20 Nov. 1936; North Ayrshire Museum
I, (4 [3 Jan.], 5 [10 Jan.], 6 [17 Jan.], 15 [20 March], 21 [1 May],
1936), VI, 41 (30 Oct. 1942)

3572 Town Crier: Magazine of the Rotherham Branch. Rotherham
    A   National Association of Local Government Officers.
Reproduced from typewriting.
    L 1951–

3573 Town Topics [193-?]. Thornaby-on-Tees, Durham; m
B   Labour Party. (Labour and Socialist International. **The Socialist Press**, 1933.)

3574 Tracer 1 (Oct. 1927)–32 (July 1935); q
A   The **Draughtsman's** 'little sister', issued as a supplement to the **Draughtsman**, (qv) and sent to all branch secretaries, and to all tracer members, chiefly woman employees in drawing and tracing offices. Written for and on behalf of tracers. Agitation for a living wage. Main contributor: Jean Fraser, Honorary Secretary, Tracers' National Sub-Committee. Then merged in the **Draughtsman**.
    L; the Union

3575 Trade Union Affairs: a Journal of Study and Criticism 1 (Winter 1960/1)–6 (Summer 1964); q; irreg
A   3s. 6d. Published by **Trade Union Affairs**, then by Union Affairs Publications. Edited by Clive Jenkins. Emphasis on matters concerning Trade-Union officers. Signed articles, documents, correspondence, reviews.
    BU; HU 1, 2, 5; LE; O; ONC†; SU; WCML† 1–5; Warwick UL

3576 Trade Union Information I, 1 (Aug. 1934)–(May 1936); m
A   1d. Published by the Trade Union Information Bureau. Included articles from the Red International of Labour Unions. Contributors: Alex Gossip, George Renshaw, W. Allan, Tom Mann, Ben Bradley etc.
    ONC† I, 1–3, 5, 7, 9–12; WCML† I, 1, 2, 8, 9, II, 6

3577 Trade Union Information I, 1 (May 1949)–   . Dublin; q
A   Irish Congress of Trade Unions.
    D; L I, 1–IX (March 1954); ONC March, April 1953; TUC; University College, Dublin, Lib.

3578 Trades Unions International of Transport, Port and Fishery Workers. **Information Bulletin** 1 (1953)–?
A   World Federation of Trade Unions.
    C; E; L

3579 Trade Union News and Tatler: Organ of All organised Workers of Ferguson Pailins, Ltd 1 (Oct. 1945)–11 (Jan. 1947). Manchester; m
A   2d. Shop stewards' paper.
    WCML†

3580 Trade Union News for Overseas: a Service of Information from the Trades Union Congress 1 [1955?] –   ; m?
A   On airmail paper.
    L 3 (2 June 1955)–   ; ONC† 126 (Jan. 1969)

3581 Trade Union News From Hungary 1 [June?] 1949—14 (Sept. 1952); bi-m
    A   Published by the Hungarian News and Information Service. Fraternal exchanges.
    TUC† 2 (Aug. 1949)—14

3582 Trade Union Propaganda and Cultural Work: Bulletin of the Agitprop Department of the RILU 1 (Oct. 1928)—14 (Nov. 1929). [Moscow]; m
    A   To assist comrades in the Red International of Labour Unions in political-cultural-educational work, eg, in the use of the media, factory papers, radio, sport. Describes work of consultation schools, and trade union schools. Reproduced from typewriting.
    L (w 10, 11); LE; MML† 1, 3

3583 Trade Union Searchlight I, 1 (Jan. 1940)—? Belfast; m?
    A   2d. Published by the Committee of the **Trade Union Searchlight**, and printed for them by R. Carswell and Son. A forum for Ulster workers of different trades and crafts, by a group of active trade unionists. Not intended to be in opposition to official trade-union journals, but to further the interests of the entire movement. 'Progressive'; 'Against bureaucracy in industry and trade unionism'. Short articles, news, women's column. None of the contributions are signed.
    ONC† 1

3584 Trade Union Unity: a Monthly Magazine of International Trade Unionism I, 1 (April 1925)—II, 6 (Aug. 1926); m
    A   2d. Published by the Editorial Board. Founded by Albert Purcell, member of the General Council of the Trades Union Congress. Editorial Board: A. A. Purcell, Edo Fimmen, George Hicks. Contributors: A. B. Swales, W. T. Kelly, Arthur Pugh, John Marchbank, John Turner, Herbert Smith etc., as well as members of the Board.
    C; L; LE I*—II, 5; O; ONC*; WCML†; Warwick UL

3585 Trade Union Worker 1 (Jan. 1916)—25 (April 1918); m
    A   1d. Organ of the Workers' Union. 'Our Special object, in a humble way, is to champion the cause of the woman worker, the labourer, and the semi-skilled worker.' Only one issue in 1918.
    L(Col); ONC† (microfilm)

3586 Trade Union World: Joint Journal of the IFTU and ITS [I], 1 (Jan. 1943)—III, 11/12 (Dec. 1945); m
    A   1s.; 1s. 6d. International Federation of Trade Unions and the International Trade Secretariats. Printed by Victoria House Printing Company for the IFTU. Extensive reports on the international trade union movement and Labour.
    L; ONC II, 5 (May 1944)—III, 7/8 (July/Aug. 1945*)

3587 Trade Unionist: a Journal Devoted to the Interests of the Working Classes I, 1 (25 Sept. 1875)–6 (30 Oct. 1875). Manchester; w

    B   1d. Printed and published for the 'Trade Unionist' Company by William Heap. Edited by Lloyd Jones. Supports principles and practice of Trade Unionism and co-operation. Reports strikes and wages movements, cases under the labour laws etc.

    LU†

3588 Trade Unionist, incorporating the Dockers' Record: a Weekly Record of the Progress of Unionism Among Workmen 1 (4 April 1891)–21 (22 Aug. 1891); then **Trade Unionist and Trades Council Record**: ns 1 (29 Aug. 1891)–30 (19 March 1892); w

    A   1d. Printed and published for the proprietors by Gree, McAllan and Fielden, Ltd., then by the Newspaper Distributing Agency. Edited by Tom Mann. To serve 'trade unionists of all grades and trades'. Very extensive coverage of union news in different industries, especially engineering, throughout the country. Follows Labour questions in Parliament, eg, for legislation for an eight-hour day,and for Labour representation. Trade union contributors from various unions. The new series contains more extensive correspondence, and runs articles in series. Merged with **Workman's Times**.

    GM i; L(Col); LE (poor condition especially 1892); LU ii 30; TUC, John Burns Lib.; Warwick UL (microfilm)

3589 Trade Unionist I, 1 (Oct. 1898)–I, 13 (Oct. 1899); m

    A   3d. Published by The Ideal Publishing Union, Ltd. Edited by Fred Maddison, MP to be a 'high-class trade union magazine' to 'represent the spirit and general advantages of trade unionism with moderation and fairness'. Supported by leaders of craft unions. Excluded party politics, but deplored the socialist influence in the TUC. Had an advisory committee elected in the Congress of 1898. Each issue features a portrait article on a trade union leader. Covers women's Trade Unionism.

    E 1; GM: L(Col)†; LE

3590 Trade Unionist I, 1 (Nov. 1915)–I, 13 (Nov. 1916); m

    A   1d. Published by Edward Loucestre Pratt. Against war, conscription, for the defence of trade union rights. Advocates policies of industrial Unionism. Opposes the 'class collaborationist' official Labour and trade union leadership. Contributors: Tom Mann, W. F. Watson, Jack Tanner, W. McLaine, J. Simpson.

    L(Col)†

3591 Trade Unionist 1 (5 Jan. 1926)–14 (5 April 1926); w

    A   1d. 'An independent weekly paper devoted to the trade union movement', and 'offers open forum for discussion between the rank and file and the officials' etc. To publicise and carry out Trades Union Congress decisions. Conducted by Richard Coppock, Jack Tanner, Fred G. Witcher, W. H. Mainwaring, W. T. A. Foot, and V. Brodsky. Inspired by the National Minority Movement.

    L(Col)† 1–12; ONC

3592 Trade Unionist: Monthly Organ of the National Trade Union Club I, 1 (Sept. 1935)–III, 4 (Dec. 1937); m

    A   Editor: W. Arthur Peacock. The Club aimed at developing social and recreational facilities for trade unionists; Chairman: Ben Tillett. The journal includes some biographical material.

    L; ONC 8 (April 1936)

Trade Unionist and Trades Council Record see **Trade Unionist, 1891**

3593 Trader: Journal of the Board of Trade Section. [19--?] –?; bi-m?

    A   Civil and Public Services Association.

    Warwick U (MRC)† Dec. 1963/Jan. 1964

3594 Trades' Advocate and Herald of Progress: Established by the Iron Trades 1 (29 June 1850)–20 (9 Nov. 1850). Manchester; London; w

    A   Published by Abel Heywood, Manchester, and James Watson, London.

    LU 3–4; MP† (w 1–3)

Trades Advocate or Scottish Trade Union Gazette see **Scottish Trades Union Gazette**

Trades and Labour Gazette see **London Trades and Labour Gazette**

3595 Trades Chronicle 1 (4 Feb. 1854)–4 (25 Feb. 1854); w

    A   4d. Published by Thomas Cannon. Printed by Samuel Taylor. An ambitious general newspaper, which focuses on the relations between Capital and Labour. Labour news from the provinces, report of proceedings of the Committee of Metropolitan Trades, and of the Labour Conference called by the Council of the Society of Arts.

    L(Col)†

3596 Trades' Examiner, or, Political and Literary Review 1 (17 Nov. 1832)–2 (1 Dec. 1832). Edinburgh; fortn?

    B   1½d. Printed and published for the proprietors by Henry Munro. 'Conducted by Benjamin Truesteel, Esq.'. . . 'being intended to advocate the interests of the Working Classes against all opposing parties.' For the repeal of taxes on knowledge, and the vote. For peaceful agitation among Edinburgh tradesmen.

    E; L

Trades Free Press see **Trades Newspaper and Mechanics' Weekly Journal**

3597 Trades' Journal: the Organ of the United Trades' Association I, 1 (4 July 1840)–12 (15 Sept. 1841). Manchester; m

    A   Publisher: Abel Heywood; Thomas Cheld for the Friendly United Smiths of Great Britain and Ireland (1–4). Editor: Alexander Hutchinson.

    MP†

3598 Trades' Newspaper and Mechanics' Weekly Journal 1 (17 July 1825)–106 (22 July 1827); then **Trades Free Press**: 107 (29 July 1827)–163 (16 Aug. 1828); then **Weekly Free Press**: 164 (23 Aug. 1828)–299 (2 April 1831); w

    A   Founded by representatives of the London and provincial trades 'who had assembled in London to watch the progress of the late Inquiry into the Combination Laws' (No. 2): 'That the Trades might have a vehicle of their own'. Committee of Management of eleven members, headed by the prominent Shipwrights' union leader, John Gast. Maintained on a joint Stock basis, shares alone held by Trades Societies of Journeymen at £5 each. Later, edited by William Carpenter.

    L(Col)†

3599 Trades' Paper [1834?]. Aberdeen

    B   'The Trades' Paper is spoken of in **The Aberdeen Shaver** (September 1834) as a paper on Radical principles about to be started in Aberdeen. Was it ever started, or did the **Shaver**'s remarks nip it in the bud?' (J. M. Bullock. 'A bibliography of local periodical literature'. **Scottish Notes and Queries**, I.)

3600 Trades' Sentinel and Workman's Guide Post (14 April 1847)–? Sheffield

    A   1½d. 'An address to the Trades of Sheffield, by a committee appointed by a meeting of Trades' Delegates, assembled . . . on . . . April 9th, 1847.' Printed and sold at the Independent Office,and by all Trades' Committees

    SP 14 April 1847

Trades Union Congress and Labour Party. **Notes for Speakers** see Labour Party and Trades Union Congress. **Notes for Speakers**

3601 Trades Unions' Magazine and Precursor of a People's Newspaper, Devoted to the Advocacy of Peaceful Combination Among the Operative Classes for the Purpose of Improving Their Social, Intellectual and Moral Condition 1 (23 Nov. 1850)–19 (10 May 1851). Salford; fortn; w

    B   1d. Printed and published by Abel Heywood, and by John Sherratt, printer, Pendleton. Edited by Rev. Thomas G. Lee, New Windsor Chapel, Salford, a Congregational pastor; 'advocate of Labour's rights'; supports and chronicles the activities of workers' co-operatives in the Manchester/Pendleton area. Recommends associative labour in place of strikes. Reports the Pendleton weavers' strike of 1851.

    HU (Photocopy); LU (w 19); Salford PL; WCML† (photocopy)

3602 Trades Weekly Messenger 1 (20 May 1848)–?; w

    A   1d. Published by Arthur Stereke, Secretary of the Committee of Metropolitan Trades, whose organ the paper was. Printed by William Stevens. 'An organ of Progress, vindicating the Claims of Labour, without assailing the rights of Property.' Supports universal suffrage. Articles on economics, and the history of labour legislation.

    LU 1–3, 5, 7–13 (1848)

3603 Tradesman: a Glasgow Weekly Journal. 1 (28 Dec. 1833)–(31 May 1834). Glasgow; w

A   1½d. Published, printed and edited by Alexander Campbell, successor to the **Scottish Trades Union Gazette**. 'A working-class newspaper that agitates on behalf of the trades unions and co-operative movements, and for the repeal of the union with Ireland' (Wiener). Reports Glasgow strikes (No. 6).

GM† 16; Harvard UL 1–20

3604 Tradition: a Quarterly Journal of Interest to Co-operators, Trade Unionists and Social Reformers I, 1 (Aug. 1934)–V, 3 (Dec. 1939). London; Manchester; Newcastle; q

A   6d. Published by the Co-operative Printing Society. House journal of the Co-operative Printing Society. Illustrated, articles, some by life-long co-operators, with historical value.

L

3605 Train [c1867]

A   Engine Drivers' and Firemen's United Society. Started by Edwards, J. Thompson and J. O. Putley. Short-lived (G. W. Alcock, **Fifty years of Railway Trade Unionism**, Co-operative Printing Society 1922, p. 29).

3606 Train: a Journal for the Railway World, and for All Who Use Railways – Travellers, Traders, Tourists, Excursionists etc. 1 (4 April 1884)–(27 Jan. 1886); w; fortn; m

B   1d. Started by F. W. Evans after he had vacated the Secretaryship of the Amalgamated Society of Railway Servants, but still supported the cause of the railway workers. The result of Evans's protecting his copyright against Harford's **Mail Train** was a complexity of dating and numbering. Later has infrequent news of railway servants. See Alcock for further details of early history (G. W. Alcock, **Fifty Years of Railway Trade Unionism**, Co-operative Printing Society 1922, pp. 264–5).

L(Col)†

3607 Tram and Bus Gazette: the Official Organ of the General Tram and Bus Workers' Union. 1 (28 Sept. 1899)–10 (8 Dec. 1899); w

A   ½d. Printed and published for the proprietor by S. C. Slade and Company. Covers agitation by London County Council bus and tram employees. Airs drivers' grievances, upholds Trade Unionism. Also provides instruction and amusement.

L(Col)†

3608 Tramway and Vehicle Worker 1 (Nov. 1905)–20 (31 March 1906). Salford; w

A   Organ of the Amalgamated Association of Tramway and Vehicle Workers. Editor?: George T. Jackson.

Transport and General Workers' Union 1905

3609 Tramwayman I, 1 (Jan. 1909)–VI, 3 (July 1914). Leeds; q

A   Organ of Leeds City Tramway Employees' Social and Athletic Society. Covers social and sports activities, and sick benefit.

LdP† (w VI, 1, 2)

Transport and General Workers' Record see **Record. 1921–1939**

Transport Salaried Staff Journal see **Railway Clerk**

Transport Topics and Accident Review see **Control**

3610 Transport Worker I, 1 (Aug. 1911)–I, 8 (March 1912). Liverpool; m

B   1d. Published and edited by Tom Mann. To organise the different trades in Liverpool and District into the National Transport Workers' Federation. For direct action and industrial Unionism. Organ of the transport workers' strikes in 1911 in Liverpool. Later agitates for an eight-hour day. Contributions by leading militants. 'Circulation 20,000'.

L(Col)†

3611 Transport Workers Link the World I, 1 (Jan. 1940)–V, 1/2 (Jan./Feb. 1944); then **International Transport Workers' Journal**: V, 3/4 (March/April 1944)–? Kempston; Bedford; London; m

A   Published by the International Transport Workers Federation, 'to keep transport workers conversant with the life and struggles of their fellow workers all over the world, so as to maintain and strengthen their international spirit.'

L I, 1–VI, 9/12 (Sept./Dec. 1945); ONC† II, 8–12, (Aug.–Dec. 1941)–XIV, 6 (June/July 1954*); Warwick U (MRC)*

3612 Transport Workers of the World: Quarterly Review of the Trade Unions International of Transport, Port and Fishery Workers 1 (Jan.–March 1958)–   . London; Prague; q

A   Published by WFTU [World Federation of Trade Unions] Publications, Ltd. Illustrated chronicle of the life and struggle of transport, port and fishery workers, internationally.

L; O 1958–70*

3613 Transporter: the Paper for All LPTB Workers 1 ([April?] 1940)–20 (Feb./March 1942); m

A   Published by the Transporter Publishing Company (J. Brent). For employees of the London Passenger Transport Board. Dealt with problems and issues concerning the various sections of London transport workers, and those in the Transport and General Workers' Union.

MML† 2 (May 1940), 4–7, 20; WCML† 15 (Sept. 1941)–20

3614 Travel Log: an Occasional News Sheet Issued by the Workers' Travel Association 1 (24 July 1926)–   ; w (1–3); q

    A   Published by the Association, a Friendly Society founded and directed by activists in the workers' movement to provide cheaper holidays abroad and promote international contacts in the interests of peace. Records travel excursions. From 1967 published by Galleon World Travel Association.

    L; O XVI, 1948–

3615 Traveller 1946–?; m

    A   3d. (1955). Union of Post Office Workers. (Mitchell, 1955.)
    CoU 2–

3616 Travelling On: Quarterly Journal of the National Union of Commercial Travellers, Representing the Interests of the Man on the Road 1 (Autumn 1961)–12 (Spring/Summer 1966); q

    A   Published by the Union. Editor: John Horrocks. Covers professional matters, Union and Labour affairs in own sphere of employment and in other industries, and generally.

    E; L; O 2 (Winter 1962)–12

3617 Tredegar Co-operative Citizen 1 (Jan. 1934)–? Tredegar

    B
    L(Col) 1

3618 Tribunal. 1 (8 March, 1916)–182 (8 Jan. 1920); w

    B   ½d. etc. Published by the No-Conscription Fellowship (set up by the Independent Labour Party). Printed by the National Labour Press. Chairman of the Fellowship: Clifford Allen; Honorary Secretary: Fenner Brockway. Edited by W. J. Chamberlain, then by B. J. Boothroyd during the former's imprisonment. 'The object of the **Tribunal** will be to acquaint our members and the general public with those facts concerning the Military Service Act which receive scant attention from the daily press just because they provide the gravest indictment of that Act.' Smaller for a time in 1918–19 when printed by Joan Beauchamp 'on our secret press' (153), then when no longer underground (24 April 1919–   ), printed by Headley Bros.

    BP*; BS 2–165*; C; L(Col)† (No. 145 Xerox); LE 1916–19*; LFS; LU 1–138; O 1916–19; Warwick UL (microfilm)

3619 Tribunal: Monthly Organ of the Fellowship of Conscientious Objectors 1940–3; m

    B   Includes cases of objection by pacifists and socialists.
    L

3620 Tribune I, 1 (14 March 1795)–III, 50 [22 April?, 1796] ; w

    B   3d.? 'Consisting chiefly of the political lectures of J. Thelwall' (cover of Vol. I). To 'communicate among the oppressed and industrious orders of society'. Printed for the author. Consists of public lectures on democratic politics, revised by Thelwall for publication.

    C I; L; LGU 1–7, 18–25; O I, 5–III, 50

3621 Tribune: Labour's Independent Weekly. I, 1 (1 Jan. 1937)–   ;
fortn; w

B   Editors include George Orwell, Michael Foot, Richard Clements.
BP 1947–   ; C; E; L(Col); LII (29 May 1942)–   ; LabP; ONC (19
Aug. 1949)–(4 Feb. 1955) (w 13 Feb. 1953)

3622 Tribune: the Magazine of the Trent River Board Branch of NALGO.
1960?–   . Nottingham

A   National and Local Government Officers' Association.
Reproduced from typewriting.
     L 1960–

3623 Tribune Libre: Organe International, Socialiste-
Révolutionnaire-Anarchiste I, 1 (15 Nov. 1890)–I, 4 (March 1891).
London; m

B   10 cents. Printed by J. Olivon. French anarchist propaganda
journal. Discussion of situation in France. In French.
     L 1–2; L(Col) 1

3624 Tribune of the People 1 (17 June 1832)–3 (1 July 1832); w

B   2d. Published and edited by William Benbow. Printed by
Richard E. Lee. 'A radical miscellany that advocated a general strike to
enforce democratic political demands.' (See N. Carpenter. "William
Benbow and the origin of the General Strike". **Quarterly Journal of
Economics**, XXXV, 1920–1, pp. 491–9; and R. E. Lee. **Victimization, or
Benbowism unmasked, addressed to the National Union of the Working
Classes.** R. E. Lee, 1832.)' (Wiener).
     L (destroyed)

Trotter see **Bolton Trotter**

'Trotter' Christmas Annual see **Bolton Trotter**

3625 True Scotsman 1 (28 Oct. 1838)–128 (27 March 1841); 1842–3.
Edinburgh; w

B   Printed and published by John Fraser. An organ of 'moral force'
Chartism and temperance.
     GM (microfilm of holdings in Paisley PL); L(Col) (microfilm of
holdings in Paisley PL; Paisley PL† 1838–41 (w 8, 96–8, 119)

3626 True Sun 1 (5 March 1832)–ns 442 (23 Dec. 1837); d

B   7d. Stamped. Proprietor: Patrick Grant. Printed and published
for him by John Ager. A daily evening paper with political/radical content.
Extensive coverage of Political Union agitation, and covers meetings of the
National Union of the Working Classes. Later agitates for an unstamped
press, and includes snippets of radical/political news and trade union news
taken from provincial papers.
     L(Col)†

3627 Trumpet: a Monthly News Letter I (1958)– . Boston,
Lincolnshire; m
    A   National and Local Government Officers' Association, Boston
Borough Branch. Reproduced from typewriting.
    L

Trumpet of Wales see **Udgorn Cymru**

3628 Truth! 1 (22 Aug. 1832)–2 (29 Aug. 1832); w
    B   1d. Published by William Strange. Printed by Henry
Hetherington. 'A political miscellany that attacks factory and judicial
abuses, capital punishment,and moderate reformers' (Wiener).
    O 1

3629 Truth: a Weekly Radical Christian and Family Newspaper I, 1 (10
Feb. 1833)–5 (10 March 1833); w
    C   7d. Published by William Oliver. Printed by C. Ellott. '. . . our
principles are most decidedly liberal, radical and Christian.' A
parliamentary and political review from the independent Liberal
standpoint. Sympathises with the grievances of the labouring population.
Advocates the removal of 'taxes on knowledge' and legislation against
child factory work.
    L(Col)†; O 1

3630 Tudorose: Journal of the Westminster Branch of NALGO I, 1 (Dec.
1956)– .
    A   National and Local Government Officers' Association.
    L

3631 Twickenham Citizen [c1935–40] ; m
    B   Gratis. Published by the London Co-operative Society (Mitchell,
1935, 1940).

3632 Twickenham Clarion [194-?] – ; m
    B   Local Labour Party paper.
    L(Col) 199 (Sept. 1959)– ; LabP 1965–70*

3633 Twisthand [190-?] –?
    A   Published by the Lace Makers' Society, 'for a short period
around the turn of the nineteenth century'. There is reference to the issue
of Jan. 1906. (N. H. Cuthbert, **The Lace Makers' Society**. Nottingham;
Amalgamated Society of Operative Lace Makers and Auxiliary Workers,
1960. P. 114.)

Twopenny Trash see **Cobbett's Penny Trash**

3634 Typist: Britain's Brightest Office Magazine I, 1 (Dec. 1939)–I, 4 (1 March 1940). Ilfracombe; m

B   3d. Managing Director: J. Radford-Evans. Articles describing the work and interests of office workers. Urges the formation of a National Union of Typists.

L

3635 Typographical Circular: a Journal Devoted to the Interests of the Printing Profession 1 (1 April 1854)–55 (22 Sept. 1858); then b **London Press Journal and General Trades Advocate**: 1 (1858)–4 (1859); m

A   1d. Published by George Berger and Messrs. Piper. Printed by Samuel Whitwell. Conducted by the London Society of Compositors. Reports LSC meetings, trade news, provincial intelligence. Correspondence, discussion on strikes, trade unions, 'free' press (ie unstamped).

LSF† (b mislaid)

Typographical Circular, 1877–1963 see **Typographical Societies' Monthly Circular**

3636 Typographical Gazette 1 (April 1846)–16 (May 1847); m

A   2d. Published by William Strange. Concerned with wages disputes. Promotes the newly-formed National Typographical Association. Extensive correspondence and news on working conditions and disputes.

LSF†

3637 Typographical Protection Circular 1 (Jan. 1849)–59 (Nov. 1853); m

A   1d. Printed and published by John Catchpool, later edited . printed and published by James Luke Hansard. Contains reports of the Typographical Association, London and provincial branches, and correspondence. Support for 'wages increases and modification of the scale'.

LSF; O 1–36 (not traced in Cat.)

3638 Typographical Societies' Monthly Circular 1 (1852)–273 (June 1875); then **Provincial Typographical Circular**: 274 (July 1875)–297 (June 1877); then **Typographical Circular**: 298 (July 1877)–1132 (Nov./Dec. 1963). Manchester; m

A   Provincial Typographical Association, then Typographical Association. Towards the end of the 19th Century contents were extended to include topics of general working-class interest, particularly Labour legislation, eight-hour day, workmen's compensation, housing, pensions, Labour representation. The Typographical Association amalgamated with the London Typographical Society in Jan. 1964 to form the National Graphical Association, whose organ was **Graphical Journal**.

L 151–239; L(Col)† 269 (Feb. 1875)–1132 (w 1883, 1994); LE*; LSF 265, 290– ; ONC Nov. 1949– ; Warwick UL Oct. 1952–; Warwick U (MRC) 1, (1852–9), 1861–75; then 1877–1963; then 1964–7

3639 UDC I, 1 (Nov. 1915)–IV, 8 (June 1919); then b **Foreign Affairs: a Journal of International Understanding**: Official Organ of the Union of Democratic Control I, 1 (July 1919)–XIII, 7 (April 1931); m

   B   1d. Etc. Published by the Union of Democratic Control. Printed by the National Labour Press. Articles on international affairs, foreign policy, activities of the UDC; book reviews. Emphasis on the need for the people to know what is happening, against secret diplomacy, for negotiation. Sees an opportunity for Labour to further these aims. Contributors: Charles Roden Buxton, E. D. Morel, F. W. Pethick Lawrence, Charles Trevelyan, H. N. Brailsford. **Foreign Affairs** has pages for Labour, and special contributions from leading Labour and trade union figures. Edited by Norman Angell.

   C b; CPE b I–CIII; L; LE b; LU a; MP a, b I–II; O b II, 12–XIII; ONC† a; SwU b

3640 ULF Pamphlet [19--?–1946?]. Cambridge
   B   University Labour Federation.
   C 6 (1941)–16 (1946); L 7–

3641 URS Opinion: the Official Organ of the Union of Railway Signalmen [19--?]–? Brierfield, Lancashire; m
   A   3d. (1955).
   TUC 4 nos. between April 1947 and July 1951 (not traced on shelf)

3642 Udgorn Cymru [Trumpet of Wales] 1 (March 1840)–40 (22 Oct. 1842). Merthyr Tydfil; fortn
   B   3d. Printed by and for David John, junior, and Morgan Williams. Chartist. In Welsh, with some contributions in English.
   L(Col)† (27 [9 April], 40 [22 Oct.] 1842)

3643 Ulidian I, 1 (Michaelmas 1950)–? Belfast; termly?
   B   6d. Published by Queen's University Labour Group; 'to be devoted to the discussion of current problems in politics and literature affecting the people of Northern Ireland'. General Editor: David Bleakley. Articles, reviews, short story.
   BlU; LabP† I, 1

3644 Una Voce: the Journal of the English Chiropodists Association I, 1 (May/June 1967)– . [Cambridge?] ; bi-m
   A   15s. per annum etc.
   The Association?

3645 Undeb: Journal of the National Union of Teachers of Wales. 1 (1948)–13 (1950); 1953–4
   A
   CrU; SwP 4–8

3646 Under the Clock I, 1 (Feb. 1937)—III, 9 (July 1939). Southport; irreg
    A   National Association of Local Government Officers, Southport Branch.
    SptP

Under the Dome see Civial Service Clerical Association. British Museum Branch. **Bulletin**

Understudy see **No Name**

3647 Unemployed Demonstrator 1 (4 Aug. 1933)—3 (2 Sept. 1933). Lochgelly, Fifeshire; fortn
    A   1d. Issued by West Fife District Council of the National Unemployed Workers' Movement. Reproduced from typewriting.
    MML†

3648 Unemployed Drama News Introductory issue. 1936
    C   1d. Published by Kathleen Edwards for the Unemployed Drama Group. A projected experiment for the unemployed 'discovering the use of leisure' by making plays.
    L

Unemployed Leader see **Unemployed Special**

3649 Unemployed News 1 (3 Dec. 1928)—2 (17 Dec. 1928); fortn
    A   1d. Published by the NAC, National Unemployed Workers' Committee Movement. Contributors: Wal Hannington, National Organiser, Tom Mann. Records activities of branches in the rest of the country. To stimulate militant action by unemployed workers. Preparation for National March to London.
    L(Col)†

3650 Unemployed News 1939
    A   Single sheet reproduced from typewriting, issued by 'the Footscray Branch of the CUC'. Apparently intended to be on-going. Joint Campaigns on housing and unemployment issues.
    MML† 16 June 1939.

3651 Unemployed Special: Official Organ of the National Unemployed Workers' Movement. 1 (July 1932)—5 (27 Oct. 1932). then **Unemployed Leader**: 6 (Nov. 1932)—III, 19 (Nov. 1935); m; fortn; m
    A   1d. Published by the NUWM. Printed by the Utopia Press. Contributors: Wal Hannington, Harry Pollitt, Sid Elias, Harry McShane.
    L(Col)†; ONC 4 (Oct. 1932).

3652 Unemployed Worker 1 (24 Nov. 1923)—2 (8 Dec. 1923); fortn

A   1d. Published by the National Administrative Council of Unemployed, National Unemployed Workers' Committee Movement. Campaigns with the Labour and Trade Union Movement for 'Work or Full Maintenance' for unemployed workers. Campaigns also for a united front to secure the return of a socialist Labour government at the forthcoming election. Incorporates **Out of Work**.

L(Col)†

3653 Unemployed Worker 1 (25 June 1925)—?

A   Free. Paper of the unemployed workers of St Pancras; 'started as a local news sheet, to which the unemployed men and women of St Pancras can send an account of their troubles', and as an organiser. Urges readers to join the National Unemployed Workers' Committee Movement. Reproduced from typewriting.

O(JJ)† 1

3654 Unemployed Worker: Official Supplement of the NUWCM (4 Oct. 1929)—(5 Feb. 1933); w

A   Issued as one page in **The Worker** (qv), for the National Unemployed Workers' Committee Movement, later National Unemployed Workers' Movement (NUWM). From 4 July 1931 the description 'Supplement' was dropped but the page continued to be devoted to news of the unemployed movement.

3655 Unemployment Research and Advice Bureau. Bulletin 1 (7 March 1938)—80 (May 1942); w

A   The Bureau was originally the Legal Department of the National Unemployed Workers Movement. Issued to affiliated organisations. Stated the law as regards unemployment benefit, with current reports on cases. Reproduced from typewriting.

L

3656 Unemployment Research and Advice Bureau. Notes and Information 1 (8 Feb. 1939)—2 (10 March 1939); m

A   Information and statistics. Reproduced from typewriting.

L

3657 Unemployment Research and Advice Bureau. Report. March—Sept. 1938

A   A report of cases over the six-month period. Reproduced from typewriting.

L

3658 Unicorn I [1955?]— . Bristol; m?

A   National and Local Government Officers' Association, Bristol and District Branch. Reproduced from typewriting.

L IV, 5 (May 1958)—

3659 Union 1 (26 Nov. 1831)–10 (28 Jan. 1832); w
    B   2d. Printed and published by John Smith [ie Richard Carlile].
'It functions as the organ of communication for various political unions by
printing accounts of their meetings and related information. Advocates
parliamentary reform and urges a union between working-class and
middle-class reformers' (Wiener). Reports meetings of the National Union
of Working Classes at the Rotunda.
    LRO 1, 3–10; LU; NwP 1–2; O 1; ONC 2, 4, 6–7

3660 Union: a Monthly Record of Moral, Social, and Educational Progress
1 (1 April 1842)–10 (1 Jan. 1843); m
    B   Edited by G. A. Fleming. Theoretical, rationalist, anti-political
economy.
    BP; Co-op. Coll.; L 1; LE; LU†; MP; Warwick UL (microfiche);
Greenwood reprint and microfiche: microfiche distributed in Britain and
Europe by the Harvester Press Ltd

3661 Union and Higher Education 1 (1924)–22 (1935); then b **Higher
Education Report**: (Dec. 1936)–?; irreg?
    A   Published by the National Union of Teachers for members
serving in higher education institutions.
    L   a 2–8, 10–18, 21–2, b Dec. 1936–Dec. 1938

3662 Union Démocratique 1 (Jan. 1872)–249 (3 Oct. 1872). London; d
    B
    L(Col) 83 (25 March 1872)–249

3663 Union Exchange Gazette 1829
    A   2d. Published by the Union Exchange Society, which was
founded by W. King. (H. S. Foxwell, 'Bibliography of the English Socialist
School' in A. Menger, **The Right to the Whole Produce of Labour** 1899,
Appendix II.)

3664 Union Magazine: the Official Organ of the National Union of Ships'
Stewards, Cooks, Butchers and Bakers I, 1 (July 1909)–II, 10 (April
1911); then **Marine Caterer**: ns I, 1 (May 1911)–XII, 6 (Dec. 1921); then
b **Marine Worker**. I, 1 (Feb. 1922)–V, [6?] (June 1926). Liverpool; m
    A   1d. Published by the Union. Early editor: Frank Pearce.
Militant; gives support to the idea of industrial Unionism (1911). Opposed
to Havelock Wilson (1921); the record of an expanding Union. From
February 1922 the organ of the Amalgamated Marine Workers' Union.
    L(Col)† a; LE b I–IV (IV*); TUC*

3665 Union News I (1958)–?
    A   Joint Shop Stewards, Armstrong Siddeley, Ltd.
    Warwick U(MRC) I, 1–3 (1958)

3666 Union Observer I, 1 (Jan. 1895)–XI, 12 (Dec. 1905); then **Civil Service Observer**: XII, 1 (Jan. 1906)–XXV, 5 (Sept./Oct. 1919); m

    C   1d. Published by V. P. Peacock. Junior Civil Service Prayer Union.

    L

Union of Construction, Allied Trades and Technicians **Journal** see Amalgamated Society of Woodworkers **Monthly Journal**

3667 Union of German Socialist Organisations in Great Britain. **News Letter** 1 (May 1941)–2 (Aug. 1941)

    B   Published by the Union which consisted of the Executive of the German Social-Democratic Party, the Committee of the Socialist Labour Party in Great Britain, the Executive of the International Union of Militant Socialists, and the Overseas Bureau. Brief news from Germany and other occupied areas. Reproduced from typewriting.

    L

3668 Union of Post Office Workers. Edinburgh and District. **Branch Notes** [19--?] –? Edinburgh; m?

    A
    TUC May 1924

3669 Union of Post Office Workers. London Central Branch. **Bulletin** [19--?] –?

    A   (W. Dunlop, 'Local journals'. **Belpost**, IV, 5 [May 1965].)

3670 Union of Post Office Workers. **South West District News-Sheet** [19--?] –July 1949

    A   'Started by Bob Bishop'. (**Mets Journal**, XXI, 3 [May 1950].)

3671 Union Pilot, and Co-operative Intelligencer I, 1 (14 Jan. 1832?)–17 (5 May 1832). Manchester; w

    B   2d.? (1–8); 1d. (9–17). Published and printed by H. N. Bullock for the Manchester operatives. 'It agitates for such factory legislation as Sadler's ten-hours' bill, and prints extensive accounts of trades union and co-operative activities in Lancashire' (Wiener).

    MP† 9 (March 10–17)

3672 Union Unity: the Paper of the Battersea Red Trade Unionists [192-?] –?

    A   Minority Movement. News of activities in local union branches. Reproduced from typewriting.

    O(JJ)† Oct. [1925]

3673 Union Voice: a Socialist Voice for Peace and Prosperity Feb.
1963—Oct. 1963; then **Voice of the Unions, for Peace and Socialism,
Comprising 'Labour's Voice' and 'Union Voice'**: Nov. 1963—   ; m
    B 6d. Published by the Workers' Northern Publishing Society.
February 1963 published in Beckenham. 'A new monthly paper to
campaign for the immediate return of a Labour Government,
implementation of Clause 4, world peace and socialism.' It 'will speak for
all those in the trade unions and the Labour Party who are storming the
citadels of capital and are actively changing society.' Supports industrial
democracy. Contributors include: Ken Coates, Walter Kendall, A.
Greenwood, Fenner Brockway.
    L(Col)†; LE 1964—*; ONC Nov. 1965—*

3674 Unionist and Labour Advocate: Official Organ of the Middlesbrough
Trades Council 1 (17 Sept. 1881)—? Middlesbrough; w
    A
    Middlesbrough PL 1—11 (w 3—4)

3675 United: the Good Team Paper for the Thinking Worker 1 [Oct.
1958]—32 (July/Aug. 1961); m
    A 4½d. Published by the Association of Liberal Trades Unionists.
Organ of those Liberal trade unions outside the Trades Union Congress.
Campaigns to free the trade union movement from compulsory political
levy to the Labour Party. Promotes Liberal Party policy; advocates
'co-ownership' of employer and worker. Nos. 1—4 are undated.
Incorporated with **Liberal News**.
    L(Col)†; TUC

**3676 United Builders' Labourers' Union Trade Circular and Monthly
Report** [18--? 19--?]?
    A   (S. Webb and A. Freeman eds., **Seasonal trades**, 1912.)

3677 United Builders' Labourers' Union. Quarterly Report [19—?]—?; q
    A   (R. W. Postgate, **The Builders' History**, London: National
Federation of Building Trades Operatives, 1923.)

3678 United Clerks' Journal: a Monthly Representative Journal for Clerks
I, 1 (15 Jan. 1883); [ns], I, 1 (21 March 1883)
    A   2d. Printed and published by Joseph T. Smith. Organ of the
newly formed United Clerks' Association urging the advantages of
combination among an 'underpaid body of workers'.
    L(Col)†

3679 United Irishman 1 (12 Feb. 1848)—16 (27 May 1848). Dublin; w
    B 5d. Proprietor, printer and publisher: John Mitchell. Newspaper
advocating freedom by means of mass insurrection, not as in 1798, in a
secret conspiratorial manner. Irish Chartist organ. Succeeded by **The Irish
Felon**.
    D; L(Col)†

3680 United Kingdom Society of Coachmakers. **Quarterly Report and Journal** I [1834?]—282 (April 1919). Manchester; q

A   For members only. Internal matters. The Society was amalgamated into the National Union of Vehicle Builders.

GM† 266 (April 1915)—282

3681 United Labour: a Labour Newspaper I, 1 (1 May 1890)—2 (Aug. 1890); irreg

B   1d. No. 1 printed and published for the proprietor at the Labour Press, Ltd. No. 2 printed and published by J. L. Mahon. Each number is a single sheet. No. 1 is, by a series of Biblical quotations, a justification of the principles of Socialism; No. 2 has four items of Labour news.

L(Col)†

3682 United Patternmakers Association. **Monthly Trade Report** [18--?]—Dec. 1968; then **APAC Progress**: Jan. 1969—April 1972; then **Patternmaker**: May 1972—   ; m

A   For members only. Coverage is gradually extended. First title varies: sometimes **Monthly Report**. Association later called Association of Patternmakers and Allied Craftsmen.

ONC† Jan. 1925—Dec. 1938; Jan. 1950—   ; the Association 1892?—

3683 United Rubber Workers of Great Britain. **News Letter** [19--?]—? [Manchester?]

A   October 1951 is one sheet, reproduced from typewriting.

TUC† Oct. 1951

3684 United Socialist Oct. 1934. Glasgow

B   1d. Edited and published by Guy Aldred. Organ of the United Socialist Movement. To agitate for the social revolution. Viewpoint of the Anti-Parliamentary Socialist Group. Led by Aldred, and having links with London and Leeds anarchists. Argues that Russia has become State capitalist. 'If you want this paper to continue, you must order quantities; become a personal subscriber; and send a donation to the press fund. We are in urgent need of funds to keep going.'

L(Col)†

3685 United Society of Boilermakers and Iron and Steel Ship Builders. **Monthly Report** [18--?]—   . Newcastle-upon-Tyne; m

A   The name of the union varies: United Society of Boilermakers, Shipbuilders and Structural Workers (1953—62); United Society of Boilermakers, Blacksmiths, Shipbuilders and Structural Workers (1962—3); Amalgamated Society of Boilermakers, Shipwrights, Blacksmiths and Structural Workers (1963—).

L ns 246 (Jan. 1893)—*; NU 993 (1955)—July 1965, July 1967—   ; ONC 1919—38, Dec. 1949—; TUC 930 (Jan. 1950—)

3686 United Trades' Co-operative Journal 1 (6 March 1830)—31 (2 Oct. 1830). Manchester; w

    A   2d; 2½d. Unstamped. Printers: M. Wardle (1—26), Alexander Wilkinson (27—31). Published by John Doherty's National Association for the Protection of Labour. It serves as the organ of the Lancashire trade unions and co-operative societies. Advocates factory legislation, abolition of the truck system, repeal of 'taxes on knowledge' (Wiener). Succeeded by the stamped paper, **The Voice of the People**.

    HO 64/18 21—5. MP†

Unity, 1877—1916 see **Labour and Unity**

3687 Unity [19--?]—? Birmingham

    A   Union of Post Office Workers, Birmingham Amalgamated DOs and SDOs Branch. (W. Dunlop, 'Local journals'. **Belpost**, IV, 5 [May 1965].)

3688 Unity [19--?]—? Cardiff

    A   Union of Post Office Workers, Cardiff Uniform Branch. (W. Dunlop. 'Local journals'. **Belpost**, IV, 5 [May 1965].)

3689 Unity [19--?]—; bi-m

    A   National Union of Insurance Workers, London and Manchester Section. The issue for June 1974 was Vol. XLII, No. 2.
    The Union?

3690 Unity I, 1 (Feb. 1919)—XV, 3 (July 1939); m

    C   3d. Published by the National (Industrial) Alliance of Employers and Employed.

    C V, VII—IX, XI—XIV; L(Col); LE*; LdU VII*— ; MP VII—XIII

3691 Unity I (1961)— . Belfast; w

    B   First published by the Communist Party, Northern Ireland, then 'In 1970 a statement **Reconstitution of the Communist Party of Ireland** appeared which announced the amalgamation of several Communist parties in Ireland to form the Communist Party of Ireland. They took over publication of **Unity** . . . ' (P. Howard. 'The paper war: Communism and Socialism'. **Fortnight**, 78 [22 Feb. 1974].)

    Belfast PL VII (1968)—*; D VII, 1969— ; Linen Hall Library, Belfast VIII (1969)—

3692 Unity; For Socialism, Peace, Democracy 1 [1961? 1962?]—? Cambridge

    B   3d.
    Warwick UL† 2 (1962)

3693 Unity 1968?— . Solihull

    A   National and Local Government Officers' Association, West Midlands Gas Board Headquarters Branch. Reproduced from typewriting.
    L 1963—

3694 Unity: the Official Journal of the Rossendale Union of Boot, Shoe, and Slipper Operatives I, 1 (Jan. 1926)–(May 1971). Waterfoot, Rossendale; q

    A   Printed at Rawtenstall. Wide-ranging contents: politics, trade union news, children's corner etc. Not published continuously.

    TUC†

Unity, 1948–1954 see **Undeb**

3695 Unity Call [19--?] –? [Nottingham?]

    A   Nottingham Trades Council.

    TUC† May 1951, May 1956

3696 Unity Journal 1868–?; m

    A?   Editor?: T. Williams. For Friendly Societies. (**Reformers' Year Book**, 1903; **Handy Newspaper List**, 1890)

3697 Universities and Left Review I, 1 (Spring 1957)–I, 5 (Autumn 1958). Oxford; q

    B   3s. 6d.; 4s. No. 1 published by R. Prince (Business Manager), Magdalen College, Oxford, and printed by the Abbey Press, Abingdon; Nos. 2–5 printed by A. Quick and Company, Clacton-on-Sea and London. Editors: Stuart Hall, Gabriel Pearson, Ralph Samuel, Charles Taylor. Socialist theory, arts criticism, university opinion, international socialist exchange. Sponsored universities and Left Review Club for meetings and discussion. Incorporated in **New Left Review**.

    C; E; L; LU; LdP; O

Universities Review see **University Bulletin**

3698 University Association of Women Teachers. **Journal** 1 (July 1892)–10 (Nov. 1895); 3-yr

    A   3d. Published by Miss G. Elder. Founded to combat apathy (No. 1). Discussion of salaries, conditions, safeguards of status, registration and training. News and correspondence.

    L

3699 University Bulletin: the Organ of the Association of University Teachers I, 1 (Jan. 1922)–VII, 1 (April 1928); then **Universities Review**: I, 1 (Oct. 1928)–XXXXIV, 2 (Feb. 1962). Leeds etc. 3-yr., bi-a

    A   6d. etc.

    AU; AbU; BU; BrU; CrU; ExU; GU; L; LE; LU; LdU; MU; NwA; O; SwU; see BUCOP for further locations

University Forward see **Oxford Forward**

3700 University Labour Federation. **Bulletin** (1[July 1942?])–14 (3 March 1945). Cambridge; irreg

    B   1d.; 2d. To record and co-ordinate work among branches, and with the International Student Movement. Reproduced from typewriting.

    MML† July 1942–14

3701 University Labour Federation. **Weekly Bulletin** 1 [1934?]–?; w

    B   Reproduced from typewriting.

    TUC† Year 5, 23 (26 Oct. 1938)

3702 University Labour News: Terminal Bulletin of the University Labour Federation 1 (Feb. 1928)–[1932?]. Oxford; termly

    B   Reproduced from typewriting.

    TUC† 1, 2, 4, 13 (Feb. 1932)

3703 University Letter 1 (Spring 1962)–4 (Summer 1963); termly

    B   1s. Published by the Communist Party of Great Britain. Editors: L. Munby; A. Kettle. Aim: 'that Communist members of university staffs give colleagues the opportunity to read and discuss the Communist Party's views'. To 'discuss general political issues as they affect university staffs, professional matters and wider aspects of university life'.

    MML†

3704 University Libertarian: an Independent Journal of University Anarchism 1 (Dec. 1955)–11 (Summer 1960). Prestwick; London; termly

    B   10d.; 1s. Published by Victor Hayes, then by The University Libertarian, London. Edited by V. Hayes. 'An independent termly for university anarchists, rationalists and humanists.' Discussion articles and reviews. Contributor: George Woodcock.

    L 1–10; O 2–11

3705 University Socialist: Journal of the University Socialist Federation I [1913?]–?; termly?

    B   6d. Published for the Federation by Clifford Allen, Chairman. Editor: M. Dobb (1922).

    L I, 2 (Michaelmas 1913), June 1922, Nov. 1923

3706 University Socialist Federation. **Bulletin** 1 (Spring 1915)–? Oxford; irreg?

    B   3d. Reports from the universities; articles by Dutt, Cole etc. Revolutionary socialist.

    L 2 (May 1915)–(May 1921) (occ. nos only); MML May 1921

3707 Unzer Veg: Organ fun der Yidisher Sotsialistisher Arbaiter Prtai Po'ale-Siyyon in England. [Our Road: Organ of the Jewish Socialist Workers' Party Po'ale Siyyon in England] I, 1 (1 May 1919)–I, 12 (19 Dec. 1919); 1 (1 Feb. 1923)–3 (10 April 1923). London; fortn

    B   2d. Yiddish.

    L(Col)†

3708 Upholder I, 1 (Jan. 1927)–II, 12 (Feb. 1929); then **Upholder and Industrial Review**: III, 1 (March 1929)–V, 11 (Jan./Feb. 1932); m
    A   1d. Organ of the Amalgamated Union of Upholsterers.
Industrial Review is an issue of the journal produced by the Trades Union Congress, inserted in the main journal.
    TUC†

Upholder and Industrial Review see **Upholder**

3709 Upton (West Ham) Citizen 1 (Oct. 1932)–44 (July 1936); m
    B   Gratis. Published by the London Co-operative Society's Political Committee.
    L(Col)

3710 Urmston Voice [194-?]. Urmston, Manchester; m
    B   2d. Published by **Voice**. Labour Party. (Labour Party. **Your own Journal**, 1948.)

3711 Us 1962?–
    A   National and Local Government Officers' Association, Central London Teaching Hospitals Branch. Reproduced from typewriting.
    L 1962–

3712 Useful Hints for the Labourer [183-?] –? m
    C   Published by the Labourers' Friend Society. Hints and advice on gardening, cooking, dress, domestic economy. Also reflections of a religious nature, or moral exhortation. Often extracted from other publications. Bound with **The Labourers' Friend Magazine**, probably circulated with it.
    LU† 61, 70–86, 91–2, 95–139, 1843; ONC† 80 (Jan. 1839)–86, 91–3, 95–103 (Dec. 1840)

3713 Uses: a Monthly New-Church Journal of Evolutionary Reform. I, 1 (22 March 1896)–V, 60 (March 1901). [Manchester? Leeds? Clitheroe?] ; m
    B   1d. Organ of the New-Church Socialist Society. Editor: T. D. Benson, Clitheroe. Secretary: S. J. Cunnington Goldsack, Keighley. Christian Socialist. Contributors: Rev. Thomas Child, G. Trowbridge, T. D. Benson.
    L

3714 Usksider I, 1 (July 1938)–I, 3 (Jan. 1939). Newport; irreg
    A   National Association of Local Government Officers, Newport Branch.
    NpP

3715 Uxbridge Citizen ns 1 (Jan. 1947)–36 (Dec. 1949); then **Uxbridge, Yiewsley and West Drayton Citizen**: 37 (Jan. 1950)– ; m
    B   Gratis. Issued by the Political Committee of the London Co-operative Society.
    L(Col)

3716 Uxbridge Parliamentary Division Citizen 1 (April 1932)–83 (Sept. 1939); m

    B   Published by the London Co-operative Society's Political Committee.

    L(Col)

Uxbridge Spirit of Freedom see **Spirit of Freedom**

Uxbridge, Yiewsley and West Drayton Citizen see **Uxbridge Citizen**

3717 Vanguard: a Weekly Journal of Politics, Biography and General Literature 1 (Jan. 1853)–7 (4 March 1853); w

    B   Publisher: J. P. Crantz. Editor and proprietor: G. J. Harney. Political editorials, but Harney's despondent mood reflects the low ebb of Chartism. Chiefly literary. Extracts from Louis Blanc's **History of ten Years**, serialised Lamartine's **Graziella**. Harney's co-worker was Alexander Bell.

    E; L; LE†; LU; MP 1–6; O(JJ)

3718 Vanguard [19--?] –?

    A   Union of Post Office Workers, South Midlands District Council No. 1. (W Dunlop, 'Local journals'. **Belpost**, IV, 5 [May 1965].)

3719 Vanguard: Organ of the British Socialist Party, Scottish Branches 1 [May?] 1913–? Glasgow; m?

    B   Published by the Twentieth Century Press and published by the Scottish District Council of the British Socialist Party. Marxist propagandist organ.

    E 3 (July), 5 (Sept.) 1913

3720 Vanguard 1 [Sept.?], 1915–1920. Glasgow; m

    B   1d.; 2d. Issued by the Glasgow District Council of the British Socialist Party. Printed by the Socialist Labour Press, then published by John Maclean. Editors: James D. Macdougall; John Maclean. There was a gap in publication between 1915 and 1920. Proclaimed Marxist proletarian internationalism against the Imperialist War.

    E 2 (Oct. 1915), 3, 4 (Dec. 1915), 6 (May 1920), 8–10, 12–13

3721 Vanguard: Journal of the British Section of the Militant Socialist International (MSI) I, 1 (Jan.–March 1934)–I, 9 (Jan.–March 1936); then **Socialist Vanguard**: II, 1 (June 1936)–VI, 6 (June 1940); then Socialist Vanguard Newsletter Service. **Bulletin**: [1] –4 [1940] ; then **Commentary**; 5 (6 Sept. 1940)–29 (2 Oct. 1941); then **Socialist Commentary**: 30 (23 Oct. 1941)– ; q; m

    B   2d. etc. Long-serving editor: Allan Flanders. For a period, 1940–2, reproduced from typewriting.

    GM 1958– ; L; LU; LabP June 1936– ; ONC 1942– ; Warwick UL 1942–

3722 Vanguard: Organ of the Barton Hall Workers 1 (Sept. 1943)—33 (Jan. 1947). Eccles; m

    A   2d. Published by the Shop Stewards' Committee at Messrs L. Gardner's Diesel Engine Works.

    WCML† 27 (July 1946)—29, 31—3

3723 Vanguard: a Communist Periodical I, 1 (Feb. 1964)—IV, 1 (Jan./Feb. 1967); m; bi-m

    B   Organ of the Committee to Defeat Revisionism, for Communist Unity. Described as containing politics, economics, world news, literature and polemics. The Committee was composed of ex-members of the Communist Party, supporters of Mao Tse Tung. Secretary and co-editor: Michael McCreery. From March/April 1966 reproduced from typewriting.

    WCML†

3724 Vanguard: Journal of the League for Worker's Vanguard 1969—[1970?]. [Belfast?]

    B   League for Worker's Vanguard, Northern Ireland.

    Linen Hall Library, Belfast I, 1—2 (1969), one issue 1970

3725 Vauxhall Citizen ns 1 (Oct. 1949)—4 (Jan. 1950); m

    B   Issued by the Political Purposes Committee of the Royal Arsenal Co-operative Society.

    L(Col)

3726 Vehicle Worker: Weekly Organ of the Amalgamated Association of Tram and Vehicle Workers (London District), London Cabmen's Trade Union, and All Workers on Vehicles 1 (4 Jan. 1909)—127 (8 June 1911); then **V. W. Cab Trade News and Owner Driver**: 128 (15 June 1911)—207 (19 Dec. 1912); then **Vehicle Worker**: ns 1 (Jan. 1921)—8 (Aug. 1921); w

    A   ½d.; 2d. Detailed news from London and provincial branches, but predominantly London. Correspondence. With No. 128 the first series gives more emphasis to cabmen and taxi drivers, as well as bus and tram workers. For militant and strong Trade Unionism. The new series was an organ of the National Union of Vehicle Workers. Then the Union amalgamated with the Transport and General Workers Union.

    L(Col)†

Venture see **Empire**

3727 Venture: the Magazine of the London Joint City and Midland Bank Staff Association I, 1 (March 1920)—I, 2 (April 1920); then **L.J.C. and M. Venture**: I, 3 (May 1920)—IV, 48 (Feb. 1924); then **Midland Venture**: V, 49 (March 1924)—XXXI, 374 (April 1951); then **Midland Chronicle**: the Midland Bank Staff Magazine: I 1951—   ; m

    A   Midland Bank Staff Association

    L; O V, 49—XVII, 195

3728 Veritas: the Official Magazine of Durham County Council Branch of NALGO 1967?–   . Durham
   A   National and Local Government Officers' Association.
   L 1967–

3729 Vermersch Journal 1 (17/18 Dec. 1871)–82 (23 March 1872); then **Union Démocratique**: 83 (25 March 1872)–249 (3 Oct. 1872) d
   B   1d. Editor: Eugène Vermersch. French republican democratic paper. Supporter of the Commune. News and analysis. In French.
   L(Col)

3730 Vermin's Journal 1 (March 1949). Hayes
   C   3d. Published by the Society for the Advancement of Political Knowledge. 'Edited by Claudius Verminus.' Consists of a 16-page leaflet on 'The evils of Communism. I'. Anti-communist and anti-socialist. The author says he is a worker himself, and opposes Communism as being based on force, and as being irreconcilable with the freedom of the individual. States that he is a clerk, the son of a journeyman tailor, self-educated, and has lived with workers all his life. Opposes the socialists in Great Britain as paying lip-service to the doctrines of communism which is a danger to the constitutional method of government. Was a 'sentimental socialist' himself when young, 'but contact with socialist leaders like Mr Fenner Brockway, the late Mr Ramsay MacDonald and others soon made me realise that I was not cut out for a Socialist', as he would not 'toe the party line'.
   L; O

3731 Vickers Combine News [Feb. 1944?–Aug. 1946?]. Sheffield
   A   Shop stewards' paper, English Steel Corporation.
   (E. Frow.)

3732 Victoria Gazette: the Official Organ of the Liverpool Victoria Employees' Union. I, 1 (June 1915)–   ; m
   1d. etc. Now sub-titled 'The Official Organ of the National Union of Insurance Workers, Liverpool Victoria Section'.
   The Union?

3733 Victoria Signal 1 [1925?]–? fortn
   A   Issued by the Signal Communist Group, Victoria Station. Reproduced from typewriting. Minority Movement and Communist Party.
   O(JJ)† (32 [25 June], 35 [9 July], 37 [6 Aug.] 1926)

3734 'Victory for Socialism' Campaigner: Organ of the Labour Party's Victory for Socialism Campaign 1 (June 1934)–4 (March/April 1935); irreg
   B   To further the campaign for the return to power of a socialist Labour government. Contributor: Jim Blunt.
   E 3–4; L; O(JJ) 1–2

3735 Viewpark Clipper
 A   Pit paper? Printed and published at 78 Main Street, Bellshill, Glasgow. (R. G. Neville.)

3736 Viewpoint: a Critical (Marxist-Leninist) Review I, 1 (April 1934)–I, 2 (Sept. 1934). Croydon; q
 B   1s. A 'revolutionary review of the arts'. Merged in **Left Review**.
 E 1; L

3737 Viewpoint: the CSCA Monthly Magazine, Ministry of National Insurance Section. I, 1 (March 1947)–VIII, 6 (Feb. 1954?); m
 A   Civil Service Clerical Association.
 L I, 1–5, VI, 7–VIII, 6

3738 Viewpoint: Magazine of the Barry and Barry Gas Branches of NALGO I, 1 (Summer 1953)–   . Barry
 A   National and Local Government Officers' Association. Reproduced from typewriting.
 L

3739 Viewpoint 1 [Dec.?] 1955–5 (Nov./Dec. 1957). Southsea; Portsmouth; s-a
 B   Journal for the newly created St Jude's Ward Labour Party, Southsea. Reproduced from typewriting.
 L

Viewpoint, 1971– see **ASW Viewpoint**

3740 Viewpoint News-Letter I (1959)–   ; Barry
 A   National and Local Government Officers' Association, Barry Branch.
 L

3741 Views 1 (Spring 1963)–11 (Summer 1966); q
 B   5s. Printed by Narod Press. Editor: Sabby Sagall, with Editorial Board. Socialist political and cultural review. Substantial articles, poems, reviews, correspondence.
 ONC†

3742 Vigilance Gazette: a Monthly Journal Devoted to the Interests of the London Society of Compositors 1 (May 1888)–6 (Feb. 1889); then **London Printer's Circular and Vigilance Gazette**: 7 (May 1889)–11 (May 1890); irreg
 A   1d. Organ of the London Society of Compositors Vigilance Association. To promote and strengthen Trade Unionism among compositors to its 'proper position as the leading combination of workmen in the first city of the world'. Reports of meetings, short articles, important correspondence.
 L 1–3; LSF†.

3743 Vigilant [1930?]. [Normanton?]

A   Published by the Normanton Branch of the National
Unemployed Workers Movement. Editor: T. Coleman. Reproduced from
typewriting.

E 2 undated numbers (Xerox)

3744 Vigilant 1 (July [1933])−2 (Aug. 1933). Blantyre; m

A   1d. Organ of the Blantyre branch of the National Unemployed
Workers Movement. Fighting means test and slum housing. Reproduced
from typewriting.

MML†

3745 Village Crier [193-?]−? [Scotland]; w

B   Scottish Independent Labour Party.

ILP (11 June 1937), (11 March 1938), (26 April, 3 May 1940)

Village Search Light see **Oxted Searchlight**

3746 Vocational Education Bulletin: Official Organ of the Vocational
Education Officers' Organisation. 1934−   . Wexford; 3-yr

A

D 1946−52; L 1953−

3747 Voice I, 1 (Feb. 1936)−7 (Aug. 1936). Sheffield; m

B   2d. Issued by Attercliffe Socialist Christian League. Editor: G.
Fullard. Anti-war (including 1914−18) and Militarism (Eg arms
expenditure) and Imperialism. For People's Peace Movement. Opposed
means test. The title first chosen for the paper was **Searchlight**, but
changed to **The Voice** when the first sheets had been printed. First issue
did appear as **The Voice**, but a few sheets are headed **Searchlight**.
Contributors: W. G. Robinson, Councillor, George Fullard, Victor
Streeter, Cecil H. Wilson, MP, and contributions from class members at the
Christian Socialist League class meeting at Labour Hall, Darnall.

SP†

3748 Voice [195-?]−? Dagenham

A   Published by the Briggs and Ford Joint Shop Stewards'
Committee.

WCML† III, 1 (Jan. 1957)

3749 Voice from the Commons [1], 23 April 1836–[6], 28 May 1836; w

    B   2d. By Thomas Wakley, MP. Published by G. Churchill. Issued as a series of pamphlets each a 'perfectly distinct work', as did Roebuck, to evade the Stamp Act. In pursuance of the freedom of the press, and to inform the people of events in Parliament and associated issues. Wakley seeks among other things, total abolition of stamp duty on newspapers, system of national education, equal representation of the people, vote by ballot, abolition of taxes on bread, malt and soap, reduction of salaries of over-paid public officers, abolition of church rates, abolition of flogging, of overwork in factories by children, and the enactment of a Ten-Hours' Bill.

    L; MP 22 May; ONC†

3750 Voice of Briggs Workers: Official Organ of the Briggs Shop Stewards Committee I, 1 (Jan./Feb. 1951)–III, 3 (Nov. 1954). Dagenham; irreg?

    A   Editor: Sid Harraway, with editorial board. The Committee covered Dagenham, Croydon, Romford, Doncaster, Southampton.

    WCML† II, 5, 7, 9–12, III, 1–3

3751 Voice of East London 1 (Jan. 1939)–2 (May 1939)

    B   Published by the Co-operative Press.

    L(Col)

3752 Voice of Ford Workers 1 (May 1964)–? m

    A   6d. The first factory edition of a **Voice** paper. Published by the 'Voice of the Unions'. Two pages under the complete control of Ford workers. For workers' participation etc.

    L(Col)† 1–Jan./Feb. 1965; WCML† Spring 1965

3753 Voice of Labour: a Weekly Paper for Those Who Work and Think 1 (18 Jan. 1907)–36 (21 Sept. 1907); [ns], I, 1 (1 May 1914)–(28 Dec. 1916); then **Labour's Voice**: May 1920; ? w; m (1914–16)

    B   1d.; ½d.; 1d.; 2d. Printed and published for the proprietors by T. H. Keill; the for 'Voice of Labour Group'. First editor: John Turner. 'Continuation of effort made by George Dallas in Glasgow in 1905. Advocated educating workers for direct action and to rely on their own powers and organization rather than upon the state. Resumed May 1914 advocating freedom, anarchy, social revolution' (Brophy). Anti-parliamentary, anarcho-syndicalist, advocated industrial Unionism. Coverage of movement in America and Europe. Contributors: G. Aldred, S. Carlyle Potter, H. Kelly, L. A. Motler. The number for May 1920 was edited by L. A. Motler for the Liberty Group. A special issue for May Day, the editorial stated that it was 'intended to be a continuation of the **Voice of Labour** suspended in 1916'. Published by the Satire Press

    L(Col)† 1907, 1914–(15 Aug. 1916), May 1920; LE 1907; TUC, John Burns Lib. 1907

Voice of Labour, 1918–1919 see **Irish Opinion**

3754 Voice of Labour in North Herts Feb. 1962–July 1962; Hitchin
    B   Published for Hitchin Constituency Labour Party
    L(Col); LabP† July 1962.

3755 Voice of the Guild: Official Organ of the National Guild of Civil
Servants I, 1 (Feb. 1954)–? m
    A   3d. Concerned with pay and conditions. Political stance:
anti-Fascist and anti-Communist. Replaces **Live Wire**.
    L 1

3756 Voice of the People, by an Association of Working Men I, 1 (1 Jan.
1831)–II, 13 (24 Sept. 1831). Manchester; w
    A   7d. Stamped. Organ of the National Association for the
Protection of Labour. Modelled on **The Times**, with parliamentary and
general news. Advocates universal suffrage and co-operation. Contributor:
Doherty.
    L(Col)† II, 1 (2 July 1831)–II, 13; MP I (microfilm); Warwick UL
(microfilm)

3757 Voice of the People: a Supplement to All Newspapers 1 (22 April
1848)–4 (13 May 1848); w
    B   3d. Stamped. Published by Charles Knight. Editors: Charles
Knight and Harriet Martineau. Anti-Chartist. Bound and sold with **Rights
of Industry**.
    L 1–2; L(Col)† 3–4

3758 Voice of the People I, 1 (13 Oct. 1883)–7 (24 Nov. 1883). Glasgow;
w
    B   1d. Printed and published for the proprietors by Dunn and
Wright. Radical. Published on Saturdays 'on the day when the working
classes have most leisure'; 'conceived in the hope that the labouring classes
will look upon it as their own'. Working towards the social and political
advancement of the people. Support for land nationalisation. Brief but
sympathetic coverage of Trade Unionism. On 10 Nov. published the
manifesto of the Democratic Federation, 'Socialism made Plain' although
we 'in no way stand pledged to the statements contained in it', but invite
discussion. Correspondence from working men on social and political
issues.
    GM; L(Col)†

3759 Voice of the People, and Labour Advocate 1 (12 Dec. 1857)–?
Bradford; w?
    B   1d. Published by Edward Smith. Printed by Michael Nelson.
    ·   BdP 1

Voice of the Unions, for Peace and Socialism see **Union Voice**

3760 Voice of the West Riding 1 (1 June 1833)—53 (7 June 1834).
Huddersfield; w

    B   1d. Publisher, printer, editor: Joshua Hobson; John Francis
Bray when Hobson was in prison from October 1833. 'A widely-circulated
working-class newspaper that agitates for universal suffrage, annual
Parliaments, repeal of stamp duty on newspapers, and, most strongly, for
factory legislation' (Wiener).

    HO 64/19 39, 41—2, 45; L(Col) (microfilm); LU 1, 3—4, 6—9, 11,
26; Tolson Memorial Library, Huddersfield; Warwick UL 1—51
(microfilm)

3761 Volunteer for Liberty: Organ of the International Brigades I, 1 (24
May 1937)—II, 35 (7 Nov. 1938). Madrid; Barcelona; w

    B   Contained news about the war in Spain, government and
military affairs. Much space devoted to Brigades' affairs, progress of the
war, letters and news about individual Brigades.

    WCML† I, 1—II, 35 (reprint); 16 occ. nos (original)

3762 Volunteer for Liberty I, 1 (Jan. 1940)—VI, 8 (June 1946); then b
Spain Today and Volunteer for Liberty: I, 1 (July 1946)—(Dec. 1947); m

    B   3d. Published by the International Brigade Association (British
Battalion). Official journal, 'to build an organisation which shall be able to
keep the Brigades together in the same type of unity which carried us
through in Spain'. To fight the threat of Fascism at home and abroad and
prepare for the victory of Socialism.

    C; L (w a I, 12, III, 1, IV, 1); MML†; O b

3763 Vox Pop, Incorporating Jazz Record and LLCU News Letter:
Journal of the Workers' Music Association. I (1944)—II, 6 (June 1945);
then b **Keynote**: the Progressive Music Quarterly: I, 1 (Autumn 1945)—ns
II, 8 (Oct./Nov. 1947); m; q

    B   6d.; 1s. Issued by the Workers' Music Association, 'a co-operative
society', founded in 1936 to co-ordinate the musical activities
of working-class organisations. Editor: H. G. Sear. Aim 'to encourage music
in all its forms and its appreciation among the British people, so as to
enrich and develop our musical heritage by giving the widest section of the
community the opportunity of participating in musical activity'. To 'foster
and further the art of music on the principle that true art can move people
to work for the betterment of society'. Discusses and promotes jazz and
folk music, and provides recreation and entertainment for war-workers and
the forces.

    L a II, 1, 3—b ns II, 3 (April 1947); O b

3764 WDU Notes: the Official Organ of the Workers' Defence Union 1
(March 1910)—3 (May 1910); then **Worker**: 4 (June 1910)—23 (Jan.
1912); m

    C   ½d. Produced by a body, virulently anti-socialist, which
promotes tariff reform and patriotic endeavour. Addressed to
working-men. Devoted to Imperialism and Protectionism as the best means
of securing a good standard of living for the British worker.

    L O 5—23

WEA Education Year Book see Workers' Educational Association. Year
Book

3765 WEA News I, 1 (Autumn issue, 1969)–   ; s-a
    C   Workers' Educational Association.
    L

3766 WIN: Workers Illustrated News I, 1 (13 Dec. 1929)
    B   2d. Published by Workers' Publications, Ltd. 'To translate the
politics of revolutionary class struggle into pictures. That is the task of
WIN, the first workers' picture paper.' Mainly photographs, some chat and
verse; reviews by T. A. Jackson, and Henry Dobb. Sports pages.
    L(Col); O(JJ); ONC†

3767 WSM News Bulletin [pre-1915]
    B   Published by the World Socialist Movement. Precursor of the
Socialist, later **World Socialist** (qv).

3768 WUEA Review 1 (July 1921)–59 (June 1928); then **Western Union
Employees' Association Review**: 60 (Sept. 1928)–83 (June 1935); then b
Bulletin: the Official Organ of the WUEA, European Division. I, 1
[1935?]–XVIII, 5 [1951?]. London; irreg?
    A   Later title was **News and Views**. Later name of Association was
Western Union Cable Employees' Association, European Division.
    L a 1–83, b XII–XVIII

Wage-Earners' Weekly and Friendly Societies' Recorder see **Oddfellows'
Recorder and Friendly Societies. Journal**

3769 Waiters' Record: the Organ of the Amalgamated Waiters' Society 1
(Feb. 1900)–23 (Dec. 1901); m
    A   1d. Secretary of the Society; Paul Vogel.
    L(Col)†; O(JJ)† 10/11 (Nov./Dec. 1900)

3770 Wakefield Echo: West Yorkshire District News and General
Advertiser 1 (25 Oct. 1876)–XXX, 1375 (20 July 1906). Wakefield; w
    B   ½d. A general newspaper until 5 May 1905, when it became the
organ of the Labour Party in Wakefield, under Stanton Coit. Editor: G. E.
O'Dell.
    L(Col)† 17 March, 29 Sept. 1882–20 July 1906; Wakefield PL
1876–91

3771 Wakefield Forward [1931?]–102 (Dec. 1939). Wakefield; m
    B   Gratis. Published by Wakefield Labour Party. Editor and main
contributor: Joe Walker.
    L(Col)† 43 (Jan. 1935)–102

3772 Wakefield Monthly Bulletin [194-?]. Wakefield; m
    B   Labour Party. Duplicated. (Labour Party. **Your own Journal**,
1948.)

3773 Wales Radical Cymru 1 [Nov. 1970?] — . Cardiff; m
    B   9d.; 4p. 'Radical is published by the Welsh Council of Labour as an open forum of news, discussion and opinion for all sections of the Labour movement in Wales.'
    LabP† 2 (Dec. 1970)

3774 Wallasey Citizen ns 1 (Aug. 1949)—21 (July 1951); m
    B   Issued by the Wallasey Trades Council and Labour Party and the Wallasey Constituency Co-operative Party.
    L(Col)

3775 Wall-paper: the Quarterly Journal of the Wallpaper Workers' Union I, 1 (Jan. 1939)—? Manchester; q
    A
    TUC† I, 1—VIII, 1 (March 1953*)

3776 Walsall Anarchist 1 (27 Feb. 1892)—3 (12 March 1892). Walsall; w
    B   1d. Printed and published by George Cores. Discusses the case of the Walsall bomb scare in which police arrested anarchists. The paper vindicates Anarchism and exposes ruling-class methods. Anarchist news in Britain and abroad. Criticism of Fabianism and of Social Democracy. Contributor: David Nicoll.
    LE† (w 2)

3777 Walsall and District Citizen 1 (Jan. 1932)—4 (April 1932); m
    B   Published for the Walsall Co-operative Society's Political Committee.
    L(Col)

3778 Walsall and District Co-operative Society Co-operative Party Citizen 1 (Dec. 1939)
    L(Col)

3779 Walsall and District Monthly Record 1 Jan. 1910—? m
    A   'On January 1st, 1910, a more ambitious venture was launched [ie than the local pages in the **Wheatsheaf**], the **Walsall and District Monthly Record**, which confined itself to the affairs of the Society. The **Record** stated on its front page that it was issued by the Educational Committee. Evidently the cost of an independent magazine was too great, or there was some other cause which led to the **Wheatsheaf** being again adopted as the medium of monthly communication with the members as it remains to-day' (F. Hall, **From Acorn to Oak, being the History of the Walsall and District Co-operative Society, Ltd., 1886—1936**, Birmingham 1936, pp. 162—3).

3780 Walthamstow Democrat 1 (Feb. 1922)–10 (Nov. 1922); m

    B   Published by the Walthamstow Democratic and Labour Party. Provided an alternative to the socialist policies of the Labour Party. For sane Trade Unionism, lower rates, lower taxes and rents, and a 'square deal for all' including the private employer. Concerned with abolishing unemployment and raising pensions, and with the transfer of surplus population to the Dominions.

    L(Col)†

3781 Walthamstow Municipal Gazette 1 (18 March 1921)–? w

    B   Gratis. Local Labour Party paper. (**Labour Organiser**, April 1921.)

3782 Walthamstow Observer 1 (March 1928)–?; Oct. 1937–June 1938; m

    B   Published by W. G. E. Robinson. Propaganda news sheet of Walthamstow Labour Party. Contributors: V. L. McEntee, M.P., H. W. Wallace, Labour candidate.

    L(Col)† March 1928–Sept. 1929; Feb. 1932–July 1934; Oct. 1937–June 1938

3783 Walthamstow Recorder, Radical and Labour: a Weekly Journal Devoted to Active Progressive Radicalism and Labour Interests. 1 (23 Oct. 1903)–ns 666 (29 June 1906); w

    B   ½d. Editor: J. J. McSheedy. Radical, Lib./Lab. viewpoint. Includes 'Labour notes'. Appears to succeed **Walthamstow Reporter**.

    L(Col)†

3784 Walthamstow Reporter: a Weekly Journal Devoted to Active Progressive Radicalism and Labour Interests I, 1 (26 Oct. 1894)–X, 5 (16 Oct. 1903); then **Walthamstow Reporter and Gazette**: ns 1 (1 Jan. 1904)–234 (3 July 1908); w

    B   ½d. Liberal/Radical. 'Organ of the working classes of Walthamstow and district.' Includes 'Labour notes'.

    L(Col)† (w 155–207)

Walthamstow Reporter and Gazette see **Walthamstow Reporter**

3785 Walworth News [193–?]; m

    B   Labour Party. (Labour and Socialist International. **The Socialist Press**, 1933.)

3786 War: Monthly Bulletin of the British Anti-War Council 1 (15 Dec. 1932)–II, 2 (Feb. 1934); then **Fight War and Fascism**: II, 3 (March 1934)–II, 10 (Nov./Dec. 1934); m

    B   1d. Published by the Council. Organ of the anti-imperialist, anti-war movement, for a united front. Officers: John Strachey, R. G. Willis.

    L(Col)†

3787 War Commentary I, 1 (Nov. 1939)–VI, 21 (11 Aug. 1945); then
Freedom Through Anarchism: VI, 22 (25 Aug. 1945)–VII, 30 (14 Dec.
1946); then **Freedom: an Anarchist Fortnightly**: VIII, 1 (4 Jan. 1947)– ?
fortn
    B   Published by Freedom Press.
    C VII, 6– ; L (temporarily mislaid); LE 1939–45; ONC III–V*

3788 War Emergency Circular 1 (7 Sept. 1939)–1185 (31 Dec. 1945);
then **Co-operative Gazette**: I, 1 (1 Jan. 1946)– . Manchester; d; irreg
    A   Published by the Co-operative Union for the information of
members. Notes on legislation and war-time arrangements, eg, rationing.
Arranged in numbered paragraphs for reference. Similar information in the
Co-operative Gazette, which is internal and confidential.
    Co-op. Union†

War Resister see War Resisters' International. **Bulletin**

3789 War Resisters' International. Bulletin 1 (Oct. 1923)–10 (Christmas
1925); then **War Resister**: 11 (March 1926)– . Enfield; London;
Brussels; irreg; q
    B   1d. etc. To make and maintain effective contact between
various anti-war groups, including working-class organisations, eg, the
Independent Labour Party. Advocates disarmament. Current title: **War
Resistance**.
    C 48 (1942)– ; L*; LFS 43 (1937)– ; O 48–

3790 War-Worker: a Monthly Magazine. I, 1 (June 1917)–II, 2 (May
1919); m
    C   1d. Published for the War Workers' League by the Society for
Promoting Christian Knowledge. Editor: Canon Masterman. Addressed to
the 'great army of women and girls who have taken up munition work and
other forms of national service to assist our country in time of need'.
Rules of the League: pray to God every day; fight for the right; help our
fellow workers.
    L

3791 Ward and Goldstone Spark 1 (1 July 1930)–3 (24 July 1930).
Manchester; m
    B   Issued by the Manchester Young Communist League.
Reproduced from typewriting. Ward and Goldstone was a Salford factory
which in the 1930s employed many young men and girls on electrical
accessories and cable work.
    WCML† 1, 3

3792 Ware Patriot 1 (16 Feb. 1833)–12 (1833); then **Hertford and Ware Patriot**: ns 13 (1833)–67 (1834); then **Radical Reformer and Hertford and Ware Patriot**. 68 (1834)–84 (1835). Hertford; w

    B   2d. Edited, printed and published by John Thacker Saxton. Designed to 'fight the people's battle with lion heart and empty coffers'. Advocates household suffrage, triennial parliaments and secret ballot. Emphasis on political Radicalism. Champions Tom Duncombe, Radical MP.

    L (w 39, 46)

3793 Warrington and District Labour News 1 (25 Oct. 1924)–833 (19 June 1954). Warrington; fortn

    B   1d. Published by Warrington Trades Council and Labour Party.

    L(Col) (microfilm); Warrington PL†

3794 Warrington Citizen 1 (Aug. 1932)–3 (Oct. 1932); then **Warrington Co-operative Citizen**: 4 (Nov. 1932)–17 (Dec. 1933). Warrington; m

    B

    L(Col)

Warrington Co-operative Citizen see **Warrington Citizen**

3795 Washington Labour News 1 (29 Sept. 1922)–44 (April 1926); 45 (8 April 1927)–47 (17 June 1927). Washington, Co. Durham; m

    B   1d. 'Owned, written and published by workers.' Published by the joint branches of the Usworth and Washington Independent Labour Party. Suspended for eleven months because of financial difficulties. Labour paper in a mining area. Contributor: J. J. Lawson, MP.

    L(Col)† (w 44)

3796 Wasp I, 1 (14 July 1832). Birmingham

    B   1d. Printed and published by Joseph Allday, for Richard Jenkinson. For a 'Union of the Working Class, since the Birmingham Political Union has been under the guidance of the Ministers ever since the second reading of the Reform Bill'. Radical miscellany, opposed to the leadership of Attwood and other middle-class reformers in the Birmingham Political Union.

    BP†

3797 Wasps 1959?– . Worksop

    A   National and Local Government Officers' Association, Worksop and District Branch. Reproduced from typewriting.

    L 1959–

3798 Watchman 1 (28 March 1835). Birmingham; m?

    B   3d. Printed and published by Richard Jenkinson. Edited by Joseph Allday. 'A full sized radical newspaper that repeatedly attacks the middle class "monetary oligarchy" ' (Wiener).

    BP†

3799 Watchman: Western Labour and Socialist Monthly 1 (Feb. 1924)–95 (Dec. 1931). Devonport, Plymouth; m

     B   2d. Sponsored by the Devonport Constituency Labour Party. Dealt with local Party matters, Plymouth City Council affairs, as well as wide socialist matters. Distributed through the Party organisation; not subsidised.

     L(Col)

Watchword see **Irish Opinion**

Watchword of Labour see **Irish Opinion**

3800 Watco NALGO Times 1960?–   . North Shields

     A   National and Local Government Officers' Association, Sunderland and South Shields Water Company Branch. Reproduced from typewriting.

     L 1960–

3801 Waterfront: the Paper for the Port I, 1 (July 1960)–6 (Dec. 1960). Dublin; m

     A   2d. Written by workers, voluntary and unpaid, to air grievances among dock and port workers, and to provide a vehicle of expression. Discusses port questions and work relations, eg, containerisation.

     L

3802 Waterman: Organ of the Seamen and Boatmen's Friendly Society I, [18--?]–ns LXVII, 1 (March 1948). Birmingham; m? w?

     A   Incorporated Seamen and Boatmen's Friendly Society.

     BP ns I–LXVII (w Oct.–Dec. 1947); L(Col) XIII, 1 (Jan. 1894)–LXVII

3803 Waterproof Garment Workers' Bulletin I, 1 (12 Nov. 1934)–I, 2 (1 Dec. 1934). Manchester; m

     A   1d. Published by the Editorial Committee of the Waterproof Garment Workers' Bulletin. Organ of the Solidarity Committee. Rank-and-file paper, campaigns for solidarity and mass action throughout the trade in London and Manchester shops, in support of the strike at Satinoff's, London, and against sweated labour, wage reductions and attempts to smash union organisation.

     L(Col)†

3804 Waterside Worker [192-?]–[1926?]

     A   See the **Dock and River Worker**, which 'is a new form of the **Waterside Worker** which used to make a regular appearance in and about the South Side Dockland'.

3805 Waterworks Officers' Journal 1945–   . Croydon; Shortlands, Kent; q

     A   Association of Waterworks Officers. (Mitchell, 1965; **Willing's Press Guide**, 1970.)

3806 Watford Citizen ns 1 (June 1957)–36 (June 1964); irreg

    B   Published by the Co-operative Press.

    L(Col); LabP† 23, 27, 28, 34

3807 Watford Critic I, 1 (April 1902)–? Watford; m

    B   I, 9 has sub-title: 'An Organ of Democracy'. III, 2 has statement of aims: 'The "Critic" honestly endeavours to voice the just demands of labour. It represents no organisation in particular but appeals for the support of all who desire to serve the common weal. To inculcate good citizenship and to foster independence, faith in their own strength among the workers, and so to secure unity – these are our aims'.

    Watford PL. I, 1–V, 9 (Sept. 1906*)

3808 Watford Labour News: Official Organ of the Watford Divisional Labour Party I, 1 (June 1937)–? Watford; m

    B

    Watford PL I, 1–II, 9 (Feb. 1939)

3809 Watford Socialist: Pamphlet of the Watford Fabian Society 1 (Jan. 1943)–?

    B

    Watford PL 1

Waverley see **Waverley Journal**

3810 Waverley Journal, for the Cultivation of the Honourable, the Progressive and the Beautiful I, 1 (Feb. 1856)–1857; then **Waverley**: Nov. 1857–? Edinburgh; London; fortn

    B   First published for the proprietors by Eleanor Duckworth; then by W. Winter; then by Thomas and Robert Bowie. 'Edited and published by Ladies.' Its aim was the defence of women's rights. Later, under new management, it is described as **The Waverley: a Working Women's Journal**, with object the 'moral, social and industrial position of women'. (**Scottish Notes and Queries**, June 1903, p. 182.)

    L 1 Jan., 15 Jan. 1858

3811 Way, for Women and Youth 1 (Oct. 1963)– ; irreg

    A   Newspaper published by the Amalgamated Engineering Union, for women and young members. 'Towards more active women and youth membership. Also features on sport, entertainment, humour, clothes, and other items of interest to women and young people.' Book reviews, correspondence.

    L; ONC†

3812 Weavers' Journal 1 (31 Oct. 1835)—18 (1 April 1837); then b
Glasgow and Paisley Weavers' Journal: 1 (4 April 1838)—2 (29 May 1838).
Glasgow; m

    A   1d. Printed and published by W. and W. Miller for the Three
Unions of the Hand Loom Weavers of Scotland (ie Paisley Harness Union,
Glasgow Harness Union, and the General Protecting Union). Edited by
William Thomson, Secretary of the General Protecting Union. Highlights
grievances of weavers, and contains union reports, addresses,
correspondence.

    BP†; GM 1, 3—18

3813 Weavers' Magazine and Literary Companion I, 1 (Sept. 1818)—II, 12
(Aug. 1819). Paisley; m

    C   Printed by John Neilson. A literary miscellany for the weaving
community of Paisley. Includes notes on the state of the trade in the
country, poetry, extracts, letters, including some from emigrant weavers in
America.

    E; GM; L I, 1—6

3814 Wednesbury, West Bromwich and Darlaston Examiner 1 (19 Sept.
1874)—159 (6 Jan. 1877). Wednesbury; w

    B   1½d. Published by William Owen. Printed for the proprietors by
the Co-operative Newspaper and General Printing Society, then by Owen
and Jeffrey. First editorial declared it to be the 'special mouthpiece of
trade union and labour organizations, [covering] all that affects the
Interests of Labour, being the recognised organ of the Trades Unions of
the district', primarily colliers and iron workers. Interesting
correspondence on Labour issues, with contributions by working-men.
Incorporated in the **Midland Examiner and Times**.

    L(Col)†

3815 Week 1 (29 March 1933)—400 (15 Jan. 1941); ns 1 (23 Oct.
1942)—211 (Dec. 1946); w

    B   Payment by yearly and half-yearly subscription. Printed,
published and written by Claud Cockburn. Review of international
politics; outspoken, socialist. Suppressed by Government order at No. 400,
then restarted. Reproduced from typewriting.

    C i 3—ii 161*; E i 35—400, ii; GU i 133—ii 140*; L(Col)†; O i 16,
55—400, ii

3816 Week: a News Analysis for Socialists I, 1 (Jan. 1964)—IX, 13 (March
1968). Lenton, Nottinghamshire; w

    B

    BP III—   ; E III, 8 (1965)—   ; LE; ONC II, 9 (16 Sept. 1964)—IV,
5 (5 Aug. 1965*)

3817 Weekly Chronicle [18--?]—June 1858. Glasgow; w

    B   Edited by Alexander Campbell. 'A rather obscure journal
mostly devoted to trade union affairs. Absorbed June 1858 by **Glasgow
Sentinel**. Proprietor, Robert Buchanan, former Owenite.' (J. Bellamy and
J. Saville, eds., **Dictionary of Labour biography**, Vol. I, 1972, p. 66).

Weekly Citizen see **Leeds Weekly Citizen**

3818 Weekly Echo 1 (18 Nov. 1893)–64 (2 Feb. 1895). Glasgow; w
    A   ½d. Printed and published by John Eddy for the **Glasgow Echo** Newspaper Company. Democratic, supporting the claims of Labour, and culture for the working class. Review of politics and literature, serial stories. Succeeded **The Echo**, 1893.
    GM†

Weekly Free Press see **Trades Newspaper and Mechanics' Weekly Journal**

3819 Weekly Herald 1 (3 July 1836)–10 (4 Sept. 1836); [ns], 1 (18 Sept. 1836)–9 (13 Nov. 1836); w
    B   2½d.; 3d. Unstamped. Printed and published by 'Benjamin Franklin', ie Benjamin Cousins. Radical, democratic.
    L(Col)† i 1, 5–10, ii

3820 Weekly Telegraph: the Union of Classes and the Liberty of Man 1 (25 Feb. 1860)–2 (3 March 1860); w
    B   2d. Proprietor and editor: Ernest Jones. For manhood suffrage and middle-class alliance. Distributed with **The Penny Times**.
    L(Col)†

3821 Weekly Times 1 (13 Sept. 1835)–53 (11 Sept. 1836); then **London Weekly Times**: ns 1 (18 Sept. 1836)–13 (18 Dec. 1836); w
    B   2d.; 2½d; 3½d. Printed and published by George Johnson (1–27), William Wilkin (28-53), then published by the proprietor Robert Harding. 'Contains extensive accounts of police intelligence and of radical activities. It attacks the Church of England and its clergy, supports Irish reform and repeal of the newspaper duty. Describes itself as "the largest and the best unstamped newspaper" ' (Wiener). The **London Weekly Times** was stamped, and from No. 10 was sub-titled: 'Devoted to the Service of the Unrepresented Millions'.
    L(Col)† 16, 26, 28, 34–5, 37–9, 43–4, 48–53, ns 1–13

3822 Weekly Times 1 (24 Jan. 1847)–2017 (27 Sept. 1885); then **Weekly Times and Echo**: 2018 (4 Oct. 1885)–3437 (29 Dec. 1912); w
    B   1d. Relevant from the early 1890s until about 1910. Standpoint of the New Liberalism, recognising the claims of Labour. Regular columns of Labour and trade union news, Independent Labour Party notes etc. Many Labour contributors including Morrison Davidson, J. C. Kenworthy, Katherine Glasier, Allen Clarke. In 1904 there was discussed the possibility of the paper's becoming an organ of the Labour Representation Committee. Amalgamated with **Reynold's Newspaper**.
    L(Col)† (w [4 Feb.]–[25 March]; [25 Nov.]–[16 Dec.] 1849)

Weekly Times and Echo see **Weekly Times, 1847–1885**

3823 Weekly Tracts [18--?] –? w
    C   1s. 6d. per 100. Published by the Weekly Tract Society for the Religious Instruction of the Labouring Classes.
    L 634–59 (w 639–42, 646–7, 658) [1860?]

Weekly Tribune, 1849–1850 see **Spirit of the Times**

3824 Weekly Tribune 1 (6 Feb. 1904)–17 (28 May 1904); w
    B   1d. Printed by the Co-operative Printing Society. Started under the direction of Richard Bell, MP and Edmond Browne, member of the London County Council. To provide common ground for all shades of opinion in the Labour movement, trade unionist, co-operative, socialist etc. Given the official approval of the Parliamentary Committee of the Trades Union Congress. Supported the Labour Representation Committee. From No. 8 is sub-titled: 'The Organ of Trade Unionism and Labour'.
    L(Col); LE; ONC; TUC, John Burns Lib†

3825 Weekly True Sun 1 (10 Feb. 1833)–331 (29 Dec. 1839); w
    B   7d. Printed and published by John Ager for the proprietor. Pro-Chartist, radical and trade union newspaper and review. Became **The Statesman** in 1840, and no longer within our categories.
    L(Col)†

Weekly Worker see **Worker, 1926–1931**

Weekly Young Worker see **Red Flag, 1920**

3826 Wells-Glastonbury Labour Leader [194-?]. Glastonbury; m
    B   2d. Labour Party. (Labour Party. **Your own Journal**, 1948.)

3827 Welsh Industrial Times and Monmouthshire Labour Chronicle 1 (4 Aug. 1888)–174 (26 Dec. 1891). Swansea; w
    B   Then incorporated in **Herald of Wales**, a general paper.
    L(Col)†

3828 Welsh Labour Outlook I, 1 (Dec. 1934)–I, 7 (July 1935). Brymbo, Denbighshire; m
    B   2d. Published by Williams and Davies. 'To supplement and inspire the local work of the Labour Party.' Editor: J. Hywell Williams.
    L(Col)†

Welsh Quarryman see **Chwarelwr Cymreig**

3829 Welsh Republican. [Y Gweriniaethwr] I, 1 (Aug. 1950)–VII, 5 (April/May 1957); ns VIII, 1 (Aug./Sept. 1973)– . Cardiff; irreg
    B   3d.; etc. Published by the Welsh Republican Movement. For a 'Socialist Republic of Wales'.
    CrP; LabP† VII, 3 (Dec. 1956/Jan. 1957); SwU

3830 Welsh Schoolmaster: Journal of the Wales Committee, National Association of Schoolmasters I, 1 (March 1967)–   ; q
    A   Union and educational matters.
    BnU; E; L

3831 Wembley North Citizen ns 1 (Sept. 1949)–40 (May 1953); m
    B   Issued by the Political Committee of the London Co-operative Society.
    L(Col)

3832 Wembley South Citizen ns 1 (Nov. 1953)–22 (Dec. 1955); m
    B   Issued by the Political Committee of the London Co-operative Society.
    L(Col)

3833 Wembley South Socialist and Citizen 1 (Nov. 1960)–
    B   Published by the Co-operative Press.
    L(Col)

3834 Wendelsworth Gazette: the Official Journal of the Wandsworth Branch, NALGO [19--?]–ns II, 2 (Summer 1955); then **Gazette**: III, 1 (Oct. 1956)–VII, 3 (May 1962); then **News and Views**: 1 (July 1962)–
    A   National and Local Government Officers' Association. Reproduced from typewriting.
    L ns 8 (Jan./Feb. 1954)–(w IV, 6)

3835 Wessex Post: Official Organ of the Taunton District Council of the Union of Post Office Workers [19--?]–? Taunton
    A
    TUC† 298 (Feb. 1950)

3836 West Birmingham Labour News I, 1 (April–June 1947)–II, 1 (April–June 1948); then **Ladywood Citizen**: ns 1 (Jan.–March 1949)–2 (May–July 1949). Birmingham; q
    B   1d. Published by West Birmingham Divisional Labour Party, then by Ladywood Divisional Labour Party.
    BP†

3837 West Bromwich Parliamentary Division Challenge 1 (June 1939)–2 (July 1939); m
    B   Published by the Co-operative Press.
    L(Col)

3838 West Cent Critic [19--?]–?
    A   Union of Post Office Workers, WCDO No. 1 Branch. (W. Dunlop, 'Local journals'. **Belpost**, IV, 5 [May 1965].)

3839 West Cumberland Labour Gazette [19--?]–? Cleator Moor; w? m?

    B   Labour Party. (Labour and Socialist International. **The Socialist Press** 1933.)

    ILP 8 May 1923

3840 West Ealing Citizen ns 1 (Jan. 1947)–11 (Dec. 1947); m

    B   Gratis. Issued by the Political Committee of the London Co-operative Society.

    L(Col)

3841 West Essex Citizen 1 (June 1931)–17 (Nov. 1932); m

    B   Published by the London Co-operative Society Political Committee.

    L(Col)

3842 West Fulham Citizen 1 [1929?]–16 (Oct. 1931); ns 1 (Feb. 1954)–12 (Jan. 1955); m

    B   Published by the London Co-operative Society, Political Committee. Probably succeeded by **Fulham Citizen**.

    L(Col) 7 (April 1930)–ns 12

3843 West Fulham Labour Magazine [c 1935] ; m

    B   Gratis. West Fulham Labour Party. (Mitchell, 1935.)

3844 West Ham Citizen: a Journal for the People 1 (29 April 1899)–16 (12 Aug. 1899); 234 (19 Aug. 1899)–266 (31 March 1900); w

    B   ½d. Published by Martin Judge for the proprietors. Labour newspaper serving West Ham. For Labour representation, national and municipal, 'municipal socialism'. Edited by Martin Judge. From 5 August 1899 sub-titled: 'with which is incorporated **The West Ham Times** and **Cann Hall Review**'. Took up the numbering of one of these?

    L(Col)†

3845 West Ham Council Employee: the Official Organ of the West Ham Corporation Employees Federal Council 1 (May 1931)–? m

    A   1d. The Council was formed in 1914, a trade union co-ordinating body for council workers. Emphasis on wages and conditions, fighting against wage cuts and rationalisation. Trades Council notes and correspondence.

    WhP† 1–14 (Feb. 1933)

3846 West Ham North Citizen 1 (Nov. 1960)–   ; bi-m

    B   West Ham Labour Party and Co-operative Society.

    L(Col); LabP occ.nos 1962–4; WhP† 1–20

3847 West Ham South Citizen 1 (Oct. 1960)–   ; irreg

    B   Published by the Co-operative Press.

    L(Col); LabP 12, 16, 17

3848 West Ham Tribune I, 1 ([July?] 1901)–III, 27 (Sept. 1903); m

A ½d. Published by R. Mitchell. 'Started by a few wage-slaves, socialists by conviction', 'Champion of the People' and relentless enemy of the Alliance Party in municipal politics. Object 'to win West Ham not only to Labour politics, but to Socialism'. Organ of West Ham and District Trades and Labour Council, which had one full page per issue. News of the working-class movement in the area. Covers W. Thorne's fight for South West Ham.

WhP† (w 1–4, 15)

3849 West Harrow Citizen 1 (Jan. [1939])–9 (Sept. 1939). West Harrow; m

B 1d. Published by the Executive Committee of the West Harrow Ward of the Harrow Labour Party.

L

3850 West Islington Citizen 1 (Sept. 1930)–15 (Oct. 1931); m

B Published by the London Co-operative Society, Political Committee.

L(Col)

3851 West Lewisham Citizen 1 (Nov. 1937)–23 (Sept. 1939); m

B Published by the Political Purposes Committee, Royal Arsenal Co-operative Society.

L(Col)

3852 West Leyton Citizen 1 (Nov. 1930)–105 (Sept. 1939); m

B Gratis. Published by the London Co-operative Society, Political Committee.

L(Col); Leyton PL*

3853 West Leyton (Divisional) Labour Party. Members' Bulletin; then **Labour News**: [19--?] –?

B Was being published between 1941 and 1947.

(Mentioned in the list of Sorensen papers)

3854 West London Citizen ns 1 (Jan. 1947)–62 (May 1952); m

B Gratis. Issued by the Political Committee of the London Co-operative Society.

L(Col)

3855 West London Metal Worker's Record I, 1 (Oct. 1917)–I, 3 (Dec. 1917); m

A 1d. Published and edited by Jack Tanner. Organ of the West London Allied Engineering Trades' Organising Committee, formed after the engineers' dispute in 1917. Advocates direct action and industrial Unionism.

L(Col)†

3856 West Midlands WEA Torch [19--?]—[1932?]
    C   Incorporated in **The Highway and West Midlands WEA Torch**
(qv).

3857 West Monckton Clarion [194-?]. West Monckton, Somerset; q
    B   2d. Labour Party. Duplicated. (Labour Party. **Your own
Journal**, 1948).

3858 West of England Examiner: a Journal of General Intelligence,
Devoted to the Interests of Labour 1 (30 May 1874)—29 (12 Dec. 1874).
Bristol; w
    B   1½d.; 1d. (Nov.) Published by Thomas Thomas. Printed by the
Co-operative Newspaper General Printing Society. 'Purely and simply a
working man's paper; has no half-dealings with other classes, no
subserviency to other ranks of society.' One of the 'Examiner' series. Some
syndicated material. Full reports of workmen's meetings, union matters;
correspondence columns.
    L(Col)†

3859 West Points: West Dorset NALGO Magazine [1] April 1965—?
Bridport; bi-m?
    A   National and Local Government Officers' Association, West
Dorset Branch. Reproduced from typewriting. First issue does not bear
title.
    L [1]—[5] (Jan. 1966)

West Riding County officers' Association. News and Views see **County
Service Journal**

3860 West Wales Health Service Branch Magazine 1961?—   . Carmarthen
    A   National and Local Government Officers' Association.
Reproduced from typewriting. Title sometime **The Beacon**.
    L 1961—

3861 West Wickham Bulletin [194-?]. West Wickham; m
    B   Duplicated. Labour Party. (Labour Party. **Your own Journal**,
1948).

West Willesden Clarion see **Willesden West Clarion**

West Willesden Courier see **West Willesden Labour and Co-operative
Citizen**

3862 West Willesden Labour and Co-operative Citizen 1 (May 1930); then
West Willesden Courier: 2 (July 1930)—110 (Sept. 1939). West Willesden;
m
    B   Gratis. Published by the London Co-operative Society.
Illustrated local popular paper with Labour, trade union and co-operative
news and features. Covers local politics.
    L(Col)†

West Woolwich Citizen see **Woolwich Citizen, 1931—1932**

3863 West Yorks Teacher: Journal of the West Riding Teachers' Association 1 (Spring 1960)—10 (Spring 1963). Rotherham; 3-yr
    A   Published by the Association, a branch of the National Union of Teachers.
    LdP†

3864 Western Counter News [c1950]
    A   A local news sheet of the Union of Post Office Workers. 'A bright effort in the charge of Harry Smith.' (**Mets Journal**, May 1950.)

3865 Western Star I, 1 (3 Oct. 1840)—8 (5 Dec. 1840). Bath: w
    B   3d. Printed and published by John Crawley. For a 'broad extension of the suffrage', ballot, short parliaments. A 'Champion of the Rights of the Unrepresented Millions'. Celebrates the release from prison of Chartists Bartlett and Bolwell. Some correspondence, including a letter from Henry Vincent in No. 6. Mostly general news.
    L(Col)† 1—6

Western Union Employees' Association. Bulletin see **WUEA Review**

Western Union Employees' Association, News and Views see **WUEA Review**

Western Union Employees' Association Review see **WUEA Review**

3866 Western Valleys Labour Journal I, 1 (Jan. 1907)—I, 12 (Dec. 1907); m
    A?   Unofficial miners' group. Formerly **Monmouthshire Labour News**. Published at Six Bells, Abertillery, Monmouthshire.
    NpP 2—5, 7—9, 11—12

3867 Western Vindicator 1 (23 Feb. 1839)—41; ns 1 (7 Dec. 1839)—? w
    B   Produced by Henry Vincent. Popular among Chartists. See also **National Vindicator**.
    CrP Feb.—Nov. 1839; LabP 1839*; NpP 23 Feb.—30 Nov. 1839

3868 Westgate Bulletin [194-?]. Westgate-on-Sea; m
    B   Duplicated. Labour Party. (Labour Party. **Your own Journal**, 1948).

3869 Westminster Beacon [194-?]; m
    B   Duplicated. Labour Party. (Labour Party. **Your own Journal**, 1948).

3870 Westminster Citizen 1 (May 1932)—21 (Jan. 1934); m
    B   Published by the London Co-operative Society's Political Committee.
    L(Col)

3871 Westminster Labour Advocate I, 1 (Oct. 1903)—?

B   Printed and published for the proprietors by the Twentieth Century Press. Official organ of the City of Westminster Labour Representation Association (formed 1903) to which seven trade unions were listed as being affiliated. Promotes the six Labour candidates in the Borough of Westminster municipal election.

O(JJ)† 1

3872 Wharfedale NALGO News 1961?—. Ilkley

A   National and Local Government Officers' Association, Ilkley and Wharfedale Area Hospitals Branches. Reproduced from typewriting.

L 1961—

3873 What the TUC is Doing: a Record of Six Months Progress 1 (1935)—(1938); then **TUC in War-Time**: 1 (Dec. 1939)—12 (April 1945); then **What the TUC is Doing**. April 1946, Spring 1948—1963; s-a; q

A   Published by the Trades Union Congress General Council, 'to keep the affiliated unions in touch with the activities of the General Council and thus to afford them guidance in the framing of resolutions for the annual Congress'. 1963 is a special edition of **Labour**.

BS April 1945—   ; L; ONC 1938, 1939—45*, 1946—63; TUC

3874 What's What: the Official Journal fo the Film Artistes' Association 1 (Jan. 1947)—3 (March 1947); m

A   Published by the Association. Editor: Oby O'Byrne. A trade-union journal 'to air views, ventilate grievances' etc. 'nonpolitical, non-sectarian'. Reproduced from typewriting.

L; TUC 1—2

3875 Wheatsheaf 1 (July 1896)—600 (July 1946); then **Co-operative Home Magazine**: LI, 1 (Aug. 1946)—LXIII, 12 (Dec. 1958); then **Home Magazine**: LX, 1 (Jan. 1959)—? Sept. 1964. Manchester; m

A   Gratis. Co-operative Wholesale Society. An arrangement was made whereby local co-operative societies could insert local pages in this central magazine, for circulation in their own area, and more and more societies took advantage of this, the local pages often superseding a local journal produced by the society. Was entitled **Wheatsheaf Magazine** for a time.

Co-op. Col.*; Co-op. Union† II, 1 (July 1897)—; L(Col)*

Wheatsheaf Magazine see **Wheatsheaf**

3876 Wheel: NALGO Wallasey Branch Magazine 1 (March 1956)—? m

A   National and Local Goverment Officers' Association. Reproduced from typewriting.

L 1—20 (Aug. 1959)

3877 Wheels: the Official Newspaper of the United Road Transport Union 1963–   . Manchester; m; bi-m

    A

    The Union?

3878 Whip 1 (27 Feb. 1830)–2 (3 March 1830). Bristol.

    B   1d. Unstamped. Published and printed by J. Bennett. Radical. Offers assistance to James Acland and the Bristol Bread Association (A. Hart, **A Catalogue of Periodicals printed in Bristol, 1820–1840**, University of Leicester Victorian Studies Centre, 1972).

    BrP

3879 Whip: a Journal Devoted to the Interests of Cabmen, Bus and Tram Drivers, Conductors, Coachmen, and All Connected with the Stable 1 (16 Nov. 1895)

    C   1d. Printed and published for the proprietors by Fred. M. Hyman. A 'Watchful, energetic and sympathetic' press organ for this section of transport workers, in their fight for a fair wage for a fair day's work. 'The **Whip** is the outcome of an earnest and sincere desire to assist a worthy, industrious, honest, toiling body of men whose utility to society and to commerce is illimitable.'

    L(Col)†

Whip, 1952– see Government Minor and Manipulative Grades Association. **Bulletin**

3880 Whisper [19--?]–   . Nottingham

    A   National and Local Government Officers' Association, Nottingham Health Services Branch. Reproduced from typewriting.

    L 62/1 (June 1962)–

3881 White Dwarf or General Miscellany of Political, Moral, and Entertaining Essays 1 (29 Nov. 1817)–13 (21 Feb. 1818); w

    C   4d. Edited and published by Gibbons Merle. Conservative journal addressed to the general public to counteract the influence of the extremist **Black Dwarf**.

    L

3882 White Hat I, 1 (16 Oct. 1819)–I, 9 (11 Dec. 1819); w

    B   2d. Printed and published by C. Teulon. For annual parliaments and universal suffrage. The articles reflect the great bitterness in the immediate aftermath of the Peterloo Massacre.

    E; L

White Rose see **County Service Journal**

White Rosette see **County Service Journal**

3883 Whitehall Journalist: Bulletin of the Whitehall Branch of the National Union of Journalists I, 1 (Nov. 1951)–? Pinner; m

    A   1d. etc. Printed and published for private circulation, by the Union. Union news. Reproduced from typewriting.

    L

3884 Whitehall Worker: the Official Journal of the Whitehall Branches of the Workers' Union I, 1 (Jan. 1926)–I, 9 (Sept. 1926); m

    A   2d. Published by the Branch. 'The only organ specially catering for the Lower Grades of the Civil Service.' Features and union news.

    L

Whitehaven Miners' Monthly Gazette see **Monthly Miners' Gazette and Public Advertiser**

3885 Whitehall Journal [c1923?] –? then **Whitehall Worker**: [c1926?] –?

    A   Workers' Union, Whitehall branches. For Civil Service Minor Grades. (R. Hyman)

3886 Whitley Bulletin: the Official Publication of the National Whitley Council (Staff Side) for the Civil Service I (1921)–   ; m

    A

    DrU XXIX, 1949–   ; LE II–   ; ONC XIX, 10 (Jan. 1940)–

3887 Whosp 1965–   . Cardiff

    A   National and Local Government Officers' Association, Welsh Hospital Board Branch. Reproduced from typewriting. First two issued do not bear title.

    L

3888 Wilberforce Gazette I, 1 [1957] –II, 1 [1958]. Hull

    A   National and Local Government Officers' Association, Hull and District Branch.

    L

3889 Willesden Call: the Local Labour and Socialist Organ I, 1 (7 Feb. 1913)–VI, 21 (28 June 1918); w

    B   ½d. Printed and published by the Willesden Labour Press. Records the activities of Willesden and District Labour Party. Brief news of other socialist and trade-union organisations, and of municipal politics.

    L(Col)†

3890 Willesden Clarion [196-?] –   irreg;

    B   Issued by Willesden Labour Party.

    L(Col) 20 (Jan. 1963)–   ; LabP† 19 (Oct. 1962)

3891 Willesden Labour Monthly 1 (Dec. 1896)–([March?] 1897); m

    B   ½d. Published by R. Weston for Willesden Independent Labour Party. Localised edition of a newspaper launched by Allen Clarke in 1896 (**Labour Leader,** 27 March 1897).

    Brent PL 1

3892 Willesden West Clarion ns Sept. 1958–

    B   Issued by the Political Committee of the London Co-operative Society. Sometimes entitled **West Willesden Clarion.**

    L(Col)

3893 Wimbledon and St Helier Citizen: the Official Organ of the Wimbledon, Merton and Morden Labour Party 1 (3 Oct. 1931)–2 (10 Oct. 1931); w

    B

    L(Col)

3894 Wimbledon Citizen 1 (Feb. 1934)–67 (Sept. 1939); m

    B   Published by the Royal Arsenal Co-operative Society's Political Committee.

    L(Col)

3895 Winalgo News 1966?–   . Winsford

    A   National and Local Government Officers' Association, Winsford Branch. Reproduced from typewriting.

    L 1966–

3896 Windsor Progress [194-?]. Windsor; m

    B   2d. Labour Party. (Labour Party. **Your own Journal,** 1948.)

3897 Wireless Branch [19--?] –?

    A   Union of Post Office Workers, Wireless Branch. (W. Dunlop, 'Local journals'. **Belpost,** IV, 5 [May 1965].)

3898 Wivenhoe [194-?]. Wivenhoe, Colchester; irreg

    B   Duplicated. Labour Party. (Labour Party. **Your own Journal,** 1948.)

3899 Wodenalgo I, 1 (Autumn 1953)–   . Wednesbury

    A   National and Local Government Officers' Association, Wednesbury Branch.

    L

3900 Woking Labour News [194-?]. Woking; m

    B   Duplicated. Labour Party. (Labour Party. **Your own Journal,** 1948.)

3901 Wolverhampton Worker [1914?–1915?]. Wolverhampton

    A   Organ of the Wolverhampton Trades and Labour Council. (Mentioned in the 1915 **Year Book** of the Council.)

3902 Woman Clerk: the Organ of the Association of Women Clerks and Secretaries I, 1 (Dec. 1919)–II, 10 (Oct. 1921); ns I, 1 (Sept. 1925)–VI, 2 (Spring 1931); m; q

    A   2d. Published by the Association. The Association is a trade union 'now sufficiently numerous and solid to support its own paper'. Also serves the needs of its sister association, the Temporary Women Tax Clerks, to which is devoted a special page. (First series.) The new series is notable in that its columns are open to contributors from writers of every shade of political opinion, eg, Harry Pollitt and Lintom-Orman in 1925. Later the Association amalgamated with the National Union of Clerks to form the Clerical and Administrative Workers' Union.

    L 1925–31; L(Col)† 1919–21

3903 Woman Health Officer I (1926)–(Dec. 1963); then **Health Visitor** XXXVII, 1 (Jan. 1964)– ; m

    A   Women Sanitary Inspectors' and Health Visitors' Association; Women Public Health Officers' Association; Health Visitors' Association.

    L I, 7–(w IV, 7, 10–12); LMH XV (1942)– ; LSH VIII, 8 (1935), XXIV (1951)–*; LdU XIII, 5–XXV, 12*; TUC† 1928– ; the Association 1947–

Woman Journalist see Society of Women Journalists. **Bureau Circular**

3904 Woman Teacher I, 1 (29 Aug. 1911)–II, 13 (No. 39), (21 May 1912); w

    A   1d. Printed and published by George Tucker for 'The Woman Teacher' Press. To counter the journals controlled by and written for men teachers. For equal pay etc. 'Independent of Party-Politics'; 'Seeking only the Woman Teachers' Advancement'. Written by women teachers. Deals with salaries, conditions; advertises job vacancies; and covers wider questions of practical education, the teacher's life, in school, and at home, women's rights etc. Then merged in **Woman Teachers' Magazine**.

    L(Col)†

3905 Woman Teacher: the Organ of the National Federation of Women Teachers I, 1 (26 Sept. 1919)–XLII, 7 (April 1961); w; m

    A   1d. etc. Published by the Federation (later 'Union'). Campaigns for equality of salaries and conditions with those of men teachers. The Union and the journal were disbanded upon the achievement of this aim.

    AbU V–XI*; CrP XIV– ; L(Col)†; LIE XI, 18– ; LdU II–VIII*, IX– ; NU XXIX (1947)– ; SwU XIV, (1932/3)–

3906 Woman To-Day 1 (12 Sept. 1936)–(Feb. 1940); irreg?

    B   2d. Published by the British Section of the Women's World Committee Against War and Fascism, later the Women's Committee for Peace and Democracy. An illustrated 'Popular Front' for women's paper. Editor: Charlotte Haldane. Stands for women's interests as wage-earners, housewifes and mothers. Contributions from Professor Haldane, and from leading women in the Labour Party and the Labour Movement.

    L(Col)†

3907 Woman Today I, (1944)–(June 1959); m?

    B   Published by Tamara Rust (Jan. 1950). Communist. Political and economic affairs, education, wages, home affairs.

    L; ONC† Jan. 1950

3908 Woman Worker: a Journal of Woman's Trade Unionism [I], 1 (Sept. 1907)–IV, 30 (26 Jan. 1910); ns Jan. 1916–July 1921; m

    A   1d. Official organ of the National Federation of Women Workers. Editor: Mary R. MacArthur, Secretary of the Women's Trade Union League. Main purpose to unite in trade unions all women workers in unorganised trades. In February 1910 it merged with **Women Folk** (qv), but was revived in 1916. Contributor: Margaret Bondfield.

    L(Col)†; LE 1916–20; O 1907–10; OW 1907–9

3909 Woman Worker 1 (March 1926)–10 (Jan. 1927); m

    B   1d. 'Issued by the Women's Department, Communist Party of Great Britain.' Urges the building of a mass Communist Party and the participation of all women trade unionists in the National Minority Movement, for the overthrow of Capitalism.

    L(Col)†

3910 Woman's Angle: Featuring Items of Interest and Information for All Members of the Women's and Girls' Section of the AEU 1 (Aug. 1952)–134 (Sept. 1963); m

    A   Amalgamated Engineering Union. Sometime **Woman's Angle Newsletter**.

    L; TUC†

Woman's Angle Newsletter see **Woman's Angle**

3911 Woman's Dreadnought [Special advance number]. (8 March 1914); I, 1 (21 March 1914)–IV, 17 (21 July 1917); then **Workers' Dreadnought**: IV, 18 (28 July 1917)–XI, 13 (17 June 1924); w

    B   1d. Published by the East London Federation of the Suffragettes, later the Workers' Suffrage Federation. Founded and edited by Sylvia Pankhurst. Militant working-class organ for political and social emancipation. Agitates for a socialist commonwealth. Supported the Russian Revolution. In 1918 became an organ of the Workers and Shop Stewards' Committee Movement. Developed anti-parliamentary communist tendencies. Thoroughly internationalist.

    BP (microfilm); CPGB 1919–24*; L(Col)†; O 1920–   ; Tower Hamlets PL May 1914–Jan. 1916; Warwick UL (microfilm)

3912 Woman's Outlook 1919–June 1967. Manchester; fortn; w

    A   National Co-operative Publishing Society. A co-operative magazine for women. Close links with the Co-operative Women's Guild.

    L 1949–67

3913 Woman's Signal I, 1 (4 Jan. 1894)–XI, 273 (23 March 1899); w

C   1d. Established by Lady Henry Somerset. Edited by her and Annie E. Holdsworth in the interests of woman's work. A Christian philanthropic journal, claiming that temperance reform is the foundation of all reform, addressed to working-class women. Organ of the National British Women's Temperance Association. Occasional items on working conditions of women in London. Latterly, some support for women's Trade Unionism.

L(Col)†; OW

3914 Women and Work: a Weekly Industrial, Educational, and Household Register for Women 1 (6 June 1874)–91 (26 Feb. 1876); w

C   1d. Takes up the problem of finding work for educated ladies thrown on their own resources. 'The establishment of the Industrial and Educational Bureau from which this journal is to be published has revealed to us in a startling manner the perplexities of women who are left alone in the world, or who are dissatisfied with the monotony of an idle existence.' The paper is to be a record of industrial employments which those who want to work and those who can give it can alike consult, a reflexion of educational progress, and a compendium of miscellanea of special interest to the homekeeper and mother. 'A Special Committee will describe the various occupations in which women are engaged at home . . . we shall avoid party politics and controversial doctrines . . . '

L(Col)†

3915 Women Cleaners' Journal: the Civil Service Union Publication for Non-industrial Women Cleaners in Government Service [195-?]–March 1958; bi-m

A

TUC† 20 (Oct–Dec. 1953)–(March 1958*)

3916 Women Folk, with which is incorporated 'The Woman Worker' [I,] 1 (20 Dec. 1909)–IV, 52 (29 June 1910); w

B   1d. Edited by Winifred Blatchford, wife of Robert Blatchford. Generally anecdotal material relating to women. Mild labourite position in editorials. Supports right to female suffrage, women's Trade Unionism etc. Took over volume numbering from **Woman Worker** (qv).

L(Col)†

Women in Council News Letter see National Union of Women Workers. **Occasional Paper**

3917 Women's Industrial News [I], 1 (Oct. 1895)–XXII, 2 (April 1919); q

A   1d. Organ of Women's Industrial Council.

BS (Dec. 1904)–(1919); L(Col) I–XXII; LE (XXII*); MP XII, (1908)–XX, (1916); O 1912–19; OW 1903–19*

3918 Women's Labour News [c1900—1904]. Manchester
A? Published by Manchester and Salford Women's Trades Council. Edited by Esther Roper and Eva Gore-Booth. (Reference in Esther Roper's introduction to the **Collected Poems** of Eva Gore-Booth.)

Women's Trade Union Review see **Women's Union Journal**

3919 Women's Union Journal: the Organ of the Women's Protective and Provident League. I, 1 (Feb. 1876)—XV, 178 (15 Dec. 1890); then b **Quarterly Report and Review**: 1 (April 1891); then **Women's Trade Union Review**: 2 (July 1891)—110 (July 1919); m; q
A
BS b 89—109*; L (w a II, 16, V, 50, XI, 121, 128); LE (1910, 1917—19*); O b; OW a, b 2—39, 81—110*; TUC 1876—90, 1891—1919 (also microfilm)

Wood Green and North Tottenham Citizen see **London Citizen. Tottenham edition**

3920 Wood Green and Southgate Citizen 1 (Dec. 1930)—104 (Aug. 1939); ns 1 (Jan. 1947)—3 (March 1947); m
B Gratis. Published by the London Co-operative Society.
L(Col)

Wood Green Citizen see **London Citizen. Tottenham edition**

3921 Wood Green Clarion 1 (Sept. 1965)
B Published by Wood Green Labour Party.
L(Col)

3922 Woodcutting Machinist 1 (Winter 1963/64)—? Dublin; q
A Irish Society of Woodcutting Machinists.
TUC 1, 2 (Spring 1964)

Woodworkers' and Painters' Journal see **Amalgamated Society of Woodworkers' Monthly Journal**

Woodworkers' and Painters' Viewpoint see **ASW Viewpoint**

Woodworkers' Journal see **Amalgamated Society of Woodworkers' Monthly Journal**

Woodworkers', Painters' and Buildingworkers' Journal see **Amalgamated Society of Woodworkers Monthly Journal**

3923 Wooler's British Gazette 1 (3 Jan. 1819)–259 (14 Dec. 1823); w
    B   8½d.; 7d. Stamped. Printed and published by T. J. Wooler. A
well-conducted radical and general miscellany, with foreign news etc. For
universal suffrage, annual parliaments, election by ballot. Covers the
movement for parliamentary reform inside and outside Parliament.
Absorbed **Manchester Observer** and retained its name as part of a dual
title.
    L(Col)†

3924 Woolwich Citizen 1 (Oct. 1931)–9 (July 1932); then **West Woolwich
Citizen**: 10 (Aug. 1932)–92 (Sept. 1939); ns 1 (May 1949)–40 (March
1953); m
    B   Published by London and Royal Arsenal Co-operative Societies'
Political Purposes Committees.
    L(Col)

Woolwich and District Labour Journal see **Woolwich and District Labour
Notes**

3925 Woolwich and District Labour Notes 1 (Nov. 1898)–10 (Sept.
1899); then **Woolwich and District Labour Journal**: 11 (Oct. 1899)–13
(Dec. 1899); then **Borough of Woolwich Labour Journal**: 1 (Oct.
1901)–33 (June 1904); then **Borough of Woolwich Pioneer**: 34 (July
1904)–36 (Sept. 1904); then **Borough of Woolwich Pioneer and Labour
Journal**: 1 (14 Oct. 1904)–87 (8 June 1906); then **Pioneer and Labour
Journal**: 88 (15 June 1906)–142 (30 Dec. 1921); then **Pioneer**: 143 (6
Jan. 1922)–153 (17 March 1922); ns 1 (May Day 1922)–36 (Feb. 1926);
37 (July 1926). Woolwich; Plumstead; Woolwich; m; w; m
    B   Gratis; 1d.; 2d.; 1d. First published by Woolwich and Plumstead
Independent Labour Party; from October 1899 by 'a Joint Committee of
the Woolwich and District Trades and Labour Council and the Woolwich
Branch of the Independent Labour Party'; 1901–4 by Woolwich District
Trades and Labour Council; then printed and published by R. Pinnock,
later by William Barefoot, for the Borough of Woolwich Labour
Representation Newspaper Printing and Publishing Company,
subsequently printed and published by The Pioneer Press, and lastly
printed by the latter and published by William Barefoot. Size varies.
    GwP, Local History Library† (w occ. nos); L(Col)† 1901–26; LE 14
Oct. 1904–1920

**3926 Word; Against the World of Capitalism, Militarism, Fascism and
Dictatorship** I, 1 (May 1938)–XXV, 12 (April/May 1965). Glasgow; m
    B   1d.; 2d. Edited and published by Guy Aldred for the Bakunin
Press, later at the Strickland Press, and after Aldred's death in 1963 edited
and published by J. T. Caldwell. Organ of the United Socialist Movement.
'All unsigned matter is from the pen of the Editor.'
    E I, 1; GM†; LI, 1 (May 1939)–   ; LE; O I, 2–   ; ONC I, 2–III,
12, IV, 7,11, 12

3927 Word Quarterly I, 1 (Spring 1950)–I, 2 (Summer 1951). Glasgow; q

B 4s. 6d. pa. 'The Word Quarterly is a magazine edition of the monthly paper The Word. It will be issued four times yearly. The object of the Quarterly is to offer an intensive inquiry into a particular subject in each issue.' Issued by the United Socialist Movement. Printed and published by The Strickland Press. Edited by Guy A. Aldred. I, 1 is a 'Special Double Number' on the 'Ghandi murder trial'; I, 2 is a 'Special Anti-War Number'.

E; L; O

3928 Word Quarterly: Mightier than the Sword 1 (Winter 1965/66)–? Glasgow; q

B 6d. Issued by the United Socialist Movement. Published by the Strickland Press. Edited by John Taylor Caldwell. 'In some ways The Word (monthly) reborn.' Carries on Aldred's work, 'less personalized' and 'deals with social issues from a wider angle'. A political review, reflecting the views of the broad Anarchist-humanist Left. Reproduced some of Aldred's writings.

E; GM† ; LE; MML

3929 Work and Play, or, Help for the Night School I, 1 (Jan. 1871)–II, 19 (July 1872); m

C 1d. Printed by John and Charles Mozley. Stories and lessons for boys and young people, religious and didactic, encouraging manliness, good living, thrift.

L

Work in Wartime see **BFYC: a Year's Work**

Worker, 1898–1902 see **Arbaiter**

3930 Worker: a Monthly Socialist Journal I, 1 (March 1898)–II, 24 (Feb. 1900). Dunfermline; m

B 1d. Edited and published by William Stewart, who later joined Keir Hardie on the Labour Leader using the pen-name 'Gavroche'. Printed by John B. Rae, Alloa.

AbU II, 19 (Sept. 1899 [microfilm])); Dunfermline PL; O(JJ) II, 19 (Sept. 1899)

3931 Worker: the Organ of the Huddersfield Socialist Party 1 (21 July 1905)–852 (25 Nov. 1922). Huddersfield; m; w

B 1d. Published by F. C. Kay. Edited by James Leatham (1908–12). Local politics and affairs.

L(Col)†

Worker, June 1910–Jan. 1912 see **WDU Notes**

3932 Worker 10 Oct. 1910–? Harrogate

A? B?   (G. E. Laughton and L. R. Stephen comps. **Yorkshire newspapers.** Library Association, 1960.)

Harrogate PL 10 Oct. (no longer in stock)

3933 Worker [19--?] –? m

B   Poplar Trades Council and Labour Representation Council. ILP May 1912

3934 Worker: a Socialist and Labour Journal 1 (May 1912)–32 (Dec. 1914); then **Southern Worker**: a Labour and Socialist Journal: 33 (Jan. 1915)–48 (April 1916); 49 (May 1919)–79 (Oct./Nov. 1921). Bournemouth; m

B   1d. First issue published by the 'British Socialist Party (Bournemouth Branch) and other Women's Organizations' afterwards printed and published for the proprietors by various printers. Covers local Labour news from the Independent Labour Party, Labour Party, trade unions etc. First title varies, eg, **Bournemouth and Poole, The Worker,** and other variations containing the names of the towns covered.

L(Col); LabP†; Poole PL† (w 39, 42)

3935 Worker: Organ of the Irish Working Class Dec. 1914–Feb. 1915. Dublin; w

B   1d. Produced by Connolly after the suppression of **The Irish Worker.** Printed by the Socialist Labour Press, Glasgow. Suppressed. (Irish Transport and General Workers' Union. **Fifty years of Liberty Hall,** Dublin [1959?], pp. 57–8.)

3936 Worker: Organ of the Clyde Workers' Committee 1 (8 Jan. 1916)–402 (Aug. 1926); [ns I, 1] (28 Aug. 1926); ns [I], 1 (26 Sept. 1926)–VI, 11 (28 Nov. 1931); then **Weekly Worker**: IV, 12 (5 Dec. 1931)–VII, 24 (25 Feb. 1933). Glasgow (1–402); London; w

A   1d. Published first by the Clyde Workers' Committee, then by the National Workers' Committees and Shop Stewards' Movement, the paper became the organ of the British Bureau of the Red International of Labour Unions, then the National Minority Movement. Format varies. Contained several supplements: **The Metalworker**, 1924, 1925 (qv); **The Mineworker**, 1926–9 (qv); **The Unemployed Worker**, 1929–33 (qv).

E 1 (8 Jan. 1916)–402 (w 28 nos) (microfilm); L(Col) 5 (21 Dec. 1918)–(25 Feb. 1933); ONC† 3 (22 Jan. 1916)–ns VI, 30 (16 April 1932*)

3937 Worker [1918? 1919?] –? Sheffield

A   Printed by Jas. Neville for the Sheffield Workers Committee. Successor to the **Firth Worker** (qv).

Bill Moore, Sheffield Bookshop, 93 The Wicker, Sheffield; ns 24 (March 1920); Warwick U (MRC) ns 24 (xerox)

3938 Worker; Devoted to the Cause of All Workers 'by Hand or by Brain'.
I, 1 (16 Nov. 1921)—IV, 102 (Jan. 1930). Letchworth; w
  B 1d. Published for the Letchworth Labour Publication
Committee. News of the local Labour Party, Independent Labour Party,
municipal politics, trades council affairs, with a women's page, fiction etc.
  L(Col)†

Worker, 1936—see Irish Workers' Voice

3939 Worker 1 (1969). [Belfast?]
  B Produced by a group of communist workers in the Six Counties.
Only one issue published as the group folded.
  Linen Hall Library, Belfast.

3940 Worker Jan. 1969—   ; m; bi-m
  B 6d.; etc. Published by the Communist Party of Britain
(Marxist-Leninist). Preceded by an irregular untitled publication. A
newspaper, with analysis of home and foreign affairs.
  L(Col)†; ONC† June 1969—

Worker Esperantist see Laborista Esperantisto

3941 Worker Sportsman: Organ of the London group, British Workers
Sports Federation [1928?]—?
  A 1d. Published by G. W. Sinfield. Reproduced from typewriting.
Communist. News and events in sport.
  O(JJ)† 2 (June 1928)

3942 Workers' Action [1940?]—? Dublin
  A When Dublin Trades' Council's Council of Action started
campaigning against a wages stand-still order and the Trade Union Act,
'the propaganda section ran a periodical **Workers' Action**, which was
generally commended for the quality of its articles directed to rallying the
movement towards unity and militant effort' (J. Swift, **History of the
Dublin Bakers and others**, [Dublin]: Irish Bakers, Confectionery and Allied
Workers' Union, 1948, p. 342).
  D 21 June 1941

3943 Workers' Bomb, to Destroy Ignorance and Prejudice 1 (Nov.
1920)—2 (Dec. 1920?) Ystrad, Rhondda; m
  B 1d. Published by the proprietors, 'The Workers' Bomb' Press
Society. Common platform for all sections of the Labour Movement,
socialist and communist. News and notes, correspondence. Contributors:
T. Young, J. M. Williams, P. G. Hughes, A. J. Cook.
  ONC† 1—2; South Wales Miners' Library

3944 Worker's Child: an International Magazine with Illustrations 1 (Sept. 1926)–3 (June 1928); irreg

B   3d. Published by the International House of the Young Communist International. It 'is intended to fill a long felt need in the English speaking working class children's movement'. [It] 'attempts to give expression to the experiences of the International Movement; to express and develop the theory of Communist education; to give a lead to all workers in the Labour movement on the best methods for organising children in the interests of the workers' struggle and by means of pictures and special articles to appeal to the children themselves.' Reports activities of the Young Comrades' League and the Young Pioneers, relevant comintern resolutions. Contributions from Children's Section Leaders and Group leaders and from children.

MML† 1–2; WCML† 2–3

3945 Workers' Control Digest [1949?]–? 10-yr?

A   3d. London League for Workers Control. (Advertisement for No. 2 in **Clarion** [Common Wealth], June 1949)

3946 Worker's Cry, and Advocate of the Claims of the Labour Army 1 (2 May 1891)–20 (12 Sept. 1891); w

B   1d. Published and edited by Frank Smith. A Labour weekly which promotes full democratic rights for the working class, the unionisation of all labour, the eight-hour day, land nationalisation etc. and exposes the sweating system. Contributors: Shaw Maxwell, J. Morrison Davidson, Lady Dilke, John Burns, Dr John Moir. Amalgamated with **The Leader** to form **The Leader and Workers' Advocate**.

L(Col); LE; TUC; John Burns Lib.

Workers' Dreadnought see **Woman's Dreadnought**

3947 Workers' Educational Association. Year Book 1918; a
    C
    AbU; BP; BS; L

Workers' Fight see **Fight**

Workers' Friend, 1885–1932 see **Arbaiter Fraind, 1885–1932**

Workers' Friend, 1924 see **Arbaiter Fraind, 1924**

Workers' Friend Bulletin see **Arbaiter Fraind Buletin**

3948 Workers' Gazette: Broadsheet Produced by Members of the **Daily Worker** Staff 1941

B   Issued by the **Daily Worker** Defence League. Newspaper format, with news, notes, short articles, illustrations. Contributors: Frank Pitcairn, Jack Owen, J. B. Haldane, Harry Pollitt. Succeeded by **British Worker**, 1941.

ONC† Aug. 1941; TUC 1 undated issue

Workers' Guide see Nelson Workers' Guide

3949 Workers' Herald 1 (12 Dec. 1891)–6 (16 Jan. 1892). Aberdeen; w
    B   1d. Printed, published and edited by James Leatham, Aberdeen
Socialist Society. News of socialist movements and literature.
    AP†; L(Col)*

Workers' Illustrated News see WIN: Workers' Illustrated News

3950 Workers' International News I, 1 (18 Dec. 1937); I, 1 (1 Jan.
1938)–(Jan./Feb. 1949); m
    B   2d. Printed and published by R. Lee (18 Dec. 1937); J. R.
Strachan. Theoretical organ of the Trotskyist Workers' International
League, later, of the Revolutionary Communist Party (British Section of
the Fourth International). From September 1940 incorporates **Workers'**
Fight. The contents of 18 Dec. 1937 and 1 Jan. 1938 are identical.
    C; E I–IV; L I, 1 (1 Jan. 1938)–   ; LE; ONC*; Warwick U(MRC)

3951 Workers' International Pictorial I, 1 (May 1924)–II, 1 (May 1925);
m
    B   2d. Official organ of the Workers' International Relief; British
edition. Incorporates **Soviet Russia Pictorial**. Editor: Helen Crawford,
Secretary. Published by Helen Crawford on behalf of the British Joint
Labour Aid Committee of the Workers' International Relief.
    Buckhaven and Methil PL, Proudfoot Papers 9 (Jan. 1925); L(Col)†

3952 Workers' International Review I, 1 (Sept./Oct. 1956)–II, 3
(Sept./Oct. 1957); bi-m
    B   Organ of the Revolutionary Socialist League, Section of the
Fourth International.
    L

3953 Workers' Journal [18--? 1900?]–[1901?]. Swansea; m
    B? Gratis. Organ of the Trades and Labour Council of Swansea and
District. (**Reformers' Year Book**, 1901, 1902.)

3954 Workers' Journal: Official Organ of the RACS Joint Advisory
Council 1928–?
    A   Royal Arsenal Co-operative Society.
    L (not traced)

3955 Workers' Life 1 (28 Jan. 1927)–152 (20 Dec. 1929); w
    B   1d. Published by Alice Holland. Communist Party organ,
undertaken after the suspension of **Workers' Weekly** as a result of libel
action taken against it.
    C; L(Col)†; TUC; Warwick UL (microfilm)

3956 Workers' Monthly 1 [192-?]–142 (Nov. 1938). Guildford; m
    B   1d. Published by Southern Counties Workers' Publications, Ltd.
News of Labour Party, trade unions etc. in the region; articles, reviews.
    L(Col)† 45 (Sept. 1930)–142*

3957 Workers' News; for English Speaking Workers in the Soviet Union 4
Feb. 1931—28 April 1932. Moscow
    B   5 kopeks, 3 cents. Published by 'Ogonyok'. World-wide news;
more emphasis on the United States of America than United Kingdom.
Edited by K. S. Herald.
    L(Col)† I, 2 (9 Feb. 1931)

3958 Worker's News: Produced by Members of the Daily Worker Staff
1941
    B   Issued by the **Daily Worker** Defence League.
TUC† [Oct.] 1941

3959 Workers' News Bulletin 1954—June 1964; w
    B   2d. Published by the Workers' League. 'Towards a Workers'
Party.' Declares itself revolutionary Left. For control of production
through workers' councils. Opposes Labour Party and Communist Party;
anti-Stalinist and anti-Trotskyist. Main focus on trade-union problems and
disputes. Reproduced from typewriting.
    L IV, 16 (3 Aug. 1957)—(June 1964); LE† II, 26 (22 Oct.
1955)—(June 1964*); Warwick UL 1954—6*

3960 Workers' Pictorial [192-?] —?
    B   3d.; 10 cents. Published by the British National Committee of
Friends of Soviet Russia. Printed by Carl Sabo, Berlin. Consists mainly of
photographs of events and conditions in various countries, especially
Russia. The issue for November 1928 has one page devoted to 'Famine
conditions in the British minefields'.
    O(JJ)† Nov. 1928

Workers' Press see **Newsletter**

3961 Workers' Register of Labour and Capital 1923
    B   3s. 6d. Published by the Labour Publishing Company. Prepared
by the Labour Research Department. 'This is not a Year Book in the
ordinary sense, but aims at providing a clear record of the relations
between labour and capital since the war, and a summary of the
organizations and forces possessed by the two sides' (H. G. T. Cannons
comp. **Classified Guide to 1700 Annuals, Directories, Calendars and Year
Books**, Grafton, 1923, p. 36). Part 1. Labour; Part II. Capital and
production. Preface signed by G. D. H. Cole and Elinor Burns.
    BP; C; L; LE; O; ONC†

3962 Workers' Republic 1898–28 Jan. 1922. Dublin; w

   B   1d.; 2d. Founded by James Connolly. At first, organ of the Irish Socialist Republican Party. Not published continuously. A new series was started in 1915, printed and published by the Irish Workers' Co-operative Society at Liberty Hall, with Labour and trade-union news and comment. Covered activities of the Irish Transport Workers' Union, the Irish Citizen army, Dublin United Trades Council and Labour League. A later series, started in 1921 was the official organ of the Communist Party of Ireland.

   ILP 15 Aug. 1898; L(Col)† [ns] I, 1 (29 May 1915)–I, 48 (22 April 1916); [ns] I, 10 (10 Dec. 1921)–I, 17 (28 Jan. 1922); O I, 47 (1916), pp. 1–8 (photocopy)

3963 Workers' Republic: a Monthly Journal of Left-Wing Opinion I, 1 (May 1938)–4 (Aug. 1938). Dublin; m

   B   3d. Issued by the Communist Party of Ireland. Articles and discussion on issues of domestic and international working-class politics. Contributors: Brian O'Neill, Dennis Shaw, Betty Sinclair.

   L

3964 Workers' Republic 1 [196-?]–? Dublin q

   B   Published by the League for a Workers' Republic. Marxist theoretical journal. At first reproduced from typewriting.

   L 23 (Spring 1969)–25 (Autumn 1969)

3965 Workers' Republic: Fortnightly Newsletter [196-?]–? Dublin; fortn

   B   (Mentioned in **Workers' Republic**, 25 [Autumn 1969].)

3966 Workers' Review: Theoretical Organ of the Socialist Workers Group I [194-?]–? q

   B   Reproduced from typewriting until VII, 2.

   ONC IV, 3 (Oct.–Dec.)–VII, 2 (June–Aug. 1953)

3967 Workers' Searchlight: Issued by the Spen and Chopwell Reds 1 (30 May 1926)–? w

   A   1d. Reproduced from typewriting. 'First edition of a new weekly' (No. 1). Published in Chopwell?

   NwP† 1, 5 (27 June 1926 [xerox])

3968 Worker's Tribune: the Official Organ of the Blackburn Independent Labour Party 1 [1908?]–? Blackburn; m

   B   ½d. Printed for and published by the Blackburn Independent Labour Party. Newspaper, containing local and national news, women's column, children's column. Monthly article by Philip Snowden on front page.

   L(Col) 15 (Aug. 1909), 16 (Sept. 1909 [microfilm]); Lancashire Co. Lib. 15, 16 (microfilm); ONC† 15, 16 (microfilm)

3969 Workers' Union Midland District. **Record** 1 (Nov. 1913)–173 (Dec. 1927). Birmingham; m

    A   ½d. etc. Published by the East Birmingham 'Forward' Publishing Society, then by Workers' Union Record, Ltd. General Secretary: Charles Duncan, MP. Extensive union reports, and articles on Labour problems.

    BP†*; TUC July 1916–173

3970 Workers' Union of Ireland. **Bulletin, News and Views** [19–?]–? Dublin; m

    A   Newspaper.

    TUC† July 1957–Feb./March 1965

3971 Workers' Voice: Weekly Paper of the Syndicalist Workers' Federation I, 1 (28 Jan. 1961)–I, 19 ([Dec.] 1961); w; m?

    B   3d. Printed and published by Bill Christopher. Advocates social general strike through industrial unions, direct action of the workers, rejection of parties and vanguardism. Organ of the National Rank and File Movement. Features and news. Contributors: Brian Behan, Tom Brown, Ken Hawkes. Reproduced from typewriting.

    L(Col)†

3972 Workers' Weekly: Official Organ of the Communist Party of Great Britain 1 (10 Feb. 1923)–205 (21 Jan. 1927); w

    B

    C; CPGB; E 1–7 (24 March 1923), (1, 8 Aug. 1924); L(Col); O; TUC.

3973 Workers' Weekly 1941; w

    B   Edited by Frank Maitland, Independent Labour Party.

    ILP 23 May, 30 May 1941

3974 Workers' Weekly ns 1 (9 Dec. 1944)–? Edinburgh; w

    B   1d. Published and duplicated by W. Tait. Organ of the Revolutionary Communist Party. Ns 1 consists of a reprint of part of a pamphlet by John Maclean, **The War after the War in the Light of the Elements of Working-class Economics.**

    ONC† ns 1

Workers' Word see **Arbaiter Vort**

3975 Working Bee, and Herald of the Hodsonian Community Society 1 (20 July 1839)–46 (30 May 1840); ns I, 1 (6 June 1840)–28 (Jan. 1841); w

    B   1d.; 2d. Printed by John Green, at the Community Press, Manea Fen, Cambridgeshire, for the Trustees of the Society. Published by Henry Hetherington, London. Organ of the Community which was set up by William Hodson, inspired by Robert Owen. Discussion and correspondence on communitarian life.

    L; LU†

Working Engineer see **Engineer**

3976 Working Gentlewomen's Journal I, 1 (7 March 1906)–V, 8 (Oct. 1910); m
    C   2d. Issued by the Working Gentlewomen's Employment Guild. To help women find employment, especially as teachers, nurses, cooks, gardeners etc.
    L

Working Man see **Workman, 1861**

3977 Working Man's Advocate 1 (27 June 1835)–7 (8 Aug. 1835); w
    A   1d.; 2d. Published by G. Purkess and A. Wakklin (later Cleave). 'Under the management of the Friendly Society of Operative Printers.' 'A radical trades union miscellany that attacks the aristocracy, and advocates a consolidated general union as a prerequisite to the creation of a co-operative system. It contains regular accounts of trades union activities in the United States, reprinted from an American periodical of the same name' (Wiener).
    LU† 2, 6; Library of Congress

3978 Working-Man's Charter 1 (Aug. 1848)–? then b **Working-Man's Charter; or, the Voice of the People, Advocating Their Spiritual and Moral Improvement**: 1 (1 Jan. 1849)–?; m; w
    C   1d. Published by Partridge and Oakey. Aims: 'Sabbath-defence . . . mutual self-improvement, and . . . general edification of the labouring classes . . . ' by means of a prize essay scheme. The first numbers were for communication with intending competitors, 'Sent gratuitously to every Competitor for the Prize Essays upon "The Temporal Advantage of the Sabbath".' In January 1849 the periodical ceased to be supplied free. It was issued during the adjudication and gives information about this; also has contributions from working-men competitors: articles, essays, verse, stories. The prize essays were published as 'Supplemental series' of 'Working Men's Prize Essays, in Defence of Their Sabbath Rights'.
    L; O 1–4, [Nov.], 1848; 1 (1 Jan. 1849)–32 (1 Sept. 1849); 40 (29 Sept. 1849 [but there is no gap in pagination between 32 and 40])

Working Man's Companion or Year-Book see **Working Man's Year Book**

3979 Working Man's Friend 1 (1 Feb. 1832)–14 (14 April 1832). Bolton; w
    C   1d. Published and printed by R. Holden. 'Features abstract analyses of contemporary political events from a moderately conservative viewpoint' (Wiener).
    Bolton PL

3980 Working Man's Friend, and Political Magazine 1 (22 Dec. 1832)–33 (3 Aug. 1833); w

B   1d. Published and printed by H. Willis (1–9), James Watson (10–33). Edited by John Cleave. 'One of the best-known working-class newspapers of the decade. It repeatedly attacks factory abuses, the competitive system, and the tax on newspapers, and advocates universal suffrage' (Wiener).

BP 1–3; Bishopsgate Institute; HO 64/19 3–5, 7–14, 16, 20–2, 24, 28; L; LU 1–24; MP 18; NwP; ONC; Tolson Memorial Library, Huddersfield 1–18, 20–7, 29–33; WCML†; Warwick UL (microfilm)

3981 Working Man's Friend and Family Instructor I, 1 (5 Jan. 1850)–ns III, 78 (26 March 1853); w

C   1d. Printed and published by John Cassell. Contains essays by working men and women sent in response to the invitation of the publisher. Instruction and guidance in reading, languages, history, science, gardening etc., with some fiction, verse, biography etc. Supplementary numbers entitled **The Literature of Working Men** also appeared.

C; GM 1–4; L i; LU i I–II, IV, VII; MP; O; ONC i III, 27 (6 July 1850)–VI, 78 (28 June 1851)

3982 Working-Man's Newspaper 1 (29 Nov. 1873)–2 (6 Dec. 1873). Aberdeen; w

B   1d. Printed for the proprietors by John Nicol, Aberdeen (1), James M. Watt, Glasgow (2). To advocate the claims and interests of working-men. No. 1 declared it was owned and conducted by working-men. Columns open to employer and employed. Short items of general news, trade reports, poetry, correspondence.

AU†

3983 Working Man's Teetotal Journal, or General Temperance Library [184-?]–1844? c; fortn

C   Printed by W. Hill. Promotes teetotalism for working-men. Includes reports of various Teetotal Associations in London which appealed to them. Also stories emphasising the evils of intemperance, poetry. Emphasis on self-improvement. Unnumbered, continuous pagination.

LU† II (1844)

3984 Working Man's Year-Book 1835-6; then **Working Man's Companion or Year-Book**: 1837–40; a

C   9d, 6d. Published by Charles Knight. Printed by W. Clowes. Under the superintendence of the Society for the Diffusion of Useful Knowledge. Articles and reports on subjects of interest to working men, eg, 'The Conditions of Working men in Europe'; 'The diseases of Artisans and other Working men'; 'Operation of the Act for the Amendment of the Poor Laws'; 'Value of an Acquaintance with the fine Arts to a Working-man'.

L; LUC*; ONC† 1835–7

3985 Working Men's College Journal I, 1 (Feb. 1890)—XXII, 382 (Dec. 1932); then **Journal**: XXIII, 383 (Jan./Feb. 1933)—; m, etc.

    A 2d. etc.

    L; O 1890—1

3986 Working Men's College Magazine I, 1 (1 Jan. 1859)—III, 37 (1 Jan. 1862); m

    C   3s. per annum. Published by Macmillan. Editors: Vernon Lushington (II), R. B. Litchfield (I, III). Lectures, news of colleges throughout the country, correspondence. Subjects covered include the Labour Movement.

    C; D I—ii; L; LE I; LU; MP*; O; ONC 14 (1 Feb. 1860)

3987 Working Men's Journal, and Free Enquirer [18–?—185-?]. [Staffordshire]; w

    B?   1d. 'Published in the Staffordshire Potteries.' 'Conducted and supported solely by working men.' (Reference in a contemporary journal.)

3988 Working Woman 1 (Feb. 1927)—26 (March 1929); m

    B   1d. Issued by Alice Holland. 'Owing to the bankruptcy proceedings taken against the publishers of the **Woman Worker, Workers' Weekly** and **Communist Review**, they are no longer able to produce the **Woman Worker**. We hope that this first issue of **The Working Woman** will meet the demand for a revolutionary women's paper.' A Communist Party paper. Contributors: Kathleen Rust, Helen Crawford.

    L(Col)†

3989 Workington Beehive Industrial Co-operative Society. Record [c1909.] Workington; m

    A   Gratis. Issued and edited by the Educational Committee. Circulation 500. (**International Directory of the Co-operative Press**, 1909).

3990 Workington Co-operative Record 1 (4 Aug. 1893)—321 (Oct. 1919). Workington; m

    A   Gratis. Issued by Workington District Industrial and Provident Society. Local notes, and comment on Trade Unionism and politics. Circulation 800 (1909).

    L 228 (July 1912), 233—4, 244—8, 251—321

3991 Workman 1 (18, Aug. 1855)—(1858). Glasgow; w

    B   2d. Published and printed for the Daily Bulletin Company by William Syme. A large commercial newspaper intended for circulation among working-class readers, and respecting the interest of the class.

    GM† 140 (24 April 1858); GU 1

3992 Workman: Co-operative Newspaper. [I], 1 (21 June 1861)–3 (5 July 1861); then **Working Man: a Political and Social Advocate of the Rights of Labour**: 4 (12 July 1861)–II, 31 (Nov. 1862); II, 32 (May 1863); ns 1 (3 Jan. 1866)–[4th s 2] (17 Aug. 1867); w; m; w?

    A   1d. First series published by Job Caudwell. Conducted by a committee of working-men, including G. E. Harris, Charles Murray. For the political and social emancipation of the working class. Aimed 'not to lead, but to advise'. Columns of 'Labour news' which chronicle strikes and disputes; co-operative news. Provision for discussion by working-men of their problems. Contributors: John Parker, G. E. Harris. The second series was published by F. Farrah, and refers to the original publication, 1861–3, when 'we were compelled to silence, through public misfortune (although **The Working Man** was then a success)'. Proprietor, and editor (since 1861); Joseph Collett. Similar aims. Motto: 'Knowledge is Power, Union is Strength'. For State education, self-education and co-operative education. Supports National Reform League, and reports proceedings of the International Working Men's Association.

    L(Col)† (w II, 32 [May 1863] ; LU 3rd series; MP 1866–1867; O 22, 1862–32 (1863), 1866–7 (w 4th series)

Workman's Advocate 1865–1866 see **British Miner and General Newsman**

3993 Workman's Advocate: the Official Organ of the Colliers, Miners, Ironworkers etc. 1 (6 Sept. 1873)–48? (Aug. 1874); then **Amddiffynydd y Gweithiwr**: (Aug. 1874)–124? (Jan. 1876). Merthyr Tydfil; w

    B   1d. Printed and published by John Thomas Morgan. 'Devoted fully, heartily and exclusively to the true interests and honest claims of the working classes.' To promote the unity of the working class to combat the strong federal union of masters in South Wales. Became the official organ of trade unions in North and South Wales and the West of England. Correspondence and contributions by working-men in Welsh and English. Later, completely in Welsh.

    L(Col)† ; SwU 18–48*, 50–124*

3994 Workman's Club Journal I, 1 (15 May 1875)–III (1878); fortn

    A   1d.; ½d. Official gazette of the Working Men's Club and Institute Union. Succeeded by **Club and Institute Journal**.

    Club and Institute Union I, 1–II, 104 (5 May 1877)

3995 Workman's Expositor, and Weekly Review of Literature, Science, and the Arts 1 (7 Jan. 1832)–2 (14 Jan. 1832). Manchester; w

    B   2d. Published by Abel Heywood. Printed by Alexander Wilkinson. Edited by John Doherty. 'A radical factory journal that exposes alleged abuses of the "cotton nobility" in a weekly section entitled "The Beauties of a Cotton Factory" ' (Wiener). Succeeded by **The Poor Man's Advocate**.

    MP; L; L, Place Coll. Set 65

3996 Workman's Friend I, 1 (1 Feb. 1862)–5 (1 March 1862); w

C 1d. Published by W. Kent and Company. 'Conducted by the Rev. Charles Rogers, LLD, assisted by a large staff of popular writers.' Printed by Neill and Company, Edinburgh, for the proprietor, Charles Rogers, Stirling. For the social and mental elevation of working people. Promotes recreation, temperance, savings banks, friendly societies. For 'domestic comfort and social happiness'.

L

3997 Workman's Magazine 1 (Jan. 1873)–12 (Dec. 1873); m

C 6d. Published by W. Kent and Company. Edited by Henry Solly. Advises and actively promotes mutual collective self-help by means of Trades Halls, working-men's social clubs and institutes. Emphasis on working-class moral, social, material improvement by moral force means, education. Articles on political economy and literary sketches; correspondence from working-men. Contributor: James Hole, on 'Association'.

Bishopsgate Institute: L (destroyed); LE†; O

3998 Workman's Times I, 1 (29 Aug. 1890)–V, 200 (17 March 1894). Huddersfield; London; Manchester; w

B 1d. Editor: Joseph Burgess. 'Started as commercial venture by John Andrew of Ashton-under-Lyne. Contained news of interest to trade unionists of various industrial areas. Later advocated formation of independent labour party. In 1894 printed and owned by the Manchester Labour Press Society, Harry Henshall, manager, and endeavour growing out of North London Fabian group. Replaced by **Labour Leader** when latter became a weekly in 1894' (Brophy). Local editions were produced for a time in Birmingham, Hull, Tyneside, Teeside, Sheffield, Staffordshire, Midlands. See separate entries for the Birmingham and Hull editions; other editions have not been located.

L(Col) (also Birmingham and Hull eds.); MP (microfilm); ONC (microfilm; some issues in original); Warwick UL (microfilm)

3999 Workmen's Club Journal, and Official Gazette of the Working Men's Club and Institute Union I, 1 (15 May 1875)–III, 144 (9 Feb. 1878); w

A 1d.; ½d. Organ of London and provincial working-men's clubs. Promotes education, social improvement and mutual help. Discusses some political, social and labour subjects. Contributor: Henry Solly.

L(Col)†

Workmen's Hall Messenger see **Drury Lane Workmen's Hall Messenger**

Workmen's Messenger see **Drury Lane Workmen's Hall Messenger**

4000 Workmen's National Protection Association, Magazine for 1900–1. 1900–1; then **Shield of the Workers**: 1 (Feb. 1901)–4 (Oct. 1901); irreg

   B   1d. Printed for the proprietors by the Unity Press. Edited by Frederick James Atkinson, founder and General Secretary of the Workmen's National Provident Sick Benefit Society (1897). Saw 'The Workman's Weapon' as 'trade union consciousness'. Included article on the Workmen's Compensation Act with the purpose of 'exposing its defects'. Contributor: J. Connell.

   L

4001 World Federation of Trade Unions. **Information Bulletin** Jan. 1946–March 1949; then **World Trade Union Movement: Review of the WFTU**: May 1949–   . Paris; London; m

   A

   LII; ONC 1965*, 1966–

4002 World Marxist Review: [English Edition of **Problems of Peace and Socialism**] I, 1 (Sept. 1958)–   . Prague; London; m

   B   2s. 6d.; 13p. Place of publication is given as Prague on the first page; the imprint on the last page says published by W. N. Clark, then S. C. Easton, 16 King Street, London. Distributors of the English edition: Central Books. Theoretical; articles, news of communist and workers' parties, international conferences and congresses, book reviews, letters, notes.

   O

World News see **International Press Correspondence**

World News and Views see **International Press Correspondence**

World of Irish Nursing see **Irish Nurses' Journal**

World Socialist see **Socialist, 1915**

4003 World Socialist: Journal of the World Socialist Movement 1 (Jan. 1956)–? m

   B   6d. Short articles and discussion. Contributor: G. D. H. Cole (No. 1). Succeeded **WSM News Bulletin**. With No. 5 became: **Journal of the London Group, International Society for Socialist Studies**; with No. 9, Oct. 1956, became: **Journal of the UK Section, International Society for Socialist Studies**.

   L 1–3; ONC 1–9, II, 1–2, (Feb. 1957)

World Trade Union Movement: Review of the WFTU see World Federation of Trade Unions. **Information Bulletin**

4004 World Trade Union News I (1955)–? irreg?

   A   World Federation of Trade Unions.

   E 1957–   ; L 3 (Feb. 1956)–   ; O 1957–9

4005 World Youth Review: Monthly Supplement to 'World News and Views' 1 (Jan. 1939)–? m
    B   2d. Published by H. R. G. Jefferson. Reports and analysis of the international situation and the tasks facing the Young Communist International. British and foreign contributors.
    MML† 1–9 (Sept. 1939)

4006 Worsley News Letter [194-?]. Walkden, Lancashire; irreg
    B   Free. Labour Party. (Labour Party. **Your own Journal**, 1948.)

4007 Worth-Moor: the Magazine of Keighley Branch of NALGO [1964?]– . Keighley
    A   National and Local Government Officers' Association. Reproduced from typewriting.
    L 4 (Aug. 1962)–

4008 Wrekin Labour News: Official Organ of the Wrekin Divisional Labour Party I, 1 (Aug. 1946)–3 (Oct. 1946). Wellington, Salop; m
    B   2d. To 'give an account of what Labour is doing, nationally and locally'. Joint editors: Edith E. Pargeter, Mellor Harrison. Main contributor: Ivor Thomas, MP.
    L

4009 Wrekin Wreview 1966?– . Dawley
    A   National and Local Government Officers' Association, Wrekin Branch. Reproduced from typewriting.
    L [1966]–

4010 Wrexboro: Monthly Newsheet 1961?– . Wrexham
    A   National and Local Government Officers' Association, Wrexham Borough Branch. Reproduced from typewriting.
    L [1961]–

Wycombe Beacon see National Association of Local Government Officers. High Wycombe and Beaconsfield Branch. **News Sheet**

4011 Wycombe Democrat [194-?]. Wycombe; m
    B   4d. Labour Party. (Labour Party. **Your own Journal**, 1948.)

4012 Wythenshawe Voice [194-?]. Manchester; m
    B   2d. A local edition of **Northern Voice**. (Labour Party. **Your own Journal**, 1948.)

4013 YAC Outlook [19--?]–? m
    A   Youth Advisory Committee of the Civil Service Clerical Association.
    TUC May, July, Aug. 1946

4014 YCI Review [192-?] –?

B   Published by the Young Communist League. Primarily reports of agitational work carried out by the Young Communist League sections of the Young Communist International.

MML† IV, 1 (May 1924)

4015 Yak: the Monthly News Bulletin of the London Youth Advisory Council and the Sports and Cultural Movement of the National Union of Clerks and Administrative Workers I, 1 (1935–)? m?

A   Reproduced from typewriting.

TUC† I, (2 [Oct.], 3 [Dec.] 1935)

4016 Yardley Citizen 1 (March 1962)–

B   Published by the Co-operative Press for the Yardley Labour Party.

L(Col); LabP† 1

4017 Yarmouth and Central Norfolk Citizen 1 (April 1961)–5 (Jan. 1962); irreg

B   Published by the Co-operative Press.

L(Col); LabP 5

4018 Yearbook of International Co-operation 1 (1910)–3 (1913); a

A   International Co-operative Alliance.

L; LE; LU 1, 3

4019 Yearbook of the International Socialist Labour Movement [I], 1956–7–II, 1960–1; irreg

B   £3.3s.; £4.4s. Published by Lincolns-Prager International Yearbook Publishing Company. Edited by Julius Braunthal. Under the auspices of the Socialist International and the Asian Socialist Conference. Information about international socialist organisations, and socialist and Labour parties, including principles, aims, policies, some historic documents etc.

ONC†

4020 Yeovil Labour News [194-?]. Yeovil; m

B   2d. Labour Party. (Labour Party. **Your own Journal**, 1948.)

4021 Yeovil Worker [19–?] –   . Yeovil; q

A   Published by the Yeovil Workers' Association. Reproduced from typewriting. General local concerns.

4022 'Yer Tiz', Being the News Sheet of the North Devon Branch of the National Association of Local Government Officers July 1950–? Taunton

A   Later National and Local Government Officers' Association.

L July 1950, Jan. 1952, March 1953, Autumn 1956, Dec. 1957, Sept. 1958

4023 Yiewsley and West Drayton Citizen ns 1 (Nov. 1953)–2 (Dec. 1953); m

    B   Issued by the Political Committee of the London Co-operative Society.

    L(Col)

4024 York Co-operative Citizen 1 (June 1934)–6 (Nov. 1934); [ns] 1 (Dec. 1939)–(July 1942); (Jan. 1946–March 1952); m

    B

    L(Col)

4025 York Daily Labour News 1 [1904?]–403 (18 Jan. 1906) York; d

    B   ½d. Printed and published by T. A. J. Waddington. Gleanings of Labour news. Campaigns for Labour candidate.

    L(Col)† (394 [1 Jan.]–403 [13 Jan. 1906])

4026 York Labour News: the Organ of the Local Labour Representation Committee. 1 ([Feb.?] 1904)–? York; m

    B   Gratis. Published for the York Labour Representation Committe. Editor: Fred Morley (No. 17), G. H. Stuart. Short articles, news and notes. Listed in **Reformers' Year Book**, 1907.

    ONC† (17 [June], 19 [Aug.] 1905); York PL 2 (March)–10 (Nov. 1904), (12 [Jan.], 14 [March], 22 [Nov.] 1905)

4027 York Pioneer 1 (Aug. 1894)–25 (Jan. 1895). York; fortn; w

    B   ½d. Published by T. Anderson and printed by Rusholme and Whitehead, in support of the Independent Labour Party.

    AbU (mirofilm); York PL

4028 Yorkshire Factory Times 1 (5 July 1889)–1104 (29 Sept. 1910); then **Yorkshire Factory Times and Workers' Weekly Record**: 1105 (6 Oct. 1910)–1704 (13 Nov. 1919); then **Labour Pioneer**: 1705 (20 Nov. 1919)–1836 (29 June 1922); then **Yorkshire Factory Times and Workers' Weekly Record**: 1837 (6 July 1922)–2040 (29 April 1926). Huddersfield; Dewsbury (17 Oct. 1908–7 Aug. 1924); Heckmondwike (14 Aug. 1924–); w

    B   1d. First published by J. Burgess. Labour and trade-union news especially in the woollen trade. In defence of Labour. Support for Labour Party. By 1919 is sub-titled: 'Official Organ of the General Union of Textile Workers', editor Ben Turner.

    L(Col)† (w 1896) (1911, 1912 microfilm); LdP 1910–April 1926

4029 Yorkshire Journalist: the Official Organ of the York Branch of the National Association of Journalists 1 (31 Aug. 1888). York; q

    A   2d. Reports the third annual meeting of members of the York District of the Union.

    L(Col)†

Yorkshire Mine-Workers' Quarterly Journal see **Mine-Workers' Journal**

4030 Yorkshire Miner 1 (May 1959)–? Barnsley; irreg
    A   2d. Issued by the Yorkshire Area Council of the National Union of Mineworkers.
    LdP† 1–2 (Jan. 1960)

4031 Yorkshire Record: of the Workers' Educational Association, Yorkshire District 1 (Dec. 1925)–34 (March 1932). Leeds; m
    C   Printed and published by A. Angus and Company. Incorporated in **The Highway**.
    LdP† (w 10,12); LdU

4032 Yorkshire Tribune: a Monthly Journal of Democracy and Seculariam for the People 1 (July 1855)–(Sept. 1856); bi-m?
    B   Published by Holyoake and Company. Edited by William Mitchell, author of **The Philosophy of Teetotalism** etc. 'The Official Organ of the West Riding Secular Alliance.' Advocates universal suffrage; the rights of Labour; free secular education for children; nationalisation of the land; accumulation and distribution of wealth on the co-operative principles of Robert Owen; home colonisation; rights of women; temperance, as the means of ushering in a new world to replace that of degradation and ignorance. Articles, poetry. Contributors: Ernest Jones, William Mitchell.
    L; LU; LdP

4033 You and Us: Organ of the Joint Shop Stewards Committee, Brigg's Bodies I, 1 (Jan./Feb. 1946)–[1950?]; m?
    A
    WCML† I, 4, 5, II, 1 (Jan. 1948)

4034 Young Chartist I, 1 (March)–2 (June 1951). Ashford, Middlesex; irreg
    B   Issued by the Labour Party League of Youth. Reproduced from typewriting. Campaigns for a socialist youth charter.
    L

Young Communist see **Red Flag**

4035 Young Comrade I, 1 (April 1924)–(May 1928); ns I, 1 May 1928–? m
    B   ½d.; 1d. Organ of the Young Communist League, later Young Comrades' League.
    L i (not traced in catalogue); MML† (occ. nos); O(JJ)† ns I, 1; WCML† I, 1

Young Co-operator see **Co-operative Youth**

4036 Young Guard: the Paper with the Socialist Programme for Youth 1 (Sept. 1961)–[1965?]; m
    B   4d. Organ of the Young Socialists, for Left-wing youth within the Labour Party.
    LE† 3 (Nov. 1961)–4, 9, 11–34

4037 Young International: Fighting Organ of the Young Communist International 1 (May 1921)–? London; New York

    B   2d. Published by the Executive Committee of the Young Communist International. One only?

    ONC† 1; WCML† 1

4038 Young Oxford: a Monthly Magazine Devoted to the Ruskin Hall Movement I, 1 (Oct. 1899)–IV, 48 (Sept. 1903). Oxford; m

    A   3d. No. 1 edited, illustrated, published and sold by students of Ruskin Hall. From No. 2 edited and published by A. J. Hacking. Editors: A. J. Hacking, Anne L. Vrooman. Sometimes entitled **Young Oxford and the Ruskin Hall News**. Varied articles including contributions on social and industrial problems.

    C; L; LE*; LdP I–III; O

Young Oxford and the Ruskin Hall News see **Young Oxford**

4039 Young Rebel 1917

    B   A Marxist paper for youth, edited by James Stewart, one of the founders of the Young Socialist League, later Young Communist League. Suppressed in 1917.

    WCML† 2 (June 1917)

Young Russia Today see **Youth Quarterly**

4040 Young Socialist [189-?]–[1897?] Ashton-under-Lyne; m

    B   ½d. Editor: Thomas Pennington. For Socialist Sunday Schools etc. (**Labour Annual**, 1897, 1898.)

4041 Young Socialist: a Magazine of Love and Service 1 (Jan. 1901)– London; Glasgow; m

    B   ½d. etc. Printed for the proprietor by the Twentieth Century Press, then published for the Glasgow and District Socialist Sunday School Union by W. Finlayson, later issued by the National Council of British Socialist Sunday School Unions, currently by the Socialist Fellowship. Editors: Archie McArthur; John Searson; L. L. Glasier Foster; Cunliffe R. Pearce. Contributors included Elizabeth Glasier, Keir Hardie, F. J. Gould.

    GM 1914–25; L*; LE 1901–5*; LabP 1903–29*; MML† 1901–*

4042 Young Socialist: the Organ of the Labour Party League of Youth I, 1 (July 1946)–I, 25 (July 1948); then **Labour Youth**: I, 26 (Aug. 1948)–I, 30 (Dec. 1948); then **Socialist Advance**: [I], 1 (Jan. 1949)–LXIV, (1956); m

    B   1d. etc.

    L; LE†; LabP*; O; ONC April 1949–Sept. 1956

4043 Young Socialist [c1950]. [Edinburgh?]

    B   Organ of Pentlands Constituency Labour League of Youth. (**Edinburgh and Lothians Clarion**, Sept. 1950.)

4044 Young Socialist Pioneer [1911?] –?
   B   Circulating in North Islington.
   ILP 1 (2nd ed.), 3 (Sept. 1911)

Young Socialists Communiqué see **Labour Party Young Socialists Chief Officer's Newsletter**

4045 Young Teacher: Young Teacher Newsletter of the National Union of Teachers 1 (Spring 1970)–   ; 3-yr
   A
   O Spring 1970–Summer 1971

Young Worker, 1921 see **Red Flag**

Young Worker, 1923–1926 see **Red Flag**

Young Worker, 1927–? see **Red Flag**

4046 Young Worker 1968–9. [Cork?]
   B   Published by Cork Young Socialists. (P. Howard, 'The Paper War: Communism and Socialism', **Fortnight**, 78 [22 Feb. 1974].)

4047 Your Business 1 (Oct. 1949)–2 (Nov. 1949); then **Orpington Labour News**: Official Journal of Orpington Labour Party: I, 1 (1949)–26 (Dec. 1951); Cray; m
   B   At first reproduced from typewriting (1–2), then 2d., published by E. F. Osborne, Secretary of Orpington Labour Party.
   L

4048 Your Magazine I, 1 (March 1960); then **Lamp**: [2] (30 June 1960)–. Lincoln
   A   National and Local Government Officers' Association, Lincoln and District Health Services Branch. Reproduced from typewriting.
   L

4049 Your Voice: Official Staff Magazine of the Birmingham Co-operative Society, Ltd. I, 1 (Jan. 1950)–   . Birmingham; m
   A   Issued by the Publicity Department, 'to chronicle matters and events of interest to BCS Employees'. Business and social news.
   BP†

Yousedit see **Factory News**

4050 Youth [c1936]. [Glasgow? London?]
   B   A Labour Party League of Youth paper (**Socialist Youth**, 1936.)

4051 Youth Against the Bomb; Monthly Journal of the Youth Campaign [1960?]–? m
   B   Campaign for Nuclear Disarmament.
   LE III, 1 (Sept. 1961), 1962–3*

4052 Youth Bulletin 1970–2. Dublin; fortn

    B   Published by Irish Young Socialists, NI. Then incorporated into **Worker's Struggle**, 1972–.

    D III, 1 (1972)–16 (1972); Linen Hall Library, Belfast II, 2 (1971)–III, 15 (1972*)

4053 Youth for Socialism I, 1 (Sept. 1938)–III, 8 (May 1941); then **Socialist Appeal**: Organ of Workers' International League, Fourth International: III, 9 (June 1941)–[1949?] m, irreg

    B   1d. Later organ of the Revolutionary Communist Party. Printed and published by Gerry Healy; B. French. **Socialist Appeal** edited by Ted Grant.

    E June 1941–; L I, 1–V, 3 (Dec. 1942); ONC† I, 1–69 (May 1949*)

4054 Youth Forum 1 [1934?] –?

    B   Labour Party League of Youth and Young Communist League. To link young socialists in different organisations, providing a forum for the expression of opinion on policy. Reproduced from typewriting.

    MML† 1

4055 Youth Forward: the Merseyside Magazine for All Young Socialists I, 1 (May 1937)–3 (July/Aug. 1937). Liverpool; m

    B   1d. Issued by the Merseyside Labour Party Leagues of Youth. Supports the official Labour Party programme.

    L

4056 Youth Front, Against Fascism and War ns 1 [1934?] –?

    B   1d. 'Organisational bulletin'. Reports the progress of the campaign to mobilise anti-Fascist youth rallies in Glasgow, Manchester, Sheffield and East London. Reproduced from typewriting.

    MML† 1

4057 Youth Herald 1950

    B   North St Pancras Branch, Labour Party Young Socialists (**Socialist Advance**, June 1950*a*).

4058 Youth in Struggle: Bulletin of the International Secretariat of Young Workers 1 [Jan. 1931?] –? [London?] ; m

    B   Issued by the International Youth Secretariat of the Red International of Labour Unions. Covers the political work of the Young Communist International in Germany, the Balkans, and Czechoslovakia, and youth work in trade unions. No. 3 has a report on 'Young workers in the cotton textile workers' struggle in Lancashire'. Reproduced from typewriting.

    MML† (2 [Feb.], 3 [March] 1931)

4059 Youth Militant I (1936)–II, 5 (June 1937); then b **Militant**: Organ of the Militant Group in the Labour Party: I, 1 (July 1937)–(April 1946?); m

    B   1d. At first the organ of the Youth Militant Group of the Labour League of Youth.

    L(Col)† Jan.–June 1937; ONC† a II, 3 (April 1937)–5 (June 1937); Aug. 1937–April 1946 (occ. nos only)

4060 Youth Militant: the Paper of the Youth Section of the Militant Labour League 1 (Feb. 1939)–3 (May 1939); irreg

    B   Published by the Militant Publishing Association. Organ of the Left wing in the Labour League of Youth. Reproduced from typewriting.

    L(Col)†

4061 Youth News 1 (Dec. 1939)–? m

    B   2d. Published by the British Youth Peace Assembly. Edited by H. Michael Scheier. Covers the World Youth Congress Movement, the aims and activities 'of forward looking youth'. Anti-imperialist.

    MML† 1–(Nov./Dec. 1941) (occ. nos only)

4062 Youth Quarterly 1 (Sept. 1946)–2 (Nov. 1946); then **Young Russia Today**: 3 (March 1947)–4 (July 1947); q

    B   Published by the British-Soviet Society Youth Department, formerly Anglo-Soviet Youth Friendship Alliance. **Young Russia Today** is a supplement to **Russia Today**. Preceded by **Soviet Youth News Service**.

    L(Col)†

4063 Youth Review, Incorporating 'The Young Worker' 1 (Jan. 1939)–[1940]; then b **Socialist Review, Incorporating 'Young Worker' and 'Youth Review'**: [1940]; ns 1 (Dec. 1945)–20 (Jan. 1948?); bi-m; m; irreg

    B   2d. etc. 'Reflects all shades of left wing opinion.' Editors: Joan Harris, George Noble. Contributors: K. Zilliacus, Sidney Dye, Graham Greene.

    L 8 (1940), b I, 1 NS 1–20

4064 Youth Review 1 (Oct. 1964).

    A   Issued jointly by the National Association of Teachers in association with the National Association of Youth Service Officers and the Youth Service Association. A magazine which discusses problems of youth, policy and activities.

    L

4065 Youth Unity Magazine: the Magazine of the Scottish Divisional Council of the ILP Guild of Youth [193-?]–[1934?]. Glasgow

    B   1d. Printed by The Proletarian Press, published by the Scottish Divisional Council of the Independent Labour Party Guild of Youth. 'The Voice of the Scottish Guild of Youth containing Guild news and opinion, striving towards the attainment of youth unity.' Discusses and approves of united action with the Young Communist League, and conditional affiliation to the Young Communist International. Argues the futility of parliamentary democracy.

    MML† I, 8 (April 1934), Nov. 1934

4066 Zherminal: Anarchistishes Organ [Germinal: Anarchist Organ] I, 1 (16 March 1900)–VI, 3 (May 1909). London; fortn; m (1905–9).

    B   4d. Yiddish.

    L(Col)†

Addenda: I

4067 An Dion (1926–1930?) Dublin; m
    A   Irish Post Office Workers Union.
Nat. Lib Ireland

4068 Bulletin of the Anarchist Black Cross 1968–70; (The Left in Britain – microfilm – Harvester Press Ltd.)

4069 Bulletin of the Centre for Socialist Education 1 (Jan. 1966). 1966, 16 pp. (The Left in Britain – microfilm – Harvester Press Ltd.)

4070 Campaign for Socialism. **Bulletin** 1. n.d., [1965?] (The Left in Britain – microfilm – Harvester Press Ltd.)

4071 Church and State: 1 (16 Jan. 1836); w
    B   2d. Printed and published by P. Hammond 'A radical political miscellany that repeatedly condemns the Church of England. It advocates universal suffrage and the ballot.' (Weiner)
    O

4072 Clarion: 1 (Aug. 1951)–(Sept. 1951)
    B   3d. Organ of the West Salford Labour Party League of Youth. Editors: Don Dickens, Keith Iverson and Gerald Daly.
    John B. Smethurst 81 Parrin Lane, Winton, Eccles, Manchester.

4073 Democrat: a Weekly Journal for Men and Women, I, 1 (15 Nov. 1884)–VI, 9 (1 Sept. 1890); w; m
    B   1d.; 2d. Editors: possibly Helen Taylor and William Saunders at first; William Saunders (Dec. 1887–Sept. 1888); J. E. Woolacott: Frederick Verinder (1889–1890). 'Major Emphasis on land reform and adult suffrage. In 1890 front cover regularly carried banners for land resumption, free education, eight hours labor, home rule, adult suffrage, paid Members of Parliament' (Brophy). Continued as **Labour World**.
    GM VI; L(Col); LE; TUC, John Burns Lib. I, 1–V, 133, Dec. 1889

4074 Dublin Trade and Labour Journal June–Sept. 1909. Dublin; m
    A   Organ of Dublin Trades Council.
Nat. Lib. Ireland

4075 The Fleet: 1 (May 1905)–550, (Dec. 1950); bi-m
    C   Editor: Lionel Yexley, 1905–1933. Organ of the lower deck.
    L(Col)

4076 The Forces: 1 (April 1919)–3 (June 1919); w
    A   Editor: J. C. Byrnes. Byrnes was the General Secretary of the Sailors, Soldiers and Airmens Union and **The Forces** was the organisations journal.
    L(Col)

4077 Hope: 82 (Feb. 1891)–189 (Dec. 1899). then **The Bluejacket and Coastguard Gazette** 190–300 (Jan. 1900)–(March 1909) then **Bluejacket and Soldier** 301–420 (April 1909)–(June 1920). then **The Colours** 421 (July 1920) Rye, Feb. 1891–March 1899 then London; m
    C   Editor/owner: J. M. Masters. Organ of the lower deck.
    L(Col)

4078 The Industrial Worker n.d. (1961?–1962); (The Left in Britain–microfilm–Harvester Press Ltd.)

4079 International Bulletin 1961–1962 then **The Bulletin** 1963–   ; (The Left in Britain–microfilm–Harvester Press Ltd.)

4080 International Socialism: journal for socialist theory.
1960–continuing; (The Left in Britain–microfilm–Harvester Press Ltd)

4081 Irish Front (19--?)–(1938?)
    B   Preceded **Irish Freedom** (qv)

4082 Irish Hammer and Plough 22 May 1926–16 Oct. 1926 Dublin w
    A Organ of the Workers Party of Ireland.
    Nat. Lib. Ireland

4083 Kidderminster Shuttle 12 Feb. 1870–(?). Kidderminster; w
    B   Radical and sympathetic to local carpet weavers. Founded and edited by the Rev. Edward Parry. Unitarian and Republican.
    Kidderminster Public Library

4084 The Law Clerk I (1 March 1906)–II (8 Oct. 1907) then **The Law Clerk and Municipal Assistant**, II, 9 (Nov. 1907)–VII, 9 (Jan. 1913); m
    A   1d., 2d. Journal of the Law Clerks Mutual Benefit Association. 'It will not air their (law clerks) grievances, stimulate their ambitions, voice their aspirations. It will be their medium of communication. It will endeavour to raise their status and improve their remuneration. It will seek to gather their dispersed forces under the banner of a common cause.'
    L (Col)

4085 Leeds Partisan the magazine of the Leeds Left Group (associated with the **New Left May Day Manifesto**), No. 1. Autumn 1968. 1968, 18pp (The Left in Britain–microfilm–Harvester Press Ltd.)

4086 Left: the magazine of Nottingham University Labour Club 1968–?
Nottingham. Organ of Nottingham University Labour Club. Editor: James
Harbord.
    N.U.

4087 Marxist Youth Journal n.d. (1970?) 21 pp; (The Left in
Britain–microfilm–Harvester Press Ltd.)

4088 May Day Manifesto Newsletter 1968–70; (The Left in
Britain–microfilm–Harvester Press Ltd.)

4089 Militant International Review A Marxist quarterly.
1969–continuing; (The Left in Britain–microfilm–Harvester Press Ltd.)

4090 Militant Teacher 1969–1971 (The Left in
Britain–microfilm–Harvester Press Ltd.)

4091 October. The magazine of the Brighton May Day Manifesto Group,
No. 1. 1968. 16 pp; (The Left in Britain–microfilm–Harvester Press Ltd.)

**4092 Quarterly Journal of the National Brass Workers and Metal
Mechanics** (1918?)–No. 11 Sept. 1921; Birmingham; q
    A   Preaches patriotism, democracy and solidarity in the aftermath
of the war.
    Birmingham Public Libraries, Local Studies Dept. (167.306)

**4093 Quarterly Reports of the Glass Bottle Makers of Yorkshire United
Trade Protection Society** I (187?)–XXIII (June 1911). Leeds, Castleford;
q
    A   Organ of the Glass Bottle Makers United Trade Protection
Society of Yorkshire. Edited by A. Greenwood, Central Secretary of the
Society. Includes Central Secretary's remarks on trade and other matters,
articles and statistics on the state of the trade general discussions of the
social role of trade unionism.
    LE

4094 The Radical Times of Birmingham Sept. 1876–(1877?) Birmingham;
w?
    A?   Planned as a co-operative newspaper but founded by C. C.
Cattell, secularist, republican and advocate of labour representation.
    L(Col) (one issue)

4095 Red Hand (Spring 1919–Winter 1919?) Dublin; w; irreg
    A   Issued by opponents of the leadership of the Irish Transport
and General Workers Union.
    Nat. Lib. Ireland

4096 Socialist Fight (1958–1963?); (The Left in
Britain–microfilm–Harvester Press Ltd.)

4097 Socialist Review 1950–1962; (The Left in Britain–microfilm–Harvester Press Ltd.)

4098 Socialist Youth 1 (Dec. 1950–?) bi-m
    B   1½d. Formed by a group of youth leaders of **Socialist Outlook**. Later became organ of the London Federation of the Labour Party League of Youth. Published and edited by Audrey Brown; other editors included Michael Perkins, John Hayes, Kevin Grant and John Daly.
    John B. Smethurst, 81 Parrin Lane, Winton, Eccles, Manchester. 1 (Dec. 1950)–5 (July–August 1951).

4099 Struggle 1969–continuing; (The Left in Britain–microfilm–Harvester Press Ltd.)

4100 The Week 1964–1968; (The Left in Britain–microfilm–Harvester Press Ltd.)

4101 Workers' Fight A Trotskyist journal for members of the IS group. 1967–68; (The Left in Britain–microfilm–Harvester Press Ltd.)

4102 Workers Voice 5 April 1930–(Dec. 1932?) Dublin; w; irreg then **Irish Workers Voice** 7 Jan. 1933–(1936?)
    A   Organ of the preparatory committee of the Revolutionary Workers Party. Subsequently Communist Party of Ireland.
    Nat. Lib. Ireland

Acknowledgements (The help of the following persons in compiling this list of additional items is gratefully acknowledged) D. Englander A. Hooper N. Howard I. McDougall A. Mitchell J. Osborn J. Spiers Kate Tiller

Addenda: II

4103 Di arbayter shtime 1898–1901 London. Russian.

A   The Arbayterstimme was published in Russian in London. The Yiddish version was published illegally somewhere in Russia.

(L. Prager **Studies in Bibliography and Booklore** Vol. 9 Spring 1969)

4104 British Labour Advocate: The Organ of Expression for all Societies connected with amelioration of the present depressed state of our Labour class 1, 14 June 1870–?

C   ½d. Printer and proprietor, Jason Marles. Organ of the Revivers: a Society opposed to free trade. Reports meetings of the Land and Labour League and the International, but calls for closer alliance of Labour and Capital.

L(Col)

4105 Executive Journal of the National Charter Association 1, 1 (16 Oct 1841)– 1, 4, (6 Nov 1841); w

A   1d. Official organ of the Chartists edited by Dr. P. M. M'Dougall; J. Leech, R. K. Philip; M. Williams, and J. Campbell. Printed and published at Bath. The final issue explained that members of the Executive were too busy attending meetings to ensure the transmission of manuscripts to the printers early enough for prompt publication.

L(Place Col set 56 Vol. Sept/Dec 1841)

4106 Dos fraye vort No. 1–8. (29 July–17 Sept. 1898); Liverpool

B   Edited by Rudolph Rocker with assistance of M. Yeger, who printed the periodical. Anarchist. Memoir literature contains many references to **Dos fraye vort**, but no copies have been located. See Rudolph Rocker's **In shturem** (partially translated by J. Leftwich as **The London Years**); **Dos fraye vort** is discussed on pp. 107–111 of **The London Years**.

(L. Prager **Studies in Bibliography and Booklore** Vol. 9 Spring 1969)

4107 Fraye yidishe tribune
No. 1–8; (Dec., 1943–Dec., 1948)

B   Edited by Charles S. Klinger. A Poalei Zion (i.e. Labour Zionist) literary-political journal.

L(Col)

4108 Di frayhayt
Vol. 1, No. 1—No. 28, 22 Feb., 1902—2 Jan. 1903; w

    B   Edited by L. Baron. Anarchist-factional, in opposition to **Der arhayter fraynd**

    (L. Prager **Studies in Bibliography and Booklore** Vol. 9 Spring 1969)

4109 General Parish Watchman Mar 1841—?

    C   2d

    L   (Place Col)

4110 Der idisher arbayter No. 1—17; Dec. 1896— Oct. 1904 London, Geneva and?

    A. Organ of the Bund. Illegal periodicals, published mainly in Geneva; No. 13 (Feb, 1902) and 14 printed in London.

    (L. Prager **Studies in Bibliography and Booklore** Vol. 9 Spring 1969)

4111 Der kostyum un mental arabayter (The Costume and Mantle Worker)
Vol. 1, No. 2—N.S., No. 1; Oct., 1927—May, 1929. q. English and Yiddish

    A Edited by Y. Kaplan (I. Caplan). Official organ of the United Ladies Tailors' Trade Union.

    (L. Prager **Studies in Bibliography and Booklore** Vol. 9 Spring 1968)

4112 Lever or The Power of the Press 1 (25 Jan 1851)—37(11 Oct 1851); ?w

    A   Organ of the People's Hall, Hanley. Chartist or ultra radical.

    Stp 1 *and* 37

4113 Di mental meyker shtime
Vol. 1, No. 1; June 1915. London; m

    A   Organ of the London Ladies Tailors Trade Union

    (L. Prager **Studies in Bibliography and Booklore** Vol. 9 Spring 1969)

4114 Di naye velt
Vol. 1, No. 1: April 1900; fortn (irregular)

    A   Edited by T. Rothstein and A. Beck (the latter not Jewish) "A fortnightly Social-Democratic Journal published by the Social Democratic Organization." Continued as DI NAYE TSAYT. q.v.

    (L. Prager **Studies in Bibliography and Booklore** Vol. 9 Spring 1969)

4115 Der nayer dor (The New Era)
Vol. 1, No. 1—6 May, 1920—Feb., 1921

    A   Published by the Press Committee of the Workers' Circle.

    (L. Prager **Studies in Bibliography and Booklore** Vol. 9 Spring 1969)

4116 Di proletarishe velt
Vol. I, No. 11—Vol. II, No. 2; October 1902—1903; q

    A   Edited by Mikhl Rubinshteyn. Organ of the polish Socialist Party (PPS). Published outside England before and after 1903.

(L. Prager **Studies in Bibliography and Booklore** Vol. 9 Spring 1969)

4117 Der Propagandist
No. 1–10: 1 May–29 October 1897
  B   Edited by A. Frumkin. Anarchist; private effort of Frumkin
during period that **Der arbayter fraynd** suspended publication. Nos. 1–4
appeared irregularly; 5–10 appeared weekly. See R. Rocker, **In shturem;**
A. Frumkin, **In der friling fun idishen sotsialism,** and E. Tsherikover's
article in **Historishe shriftn fun Yivo,** III.
  (L. Prager **Studies in Bibliography and Booklore** Vol. 9 Spring 1969)

4118 Di tsukunft (The Future)
No. 16–227; (7 Nov. 1884)–(4 Jan. 1889); w
  B   Edited by M. Vintshevski (Wintchevsky). Continuation of **Der
poylisher idel** (No. 1–15).
  (L. Prager **Studies in Bibliography and Booklore** Vol 9 Spring 1969)

4119 Union Advocate 1 Nov 1842–Jan 1843
  C   2d. Advocated union of middle and working classes. Printed by
R. K. Philip and published by John Cleave.
  L (Place Col)

4120 The Waker Vol. I, No. 1–Vol. II. No. 10 (12); (23 Dec 1892)–
(10, Mar 1893); London; w
  B   Editors M. Baranov and M. Vintshevski (Morris Wintchevsky)
Social-democratic, published by the "Socialist Workers' Association".
  L (Col.)

4121 Working Men's Association Gazette Jan–Mar 1839
  B   2d. Motto: "Labour is the source of all wealth". Printed and
published by H. Hetherington.
  L (Place Col)

4122 Yidish sotsialistishe shtime
No. 2, 1947; London
  A   Edited by Moshe Loketsh in 1948. Organ of the Jewish Socialist
Organization in England.
  (L. Prager **Studies in Bibliography and Booklore** Vol. 9 Spring 1969)

4123 Di yudishe frayhayt (The Jewish Library) Vol. 1, No. 1–3: April–
June 1905; m
  A   Edited by K. Marmor. Socialist-Zionist Trial No. dated July 1,
1904.
  (L. Prager **Studies in Bibliography and Booklore** Vol. 9 Spring 1969)

4124 Der Yudisher proletaryer Vol. 1, No. 1: Nov. 1905; London ?
  A   Organ of the Zionist-Socialist Labor Party. Illegally distributed
in Russia. Yivo possess both thick and thin-paper issues, the latter for
illegal use.
  (L. Prager **Studies in Bibliography and Booklore** Vol. 9 Spring 1969)

4125 Der yidisher zhurnalist (The Jewish Journalist) No. 1–2; Dec. 1960–Dec. 1961; London; Hebrew, Yiddish, and English

    A   Edited by J. Cang, J. Fraenkel. Published on behalf of the Preparatory Committee for the Establishment of a World Union of Jewish Journalists.

    L(Col)

Index of Dates

Workers' journals concerned with politics in the pre-Chartist period are
described as 'democratic', while in the post-Chartist period, if they are not
Socialist, Communist, Anarchist etc. they are described as radical.

The anti-religious literature before 1850 is described as infidel, whereas
after 1850 it is referred to as secularist.

1840–1849 'B' 21, 38, 84, 90, 158, 254, 362, 486, 506, 508, 609, 624, 656, 660, 664, 670, 685, 865, 880, 911, 938, 1007, 1035, 1041, 1067, 1079, 1152, 1282, 1384–5, 1547, 1557, 1577, 1652, 1769, 1804, 1818, 1911, 1929, 1950–1, 1960, 1975, 2045, 2047, 2090, 2109, 2115, 2206, 2208, 2287, 2299–2300, 2327, 2343, 2370, 2431, 2477, 2512, 2553, 2646, 2657, 2665, 2670–1, 2680, 2724, 2764, 2769, 2808, 2846–2847, 2918, 2927, 2967–8, 2972–3, 2980, 3007, 3050, 3102, 3117–18, 3179, 3183, 3231, 3333, 3367, 3408, 3551, 3625, 3642, 3660, 3679, 3822, 3865, 3975

1840–1849 'C' 85, 113, 178, 322, 503, 926, 1019, 1098, 1146, 1269, 1337, 1425, 1480, 1493, 1609, 1650, 1776, 1849, 2001–2, 2072, 2473, 2549, 2640, 2653, 2656, 2687, 2719, 2768, 2812, 2855, 3014, 3160, 3437, 3440, 3757, 3978, 3983, 3984, 4109, 4119

1850–1859 'A' 243, 293–4, 296, 497, 586, 725, 873, 1156, 1223, 1230, 2283, 2803, 3122, 3189, 3594, 3959, 3635, 3680, 4112

1850–1859 'B' 91, 203, 254, 376, 433, 507, 540–1, 764, 875, 882, 911, 1001, 1042, 1043, 1069, 1215, 1220, 1246, 1282, 1407, 1411, 1818, 1847, 1922, 1927, 1975, 2206, 2296, 2301, 2309, 2340, 2432, 2477, 2479, 2493, 2529, 2541, 2641, 2646–7, 2662, 2751, 2753, 2802, 2927, 2954, 2967, 2984–2985, 3008, 3021, 3022–4, 3179, 3280, 3365–6, 3601, 3717, 3759, 3810, 3817, 3822, 3987, 3991, 4032

1850–1859 'C' 129, 368, 503, 774, 957, 1019, 1073, 1098, 1146, 1221, 1333, 1576, 1715, 1776, 1899, 2001, 2100, 2308, 2656, 2659, 2716, 3156, 3160, 3440, 3981, 3986

1860–1869 'A' 131, 214, 294, 571, 586, 759, 1223–4, 1230, 1472, 1575, 1584, 1608, 1669, 2105, 2283, 2288, 2543–2544, 2548, 2796, 3011, 3067, 3105, 3122, 3482, 3605, 3680, 3696, 3992

1860–1869 'B' 214, 222, 254, 298, 775, 874, 911, 984, 1038–40, 1282, 1479, 1519, 1570, 1606, 1770, 1818, 1975, 2049, 2206, 2301, 2432, 2529, 2542, 2649, 2654, 2801, 2927, 2966, 3008, 3412, 3820, 3822

1860–1869 'C' 129, 166, 354, 355, 368–9, 567, 743, 770, 1098, 1146, 1206, 1210, 1221, 1484, 1494, 1776, 1872, 2001, 2509, 2511, 2637, 2803, 2965, 3160, 3440, 3986, 3996

1870–1879 'A' 52, 214, 294, 488, 586, 589, 738, 759, 888, 1037, 1172, 1552, 1575, 1584, 1627?, 1669, 1710, 1777, 1779, 1829, 1843, 1946, 2015, 2060, 2067, 2283, 2298, 2312, 2396, 2508, 2543–4, 2570, 2878, 2900, 3067–8, 3094, 3105, 3122, 3499, 3638, 3680, 3919, 3994–5, 4073

1870–1879 'B' 181, 214, 281, 463, 564, 721, 812, 860, 911, 984, 1108, 1218, 1282, 1320, 1523, 1571, 1747, 1814, 1975, 2074, 2206, 2301, 2432, 2449, 2514, 2529, 2651, 2801, 2804, 2835, 2927, 2981, 2983, 3008, 3178, 3203, 3235, 3314, 3319, 3346, 3400, 3489, 3493, 3587, 3662, 3729, 3770, 3814, 3822, 3858, 3982, 3993

1870–1879 'C' 42, 111, 166, 368, 434, 466, 646, 743, 770, 928, 932, 947, 1090, 1103, 1210, 1421, 1494, 1561, 1722, 1776, 1832, 2001, 2075, 2509, 2511, 2637, 2834, 2852, 3227, 3237, 3440, 3535, 3914, 3929, 3997, 4104

1880–1889 'A' 51, 81, 145, 279, 488, 586, 616, 621, 626, 738, 752, 796, 888, 942, 1037, 1135, 1225–6, 1297?, 1550, 1575, 1584, 1610, 1614, 1640, 1669, 1807, 1829, 1843, 1866, 1871, 1906, 1921, 1957, 1963, 1976, 2015, 2061, 2073, 2283, 2312, 2451, 2487–8, 2496, 2507, 2543–4, 2582, 2610, 2668, 2738, 2788, 2895–6, 2898, 2900, 3020, 3094, 3097, 3122, 3427, 3499, 3511–12, 3638, 3674, 3678, 3680, 3742, 3919, 4029, 4073

1880–1889 'B' 73, 86, 153, 181, 378, 510, 538, 542, 551, 592, 650, 657, 661, 771, 784, 860, 879, 911, 989, 1212, 1218–19, 1284, 1426, 1462, 1621, 1694, 1706–4, 1757, 1762, 1820, 1861, 1873, 1942, 1975, 2206, 2301, 2429, 2527, 2529, 2607, 2652, 2663, 2698, 2733,

1900–1909 'B' 7, 94–5, 122, 188, 192, 199, 219, 238, 262, 264, 285–6, 304, 319,
333, 374, 378, 462, 517, 519, 524, 538, 554, 596, 597, 623, 643,
658, 662, 771, 822, 844, 857, 860, 862, 868, 899, 911, 959, 961,
980, 1062, 1134, 1138–9, 1180–1, 1194, 1212, 1217, 1266, 1270,
1274, 1292, 1315, 1339, 1348, 1386, 1409, 1424, 1449, 1450–1,
1490, 1545–6, 1584, 1590, 1594, 1621, 1667, 1670, 1681, 1685,
1705, 1717, 1728?–9, 1745, 1751, 1753–4, 1758, 1781, 1857,
1900, 1965, 1972, 1975, 2041, 2119, 2302, 2336–7, 2342, 2386,
2392, 2397, 2427, 2462, 2498, 2529, 2531, 2551, 2585, 2590,
2595, 2608, 2703, 2705–11, 2728, 2844, 2920, 3004, 3008, 3018,
3027, 3028, 3057, 3070, 3176, 3203, 3223, 3240, 3246–8, 3251,
3265, 3268, 3270, 3285, 3293, 3322, 3324, 3417, 3429, 3471,
3493, 3534, 3543, 3549, 3713, 3753, 3770, 3783–4, 3807, 3822,
3824, 3844, 3871, 3916, 3925, 4108
1900–1909 'B' 3930–1, 3953, 3962, 3968, 4000, 4025–6, 4028, 4041, 4066
1900–1909 'C' 146, 166, 308–9, 368, 445, 743, 770, 932, 994, 1204, 1210, 1290,
1318, 1397, 1688, 1810, 2051, 2532, 2560, 2901, 3049, 3212,
3226, 3399, 3440, 3504, 3666, 3976
1910–1919 'A' 1, 11, 57, 60, 63–4, 117, 126?, 130, 139, 143, 145, 148, 154,
174–5, 195, 273, 279, 295, 307, 352, 358, 364, 389, 412, 424,
443, 458, 474, 483–4, 516, 527, 535, 586, 591, 607, 614, 686,
693, 716, 729–30, 736, 738–9, 750–2, 783, 840, 884, 888, 902,
915, 917, 928, 930, 943, 945, 949, 988, 1014, 1021, 1028, 1030,
1044, 1095, 1097, 1107, 1111, 1113, 1135, 1144, 1166, 1168,
1171, 1229, 1241, 1251, 1271, 1273, 1276, 1299, 1310, 1323–4,
1328, 1336, 1356, 1437, 1473, 1518, 1540, 1560, 1562–1563,
1575, 1580, 1583–4, 1602, 1605, 1614, 1616?, 1636, 1655, 1669,
1697, 1773, 1812, 1829, 1834, 1843, 1848, 1865–6, 1897, 1914,
1920, 1935, 1936, 1989, 2006, 2015, 2046, 2056, 2104, 2113,
2118, 2124, 2179, 2283, 2289, 2297, 2303, 2310–11, 2314, 2317,
2325–2326, 2329, 2393, 2399, 2421, 2485, 2487, 2496, 2507,
2520, 2523, 2543–4, 2547, 2556, 2571, 2677, 2738, 2739, 2745,
2747, 2781, 2787, 2789, 2797, 2815, 2827, 2831–2, 2856, 2862,
2876, 2882, 2894, 2957, 2996, 3039, 3056, 3094, 3096–7, 3107,
3132, 3143, 3152, 3157–8, 3167, 3177, 3181, 3191, 3281–2,
3287, 3321, 3405–6, 3431, 3458, 3475, 3477, 3480, 3496,
3500–10, 3521, 3585, 3590, 3609, 3638, 3664, 3680, 3726, 3732,
3779, 3855, 3875, 3901–2, 3904, 3905, 3908, 3912, 3917, 2919,
3932, 3936–7, 3969, 3985, 3990, 4018, 4171, 4073, 4113
1910–1919 'B' 7, 75, 95, 98, 192, 283, 285, 318–19, 339, 378, 426, 441, 538,
547, 552, 597, 623, 659, 662, 673, 747, 771, 828, 839, 843, 844,
892, 911, 961, 963?, 1048, 1056, 1066, 1085, 1182, 1208, 1212,
1262, 1280, 1292, 1329, 1366, 1382, 1386, 1424, 1444–5, 1448,
1569, 1621, 1630
1910–1919 'B' 1667, 1704–5, 1737–8, 1754, 1767, 1817, 1822, 1824, 1827,
1875, 1895–6, 1900, 1923, 1975, 1986, 1998, 2180, 2189, 2342,
2352, 2374, 2385, 2387, 2392, 2414, 2460, 2462, 2491, 2500,
2529, 2551, 2591, 2617, 2661, 2702, 2706, 2712–13, 2731, 2734,
2928, 2999, 3008 3010, 3028, 3052, 3058, 3061, 3090–1, 3176,
3223, 3240–1, 3247–8, 3263, 3265, 3284, 3322, 3332, 3380,
3401, 3469, 3493, 3553–5, 3569, 3610, 3618, 3639, 3705–7,
3719–20, 3753, 3822, 3889, 3911, 3916, 3925, 3931–3, 3935,
3962, 4028, 4039, 4044
1910–1919 'C' 166, 179, 308, 349, 368, 392, 743, 770, 869, 920–1, 994, 1034,
1076, 1109, 1210, 1216, 1290, 1318, 1434, 1810, 2098, 2103,
2532, 2560, 2833, 2871–2, 2901, 3212, 3399, 3440, 3504, 3666,
3690, 3764, 3790, 3947, 3976
1920–1929 'A' 1, 4, 17, 26, 53, 57, 60, 63, 65, 67–68, 112, 117?, 120, 130,
140–1, 143, 145, 150, 165, 201, 215, 240, 252, 272, 279–80, 320,
328–30, 347, 352, 364–6, 382–3, 390, 400, 409, 413, 420, 424,

641

429, 454, 458, 460, 522, 533, 535, 539, 544, 577, 586, 588, 607,
614, 620, 639, 648, 686, 699, 729, 732, 739, 745, 748, 751–2,
760, 852, 884, 888, 900, 902–3, 909–10, 912–13, 915, 928, 930,
945, 983, 988, 1010, 1017, 1021, 1027, 1030, 1041, 1095, 1097,
1112, 1115, 1128, 1135, 1149, 1171, 1183, 1199, 1229, 1239,
1241, 1252, 1255, 1273, 1305, 1323, 1324, 1328, 1330, 1334?,
1341–3, 1417, 1422, 1431, 1456, 1478, 1481, 1485, 1497, 1506,
1516–18, 1524–6, 1530, 1540–2, 1560, 1572, 1575, 1583, 1602,
1605, 1614–15, 1617, 1636–7, 1641, 1655–6, 1829, 1834,
1843–4, 1848, 1865–6, 1876, 1885, 1891–2, 1897, 1920,
1930–1, 1936, 1940, 1947, 1958, 1969, 1989, 2014–15, 2020,
2035–6, 2043, 2046, 2056, 2062–3, 2076–7, 2079, 2114, 2124,
2177, 2179, 2184–5, 2283, 2289, 2293, 2303, 2306–7, 2313,
2318–19, 2325–6, 2329, 2353, 2382, 2390, 2399–2400, 2485,
2487, 2492, 2496, 2507, 2521, 2589, 2544–6, 2550, 2556, 2576,
2606, 2612, 2632, 2677, 2693, 2694, 2738, 2747, 2782, 2791,
2795, 2807, 2820–3, 2830–1, 2856, 2875, 2879–80, 2882, 2894,
2897, 2911, 2912, 2936, 2947, 2949, 2952, 2987, 2991, 2996,
3039, 3041, 3056, 3072, 3074, 3085, 3094, 3096–8, 3103, 3107,
3112, 3114, 3123, 3127, 3132, 3137, 3162, 3167, 3175, 3177,
3190–3191, 3206, 3207–8, 3225, 3287, 3290, 3331, 3352–4,
3381, 3403, 3426, 3431, 3458, 3463, 3496–7, 3515, 3520, 3556,
3574, 3582, 3584, 3591, 3614, 3638, 3649–54, 3661, 3664, 3672,
3694, 3699, 3708, 3726, 3727, 3733, 3768, 3804, 3875, 3884–6,
3902–3, 3905, 3908, 3912, 3936, 3941, 3954, 3967, 3969, 3985,
4111. 4115
1920–1929 'B' 55, 79, 82, 95–6, 188, 190, 192, 229–30, 284, 285, 318–19, 332,
341, 375, 378, 393, 397, 492, 518, 529, 538, 552, 563, 597, 608,
623, 659, 662, 665–7, 672–4, 681, 715, 727, 747, 761, 771, 773,
809, 824, 826, 839, 844, 845, 854, 858, 886, 892, 931, 936, 940,
954, 962, 963?–4, 966, 1004, 1049, 1055, 1070, 1141, 1147,
1196, 1209, 1212–13, 1259, 1262, 1278, 1308, 1311, 1329,
1334?, 1346–7, 1362, 1379–80, 1392, 1424, 1427?, 1442, 1460,
1475, 1492, 1511, 1527, 1544, 1556, 1566?, 1569, 1589, 1591,
1599, 1621, 1629, 1634, 1642, 1654, 1668, 1672–3, 1675, 1691,
1701, 1705, 1716, 1721, 1723, 1730–1, 1735, 1737, 1739, 1746,
1748, 1750, 1759, 1761, 1767, 1801, 1813, 1821–2, 1840,
1854–5, 1900–1, 1904, 1912–13, 1928, 1967, 1975, 1987, 2028,
2084, 2111, 2342, 2352, 2354, 2384–5, 2404, 2423, 2426, 2463,
2482, 2497, 2529, 2537–8, 2569, 2615, 2673, 2712, 2714,
2717–18, 2736, 2828, 2845, 2922, 2931, 2938–40, 2942–3,
3008, 3015, 3028, 3033, 3076, 3079–80, 3092, 3128, 3154, 3174,
3176, 3185, 3199, 3218, 3240, 3249, 3265, 3267, 3275, 3282,
3285, 3301, 3304, 3313, 3316, 3337, 3339, 3351, 3380, 3396,
3401, 3404, 3409–10, 3430, 3432–3, 3442, 3454, 3464, 3470,
3493, 3518, 3569, 3639, 3702, 3707, 3720, 3753, 3766, 3780–2,
3789, 3793, 3795, 3799, 3909, 3911, 3925, 3931, 3934, 3938,
3943–4, 3951, 3955–6, 3960–2, 3972, 3988, 4014, 4028, 4035,
4037
1920–1929 'C' 166, 349, 368, 461, 869, 920, 1076, 1094, 1210, 1290, 1406,
1810, 1827, 1939, 2103, 2532, 2630, 2901, 3399, 3440, 3446,
3690, 4031
1930–1939 'A' 4, 63, 65, 67, 112, 120, 124, 133, 143–5, 150, 161–2, 167, 169,
186, 200, 210, 215, 225, 227, 265, 268, 278–9, 285, 301–2, 306,
311, 321, 327, 336, 338, 351, 384, 386, 403, 406, 410, 414, 416,
417, 422, 424, 436, 458, 460, 491, 513, 556, 576, 578–9, 585,
594, 614, 648, 686, 699, 719, 729, 732, 739, 745, 752, 755, 760,
762, 772, 785, 804–5, 842, 888, 918, 908, 928, 944–5, 950, 988,
1010, 1021, 1024, 1029–30, 1033, 1095, 1099, 1100, 1105, 1112,
1121, 1131, 1135, 1142, 1171, 1174, 1183, 1232, 1239, 1241–4,

1252–4, 1273, 1298, 1324, 1327–8, 1341, 1344, 1367–8, 1378, 1398, 1413, 1419, 1431, 1469, 1471, 1483, 1485, 1497, 1506, 1530, 1539, 1542, 1558, 1575, 1581, 1585, 1600, 1602, 1605, 1614–15, 1619? 1632, 1636–7, 1655, 1657, 1659, 1663, 1829, 1834, 1848, 1866, 1876–7, 1885, 1892, 1916, 1920, 1924, 1936, 1948, 1956, 1989, 2015–16, 2020, 2023, 2025, 2038, 2040, 2055–2056, 2058, 2068, 2071, 2095, 2114, 2124, 2179, 2183–2184, 2254, 2283–5, 2306, 2321–2, 2325–6, 2329, 2349, 2353, 2373, 2380, 2485, 2487, 2496, 2505, 2507, 2539, 2545–6, 2550, 2556, 2572, 2578, 2632, 2634, 2643, 2677, 2681–2, 2720, 2722, 2735, 2738, 2740, 2747, 2776, 2790, 2795, 2799, 2822–3, 2825, 2830–1, 2856, 2858, 2864–5, 2870, 2882, 2894, 2904, 2907, 2936, 2947–8, 2950, 2989, 3039, 3060, 3062, 3080, 3094, 3097–8, 3103, 3107–8, 3113–14, 3119, 3123, 3147, 3148, 3151, 3167, 3169, 3177, 3180, 3191, 3205, 3209, 3214, 3320, 3355–6, 3357, 3378–9, 3426, 3435, 3458, 3463, 3481, 3486, 3501–2, 3514, 3521, 3529, 3529, 3539, 3546–7, 3557, 3565, 3574, 3576, 3592, 3604, 3638, 3646–3647, 3654–7, 3661, 3694, 3699, 3708, 3714, 3727, 3743–4, 3746, 3768, 3775, 3788, 3803, 3845, 3873, 3875, 3902–3, 3905, 3912, 3936, 3985, 4015

1930–1939 ‘B’ 27, 30, 32, 35, 55, 83, 95, 97, 103, 151–2, 170, 188, 192, 211, 229, 284, 315, 318, 341, 350, 357, 378, 399, 402, 423, 442, 446, 450, 469–70, 481, 489, 493, 499–501, 509, 528, 530, 545, 563, 597–8, 635–6, 652, 659, 662, 669, 673, 680–1, 683, 717, 741, 771, 779–80, 793, 797, 801, 830, 837, 844–5, 859, 861, 877, 887, 893, 898, 906, 914, 927, 939–41, 946, 951–2, 954, 965–71, 981–2, 997–8, 1004, 1022, 1025–6, 1049, 1051, 1061, 1080, 1086, 1092, 1124–7, 1129, 1132, 1136, 1148, 1184, 1188, 1197, 1203, 1212–13, 1236, 1259, 1262, 1275, 1278, 1288, 1294, 1303, 1309, 1311, 1313, 1350–1, 1359, 1374, 1376, 1389, 1403, 1408, 1427?, 1429, 1435, 1440, 1458, 1513, 1527–8, 1549, 1559, 1564, 1569, 1621, 1629, 1631, 1642, 1644, 1648, 1658, 1661–2, 1664, 1666, 1668, 1674–7, 1690, 1692, 1705, 1716, 1719, 1724, 1731, 1736–7, 1740, 1748, 1761, 1767–8, 1808, 1822, 1826–8, 1830, 1836, 1838–9, 1842, 1870, 1888, 1894, 1900, 1904, 1912–13, 1915, 1928, 1933, 1937, 1943, 1966, 1971, 1993, 2008, 2042, 2054, 2059, 2086, 2088, 2092, 2112, 2342, 2344–7, 2350, 2352, 2356, 2372, 2377, 2383, 2385, 2394–5, 2401, 2403, 2405, 2407, 2409, 2423, 2424, 2430, 2434, 2436–40, 2443–5, 2448, 2452–3, 2455, 2482–3, 2495, 2503, 2524–5, 2529, 2538, 2558, 2565, 2567, 2581, 2583–4, 2592, 2593, 2602, 2605, 2609, 2615, 2620–1, 2631, 2635, 2683, 2688, 2725–6, 2743, 2778, 2816, 2839, 2867, 2924, 2944, 2956, 2971, 2998, 3003, 3008–9, 3029, 3034, 3043–4, 3054–5, 3075, 3099, 3104, 3109, 3139, 3146, 3155, 3159, 3174, 3198, 3204, 3224, 3240, 3242, 3250, 3255, 3257, 3259, 3265, 3269, 3275–6, 3288, 3294–5, 3300–1, 3304, 3312, 3315–16, 3323, 3325, 3327, 3329–30, 3347, 3349–50, 3354, 3363–4, 3389, 3392, 3398, 3401–2, 3409, 3411, 3419, 3422, 3425

1930–1939 ‘B’ 3428, 3441, 3444, 3493, 3537, 3558, 3569, 3571, 3573, 3617, 3621, 3631, 3634, 3639, 3684, 3701–2, 3709, 3716, 3721, 3734, 3736, 3745, 3747, 3751, 3761, 3771, 3777–8, 3785–6, 3787, 3791, 3794, 3899, 3808, 3815, 3828, 3837, 3841–3, 3849–52, 3862, 3870, 3893–4, 3906, 3920, 3924, 3926, 3938, 3950, 3956–7, 3963, 4005, 4024, 4050, 4053–6, 4058–61, 4063, 4065, 4070

1930–1939 ‘C’ 166, 447, 461, 1082, 1210, 1290, 1399, 1646, 2532, 2840, 3163, 3399, 3440, 3648, 3690, 3856, 4031

1940–1949 ‘A’ 2, 5, 51, 65, 120, 134, 137, 142–3, 145, 149, 162, 215, 220, 227, 234–5, 256, 266, 279, 338, 348, 387, 424, 444, 556, 580, 581,

585, 590, 593–4, 614, 686, 700, 724, 728, 732, 739, 745, 752,
755–6, 776?, 792, 804, 819?. 841, 871, 885, 888, 908, 928, 937,
976, 979, 988, 996, 1018, 1021, 1031, 1047, 1075, 1077, 1091,
1095–6, 1105, 1116, 1143, 1241, 1245, 1298, 1324, 1327–8,
1341, 1371, 1431, 1436, 1470, 1483, 1497, 1506, 1520–1, 1542,
1543, 1558, 1575, 1595, 1602, 1605, 1614, 1632, 1637, 1655,
1663, 1802, 1829, 1848, 1863, 1889, 1892, 1910, 1924, 1936,
1955, 1968, 1989, 2004–5, 2015–16, 2020, 2040, 2056, 2064,
2091, 2114, 2123, 2140, 2152, 2163, 2174, 2179, 2182, 2184,
2231, 2251–3, 2256–7, 2262–3, 2266, 2270, 2280, 2284–5,
2306, 2315, 2325, 2329, 2331, 2333, 2349, 2353, 2380, 2411,
2422, 2425, 2470, 2487, 2496, 2507, 2517, 2533, 2545, 2556, 2566,
2572–3, 2598, 2600, 2613, 2632, 2634, 2642, 2643, 2678, 2722,
2729, 2738, 2744, 2795, 2799, 2809, 2814, 2822, 2830–1, 2856,
2858, 2864, 2869, 2877, 2882, 2894, 2936, 2993, 3019, 3039,
3062, 3064, 3094, 3098, 3103, 3123, 3133–4, 3164, 3166, 3177,
3180, 3191, 3195–6, 3277–8, 3359, 3372, 3376, 3387, 3426,
3448, 3458, 3463, 3495, 3514, 3521, 3524, 3540, 3577, 3579,
3581, 3583, 3586, 3611, 3613, 3615, 3638, 3645, 3655, 3670,
3694, 3699, 3722, 3727, 3731, 3737, 3768, 3788, 3802, 3805,
3873–4, 3875, 3903, 3905, 3912, 3942, 3945, 4001, 4033, 4122

1940–1949 'B' 27, 102, 124, 147, 152, 164, 183–4, 188, 192, 196, 198, 208–9,
229, 232, 236–7, 244–5, 257, 270?, 236, 328, 334, 341, 367,
371–2, 384, 402, 408, 423, 459, 464, 472–3, 509, 514, 525,
531–2, 534, 599–601, 618, 627, 634, 653–4, 659, 675–6, 679,
681, 689–90, 701, 717, 723, 740, 799–800, 806–7, 813–14, 820,
823, 837–8, 844–5, 847–50, 4107

1940–1949 'B' 853, 855, 866, 870, 872?, 925, 934–5, 941, 954–5, 966, 969, 972,
974, 987, 997, 1004, 1006, 1008, 1011, 1022, 1058, 1063, 1072,
1088, 1106, 1117, 1133, 1140, 1169, 1185, 1198, 1214, 1250,
1259, 1262, 1278, 1289, 1294, 1296, 1304, 1312–14, 1350, 1354,
1357, 1361, 1363, 1373–4, 1377, 1393, 1403, 1408, 1410, 1418,
1423, 1427?, 1459, 1461, 1528–9, 1559, 1588, 1596–7, 1622,
1626?, 1638?, 1642, 1649, 1671, 1674, 1677, 1689, 1692, 1695,
1702, 1705, 1712, 1719, 1727, 1731, 1737, 1740, 1748, 1785,
1791, 1803, 1806, 1809, 1822, 1825, 1827–8, 1838, 1867, 1869,
1888, 1890, 1894, 1900, 1912–13, 1915, 1928, 1949, 1966, 1971,
1996, 2008, 2029, 2052, 2057, 2086–7, 2089, 2092, 2108, 2126,
2128, 2334, 2338–9, 2351–2, 2356, 2364, 2368–9, 2409, 2433,
2435, 2439, 2442, 2447, 2459, 2464, 2466, 2482, 2484, 2490,
2495, 2503, 2529–2530, 2563–5, 2574, 2579, 2583, 2586, 2603,
2622, 2624, 2633, 2726, 2748, 2777, 2891, 2909, 2960, 2992,
3000–1, 3008, 3012, 3016, 3026, 3029–30, 3035, 3042, 3048,
3051, 3054–5, 3066, 3041, 3073, 3078. 3084, 3100–1, 3136,
3155, 3168, 3182, 3200–1, 3233, 3240, 3243, 3244, 3256,
3258–9, 3261–2, 3271, 3274, 3294, 3301–3, 3306, 3311, 3328,
3335–6, 3343–5, 3362, 3385, 3391, 3409, 3424, 3434, 3443,
3450, 3457, 3460–2, 3467, 3488, 3494, 3498, 3516, 3525, 3531,
3562, 3564, 3567, 3569, 3619, 3631, 3632, 3634, 3640, 3667,
3700, 3710, 3715, 3721, 3725, 3762–3, 3772, 3774, 3787, 3809,
3815, 3826, 3831, 3836, 3840, 3842, 3854, 3861, 3868–9, 3896,
3898, 3900, 3906–7, 3920, 3924, 3926, 3948, 3958, 3966,
3973–4, 4006, 4008, 4011–12, 4020, 4024, 4042, 4047, 4053,
4062–3

1940–1949 'C' 166, 934, 1290, 1372, 1399, 1902, 2532, 2905, 2908, 3399, 3440,
3730

1950–1959 'A' 2, 10, 36, 69–71, 88–9, 99, 127, 132–3, 136, 145, 157, 162, 173,
194, 205, 212, 215, 226, 234, 256, 279, 338, 356, 379, 380, 387,
394–5, 401, 415, 431, 448, 482, 487, 494, 546, 582, 594, 602,
612, 614, 686, 703, 727–8, 732, 739, 745, 755–6, 776?, 778, 785,

789?, 835, 850, 863–4, 891, 894, 916, 948, 978, 1016, 1021,
1047, 1075, 1078, 1095–6, 1110, 1130, 1159, 1164, 1167, 1170,
1176–8, 1187, 1233–4, 1237–8, 1241, 1245, 1256, 1258, 1285,
1298, 1307, 1317, 1322, 1324, 1326–8, 1341, 1353, 1391, 1431,
1468, 1483, 1491, 1497, 1500–2, 1504, 1506, 1508, 1514, 1522,
1524, 1558, 1575, 1595, 1602–5, 1614, 1620, 1633, 1637, 1655,
1829, 1848, 1852–3, 1878–9, 1892–3, 1905, 1924, 1936, 1989,
2016, 2021–2, 2040, 2056, 2065, 2069, 2083, 2114, 2127, 2130,
2140–3?, 2153–4, 2156–7, 2159, 2161, 2164, 2169, 2171, 2173,
2176, 2186, 2190, 2192, 2194, 2196, 2197, 2199, 2201–4, 2210,
2212, 2214, 2217–18, 2221–3, 2225–6, 2228, 2233, 2235–6,
2246, 2249–51, 2259, 2261, 2263–8, 2271–2, 2275–7, 2284,
2306, 2315–16, 2325, 2329, 2331, 2349, 2353, 2380, 2406,
2410, 2487, 2507, 2518, 2526, 2545, 2556, 2566, 2573, 2596,
2600–1, 2613, 2623, 2632, 2634, 2676, 2679, 2685, 2690, 2727,
2729, 2742, 2746, 2775, 2783, 2793, 2822, 2826, 2829–31, 2856,
2858, 2863–4, 2868, 2882, 2894, 2936, 2958, 2988, 2994, 3006,
3013, 3017, 3032, 3039, 3062, 3064, 3086, 3088, 3094, 3098,
3103, 3111, 3120, 3164, 3166, 3188, 3277–9, 3338, 3348,
3359–61, 3382, 3386, 3413, 3436, 3448, 3452, 3458, 3463, 3495,
3503, 3507, 3514, 3519, 3524, 2536, 3548, 3550, 3568, 3578,
3580–1, 3612, 3627, 3630, 3638, 3645, 3665, 3645, 3694, 3699,
3727, 3737–8, 3740, 3748, 3750, 3755, 3768, 3797, 3834, 3857,
3864, 3873, 3875–6, 3883, 3888, 3899, 3903, 3905, 3910, 3912,
3915, 4004, 4022, 4030, 4033, 4049

1950–1959 'B' 18, 54, 182, 192–3, 232, 249, 269, 316, 344, 371, 430, 452, 509,
600, 644, 655, 663, 678, 681, 702, 723–4?, 740, 795, 816, 827,
844–7, 866, 881, 904, 929, 958, 974, 997, 1004, 1006, 1008,
1011, 1020, 1022, 1052, 1054, 1058, 1083–4, 1088–9, 1102,
1114, 1117, 1186, 1235, 1247, 1278, 1294, 1296, 1350, 1374,
1377, 1394, 1404, 1415–16, 1427?–8, 1464, 1477, 1515, 1528,
1532–4, 1537, 1596, 1625?, 1689, 1702, 1709, 1714, 1718–19,
1731, 1742, 1744, 1748, 1755, 1760, 1783, 1786–7, 1788–91,
1806, 1822, 1827, 1850, 1894, 1900, 1912–13, 1928, 1953, 1966,
1971, 1990–1, 1994, 2000, 2008, 2026, 2029–30, 2085, 2092,
2122, 2341, 2352, 2357, 2360, 2365, 2381, 2412, 2416–14, 2439,
2441–2, 2447, 2475, 2482, 2495, 2559, 2575, 2586, 2633, 2664,
2715, 2780, 2866, 2926, 3008, 3012, 3029, 3045, 3054–5, 3123,
3136, 3197, 3240, 3252, 3254, 3262, 3266, 3273, 3294, 3296,
3301, 3303, 3307–9, 3318, 3362, 3371, 3409, 3445, 3451, 3460,
3476, 3488, 3490, 3516, 3527, 3538, 3545, 3559, 3566, 3569,
3643, 3697, 3704, 3715, 3739, 3774, 3806, 3829, 3831–2, 3842,
3892, 3907, 3924, 3926–7, 3952, 3959, 4002–3, 4019, 4023–4,
4034, 4042–3, 4047, 4057, 4068, 4074

1950–1959 'C' 104, 166, 483, 977, 1290, 1369, 1399, 2359, 2506, 2532, 2811,
3399

1960–1970 'A' 6, 9, 10, 12–14, 24, 41, 70, 88, 101, 124, 135, 137, 145, 163, 171,
177?, 187, 197, 202, 206, 212, 216, 221, 228, 234, 277, 279, 300,
310, 324–5, 381, 387–388, 396, 419, 428, 451, 455, 495–496,
498, 512, 573, 595, 603, 614, 641–642, 684, 704, 706–14, 731,
735, 739, 749, 754, 756, 767, 776, 778, 785, 814, 825, 829, 975,
1013, 1015, 1021, 1032, 1036, 1047, 1059, 1060, 1074, 1150,
1151, 1153, 1157, 1159–61, 1164–5, 1191, 1234, 1238, 1241,
1245, 1264, 1291, 1301–2, 1324, 1326, 1335, 1431, 1441, 1443,
1453, 1463, 1465–4, 1482–3, 1497, 1503, 1506, 1509, 1538,
1542, 1555, 1568, 1592–3, 1595, 1605, 1614, 1829, 1831, 1860,
1880–4, 1936, 1952, 1982–3, 1988, 2007, 2009, 2011–12, 2016,
2065–6, 2069, 2078, 2097, 2114, 2131–2, 2135, 2137, 2144–50,
2155, 2158–60, 2162, 2165–8, 2172, 2175, 2178, 2181?, 2186–7,
2191, 2193–5?, 2198, 2200, 2205, 2209, 2211, 2213, 2215,

2219–20, 2224, 2227, 2229–30, 2232, 2234–5, 2247, 2239–45, 2247–8, 2255, 2258, 2260, 2268, 2269, 2272–4, 2278–9, 2281–2, 2284, 2306, 2315–16, 2320, 2324–5, 2329–30, 2348, 2353, 2355, 2362, 2380, 2389, 2408, 2413, 2418, 2469, 2471, 2486, 2499, 2502, 2504, 2510, 2515, 2534, 2545, 2554, 2566, 2568, 2597, 2600, 2604, 2613, 2632, 2636, 2643, 2684, 2691, 2729, 2746, 2773, 2779, 2806, 2830–1, 2837?–8, 2843, 2850, 2856–61, 2864, 2875, 2881, 2913–15, 2921, 2932, 2936, 2955, 2997, 3037–9, 3046–7, 3062–4, 3094, 3098, 3115–16, 3120, 3135, 3141, 3150, 3153, 3165, 3188, 3213, 3219–21, 3283, 3310, 3317, 3334, 3373–5, 3377, 3383, 3407, 3413–15, 3438–9, 3452, 3458, 3479, 3491–2

1960–1970 'A' 3509, 3514, 3524, 3532, 3568, 3575, 3616, 3622, 3638, 3644, 3675, 3682, 3693–4, 3699, 3711, 3728, 3752, 3800–1, 3811, 3830, 3834, 3859–60, 3863, 3872–3, 3875–7, 3887, 3895, 3903, 3905, 3910, 3912, 3933, 4007, 4009–10, 4045, 4048, 4064, 4125,

1960–1970 'B' 2–3, 22, 25, 33, 45, 47, 76, 78–9, 156, 192, 232, 239, 249, 261, 288, 398, 457, 520, 536, 562, 566, 644–5, 668, 671, 678, 682, 705, 718, 740, 777, 791, 836, 844–5, 896, 905, 929, 993, 1004, 1011, 1022, 1058, 1064, 1081, 1117, 1137, 1162, 1189, 1193, 1200, 1278, 1306, 1316, 1345, 1366, 1375, 1396, 1399, 1416, 1420?, 1427?, 1438–9, 1495–6, 1507, 1512, 1528, 1554, 1567, 1574, 1624, 1645, 1668, 1686, 1696, 1714, 1719, 1726, 1731–4, 1741, 1743, 1748, 1752, 1755–6, 1760, 1765, 1789, 1791, 1794, 1798–9, 1822, 1827, 1837, 1841, 1859, 1864, 1900, 1913, 1919, 1928, 1938, 1964, 1966, 1977, 1992, 1995, 1999, 2008, 2017, 2026, 2030, 2032, 2053, 2080, 2290–1, 2341, 2352, 2416–17, 2450, 2476, 2482, 2494, 2501, 2522, 2535, 2555, 2587–9, 2594, 2618–19, 2639, 2648, 2730, 2737, 2910, 2925, 2929–30, 2937, 2945–6, 2951, 2953, 2959, 2986, 3008, 3012, 3029, 3055, 3083, 3089, 3149, 3211, 3234, 3245, 325~ 3260, 3264, 3272, 3299, 3301, 3303, 3305, 3341, 3358, 3362, 3449, 3460, 3466, 3472, 3488, 3506, 3524, 3526–8, 3545, 3563, 3673, 3691–3692, 3703–4, 3723–4, 3741, 3754, 3773, 3806, 3816, 3829, 3833, 3846–7, 3890, 3922, 3926, 3928, 3939–40, 3959, 3964–5, 3971, 4016–17, 4019, 4036, 4046, 4051–2, 4072

1960–1970 'C' 104, 297, 2506, 2532, 3399, 3765

Subject Index

Aberavvon, 15

Aberdare, 16, 1333, 2880, 3493

Aberdeen, 17–21, 109, 365, 607, 643, 1120, 1232, 1492, 2350, 2466, 2481, 2517, 2547, 3092, 3107, 3167, 3385, 3599, 3949, 3982

Aberystwyth, 636

Abingdon, 22

Accrington, 1704

Actors' Association SEE ALSO Equity, 1, 351

Addingham, 1553

Agricultural and Horticultural Association, 743

Agricultural Organisation Society, 7, 747, 2560

Agriculture, 48, 87, 743, 747, 779–80, 850, 1037, 1103, 1710, 1771–1775–9, 1812, 2732, 3049, 3107–8

Aircraft Workers, 700, 2380

Aldershot, 101

Aldred, G., 151, 665, 666, 1386, 1440, 2383, 2407, 2939, 2971, 3380, 3684, 3926–8

Allerton, J. W., 1699

Allied Ex-Service Association, 2992

Alloa, 52

Allotments and Small Holdings Association, 1811

Allotments Organisation Society and Smallholders Ltd. 727

Alnwick, 54

Altrincham, 55

Alyth, 1707

Amalgamated Association of Tramway and Vehicle Workers, 3608, 3726

Amalgamated Brassworkers and Metal Mechanics 2303

Amalgamated Cab-Drivers Society, 488

Amalgamated Danish Seamen's Union, 841

Amalgamated Labour League, 1710

Amalgamated Marine Workers' Union, 3664

Amalgamated Musicians' Union SEE Musicians' Union

Amalgamated Society of Carpenters & Joiners, 56, 477

Amalgamated Society of Coopers, 57

Amalgamated Society of Dyers, Bleachers, Finishers and Kindred Trades, 2546

Amalgamated Society of Engineers, 58, 2541

Amalgamated Society of Farriers and Blacksmiths, 59

Amalgamated Society of Gas, Municipal & General Workers, 60

Amalgamated Society of Home Decorators, 61

Amalgamated Society of Leather Workers, 62

Amalgamated Society of Lithographic Printers of Gt. Britain & Ireland, 1889

Amalgamated Society of Painters and Decorators, 2306

Amalgamated Society of Pharmacists, Drug and Chemical Workers, 930

Amalgamated Society of Railway Servants SEE National Union of Railwaymen

Amalgamated Society of Tailors, 63, 1252, 1612

Amalgamated Society of Telephone Employees, 11

Amalgamated Society of Woodcutting Machinists, 64

Amalgamated Society of Woodworkers & Painters, 13, 65, 387

Amalgamated Union of Building Trade Workers, 67–9, 381

Amalgamated Union of Cabinet Makers, 1616

Association of Broadcasting Staffs, 2
Association of Cine Technicians, 133
Association of Cinematograph, Television & Allied Technicians, 133
Association of Civil Service Designers & Draughtsmen, 134
Association of Dispensing Opticians, 908
Association of Engineering & Shipbuilding Draughtsmen, 135–6, 494, 928
Association of European Civil Servants, 2421
Association of Ex-Service Civil Servants, 1075, 1077
Association of Executive Officers & other Civil Servants, 588
Association of First Division Civil Servants, 137
Association of Government Supervisors and Radio Officers, 2094
Association of Head Postmasters, 2492
Association of H.M. Inspectors of Taxes, 138
Association of Irish Post Office Clerks, 1572
Association of Liberal Trades Unionists, 3675
Association of Local Government Engineers & Surveyors, 5
Association of Local Government Financial Officers, 6, 139
Association of Medical Record Officers, 2004
Association of National Insurance Clerks, 2297
Association of Officers in the Ministry of Labour, 140
Association of Post Office Controlling Officers, 3458
Association of Post Office Women Clerks, 130
Association of Professional, Executive, Clerical and Computer Staff, 614
Association of Professional Fire Brigade Officers, 141
Association of Scientific, Technical & Managerial Staffs, 9–10
Association of Scientific Workers, 9, 142, 3098
Association of Secondary Teachers, 1562, 3153
Association of Sorting Assistants, 3290
Association of Supervisory Staffs, Executives and Technicians, 3448
Association of Tax Clerks, 3496
Association of Teachers in Secondary Schools in Scotland, 3152
Association of Teachers in Technical Institutions, 143
Association of Teachers of Domestic Science, 1422
Association of Temporary Women Tax Clerks, 3497
Association of Tutors in Adult Education, 144
Association of University Teachers, 14
Association of Waterworks Officers, 3805
Association of Wireless & Cable Telegraphists, 3206
Association of Women Clerks and Secretaries, 3902
Asylum Workers' Association, 148
Atheism, 510
Atherton, 2837
Auden, W. H., 450
Austria, 152, 1528, 1544
Aveling, E. M. and E. 1277
Aviation Workers, 200
Aylesbury, 1013, 2218, 2219, 3346

BMS Publications, 398, 1995
Babcock and Wilcox Staff Association, 558
Bacup, 164, 3438
Baines, E., 106, 867
Bakers, 166–7, 1614, 3123
Bakunin Press, 665–6, 801, 1386, 2939, 3380, 3926
Bala, 1902
Balfour, H., 654
Banbury, 172, 817, 2476
Banda, M., 1193
Bangor, 553
Bank Employees, 174–5, 567, 781, 1903, 2329, 3727

Blaydon-on-Tyne, 273
Blind, 275, 323, 1414
Blyth, 278, 2043
Boilermakers, 280, 3685
Bolton, 29, 173, 174, 282–8, 467, 1065, 1685, 1713, 1819, 2121, 2205, 2658, 3504, 3979
Bookbinders, 290–6
Bookbinders' and Machine Rulers' Consolidated Union, 290, 295
Bookbinders' Consolidated Union, 291–2
Bookbinders' Provident Asylum Society, 293
Boot and Shoemakers, 3067
Bootle, 105, 1869, 1883
Boston, 1710, 3387, 3627
Bournemouth, 546, 550, 715, 3934
Bowman, G., 1486, 3475, 3477
Boxers, 306
Bracknell, 310
Bradford, 292, 311–19, 333, 980, 1181, 1703, 1763, 2058, 2546, 3549, 3759
Bradford Labour Union, 1763
Brailsford, H. N., 1705
Brecon, 326
Brentford, 327–8, 2166
Bridgend, 547
Bridgewater, 332
Bridport, 3859
Brierfield, 3641
Brighton, 121, 334–5, 337, 395, 437, 754, 758, 1893, 2190, 2215, 2610, 4091
Brighton Radical Registration & Patriotic Association, 335
Bristol, 76, 80, 338–46, 700, 733, 776, 961, 1159, 2216–17, 2553, 2745, 2827, 3299, 3658, 3858, 3878
Britannic Field Staff Association, 347
British Advocates of Industrial Unionism, 1487
British and Foreign Sailors' Society, 2695
British and Irish Communist Organisation, 668, 671, 1554
British Anti-War Council, 3786
British-Asian Socialist Fellowship, 958, 1714
British Association for Promoting Co-operative Knowledge 1961
British Association of Colliery Management, 348
British Broadcasting Corporation Staff Association, 2
British Committee for the Defence of Leon Trotsky, 350
British Council Staff Association, 2408
British Dental Association, 712
British Diamond Workers' Union, 900
British Federation for the Emancipation of Sweated Women, 1434
British Federation of Co-operative Youth, 162, 755
British Friends of the Algerian Revolution, 1200
British Gardeners' Association, 352
British Gas Staff Association, 3524
British Medical Association, 163
British Seafarers' Union, 358
British Socialist Party, 441, 1056, 1704, 2392, 2702, 3247, 3263, 3268, 3553, 3719, 3720, 3934
British Society for the Creation of the New Man, 2368
British Soviet Friendship Society, 3054–5, 4062
British Steel Smelters Amalgamated Association, 363
British Workers' National League, 349
British Workers Sports Federation, 3941
British Youth Peace Assembly, 4061
Brockway, F., 538, 717, 1445, 3618
Bromley, 375, 1021, 2348

Brotherhood Association, 122
Brotherhood Trust, 821
Brotheton, J., 1680
Brownhills, 835
Brussels, 1668, 1814, 3789
Buchanan, R., 1282, 2343
Buckhaven, 3557
Buckingham, 2047
Building and Monumental Workers' Association of Scotland, 382
Building Trade, 67–9, 381–90, 2025, 2543–5, 2696, 2914, 3676, 3677
Building Workers' Charter, 388
Building Workers' Industrial Union, 389–90, 3287
Burgess, J., 640, 771, 1179, 1433, 2527, 3998, 4028
Burnley, 402–5, 1034, 1704, 2702, 3247
Burton-on-Trent, 57, 890
Bury, 407, 1868, 2193
Bury-St-Edmunds, 408
Business Girls' League, 412
Busmen, 395, 409–11, 413–17, 1372, 3491, 3607
Butchers' Federation of Gt. Britain, 1615

C.W. Publishing Ltd., 653–4
Cabinet Makers, 1616
Cabmen, 434–9, 488, 715, 1307, 1865
Caernarfon, 902
Caernarvon, 2221
Caldwell, J. T., 3926, 3928
Camborne, 2535
Cambridge, 448–53, 877, 1036, 1073, 1207, 1778, 2549, 2583, 2840, 3640, 3644, 3692, 3700
Cambridge Colony, 3229
Campaign for Democratic Socialism (CDS), 457
Campaign for Nuclear Disarmament, 3089, 4051
Campbell, A., 1282, 1389, 3603, 3817
Canal Boatmen, 461
Cannock, 464
Canterbury, 1633, 2631
Card and Blowing Room and Ring Frame Operatives' Association, 467–8,
Cardiff, 365, 447, 469–72, 553, 639, 711, 836, 1018, 1745, 1750, 2064–5, 2071, 2098, 2222, 2331, 2552, 2897, 2902, 3191, 3210, 3317, 3319, 3688, 3773, 3829, 3887
Cardiff Socialist Party, 1745
Carlile, R., 475–6, 879, 897, 1265, 1295, 1300, 1887, 2010, 2107, 2402, 2689, 2759, 2847, 2979, 3130, 3659
Carlile, R., Jr., 769
Carlisle, 298–9, 603, 830, 874
Carmarthen, 2022, 3860
Carpenter, W., 478–80, 504, 549, 2749, 2755–6, 2762, 3217, 3598
Carpenters, 56, 125, 477, 1272
Carshalton, 481, 2223
Carters' Association 3570
Castle Douglas, 1250
Castleford, 2293 4093
Caterers Employees Union, 3005
Catering Trade, 483–4, 1524, 1921, 3005
Catholic, 485, 539
Catholic Social Guild, 539
Central European Democratic Committee, 1042
Central London Postmen's Association, 490
Central Printing and Publishing Offices, 1340

Ceramic & Allied Trades Union, 2806
Chain Makers' Trade Union, 497
Champion, H. H., 19, 542, 650, 1120, 1694
Chartist and Near-Chartist, 21, 84, 158–9, 172, 254, 335, 362, 377, 399, 433, 486,
    502, 504–8, 764, 865, 873, 880, 926, 938, 1000, 1035, 1041–2, 1067, 1769,
    1847, 1911, 1917–18, 1960, 2207–8, 2296, 2300, 2309, 2431, 2446, 2465,
    2477, 2493, 2512. 2540, 2662, 2724, 2769, 2808, 2968, 2973, 2980, 3007–8,
    3102, 3117, 3126, 3183, 3231, 3333, 3625, 3642, 3679, 3825
Chatham, 31, 509
Chatterton, D., 510
Chauffeurs, 2832
Cheadle, and Gatley, 512
Chelmsford, 514–15, 1116, 2042, 2155, 2231, 2388, 2400, 3151
Cheltenham, 521, 707, 3240
Chemical Workers', 522–3
Chemists, 524, 2864, 2881, 3063
Chemists Assistants Association, 524
Chemists' Assistants Union of Gt. Britain, 524
Chepstow, 528
Chester, 85, 526, 2161
Chesterfield, 891, 1121, 2435
Chichester, 1160, 1176
China Campaign Committee, 528
Chingford, 529–31
Chippenham, 532
Chiropodists, 1036
Chorley, 534–5, 2798
Christchurch, 2224
Christian Post Office Association, 2873
Christian Social Union, 994
Christian Socialist, 378, 485, 540–3, 551, 821, 1070, 1292, 1409, 2352, 2734,
    3340, 3429, 3713, 3747
Christian Socialist Fellowship, 543
Christian Socialist Society, 542
Church of England, 360, 550, 4071
Church of England Working Men's Society, 550
Church Socialist League, 552, 2551
Circle Co-operative Printing Co., 378, 784
Citizen Publishing Society, 14
City Waiters' Provident Society, 571
Civil Defence League, 652
Civil Service, 134, 137–8, 140, 154, 277, 307, 323, 424, 428, 458, 572–93, 818,
    833–4, 917, 1013, 1075, 1077, 1298–9, 1498–1504, 1618, 1892, 2021, 2421,
    2516, 2550, 2685, 2879, 2957, 3132, 3162, 3277–9, 3402–3, 3496–7, 3666,
    3737, 3755, 3884–6
Civil Service Association, 585
Civil Service Clerical Association, 323, 424, 576, 578–84, 593, 1371, 2373, 2533,
    2573, 2957–8, 2993, 3207, 3737, 4013
Civil Service Executive Association, 590
Civil Service Socialist Society, 591
Civil Service Union, 3132
Civil Service University & Professional Association, 3402
Claimants Union, 2290 2291
Clarion Newspaper Co., 591, 597, 1639, 1670, 3131
Clarion Publishing Society, 997
Clarke, A., 287, 1685, 3504
Clayton, J., 1684, 1818
Cleave, J., 549, 609–10, 1007, 1035, 2109, 2343, 3217, 3229, 3980, 4119
Clerical and Administrative Workers' Union, 611–12, 614, 792, 1096, 1802, 1910,
    2461, 2517–18, 2642, 3133–4

Cousins, B. D., 811, 2110, 2371, 2640, 2696, 2846, 3184, 3819
Coventry, 136, 456, 642, 783, 791–800, 1404, 1436, 2075, 2227, 3086
Cowie & Strange, 118, 251, 549, 758, 1925, 2519, 2629, 3138, 3217, 3333
Craftsmen's Club, 803
Credit Workers' Association, 805
Cremer, W. R., 100
Crewe, 807–9
Croxley Green, 820
Croyden, 380, 444, 821–7, 1048, 1082
Cuffley, 1026
Cumming, J., 2101, 3126
Cumnock, 2061
Customs and Excise Federation, 1605
Customs and Excise Group, 833
Customs and Excise Preventive Staff Association, 834
Czechoslovakia, 837–8, 881, 1515, 1538, 3345, 3503, 3612, 4002

Dagenham, 1170, 2857, 3748, 3750
Daily Bulletin Company, 3991
Daily Herald League, 1382, 1824
Daily Herald Printing & Publishing Society, 1066
Daily Worker, 367, 3948, 3958
Dalmacoulter, 3107
Darley Abbey, 853
Darlington, 605, 854, 1584, 2119, 2160
Dartford, 487, 855, 1167, 1186
David, J., 1023
Davison, T., 465, 2010
Dawdon, 950
Deal, 863
Democrat, 628–30, 632–3, 1295, 1586, 1833, 1961, 1970, 1975, 1979, 2010,
    2048, 2294, 2376, 2378, 2472, 2627–9, 2638, 2645, 2667, 2749, 2752, 2756,
    2763, 2847, 2883, 2887–2888, 2969, 2979, 2982, 3624, 3626, 3628, 3878,
    3923
Democrat (pre– 1832), 28–9, 110, 170, 213, 231, 253, 260, 271, 276, 335, 346,
    370, 465, 475, 480, 506, 628–30, 651, 769, 810, 876, 878, 999, 1003, 1412,
    1430, 2611
Democratic and Radical (1832–1848), 44, 46, 106, 109, 160, 289, 345, 548, 610,
    628, 631, 769, 867, 1265, 1396, 1430, 1547, 1816, 1856, 1918, 1926, 1934,
    1951, 2081, 2101, 2363, 2366, 2379, 2391, 2467, 2655, 2665, 2674–5, 2687,
    2723, 2757–60, 2762, 2765–7, 2884, 2889, 2963, 2976–7, 3082, 3102, 3217,
    3369, 3792, 3796, 3798, 3819, 3821, 3995
Democratic Socialism, 457
Denmark, 841
Dentists, 712, 884–5, 2829
Derby, 462, 606, 842, 878, 887, 889–90, 894, 1657, 1810, 1880, 2228, 2505, 2751,
    3135, 3357
Devizes, 1771
Dewsbury, 898–9, 3364, 4028
Disabled, 420
District Agricultural Union, 1103
Dobb, M., 450, 1209
Dock, Wharf and General Workers' Union of Gt. Britain and Ireland, 915
Dockers, 912–16, 2023–4, 2176, 2876, 3081, 3801, 3804
Doctors, 163, 2006, 2534
Doherty, J., 688, 1388, 2766, 3995
Dolby, ?, 878, 918
Dolgellau, 2418
Domestic Servants' Association, 920
Domestic Servants Insurance Society, 920

Domestic Servants' Union, 922
Domestic Workers, 920–3, 1118, 3160–1, 3163, 3915
Domestic Workers' Friendly Society, SEE Domestic Servants Insurance Society
Doncaster, 149, 925, 1465, 1886, 2078, 2492
Dorchester, 1604, 3219
Douglas, Isle of Man, 90, 486, 1385, 1708, 1987, 2070, 2286, 2300, 2670
Douglas Water, 1100
Dover, 927
Draughtsmen, 134–6, 494, 928, 3574
Draughtsmen's and Allied Technicians Association, 135–6, 928
Droylsden, 929
Dublin, 167, 171, 291, 540, 564, 576, 590, 624, 747, 903, 910, 933, 1189, 1316,
    1319, 1356, 1443, 1464, 1555, 1557, 1558, 1560–6, 1568–70, 1572–7,
    1579–80, 1582, 1724–5, 1727, 1863, 2117, 2206, 2390, 2542, 2649, 2688,
    2714, 2953, 3090, 3153, 3459, 3558, 3577, 3679, 3801, 3935, 3942, 3962–5,
    3970, 4052, 4067, 4074, 4095, 4102
Dudley, 934, 2628
Dukes, C., 1697
Dumbarton, 1853, 2229
Dundee, 259, 320, 607, 937–45, 2654, 3115, 3520, 3543
Dunfermline, 946, 2062, 2167, 3930
Dunning, T. J., 294, 1479
Dunstable, 1501
Durham, 2611, 3573, 3728
Durham, Co., 561, 691, 947–50
Durham Miners' Association, 949, 950

Early Closing Association, 957
East Bowling, 960
East London Communist-Anarchist Group, 77
East London Federation of the Suffragettes, 3911
Eastbourne, 1502, 2132, 2200, 3245, 3568
Eastwood, 987
Eccarius, J. G., 354
Eccles, 988–9, 2332, 3722
Economic Housing Association, 1082
Economic League, 2359
Edinburgh, 39, 76, 110, 168, 357, 499, 757, 992, 996–1001, 1180, 1480, 1503,
    1659, 1682, 1759, 1770, 1885, 2169, 2197, 2367, 2422, 2431–2, 2570, 2627,
    2732, 2853, 2907, 2931, 2943, 2966, 2975, 3064, 3068, 3095, 3111, 3120,
    3122, 3125, 3152, 3240, 3485, 3596, 3625, 3810, 3974, 4043
Edlington, 1002
Edmunds, G., 253, 432, 1003
Educational Association, 273
Education Workers' International, 3501–2
Education Workers' League, 1010
Edwards, J., 1670, 1711
Egham, 1011
Electrical Power Engineers' Association, 1014
Electrical Trades Union, 1015, 1017, 1150, 2600, 2807
Electricians, 206, 1014–15, 1017, 1150, 2807, 2809
Eleventh Hour Group, 2347
Ellesmere Port, 1020, 3397
Elliot's Literary Salon, 432
Elswick, 1331
Engels, F., 1652
Engine Drivers and Firemen's United Society, 3605
Engineer Surveyors' Association, 1028–31
Engineers, 5, 58, 135–6, 460, 494, 695, 704, 928, 1014, 1027–34, 1514, 1602,
    1633, 2541, 2783, 3556

English Chiropodists Association, 1036, 3644
English National Brotherhood, 1409
Enterprise Club, 1044
Epping, 1046
Epsom, 234, 705
Equity, 351, 1047
Erith, 1051–1056
Esher, 41, 1058–9
Esperanto, 1662
Essex, 1061–2, 1107, 1117
Eton, 1063, 2171
Eversley, 2259
Evesham, 2232
Exeter, 832, 1071–2, 1218, 1585, 2073, 2150
Ex-Naval & Military Civil Servants' Association, 3157
Ex-Service Press, 516
Ex-Servicemen, 34, 201, 392, 420, 458, 516, 527, 840, 1076, 1078, 1128, 2393, 2992

Fabian Society, 828, 1022, 1083–8, 1198, 1681, 1703, 1820, 1904, 2356, 2585, 2591, 2810, 3531, 3809
Falkirk, 1096
Fareham, 1234
Farmers' Defence Association, 1103
Farnham, 401
Farrah, F., 1038–9, 1606
Farringdon Press, 524
Fawcett Association, 2781
Fazakerley, 611
Federal Union of Agricultural & General Labourers, 1777
Federalist Congress of the International Workingmen's Association, 1108
Federated Productive Societies of U.K., 3427
Federated Teachers' Association, 1107
Federation of Greek Maritime Unions, 2331
Federation of Women Civil Servants, 2550
Federation of Working Men's Social Clubs, 1109, 1111
Federation of Yiddish Speaking Anarchists, 95
Felixstowe, 861
Fellowship of Conscientious Objectors, 3619
Fellowship of the New Life, 3340
Fielden Society, 503
Fife, 272, 1099, 3208, 3354, 3381
Fife, Kinross, Clackmannan Miners' Association, 2062
Film Artistes' Association, 1130, 3874
Finishers' Friendly Association, 296
Finsbury Communist Association, 1137
Fire Brigade SEE ALSO Fire Brigades Union, 141, 235, 985, 1595, 1620
Fire Brigades Union, 1131, 1142–3, 2988
Fishermen, 1145–6
Fleetwood, 418
Ford, I., 1179
Fordingbridge, 866
Forest of Dean, 1173
Foundry Workers, 70, 1190, 1227
Fourier, C., 1929
Foxwell, S. H. E., 1965
Fraternal Democrats, 203
Free Labour Society, 1206
Freedom Defence Committee, 1214
Freedom Group, 1129

Great Northern Radical Union, 1979
Great Wakering, 1304
Greece, 1018, 2331, 2333
Greek Maritime Co-operating Unions, 1018
Greening, E. O., 155, 1484
Greening, E. W., 3427
Greenock, 1309—12
Greenwood, J., 1640
Grimsby, 1317, 2358
Groombridge, R., 223, 1098
Groves, F., 517, 519
Groves, R., 443
Guild of Insurance Officials, 1506
Guild of Nurses, 1325
Guild of Postal Sorters, 2795
Guild of Public Pharmacists, 2864
Guild of Sorting Clerks & Telegraphists, 3060
Guild of Youth, 530, 1147
Guild Socialist, 383, 2342, 2347, 2491
Guildford, 496, 713, 762, 2423, 3463, 3956
Gunpowder Press Association, 652

Hadleigh, 3451
Hailsham, 1335
Hairdressers, 1336
Hales, S., 1681
Halifax, 1339—40, 2381, 2933
Hanbridge, L. L., 1102, 1296
Hanley, 2803—4, 3148, 3393—4, 4112
Hannington, W., 53, 1027, 3649
Hansard, T. C., 632
Hardie, J. K., 1448, 1647, 1705, 2061
Harlow, 1353, 1500, 2135
Harmonious Industrial College, 2343
Harney, G. J., 880
Harpenden, 1357
Harrison, F., 354
Harrogate, 1358, 2172, 2247, 3383, 3932
Harrow, 1359—1360
Hartlepools, 1361—3
Hartwell, R., 214, 504
Haslam, J., 771, 2831
Haslington, 1413
Hastings, 23, 1903, 2235, 3015
Hatfield, 3479
Hayes, 1021
Haywards Heath, 703
Hazel Grove, 2915
Head Postmasters' Association, 2798
Headlam, S. D., 551
Headmasters' Association, 1370
Health Visitors' Association, 3903
Hebden Bridge, 608, 3341
Hednesford, 463
Helensburgh, 936
Helmsley, 1165
Hemel Hempstead, 202, 2875
Henderson, F., 1660
Henderson, F. R., 462
Hendon, 1024, 1378—80, 2236

3324, 3411, 3418, 3518, 3530, 3549, 3571, 3795, 3891, 3925, 3968, 3973, 4027
Independent Labour Party Guild of Youth, 3275, 4065
Independent Labour Party Young Socialist League, 2360
India, 2000
Indian Socialist Group, 1477
Indian Workers' Association, 2000
Industrial Alliance, 2911
Industrial Democracy League, 3287
Industrial League, 1094, 1490
Industrial Newspaper Co., 354
Industrial Participation Association, 1688
Industrial Syndicalist Education League, 3475
Industrial Workers of Gt. Britain, 1487
Industrial Workers of the World, 1488, 2932
Infidel, 84, 475–6, 537, 549, 897, 1887, 2553, 3523
Inland Revenue Staff Federation, 3496
Inner London Teachers' Association, 279, 495
Institute for Workers' Control, 1495–6
Institute of Journalists, 1497
Institution of Professional Civil Servants, 1013, 1498–1504, 2685, 3403
Institution of Women Shorthand Typists, 412
Insurance, 145–6, 1112, 1199, 1506, 1669, 1866, 2632, 2856, 2880, 3040–1, 3158, 3357, 3689
Inter-Hospital Socialist Society, 1419
International Arbitration League, 100
International Brigades, 3761–2
International Chemical Workers Committee for Propaganda and Action, 522
International Class War Prisoners' Aid, 1442, 1691, 2828
International Confederation of Free Trade Unions, 1522
International Co-operative Alliance, 482, 1517–18, 4018
International Co-operative Printing Office, 1519
International Council of Social Democratic Women, 1537
International Council of Trade and Industrial Unions, 1525
International Federation of Trade Unions, 1520, 3586
International Federation of W.E.A.'s, 1515
International Labour Defence, 1690
International Libertarian Group of Correspondence, 1270
International Marxist Group, 2951
International Needle Workers, 2952
International Peace Campaign, 2377
International Printer, 3542
International Propaganda Committee of Revolutionary Transport Workers, 1530, 1541
International Publishing Co., 73, 153
International Secretariat of the League Against Imperialism, 82–3
International Socialist Conference, 3274
International Socialists, 1306, 1765, 4080, 4101
International Transport Workers' Federation, 1105, 1453–4, 3611
International Union of Journeymen Hairdressers of London, 1336
International Working Men's Association, 214, 904, 984, 1519, 1523, 4104
International Workingmen's Educational Club, 95
Ipswich, 907, 1060, 1184, 1391, 1549–52, 1784, 2384, 3145, 3215, 3449, 3451–2
Ireland, 28–29, 69, 167, 275, 291, 387, 540, 564, 576, 590, 624, 668, 671, 747, 903, 910, 933, 1041, 1050, 1189, 1316, 1319, 1356, 1443, 1464, 1554–82, 1724–5, 1727, 1766, 1863, 2014, 2117, 2206, 2390, 2542, 2649, 2688, 2714, 2953, 3090, 3153, 3332, 3459, 3558, 3577, 3679, 3801, 3922, 3935, 3942, 3962–5, 3970, 4052, 4081, 4082
Irish Agricultural Organisation Society, 1555, 1560
Irish Bakers', Confectioners & Allied Workers Amalgamated Union, 167, 171

Irish Christian Left, 1316
Irish Communist Organisation SEE British and Irish Communist Organisation
Irish Journalists Association, 1563
Irish Labour Party, 1464, 1565–6, 1569, 1724–5, 1727, 2714
Irish Labour Printing and Publishing Co., 1564
Irish Local Government Officials Union, 1443
Irish Medical Association, 1558
Irish Mental Hospital Workers' Union, 2014
Irish National League, 1578, 3459
Irish National Teachers' Organisation, 1575, 2117
Irish National Union of Vintners, Grocers & Allied Trades Assistants, 171
Irish Nurses Organisation, 1568
Irish Post Office Workers Union, 4067
Irish Press Co. of Gt. Britain, 1578
Irish Revolutionary Youth, 2953
Irish Self-Determination League, 1556
Irish Socialist Republican Party, 3962
Irish Society of Woodcutting Machinists, 3922
Irish Trade Union Congress, 1566, 1569, 2714, 3577
Irish Transport and General Workers' Union, 1569, 1863
Irish Union of Distributive Workers and Clerks, 910
Irish Young Socialists, 4046, 4052
Iron and Steel, 126, 297, 363, 1583–4, 1762, 3406–7, 3731
Iron and Steel Trades Confederation, 1583
Isle of Ely, 2032
Italy, 281, 369, 438–4, 1274, 1546, 3018, 3280

Jackson, T. A., 1080, 1125
Jarrow, 1594
Jenkins, C., 1247, 3573
Jewish Social Democratic Organisation, 98, 2189, 3293
Jewish Socialist Workers' Party, 3707
Jewish Workers, 94–8, 555–6, 1194–7, 1211, 1455, 1596, 1597, 2741, 3707
Johnson, F., 1134, 1449
Johnston, T., 940
Johnston, W., 121, 549
Joiners, 56, 125, 1272
Jones, E., 433, 507, 874, 1069, 1927, 2493, 2641, 2662, 3820
Jones, L., 214, 1282, 2074, 3578
Journalists, 1497, 1610, 2310, 3282, 3883
Jowett, F. W., 314, 318
Junior Civil Service Prayer Union, 3666
Junior (Fire Brigade) Officers Association, 1620
Junior Hospital Doctors Association, 2534
Jute and Flax Workers' Union, 937, 944–5

Kalamazoo Workers' Alliance, 1623
Kamiowski, J., 94, 1266, 3471
Keele, 1624
Keighley, 1447, 1626–7, 4007
Kempston, 1105, 1542
Kenworthy, J., 462, 821
Kettering, 1635–6
Kidderminster, 1638, 4083
Kilmarnock, 159–60
Kinema Projectionists' and Engineers Association, 2842
King, W., 758, 995
Kingsbridge, 712
Kingston-upon-Thames, 2244–5, 2419, 3340
Kinning Park, 1647

Kirkcaldy, 924, 1723
Kirkdale, 1648
Kitchen Workers' Union, 483
Kitz, F., 657, 1219
Klingender, F. D., 1080
Knebworth, 1649
Knee, F., 1424
Knight, C., 129, 1650, 3014, 3757, 3984
Kropotkin, P., 1212, 1654
Kydd, S., 1407

Labour Agency & Employment Inquiry Office, 1722
Labour Book Service, 1671
Labour Chronicle Publishing Co., 1680
Labour Church, 1104, 1684–5, 1693, 1703, 1729, 3534
Labour Committee for Europe, 1064
Labour Co-partnership Association, 1688, 2833
Labour Educational League, 262
Labour Electoral Association, 650, 1762
Labour Housing Association, 1424
Labour Journal Co., 1703
Labour League, 1407
Labour Literature Society, 1277, 1672
Labour Newspapers Ltd., 843
Labour Party, 18, 22, 54–5, 102–3, 147, 164, 183–4, 188, 190–1, 196, 198,
    208–9, 211, 220, 229–30, 237, 245, 257, 266, 270, 284, 288, 316, 318, 326,
    328, 332, 334, 341, 372, 408, 446, 448, 457, 459, 464, 472–3, 481, 492–3,
    500, 514, 518, 520, 525, 531–2, 534, 536, 545, 547, 563, 565–6, 598, 600,
    618, 627, 635, 663, 705, 733, 773, 777, 794, 797, 799–800, 806–7, 809,
    813–15, 820, 822–4, 826–7, 830, 843, 853–5, 858–9, 861, 870, 872, 892,
    898, 925, 929, 934–6, 939, 955, 961–3, 966, 969, 972, 979, 987, 989, 993,
    997, 1011, 1020, 1026, 1046, 1049, 1052, 1054, 1058, 1063, 1072, 1081, 1089,
    1106, 1116, 1133, 1140–1, 1148, 1162–3, 1182, 1184–5, 1188, 1236, 1247,
    1250, 1259–61, 1280, 1288–9, 1293–4, 1296, 1304, 1308, 1312, 1314,
    1346–7, 1354, 1357, 1359, 1362, 1373–4, 1377, 1392–3, 1395, 1400–1, 1404,
    1410, 1415–16, 1418, 1420, 1424, 1427, 1457, 1459–61, 1544, 1588–90,
    1594, 1626, 1629, 1631, 1634, 1638, 1642–3, 1646, 1648–9, 1671, 1673–7,
    1683, 1689, 1695–6, 1712, 1716, 1719, 1723, 1726, 1731–4, 1737–40, 1748,
    1751–2, 1754, 1756, 1761, 1764, 1767, 1773, 1784, 1793, 1799, 1803,
    1808–9, 1813, 1822, 1825–6, 1850, 1854–5, 1869, 1890, 1896, 1904, 1923,
    1928, 1936, 1938, 1949, 1953, 1966–7, 1977, 1996, 2030, 2032, 2042, 2052,
    2059, 2085, 2088, 2099, 2108, 2112, 2126, 2334, 2338–9, 2341, 2351, 2358,
    2369, 2374, 2384, 2386–7, 2388, 2400–1, 2403–5, 2409, 2412, 2417, 2433,
    2435–6, 2440–1, 2448, 2453, 2459–60, 2475–6, 2483–4, 2490, 2522, 2525,
    2530, 2562–3, 2571, 2579–80, 2593, 2602–3, 2607, 2615, 2618, 2624, 2664,
    2706, 2736–7, 2777, 2816, 2891, 2922, 2925, 2960, 3009, 3012, 3015, 3030,
    3033, 3042, 3051, 3066, 3071, 3073, 3076, 3078, 3084, 3155, 3159, 3168,
    3197, 3199–3201, 3211, 3216, 3245, 3252, 3254, 3256, 3262, 3284, 3295–6,
    3299, 3305, 3307–9, 3311–12, 3318, 3325, 3328, 3335, 3337, 3341, 3362,
    3364, 3389, 3391, 3398, 3419, 3424, 3430, 3432–4, 3449–51, 3457, 3460–2,
    3467, 3470, 3488, 3490, 3494, 3498, 3505–6, 3525, 3527, 3537–8, 3545,
    3555, 3559, 3561, 3563–3564, 3566, 3569, 3573, 3632, 3710, 3734, 3754,
    3770–2, 3774, 3781–2, 3785, 3793, 3799, 3808, 3826, 3828, 3836, 3839,
    3843, 3846, 3849, 3853, 3857, 3861, 3868–9, 3889–90, 3893, 3896, 3989,
    3900, 3921, 4006, 4008, 4011–12, 4016, 4020, 4047
Labour Party League of Youth, 32, 702, 1361, 1735–6, 1768, 2345, 2372, 2575,
    2909, 3243, 3271, 4034, 4042–3, 4050, 4054–5, 4059–60, 4072, 4098
Labour Party Young Socialists, 777, 1709, 1741, 1837, 2017, 2053, 2589, 2930,
    3371, 4057
Labour Peace Fellowship, 1742–4

Labour Press Society, 1446, 1670
Labour Protection League, 2651
Labour Publishing Co., 1721, 2571, 3262, 3961
Labour Representation Committee, 1781, 2706, 2708, 3417, 3871, 4026
Labour Research Dept., 1658, 1740, 3225, 3233, 3961
Labour Standard Printing & Publishing Society, 1759
Labourers' Friend Society, 1093, 1776, 3712
Lace Makers' Society, 3633
Lanark, 1100
Lancaster, 148, 1807−9
Land and Labour League, 2981, 4104
Land Nationalisation Society, 1810
Land Reform Union, 542
Lansbury, G., 552, 844
Lapworth, C., 844
Larkin, J., 1580
Law and Liberty League, 1873
Law Clerks Mutual Benefit Association, 4084
League Against Imperialism and for National Independence, 1821
League for a Workers' Republic, 3964
League for Shortening the Hours of Unnecessary Labour, 3222
League for Workers' Vanguard, 3724
League of Social Progess, 3367
League of Socialist Freethinkers, 1125
League of the Jewish Social-Democratic Associations in England, 2189
League of Young Socialists, 2537
Leamington Spa, 1825−6
Leatham, J., 643, 1262, 1339, 3931
Leatherhead, 2406
Lee, F., 1247
Lee, R. E., 1970, 2363, 2379, 2655, 3624
Lee Green, 1248
Leeds, 62−3, 142, 271, 353, 399, 406, 420, 559, 619, 716, 867, 919, 1067, 1175,
    1179, 1201, 1252, 1254, 1328, 1385, 1665, 1679−80, 1827−36, 1841, 2246−7,
    2323, 2360, 2370, 2386, 2477, 2555, 2571, 2639, 2646, 2657, 2708, 2872,
    2906, 2967−8, 3149, 3229, 3253, 3358, 3486, 3609, 3713, 4031, 4073, 4085,
    4093
Leeds Industrial Co-operative Society, 1829
Leeds Labour Publishing Society Ltd., 1827
Leeds University Socialist Society, 1841
Left Book Club, 1838
Legge, J., 20, 2481
Leicester, 321, 450, 462, 606, 664, 745, 970, 1079, 1208, 1354, 1463, 1466, 1642,
    1842−7, 1860, 2045, 2049, 2248, 2706, 3050, 3167, 3373
Leigh, 1848−9
Leigh-on-Sea, 3330
Leith, 1850
Lenin, V. I., 1587
Leno, J. B., 87, 2309, 3067, 3365
Lenton, 1851, 3816
Lerwick, 3185
Letchworth, 378, 1251, 1329, 3286, 3938
Lewes, 1057
Liberal Labour League, 1857
Liberal Party, 3453
Libertarian League, 1867
Libertarian Teachers' Association, 1860
Liberty Press, 3128
Liberty Publications, 2748
Limavady, 378, 784

Long Eaton, 1943–6
Lorry Drivers, 1948
Lorymer, J. H., 289, 1816, 2758, 2883, 2963, 2982
Loughborough, 431, 724, 728, 756, 1949, 3361
Loughton, 3532
Lovett, W., 506, 734, 1007, 1035, 1425
Ludlow, 3312
Ludlow, J. M., 541
Lumphinnans, 2612
Lund, 1512
Luton, 840, 1953, 2586, 3271
Lymington, 1954
Lyndhurst, 790, 2260

MacAnna, J., 1567
McCallu, Peter & Co., 166
Macclesfield, 1959
Machine Managers' Trade Society, 2823
Macintosh, W., 42, 1146
Mackay, G. 20, 21
Maclean, A. W., 2367, 2595
Macmillan, V., 155, 538
McPhun, W. R., 1281, 1951, 2752, 2975
Madeley, 3202
Madrid, 3761
Maguire, T., 1679–80
Mahon, J. L., 1462, 1539
Maidenhead, 2503
Maidstone, 1467, 1632, 1777, 1962
Malatesta, E., 1546
Malcolm, R., 3102, 3117
Maldon, 2400
Maltby, 1969
Manchester, 3–4, 43, 56, 63–5, 81, 103, 114, 127, 144–5, 156, 161, 263, 265–6,
    269?, 273, 275, 287, 292, 295, 316, 339, 365, 383, 410, 415, 425, 503, 536,
    544, 560, 569, 597, 604, 640, 687–8, 696?, 729–30, 732, 735, 738–9, 748–52,
    756, 759–61, 771, 778, 843, 856, 914, 1014, 1016, 1021, 1028–31, 1041,
    1091, 1095, 1148, 1150, 1166, 1201, 1220, 1283, 1291, 1306, 1324, 1345,
    1387, 1388, 1439, 1446, 1448–50, 1484, 1487, 1571, 1607, 1661–2, 1670,
    1719, 1726, 1729, 1755, 1767, 1783, 1786–9, 1791–2, 1794–1800, 1804–6,
    1817, 1819, 1866, 1877, 1889, 1956, 1958, 1960, 1972–86, 2056, 2111–12,
    2115, 2121, 2124, 2146, 2153, 2163, 2179, 2209, 2255–7, 2263, 2264, 2289,
    2306–7, 2325, 2357, 2362, 2370–1, 2474, 2482, 2501, 2556, 2562, 2566,
    2575, 2626, 2652, 2673, 2709–11, 2719, 2722, 2766, 2782, 2789, 2848, 2865,
    2914, 2918, 2973, 2995, 2997, 3023, 3051, 3053, 3081, 3169, 3174, 3193,
    3194, 3196, 3209, 3229, 3279, 3351, 3379, 3388, 3405, 3408, 3426, 3447,
    3504, 3517, 3533, 3559, 3579, 3587, 3594, 3597, 3601, 3604, 3638, 3671,
    3680, 3683, 3686, 3689, 3710, 3713, 3756, 3775, 3788, 3791, 3803, 3877,
    3912, 3918, 3995, 3998, 4012
Manchester Alliance of Operative House Painters, 1973–4
Manchester Citizen Newspaper and Publishing Co., 560
Manchester Unity of the Independent Order of Odd Fellows, 1601
Mann, T., 53, 361, 915, 1080, 1449, 1474, 1486, 2055, 3576, 3588, 3610, 3649
Manning, J. C., 1204
Mansfield, 2596
Margate, 1988
Marine Engineers' Association, 1989
Martin, K., 654
Marx, K., 1219, 2493
Marx Memorial Library, 1513

Marxist, 398, 1942, 1990–2, 1995, 2999, 3125, 3964, 4002, 4039, 4087, 4089
Marxist League, 1993, 2944
Marxist-Leninist Organisation, 2946, 2959
Massey Ferguson Joint Shop Stewards Combine Committee, 642
Master Bakers' Association, 166
Mathison, A., 1680
Matlock, 2178
Maurice, F. D., 541
Maxton, J., 82
Mazzini, G., 1039, 1042
Mechanics, 108, 118, 223, 1281, 1493, 1494, 1613
Mechanics' Institutes, 1849, 1856, 1925, 1951, 2001, 2803
Medical Association of Eire SEE Irish Medical Association
Medical Superintendents' Society, 2005
Mellor, W., 295, 1426
Members' Rights Movement, 2095
Mendlesham, 780
Mental Hospital and Institutional Workers' Union, 2179
Mercantile Marine Service Association, 2015
Mercer, T., 739, 748, 758
Merchant Navy and Airline Officers' Association, 3188
Merthyr Tydfil, 38, 1332 2712, 2938, 3322, 3400, 3642, 3993
Merton, 3038
Metal Trades Federation, 2033
Metalworkers, 127, 320, 1245, 1271, 1514, 1516, 2033–6, 2320
Metropolitan Board Teachers' Association, 279
Metropolitan Drapers' Association, 3440
Metropolitan Water Board Staff Association, 93
Metropolitan Working Men's Union, 2650
Middlesbrough, 2039, 2067, 2449, 3674
Middleton, 1381, 2041
Militant Socialist International, 3721
Mill, J. S., 725
Miller, W. and W., 3118, 3121
Miners' Association of Gt. Britain & Ireland, 2070
Miners' Federation of Gt. Britain, 2063, 2068
Mineworker Publications, 3112
Mitcham, 2084–9, 2099, 3037
Mitchell, J., 271
Modern Books, 1529
Moffat, A., 421
Monotype Casters' and Typefounders' Society, 2097
Morecambe, 2108
Morris, W., 657, 1349
Morrison, H., 773, 1923, 1928
Morrison, J., 2696
Moscow, 443, 673, 1516, 1525–6, 1888, 3582, 3957
Mosley, O., 977
Most, J., 1218
Motor Cab Trade Protection Society, 1307
Motor Industry, 1170, 1436, 3748, 3752
Mowbray, C. W., 657
Mudie, G., 39, 995, 1268, 2750
Muggeridge, H. T., 822, 824
Municipal Workers, 5–6, 23–4, 36, 41, 88, 99, 101, 105, 139, 149, 194, 202,
    205–6, 212, 216, 226, 234, 300–1, 310, 324–5, 373, 379–80, 394, 396, 401,
    418, 444, 451, 455–6, 487, 512, 546, 594–5, 603, 641, 703, 706–11, 713–14,
    767, 785, 787, 789–90, 808, 817, 819, 832, 835, 864, 894, 901, 943, 948, 975,
    978, 1016, 1024, 1057, 1059–60, 1074, 1151, 1153, 1160–1, 1164–5, 1176,
    1187, 1191, 1233–4, 1237, 1257–8, 1263–4, 1285, 1301, 1317, 1322–4,

1326–8, 1330, 1335, 1344, 1353, 1391, 1443, 1463, 1465–9, 1491; 1508–10,
    1592–3, 1604, 1632, 1651, 1653, 1655, 1659, 2118, 2120–1, 2313, 3845
Munitions Workers, 1473
Murphy, J. T., 53
Music Hall Artistes Association, 1957
Musicians, 195, 2123–5
Musicians' Union, 2123–5
Musselburgh, 2126, 2127
Muthill, 2128

Napoleon, L., 91
National Administrative Council of Unemployed, 2569
National Agricultural Labourers' Union, 1037, 1772–3, 1812
National Alliance of Employers and Employed, 3690
National Amalgamated Furnishing Trades' Association, 1243
National Amalgamated Sailors' and Firemen's Union, 1531, 3142
National Amalgamated Union of Life Assurance Workers, 145
National Amalgamated Union of Stevedores and Dockers, 2176
National Ambulance Services Association, 71
National Association for Promoting the Political and Social Improvement of the
    People, 2208
National Association for the Promotion of Social Science, 1221
National Association for the Protection of Labour, 3686, 3756
National Association of Assessors and Collectors of Taxes, 112
National Association of Bank Clerks, 174
National Association of Card, Blowing Room and Ring Frame Operatives, 2209
National Association of Discharged Sailors and Soldiers, 201
National Association of Employment and Clerical Officers, 117
National Association of Fire Officers, 1595, 1620
National Association of Grocers' Assistants, 1318
National Association of Head Teachers, 1365–6, 3500
National Association of Industry, Humanity & Knowledge, 2371
National Association of Iron, Steel, Tin, Blastfurnace and Other Workers, 1584
National Association of Journalists, 1610, 4029
National Association of Labour Agents, 1731
National Association of Labour Student Organisations, 600
National Association of Local Government Officers, 23–4, 36, 41, 88, 99, 101, 105,
    149, 157, 173, 177, 194, 197, 202, 205, 212, 216, 226, 234, 300, 310, 324–5,
    373, 379–80, 394, 396, 401, 418, 444, 451, 455–6, 487, 496, 512, 546, 594–5,
    603, 641, 703, 706–11, 713–14, 767, 785, 787, 789–90, 808, 817, 819, 825,
    832, 835, 864, 894, 901, 943, 948, 975, 978, 1016, 1024, 1057, 1059–60, 1074,
    1151, 1153, 1160–1, 1164–5, 1176, 1187, 1191, 1233–4, 1237, 1256–8, 1263,
    1264, 1285, 1301, 1317, 1323, 1326–8, 1330, 1335, 1353, 1391, 1463,
    1465–9, 1491, 1508–10, 1592–3, 1604, 1632, 1651, 1653, 1655, 1831,
    1852–3, 1878, 1880–3, 1893, 1905, 1954, 1988, 2009, 2011–13, 2022, 2083,
    2130–74, 2181, 2190–2205, 2210–82, 2348, 2355, 2399, 2410, 2413,
    2418–19, 2425, 2471, 2486, 2499, 2502, 2510, 2526, 2568, 2596–8, 2604,
    2623, 2636, 2679, 2684, 2691, 2727, 2742, 2744, 2773, 2775, 2826, 2837–8,
    2843, 2850, 2857, 2859–62, 2868, 2875, 2955, 2994, 2997, 3006, 3013, 3017,
    3032, 3037–8, 3046–7, 3114, 3135, 3150–1, 3165–6, 3177, 3215, 3219, 3221,
    3310, 3334, 3338, 3348, 3359–60, 3373, 3377, 3382–3, 3386–8, 3414–15,
    3436, 3438–9, 3452, 3479, 3495, 3524, 3532, 3536, 3550, 3568, 3572, 3622,
    3627, 3630, 3646, 3658, 3693, 3711, 3714, 3728, 3738, 3740, 3797, 3800, 3834.
    3859–60, 3876, 3880, 3887–8, 3895, 3899, 4007, 4009–10, 4022, 4048
National Association of Labour Teachers, 1760, 2091, 3234
National Association of Men Teachers, 3096
National Association of Nut & Bolt Makers, 2508
National Association of Old Age Pensioners, 2643
National Association of Operative Plasterers, 2283
National Association of Plasterers, Granolithic and Cement Workers, 2284

National Association of Postmen, 2799
National Association of Probation Officers, 2175
National Association of Registration Officers, 104
National Association of School Attendance Officers, 3093
National Association of Schoolmasters, 187, 2285, 2382, 3213, 3830
National Association of Supervising Electricians, 699
National Association of Teachers, 4064
National Association of Temporary Postal Employees, 3480
National Association of Theatre Nurses, 2178
National Association of Theatrical Employees, 72, 2177, 2469, 3522
National Association of United Trades, 92, 1708, 1769, 2286
National Association of Youth Service Officers, 4064
National Asylum-Workers' Union, 2179
National Brass Workers and Metal Mechanics, 4092
National British Women's Temperance Association, 3913
National Building Guild, 383
National Charter Association, 1035, 2287, 2477, 2662, 4105
National Clerks' Journal Company, 616
National Committee for the Prevention of Destitution, 828
National Commonwealth League, 661
National Confederation of Labour, 1129
National Co-operative Managers' Association, 736, 739, 755
National Co-operative Men's Guild, 732, 2289
National Council of Labour Colleges, 2731
National Council of Women of Gt. Britain, 2326
National Democratic and Labour Party, 349
National Democratic League, 868, 1758
National Dental Association, 884
National Ex-Service Men's Union of Temporary Civil Servants, 1892
National Federation of Assistant Teachers, 606, 1914
National Federation of Associated Employers of Labour, 466
National Federation of Blastfurnacemen, 2033
National Federation of Building Trades Operatives, 381, 384, 684, 2545
National Federation of Caretakers, 474
National Federation of Claimants Unions, 2290–1
National Federation of Discharged and Demobilised Sailors & Soldiers, 392, 516,
    527, 840
National Federation of Fishermen of Gt. Britain & Ireland, 1145
National Federation of Foremen Tailors' Societies, 3484
National Federation of Pearl Officials, 1112
National Federation of Postal and Telegraph Clerks, 2795
National Federation of Professional Musicians, 195
National Federation of Shipworkers, 2292
National Federation of Shop Stewards, 240
National Federation of Sub-Postmasters, 3447
National Federation of Tenants' and Residents' Associations, 1408
National Federation of Women Teachers, 3905
National Federation of Women Workers, 3908
National Flint Glass Makers' Friendly Society, 1156
National Foremen's Association, 1171
National Fraternal Association of Life Insurance Officials, 1199
National Free Labour Association, 1204–5
National Glass Workers Trade Protection Association, 2293
National Graphical Association, 1302
National Guild of Civil Servants, 3755
National Guild of Telephonists, 3514
National Guilds League, 1329
National Home Reading Union, 2295
National Industrial & Provident Society, 2288
National Labour Alliance, 2751

National Labour Housing Association and Federation of Tenants Leagues, 1424
National Labour Press, 339, 400, 591, 717–18, 1115, 1182, 1383, 1448–50, 1456,
    1967, 1986, 3397, 3400, 3618, 3639, 3681
National Land and Building Association, 656
National Land League, 564
National League for the Blind of Gt. Britain and Ireland, 275, 1414
National Liberation Front, 1018
National Minority Movement, 165, 280, 320, 386, 413, 454, 522, 533, 909, 913,
    1027, 1033, 1149, 1242, 1343, 1530, 1541, 1641, 1656, 1801, 1940, 1947,
    2035, 2076, 2077, 2095, 2790, 2821, 2825, 2947, 3209, 3672, 3733, 3936
National Non-Partisan League of Socialism, 2426
National Political Union for the Obtainment of the People's Charter, 2309
National Press Agency, 812, 2657
National Progressive Democrats, 1189
National Provincial & Union Bank Staff Association, 2329
National Sailors & Firemen's Union, 3144
National Seamen's Reform Movement, 1157
National Shop Assistants' Union, 3193
National Society of Amalgamated Brass Workers and Metal Mechanics, 2034
National Society of Drillers & Holecutters, 2304
National Society of Electrotypers & Stereotypers, 3413
National Society of Metal Mechanics, 2305
National Society of Operative Printers and Assistants, 2330, 3819
National Society of Operative Printers Graphical and Media Personnel, 2411
National Society of Painters, 2306–7
National Society of Pottery Workers, 2806
National Society of Telephone Employees, 3513
National Sunday League, 1210, 2308
National Trade Union Club, 3592
National Trade Union Defence Campaign, 366
National Unemployed Workers Movement, 2870, 2991, 3147–8, 3404, 3647, 3649,
    3651–5, 3743–4
National Union for Combating Fascism, 608
National Union of Auxiliary Postmen, 154
National Union of Bank Employees, 175
National Union of Bookbinders, and Machine Rulers, 295, 2311
National Union of Boot & Shoe Rivetters, 2312
National Union of Boxers, 306
National Union of Catering Workers, 484
National Union of Clerks, 614, 616, 4014
National Union of Commercial Travellers, 648, 3616
National Union of Co-operative Insurance Society Employees, 2505, 3357
National Union of Co-operative Officials, 739
National Union of Corporation Workers, 2313
National Union of County Officers, 786, 2182–3
National Union of Disabled Ex-Servicemen, 420
National Union of Distributive and Allied Workers SEE Union of Shop, Distributive
    and Allied Workers
National Union of Dock Labourers, 2024
National Union of Docks, Wharves, and Shipping Staff, 2876
National Union of Drug and Chemical Workers, 523
National Union of Dyers, Bleachers and Textile Workers, 944, 3521
National Union of Ex-Servicemen and Women, 1128, 2393
National Union of Funeral and Cemetery Workers, 1238
National Union of Funeral Service Operatives SEE National Union of Funeral and
    Cemetery Workers
National Union of Furniture Trade Operatives, 1241
National Union of General and Municipal Workers, SEE General and Municipal
    Workers, Union
National Union of Gold, Silver & Allied Trades, 885, 2314

National Union of Horticultural Workers, 352
National Union of Insurance Workers, 2632, 2856, 2880, 3040–1, 3158, 3689, 3732
National Union of Journalists, 2310, 3883
National Union of Labour Students, 2574
National Union of Life Assurance Agents, 145, 1866
National Union of Mineworkers, 891, 2065–6, 2315–16, 3111, 4030
National Union of Newsvendors, 3435
National Union of Packing Case Makers, Box Makers, Sawyers, and Mill Workers, 2317
National Union of Police and Prison Officers, 400, 2745, 2747
National Union of Portworkers, 2779
National Union of Press Telegraphists, 2814
National Union of Printing, Bookbinding & Paper Workers, 2318, 2613
National Union of Public Employees, 1344, 2858
National Union of Railwaymen, 2897–2900, 3208
National Union of Sanitary Inspectors, 3087
National Union of Scalemakers, 2319
National Union of Scientific Workers, 3098
National Union of Seamen, 3140
National Union of Sheet Metal Workers and Braziers, 1245, 2320
National Union of Ships' Stewards, Cooks, Butchers and Bakers, 3664
National Union of Shop Assistants, Warehousemen & Clerks, 3191, 3194
National Union of Teachers, 279, 495, 498, 606, 804, 976, 1107, 1135, 1155, 1159, 1207, 1341, 1834, 1844, 1876, 1914, 1982–3, 2040, 2184–7, 2321–4, 2913, 3094, 3204, 3548, 3645, 3661, 3863, 4045
National Union of Textile Workers, 3521
National Union of the Working Classes, 170, 479, 769, 2638, 2762
National Union of Theatrical Stage Employees, 3395
National Union of Vehicle Builders, 1368, 2188, 2325
National Union of Vehicle Workers, 2113, 3726
National Women's Labour League, 1822
Nationalization of Labour Society, 378, 2328
Navigators and Engineers Officers' Union, 2016
Navvies' Bricklayers' Laborers and General Laborers' Union, 2332
Navvy Mission Society, 2871
Navy, Royal, 4075, 4077
Nelson, 2226, 2334–7
Neston, 2338
Netherlands, 369
Netley Abbey, 2339
New Age Press, 2551
New Builders Leader Ltd., 2349
New Church Socialist Society, 3713
New Leader Ltd., 2063
New Malden, 430, 3462
New Park Publications, 1755
New World Publishing Co., 2393
New York, 1218, 2361, 4037
Newark, 2009
Newbury, 2868
Newcastle-under-Lyme, 1651
Newcastle upon Tyne, 365, 374, 497, 583, 612, 625, 653, 841, 1371, 1578, 2070, 2072, 2100, 2185, 2395–9, 2462, 2465, 2467, 2469, 2472, 2475, 2479, 2485–6, 2549, 2860, 2984, 3186–7, 3396, 3604, 3685
Newcastle West (Ireland), 3332
Newlove, J. C., 591
Newnham, 1173
Newport, 553, 1781, 2261–2, 2403–4, 2965, 3032, 3560, 3714
Newport Pagnell, 1494
Newport Publications, 2564

Newquay, 767
News Agents, Publishing Co., 166
Nicoll, D. J., 74, 657, 658
Nigeria, 2421
Nitshill, 1423
No-Conscription Fellowship, 426, 2180, 3618
No More War Movement, 2394, 2423–4, 2743
Noel, C., 485, 552, 1209
Normanton, 3743
North Shields, 2451, 3800
North Wales Quarrymen's Union, 554
Northampton 2457–9
Northern Ireland, 217–9, 221, 668, 896, 1005, 1068, 1622, 1666, 1678, 1782, 2456, 2461, 2464, 2478, 2576–7, 2910, 3016, 3213, 3260, 3583, 3643, 3691, 3724, 3939
Northern Ireland Communist Party, 3691
Northern Ireland Labour Party, 1678, 2464, 2910, 3016, 3260
Northern Typographical Union, 2480
Northern Union of Literary and Mechanics Institutions, 2100
Northfleet, 1151, 2484
Northwood, 2623, 2811
Norwich, 860, 871?, 986, 1773, 2170, 2265, 2427, 2487–9
Nottingham, 348, 702, 1495–6, 1693, 2054, 2266, 2494–2501, 2720, 2862, 2864, 2937, 3006, 3309, 3416, 3622, 3695, 3880, 4072
Nottingham Tribune Co., 2500
Nottingham University Labour Club, 4086
Nuneaton. 37, 2672
Nurses, 1325, 1568, 1968, 2014, 2178, 2179, 2507, 2921, 3220
Nut and Bolt Workers, 1762, 2508

Oastler, R., 106, 113, 503, 610, 1152, 1407
O'Brien, B., 362, 376–7, 506, 895, 1396, 1926, 2048, 2300, 2540, 2767, 2769, 2808, 3231, 3333
O'Brien, W., 3459
O'Casey, S., 1559
O'Connor, F., 1035, 1067, 2296, 2477
Odhams Press, 1376, 1676, 1813
Oldham, 468, 1769, 2209, 2523–1
Open Door International, 2538
Operative Bleachers, Dyers & Furnishers Association, 274
Operative Bricklayers' Society, 2543–4
Operative Potters' Union, 2805
Operative Society of Masons, Quarrymen and Allied Trades SEE Operative Stone Masons' Society
Operative Stone Masons' Society, 1229, 1607
Opticians, 908
Orage, A. R., 1179
Order of Oddfellows, 2719
Organisation of the Journeyman Tailors and Machinists, 86
Orpington, 379, 813, 1410, 2742, 3046, 4047
Orwell, G., 1214
Our Time Publications, 2564
Owen, R., 255, 734, 811, 2082, 2370, 2371, 2917–2918, 2973, 2975, 3021–4, 3229–30, 3367
Owen, R. D., 811
Owen, W., 463, 890, 1172, 1747, 2102, 3314, 3393–4, 3489, 3814
Oxford, 539, 550, 600, 886, 1504, 1696, 2225, 2267, 2318, 2374, 2578–94, 2725, 2731, 3052, 3697, 3702, 3706, 4038
Oxted, 2595

Paddington Society for Promoting Christian Knowledge among Canal Boatmen, 461
Padiham Advertiser Ltd., 402, 2607
Painter, 12, 61, 1973–4, 2306–7, 3116
Paisley, 158, 951, 1329, 1700, 2608–9, 2890, 3126, 3813
Palme-Dutt, R., 1701
Pankhurst, S., 1435, 3911
Paraguay, 768
Pare, W., 251, 255
Paris, 82, 1308, 1521, 1814, 3501, 4001
Parkstone, 962
Parmel, P., 91
Parnell, 564
Pately Bridge, 2624
Paton, J., 1329
Paul, W., 1525
Peacehaven, 3329
Pease, E., 1085
Pendlebury, 2703, 2710
Pendleton, 2634
Penge, 2635
Penny, C., 2366, 2666
Penny, J., 2728, 3176
Penrith, 2322
Penygraig, 3009
People's Newspaper & General Publishing Co., 2651
People's Party, 2652
People's Press Printing Society, Ltd., 846–847
Perth, 570, 1256, 2679–81
Peterborough, 2520, 2682–3
Petersfield, 300, 2684
Pethick–Lawrence, F. W. 1670
Petrograd, 674
Petts Wood, 1743
Piano Workers, 26, 2693
Pianoforte Tuners' Association, 2692
Pioneer Press, 1299, 2710–11, 3925
Pioneer Publishing Association, 2052
'The Pioneer' Publishing Co., 2698
Pioneer Socialist League, 1823
Plimsoll, S., 1531
Plumbing Trades Union, 1021
Plunkett, H., 747
Plymouth, 104, 2597, 2736–9, 3238, 3467, 3799
Poland, 97, 238, 369, 882, 1266, 2616, 2741, 2748, 3025–3026, 3471
Police, 400, 1934, 2745–7
Police Federation, 2746
Polish Socialist Party, 94, 1266, 3471
Pollitt, H., 53, 280, 1080
Pontypridd, 3010
Poole, 1301, 2230
Poor Law Workers' Trade Union, 2104
Poor Man's Guardian Society, 2768
Port Talbot, 15
Portsmouth, 1684, 2140, 2324, 2704, 2777–8, 3739
Post Office Engineering Inspectors, 3062
Post Office Engineering Union, 460, 704, 1602, 1633
Post Office Workers, 50, 130, 154, 221, 242, 309, 337, 429, 460, 490, 553, 568,
    584, 704, 716, 788, 889, 903, 953, 983, 1101, 1115, 1175, 1183, 1232, 1248,
    1321, 1360, 1548, 1572, 1585, 1602, 1619, 1633, 1874, 1930, 2552, 2571,
    2599, 2781–800, 2873, 2877, 2950, 3062, 3281, 3480, 3510–14

Postal and Telegraph Christian Association, 309, 1248
Postal Clerks' Association, 2786, 2789
Postal Inspectors' Association, 2793
Postal Telegraph and Telephone Controlling Officers' Association, 716
Postal Telegraph Clerks' Association, 3510—11
Potter, G., 214, 774
Potters, 2805—6
Power Loom Tenters' and Under Tenters' Society, 944
Prague, 1515, 1538, 3503, 3612, 4002
Preston, 789, 810, 1809, 2070, 2108, 2707, 2815—16, 2859, 2955, 3437
Priestley, J. B., 528
Prince Town, 2414
Printers, 40, 685, 990, 1097, 1302, 1608, 1889, 1898, 1936, 2318, 2330, 2411,
    2480, 2570, 2613, 2817—25, 2830, 2878, 3635—8, 3724
Printers' Protection Society, 40
Printers' Watchwork Propaganda Society, 2820
Prison Officers 400, 2745, 2747, 2827
Prison Officers' Association, 2827
Progressive Book Society, Ltd., 1174
Progressive League, 283, 2726
Progressive Press, 2608, 2740
Progressive Publishing Co., 2835
Proletarian Press, 2845, 2940
Prudential Staff Union, 2856
Public Services Temporary and Unestablished Clerks' Association, 3515
Pudsey, 1699

Quelch, H., 899, 1621
Quelch, T., 53, 1113
Quigley, J., 159, 1561

Radcliffe, 2882
Radek, K., 1080
Radical (Post—1848), 192, 488, 784, 812, 868, 879—80, 986, 1039, 1065, 1215,
    1286, 1606, 1818, 1861, 1927, 1941, 2047, 2061, 2206, 2301, 2429, 2449,
    2479, 2647, 2651, 2653, 2698, 2700, 2885—6, 2890, 2954, 2961, 2981,
    2983—4, 3077, 3393—4, 3758, 3783—4, 3818, 4073, 4083, 4094
Radical Registration and Patriotic Association, 335, 3333
Radical Workingmen's Clubs, 2886
Radlett, 2891
Radnor, 326
Railway Clerks' Association, 2894, 2896
Railway Nationalisation Society, 3401
Railwaymen, 329—30, 334, 356, 454, 460, 1276, 1305, 1417, 1478, 1541, 1617,
    1640—1, 1656, 1963, 2390, 2454, 2521, 2532, 2606, 2668, 2893—2908,
    3209—10, 3352—3, 3381, 3477, 3606
Railwaymen's Vigilance Movement, 2904
Ramsgate, 2271
Rank and File League, 2912
Rational Society, 2927, 2972
Rawdon, 1074
Rawtenstall, 772, 2920
Reading, 227, 394, 719, 726, 1326, 1406, 2685, 2922—5, 2994, 3538
Rebel Press, 2928
Red Cross, 96
Red International of Labour Unions, 53, 1526, 1530, 1539, 2947—9, 3225, 3582,
    3936, 4058
Redcar, 2960, 3506
Redemption Society, 1385
Referees' Association, 1167

Sailors', Soldiers and Airmen's Union, 1168
Saint-Helier, 1411
Salaried Pharmacists Union, 2881, 3063
Salford, 914, 1157, 1491, 1794, 1805, 2273, 2991, 3081–2, 3519, 3601, 3608,
    4068, 4072
Salisbury, 373, 3083–4
Saltcoats, 3571
Samuels, H. B. 657

Satirical Publications, 276, 432, 609, 867, 1816, 1817, 2363, 2467, 2640
Schoolmistress Newspaper Printing Co., 3097
Scotland, 17–21, 28, 30, 35, 44, 52, 57, 123–6, 151, 157–60, 168, 259, 272, 290,
    292, 320, 331, 357, 365, 382, 421, 459, 499, 506, 570, 594, 607, 615, 638, 643,
    665–66, 689, 757, 801, 806, 839, 851, 924, 928, 937–46, 951, 990, 992,
    996–1001, 1096, 1099, 1100, 1129, 1180, 1190, 1232, 1256–7, 1276–82,
    1309–12, 1329, 1367, 1389, 1398, 1423, 1440, 1480, 1503, 1511, 1670, 1682,
    1700, 1707, 1759, 1770, 1803, 1850, 1853, 1858, 1874, 1885, 1951, 1989,
    1996–7, 2036, 2052, 2057, 2060–1, 2063, 2101, 2126–8, 2167, 2169, 2197,
    2198, 2229, 2350, 2367, 2375, 2378, 2383, 2393, 2407, 2422, 2431–2, 2466,
    2481, 2515, 2517, 2547–8, 2570, 2608–9, 2617, 2627, 2654, 2679–81, 2698,
    2701, 2732, 2752, 2797, 2852–3, 2877, 2880, 2887, 2890, 2907, 2939–40,
    2943, 2966, 2969, 2971, 2975–7, 2999, 3064, 3068–9. 3072, 3088, 3092,
    3095, 3099–129, 3152, 3167, 3172, 3185, 3212, 3218, 3269–70, 3313, 3356,
    3369, 3375, 3378, 3415, 3442, 3485, 3520, 3543, 3596, 3599, 3603, 3625,
    3647, 3684, 3719, 3720, 3745, 3758, 3810, 3812–3813, 3818, 3926–8, 3930,
    3936, 3949, 3974, 3982, 3991, 4041, 4050, 4065
Scottish Assistant Teachers' Association, 607
Scottish Class Teachers Federation, 607
Scottish Clerks' Association, 615
Scottish Commercial Motormen's Union, 1398
Scottish Co-operative Wholesale Society, 3106
Scottish Farm Servants Union, 3107–8
Scottish Horse and Motormen's Association, 1398
Scottish Independent Labour Party, 3745
Scottish Land Restoration League, 331, 3212
Scottish National Operative Plasterers Federal Union, 3115
Scottish Painters Society, 3116
Scottish Schoolmasters' Association, 3119
Scottish Secondary Teachers Association, 3064, 3120
Scottish Socialist Federation, 1682, 1707
Scottish Socialist Party, 3100, 3109, 3276
Scottish Socialist Union Congress, 3103, 3127
Scottish Typographical Association, 3122
Scottish Union of Bakers & Confectioners, 3123
Scottish United Operative Masons, 3124
Scottish Workers' Republican Party, 3128
Scrymgeour, E., 940
Scunthorpe, 2141, 3136
Seamen, 358–60, 392, 841, 1018, 1157, 1530–1, 2015–16, 2331, 2333, 2393,
    2473, 2695, 3065, 3137, 3138, 3140–4, 3802
Search Publishing Co., 2347
Secular Reformers Society, 3412
Secularism, 1038, 1040, 1215, 1922
Selby, 1864
Servicemen, 1168
Settmakers' Union SEE Amalgamated Union of Quarryworkers and Settmakers
Sevenoaks, 24, 3168
Sexton, J., 1437
Seymour, H., 1202, 3002
Sharp, C. D., 828, 1670

Shaw, Frederick & Co., 1810
Shaw, G. B., 73
Sheerness, 3172
Sheffield, 74, 297, 336, 658, 788, 804–5, 815, 1123, 1144, 1177, 1322, 1341–2,
    1615, 1856, 2013, 2033, 2311, 2615, 2653, 3147, 3164, 3173–83, 3235, 3384,
    3507, 3600, 3731, 3747, 3937
Sherborne, 1103
Shieldhall, 851
Shipbuilding, 135, 320, 494, 3685, 3936
Shipconstructors' and Shipwrights' Association, 3186
Shipley, 598, 3085
Shipyard Communist Group, 320
Shop Workers, 1318, 3191–4
Shorter, R., 541, 3523
Shrewsbury, 1258, 2143 2202–3, 3203
Sign and Display Trades Section SEE National Society of Operative Printers Graphic
    and Media Personnel, 2411
Sims, J., 282, 1685
Singapore, 1504
Sinn Fein, 3090
Sittingbourne, 1106, 2412, 2436, 2743
Skipton, 3216
Slough, 1063, 2727
Snowden, P., 538, 1447
Social Democratic Club, 1219
Social Democratic Federation, 303, 643, 857, 899, 1621, 2427, 2457, 2702, 3224,
    3247–8, 3251
Social Democratic Party, 597, 1062, 1621, 2392, 3061, 3248
Social Institutes' Union, 1109, 3226
Social Service League 2556
Socialism other than mainstream – for mainstream SEE main
    headings e.g. Labour Party, Communist Party, etc., 45, 168, 259, 283, 361, 374,
    399, 462, 523, 1056, 1062, 1064, 1068, 1070, 1128, 1138, 1177, 1197, 1209,
    1231, 1262, 1266, 1277, 1348–9, 1419, 1532–4, 1817, 1875, 1950, 2110,
    2350, 2368, 2381, 2426, 2551, 2555, 2567, 2586–8, 2590, 2704–5, 2725,
    2928, 2937, 3010, 3027, 3131, 3185, 3235, 3236, 3241–2, 3253, 3264,
    3266–7, 3270, 3358, 3543, 3721, 3741, 3767, 3815–16, 3931, 3943, 3949,
    4040–1, 4070, 4078, 4079, 4080, 4088, 4096, 4097, 4099, 4100
Socialist Anti-War Front, 442
Socialist Clarity Group, 1692
Socialist Current Publications, 3252
Socialist Education, Centre of, 4069
Socialist Educational Association, 3234
Socialist Fellowship, 1114, 3262
Socialist Information and Liaison Office, 3274
Socialist International, 644, 1535–6, 4019
Socialist Labour League, 1193, 1755, 2416
Socialist Labour Party 499, 3240
Socialist Labour Press, 499, 1276, 2999, 3720, 3935
Socialist League, 657, 1706, 1820, 3250, 3257
Socialist Medical Association, 2008, 3255, 3258, 3259
Socialist Newspaper Society, Ltd., 1339
Socialist Quaker Society, 2734
Socialist Review Publishing Co., 1765, 2914, 3266
Socialist Round Table, 3267
Socialist School, 2999
Socialist Union, 3236
Socialist Union of Central-Eastern Europe, 1785
Socialist Workers' Group, 3273, 3966
Socialist Workers' National Health Council, 1126

Socialist Workmen's Association, 1211
Society for Promoting Christian Knowledge, 3790
Society for Promoting National Regeneration, 1388
Society for Promoting Working Men's Associations, 541
Society for the Advancement of Political Knowledge, 3730
Society for the Diffusion of Useful Knowledge, 3984
Society for the Encouragement of Socialist and Democratic Literature, 2090
Society for the Union of Benevolence, 2855
Society of Anarchist Press, 1194
Society of Civil Servants, 588, 833–4, 2879, 3277–9
Society of Friends of Italy, 3280
Society of Graphical and Allied Trades, 3282
Society of Lithographic Artists. Designers Engravers (SLADE), 2830
Society of Post Office Engineers, 2783–4, 3281
Society of Registered Male Nurses, 1968
Society of Technical Civil Servants, 134
Society of Women Journalists, 3282
Soldiers, 3285
Solidarity Press, 3287
Solly, H., 214, 649, 3997, 3999
Somerville, A., 769, 2759
Sorter Tracers' Association, 2996
South Essex Printing Co., 1062
South Shields, 1852, 2413
South Wales Labour Press Association, 3322, 3470
South Wales Miners' Federation, 639, 2064, 2071
Southampton, 358, 1102, 1264, 1684, 1905, 2138, 2554, 3073, 3261, 3328,
    3518
Southborough, 2278
Southend-on-Sea, 2156, 2563, 2774, 3330
Southern Counties Workers' Publications, 3956
Southport, 356, 647, 3536, 3646
Southsea, 1226, 2140, 3739
Sowerby Bridge, 2636
Spanish Publications, 1520, 2509
Spanish Civil War, 801, 2407, 2558, 3349–50, 3761–2
Spenborough, 3363
Stafford, 324, 3389–91, 3393
Standring, G., 1085
Stansfield, W. D., 1052
State Medical Service Association, 2006
Staveley Tenants Defence Committee, 3404
Steam Engine Makers' Society, 3405
Steel Smelters' Association, 3406
Steill, B., 2724, 2874
Stephens, J. R., 113, 503, 3408
Stevenage, 3439
Stevens, W., 926
Stewart, M., 1247
Stirling, 1874, 2877, 3107, 3415
Stockport, 200, 706, 3417–22
Stockton-on-Tees, 3422–3, 3505
Stoke Hammond, 2433
Stoke-on-Trent, 704, 1747, 2453, 2802, 2806, 3424
Stonemasons, 1228–9, 1607, 2547, 3124
Stowmarket, 1081
Strange, W., 479, 1961, 2376, 2519, 2629, 2723, 2749, 2762, 3628, 3636
Strickland Press, 3926–8
Strines, 2369
Stroud, 440, 1289

Students' Anti-War Council, 3441
Suffolk, 1061
Summerbell and Johnson, 3237
Sunbury, 226
Sunderland, 1531, 1605, 2277, 3189, 3237, 3455–7
Superannuation Rights Association, 2539
Surbiton, 1344
Surveyors, 5, 1637
Sutton, 2162
Swann, E., 552
Swansea, 710, 1489, 2137, 3322, 3468–70, 3495, 3827, 3953
Sweden, 397
Swindon, 858, 1879, 2454, 3472
Swinton, 2199, 2703
Switzerland, 1012, 1587, 1668, 3342
Syndicalist Workers' Federation, 904–5, 3971
Syndicalists, 47, 75, 904–5, 1486–8, 1864, 2062, 2591, 3475–7, 3971
Syndicat des Cuisiniers, Patissiers, Glaciers, Confisiers de Londres, 483

Tailors, 63, 1252, 1611–12, 2548, 3482–7
Tailors and Garment Workers' Trade Union SEE Amalgamated Society of Tailors
Tailors' Publishing Association, 3487
Tamworth, 2355, 3489–90
Tanner, J., 1027
Taunton, 2133, 2274, 3494, 3835, 4022
Taxes Left Wing Group, 2373
Taylor, E., 873
Taylor, John, 160, 506
Taylor, Joseph, 1337
Teachers SEE ALSO National Union of Teachers, 14, 119–20, 131–2, 143–4, 150,
    607, 924, 1005–6, 1010, 1297, 1365–6, 1370, 1422, 1494, 1515, 1538, 1562,
    1573, 1575, 1760, 1860, 1897, 1914, 1920, 1931, 2040, 2091, 2117, 2285,
    2377, 2382, 2478, 2572, 2735, 3064, 3096–7, 3119–20, 3152–3, 3213, 3234,
    3463, 3499–3503, 3698, 3830, 3904, 3905, 4090
Teachers' Anti-War Movement, 2735
Teachers' Labour League, 1010
Teachers' Peace Publications, 2735
Teddington, 2040
Telecommunications Sales Superintendents' Association, 3507–3508
Telegraph Messengers Christian Association, 308
Telephone Contract Officers Association, 2722
Temporary Sorters' Association, 3480
Textile Machinery Makers, 3519
Textiles, 688, 771–2, 937, 944–5, 2058, 2528, 3520–1
Thames Conservancy Staff Association, 3017
Thames Valley Publishing Society, 3305
Theatrical Employees, 72, 2177, 2469, 3522
Thelwall, J., 3620
Theydon Bois, 3525
Thomas, A. A., 847, 849
Thomas More Society, 886
Thompson, E. P., 2381
Thompson, R., 685, 2393, 2818
Thomson, W., 506
Thorne, 3529
Thornhill, T., 1152
Thornhill Lees, 3530
Thornton Heath, 1048
Thurrock, 2410
Tillett, B., 361

Tinplate Workers' Union, 1489
Tipton, 36
Tobacco Workers' Union, 3540
Toddington, 2321
Toolmakers, 66
Topham, E., 732, 748
Torquay, 2279
Tory Radical (up to 1860 approx.), 113, 895
Trade Societies Printer, 1145
Trade Union Affairs, 3575
Trade Union Co-operative Publishing Society, 2055
Trade Union Information Bureau, 3576
Trade Union, Labour, Co-operative Democratic History Society, 3526
'Trade Unionist' Company, 3587
Trade Unions, 214, 364, 1473, 2541, 2544, 2729, 2912, 3121, 3575−7, 3579−92,
    3675, 3814, 3977, 3998
Trades and Labour Council, 15, 17, 31, 207, 402, 405, 941, 1697, 1703, 3028, 3074,
    3175, 3328, 3848, 3901, 3918, 3925, 3953
Trades' Committee of Glasgow, 1389
Trades Council SEE ALSO London Trades Council, 214, 217, 219, 247, 256, 318,
    448, 518, 863, 892, 1113, 1259−61, 1334, 1431−2, 1681, 1756, 1758, 2681,
    3430, 3468, 3674, 3695, 3774, 3793, 3933, 3942, 4074
Trades Newspaper Co., 214
Trades Union Congress, 364−365, 843, 1481−3, 1485, 1540, 1663, 1675, 1716,
    1737, 1767, 3481, 3580, 3873
Transport and General Workers' Union, 438, 850, 1398, 1470, 1916, 1948, 2776,
    2936, 3019, 3137
Transport Workers, 395, 409−11, 413−17, 434−9, 488, 715?, 1307, 1369, 1372,
    1437, 1453−4, 1530, 1541, 1865, 1924, 1948, 2729, 2865, 3019, 3180,
    3491−2, 3607−13, 3726, 3879
Transporter Publishing Co., 3613
Travis, H., 3021
Trevor, J., 1685
Tropical Emigration Society, 2109
Trotsky, L. and Trotskyists, 350, 357, 1127, 1192−3, 1625, 1755, 1994, 2078,
    2780, 2945, 3244, 3273, 3950, 3974, 4053, 4101
Troup, G., 214
Trowbridge, 419, 2174
Truelove, E., 2983, 3023
Truscott, J., 93
Tunbridge Wells, 2826
Tupling, J., 541
Turner, J., 370, 1212−13
Turrif, 1262
Twentieth Century Press, 648, 900, 1017, 1449, 1587, 1823, 1857, 1875, 1935,
    2084, 3223, 3248, 3263, 3513, 3522, 3719, 3871, 4041
Typists, 412, 3634
Typographical Association, 902, 1608, 2570, 3636−8

U.S.A., 675, 1218, 1529, 1971, 2361, 4037
Unemployed, 513, 842, 2569, 2870, 2991, 3647−57, 3743−4
Union Exchange Society, 3663
Union of Construction, Allied Trades & Technicians, 13
Union of Democratic Control, 3639
Union of German Socialist Organisations in Gt. Britain, 3667
Union of Greek Seamen in Britain, 2333
Union of Latvian Social Democrats, 2844
Union of Post Office Workers, 50, 221, 242, 337, 429, 553, 568, 697, 788, 889,
    903?, 953, 983, 1101, 1115, 1175, 1183, 1232, 1321, 1360, 1548, 1585, 1619,
    1874, 1930, 1958, 2018−20, 2038, 2114, 2116, 2415, 2468, 2470, 2520, 2571,

Walton-Newbold, J. T., 53
War Workers' League, 3790
Warbey, W., 1247, 1692
Wardle, G. J., 1447
Warley, 2522
Warrington, 736, 1697, 2201, 3793–4
Warsash Press, 1102
Warwick, 37, 2280
Washington, Co. Durham, 3795
Watford, 51, 1392, 1876, 3154, 3531, 3806–9
Watkins, N., 53, 2076
Watson, J., 84, 486, 541, 734, 764, 865, 880, 1035, 1042, 1215, 1708, 2090, 2109,
    2207, 2549, 2646, 2753, 2927, 2980, 3021, 3023, 3594, 3980
Weavers, 1352, 3370, 3812–13
Webb, B., 662, 828
Wednesbury, 3314, 3814, 3899
Weekly Tract Society, 3823
Wellingborough, 500
Wellington, 1753, 4008
Welsh Council of Labour, 3773
Welsh Republican Movement, 3829
Wertheim & Macintosh, 1407
West Bridgford, 565
West Bromwich, 1762, 3534, 3837
West Drayton, 2241
West Wickham, 3861
Western Union Employees Association, 3768
Westgate-on-Sea, 3868
Westhoughton, 1719, 2282
Westley and Parrish, 2003
Wexford, 3746
Whitehaven, 2103
Whiteley, Wilfred, 2405
Widnes, 1187, 2196
Wigan, 1191, 1849, 2854
Wilkinson, E., 53, 1080
William Morris Press, 1958
Williams, M., 38, 1332, 4105
Wilson, J. H., 1531
Winchester, 819, 2510
Windsor, 714, 2178, 3896
Winsford, 3895
Wintringham, T., 1839
Wokingham, 1164
Wolverhampton, 146, 396, 890, 1747, 2019, 3901
Women, 130, 132, 180, 412, 753, 920, 1044, 1109, 1118, 1216, 1334, 1434–5,
    1483, 1537, 1543, 1573, 1703, 1822, 2326, 2538, 2550, 2905, 3097, 3154,
    3156, 3160, 3171, 3183, 3282, 3497, 3698, 3810–11, 3902–19, 3976, 3988
Women's Industrial Council, 3917
Women's International Matteotti Committee, 1435
Women's Protective and Provident League, 3919
Women's World Committee Against War and Fascism, 3906
Woodbridge, 864
Woodcock, G., 866, 1214
Woodcraft Folk, 2720
Woodstock Press, 306
Woodworkers, 13, 56
Wooler, T., 260, 1979, 3923
Worcester, 595, 1731, 2154, 2351
Worker Newspaper Society, 2520